or why or how, to give him or her a grip,
so Irma said fine, let's do a visual introduc-
uperfluous, images that announce the things
lisher insisted that we need Petra's voice to
ested starting a sentence on the front cover
er a river of words, beautiful idea, exactly
sking ourselves some questions about why
atterns of the past primitive classic modern
softer richer methods that. . .

. . .invite unpredictability, finiteness and change and why they associate it with luxury or decoration when our work is actually scientific, technical, rational and physical, while addressing context and necessities, within a framework of time, money and culture, art, architecture and social and political structures, in the meantime certainly referring to life and memory and. . .

Inside Outside
Petra Blaisse

. . .beauty and consolation, instinct and emotion but still unbelievable how hard it is to give the work, that is to say an object of beauty – depending on how you look at it – its right of existence in this era that we live in, as if beauty is less important than necessity, then grey concrete pavement and plastic window frames or donor walls and café corners, so. . .

The Monacelli Press
New York

. . .in the sense of being considered as a useful tool of a certain value and you wonder sometimes why the devotion and the loss of things and time and you know it is this flexible flowing form of architecture and nature that lives and moves, glows and blooms, dies and surprises, triggers excitement and love of novelty and curiosity that urges us on and on, up and down, deeper in and why. . .

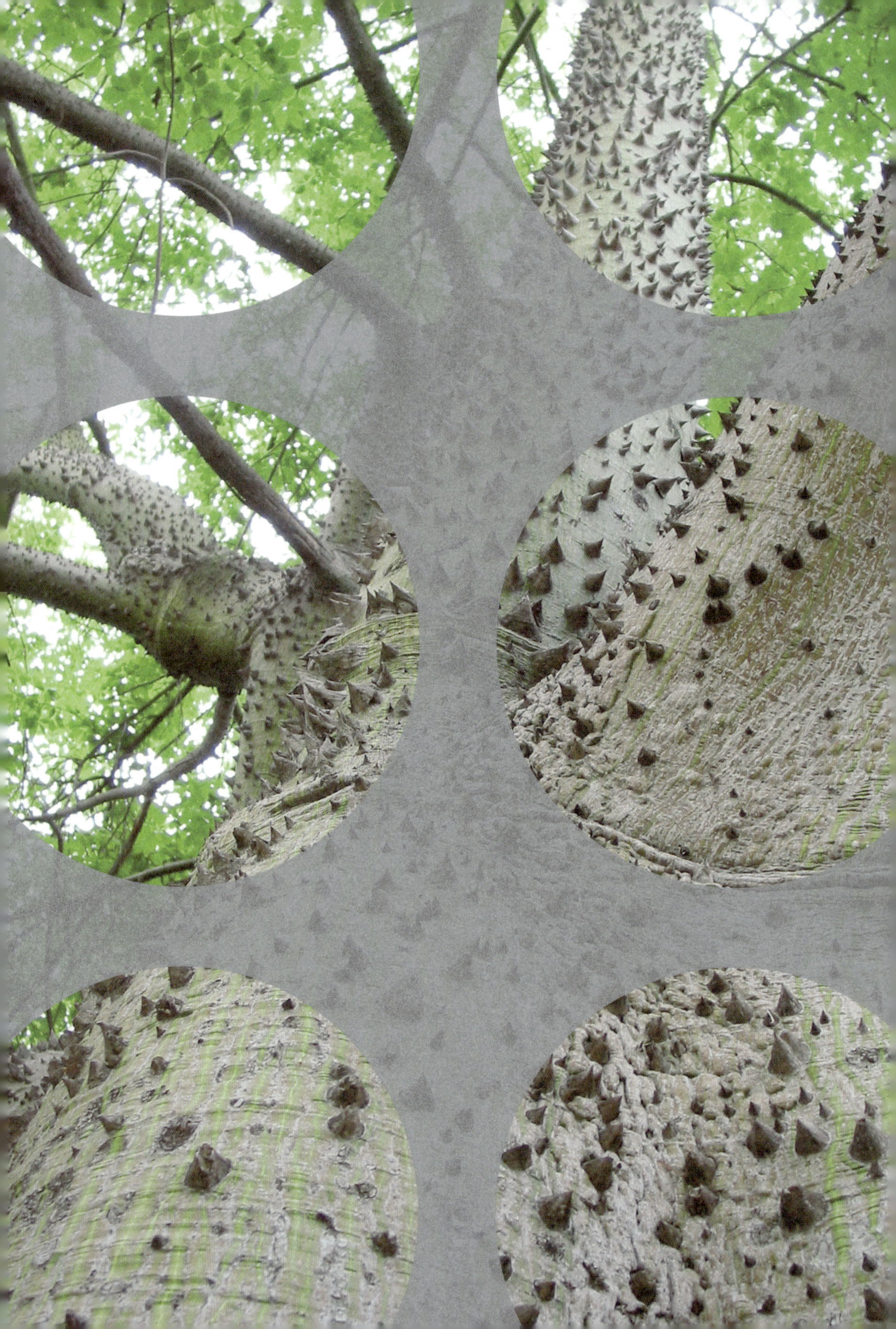

. . .then, this book that does exactly what we don't do, namely framing, labeling, freezing phenomena, thoughts, ideas, things in movement and certainly not on paper although it is like cloth folding, tearing, paging, breathing the medium of life and memory and thought and learning and although we thought of adding dvds, ftps, pdfs, cds, websites, films, train and flight tickets to. . .

To Wim Blaisse (1923–2005)
This book is both a testimony to his unfailing
support and to the luxury and freedom of thinking,
doubting and creating, whatever the field.

....lead everyone to the touch, the smell, the movement, the real thing – all the real things – but this is what lies now in front of you like all lies in front and behind us – the weave of things, one thing leading to another, but here just about work and processes within a certain field and time; stories deriving from interviews by Kayoko and conversations with others in different places around the globe....

Petra Blaisse
June 2006

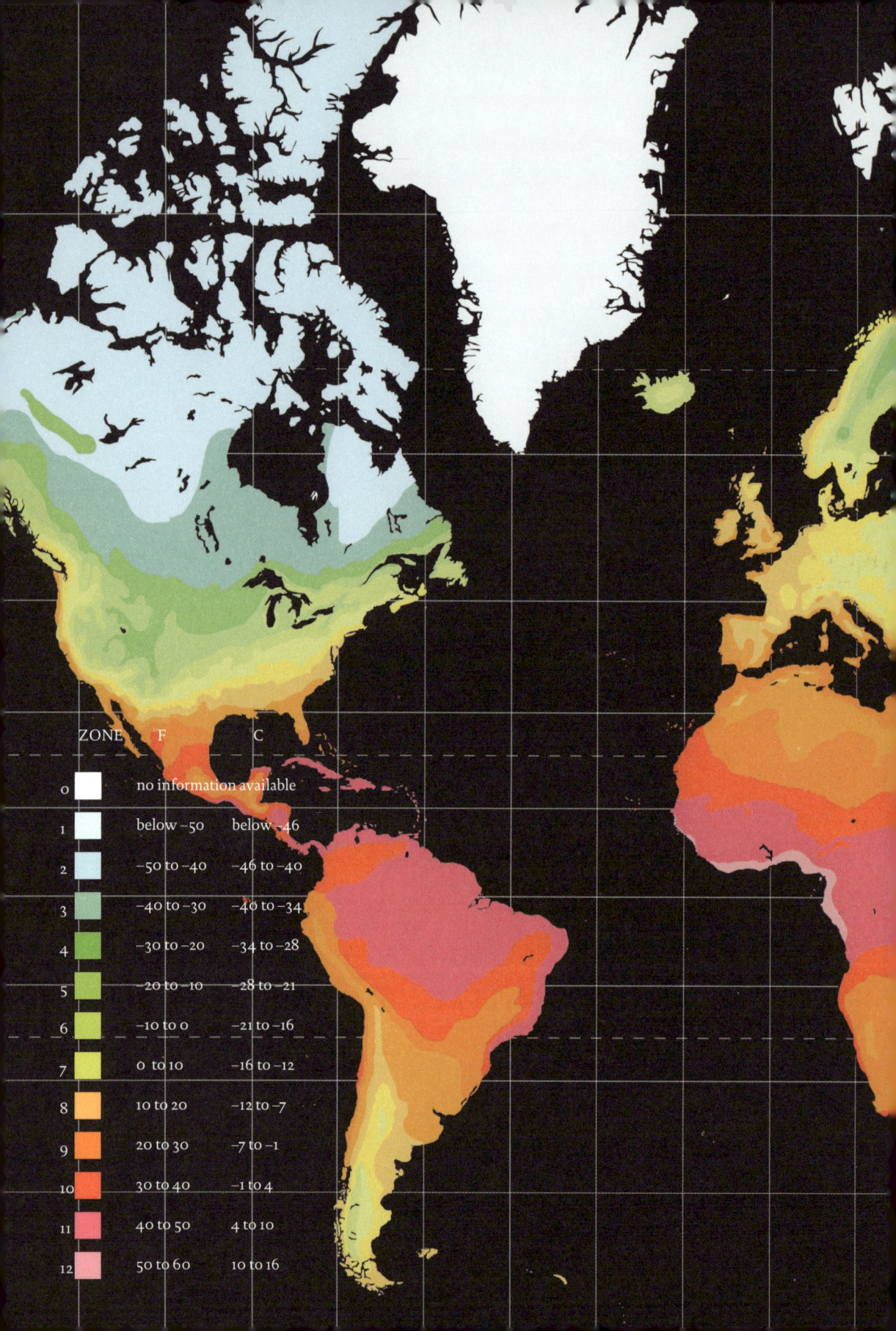

ZONE	F	C
0	no information available	
1	below −50	below −46
2	−50 to −40	−46 to −40
3	−40 to −30	−40 to −34
4	−30 to −20	−34 to −28
5	−20 to −10	−28 to −21
6	−10 to 0	−21 to −16
7	0 to 10	−16 to −12
8	10 to 20	−12 to −7
9	20 to 30	−7 to −1
10	30 to 40	−1 to 4
11	40 to 50	4 to 10
12	50 to 60	10 to 16

Hardiness Zones

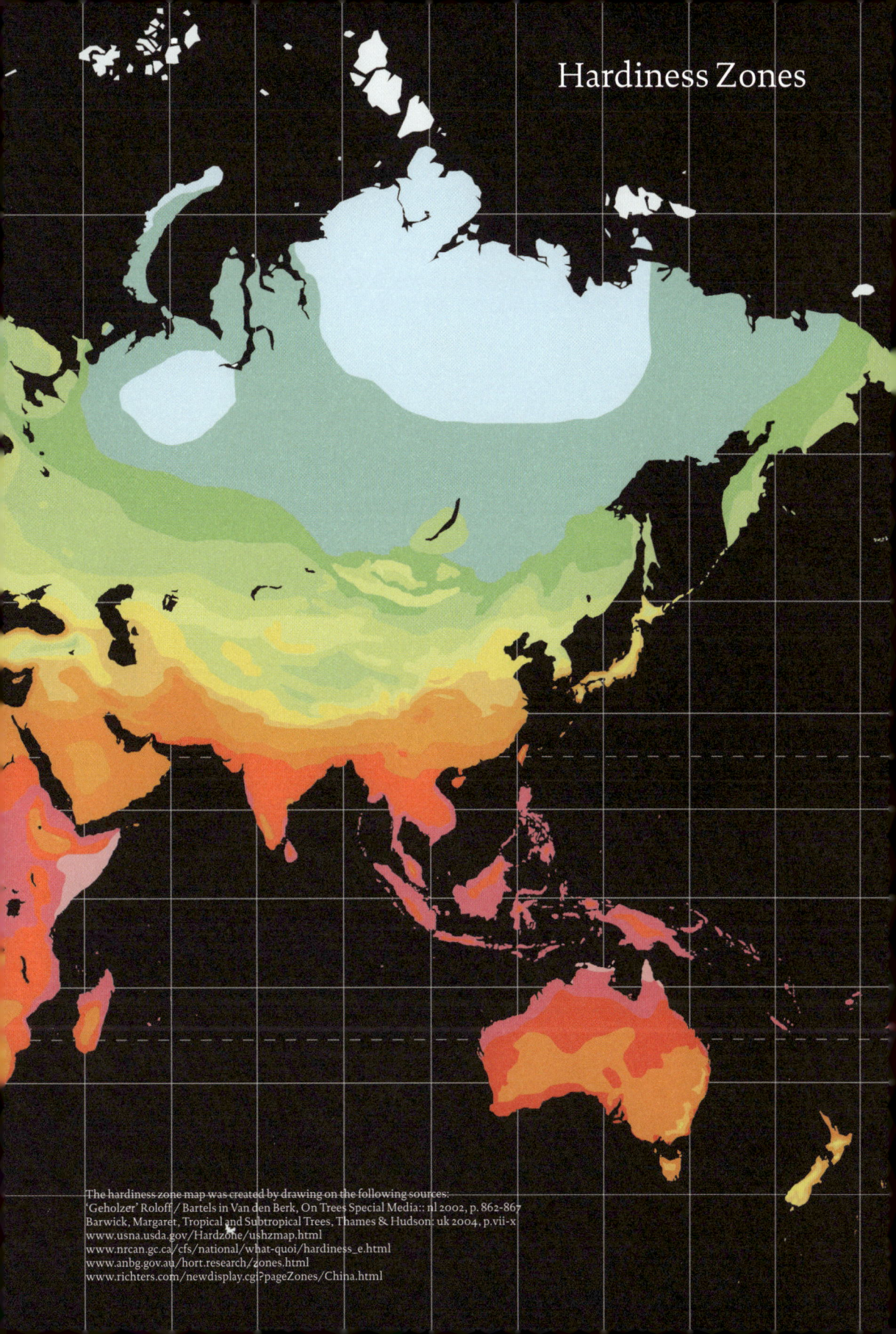

The hardiness zone map was created by drawing on the following sources:
'Gehölzer' Roloff / Bartels in Van den Berk, On Trees Special Media:: nl 2002, p. 862-867
Barwick, Margaret, Tropical and Subtropical Trees, Thames & Hudson: uk 2004, p.vii-x
www.usna.usda.gov/Hardzone/ushzmap.html
www.nrcan.gc.ca/cfs/national/what-quoi/hardiness_e.html
www.anbg.gov.au/hort.research/zones.html
www.richters.com/newdisplay.cgi?pageZones/China.html

Trajectories
Inside

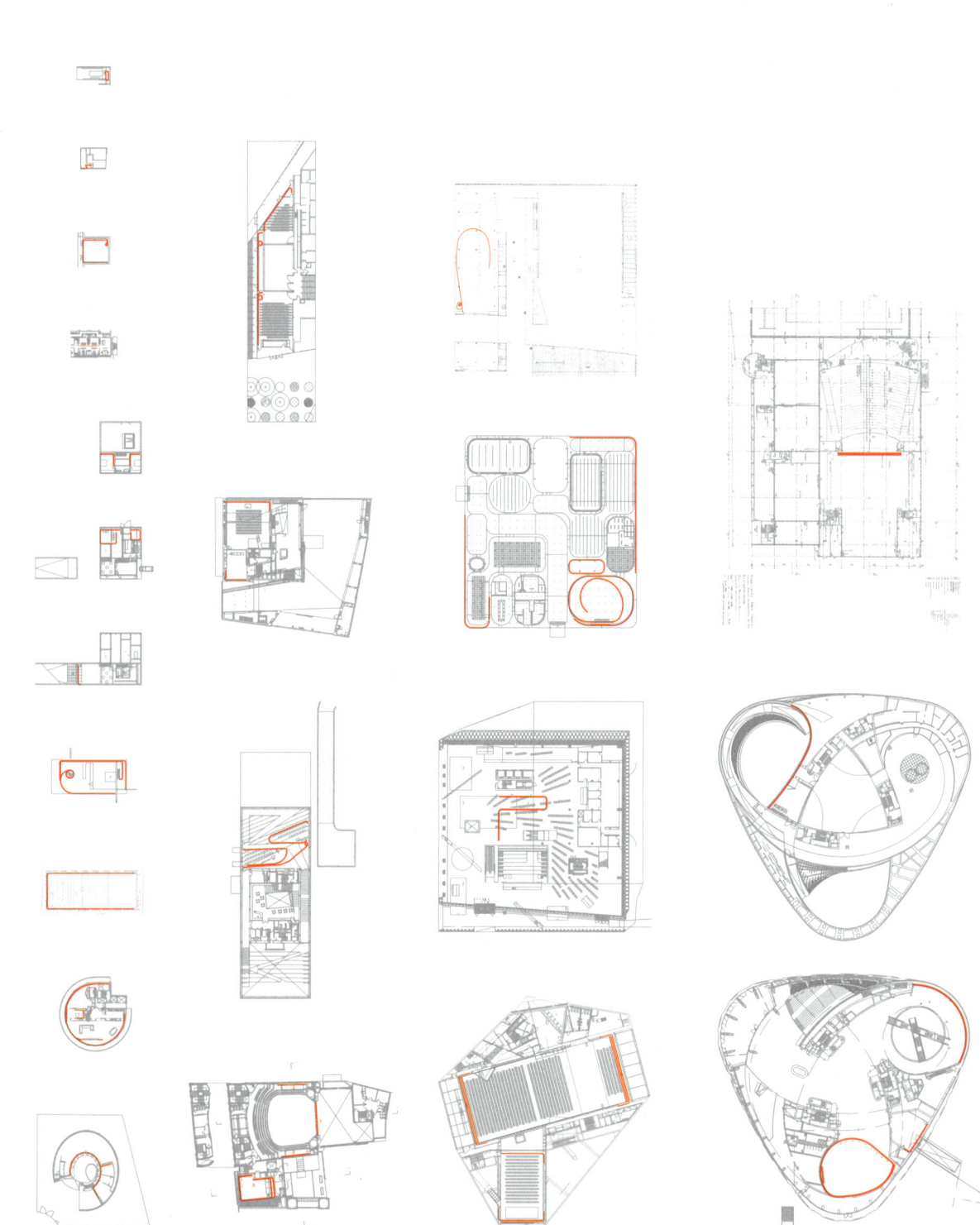

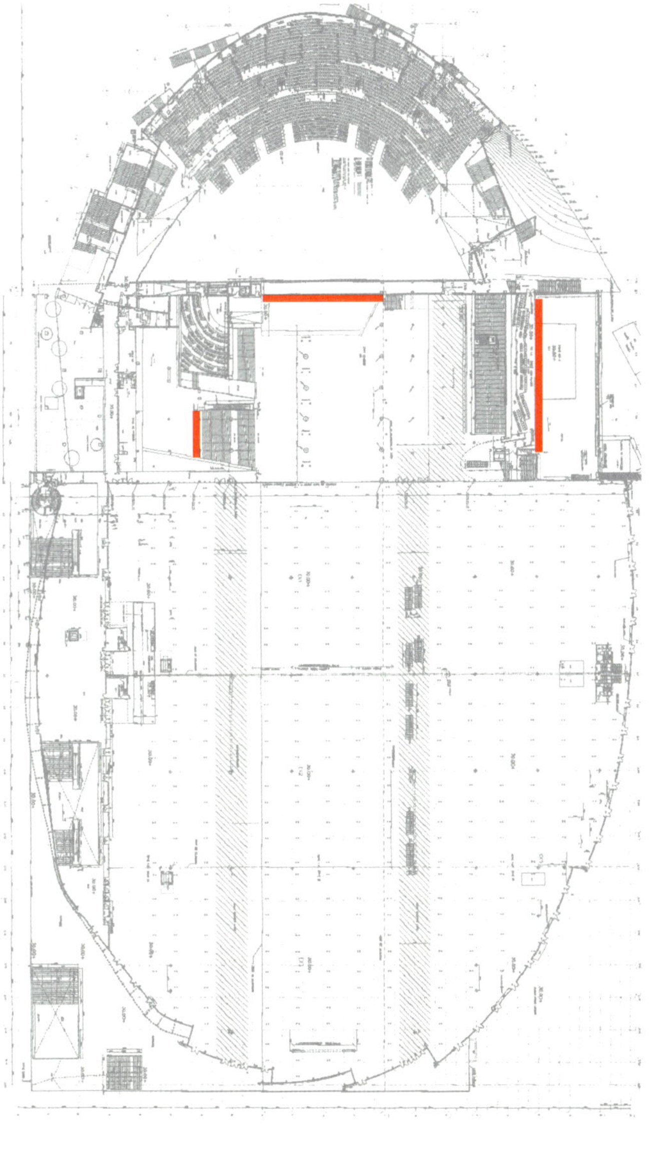

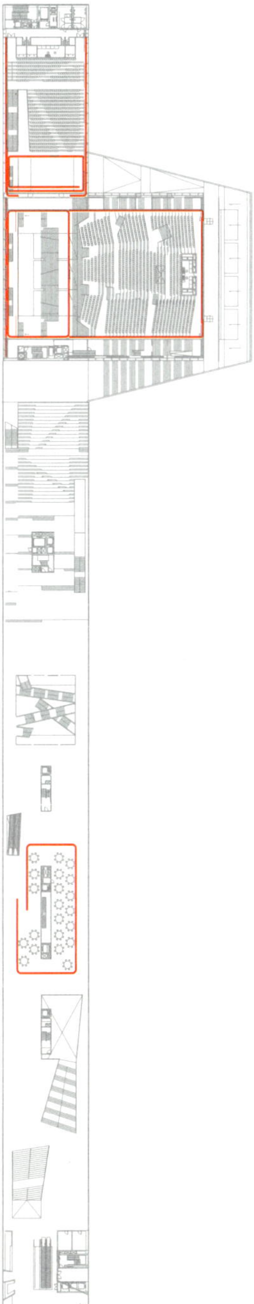

Trajectories
Outside

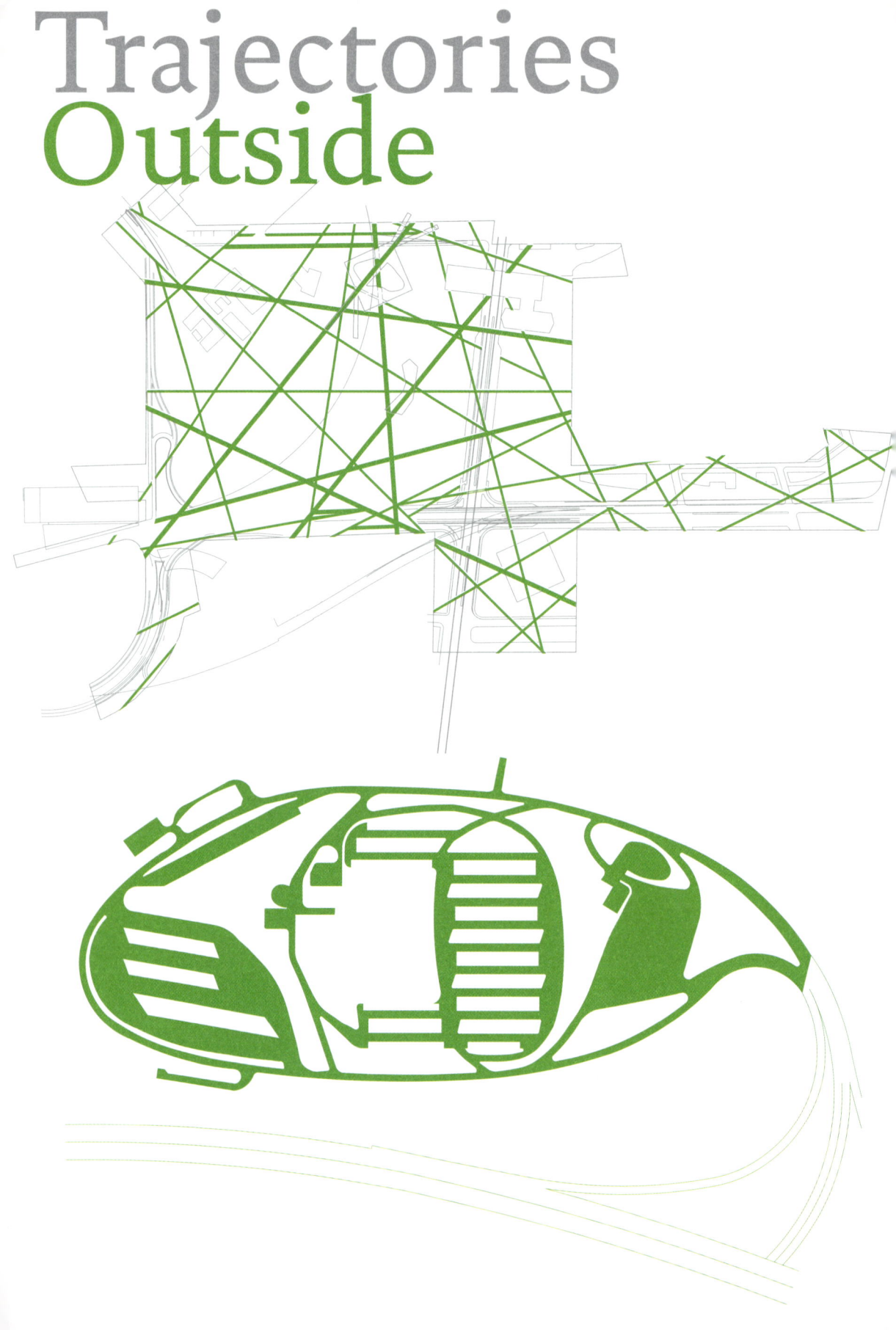

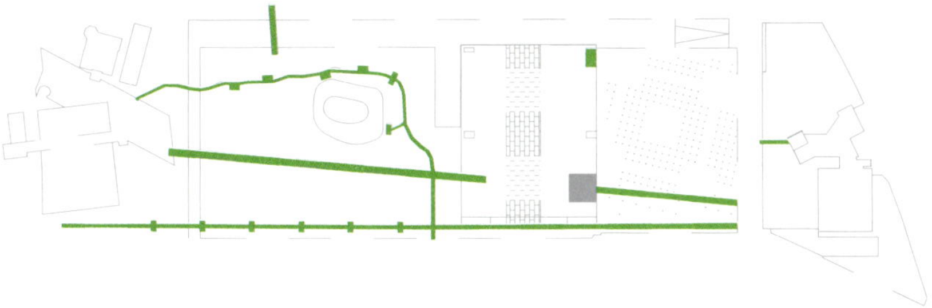
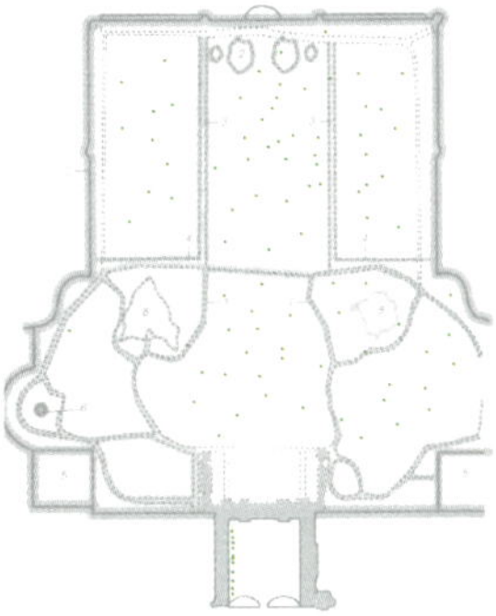
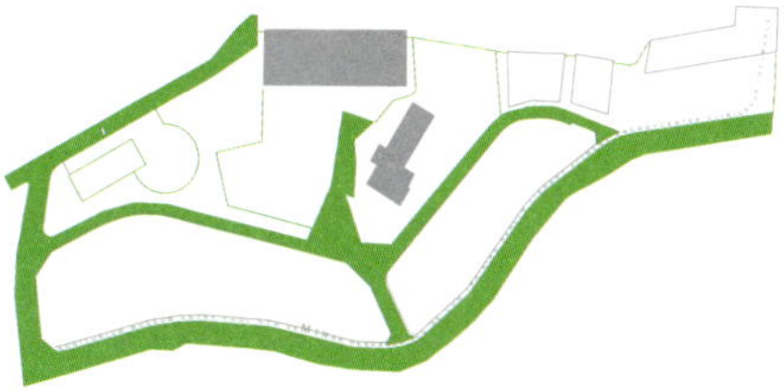
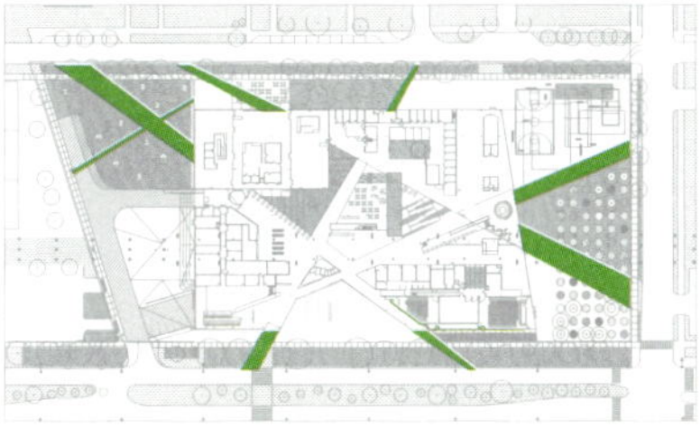
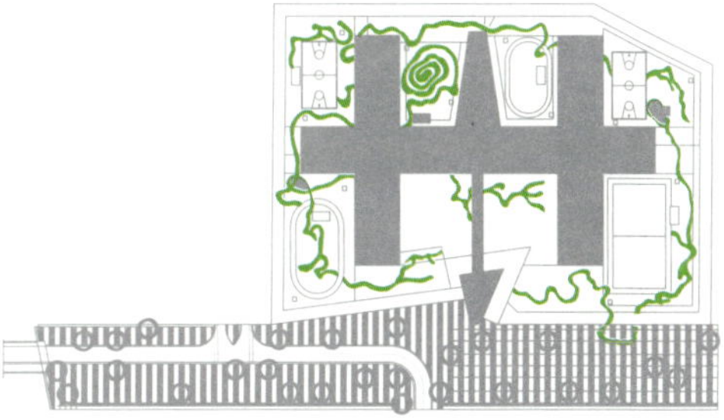
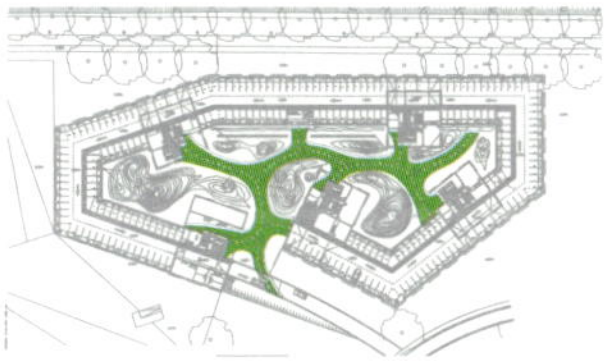
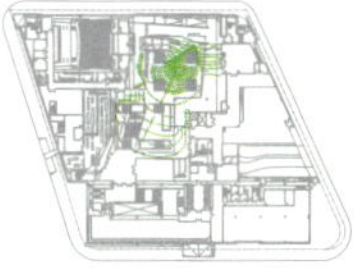
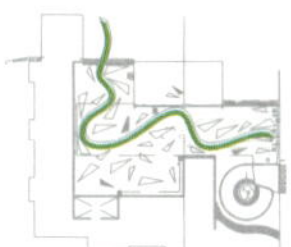
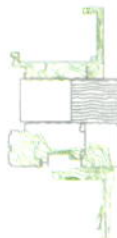

Contents

Part 1

Invisible Presence
- 18   The Glass Pavilion, Toledo, USA
Petra Blaisse

- 46   *Die Welt ist alles, was der Fall ist –
The Limits of the World are also its Limits*
Chris Dercon

Reflection
- 52   Cloudy Sky, Delft, NL
- 54   Vla-Flip, Lille, FR
- 56   Rifletutti, Codroipo, IT
- 60   Mass, Amsterdam, NL
- 62   Silk, Lawn, Paris, FR
- 64   Radial Views, London, UK
- 66   Reflection, Chicago, USA
- 72   OMA Retrospective, Barcelona, ES

Restoration Revised
- 74   Hackney Empire Theatre, London, UK
Petra Blaisse

- 102   The Effect of Curtains
Tim Ronalds

Branding
- 104   Shifting Layers, Dartford, UK
- 106   Milky Way, Lille, FR
- 108   Liquid Gold, The Hague, NL
- 112   Powder Gold, The Hague, NL
- 114   Angel Root, Berlin, DE
- 120   Noise Dress, Flower Field, Rotterdam, NL
- 124   Façade Curtain, New York, USA
- 126   Fin de Siècle, Paris, FR

Complex Urban Park
- 128   Giardini di Porta Nuova, Milan, IT
Petra Blaisse

- 152   Nature at a Glance: The Urban Scenery
in the Work of Inside Outside
Gaston Bekkers

Production
- 156   Windy Zero, Rotterdam, NL
- 158   Radial Views, London, UK
- 160   Reflection, Chicago, USA
- 162   Smallest Parcel, Sub-Saharan Countries
- 164   Whipped Cream with Mesh, Beverly Hills, USA
- 166   Sound Sock, New York, USA
- 168   Reflection, Chicago, USA
- 170   Mass, Amsterdam, NL
- 172   Hairs, Fins, Sauerkraut and Furs, Stuttgart, DE
- 174   Touch, Long Island, USA
- 180   Reflection, Chicago, USA
- 182   Angel Root, Berlin, DE
- 184   Rifletutti, Codroipo, IT
- 188   Inside Outside Architecture, Amsterdam, NL
- 190   Workshop, Amsterdam, NL
- 192   Lunch, Amsterdam, NL

Undoing Boundaries
- 194   Seattle Central Library, Seattle, USA
Petra Blaisse

- 220   Design Issues of Acoustics
Renz van Luxemburg

- 237   Living with Curtains
Hélène Lemoine

Windows
- 230   Water Fleece, Bordeaux, FR
- 234   Bedroom Terrace Mirror, Bordeaux, FR
- 236   Pink Bathrobe, Bordeaux, FR
- 240   Sun and Moon, Leefdaal, BE
- 246   Window Windows, Amsterdam, NL
- 248   Dutch, Amsterdam, NL

The Path as Spatial Tool

250 State Detention Centre, Nieuwegein, NL
Petra Blaisse

280 A Choreography of Reciprocities
Dirk van den Heuvel

Gardens

284 Distant Recipe, Seoul, KR
288 Arteries, Breda, NL
292 Municipal Restoration: Previous, Rotterdam, NL
293 Municipal Restoration: Current, Rotterdam, NL
294 Oil Pressure, Los Angeles, USA
296 False Horizons, Chicago, USA
300 View, Movement, Protection, Bordeaux, FR
304 Cool Inlays, Dubai, AE
306 Shade, Honey, Holten, NL
310 Riga Port City, Riga, LV
316 Piranesi Pixel, Beijing, CN

Connective Green

320 Landscape Design for 'H-Project', Seoul, KR
Petra Blaisse

352 Collaboration with Inside Outside and Petra Blaisse
Bernd Baumeister

Structures

344 Silk Rock, Sunset, Breda, NL
348 Garage Door, New York, USA
354 Sound Sock, New York, USA
360 Whipped Cream, New York, USA

Curtain as Architecture

364 Casa da Música, Porto, PT
Petra Blaisse

406 Dialectics of the Tangible and the Intangible
Cecil Balmond

Part 2

409 The Glass Pavilion, Toledo, USA
416 Hackney Empire Theatre, London, UK
424 Giardini di Porta Nuova, Milan, IT
432 Seattle Central Library, Seattle, USA
440 State Detention Centre, Nieuwegein, NL
446 Landscape Design for 'H-Project', Seoul, KR
454 Casa da Música, Porto, PT
460 Emancipation, Birsfelden, DE
462 Sound Sock, New York, USA
463 Whipped Cream, New York/Beverly Hills, USA
464 Radial Views, London, UK
466 Silk Rock, Sunset, Breda, NL
468 Window Windows, Amsterdam, NL
469 Shadows of Nothing, Groningen, NL
470 Unweaving the Heart, Scientific American
Michael Shermer
471 Shifting Layers, Dartford, UK
472 Gradiant Voiles, Haaksbergen, NL
473 Angel Root, Berlin, DE
474 Garage Door, New York, USA
476 Hairs, Fins, Sauerkraut and Furs, Stuttgart, DE
478 Reflection, Chicago, USA
479 Windy Zero, Rotterdam, NL
480 Multiple Choice, Amsterdam, NL
482 Taiwan Sketches, Chen Sui, TW
484 Cool Inlays, Dubai, AE
486 Job Creation, Abuja, NG
488 Black-and-White Landscape, Dubai, AE
490 Smallest Parcel, Sub-Saharan Countries
492 Project Credits
494 Project List of Inside Outside
496 Photo Credits
498 Biographies

500 The Garden and the Veil
Sanford Kwinter

Credits

The first edition was made possible thanks to the generous support of the Netherlands Foundation for Visual Arts, Design and Architecture (Fonds BKVB), the Netherlands Architecture Fund, the HGIS Culture Fund, the Graham Foundation and the Mondriaan Foundation.

We would like to express our special gratitude to the following firms and individuals for their donations: Ahrend de Winter Groen-Projecten, Architectura & Natura, Gerriets GmbH, Lehmann Maupin Gallery, Office for Metropolitan Architecture, Theatex, Twentebelt/Twentynox, Vertical Vision.

Text: Petra Blaisse

Contributions: Cecil Balmond, Bernd Baumeister, Gaston Bekkers, Chris Dercon, Dirk van den Heuvel, Sanford Kwinter, Hélène Lemoine, Renz van Luxemburg, Tim Ronalds

Edited by: Kayoko Ota

Design: Irma Boom Office
Image Editing: Lieuwe Conradie, Marieke van den Heuvel (Inside Outside)
Translations: Brian Holmes, Andrew May, Mark Speer, Laura Watkinson
Text editing: D'Laine Camp

Cooperation: Rosetta Elkin, Karin Falkenhagen, Peter Niessen, Alexandra Pander (Inside Outside); Minsuk Cho (Mass Studies); Robert Kater (Kennemer Valley); Jan Knikker, David van der Leer, Nuno Rosado, Guus Staats, Michael Zwiers (OMA); Todd Reisz (AMO); Lindy Roy (ROY Co. design)

Acknowledgement

I would like to thank the following persons for their investment, intelligence, creativity, advice, knowledge, support and sense of humour:
Gaston Bekkers, Riny Blaisse, Tineke Blok, Cini Boeri, Irma Boom, Anna van Dorp, Brian Eno, Tijs Goldschmidt, Rebecca Gomperts, Rem Koolhaas, Sacha Marlisa, Herbert Muschamp, Hans Ulrich Obrist, Kayoko Ota, Piet Oudolf, Alwin van Steijn, Julius Vermeulen, Ien Wiegers.
Petra Blaisse

Copyright © 2007 by Inside Outside

All rights reserved. Published in the United States in 2009 by The Monacelli Press, a division of Random House, Inc., New York.

This work was originally published in The Netherlands by NAi Publishers, Rotterdam, in 2007.

The Monacelli Press is a trademark and the M design is a registered trademark of Random House, Inc.

For works of visual artists affiliated with a CISAC-organization the copyrights have been settled with Beeldrecht.
© 2004, c/o Beeldrecht, Amsterdam

Library of Congress Cataloging-in-Publication Data
Blaisse, Petra.
Inside outside / Petra Blaisse.
p. cm.
Originally published: Rotterdam : NAi Publishers, 2007.
ISBN 978-1-58093-258-5
1. Blaisse, Petra. 2. Inside Outside (Firm)
3. Interior architecture—History—21st century.
4. Interior decoration—History—21st century.
5. Landscape architecture—History—21st century.
I. Title.
NA1153.B538A4 2009
720.92—dc22   2009027480

Printed in Italy

www.monacellipress.com

10 9 8 7 6 5 4 3 2 1

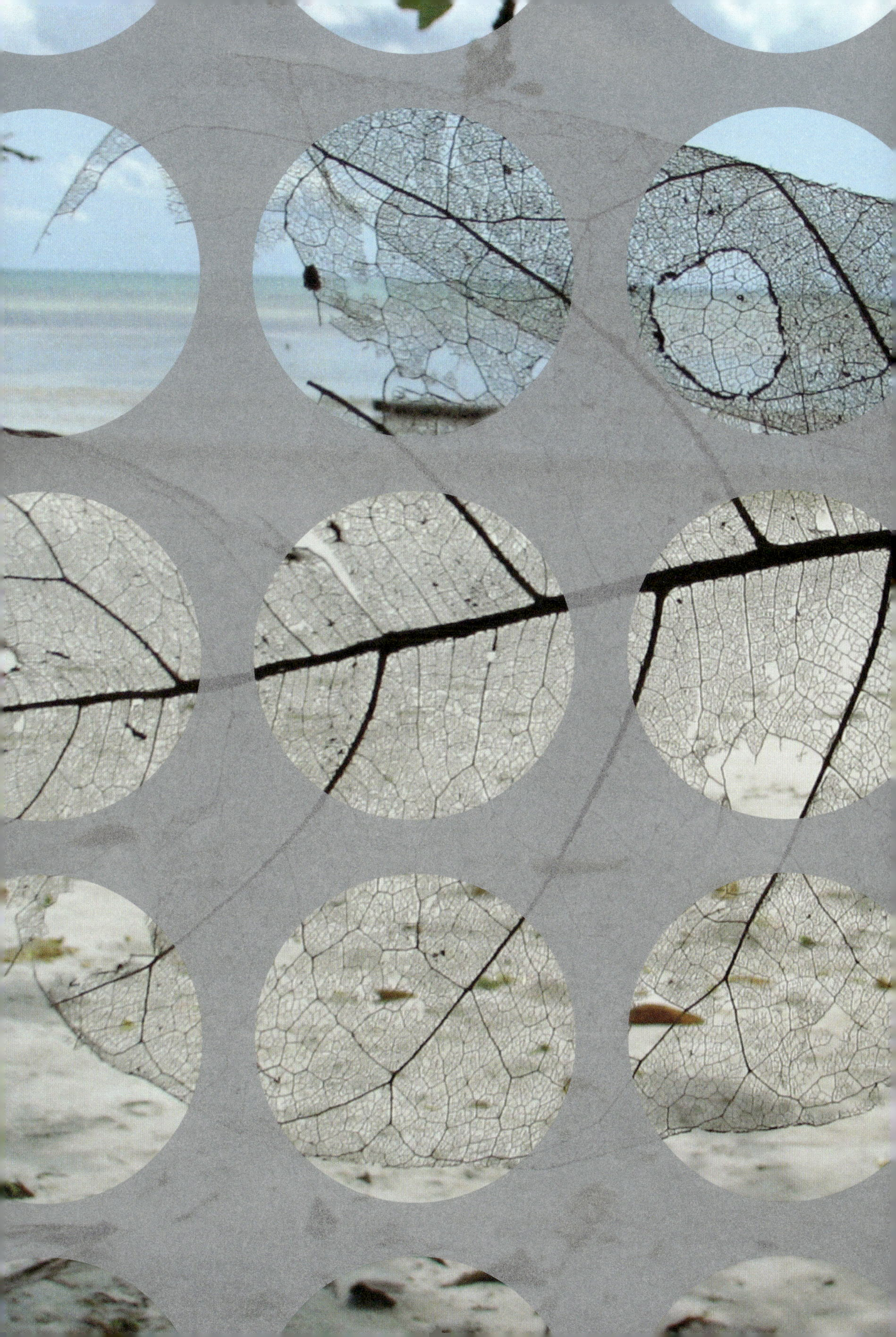

Invisible Presence

The Glass Pavilion, Toledo, USA 2002–2005
Light- and sound-regulating curtains and veils

Japanese Architects Come to Visit

One day in the summer of 2003, Kazuyo Sejima and Ryue Nishizawa walked into our studio with suitcases, straight from Amsterdam's Central Station. The two architects from Japan said, 'We are designing a pavilion for the Museum of Art in Toledo. The façade is entirely made of glass and we'd like you to create a curtain for the multipurpose room. We want a Petra curtain.'

We were delighted to be invited by SANAA, whose work I had followed closely over the years. I like their early projects – the very thin apartment slabs of Saishunkan Seiyaku Women's Dormitory, where each apartment reaches from the front to the back façade, and the Forest House, a tiny raised block between the trees – and respect the refined buildings that their office has produced since then.

Soon, we were looking at countless plans, drawings and photographs of the architectural models, and saw that the key concepts for this building were transparency and weightlessness. It was truly an ethereal building: a one-storey, square pavilion with rounded corners and a very thin, flat roof. Most of the interior volumes – exhibition spaces, restaurant, entrance hall and workshop – were transparent glass rooms, large bubbles enveloped by a continuous glass façade, with no visible frame or division of any kind. The organically shaped residual space between the interior glass bubbles contains the entrance hall. With the exception of a few technical rooms and storage spaces, the architects managed to keep the entire building transparent.

The Curtain's Role

When we start a project, we study the general situation first: the country, the region, the city, the area, the site. It's important for us to understand as much as possible about the conditions that surround the project – like invisible rings, they will influence the ideas that develop in the course of a commission. These conditions can be political, cultural, economic or social, but they are also about issues such as climate, light, sound, planting, local fashion, music, traffic behaviour, architecture or language. And, of course, the scale and character of the building in question and the future agenda for the spaces that are planned.

The building was projected in the middle of a small park with a very green lawn and elegant oak trees that will cast shadows over the building in spring and summer, less in autumn and winter when the trees are bare. This ethereal and transparent structure would be exposed to harsh climatic conditions and our worry was that all conventional methods to deal with issues such as glare, heat gain and insulation would typically undermine the elegance and fragility that would make the Glass Pavilion so unique.

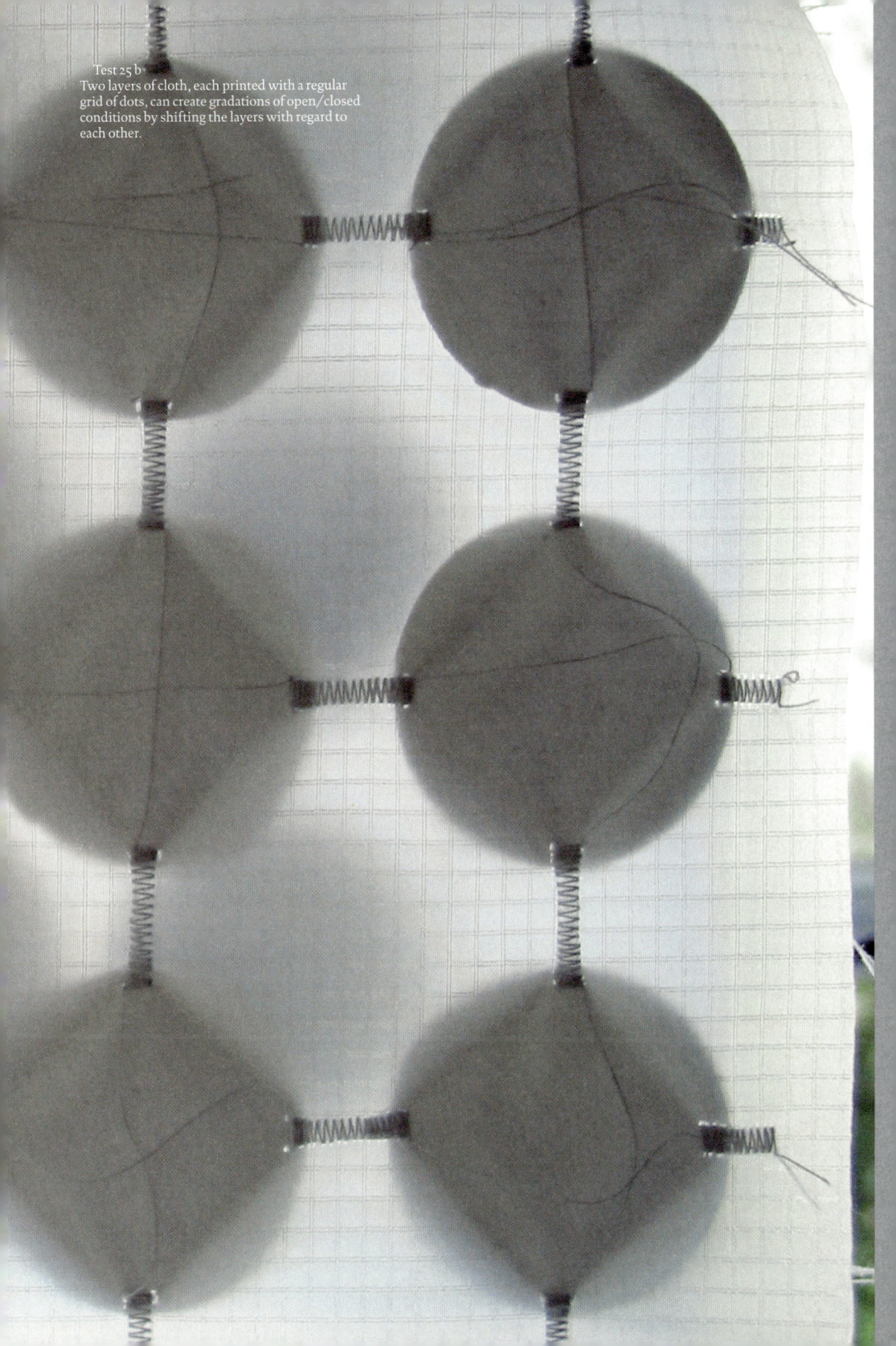

Test 25 b
Two layers of cloth, each printed with a regular grid of dots, can create gradations of open/closed conditions by shifting the layers with regard to each other.

In their public buildings with transparent façades, SANAA had solved climatic and lighting problems in a beautiful and effective way, using burnt, etched or printed glass. But for this museum in Toledo we understood, in the wordless communication that we would soon get accustomed to, that the architects were indeed searching for a new way to solve these issues.

Getting Acquainted

What is the range of possibilities and impossibilities that textile introduces? How dependent or independent will its performance be of the architecture?

Architects struggle to find materials that fit their design. They cringe at the idea of having to implement acoustic panels into the interiors, or put enormous air-conditioning systems into thin ceilings and walls; they shiver at the idea that a curtain's weight, tracks and motor systems will impose adjustments to the building's structure.

Curators have a phobia about ultraviolet radiation, light patches and vertical or horizontal lines – however thin and translucent – everywhere, especially when glass is used for the façades. They dislike any accidental shadow, colour or reflection cast by the surroundings that may disturb displays and threaten the collections. They will always choose museum grey, real walls and artificial light over 'openness' and daylight. Museum directors are burdened with their own issues to think of: the staff, the working circumstances, the collection and its growth and safety, the storage systems, their sponsors, the good name of the museum, its income flow, its political agenda, and so on. They need to force themselves to think generally, diplomatically and economically – both locally and globally.

Everybody has so many problems to solve and yet it seems to remain difficult for all the other parties involved in the project to envision the value of having cloth-covered façades, windows and openings, or to imagine that curtains can create extra spaces, form flexible walls and change the acoustics and the entire atmosphere. The truth is, textiles do solve a number of architectural issues in a simple and economic way. They answer many and varied demands and unveil many unconscious dreams. They can represent the city, the institution as much as the architecture itself, act like a real diplomat, changing face and tone according to the context, whether appearing powerful or almost inexistent. I felt that perhaps Inside Outside would be able to contribute a little more to this project than I had initially thought.

Multipurpose Curtains

In any case, we at Inside Outside concentrated on our multipurpose room commission, building a study model of the Glass Pavilion in its setting and concentrating on what the curtain could become. We flirted with the building's rounded corners, its thin roof, its two patios and the park.

In general, a curtain for a multipurpose room must perform many different tasks. At some times the room has to be dark, at others it needs bright daylight; at one time there is only one event, on another day there are two parties

Test 27-b
Thin fins of reflective material placed on transparent voile can shade an interior space to different levels, depending on their angle (direction of reflection and degree of openness) and width (reflective surface in relation to non-reflective surface).

Floor plan with representation of
technical demands per volume.

PRIMEX 1

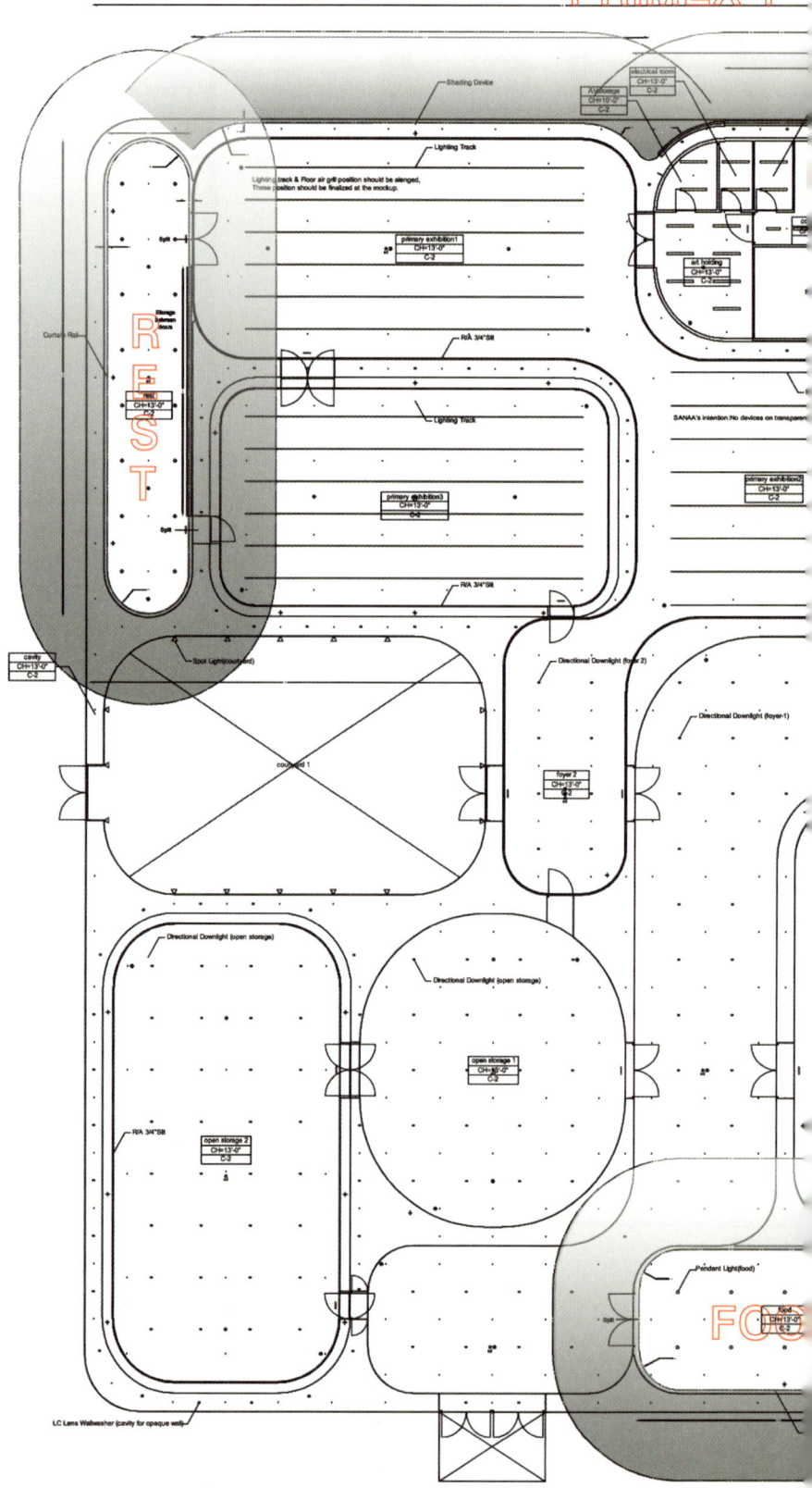

REST

FOO

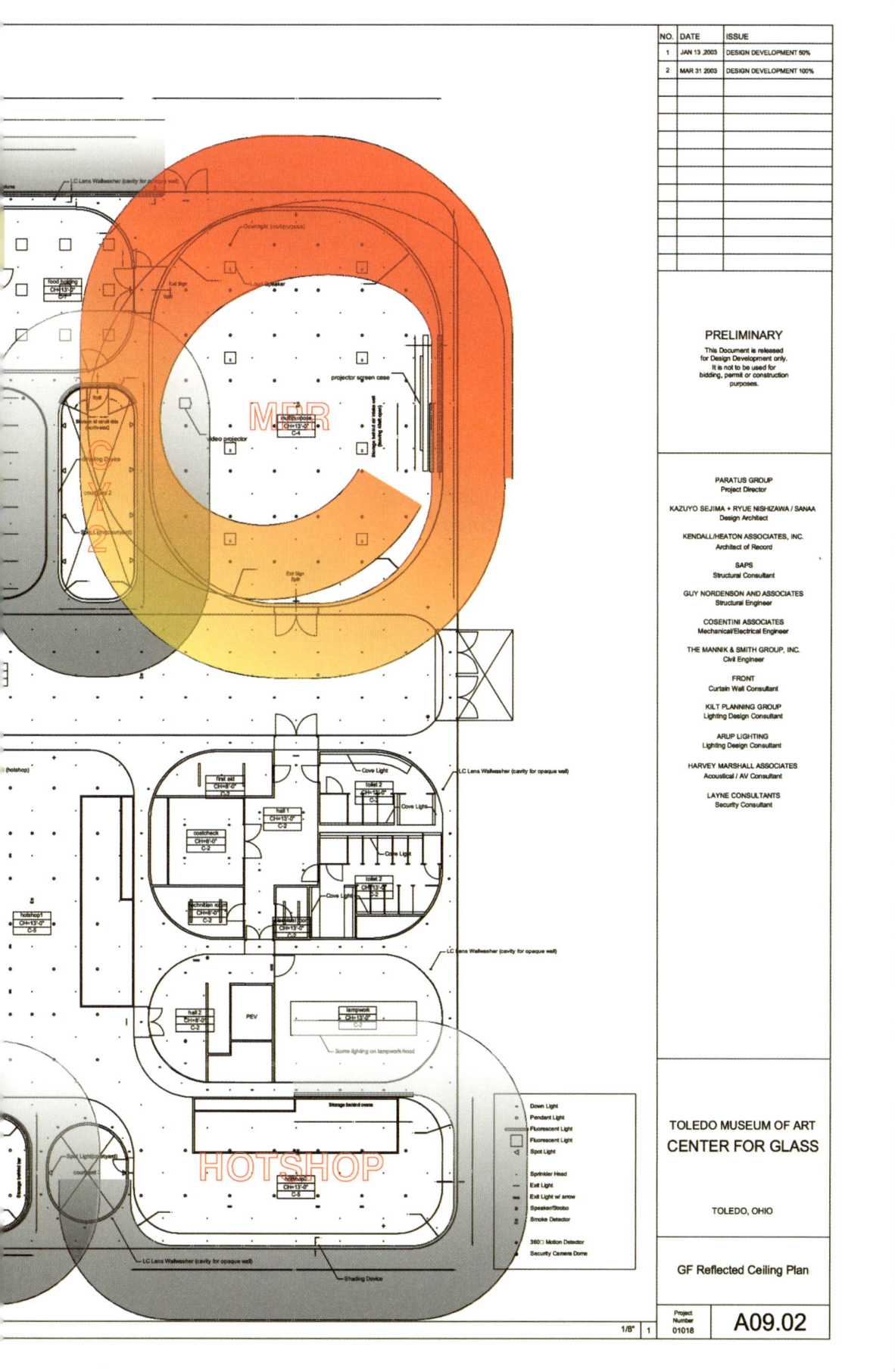

NO.	DATE	ISSUE
1	JAN 13, 2003	DESIGN DEVELOPMENT 50%
2	MAR 31 2003	DESIGN DEVELOPMENT 100%

PRELIMINARY

This Document is released
for Design Development only.
It is not to be used for
bidding, permit or construction
purposes.

PARATUS GROUP
Project Director

KAZUYO SEJIMA + RYUE NISHIZAWA / SANAA
Design Architect

KENDALL/HEATON ASSOCIATES, INC.
Architect of Record

SAPS
Structural Consultant

GUY NORDENSON AND ASSOCIATES
Structural Engineer

COSENTINI ASSOCIATES
Mechanical/Electrical Engineer

THE MANNIK & SMITH GROUP, INC.
Civil Engineer

FRONT
Curtain Wall Consultant

KILT PLANNING GROUP
Lighting Design Consultant

ARUP LIGHTING
Lighting Design Consultant

HARVEY MARSHALL ASSOCIATES
Acoustical / AV Consultant

LAYNE CONSULTANTS
Security Consultant

TOLEDO MUSEUM OF ART
CENTER FOR GLASS

TOLEDO, OHIO

GF Reflected Ceiling Plan

Project Number 01018

A09.02

sharing the same space. So a curtain for a multipurpose room needs to have complex acoustic, architectural and atmospheric qualities and robust physical characteristics to be able to perform during openings, concerts, presentations, dinners and many other activities for at least twelve to fifteen years.

Since the entire building would be made of glass, the multipurpose room curtain would define a considerable part of the Glass Pavilion's identity. We had to invisibly integrate numerous technical demands inside one glamorous and festive device that would represent the institution and, at the same time, complement this building's very special qualities.

Expanded Role

In 2003, I was invited to New York to present my work to the museum's director, Roger Berkowitz, the financial coordinator Andrew Klemmer, the architects and the lighting, acoustic and climate engineers. After my presentation, the director and the architects realized that, although the museum had anticipated a beautiful textile addition to the interior of its new Glass Pavilion, the project could also benefit from our experience with using textiles to create shading, filtering and cooling solutions. They understood that textiles can be used for flexible and changeable solutions, as opposed to the static techniques that SANAA had used in their glass buildings before.

I suggested that Inside Outside act as technical advisor. We could present a series of possible curtain solutions that would respond to the needs of the building's light and climate conditions, as well as to their curatorial wishes.

This would not only entail studies of textiles and specific techniques with which to complement the building's transparency and weightlessness, but also a search for original solutions with respect to their 'behaviour': the way these functional curtains would move along the façades and surround interior spaces, how they could appear and disappear, both literally and visually, through their level of transparency or opacity. This study would also include the configuration of the curtain tracks and the way in which they could be integrated into the architecture: recessed in ceilings, into walls or inside cavities.

The museum agreed and we became part of the existing research team, along with the engineers and the architects.

A Peripheral, Yet Central Issue

The museum would use the new pavilion to exhibit their antique and contemporary glass collection and to house temporary exhibitions. During a visit to Toledo, we were shown their collection, which ranged from the tiniest fragile vases from the prehistoric era to huge, colourful, contemporary objects. All of the exhibits had to be protected from ultraviolet rays and temperature swings. Daylight had to be filtered or dimmed to much lower, specified levels, so that the objects can be exhibited in precisely orchestrated conditions.

A thin and transparent or translucent sun-screening curtain can be an attractive solution as it can escape from – be independent of – the façade and literally disappear into cavities between volumes or inside walls. Also, by using

Test 38 a
Dramatic effect with minimal action: making a flat plane three-dimensional.

motorized systems, the density of each curtain can be programmed according to necessity: stretched for more transparency and light penetration; folded for a more opaque result. So we imagined we could solve nearly all problems with curtains that are completely transparent or translucent, colourless, flexible and elegant. And that without taking over the building or the artefacts – something that preoccupies architects and curators!

We also looked outside, to nature, for answers: to what extent could the trees relieve the lighting and cooling problems of this thin-roofed and glazed building? Shading is, after all, the simplest, most cost-effective way to cool an interior and reduce energy use. Especially deciduous trees like oaks, because they shade in summer when the sun is at its strongest, while allowing light and radiant heat to pass through in winter. But in winter, the sun is also at its lowest, penetrating deeper into the building. We made a study of the existing trees and, in order to protect the lower area of the building, suggested the placement of strategically positioned additional trees and shrubs of various heights and densities, both in the park and in the two patios inside the building.

The whole effort made me think of the OMA exhibitions I designed with photographer Hans Werlemann and sound technician Claudi Cornasz in the early nineties. In these installations, we simulated exactly what we needed to prevent in the Toledo project: natural sunlight. We installed huge lamps outside on the roof to inject light through the existing skylights or on the other side of the street to beam light inwards through the gallery windows, as a means to light the exhibition spaces. This had the astounding effect of bright, sunny daylight, sometimes casting shadows, sometimes just booming up the atmosphere – very optimistic and beautiful – adding materiality to the objects and giving more radiance to OMA's work: exactly what we wanted to add to their architecture!

A few months into the Toledo project, the museum director and the architects became so intrigued by the concept of 'curtain' that, together with the financial director of the project, they visited our studio in Amsterdam several times. They seemed totally excited and charmed by the idea that you can combine the beauty of textiles with technical performance.

Life-Size Testing

After studying all the drawings and reading every technical report, we started to make a systematic series of samples, searching for subtle solutions for the lighting, air and cooling demands of the engineers. We tried out different shades of colour, greys, silvers and golds, together with all kinds of techniques. We tried to imagine the space, the objects, the feel of the materials, the shadow play of the trees, the weather, light changes and the visitor's mentality.

We studied the colour and thickness of the glass panels, the shades added by filters within the glass. We measured and analysed the distances between layers of glass, between façade and inner volumes, between lamps and curtains. We examined the colour and finish of concrete floors, ceiling and walls, doors and signage. We studied the temperatures of heaters and coolers, the placement

Test 25 h
Dictated percentage of reflecting surface translated into form.

Initial model with trees to check impact on
interior shading; first curtain colour studies.

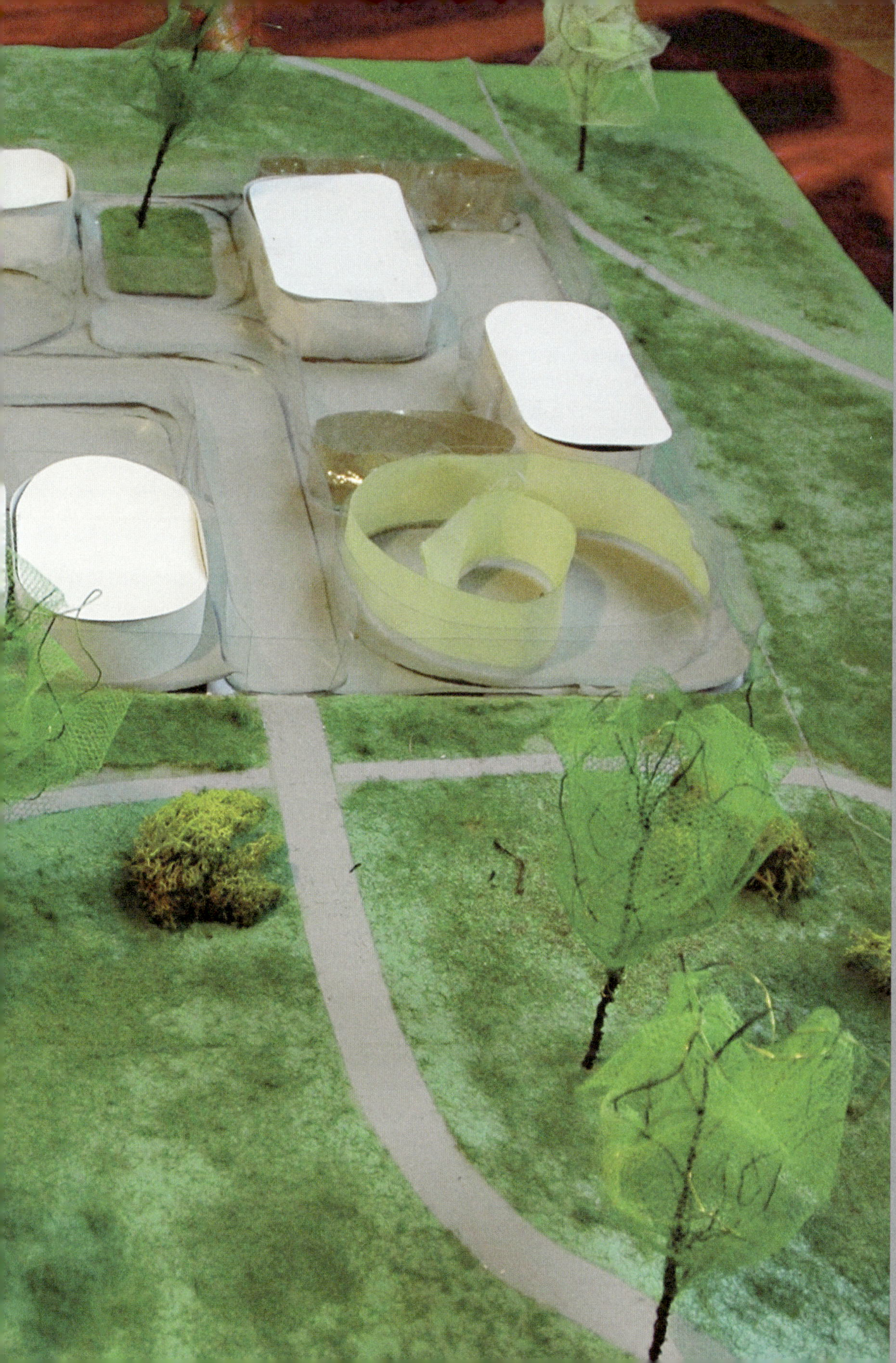

and sizes of sprinklers, sound boxes, columns and exit signs. And of course we took the form and sizes of the museum's showcases into consideration. Through testing, manipulating and layering materials and techniques, we found a series of solutions that we thought could work technically and at the same time embellish both the spaces and the museum's glass collection.

During the construction drawing (CD) phase, the Museum constructed a one-to-one (1:1) mock-up of the building, close to the site. This was incredibly luxurious and useful. It included a typical piece of the glass façade, the roof equipped with an exterior lighting system, one transparent and one opaque interior volume, the actual ceiling with the lights, the rounded curtain tracks, and even a few versions of the concrete floor! So every element was installed 'for real', down to the thin silicone connection injected between the glass panels. They were all to be critically studied and commented on by the entire team. Everyone – the director, architects, consultants and builders – was there to review it, and the curtains were as carefully reviewed as all the other architectural elements and details.

The mock-up was really a fantastic testing tool. The interesting thing was that, in our studio, we always produce 1:1 mock-ups – fragments of the real thing – but we had never seen architects do the same. With architects, we are used to having to wait until construction starts to do our decisive tests, on site, in helmets and boots, balancing on ladders, hanging our drapes between scaffoldings and judging them by dim construction lights – always in a hurry because we are 'holding up' the process. The rest is prediction through tiny pieces of paper or silk scraps inside the architect's models!

We can usually foresee the end result quite well. But in the 1:1 mock-up in Toledo, the effect of the sun-screening curtains proved much more sensitive than we'd initially imagined. During this first mock-up session on site, the whole relationship of the components was suddenly revealed to me: 'Okay, out, out, out! It looks quite nice but definitely not for this project.' The scrutinizing went on and on until we had only two or three examples left that might work.

Plus and Minus Theory

Our initial design proposed translucent curtains in various tones of white, silver, grey and gold. Some were layered, some were punctured and others were printed with subtle *ton sur ton*. But after our tests in the Toledo mock-up, we concluded that we should choose a very sober series of light grey voile curtains, coated with aluminium on the exterior to reflect the sun. Ideally, they should be so transparent and weightless that from the outside you would not see them as a mass, and from the inside they would leave the view of the park open without toning down the sheen and colours of the exhibits. The textiles we proposed had, in themselves, no character at all, so we combined different degrees of transparency and weave, making the material look slightly different – the cloth a bit more opaque, or the weave a bit less smooth – from area to area. We also proposed to add something very subtle to

Sample tests in 1:1 building mock-up in Toledo: Sejima-san behind Verosol 818.

the 'zero line', that is, the lower seam that runs just above the floor surface: tiny dots that mimic the grass outside. We also wanted to influence the structure of the cloth itself, for instance by having it creased beforehand to make it look like paper. Details that are barely visible may nevertheless give the textiles something extra!

Imagine yourself approaching the pavilion from the outside, seeing not only glass, but something reflecting and moving – be it colour or figure. It could be creases that perform a subtle shadow play. It could be tiny silver dots printed just along the bottom seam of the textile, looking like grass. Silver on silver, hardly visible, catching light in a very subtle way ... Then imagine yourself being inside, with that same effect but more subtle, as the light is stronger outside than inside: a barely visible play of shadow that draws your attention to the lower seam, not in the view line of the exhibited objects, but much lower, where the curtain touches the ground ... shadows of grass.

The idea of flexibility and change achieved with one single neutral cloth was appealing to the museum; the addition of subtle decoration at the lower seam, however, was not in line with the museum curator's mentality.

The Pleats' Algorithm

We normally prefer pleats to be 'free' as opposed to predetermined, due to varying acoustic demands, as they are usually an important tool in ensuring acoustic absorbance.[1] But we'd never worked with pleats as a mechanical tool with which to orchestrate light before. Here in Toledo, we wanted to use the pleat to methodically darken a space to different degrees.

One thing that excited us was that our role inside the team, as researchers of light and shade, made us move away from our normal working method. Although we were used to integrating complex and often contradictory demands into our designs, here aesthetics truly took the back seat! We developed a rational programme with the expertise of the rest of the technical team.

Our major worry was not the pleating itself, but the visual effect a pleated vertical surface of transparent or translucent textile would have on the building's interior: depending on the weather, the pleats would cast vertical, striped shadows onto the floors and the objects inside. When the pleats were closed, however, when thoroughly folded one over the other, this effect would vanish.

To measure the exact cooling and darkening degree of the textiles that we had in mind, we explored – with lighting and climate engineer Matthias Schuler – how different degrees of weaving density, combined with pleating and positioned between two layers of glass, would affect the interior. How much shading would it bring? How much would it contribute to cooling? What problems would we encounter? Nishizawa-san was fascinated by the fact that such thin cloth can perform various tasks according to the way it is pleated.

We developed a combination of mechanisms to fold the pleats in a strictly methodical way. With Gerriets GmbH in Germany we were able to shrink their smallest existing track motors (motors that run along the curtain track)

1. To achieve maximum acoustic absorbance of a thin cloth, you need heavy pleating. By doing this, however, the reflectivity level of the cloth – towards the sun – is marginalized because the surface folds sideways and inward, minimizing the reflective surface. For maximum sun reflection and cooling, you need to hang the cloth as close to the façade as possible, stretching it out to a flat to almost flat surface; this, however, gives zero acoustic absorbance.

Test 43 c
Tiny dots along the lower seam of Baumann Protect 2/colour 154. For a bit of lively but reduced reflection.

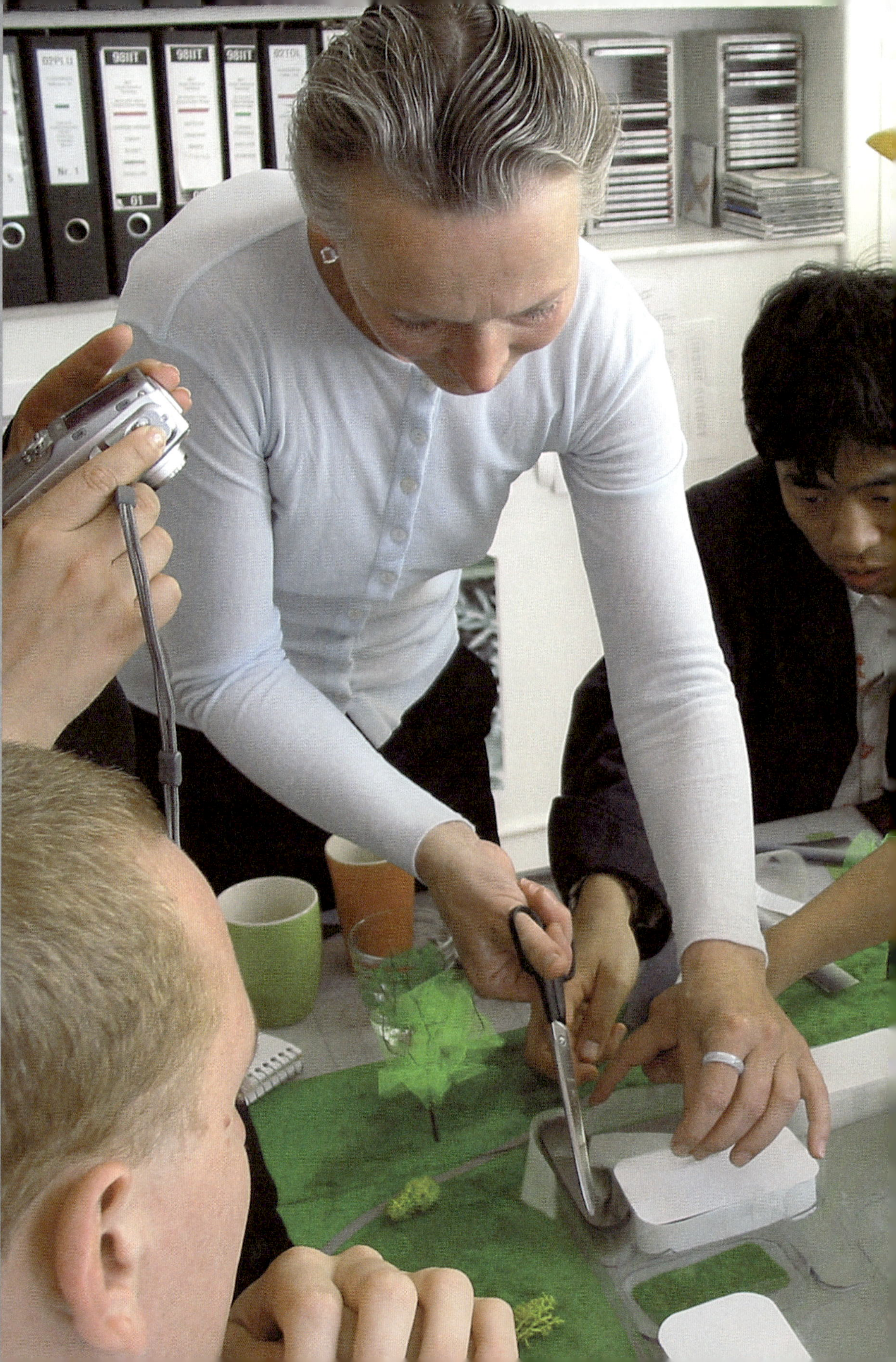

At work with architects, light engineer and museum director at Inside Outside studio: schematic phase.

to an even smaller size (and to introduce white and light grey replacements for the black carriers): we didn't want to disturb the elegance of the thin roof. By connecting the motors to both outer ends of a curtain, they could either pull or push the curtain in two directions, or more importantly, roll up or pull a metal cord loop in two directions according to a strict computerized program. This cord was to be woven through and connected to the carriers of the curtain that were themselves connected to metal 'sticks' – each as long as the pleat's depth: 12.5 cm – that were implemented inside the top seam of the curtain. By shifting the direction of these sticks through the cord that would turn the carriers, the position of the pleats would change simultaneously with equal intensity from the open position to the closed position, overlapping in such a way that no vertical shadow lines would show.

<u>The Freedom of the Perfect Zero</u>

Then Matthias measured the pleated curtain's effect on the interior temperature and found out that if you have the closed pleats that are ideal for darkening, you get air chambers that heat up, which is unacceptable. The pleats need to stay open in two directions to give the right degree of cooling, thus limiting their darkening effect and reintroducing the possibility of shadow lines. This discovery undermined our entire concept.[2]

So, at a certain point – I think it was in the spring of 2004, after two years of work – we felt we had reached the point of 'perfect nothing'. So many ideas, discoveries, tryouts, measurements, tests and counter tests and the invention of new and better solutions (from specially made tracks, motors and carriers to invisible prints, stitches, layers, seams, connections, pleats, folds, sheens, pinpoint holes, cuts, slits, weaves, threads, metals, powders and colours) all bouncing back again and again against shifting technical or curatorial reasoning. Which is fine, but it stripped us bare and left our brains and hands empty.

We wanted so much to avoid the existing, dull, unplayful, static sun reflective and darkening textiles that will simply do their job, making the building heavy and solid when they are used!

But our negativity lasted only moments, as we decided to consider our situation as the perfect zero! Everyone knows that when you reach the perfect zero, you have regained freedom. You breathe in and out deeply, renew yourself and your environment and continue on in a new direction.

And so here in Toledo, we knew that although there was seemingly nothing left for us to do but recommend the right cloth – which we had done – and hang them on the wrong tracks – which we hadn't chosen, we could certainly add something that is invisible to the normal eye but essential to that of the professional. Just invent something that adds a slight touch of beauty, a scratch of smart solution that will give each single curtain a new and unexpected quality. What an exciting notion! All our attention turned to meticulous details along the lower seam and the top edge airflow.

2. It seems we wanted to achieve the impossible: we tried to use very thin, transparent textile as a darkening tool by amassing the cloth into a heavily pleated surface when darkening was asked for; changing it from transparent to different levels of translucency and opaqueness, depending on the intensity of pleat. Conceptually this is as exciting an idea as knitting the thinnest tulle into a massive wall (test for Vitra). But we also needed its reflectivity – its cooling quality – to function, and that didn't work (see footnote 1). So we were forced to change our direction from conceptual to practical: choose a cloth that in itself is darkening to the maximum given levels (expressed in 'foot candle' measures), so that nothing was left to chance…

Translucency and light-effect test with Baumann Protect 2/colour 154.

The Real World

In Spring 2004, Inside Outside had finished their research and design proposals for sun-screening and multipurpose curtains for the Toledo Glass Pavilion as stated in their '80%' contract.[3]

After the new director was appointed in that same year and we had reached the famous zero point, an 'RFQ' (request for quote) for the Glass Pavilion curtains was formulated in October 2005. This RFQ, addressed to both Inside Outside, Amsterdam and to a New York-based curtain designer, asked us to bid for the finalization of all sun-screening curtains and a new design for the multipurpose room curtains. An anonymous commission would judge our seam-detailing qualities as well as our price value, and so we were requested to send a series of detailed samples; based on the sun-screen textiles, airflow and track configurations that we, after two and a half years of research and collaboration, had proven to be right for the Glass Pavilion.

My first instinct was that this new move, the initiative of the new director, was not to organize a fair 'tender', but was probably a purely strategic move. So I called our American 'colleague' and proposed a collaboration to confront the TMA director and his staff with our mutual professional loyalty. I think I surprised the person at the other end quite a bit! Silence ... Then he told me that his studio had been visited by the museum several times in the previous year and shocked me with the news that the images of all our work had been shown to him. I soon realized that the competitor had no faith in a creative collaboration. Indeed, he admitted that he wanted the job for himself. How naïve a moralist can one be, indeed, I asked myself ...

So Inside Outside put meticulously detailed samples in beautiful wrappings, accompanied by a carefully designed booklet that included the most economic budget proposal thinkable, and then sent the package from Amsterdam to Toledo, Ohio, by Federal Express. The story of our battle could shed light on the reality of the cultural world of today, but this would require a whole new chapter ...

3. It happens that a commission spans one to five or six years. The process of designing in itself doesn't need years, but we need to follow the entire timeline because the perspective tends to change over time: an idea that might look perfect at one point might need adjustments by the time the building starts to take shape; by the time all materials or furniture is chosen; or if there is a change in staff or a shift in economic resources. Tracks and motors (defining the positioning and the trajectory of curtains); and maximum weights and characteristics of curtains need to be decided in an early stage as these influence the building's structural organization. But the final details and colours of a cloth can be decided later in the process. That's why we agreed with the client to sign an 80%DD (Design Development) contract to pursue up to 80% of the design, so that most things could be defined and agreed to, yet leaving space for adjustments towards the completion of the project.

Test 52 f:
Everyone knows that when you reach the perfect zero, you have regained freedom. Last exchange with client: seam and stitch quality.

Test 34 d
Silk-screened white dots on one side of the white tulle (facing out), golden dots slightly shifted on the other (facing in): an elegant thin layer encircling the oval living room, but too present for this project.

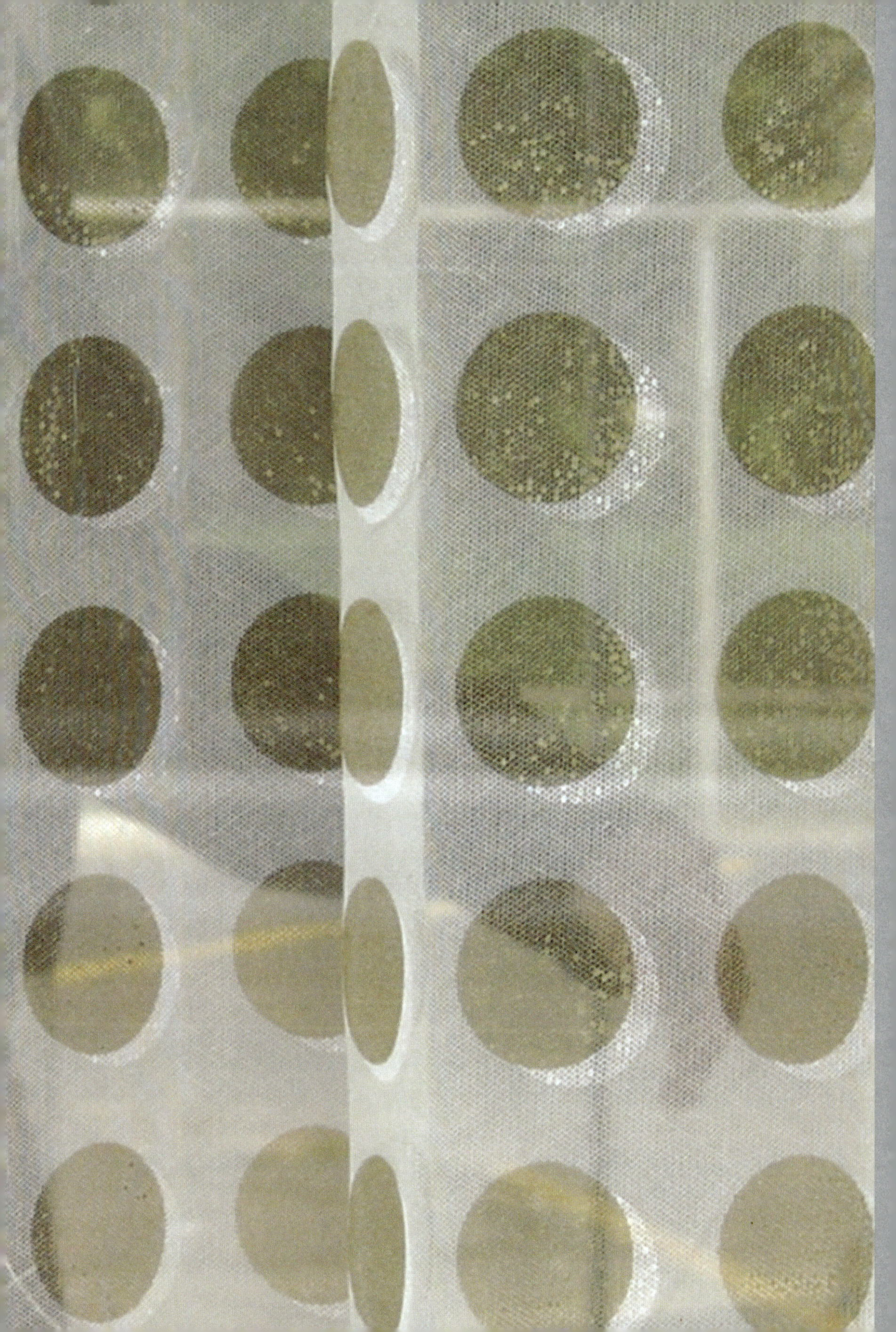

Two white/silver blackout curtain proposals side by side: schematic phase samples in 1:1 mock-up studied by the architects, favouring the large flower pattern (we would use a local flower drawing if this concept was accepted).

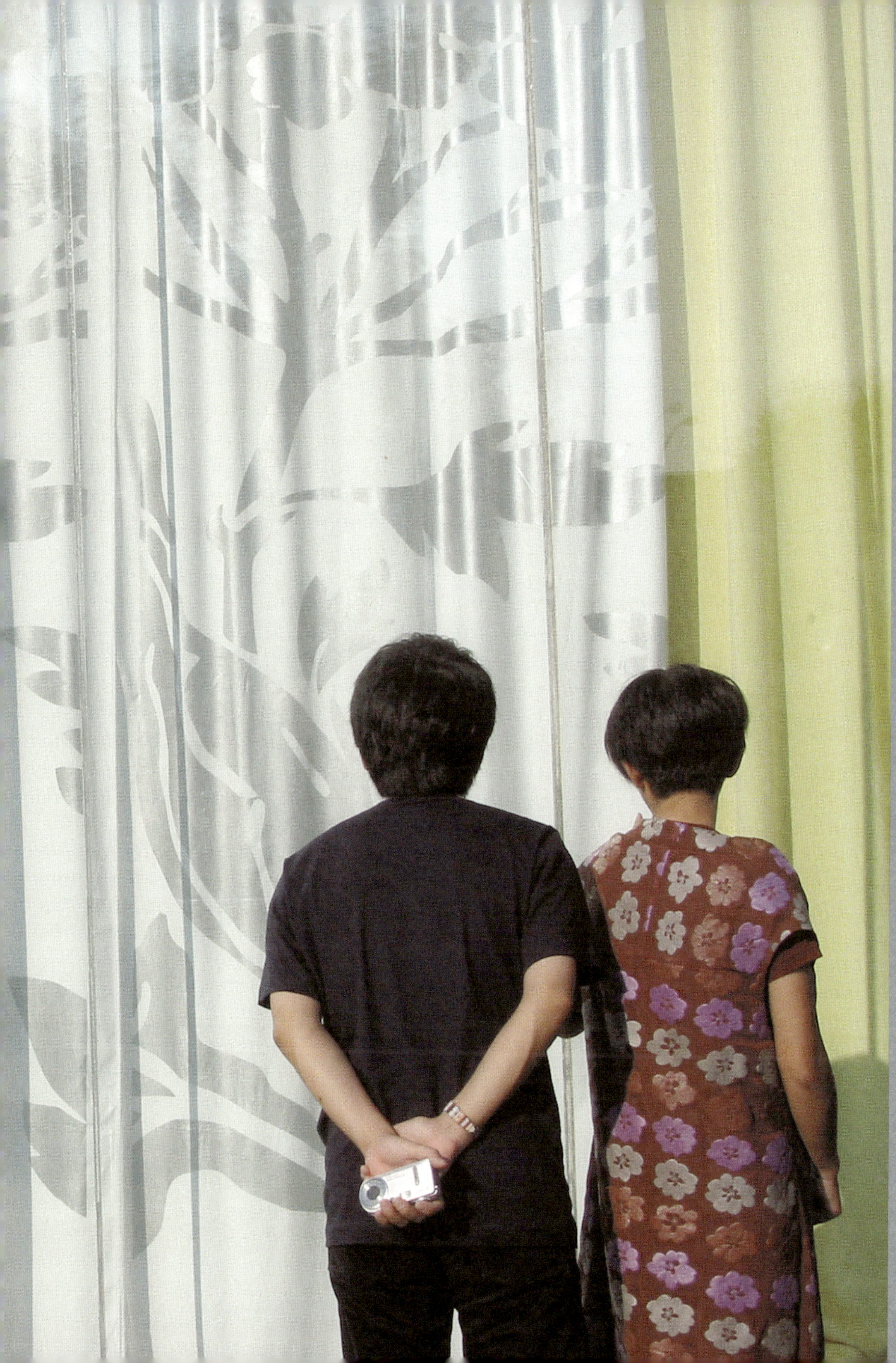

View into 1:1 mock-up interior, showing the glass 'bubbles' inside the glass volume at night. Notice the vertical seams of the glass plates and the thin columns: our voile seams needed 24 tests to prove that they were hardly visible. Standing inside, the rounded corners act like disorienting distorting mirrors at night. The team wondered how to neutralize this effect with an invisible intervention . . . a thin voile or a self-adhesive filter?

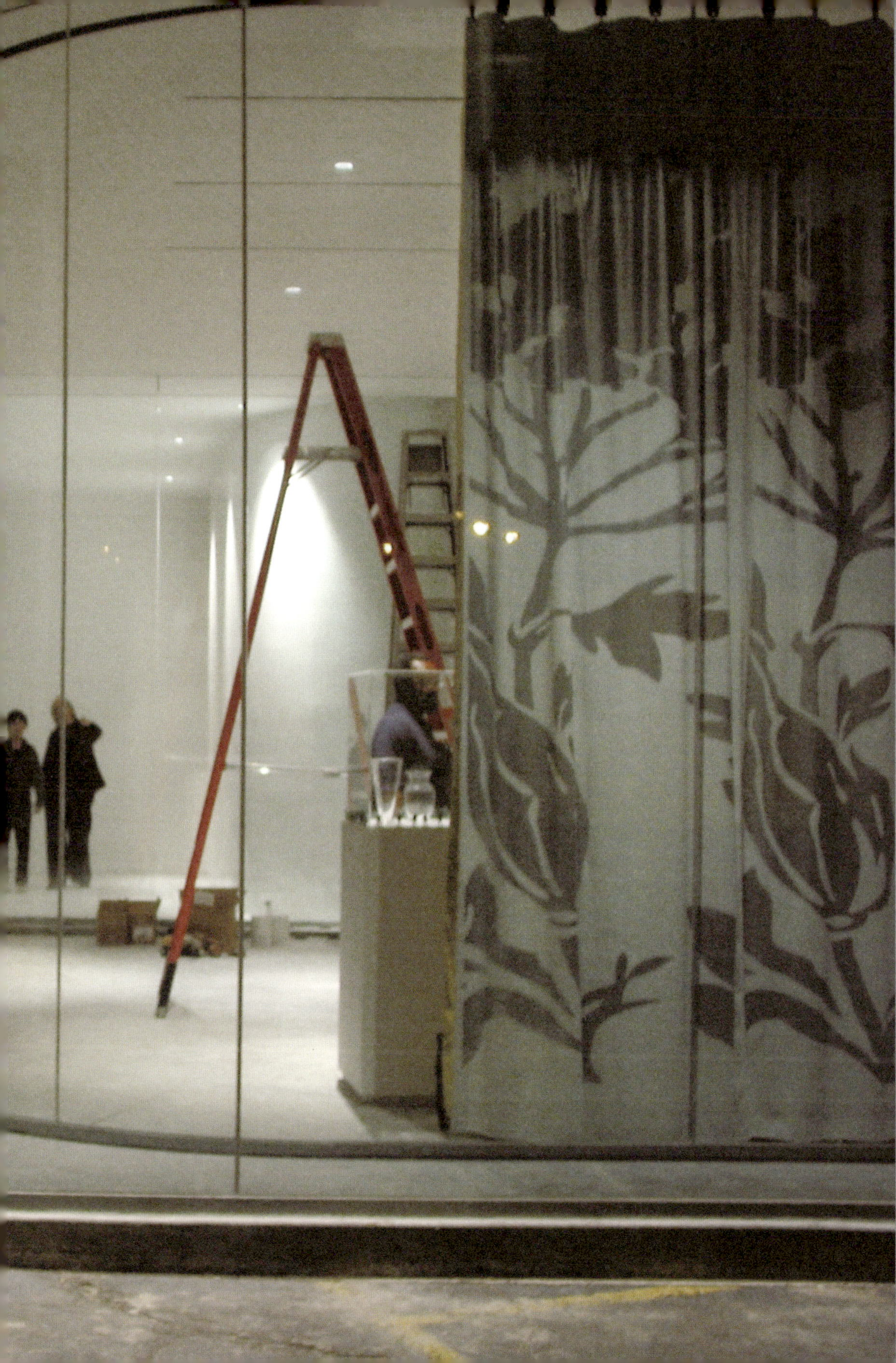

Die Welt ist alles, was der Fall ist – The Limits of the World are also its Limits
Chris Dercon

Aversion

In 1925, the fabulously wealthy Margaret Stonborough-Wittgenstein asked her younger brother Ludwig whether he could build a town house for her in the middle of Vienna. A mechanical engineer, Ludwig Wittgenstein, who was to become a world-renowned philosopher, had never had anything meaningful to say about architecture until then, and he had never designed an actual building. However, his most famous philosophical work opens with this sentence: *Die Welt is alles, was der Fall ist* – 'The limits of the world are also its limits.' From 1926 to 1928, Ludwig Wittgenstein was charged with the construction of an immense villa for his sister in Vienna's stately third *Bezirk*, between Kundmanngasse and Parkgasse. Wittgenstein expert Paul Wijdeveld has described the architectural exercise of the famous thinker as a 'purifying gesture' – here an autodidact had produced one of modern architecture's most radical structures. The influence of family friend and ornament-hater Adolf Loos is unmistakable: a severely reductive architecture, as regards exterior as well as interior work. Wittgenstein's aversion to the ornament, to every form of decorative addition, surpassed even that of Loos. Bare, 200-watt light bulbs were all that was permitted, and nothing else; certainly no curtains or other upholstery behind the many windows or between and within the large spaces. Green was all that was permitted in the garden; flowering plants were taboo. Ludwig Wittgenstein the architect would never have had any work for someone like Petra Blaisse, who is an enthusiast, designer and champion of such decorative additions and interventions. However, the pronouncement of Ludwig Wittgenstein the philosopher – *Die Welt ist alles, was der Fall ist* – perfectly describes Petra Blaisse's career and most particularly her working methods and wide-ranging oeuvre. The total architectural reduction and transparency pursued by Wittgenstein in his architecture are no myth. Perhaps his aversion to architectural concealments and disclosures – veilings and unveilings – also anticipated the concluding statement of his *Tractatus Logico-Philosophicus*: 'Whereof one cannot speak, thereof one must remain silent.'

Remaining Silent

What did the textile applications in Bauhaus architecture and the architecture of the International Style from that same era look like? In their historic proclamations and subtle interpretations concerning the concepts of 'literal and phenomenal transparency', leading architectural theoreticians like Colin Rowe and Robert Slutzky do not utter a word about such exciting and yet highly necessary textile additions as curtains. Even in photographic illustrations, such 'details' are usually avoided by these and other historians of modern architecture. In Rowe and Slutzky's comparison of the Bauhaus workshop wing in Dessau by Gropius and Le Corbusier's villa at Garches they wrote: 'Recognizing the physical plane of glass and concrete and this imaginary (though scarcely less real) plane that lies behind it, we become aware that here a transparency is effected not through the agency of a window but rather through our being made conscious of primary concepts which interpenetrate without optical destruction of each other.' To this we might add that, whereas Le Corbusier chiefly employed glass as pure surface, the curtains that are clearly visible on historical photographs by no means interfere with his cherished 'cubist' transparency. On the contrary, they add a 'primary image' to the building, an additional, diffuse transparency. Indeed, the fact that one does not preclude the other – whether actual or metaphorical transparency – is demonstrated by the results of the frequent architectural collaborations between Petra Blaisse the designer and Rem Koolhaas the architect. This is also demonstrated by the medial representations of Blaisse's material 'interventions' in the architecture of Rem Koolhaas. Are there one or more possible explanations for the embarrassment of those days? Most certainly! At the same time, such explanations also present an opportunity to better understand the 'origins' of the textile 'additions' by Blaisse.

Otherness

The radical, modernistic European architecture of the 1920s and '30s often integrated elements that directly or indirectly referred to the architectural culture of North Africa and the Middle East, as clearly demonstrated by the Weissenhofsiedlung housing estate realized in Stuttgart in 1927. There were other 'Arabizing' influences to be discovered besides the bare, white walls, ranging from flat roofs to large terraces and *pilotis*. However, when such adaptations met with criticism in pre-Nazi Germany, designers proceeded with greater discretion. The racist attacks on the 'otherness' of the Weissenhofsiedlung and its actual content were indeed a matter of course. These attacks could, for example, be seen and read in the form of caricatured collages: portraits of men and women in Arabian attire, including traditional domestic and working animals such as camels, were used to represent an Arabic village scene that was enacted in ... Stuttgart. The men traded oriental carpets – what else? – in the street, in the open air. Such caricatures of the Weissenhofsiedlung were echoed in critiques of other modernist housing projects: the housing by Ernst May in Frankfurt was derisively referred to as 'New Morocco', and the project in Pessac by Le Corbusier acquired the nickname 'the Casbah', despite the fact that his 'Mediterranean' villas near Paris were very well received. These and other housing projects were even compared with the Arabian pavilions at the large-scale world fairs and with the specialized Arabian or so-called Mohammedan exhibitions that were held in Stockholm, Paris and Munich around the turn of the twentieth century. However, the Arabian pavilions and exhibitions enjoyed plenty of support among progressive, curious, cosmopolitan and predominantly European artists, arts and crafts specialists, and architects. They discovered, for example, the 'modern' allure of age-old uses of oriental 'curtains', such as the *hajib* in the throne room of the caliph and the *sutra* that surrounds sun-drenched terraces. The most sacred Muslim pilgrim shrine, the Kaaba in Mecca, is covered with the *kiswa*, a gigantic black cloth, and – not to be forgotten – there is the sophistication of the everyday *mashrabiyya*, the perforated wooden screen, a decorated, semi-transparent window that traditionally divides and distinguishes interior and exterior space. Such material expressions of the mysterious tension between the seen and the unseen had already been commended in 1860 by Gottfried Semper in his 'Theory of Dressing' in the first volume of *Style: Style in the Technical and Tectonic Arts; Or, Practical Aesthetics*.

The 'Other'

Nevertheless, the great enthusiasm for a truly international architecture and all its derivatives soon made way for the 'enclosure' of the International Style. After the interpretation of the bare white wall as a problem of 'blood and soil', that same white wall suddenly presented the solution: the problem of identity could be glossed over by the so-called neutrality of the plain white surface. And ... the white wall was understood as a veil, to hide the severe, rational and technological basis of modernist architecture. It seems that most modern architects and architectural theoreticians, before and after the Second World War, were still afraid to go as far as Ludwig Mies van der Rohe with his Farnsworth House (1945-1950), where he introduced a much more sensuous veil. Inseparably linked with dematerialized transparency, Mies presents a materialized transparency of gauze and fabric, a kind of 'house dressing'. The same sensuousness can already be found in the German Pavilion that Mies designed for the 1929 International Exhibition in Barcelona, in the guise of a floor-to-ceiling curtain with deep folds in a warm colour. And this time the 'coverings' are also clearly identifiable in the photographs. It is also appropriate to talk about 'house dressing' in the case of the coverings and spatial subdivisions that Petra Blaisse achieves using fabrics. However, Blaisse takes this a step further, for example when she deliberately contradicts the instrumental rationality of the architectonic design by introducing generous curves, circles or ovals. This is how Blaisse creates space for 'otherness': there is no longer any fear of the exotic and sophistication, in short, for the culture of the 'Other'.

Weaving Women

The example of the encircling drapes in colourful silk and velvet for the 'Samt und Seide' cafe by Mies and his Werkbund colleague Lilly Reich, for the 1927 exhibition 'Die Mode der Dame' (Women's Fashion) at the Funkturmhalle in Berlin is always hovering in the wings. The flexible, undulating walls of pleated fabrics were an innovation of Mies and Reich: the glass wall was all of a sudden replaced by textile. It was only thanks to the frequent invitations to stage presentations at industrial exhibitions that Mies van der Rohe and Lilly Reich were able to adapt existing textile and upholstery techniques and experiment with them on a large scale. Petra Blaisse also depends to a large extent on the nature and scope of commissions in order to be able to experiment with new materials. And there is always the issue of whether clients are also interested – financially – in her surprising interventions. Even in this respect, textiles – Blaisse herself talks about 'materials' – are still about designing 'otherness' and they are still fabricated by the 'Other'.

It is nonsense to claim that there was no interest in new textile applications at the Bauhaus. Besides the well-nigh woman-unfriendly Bauhaus environment, the explanation for the 'lag' of the Bauhaus in the field of curtains and other textile coverings should primarily be sought in the sophisticated techniques and sizeable production capacity necessary for the development of functional textiles and fabrics sold by the metre, such as curtains. That everyday reality was something more than a preoccupation for the only Bauhaus 'master', Gunta Stölzl. The closure of the Weimar Bauhaus in 1925 did not prompt a positive shift in this state of affairs. Even in Dessau, Gunta Stölzl, who was in charge of the *Textilwerkstatt* ('Textiles Workshop'), could make little progress at first: her weaving women had no choice but to remain far removed from the developments in the rest of the Bauhaus. The *Textilwerkstatt* was taken more seriously only after the opening of the architecture department in 1927, which meant much more attention could be devoted to space-defining, architectural textiles. After all, the large, glass walls and bare white spaces of the new architects required effective shading from daylight and from prying eyes and, not to be forgotten, wall coverings – washable! – as well as textiles – soft! – to improve the acoustics. Oskar Schlemmer noted that the essential task in the construction and interior design of housing was to reintroduce the visual. The fabrics designed under Stölzl's supervision are rich in colour, feature coarse structured patterns, sometimes display dazzling bright sections against a dark background, and occasionally 'they sparkle like silver', as Amédée Ozenfant noted in admiration. These and other accounts reiterate what a loss it is that the textiles created by the weaving women have largely disappeared from accounts of the Bauhaus tradition. It is a pity because certain characteristics of the *Bauhaus-Vorhänge* – the Bauhaus curtains and drapes – from Gunta Stölzl's workshop could in fact be seen as precursors or examples for the way in which Petra Blaisse works with coarse surfaces, shimmering fabrics and highly distinctive combinations of diverse materials and techniques.

Chris Dercon

Ludwig Wittgenstein with Paul Engelmann, *Stonborough-Wittgenstein House*. Vienna, 1926–1928.

The Descent from the Cross (detail), Peter Paul Rubens, 1611–1614.

Wooden *mashrabiyya* screen at the entrance of a mausoleum.

Mies van der Rohe, *Farnsworth House*. Plano, Illinois, USA, 1946–1950.

Mies van der Rohe and Lilly Reich, *The Velvet and Silk Café,* Women's Fashion Exhibition, Berlin, 1927.

Gunta Stölzl, detail of wall hanging, 1923. Collection of Kunstsammlungen, Weimar.

The Fold

It is a fact that historians of modern architecture have not been very adept at handling the fold of fabrics, nor folds in general. It wasn't always like this. The notion of the 'fold' is familiar from the philosopher Gilles Deleuze's *The Fold: Leibniz and the Baroque* and, as transmitted via Deleuze, from the great universal thinker of the Baroque era, Gottfried Wilhelm Leibniz. The concept of the fold can be traced back to Leibniz and his essay, 'Principles of Nature and Grace, Based on Reason' (1714). In the margins of an unpublished manifesto from 1685, Leibniz even sketched a little drawing of *Strumpfbandknoten* – 'garter knots'. The philosopher was profoundly fascinated by everything that even resembled a fold. Leibniz wrote that one could only know the beauty of the universe in each soul 'if one could unfold all of its folds'. For Deleuze the fold is the Baroque era's greatest contribution to the arts and the core of Leibniz's philosophical principles. After all, the sensuality of the fold stimulates the representation of abstract ideas and concepts. The fold therefore embodies the transition from the 'inexplicit' to the 'explicit'. That is why the 'Theatre of Nature and Art' is regarded by contemporary scholars of visual studies such as Horst Bredekamp as a heightening – a performative staging – of the illustrative. The frequent occurrence of images of folded and pleated fabrics in Baroque art is an instance of this. However, Leibniz himself provides the most telling example: 'What we sense is only a certain resultant to which we are habituated, and we are not able to distinguish the things that enter into the resultant because of their multitude, just as when one hears the noise of the sea from afar, one does not discern what each wave does, even though each wave has an effect on our ears.' Leibniz also implies that the noise is the signal of the fold. The folds in Petra Blaisse's fabrics are no different: they make noise. They appear like folds in the soul, in the soul of a building. In *The Fold: Leibniz and the Baroque*, Deleuze tells us that what is folded is the enclosed, the inherent, and that what is folded only exists in an envelope, in what it envelops: 'A fold is always folded within a fold, like a cavern in a cavern.' For Petra Blaisse, all of this, from folds to knots, is acceptable and normal because, to return to Wittgenstein, '*Der Welt ist alles, was der Fall ist.*'

Munich, November 2005

With grateful thanks to Susanne Ehrenfried, Nicole Matthiss, Avinoam Shalem and Mathieu Wellner.

Bibliography

- Bailey, David A. and Gilane Tawadros (eds), *Veil. Veiling, Representation and Contemporary Art* (London/Oxford, inIVA/Modern Art Oxford, 2003).
- Bexte, Peter, 'Transitstrecken. Eine Philosophie der Relationen nach Michel Serres'. Lecture given at the Merve Verlag, Berlin, 5 June 1998. Also available online: MoMo-Berlin. 22 May 2001. www.momo-berlin.de/Bexte_Serres.html (12 Dec. 2005).
- Bredekamp, Horst, *Die Fenster der Monade. Gottfried Wilhelm Leibniz' Theater der Natur und Kunst*, Acta Humaniora Schriften zur Kunstwissenschaft und Philosophie (Berlin, Akademie Verlag, 2004).
- Deleuze, Gilles, *The Fold: Leibniz and the Baroque*, trans. Tom Conley (Minneapolis, University of Minnesota Press, 1993). Originally published as *Le pli. Leibniz et le baroque* (Paris, Les Éditions de Minuit, 1988).
- Harather, Karin, *Haus-Kleider, Zum Phänomen der Bekleidung in der Architektur* (Vienna/Cologne/Weimar, Böhlau Verlag, 1995).
- Leibniz, Gottfried Wilhelm, 'From the Letters to Arnauld (1686-87)', in *Philosophical Essays*, trans. Roger Ariew and Daniel Garber (Indianapolis, Hackett Publishing Company, 1989).
- Overy, Paul, 'White Walls, White Skins: Cosmopolitanism and Colonialism in Interwar Modernist Architecture', in Mercer, Kobina (ed.), *Cosmopolitan Modernisms* (London/Cambridge, Mass., inIVA/MIT Press, 2005).
- McQuaid, Matilda and Magdalena Droste, *Lilly Reich, Designer and Architect* (New York, Museum of Modern Art, 1996).
- Rowe, Colin and Robert Slutzky, 'Transparency: Literal and Phenomenal', *Perspecta*, no. 8, 1964.
- Stölzl, Gunta, *Meisterin am Bauhaus Dessau, Textilien, Textilenentwurfe und freie Arbeiten, 1915-1983* (Dessau/Ostfildern-Ruit, Stiftung Bauhaus Dessau/Verlag Gerd Hatje, 1997).

Chris Dercon

Yellow silk curtain slowly wafting in the breeze of the air machine in the Museum Boijmans Van Beuningen during OMA's 'The First Decade' exhibition, 1989.

Cloudy Sky

Poured floor in cafeteria and corridors
Faculty of Space Technology, Delft University of Technology,
Delft, the Netherlands, 2003

Installing the polyurethane floor for the faculty, representing the cloudy sky (reflective surface) and topography (matte surface) seen from the space shuttle. (Art commission, 2002)

Reflection

"The habitat of fish is organized in horizontal bands within the water's profile; some stay directly under the surface, others move about within their own specific level in the depths of the water. Fish react to wavelengths of light which are filtered through the various depths of the water. As the light intensity changes during each 24-hour cycle, species start migrating in vertical direction to find their prey, penetrating other layers and braking out of their horizontal column. This daily movement is like weaving through aquatic space."

(In conversation with Tijs Goldschmidt, 2005)

Vla-Flip

Liquid floor for Banquet Hall
Lille Grand Palais, Lille, France, 1994

The colours represent the restaurant's food: salmon (pink) with mayonnaise (yellow) in a concrete structure (grey).

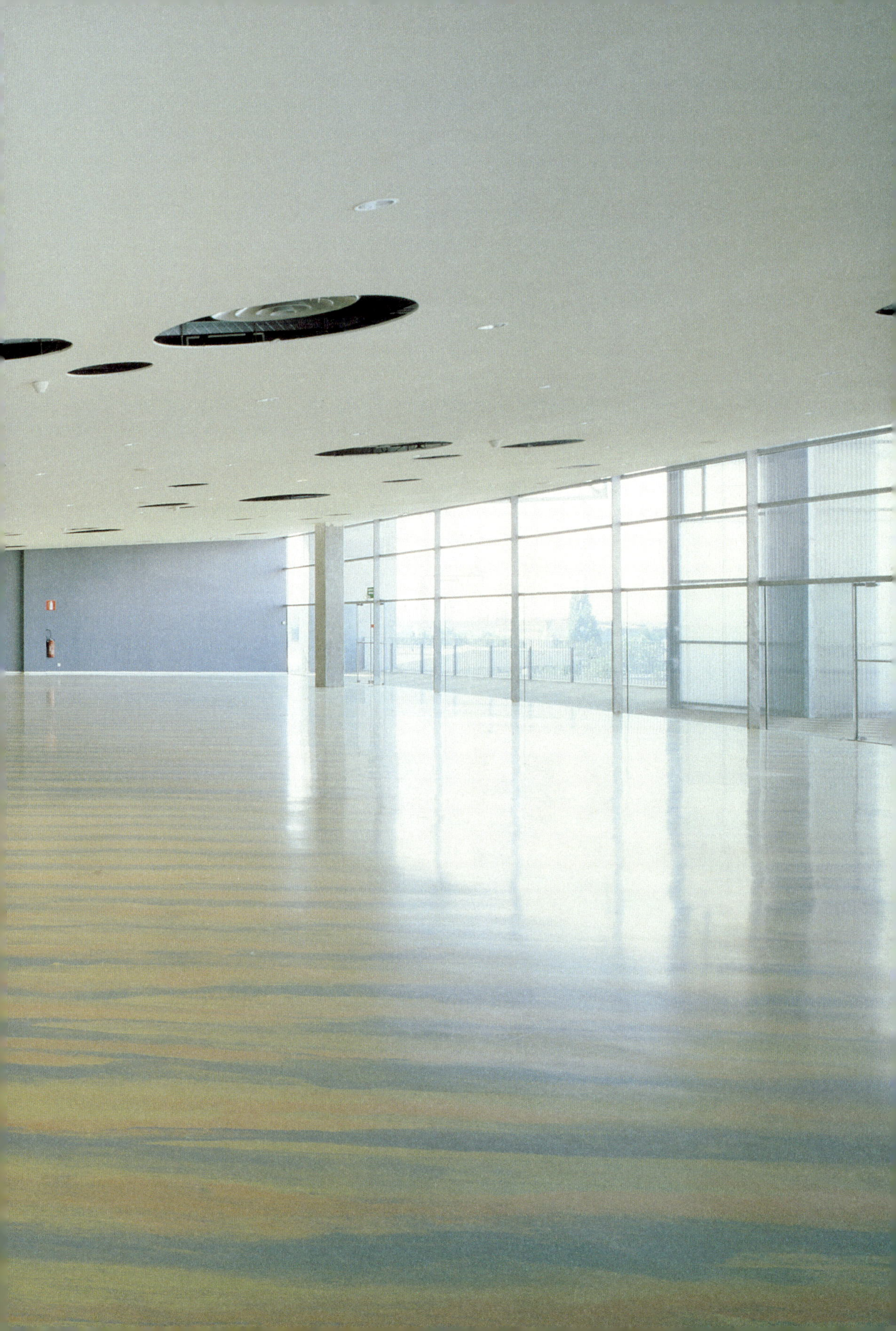

Rifletutti

Personal pavilions and mirror drop installation
Villa Manin, Codroipo, Italy, 2005

Inside Outside's installation during the Venice Biennale. Walking through the villa's gardens, visitors wore our personal, mobile pavilions: reflective and translucent parasols with integrated view points. On the way, they encountered reflective 'water drops' embedded in the landscape.

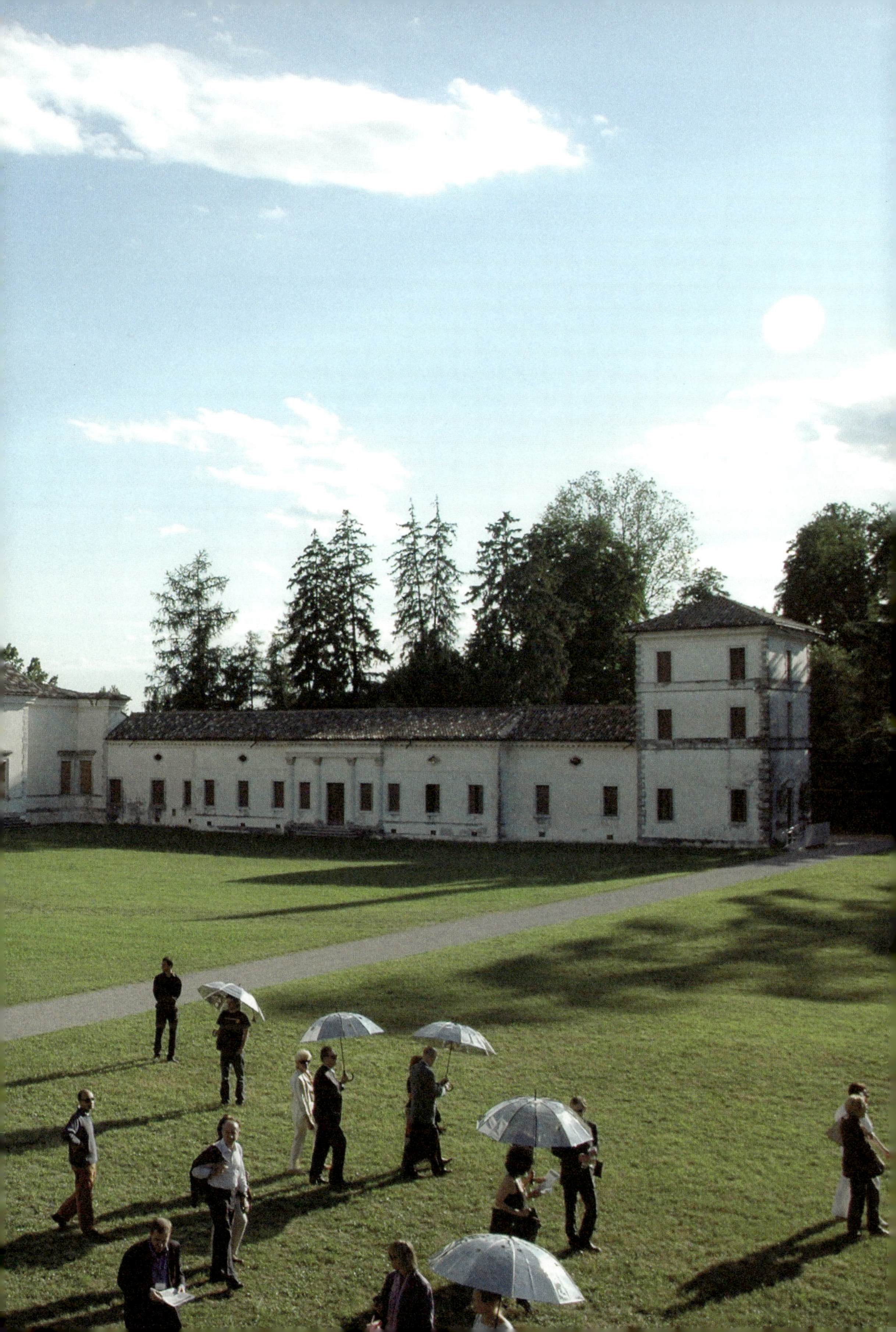

58

Stainless steel ground mirrors reflect the sky, opening up views downward. Mirrored umbrellas reflect the ground, reveal what lies behind.

Mass

Climate- and sound-regulating division wall for entry
Heemstra/Strik House, Amsterdam, the Netherlands, 2002

This curtain replaces a former wall that divided the entrance hall from the dining room and kitchen: a massive woollen curtain with a clear plastic lining that isolates cold and draught, absorbs sound and protects the children who tend to run off into the street or climb the stairs. Despite its mass, the curtain is transparent and fluid. It covers the entire wall of the entrance hall, appearing only within the frame of the opening when seen from the dining room. Green felt fins are sewn onto black voile; clear plastic lining; one slit with overlap (all materials fire-retardant).

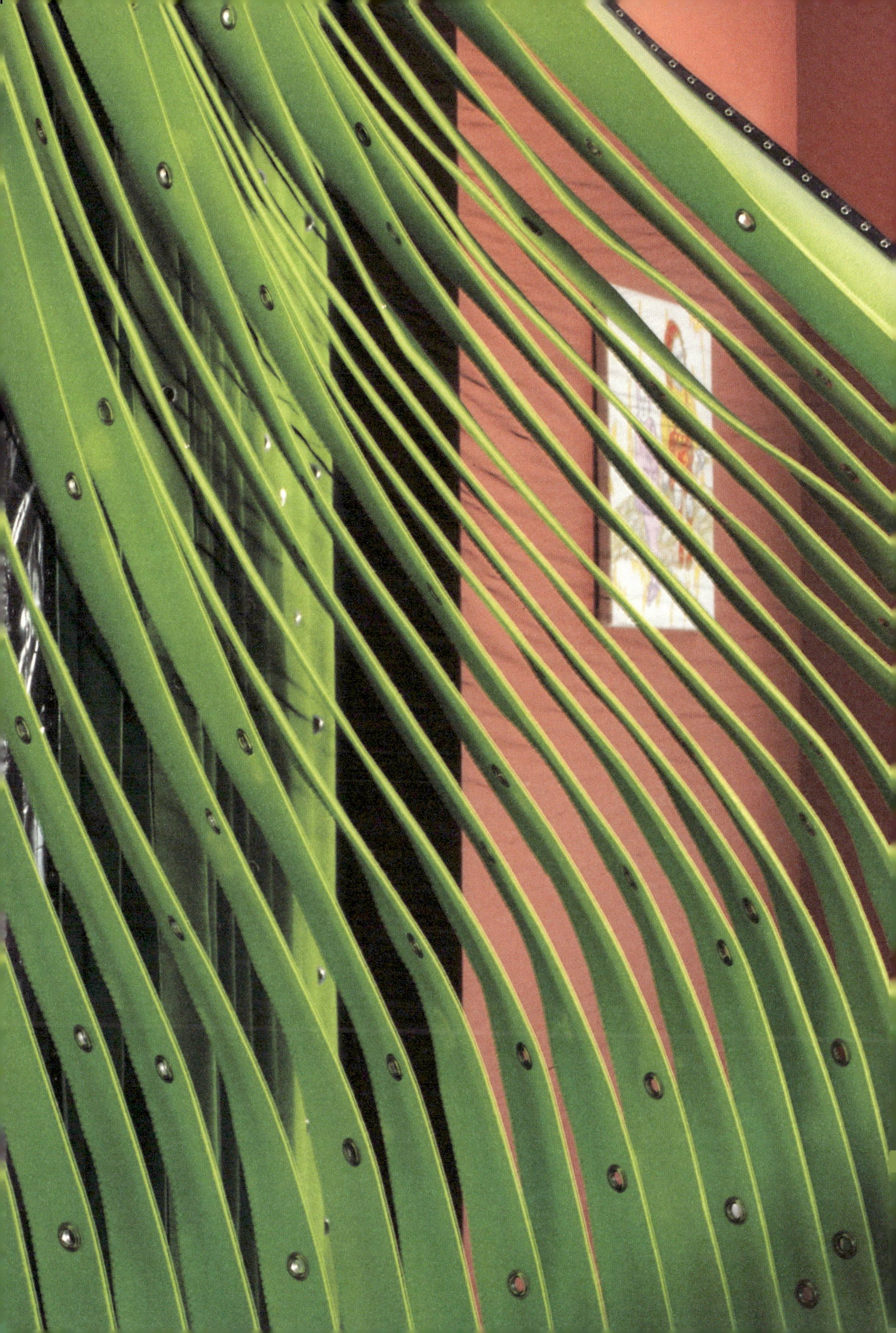

Silk, Lawn

Yellow silk room inside the living room area
Villa dall'Ava, Saint Cloud, Paris, France, 1992

Yellow silk curtain moves slowly in the wind that enters from the garden. In actuality, this curtain creates an entire room within the room, enveloping the owners within its warm yellow sheen and changing the living room's acoustic atmosphere and spatial division. When large parts of the villa's glass façades are slid open, the curtain flows out onto the lawn.

"Mammals create boundaries through visual or olfactory markings like tracks, droppings and skin oils. Birds, fish and insects, however, 'mark' their territory through movement only – moving up, down and sideways from a fixed starting point – while fighting creatures that pass through their invisible boundaries. The size and location of the territory is modified through time and according to the physical energy of the animal in question: the healthier it is, the faster the movement and the larger their territory."

(In conversation with Tijs Goldschmidt, 2005)

Radial Views

Roof garden and curtains for penthouse
Cinnabar Wharf, London, UK, 2002

Like an intermediary screen between roof garden and penthouse,
this translucent curtain extends the garden inward.

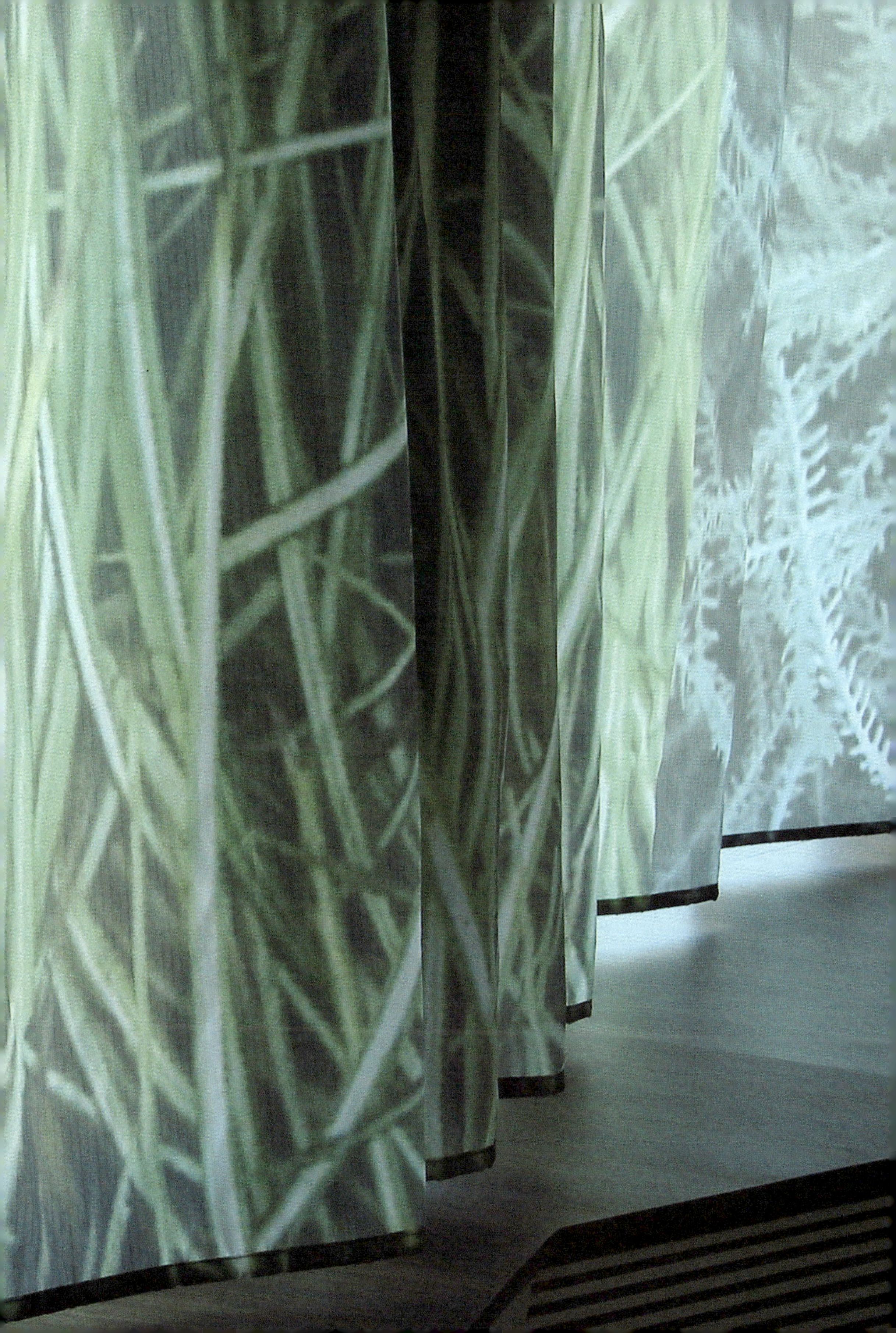

Reflection

Three light-regulating curtains
McCormick Tribune Campus Center,
Chicago, USA, 1999–2004

Precisely the point.

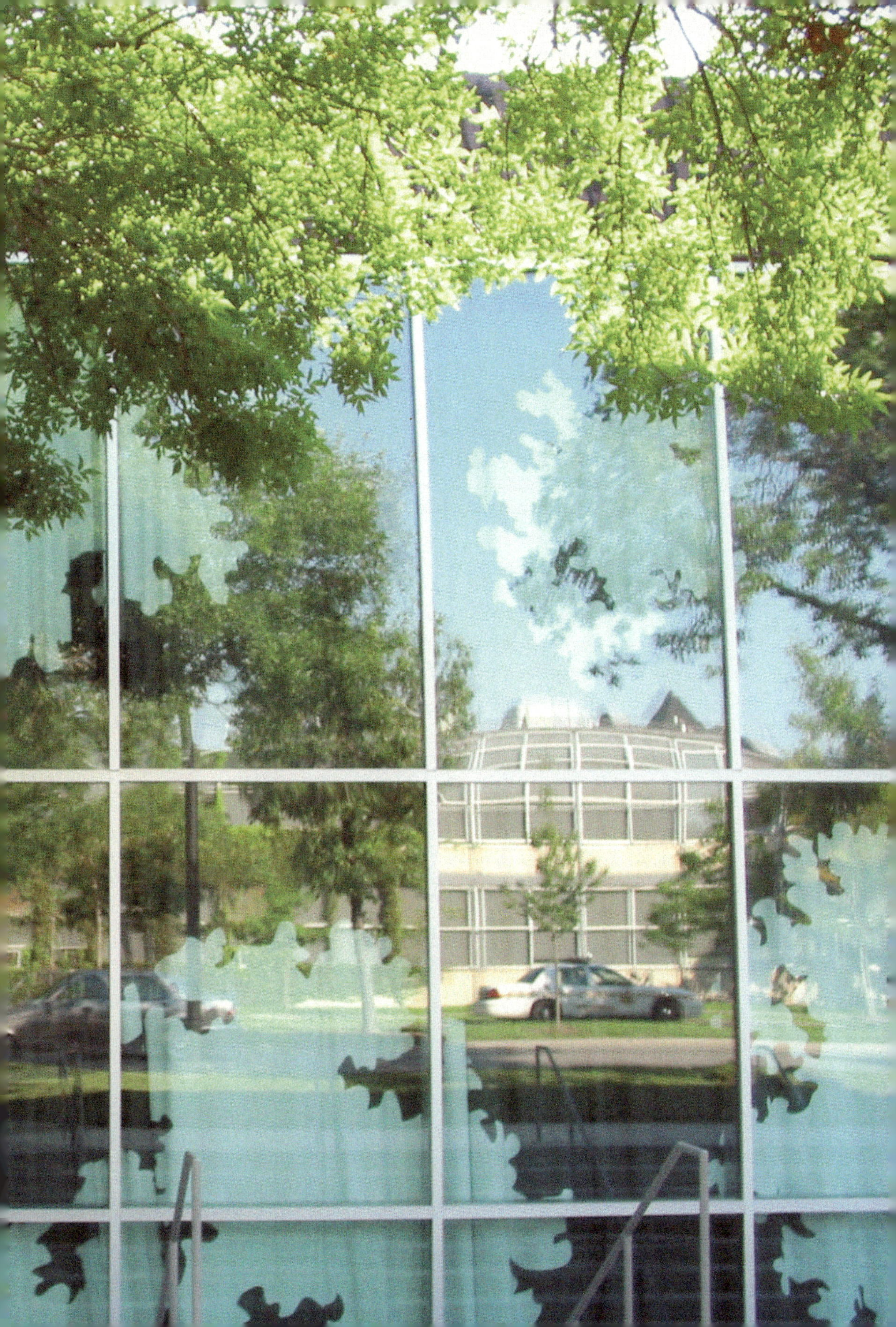

Storage position can be sensational.

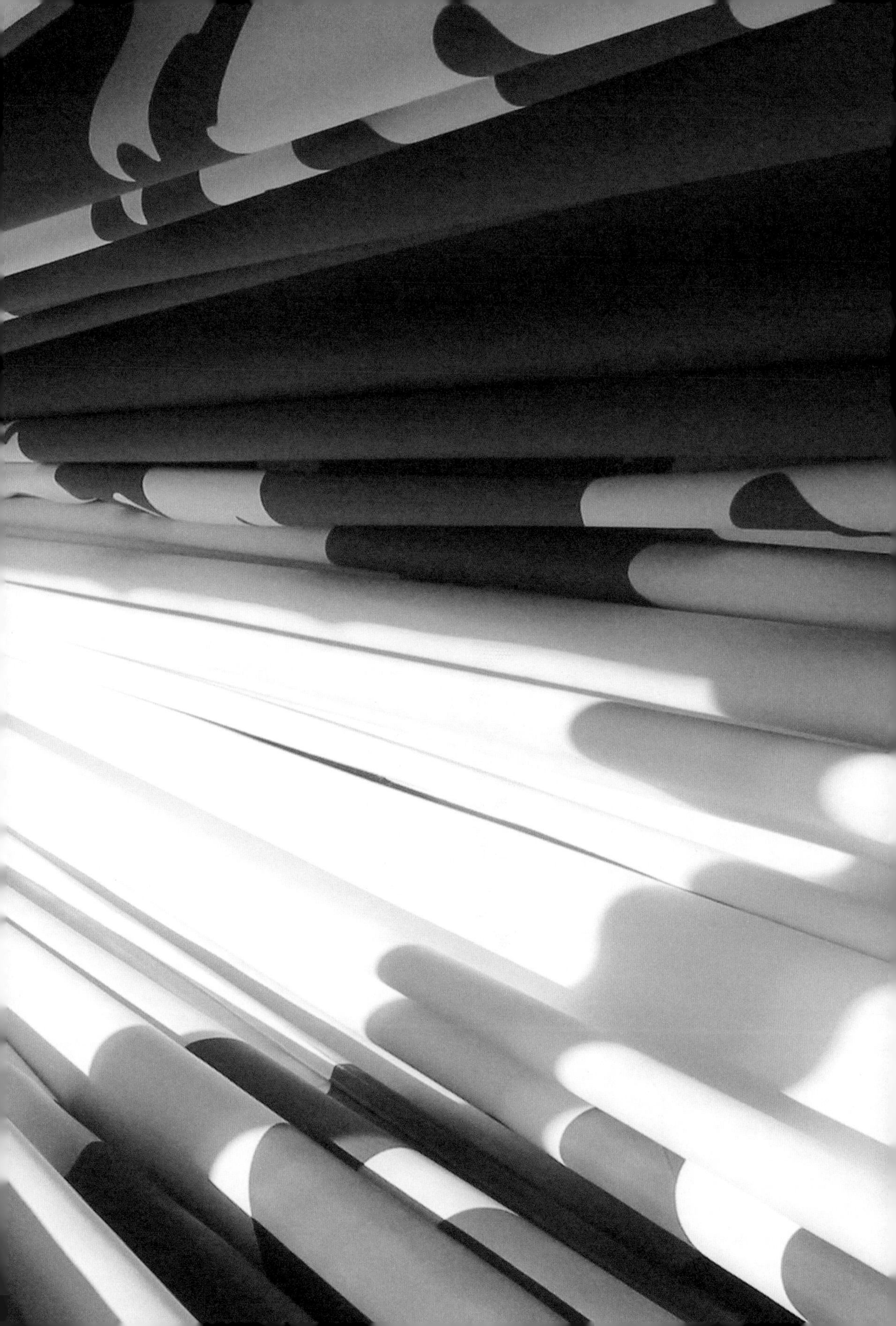

WHAT are you going to do?!
Stitch rows of holes?!...Why?!

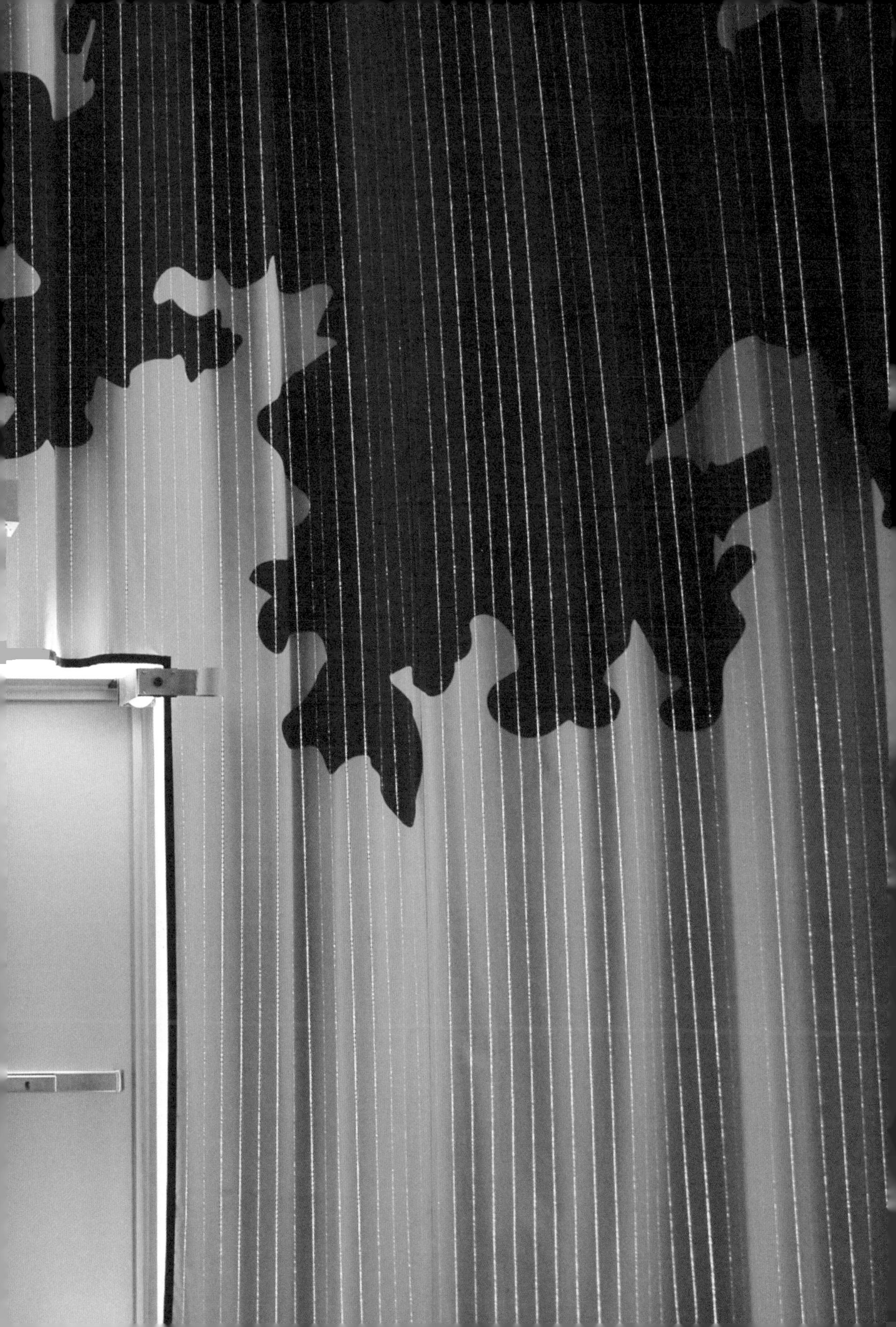

OMA Retrospective

Exhibition design for OMA
Collegi d'Arquitectes de Cataluña, Barcelona, Spain, 1991

We opened the gallery windows to the adjacent shopping streets and built tilted planes to fluidly connect them to the gallery level. To reinforce the effect of daylight and openness, we lit the exhibition with one single construction lamp (sponsored by Philips) mounted on the fence of a building site opposite the gallery: a bright sun lighting the objects in a 'natural' way by day, and directing all attention from passers-by towards our space by night.

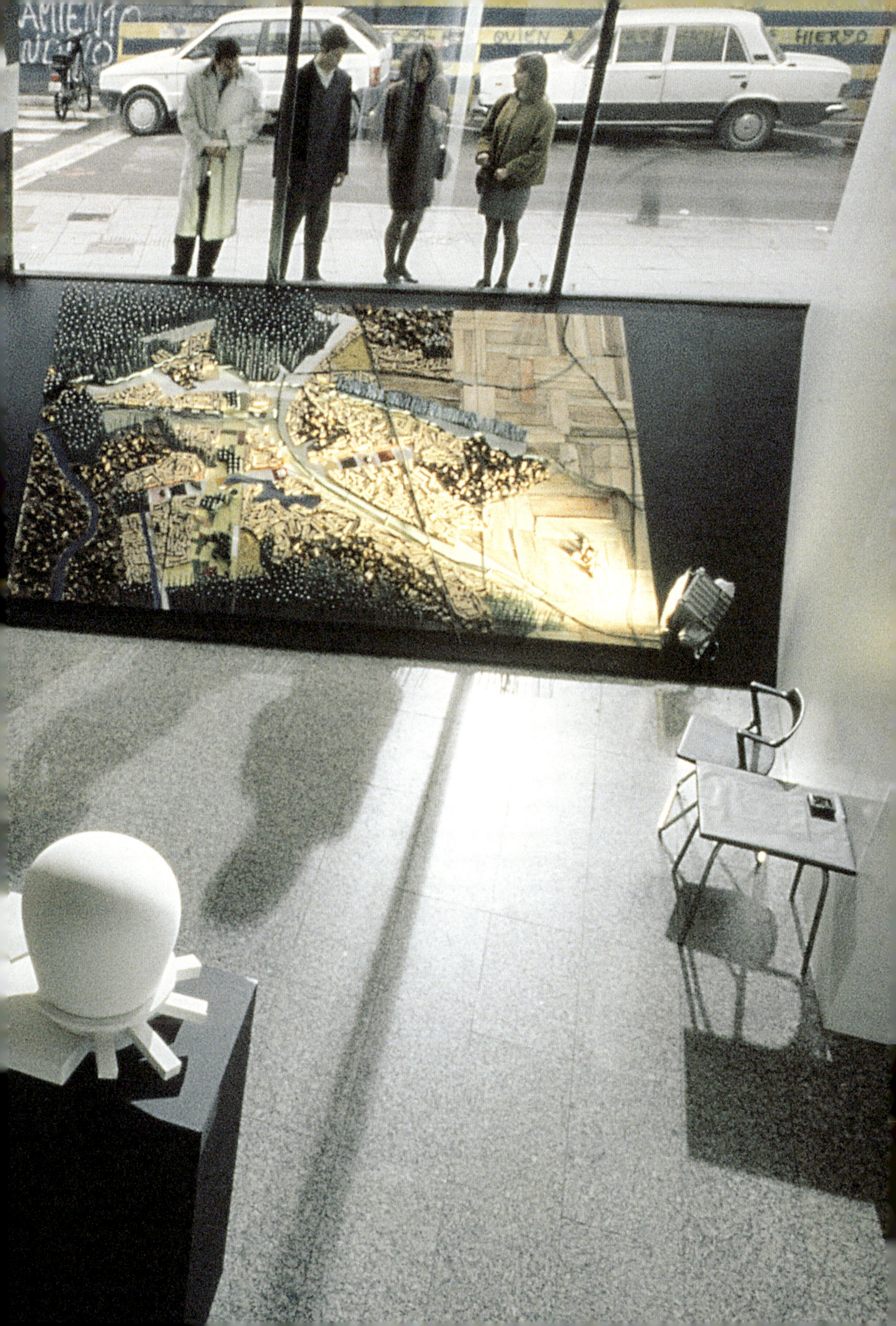

Restoration Revised

Hackney Empire Theatre, London, UK 1999–2005
Stage curtain, upper circle curtain, all curtains for the new annex

Two Flies with One Swat

The Hackney Empire Theatre commission was the second British building restoration that Inside Outside was invited to participate in 'through a different door'. Tim Ronalds, architect based in London, asked Inside Outside to collaborate as an 'artist', rather than as part of the architectural team. Quite a smart move, I thought. His initiative enabled our 'applied' work to be labelled as art, thus adding the arts budget to the interior finishing budget. Killing two flies with one swat, as we say in Holland.

We first collaborated with Tim on the Mick Jagger Centre in Dartford, where he turned a Victorian school building into a modern (pop) concert hall with sound and rehearsal studios, gallery spaces and an entrance foyer. We worked on light- and sound-regulating curtains for the new concert hall, using pink and yellow velvets that change colour through layers of muting fleeces.

Now we were selected for the Hackney Empire Theatre in London, a totally different and much more complex environment. This popular, turn-of-the-century theatre needed serious restoration. Inside Outside was asked to propose new designs for the auditorium curtains (stage, upper circle and balconies) and wallpaper; and for all curtains in a new annex – a small vertical block replacing the old corner building – in which a pub, a 'hospitality space' and a theatre studio were to be housed.

The Hackney Empire Theatre is located in an intense, multicultural area of East London. Since it was designed by the English architect Frank Matcham and built in 1903, it has always been a truly populist theatre, hosting slapsticks, musicals, pop, hiphop and jazz concerts, gospels, operas, children's events in the afternoons and even bingo evenings for adults. It is the entire society's machine at work, day and night, day after day. Londoners of all ages, all nationalities and all cultural backgrounds know this theatre, and every Londoner goes there at least once in their life. We were told that Charlie Chaplin performed there more than once in his time! And that the internationally loved Mister Bean – Rowan Atkinson – is one of its most enthousiastic supporters.

In the decades following its birth, the Hackney Empire's interior was redone several times in a variety of ways, each time with new colours, materials and symbols, according to the fashion and the cultural and social expectations of the day. This led to a cacophony of colours and a plethora of different types of lampshades, chandeliers, carpets, upholsteries, paints, tiles, wallpapers, gadgets and sculptures – quite ugly but great fun – crossed with a layer of different sign languages and letterings, as if dozens of cultures had passed through and left their mark: African, Indian, Chinese, English, Russian, baroque, Zen, jazz, Biba, hippy, pop, posh and kitsch. You could imagine a bit of everything hidden inside the Hackney's belly.

Amnesia

For Inside Outside, the project started in November 1999, but it was not until 2005 that we installed our last curtains. At the beginning, we had no idea how important this project would be and how much we would learn from the working process. Looking back, we see that it inspired a new kind of intelligence – a new design language, if you like.

In a way, the task was to find the right answer to a cultural dilemma. Not only were we designing for an old building spotlighted as a 'National Restoration Project',[1] but we also wanted to visualize what 'restoration' actually entails. Bringing the original features of this building's interior back to life? Interpreting the publics' expectations for the theatre? Does it mean introducing a new layer? And what does it imply for the future of a theatre like the Hackney Empire? So we wondered about how to deal with the most symbolic objects in a performance theatre – the proscenium and upper circle curtains – in a way that would articulate the tension between the old and the new; between the past and the future.

When we started on this project, no information about the original interior of the auditorium or the foyers was available – no images, no materials. We were introduced to a restoration project with interior amnesia.

We looked at images and drawings of other theatres designed by Matcham in the same period: cream-, brown- and gold-coloured auditorium interiors with gold leaf decorations, enriched with wall paintings of angels and composers, centred by a dark brown velvet proscenium curtain topped with a pelmet[2] and edged with a golden fringe. Refined interiors with restrained colours. The Hackney Empire was probably conceived in much the same way.

Which History to Restore?

What Tim and I like very much about this theatre is that it is quite compact and intimate, with an intricate route through the building. Matcham seems to have been good at creating enormous complexity in limited spaces, making small buildings appear large. For example, he fit an enormous amount of chairs onto the balconies in a very steep setting, opening up intriguing perspectives from every position.

Another charming feature of this theatre is the fact that the auditorium has three round windows that can be opened: one in the centre of the auditorium dome, which slides open along large tracks on the roof; and one stained glass window on each side, on the upper circle balcony level. Mind you: the audience is still allowed to drink and eat during performances, as always, but in the past they were also permitted to smoke. Since there were no airflow or air-conditioning systems, the roof and side windows were opened for ventilation. The large skylight is one of the most beautiful features of the theatre. It is such an exciting idea to be able to look up and see the sky at night and have air and rain literally come in from outside into the innermost interior space!

---

1. The restoration was financed by the National Lottery Fund.

2. A pelmet is an adjustable element covering the stage curtain along the top of the proscenium opening. Together with the 'side slips' the pelmet enlarges or diminishes the stage opening's size by sliding up or down.

Every floor has its own bar connected to the auditorium. Each bar has a different window configuration – some have a balcony, too – and all of them look out over the city of London. You can sneak out of a performance to get a drink, chips or to smoke, and, over the bartender's head, look at the city spread out in front of you. What a present!

To which of the Hackney's multiple layers should an interior restoration in the year 2000 refer? Should one simply go back to the past, holding on to it, basically mimicking it? Or can one create a visual bridge from a past era to the next, even in the most historic spaces? Can one, without necessarily undermining the beauty and importance of the past, integrate elements that show the present, or even project the future?

We studied the architect's designs and models, visited the building site, met the theatre's staff and let all of the implications of the project sink in for a while. Then we proposed two completely opposite approaches. One was to reach way back and restore the general interior to its 1903 state: the refined and classic version, with soft colours and a few highlights. In this scenario we could imagine implementing rich and colourful curtains and wallpaper. The other approach was to exaggerate the existing general interior condition by polishing the current cacophony of colours to an even more ecstatic intensity. In this case we would implement a layer of renewal, steering the Hackney Empire towards the future with what we imagined as simple, black-and-white colour schemes for our interventions, contrasting the oversaturated auditorium; challenging the bonbon box by introducing a form of abstraction.

The architect and the client decided on the second scenario, although they eventually reduced the cacophony of colours to a much more 'muted' palette of ochre, copper and red.

Dramatic Ideas

The Hackney's theatre stage curtain has a 'guillotine' mechanism, which moves up and down only, whereas a proscenium curtain usually opens sideways. A metal bar with a piece of cloth comes down from the fly tower hissing *shrrrr!* and goes up again. The only drama is the speed: slow, quick or an abrupt fall. We thought, okay, it might be wonderful to exaggerate that movement, prolong it and dramatize it.

We found that a horizontally striped, black-and-white proscenium curtain introduced the modern element we were searching for and that it looked appealing in this context. One of the qualities of this idea was that the white stripes would take on the colour of the projected light, changing the curtain into a chameleon.

There were two ways of interpreting this concept. One was the 'accordion', introducing elasticity. For this idea, we incorporated technical constructions into the backside of the curtain, to exaggerate the effect of elasticity. When the curtain comes down or moves up, the stripes stretch and shrink in a vertical direction, like an accordion – *shwooff shwooff* – up and down. Even when 'down', the curtain oscillates more and more slowly, until it finally shrinks

Swooooooosh – a curtain made entirely of black and white frills...

back to its original size. After lots of tests however, the system proved to be too complex, and too costly.

The other idea was a three-dimensional 'frilly' curtain: the entire curtain would be made of tonnes of frills, which would undulate while falling down, creating an enormous waterfall effect, exaggerating each movement, introducing weird counter movement – like naked male ballet dancers – and reacting to every airflow. How we loved this idea! Every test, model and collage we did looked gorgeous.

Giving Up to Take In

We pretty much convinced the architect to go along with our black-and-white 'steering the Hackney towards the future' idea, but what we were proposing was, of course, shocking. Challenging. New. Tim was understandably worried about the client's reaction.

It took a long time, a year or so I think, and a lot of discussion on the subject for the client and all parties involved to finally decide that it would be unwise to change the Hackney Empire Theatre that much. Our proposals were too modern.

The client had assumed they could be progressive and move into the future, but then they discovered that they shouldn't. That the theatre, unless it remained 'the good old Hackney Empire', would unnerve everyone, and that this would definitely mean that the theatre would lose its audience, artists and all important sources of income.

Well.

We were asked to either hand back the commission for the auditorium curtains or to agree to design a classic stage curtain that would merge with the Hackney Empire interior and fit the theatre's mentality. Of course, they would understand perfectly if we decided not to take the commission! After all, being contemporary designers, their mentality would probably not excite us very much... In fact, we *did* want to do it – such an interesting challenge not to challenge!

One good thing about a very, very long and chewy process is that you begin to understand the situation better and better. The endless pushing and pulling and waiting creates subconscious insight and breaks open hidden memories. I started to remember earlier experiences with musicians, actors and the theatre, the particular mentality that performers have. Their workspace is not about cleanliness and aesthetics. They do need a form of efficiency to function, but their work is essentially about life. You sweat, you love, you hate, you die in the theatre. Performers need a space where they can create their own world, where they can throw eggs and shout, where they can make a cocoon of total silence to slowly pull out their innermost feelings. And they want their public to do the same, see the same, feel the same. They don't want their audience to sit in an aesthetically controlled environment watching them perform. The audience has to *live* a performance. The Hackney Empire is such a workplace: a mysterious building full of illusions, inhabited with ghosts in every corner. That is what the theatre people wanted to keep, I think.

In the architecture and design world, we tend to get obsessed with intellectual reasoning and aesthetics, and we become total control freaks. We tend to think: 'We are so great, let's just convince everyone and do it and it will be a big success!' But if you step back and forget about your so-called 'originality', it could be just as fascinating to accomplish something that goes against your basic, ingrained instincts.

Stage-Sized Craftwork

How could we incorporate our earlier fantasies into this traditional 'corset' of a red velvet curtain? We were clueless at first, until I dreamt about a little girl wearing a smocked dress. She hopped from one side of the water to the other, using her arms for balance, swaying them sideways, backward and forward. And all the time I saw this accordion structure on her chest stretching and contracting with her movements. Ah, a smocked curtain!

I think this is the first time that the smocking technique has been used to create a theatre curtain; applied on such a large scale, I mean. Of course, smocking is often used in stage costumes – sleeves, men's trousers, etcetera – but what I saw in my dream of the little girl's dress was the diamond shapes that stretched out as she took a deep breath. Elasticity and three-dimensional structure combined.

Now, how could we enlarge a girl's dress to the scale of a theatre curtain? We knew we wanted to work with heavy cotton velvet, so we did all our scale studies with that material. During our step-by-step tests, however, we discovered that simply enlarging the scale of the smock through simple, parallel mathematical logic – the depth of folds and pockets; and the height and width of each diamond shape – was not working. So the enlargement of each diamond – or fold – had to be steered towards the right balance, which could only be found through manipulation; through a fascinating process of physical trial and error.[3]

You must realize that cloth in itself – in this case heavy cotton velvet – cannot change its own characteristics in the process; its weave, thickness and flexibility do not change, whatever the scale you work in. Textiles pose a unique problem, since experiments and models are made using the actual, final material, whether the scale is 1:50 or 1:1. Unlike with, for instance, architectural models, where cardboard is used as a stand-in for concrete.[4]

We had to find special techniques with which to mimic the effects in the scale that we were looking for. We exaggerated the size and thickness of the folds. We expanded the thickness of the 'embroidery thread' that connects the pleats in the rhythm that creates the right smock pattern, and where the smock pockets needed to be rigid, we inserted reinforcement to assure that the cloth was stiff enough.[5]

An environment without daylight requires a particular design mentality. Darkness and distance in an auditorium dictate a form of bluntness; a

---

3.
You would think that the depth of the diamond shapes would have to increase along with the scale of the folds and the distance of each connecting point. But no: once you find the right visual balance through scale, the material itself might not 'behave' well in that particular size – the folds become too thin, pockets that are supposed to stand out rigidly start sagging – undermining the effect that you want to trigger.

4.
We tested thickness, material, depth, structure, rhythm and, of course, the way of making it. We made the first 1:1 and scale tests ourselves until we got the feel of it.

5.
We found a technique to ensure the rigidity of the mock pockets by stiffening and fixing the two 'side walls' of each single one of them; and we used classic stuffing material to thicken the folds: wool felt cords.

From radical black-and-white contrast to red – but smocked – velvet

Fire-screen

Final design

language of exaggeration is necessary to get your intentions across. And dust that settles in the smocks' diamond-shaped pockets becomes an additional factor of three-dimensionality. This element of time further adds to the visual depth of the space. Strange, because you normally want to avoid any dust settling, but in the theatre dust can be a beautiful addition to an object.

Blowing up the diamonds step by step brought about authentic excitement, as you can imagine! Especially drawing the lower edge of the smock as an irregular horizontal line, from which an abundant waterfall of pleats would spill downward...

In the end, our curtain became an enormous structure weighing 480 kilos, measuring 10.2 m high and 10.85 m wide. Where a normal stage curtain would need 100 per cent extra fullness at the most, we needed 400 per cent more width to create a smocked plane large enough to amply cover the stage opening. But the stage tower could 'carry an elephant', Tim assured us.

Thanks to the one-to-one (1:1) mock-up based on our working drawings, made by Graham Creasey and his team, we realized that the smock structure, at this weight and size of surface, pulled the curtain's surface inward (accordion!) with enormous persistence. Involving the architect and the production guys, a stiff metal frame was designed onto which the curtain could be laced and stretched to exactly the right openness and size.[6]

Notwithstanding the client's wish for a 'classic' red curtain, we stubbornly kept proposing different colours and variations. Versions of lime green, Chinese yellow, Rembrandt brown and Russian blue appeared. But the client was not to be seduced. There was no escape from the red and gold! So we attacked the 'red and gold' question: What hue of red for the large curtain surface? Which red for the pelmet? What kind of gold sheen? What thickness for the cords? What finish for behind the centre slit?

Of course, 'our' colours needed to work with the materials and colours chosen by the architect: upholstery (red crushed velvet); carpets (red leaf pattern); walls, ceilings and decorations (brown and copper tones, red and numerous other colours, carefully chosen by a sensitive colour expert). Finally bright red and burgundy were chosen for the curtain and a sudden pink 'flash' for the cloth behind the centre slit. A bit weird.

When seen from behind, standing on stage, the curtain is also quite amazing: It's a huge plane with tons of small cushions bulging towards you! And if the strong spotlights are on...

After the Curtain Falls

Don't even *ask* how often we secretly wanted to give up! Phew! And how happy we are that we didn't! This project was, for everyone involved, a never-ending story about diplomacy, calculation, logic, labour, patience and modesty. An endless rebooting of energy: building up, aborting and starting again; building up, waiting and then continuing; in a framework that was simultaneously about reconciling political and economic conflicts of interest on

---

6.
Invisibly positioned behind the entire width of the curtain and from top down to the point where the centre slit starts, a light-weight but very strong! frame stabilizes the curtain where needed, nevertheless allowing the cloth and the millions of pleats to move naturally.

various levels and about keeping contractors and subcontractors active against all laws of nature, while finding money on the way, bit by bit.

In public projects like this, everyone and anyone – from the government, region, city, sponsors, foundations, local inhabitants to administrators; from artists, technicians, architects, engineers, historians, developers, contractors, craftsmen, colour specialists, workmen, designers, policemen, cooks to cleaners – has a role to play. And this complex network of players needs to work together without much open communication among one another. Acting under the laws of sometimes questionable logic they must somehow manage to carry the process through to the end and reach a satisfying result for *everyone*.

That's what all of us together achieved with six or more years of work. Not bad.

Positive/negative concept; black-and-white for old; colour for new.

Old golden bonbon box enveloped in a new black and white wrapper.

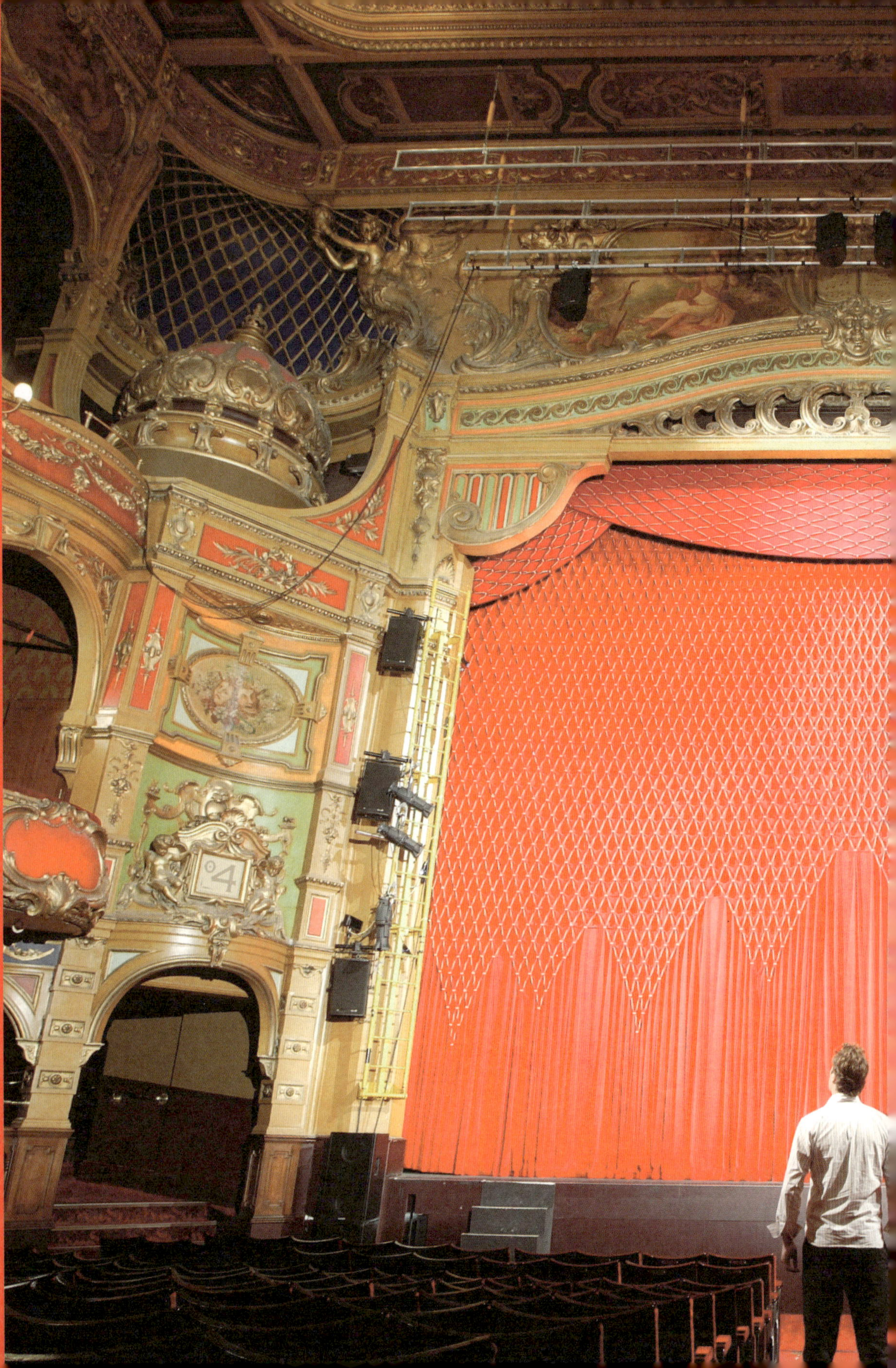

O4

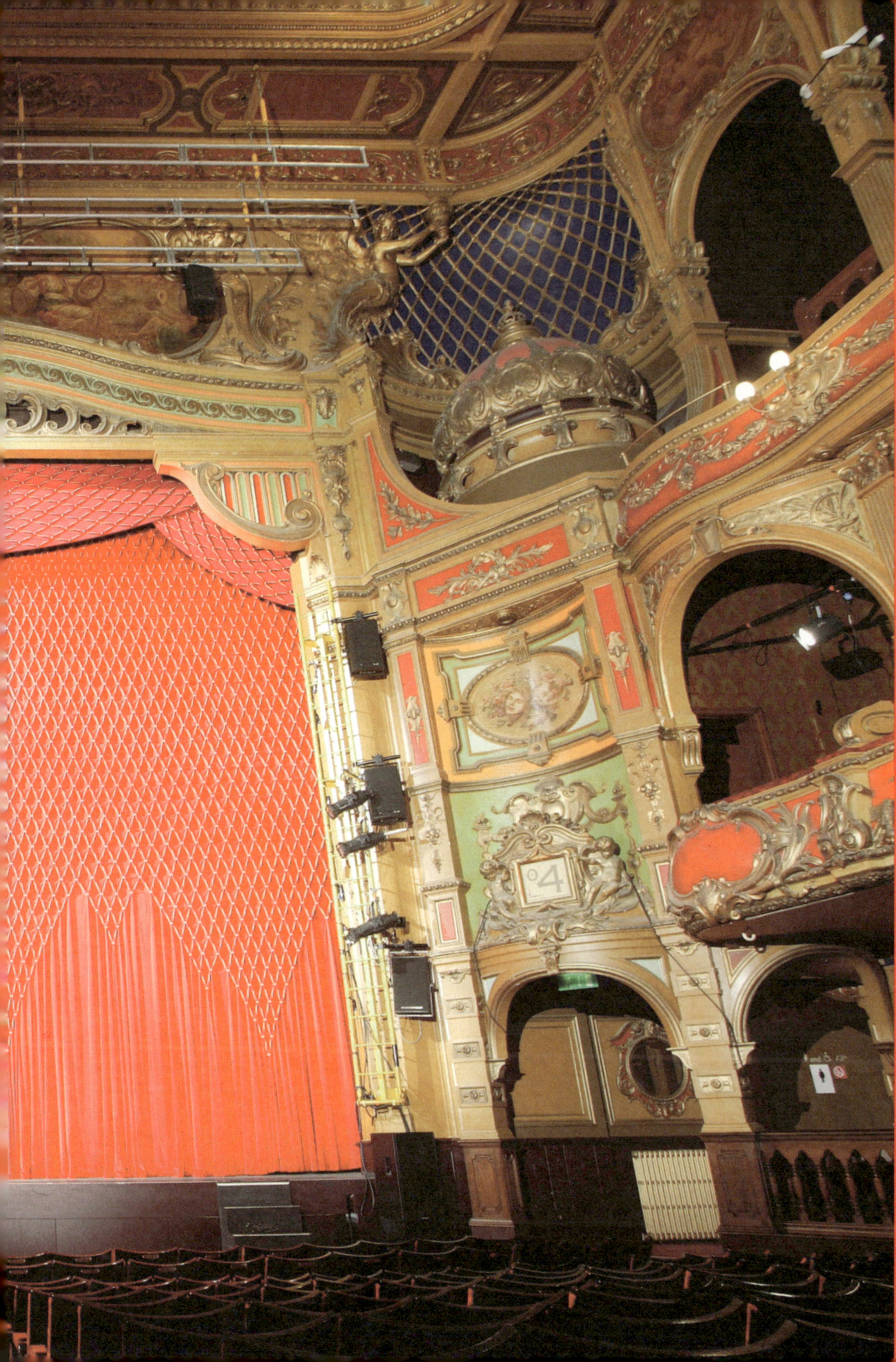

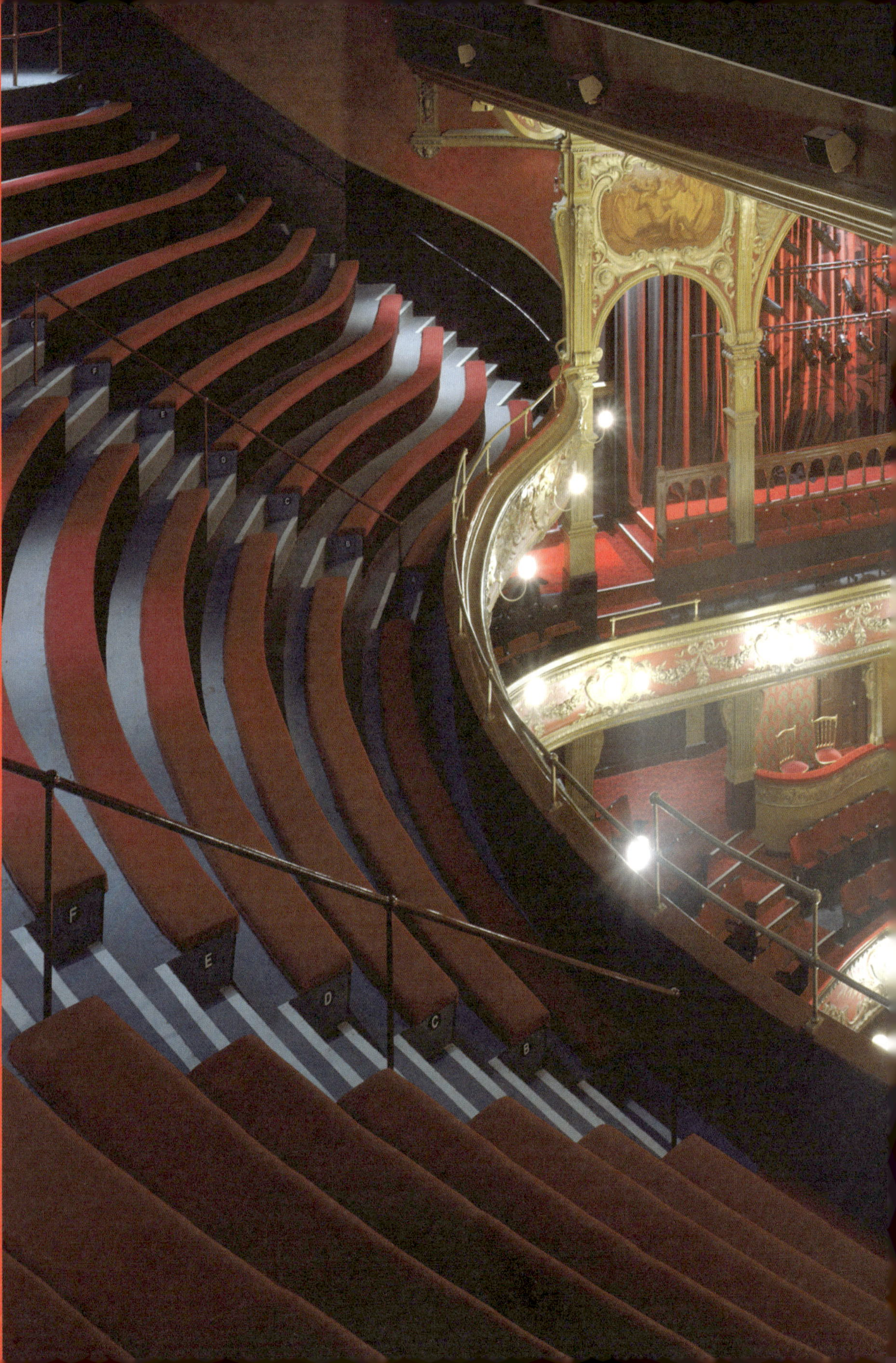

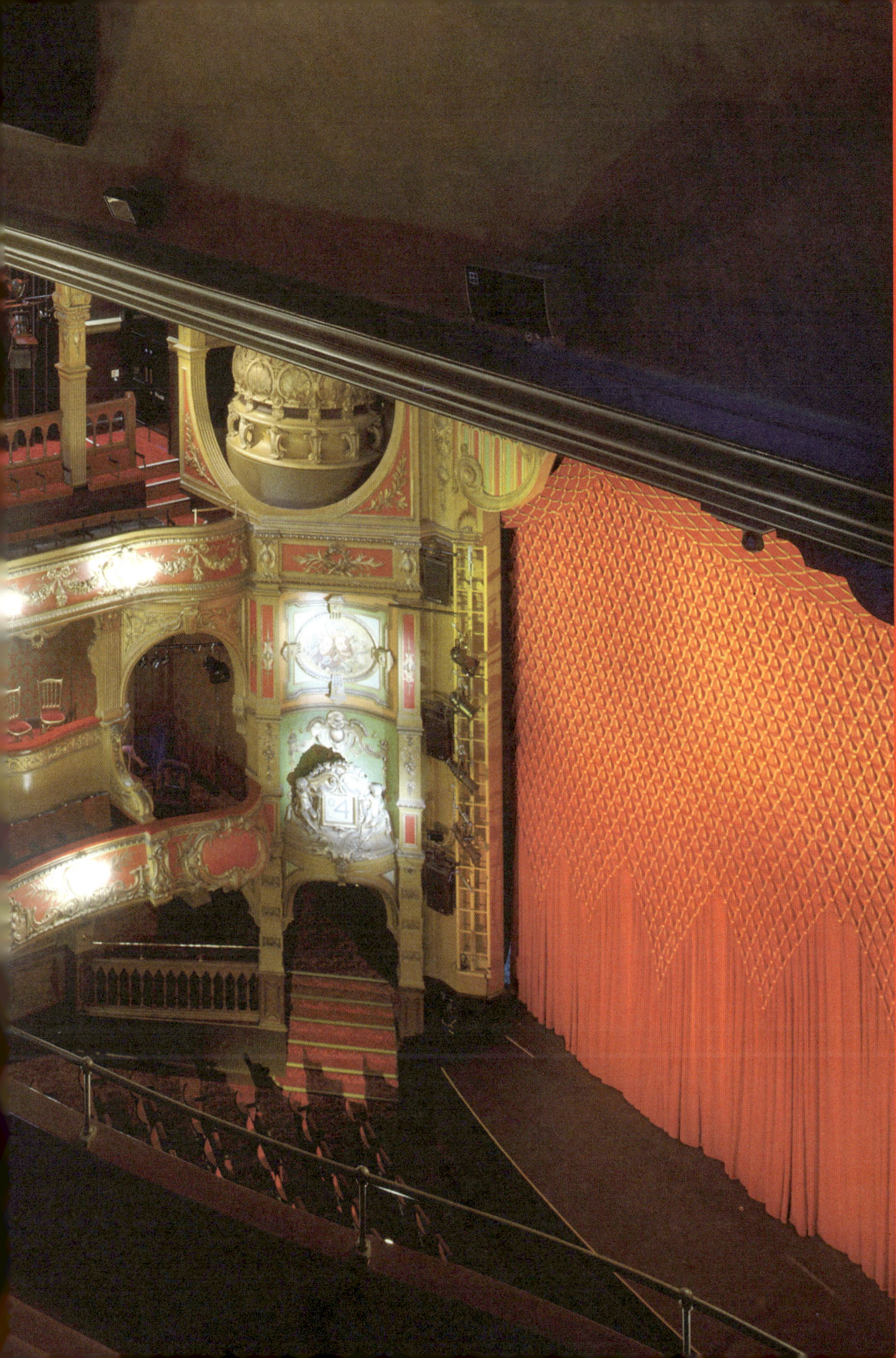

Looking up at the pelmet and the lower seam of the pulled-up curtain: two reds and heaps of pleat.

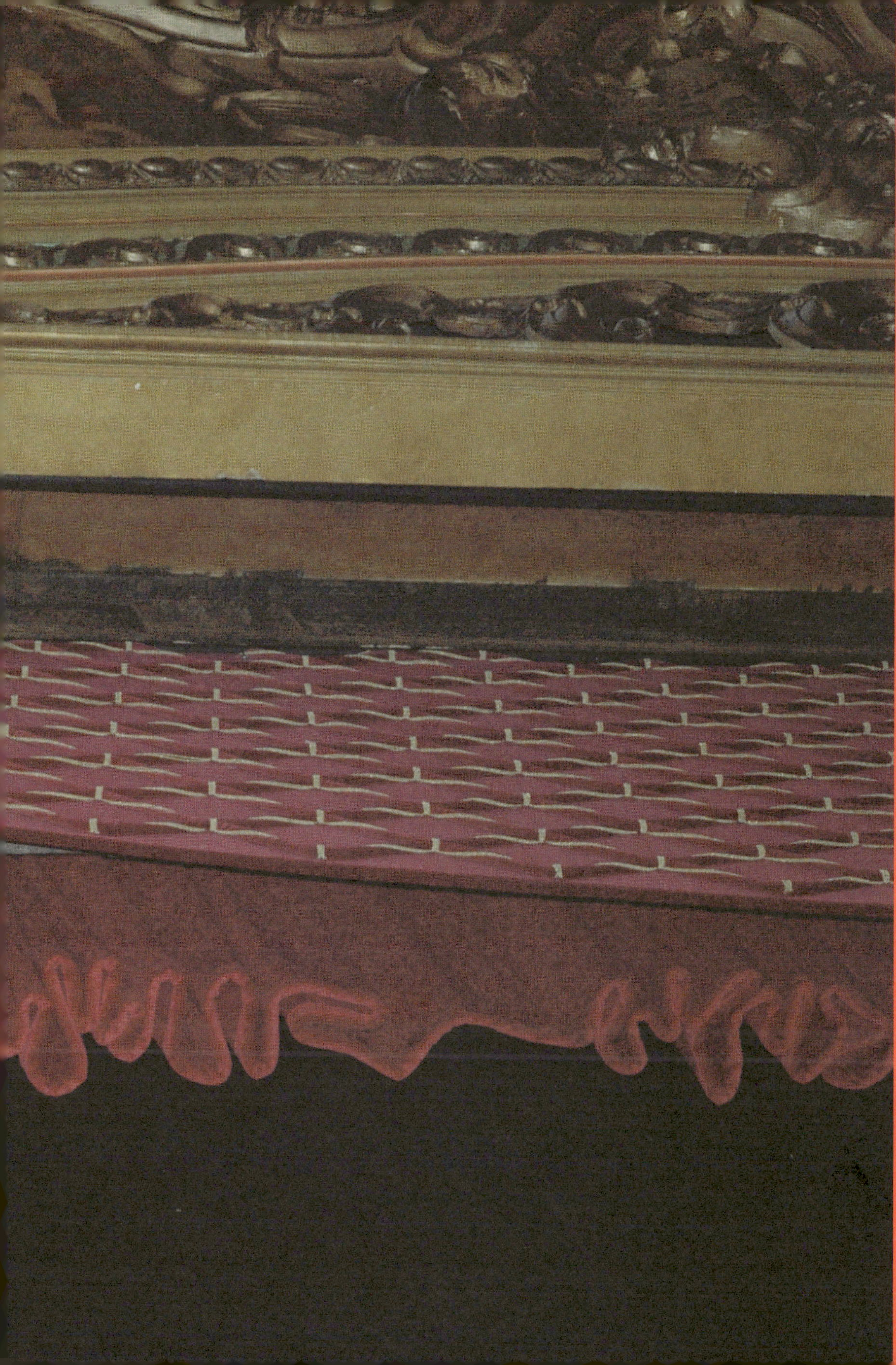

This is what you see standing on stage if the spotlights are turned on in the auditorium.

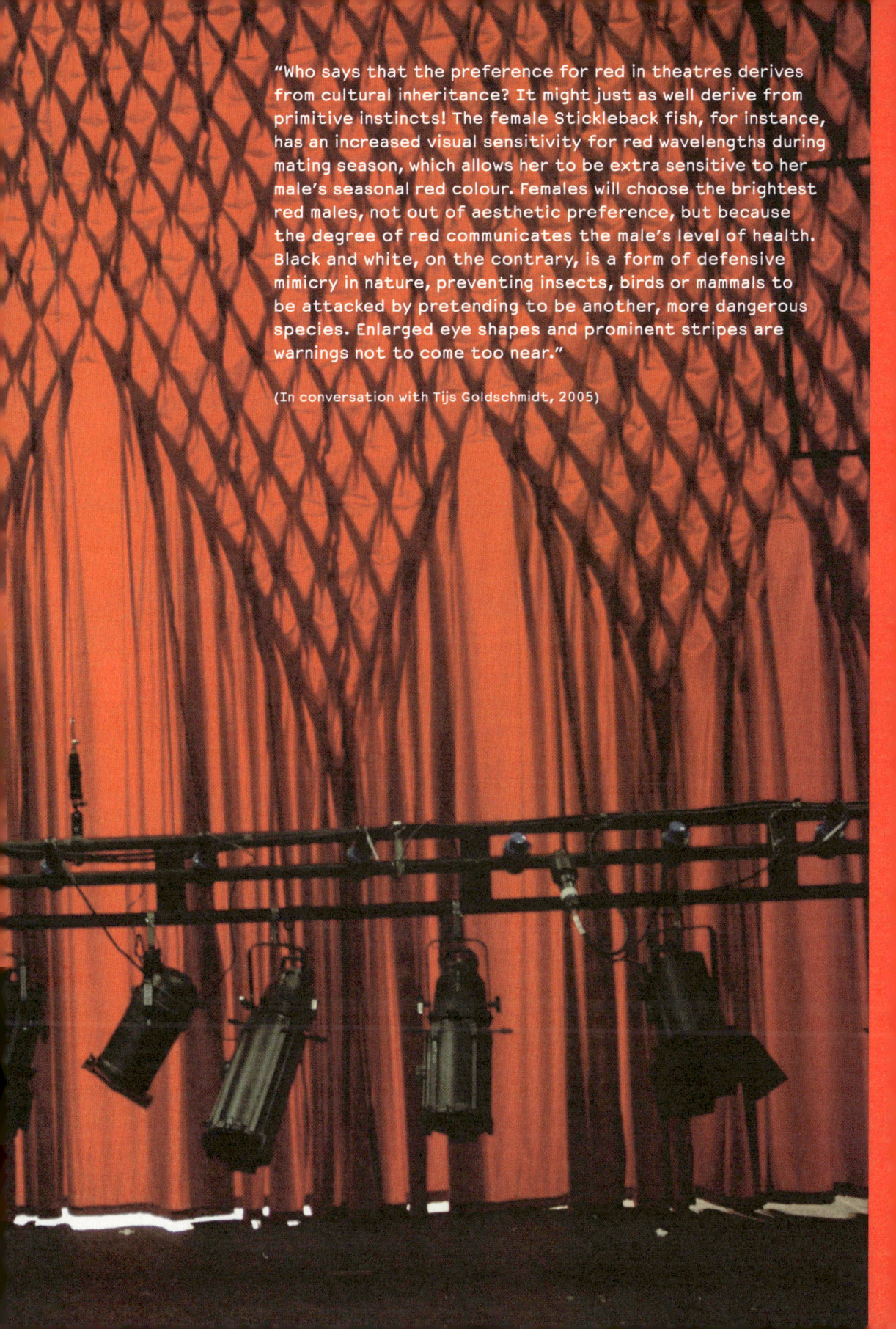

"Who says that the preference for red in theatres derives from cultural inheritance? It might just as well derive from primitive instincts! The female Stickleback fish, for instance, has an increased visual sensitivity for red wavelengths during mating season, which allows her to be extra sensitive to her male's seasonal red colour. Females will choose the brightest red males, not out of aesthetic preference, but because the degree of red communicates the male's level of health. Black and white, on the contrary, is a form of defensive mimicry in nature, preventing insects, birds or mammals to be attacked by pretending to be another, more dangerous species. Enlarged eye shapes and prominent stripes are warnings not to come too near."

(In conversation with Tijs Goldschmidt, 2005)

Pockets (left) and pleats (right).

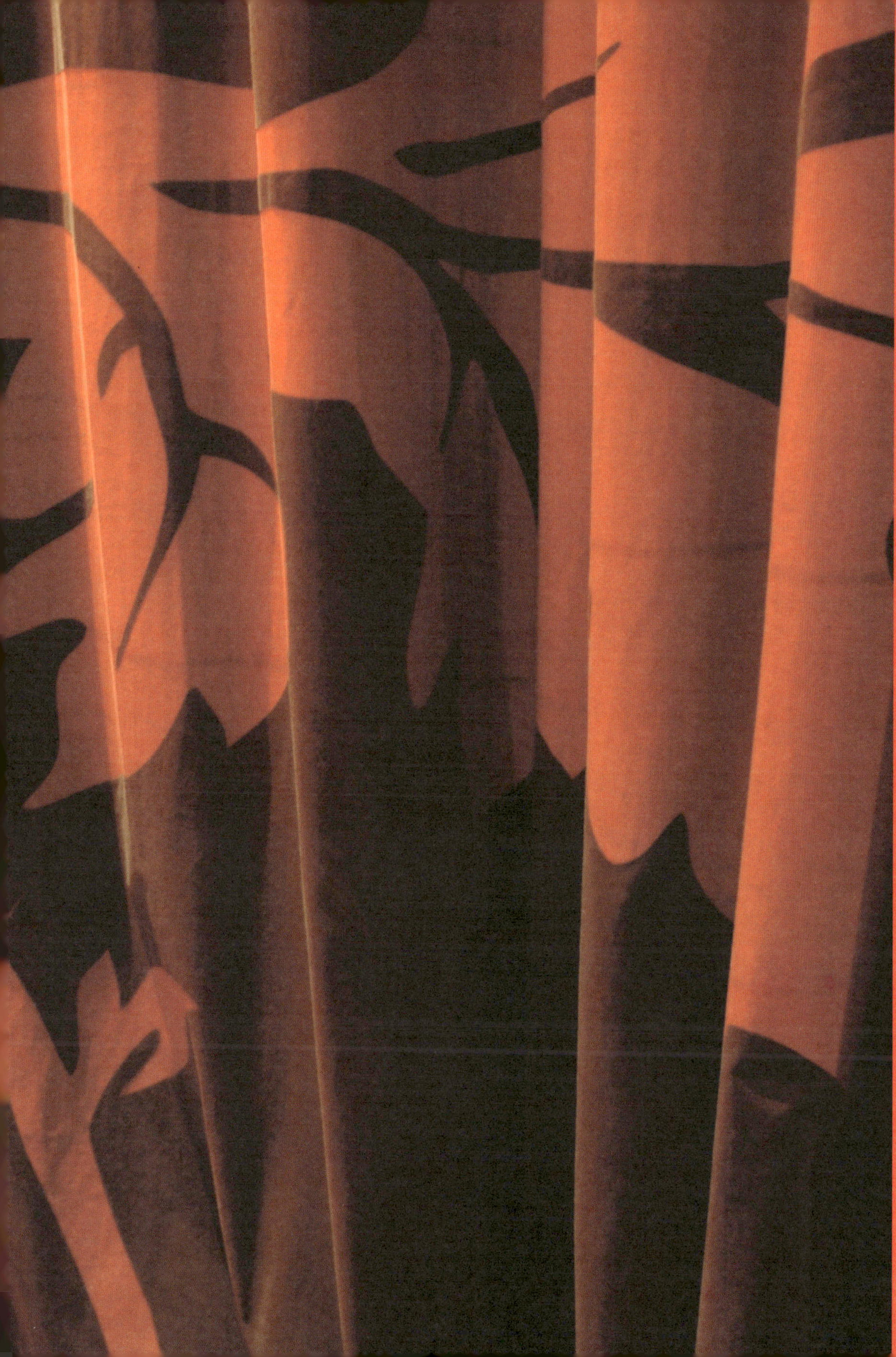

Smock (left) and print (right).

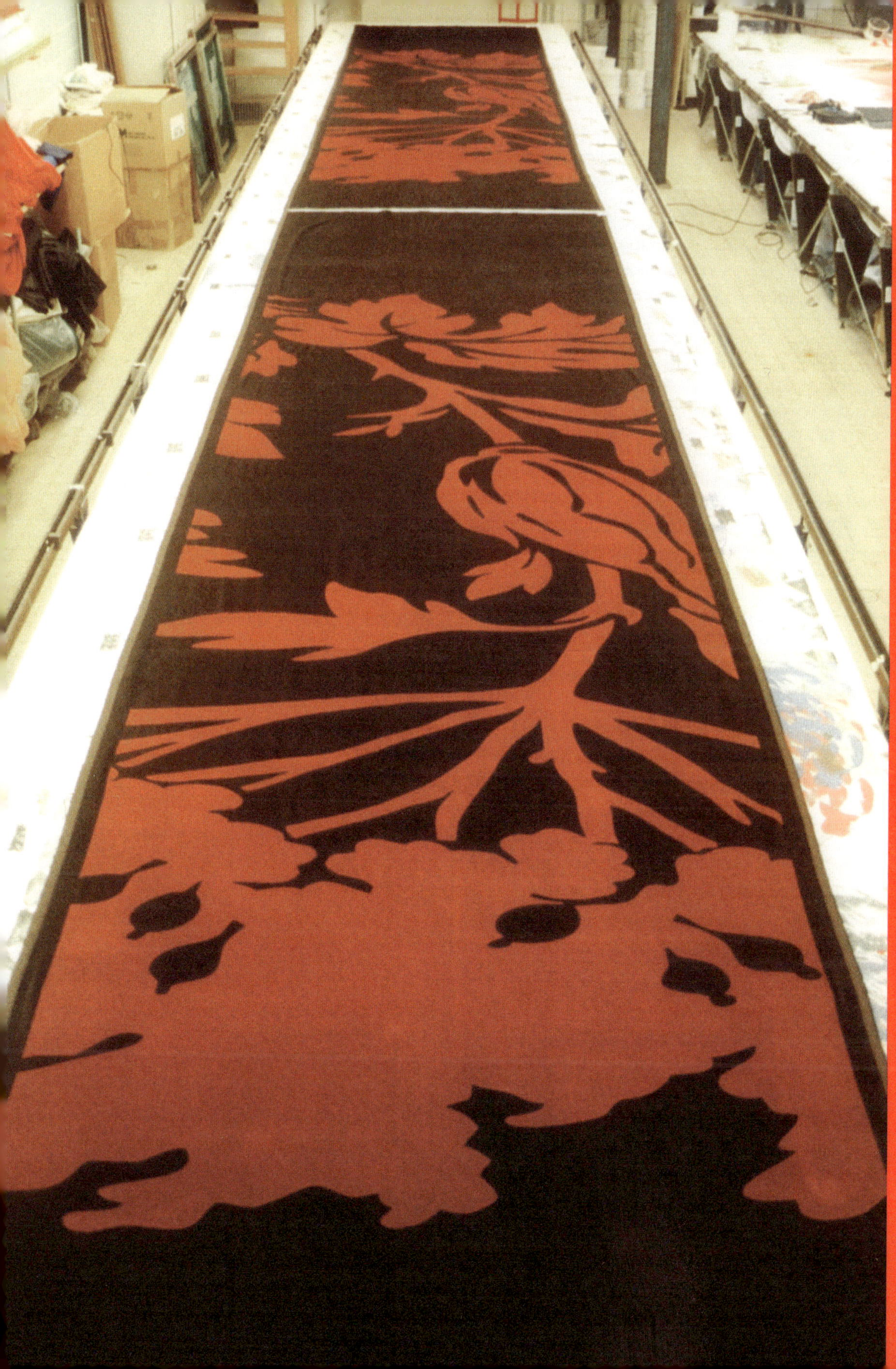

Upper Circle Curtains

In any theatre, acoustic demands differ according to the type of performance – whether a musical, pop concert or a one-man show – and to the amount of seats that are filled. At the Hackney we needed two additional curtains at the back of the upper circle balconies of the auditorium that absorb sound as well as block the daylight coming through the circular windows. Both of these curtains can be shifted and positioned along heavy tracks, organizing their acoustic effect by stretching or compressing them. Both curtains are immensely heavy, built up of three layers of cloth. The visible part is heavily pleated cotton velvet, brown in tune with the adjacent walls, imprinted with enormous red flowers. These flowers, which outgrow the theatre with their size, relate the curtains to the stage curtain and the red finishes of the auditorium, and refer to the former flowered wallpaper and to the park outside the windows that they cover.

Printing on wool or cotton velvet is a profession in itself. Not only do the fibres work against every form of manipulation (they literally push out the paint and force away the needle under the foot of the sewing machine with incredible force!) but a printer can't affix the cloth to the table when it has to be printed. Even the lightest type of glue will tear out the velvet's threads when you want to pick up the cloth again . . . so you can only pin the cloth down along its edges. And you have to print layer upon layer to build up the envisioned effect.

Since the cloth was to be pleated by 200 per cent, the actual pattern we drew was stretched out considerably larger than the form one sees in the end. The Dutch firm we work with made eighteen silk screen frames, each 135 x 175 cm, to form one flower altogether and needed three print runs to get the right paint coverage.

New Annex Curtains

For the new annex, in which a theatre pub, a hospitality space and rehearsal studios are stacked on top of each other on three floors, all curtains we made regulate acoustics and light. In Pepy's Pub, large ivory coloured velvet and satin curtains cover the south and east façades. Their lower half can be easily demounted for dry cleaning. A separate curtain made of stainless steel mesh acts as backdrop for a small removable stage. Its colour adapts to each colour of the spotlights, as the cloth behind it picks up any colour.

For the Education Space on the third floor, we designed a parallel track system that envelopes the room like a spiral; the position of two layers of curtains (one thin and one thick) can be adjusted to create a different configuration and atmosphere of room and stage at each event.

As all windows on the south side of the new annex look out onto a small square with a fountain and trees, we proposed to line the curtains on all consecutive floors with one huge flower (the upper circle curtain flower on an even larger scale): as the three floors, when added up, measure the same height as the proscenium curtain, the unifying flower form would not only reflect the park, but also show the scale of the curtain hidden inside the theatre to the world outside. But costs were adding up, and this idea did not materialize, alas!

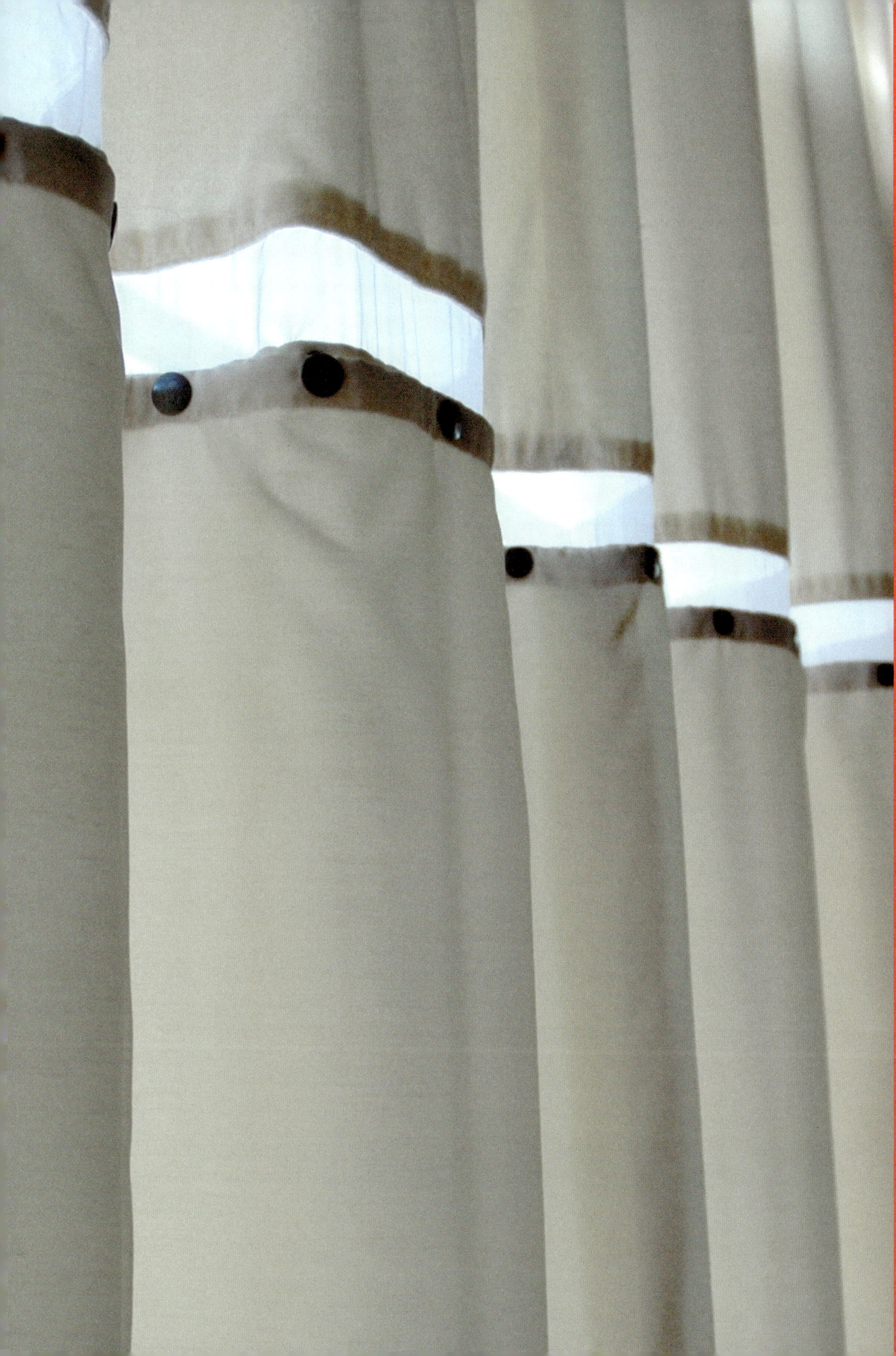

A 'rainbow' voile envelopes the space and its stage, organizing the use of the room. A thick wool-serge curtain rolls parallel to it, covering the large windows and organizing the stage into front- and back-stage areas, while influencing the acoustic quality of the room both in stored and in open position.

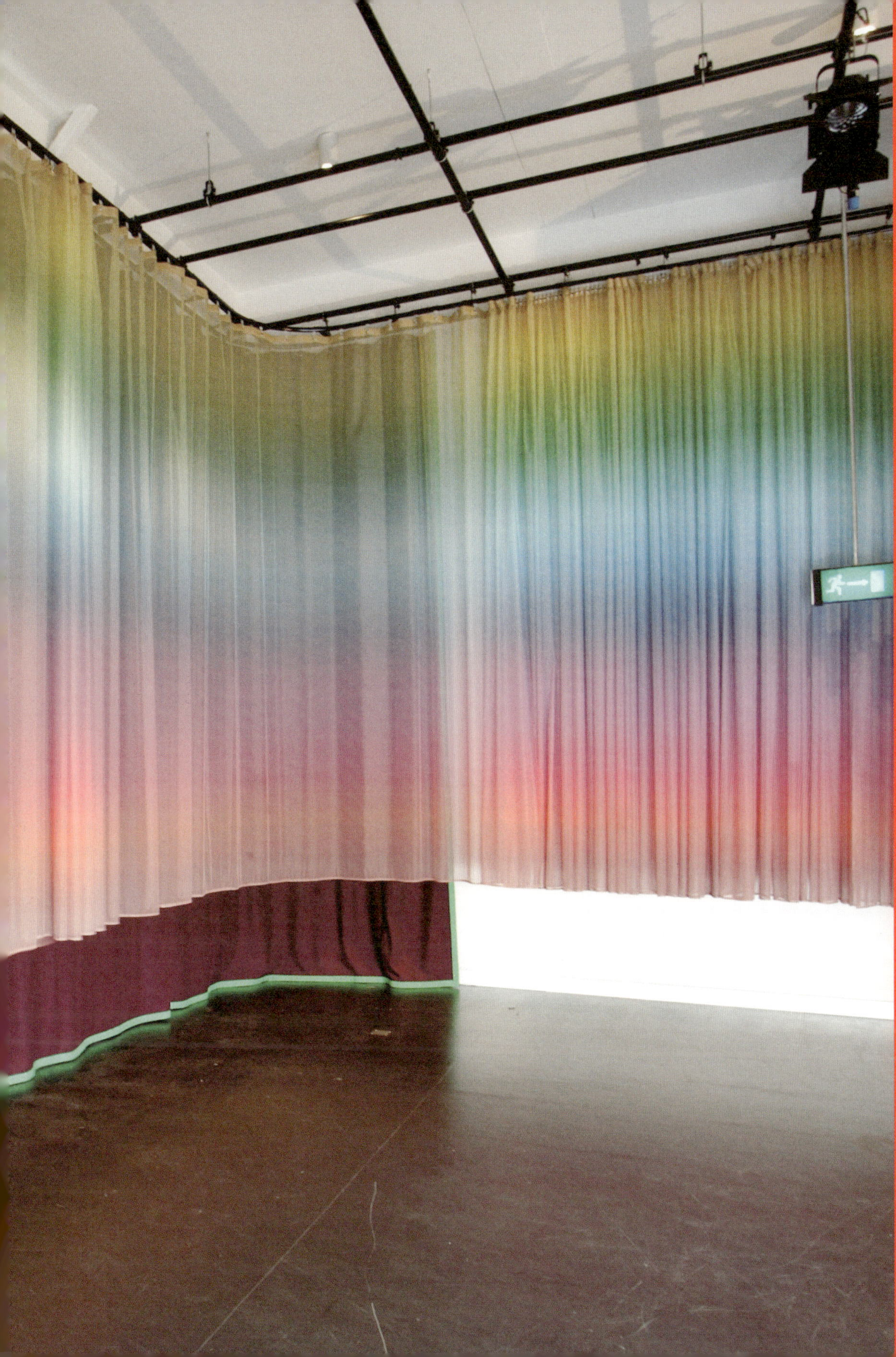

Preparing for a mid-day performance in the Education Space.

… looking out from the Education room – on the third floor – past the voile and the new HACKNEY EMPIRE façade lettering.

The Effect of Curtains
Tim Ronalds

For performance we dreamed of bare rooms, of a discovered, bare-boarded room, shutters closed, full of memories of previous occupations, but vacant now, its hard surfaces daring sound or movement. We sought found spaces, specific spaces, best of all old theatres where the form still provided focus, but the decoration had faded to leave a harder edge. The space we despised was the room with walls lined with curtains, matt wool serge that soaked up light and sound. Such rooms, we thought, had no particularity, no memory, no architecture.

That was my attitude when I first met Petra Blaisse. Now, through the experience of working with her and Inside Outside, we have learned the potential of curtains – how fabric with its colour, softness, movement, translucency, sheen, sound, can transform space and touch the emotions.

Our first collaboration with Inside Outside was on the Mick Jagger Centre: a public performing arts centre being created within the school where Mick Jagger had been a pupil. The essential challenge was how to change the spirit of its institutional spaces. Curtains were regrettably the practical requirement. An article in *de Architect* magazine prompted us to approach Petra Blaisse.

Her design for curtains in the main performing space proposed, on one side of the room, lemon yellow velvet overlaid with the finest silver grey metallic voile and, on the other side, pink velvet, overlaid with alternate vertical bands of black and white gauze. Photographs do not begin to convey the sensual qualities of the fabrics – the changes of colour as light falls on the nap of the velvet, the way the movement of the gauze changes the colour of the fabrics behind, how the translucent fabric colours the light in the space, least of all how the pretty pink and primrose is sensually charged by the slippery gauzes. I remember watching with some trepidation when the design was presented to the client – for, despite their famous pupil, this was a traditional institution that would continue to use the hall for morning prayers and assemblies. The Governors touched the samples. Not a word was said about the associations these materials triggered but perhaps all recognized that the designs embodied the essence of the difference between school and rock performance.

Curtains were part of the concept for the new spaces of our next project, the redevelopment of Hackney Empire, and Inside Outside's propositions were equally acute: cream velvet, cream silk and steel mesh bring reckless luxury to the dark spaces of a street front bar; spectral voile over burgundy serge makes a white studio rich and ethereal. Curtains bring sensuality to these hard-surfaced spaces. They make gravity visible, light apparent, they curve and move and are full of association. The curtains make a primal connection between space and people: the stuff that wraps our bodies and touches our skin becomes an element of architecture.

Making new curtains inside the historic theatre was difficult. It seemed a simple strategy: to replace the original furnishings with new to avert the dead hand of forensic restoration. But a proscenium stage curtain is not a modern thing and a textured textile surface held taut within its aperture is never allowed its own form.

Our next project is a circus school. On occasions its vast training hall is used for performance, the essential transformation of the space made with a huge curtain hung in space. I recall the sheet which is stretched to make a backdrop for a child's first play and I know now that the curtain – and not the bare room – is what makes for performance.

London, 2005

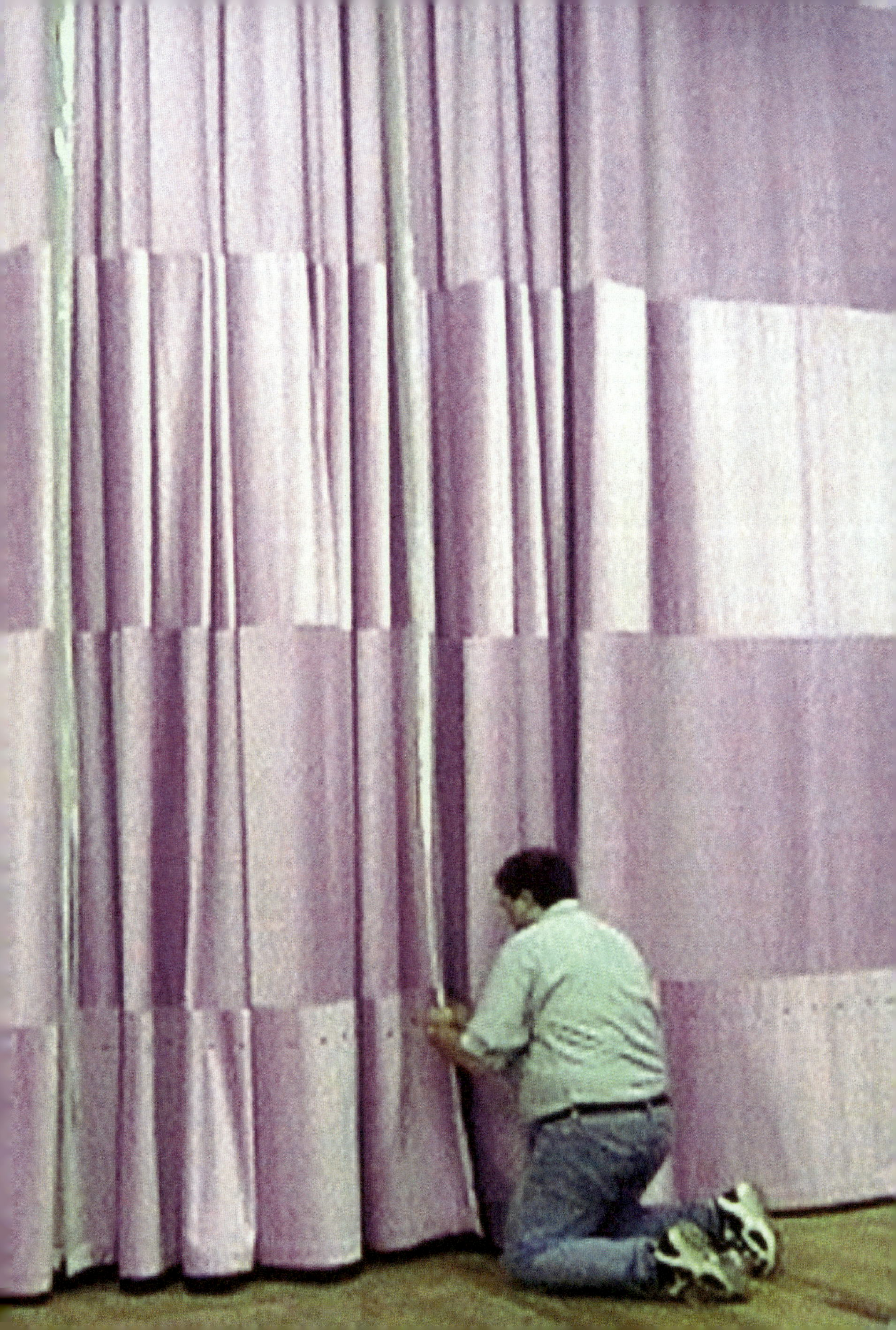

Shifting Layers

Light- and sound-regulating curtains
Mick Jagger Centre, Dartford, UK, 1998–1999

Pulling fleeces over colours.
(Installation, video camera stills)

Branding

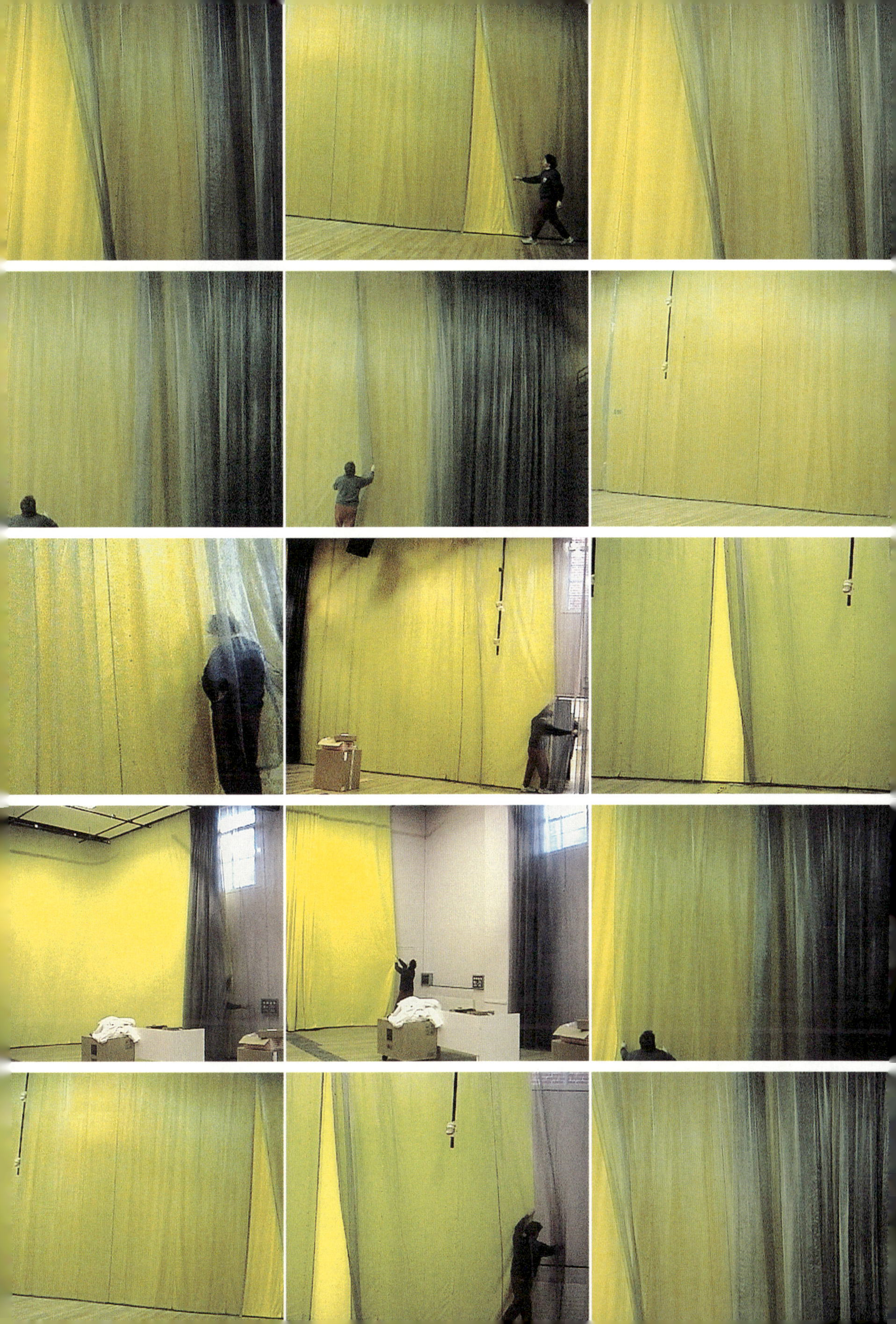

Milky Way

Stage curtain
Palais de Congrès, Lille, France, 1992–1994

Exit from left to right: light grey curtain follows purple curtain to storage behind the auditorium's corrugated plastic side wall.

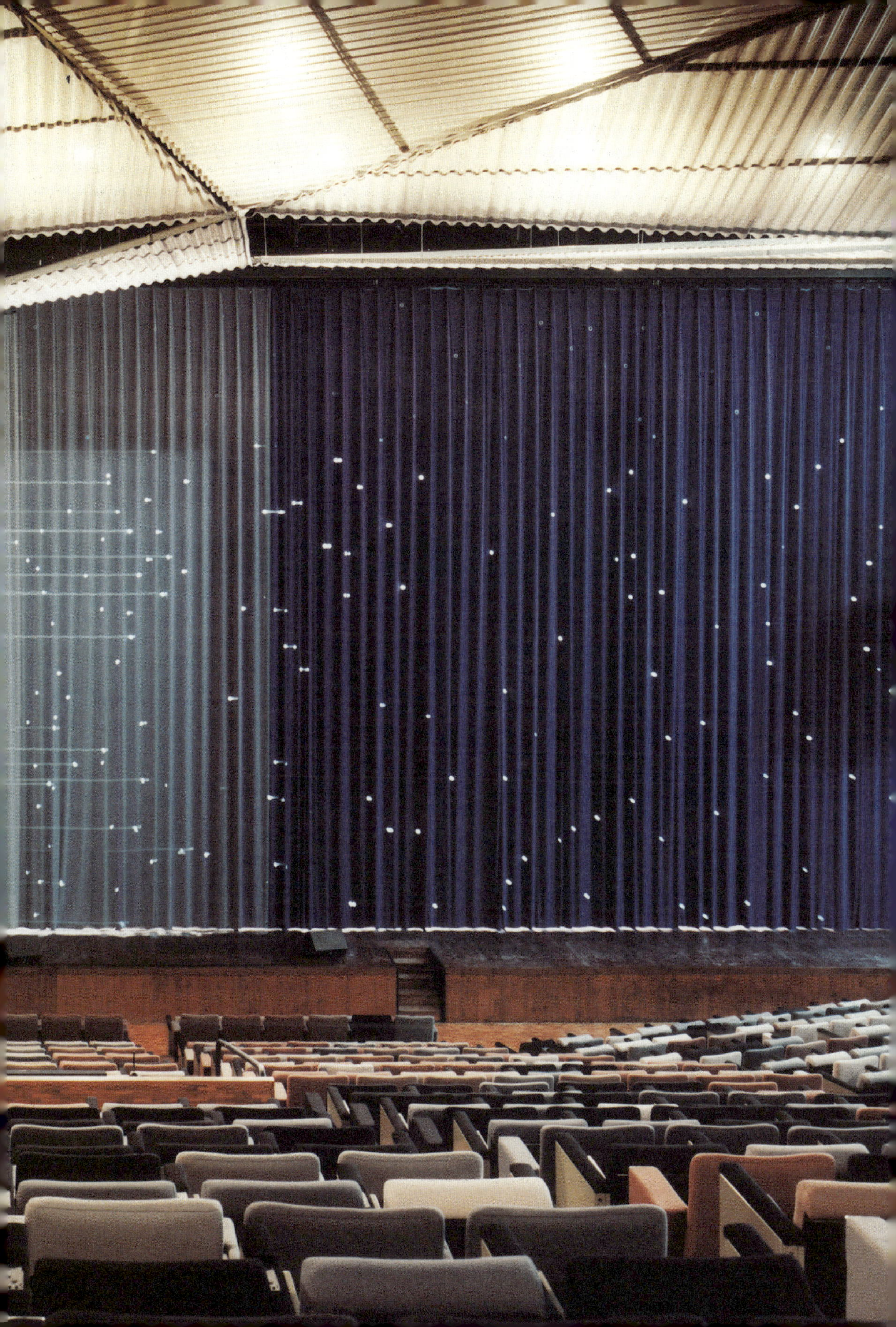

Liquid Gold

Stage curtain for Nederlands Dans Theater
The Hague, the Netherlands, 1987 & 1999

For Jirí Kylián.

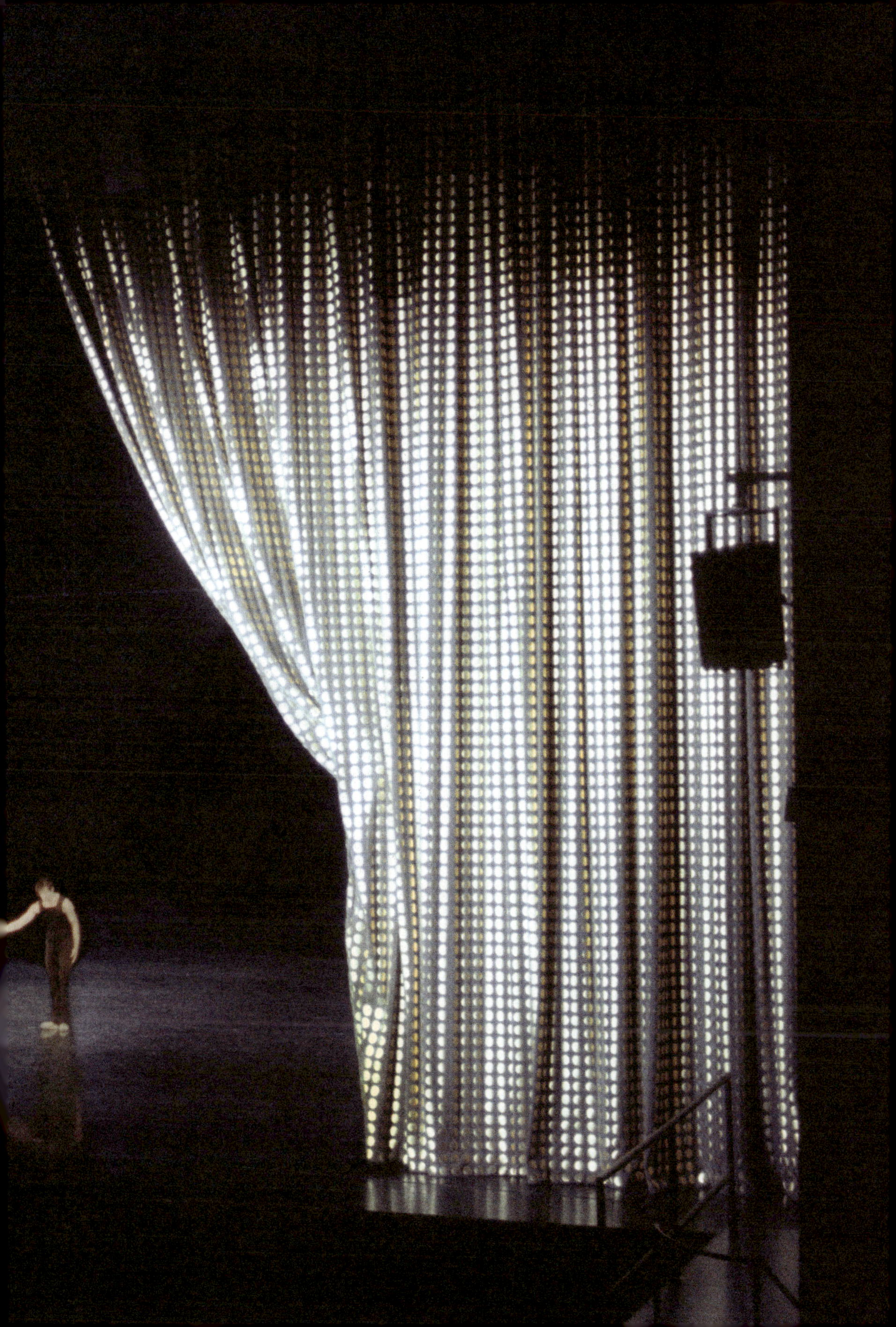

Ah! Not holes.

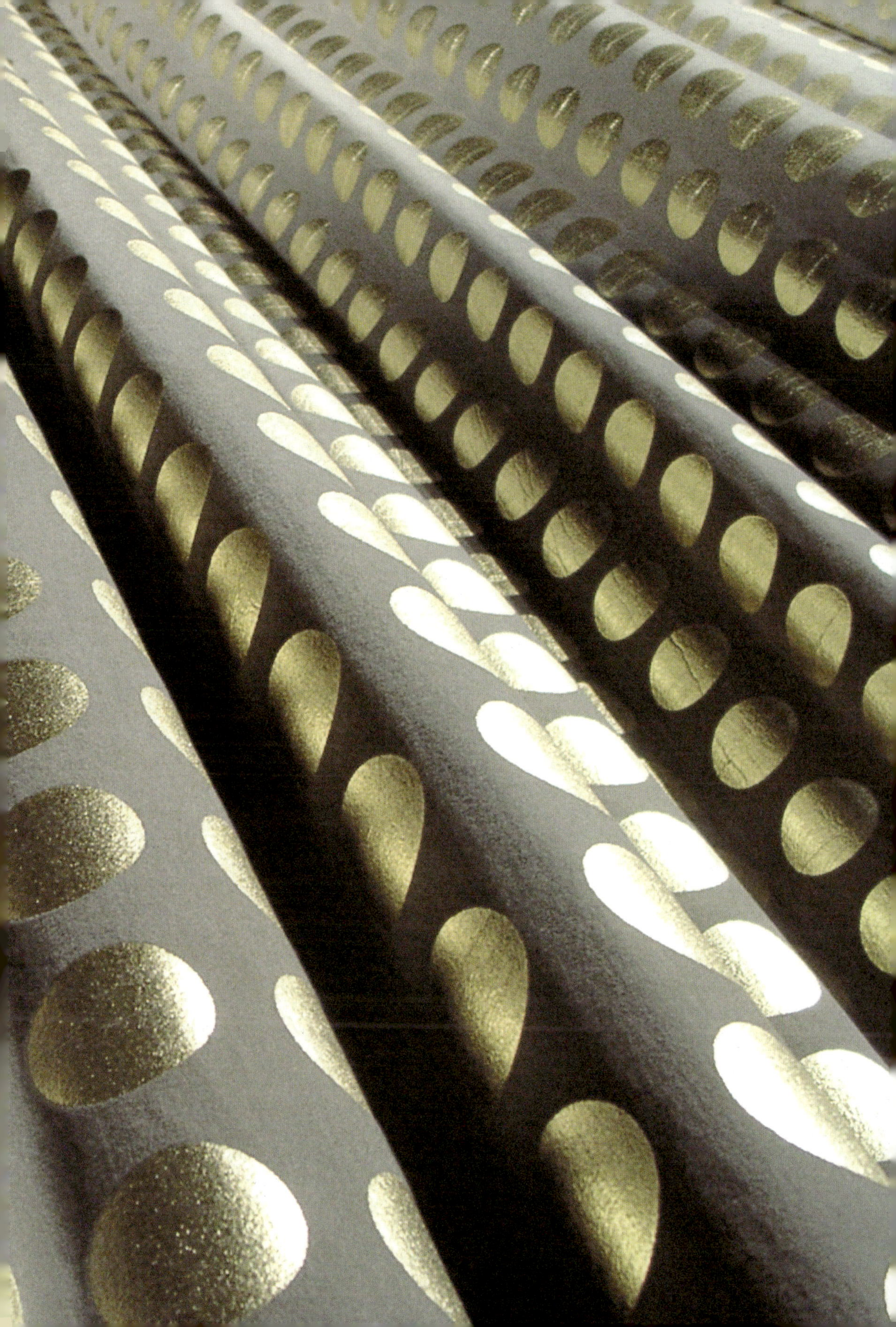

Powder Gold

Sound-reflective panels for Nederlands Dans Theater
The Hague, the Netherlands, 1987 & 1999

Tiny mirrors were used for laser beam sound tests at the time;
I asked to leave them on.

Angel Root

Light- and sound-regulating curtains
The Netherlands Embassy, Berlin, Germany, 2004

Holland in Berlin.

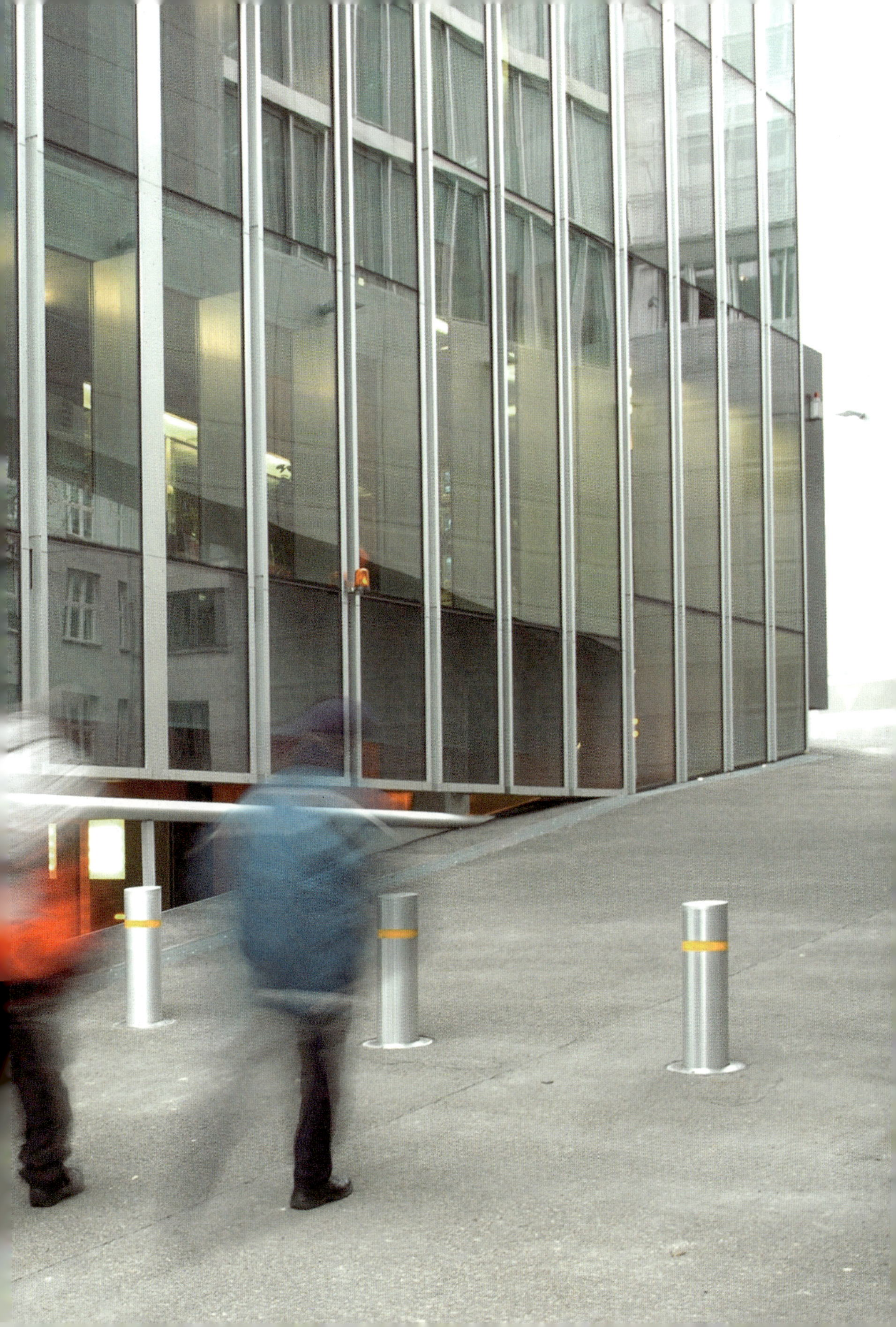

Two kinds of architecture.

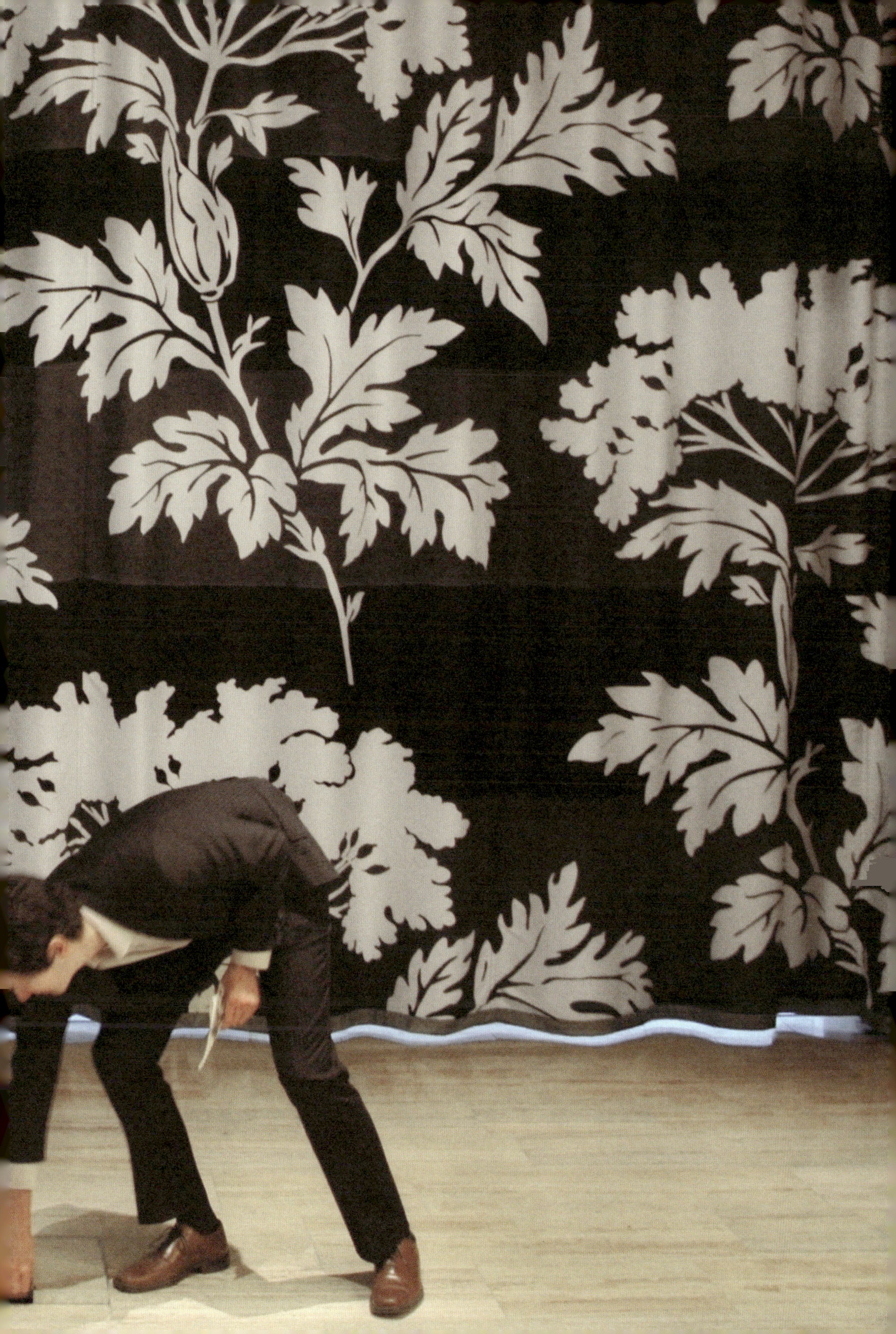

Acacia green.

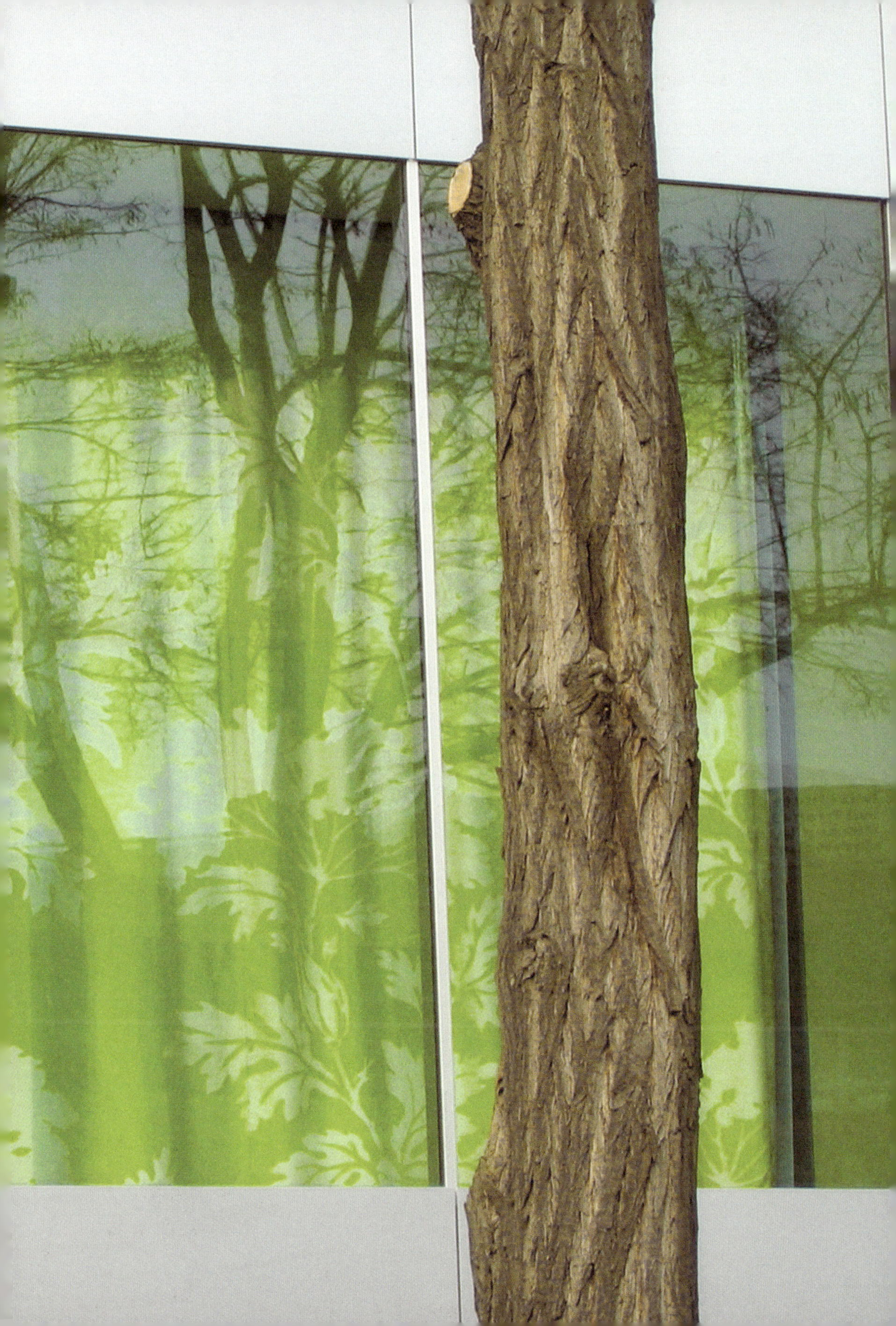

Noise Dress, Flower Field

Sound-, light- and space-creating curtain
Kunsthal, Rotterdam, the Netherlands, 1992–1994

Unrolling sound, turning the outside in.

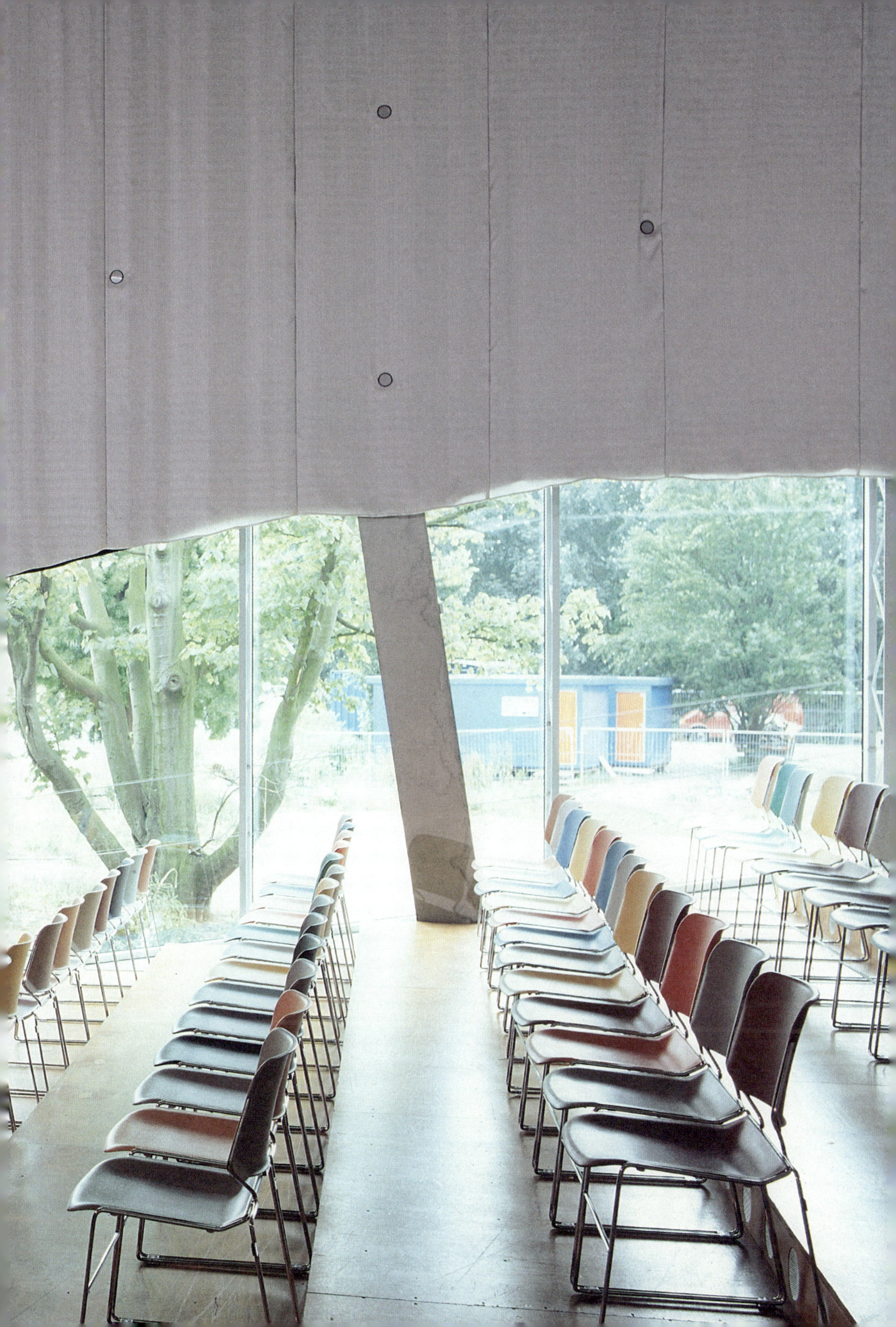

The first time that a track was placed within the matting before pouring the concrete roof (on a very hot summer day); truly part of the architecture.

Robe eats column, flirts with Metasequoia.

Façade Curtain

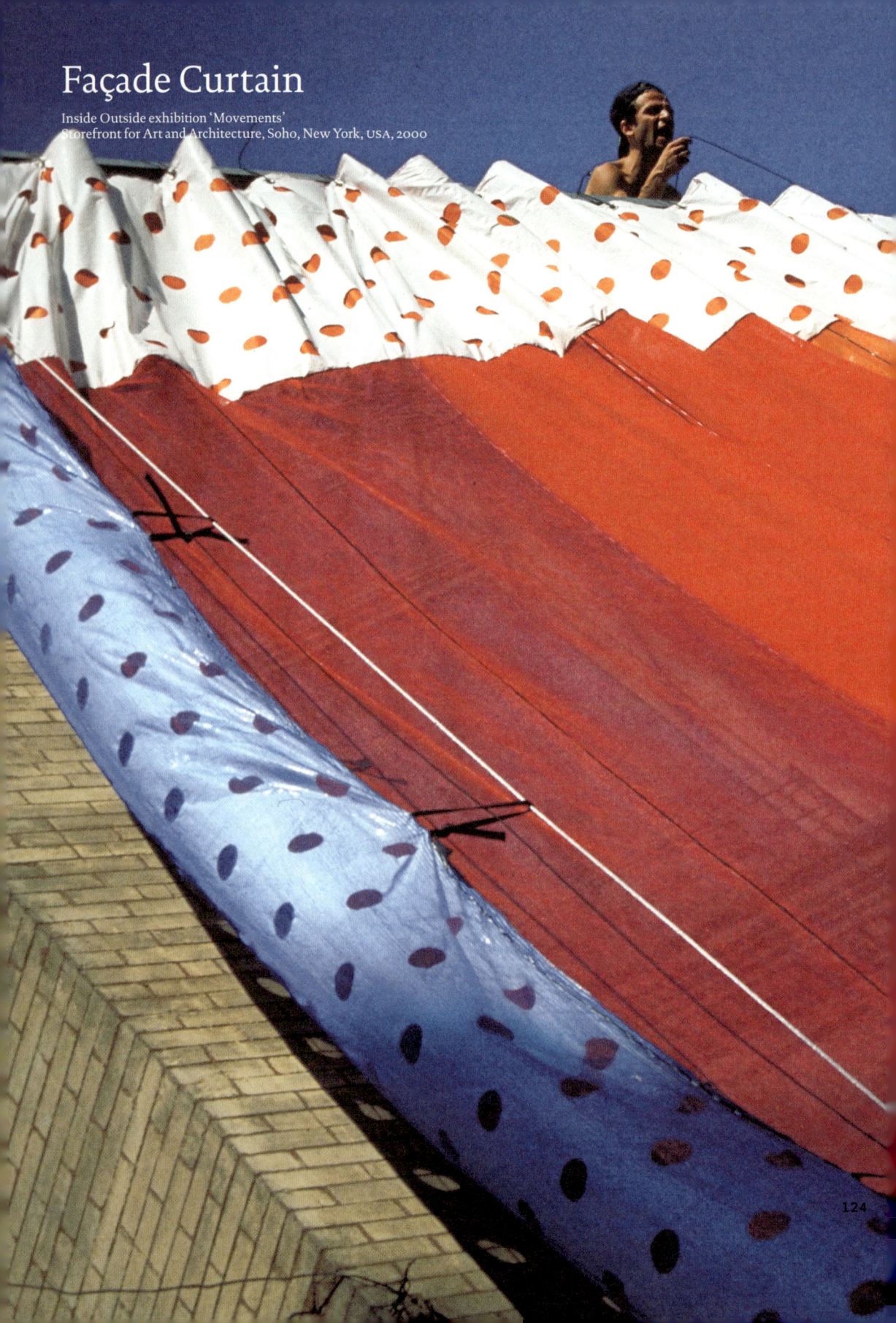

Inside Outside exhibition 'Movements'
Storefront for Art and Architecture, Soho, New York, USA, 2000

For our 'Movements' exhibition in 2000, we created a 15 m-high façade curtain to symbolize the scale in which we usually work. We made the curtain on site, sewing it on the sidewalk (Anky and I). Mountaineers helped us install the curtain in such a way that it didn't obstruct movement on Manhattan's sidewalks (contact thanks to Diller and Scofidio).

Fin de Siècle

Exhibition design for OMA
Institut Français d'Architecture, Paris, France, 1990

Introductory space mimicking Villa dall'Ava's 'bunch of columns' (in construction at the time) installed in the IFA. Spaces were tiny and intricate, so we asked to break down walls and toilets, showed OMA's mentality through images and quotes, then guided the public through a series of work spaces; each room different, from light to very dark, from square to extremely narrow, using sound, projections, scale and light effects to transmit the size and atmosphere of OMA's architectural creations.

ÉQUILIBRE

EUPHORIE

EXPLOSION

CLIENT

CROQUIS

CONTRASTE

DÉSIR

FUTUR

Complex Urban Park

Giardini di Porta Nuova, Milan, Italy
Biblioteca degli Alberi, winning project by Inside Outside Group 2003–unknown

The Requirements of an Urban Park

In February 2004 we heard that we had won the international landscape competition for the Giardini di Porta Nuova: a new park design for the city of Milan. Our entire team – from Milan to Amsterdam to Los Angeles – went berserk. Of course, we had hoped and prayed to win, but we were totally surprised and incredibly happy. Pleased also, that we had taken the job seriously, believing in our own way and everyone giving his or her best.

Almost inevitably, urban parks these days are submitted to an intricate, complex programme. A city park has cultural, political, social and economic roles. It must convey the city's prosperity and cultural status. It has to create income and jobs. It has to solve a series of infrastructural problems. It has to absorb traffic, tunnels, parking lots, waste or city plumbing. And it has to connect different areas, both mentally and physically. The city of Milan expected all of these things of the future Giardini.

The site of the Giardini di Porta Nuova – literally 'the gardens of the new city gate' – is a hundred thousand square meters, or ten hectares of land, in the heart of Milan, hardly developed since the Second World War. Quite something. Irregular in shape, the site is embedded in a dense urban situation. Connected to the Garibaldi Station to the northwest, tunneled by train tracks and encircled by four- to six-lane traffic roads, tram and metro lines, parking lots and pedestrian crossings, the site itself looks chaotic and unkempt, scarcely protected by damaged fences covered in graffiti. The site is partly inhabited – small clusters of old buildings – and partly used for the storage of building materials and temporary structures like sheds and circus tents.

The train tunnel underneath the park creates a long topographical hump that divides the park in two. Plans to extend the train tracks and construct underground traffic tunnels in the future demand 'accessibility at all times' from the park surface down. Built areas within the park that are still privately owned will remain 'no go' areas to us for at least another fifteen years.

Along the Giardini's edges, the city is developing large high- and medium-rise building projects: the huge Cità della Moda project with Hines Developers and architect Cesar Pelli to the west; the Regional Tower of Pei Cobb Freed & Partners to the east; new residential apartment blocks in the 'Isola' area to the north; and an extension to the municipal office buildings by an Italian architect in the direction of the Central Station.

So we had a list of 'additional issues' that went on and on. But we didn't mind – we thought they would make the site all the more intriguing.

Inside Outside had never entered this kind of competition before. It wasn't the scale that was new to us. I'd worked on the Downsview Park competition in Toronto with Bruce Mau, Rem Koolhaas and Oleson Worland Architects, winning the first prize, and had composed a 'green plan' for a much larger-scale Vinex Location project near Utrecht. What was new was that *we* were the invited party, *we* had to select and lead the team of architects, designers and engineers and take on the paperwork.

The Team

When Inside Outside was invited to join this competition, we were asked to present a team and a working method. So first we brainstormed among ourselves, in order to understand the implications of the situation and the city's requests. Then we sketched and formulated our first ideas – a web of connective paths, the topography and the system of irregular plots – and then assembled a team.

What I like about Inside Outside is that it is so small and yet is able to address such complex issues. That is why it needs to attract staff with multiple talents. Every single person in the studio has his or her basic profession, but only uses their specialty as a starting point for further exploration. Why limit your perspective and know-how, why not go further and learn more in different fields?

For this competition our team consisted of: architect alias photographer Lieuwe Conradi, team coordinator alias strategic talent Mathias Lehner, designer and cultural anthropologist Marieke van den Heuvel, office manager alias handyman and computer technician Jaap de Vries and myself. Around this core of members of Inside Outside, in view of the complexity of the competition's demands, the team was reinforced with people from various fields, who work on different scale levels.

Mirko Zardini is an Italian urban planner, architect and thinker based in Milan, whose written work on the contemporary city is influential. His perspective on the city of Milan, his knowledge of the local language and culture – the Milanese traditions and contradictions – and his understanding of the political aspects of the project seemed essential to support our work in the context.

I got to know Michael Maltzan, an American architect from Los Angeles, when working on competitions and on the Hammer Museum project in LA. He has designed very contemporary museum spaces and private houses, but I also value him for his strategic and diplomatic talent. Which is something I thought would be valuable both within the team – to mediate among opposing viewpoints – and in case we had to find the right protocol for presenting less than obedient plans to the city – something, knowing our working method, that I expected us to be heading for!

I had worked with the Dutch graphic designer Irma Boom on our 'Movements' exhibition catalogue for Storefront for Art and Architecture in New York's Soho in 2000. I knew how deeply she enjoys creating beautiful, layered and physically engaging books, weaving text, images and hidden information. When I imagined the paths of the park as surfaces inscribed with text, I thought of Irma as the best designer for the job. And I was sure she would

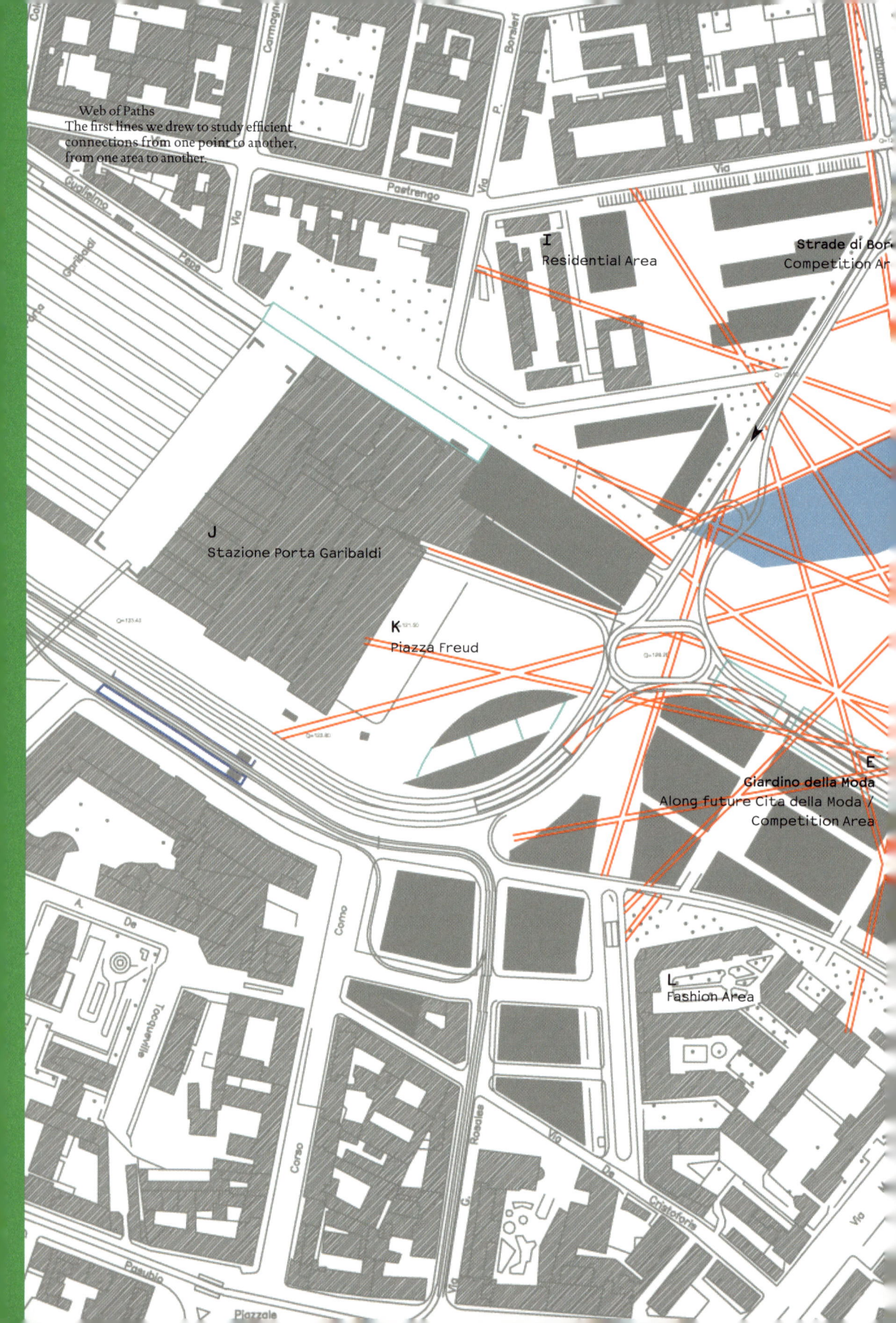

Web of Paths
The first lines we drew to study efficient
connections from one point to another,
from one area to another.

I
Residential Area

Strade di Bor
Competition Ar

J
Stazione Porta Garibaldi

K
Piazza Freud

E
Giardino della Moda
Along future Cita della Moda /
Competition Area

L
Fashion Area

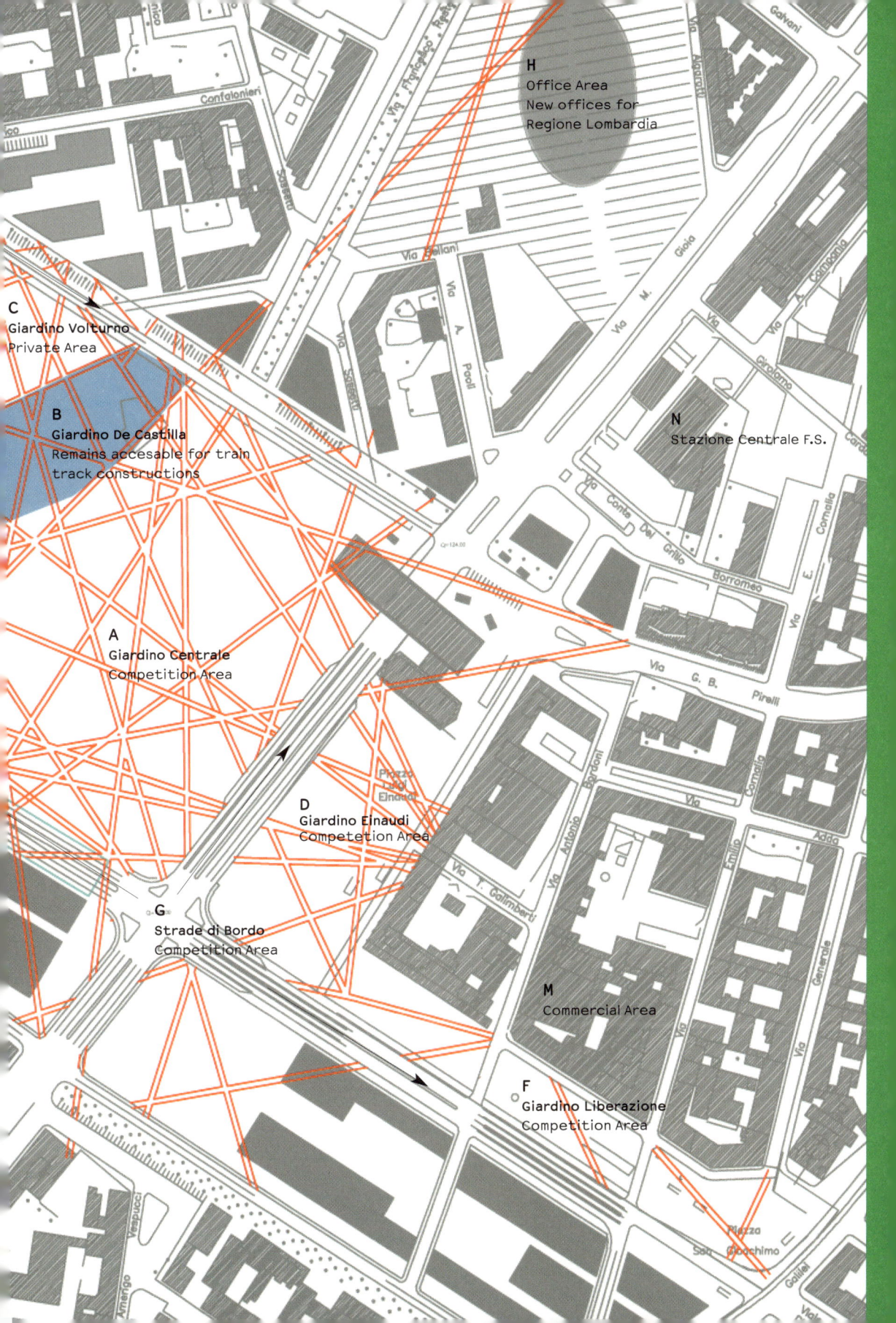

H
Office Area
New offices for Regione Lombardia

C
Giardino Volturno
Private Area

B
Giardino De Castilla
Remains accesable for train track constructions

N
Stazione Centrale F.S.

A
Giardino Centrale
Competition Area

D
Giardino Einaudi
Competetion Area

G
Strade di Bordo
Competition Area

M
Commercial Area

F
Giardino Liberazione
Competition Area

be inspired by the thought of working outside, away from the paper surface!

Piet Oudolf, renowned Dutch horticultural master planner, developed a new way of using plants and designing gardens that mimicked their natural habitat, together with other Dutch garden and planting designers in the eighties and nineties. Gardens in the city today have become more like rigid urban sculptures, lacking movement and hidden surprises. I wanted to reintroduce seasonal, rich planting in the urban park and Piet is a professional who can implement that romantic, sensual layer with authority and experience.

And, last but not least, Rob Kuster, landscape engineer with a vast technical know-how and a flexible mind, is a must-have for a team that wants to reinvent the wheel at every turn!

The Park as a Connector

In classic French gardens, paths played a crucial role. They were straight lines, like axes in city plans, opening up perspectives, creating connections and orchestrating efficient movement. Paths can function not only as a connector, but also as an instrument that organizes the whole environment: they define spaces, creating squares, gardens, fountains; they locate pavilions or monuments, areas for reading or meditating. Working with paths is like tracing lines with a pencil.

As we looked at ways in which this park could become an efficient interface, we started with literal connections, tracing straight lines from one important point to another, or from one city area to another. A web of paths now covered the site, with irregularly shaped plots left between the lines. The graphic strength of the connective web was evident.

The model of the 'web' has a certain robustness, and doesn't need to be complete to work. It will remain obvious during any intermediate phase that this park's realization inevitably entails. Also, the path's web model allows the edges of the park to remain frayed, in other words 'flexible'. A jagged edge will allow changes according to necessity until the park's boundaries really 'settle' and the areas in between the paths can be filled in.

The paths themselves are not only for walking, jogging, meditating, studying, eating and interacting, but can also be used for events such as fashion shows, markets and exhibitions, public gatherings and social or cultural events. Their intersections can become plazas or marketplaces. They will be built with different materials in different colours for different functions. Moving through diverse conditions, the paths will take you through a series of sensual experiences, climates and atmospheres – a kind of new haven in the city.

Height differences (between park and city; between park and buildings; within the park itself) can be overcome by lifting or sinking the paths. So paths turn into bridges, walls, tunnels and even furniture in the designing process.

Walking in the park, enjoying the scents and sounds, you'll find various texts written on the path, like pages of a book. I thought it might be interesting to walk over the text, to read a text while moving, as if walking in a film.

The text can be anything: poetry, botanical names, wayfinding information, announcements, stories – readable from up close and from the windows of buildings nearby.

Then Irma showed me etchings and drawings of garden plans and mazes from centuries ago, which depict poems and texts written on the paths. Inscriptions in the garden: exactly as we envisioned them and fantastically beautiful. None of us knew if these drawings were actually ever realized.

Manipulating Views

European aristocratic gardens have patterns and profiles designed to be viewed from the interior, through the windows of the mansion or castle. They create illusions of depth and perspective, treating the garden like a continuation of rooms, with carpet-like patterns of trimmed shrubbery and colourful plants. Also, these gardens dared to turn a garden into 'a land of illusions',[1] its complexity depending on the fantasy of the landscape designer and the owner. Some gardens were filled with grotto's, fountains, architectural structures and fake nature, even escalating to representations of the world, as if 'uniting in one garden all times and places', as the eighteenth-century French landscape designer Carmontelle described his design for the Parc de Monceau in Paris.

Now, there are multifarious points of view in our design for the Giardini. The first conceptual sketch shows both the complex section of the park – with the levels below ground – and the many positions from which the public will be able to experience the park visually: from cars, busses, sidewalks, trains, airplanes, helicopters. There's a different view from every level and angle.

From within the park the topography creates views downward or upward over the park and towards the city. That same system of folds and slopes will protect the visitor – and the surrounding residential areas – from the noise and smell of the surrounding traffic.

By folding some of the plots downward, we created sloping gardens which at their lowest point open the visitor's view to the subterranean canal that runs right through our site, or to the trains passing by underground. A kind of new metropolitan grotto experience.

We also wanted to manipulate planting heights and levels of opacity. You can make screens with vegetation in the same way that you use curtains on a stage. When you walk through the park, you experience layers of screens, from translucent to opaque, from thin to thick, giving a feel of dense complexity, although the garden's organization is actually really simple. And speaking of curtains, we also planned a real curtain made of stainless steel that closes off an area in the heart of the park at night.

This three-dimensionality of the park, combined with the rich planting compositions, will entertain the Milanese who visit the park, the Milanese that look onto the park and certainly those who circle around the park at different speeds!

---

1. Allen S. Weiss's book, *Unnatural Horizons* (New York, Princeton Architectural Press, 1998), contains many paragraphs that could describe our park. Weiss: heterogeneity is valorized as a function of pleasure, seduction, and libertinage, not of the totalizing effects of the Enlightenment egalitarianism or universal reason; taste follows both fashion and the sundry demands of the passions.'

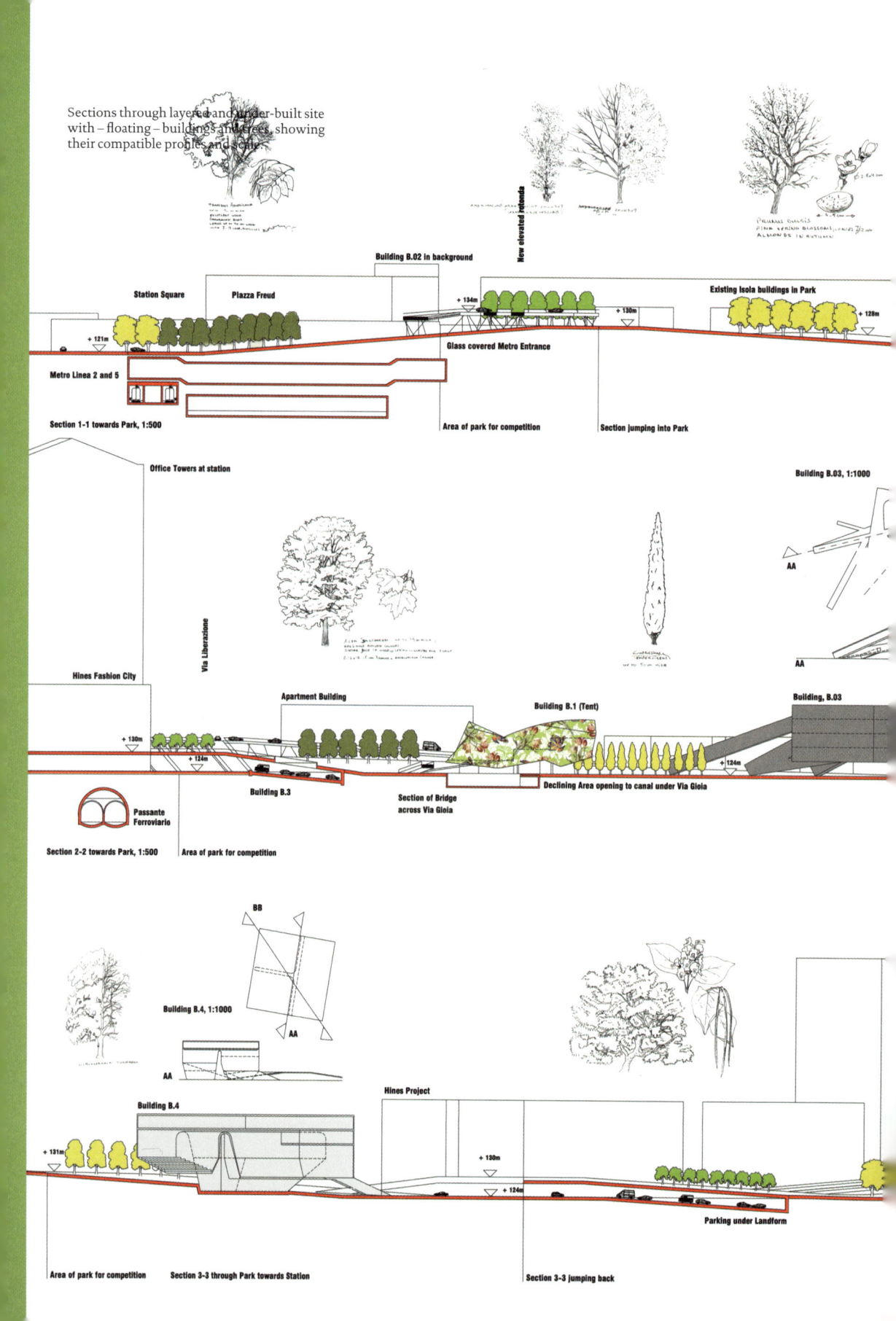

Sections through layered and under-built site with – floating – buildings and trees, showing their compatible profiles and scales.

Section 1-1 towards Park, 1:500

- Station Square
- Piazza Freud
- Building B.02 in background
- New elevated rotonda
- Existing isola buildings in Park
- +121m / +134m / +130m / +128m
- Metro Linea 2 and 5
- Glass covered Metro Entrance
- Area of park for competition
- Section jumping into Park

Section 2-2 towards Park, 1:500

- Office Towers at station
- Building B.03, 1:1000
- Hines Fashion City
- Via Liberazione
- Apartment Building
- Building B.1 (Tent)
- Building, B.03
- +130m / +124m / +124m
- Building B.3
- Passante Ferroviario
- Section of Bridge across Via Gioia
- Declining Area opening to canal under Via Gioia
- Area of park for competition

Section 3-3 through Park towards Station / Section 3-3 jumping back

- Building B.4, 1:1000
- Building B.4
- Hines Project
- +131m / +130m / +124m
- Parking under Landform
- Area of park for competition

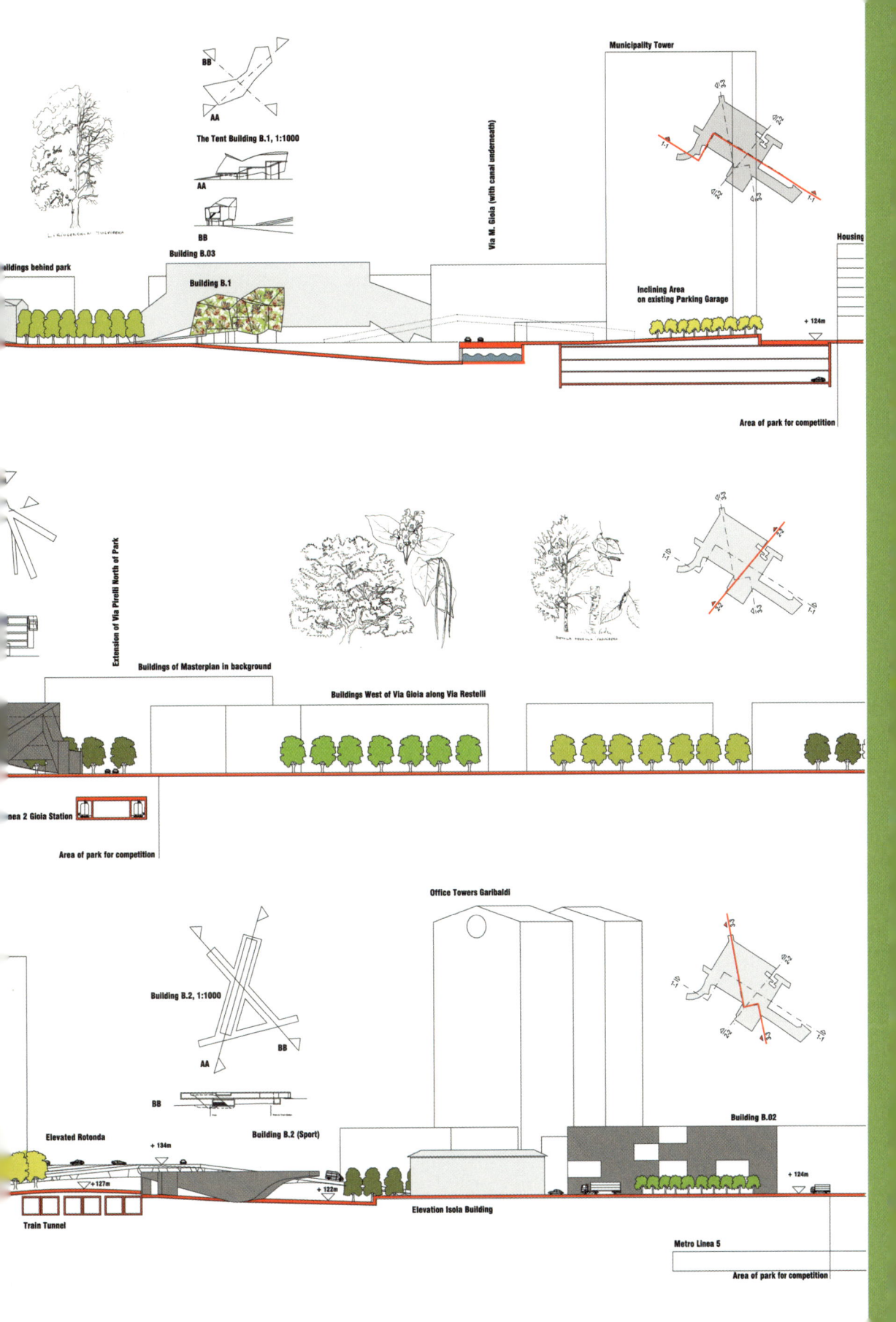

BB
AA
The Tent Building B.1, 1:1000
AA
Building B.03
BB

Municipality Tower

Buildings behind park
Building B.1

Via M. Gioia (with canal underneath)

Inclining Area
on existing Parking Garage

Housing

+ 124m

Area of park for competition

Extension of Via Pirelli North of Park

Buildings of Masterplan in background

Buildings West of Via Gioia along Via Restelli

Linea 2 Gioia Station

Area of park for competition

Building B.2, 1:1000
AA
BB
BB

Office Towers Garibaldi

Building B.02

Elevated Rotonda
+ 134m
+ 127m
Building B.2 (Sport)
+ 122m
Elevation Isola Building

+ 124m

Train Tunnel

Metro Linea 5

Area of park for competition

Library of Trees

In Holland, where the landscape is so synthetic, we plant everything in straight rows – our country's only openly military form of expression! Like bulb fields and tree nurseries, the system suddenly becomes dynamic when you move past at a certain speed. Such a beautiful effect. And considering how much traffic passes the Giradini, I wanted this park to have a nursery-like planting system from very early on. Also, hearing that Milan's old botanical garden in the northern area of the city called Brega doesn't function anymore – it is in bad shape and closed down – the idea of creating a new botanical garden fell into place.[2]

Botanical gardens have always been intriguing because of their simple and systematic organization. They have the visual attraction of the mathematic logic of partitions, groupings, placement and nametags; the smells of glass houses, herb gardens and water gardens; the authority of age-old trees; the separate areas for 'mother plants'; the synthetic interventions that make miniature biotopes. And there is always something bizarre about botanic gardens. Like in nurseries, plants are collected in a 'subjective-objective' way, it seems, and that is fascinating. It is science driven by personal obsession, and not one botanical garden or nursery is the same as any other.

I wondered how we could translate these favourite ingredients into a more contemporary form of botanical garden. We realized that our botanical garden would not be protected by walls – as is traditional – but would lie naked in the embrace of a very busy city centre; and that it would certainly never be maintained in a very careful manner.

Instead of a garden that exhibits plants and trees as unique specimens, we proposed fields of plants and trees, which create diverse environments. The park's collection of irregular plots clearly lent itself for this concept: you can just see the park as a mosaic of plots filled with flower gardens and water gardens, trimmed or wild shrub gardens, prairies and lawns, orchards and nurseries ... Piet would compose these gardens in the most beautiful way! And then there would be sports fields, playgrounds and picnic areas.

We scattered circular forests – interior spaces covered by translucent vegetal canopies – across the park. We mainly chose trees that Milan uses in its parks and along its streets, complemented by fruit trees that refer to Milan's agricultural tradition. You go in and out of these little forests of 20, 40 or 70 trees, all of a different kind. Trunks are different, colours are different, and the way the foliage covers you differs according to the season. Some stay green all year, others are naked in winter; some are fruit trees, some are blossoming trees. As you move on, different worlds unfold at different levels.

The proposal we delivered was called 'The Library of Trees', and this became the name of the design. This decision turned out to be quite a strategic one: Mirko brought us the news that not only the jury but many people he met in Milan after the competition remembered the name of our project – not so much the name of our team! – and felt very enthusiastic about the idea of a Library of Trees for Milan.

[2]. The idea of the nursery has two reasons: first of all, that the park's developement mus be phased over many years, which asks for an immediate and attractive effect. Apart from constructing the web of paths and seeding the entire site with grasses and wild flowers, a nursery should be immediately included for visual effect and mental optimism. Secondly most people enjoy plants or working with them, and a nursery symbolizes health and the creation of a future, while also organizing income and work. With an active nursery on site, local inhabitants can help build this park, make it part of their daily life; thus securing the park's future.

136

Giardini di Porta Nuova

path orientation and planting list

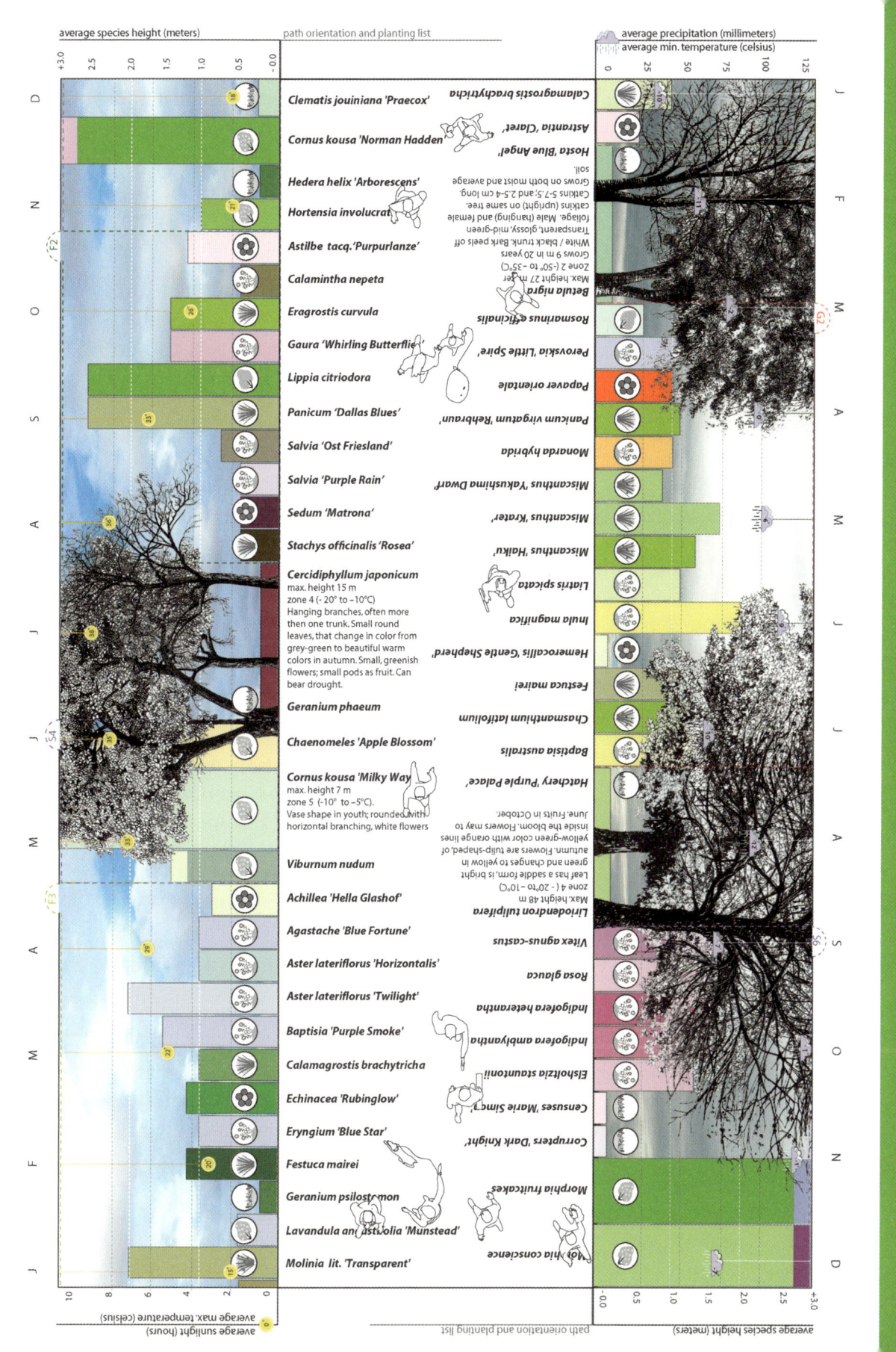

Left column (average species height, meters)

- Clematis jouiniana 'Praecox'
- Cornus kousa 'Norman Hadden'
- Hedera helix 'Arborescens'
- Hortensia involucrata
- Astilbe tacq. 'Purpurlanze'
- Calamintha nepeta
- Eragrostis curvula
- Gaura 'Whirling Butterflies'
- Lippia citriodora
- Panicum 'Dallas Blues'
- Salvia 'Ost Friesland'
- Salvia 'Purple Rain'
- Sedum 'Matrona'
- Stachys officinalis 'Rosea'
- Cercidiphyllum japonicum
  max. height 15 m
  zone 4 (−20° to −10°C)
  Hanging branches, often more than one trunk. Small round leaves, that change in color from grey-green to beautiful warm colors in autumn. Small, greenish flowers; small pods as fruit. Can bear drought.
- Geranium phaeum
- Chaenomeles 'Apple Blossom'
- Cornus kousa 'Milky Way'
  max. height 7 m
  zone 5 (−10° to −5°C)
  Vase shape in youth; rounded with horizontal branching, white flowers
- Viburnum nudum
- Achillea 'Hella Glashof'
- Agastache 'Blue Fortune'
- Aster lateriflorus 'Horizontalis'
- Aster lateriflorus 'Twilight'
- Baptisia 'Purple Smoke'
- Calamagrostis brachytricha
- Echinacea 'Rubinglow'
- Eryngium 'Blue Star'
- Festuca mairei
- Geranium psilostemon
- Lavandula angustifolia 'Munstead'
- Molinia lit. 'Transparent'

Right column (average precipitation / temperature)

- Calamagrostis brachytricha
- Astrantia 'Claret'
- Hosta 'Blue Angel'
  Transparent, glossy, mid-green foliage. Male (hanging) and female catkins (upright) on same tree. Catkins 5–7.5, and 2.5–4 cm long. Grows on both moist and average soil.
- Betula nigra
  Max. height 27 m
  Zone 2 (−50° to −35°C)
  Grows 9 m in 20 years
  White / black trunk. Bark peels off
- Rosmarinus officinalis
- Perovskia 'Little Spire'
- Papaver orientale
- Panicum virgatum 'Rehbraun'
- Monarda hybrida
- Miscanthus 'Yakushima Dwarf'
- Miscanthus 'Krater'
- Miscanthus 'Haiku'
- Liatris spicata
- Inula magnifica
- Hemerocallis 'Gentle Shepherd'
- Festuca mairei
- Chasmanthium latifolium
- Baptisia australis
- Hatchery 'Purple Palace'
  Leaf has a saddle form, is bright green and changes to yellow in autumn. Flowers are tulip-shaped, of yellow-green color with orange lines inside the bloom. Flowers may to June. Fruits in October.
- Liriodendron tulipifera
  Max. height 48 m
  zone 4 (−20° – −10°C)
- Vitex agnus-castus
- Rosa glauca
- Indigofera heterantha
- Indigofera amblyantha
- Elsholtzia stauntonii
- Censuses 'Marie Simon'
- Corrupters 'Dark Knight'
- Morphia fruitcakes
- Mohnia conscience

Everyone understands what a library of trees is and it immediately triggers a vision of a respected, classic environment where one can learn and relax at the same time, while, unnoticed by many, the city fumes are being filtered and recycled into life-enhancing oxygen.

The Challenge

Initially, the brief asked that we incorporate pavilions and reuse some of the existing buildings. But after being selected along with nine other landscape architects for the final phase, we were suddenly confronted with a new situation: an area as large as one third of the entire project site had been allocated for a large fashion-museum building, diminishing the site to two thirds of its initial size. We were all astonished.

We decided that we would not accept having this park suffer as the 'doormat' of the developer's buildings! So we threw our obedience overboard, took the given volume, chopped it in pieces, added more programmes and integrated them as separate buildings into the park.

Michael's office created beautiful volumes for each element and we placed some on the edge and some inside of the park; sometimes crossing avenues like bridges and allowing paths to cross through them, making fluid connections.

This reminds me of the Kunsthal project in Rotterdam, where the Museumpark (the public park that surrounds the Kunsthal in Rotterdam) flows into the building, turns into tree trunk columns, a group of colourful chairs and a trunk-like curtain, and reappears as a garden on the sloping roof. Like the Seattle Library, where the landscape turns into 'garden carpets' in its interior, many of our plans consider the garden and the building as one narrative.

So by 'chopping', we introduced a fashion museum, a fashion and design school, a sports building and a community centre as new architectural elements to the park, in addition to the Museum of Flowers and Insects that we housed in one of the empty old buildings and the textile pavilion that were both part of the competition brief – the latter of which Michael and I virtually designed over the phone. 'Why don't we make a textile pavilion?' 'Great idea!' 'Can we imprint it with huge flowers?' 'Fantastic, send me images of flowers!' After which Michael's team went on to create a two-storey caterpillar tent, hovering over paths and gardens! Placing these buildings throughout the site unites them with the park and intensifies the use of the park; animates it. We believe that the building volumes, together with the circular forests, will create equilibrium between the park and the city.

Three important things that were required for the park were: flexibility, connectivity and a workable phasing strategy. I think our simple, graphic approach generated visual strength and flexibility. The concept also seemed capable of allowing the park to be built up step by step from the simple to the complex elements – or from sober to rich – over a time span of years, without losing its rigour.

It was a nice revelation that our first instinct remained convincing in all the phases of the design process: surviving the team's thorough studies and argumentations. While we became more and more knowledgeable about the political expectations, the tensions within the city, the economic possibilities, the driving forces behind decisions, the money flow and the influence of the developers, our basic ideas still fit the requirements, and remained doable within the given budget of 20 million euros for the park plus 6 million euros for the pavilions – that is, 200 euros per square metre!

We felt very free doing our own thing for the competition. Maybe it was beginner's innocence – 'Let's do it! How much fun!' – daring to be more dynamic than reasonable and never imagining that we would win, considering that we were up against landscape architects like Peter Walker, Gustavson, Adriaan Geuze, and the late Giancarlo de Carlo. This freedom did allow us the inventiveness that brought us to the answers that we wanted to find, the quality that we wanted to achieve for this large city park.

The Park as a Political Arena

The competition for the Giardini was actually one of three or four major ones held by the city government of Milan around the same time. The others were also for large-scale developments, containing a number of new parks that are currently under way, marking a new era for Milan.

After winning the competition, we continued to look at what we could add to the park to strengthen its political position and how we could defend our park throughout election periods, territorial conflicts, financial shortages, social tensions and long after that. We never stopped thinking of how we could see to it that the park would survive, would be cared for and maintain its growth, health and use, constantly stimulated to be enjoyed for generations to come.

A city like Paris has a very high ambition level when it comes to its parks. Developers were less powerful at the time of their conception; or perhaps the city was less dependent on income coming from that direction, who knows. The city of Paris protects its parks well during construction. The entire site of the Parc Citroën Cevennes, for instance, was closed off with an enormous fence until the garden had settled, so that the public could not enter it for three years. An extremely luxurious situation, but an effective one!

Although a team can win a competition, the site's development is in the hands of the city, the investors and the developers. This particular park is financed by the developers who work around the park: each developer is requested to reserve a certain percentage of their building budget, which is then put in the 'city purse' for the park. Twenty-four million euros so far. So the influence is heavily weighed in favour of the developers, not the city – and certainly not the designers.

In the two years since we won the competition, the city of Milan has not offered us a contract yet – but they keep announcing it. With elections coming up, a park is an important initiative to advertise.

In the meantime, developers keep buying up pieces of the Giardini di Porta Nuova site: the city doesn't seem to oppose to this, allowing the original competition site to continue to shrink and change form. They also allow the five building sites around the park to use the Giardini as a construction yard, proposing to delay the construction of the future park by at least four years. They choose to ignore the fact that the construction sites can actually be integrated within the 'web' and plot structure of our design – and that they could easily fit the first phase into the general phasing plan that we suggested.

Initiating a competition for a park is easy. Developing a park is much more difficult, demanding a lot from the city and all parties involved. Besides money, trained workers and a strict organization, a park needs attention and time, patience and perfectionism. And one more important thing: a form of visionary optimism. The park can grow, get more and more rich and beautiful, and live for hundreds of years, but only if the city and all its inhabitants – including the press – fight for it together. (And yes: where *is* the press? We will have to activate them!)

The residential community is not sure if the city can maintain such an ambitious plan. Neither are we, but political strategies aside, we'll continue to look for the best solutions under the changing circumstances, asking ourselves how we can maintain the important qualities and functions of the park; how the park can still help improve the adjacent conditions and the city as a whole – not only from an environmental perspective, but also from a 'human interest' standpoint; and how to ensure that both specialists and residents are involved in the park's realization. After all, being resilient is one of the winner's jobs.

Trees for colour, sound, scent, profile and scale but also for screening, wind breaking, sound absorption and air filtering.

Bottom:
Groupings of trees form interior spaces with vegetal roofs.

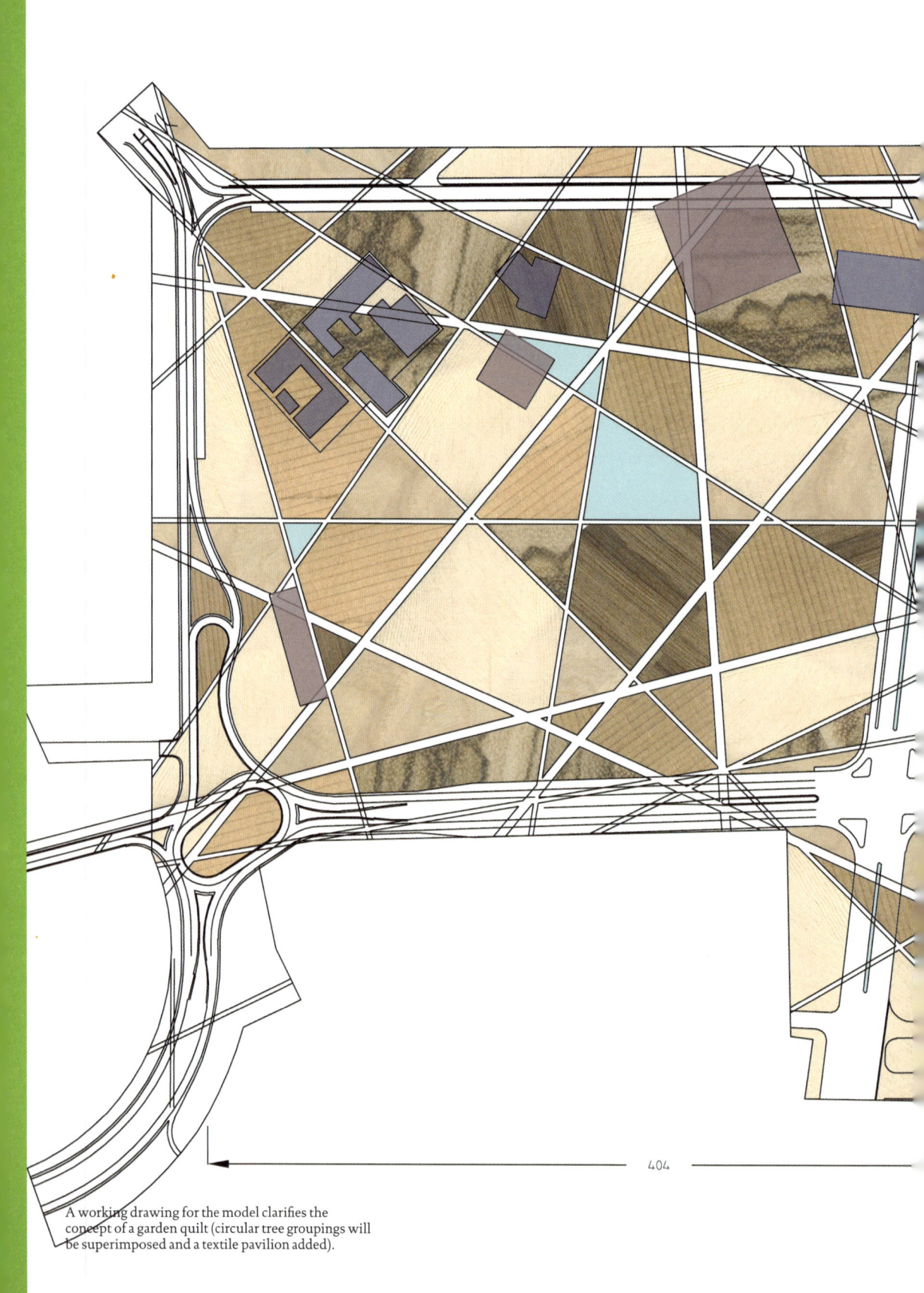

A working drawing for the model clarifies the concept of a garden quilt (circular tree groupings will be superimposed and a textile pavilion added).

Grasses (colour, air)

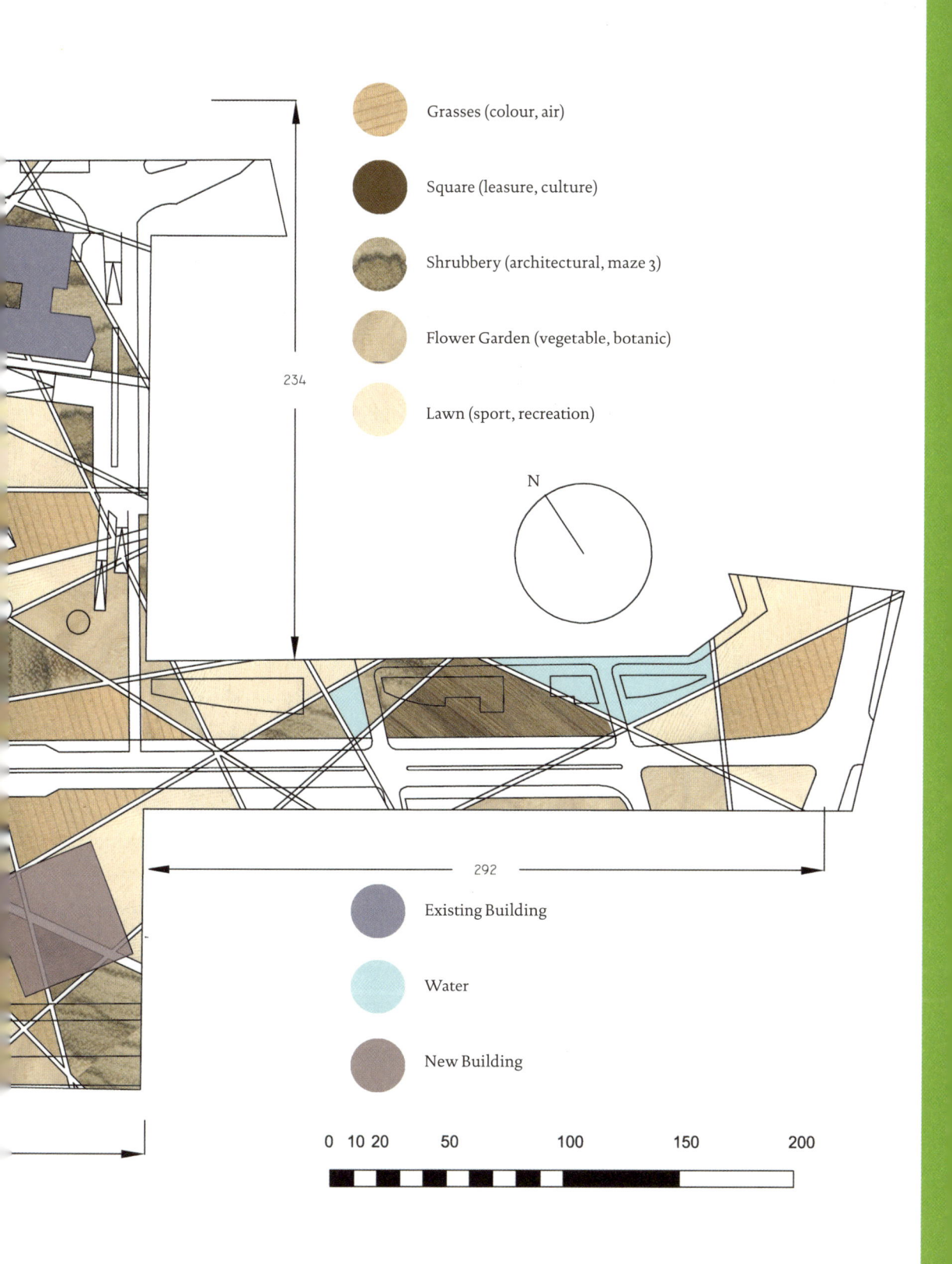

Square (leasure, culture)

Shrubbery (architectural, maze 3)

Flower Garden (vegetable, botanic)

Lawn (sport, recreation)

N

234

292

Existing Building

Water

New Building

0 10 20   50   100   150   200

The model at Inside Outside studio before take off to Milan!

VIA MELCHIORRE GIOIA

Biblioteca degli Alberi embedded in city.
Building volumes on left foreground:
Cita della Moda envelopes.
Within park: Fashion Museum;
Textile Pavilion; Fashion Academy.

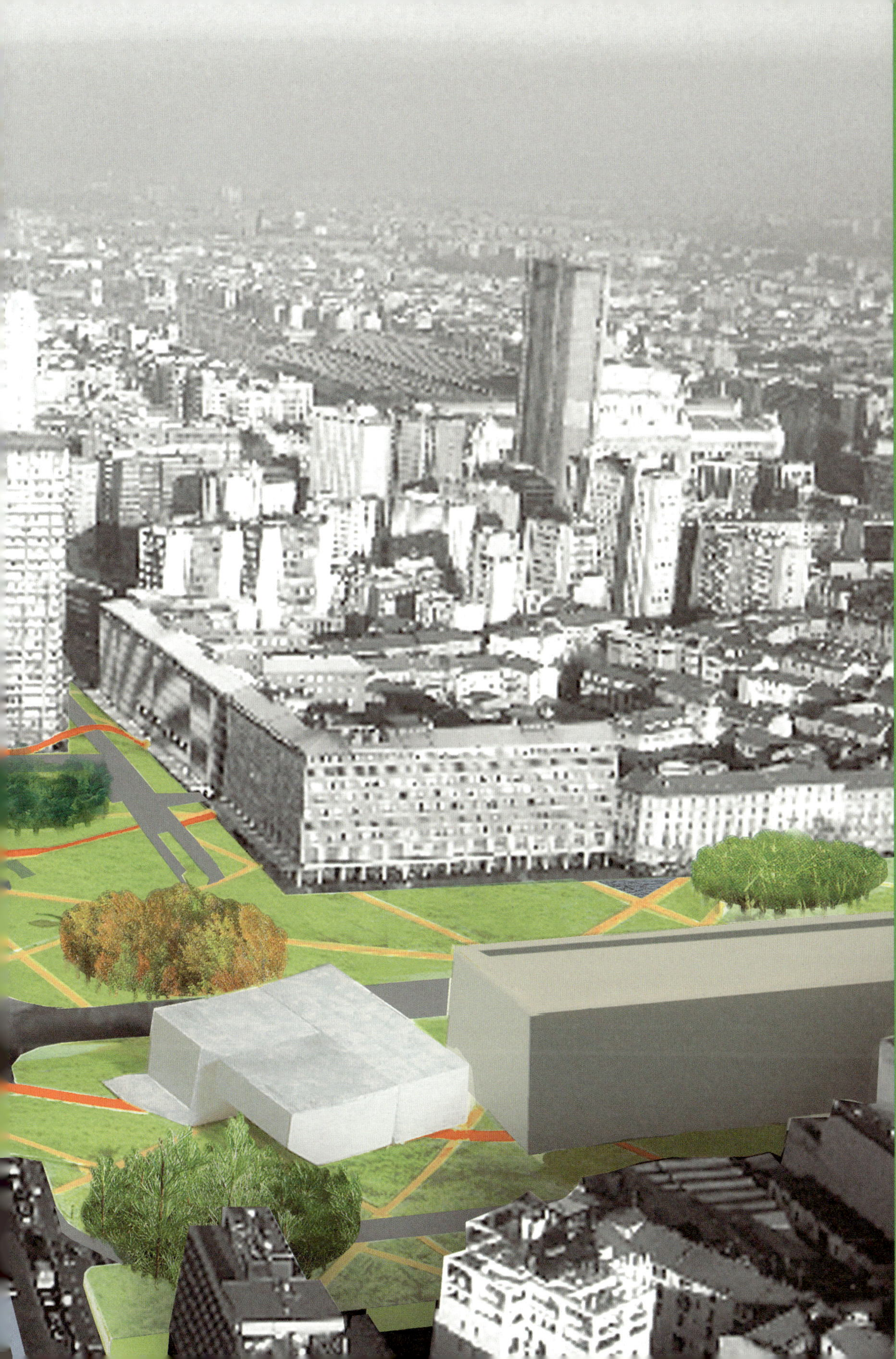

The smell of autumn leaves.

Four different gardens intersect.

One of our presentation collages, showing the diversity of planting and treatment, lettered paths and vegetal screening towards city.

Circular bosques. Path as scrolls of text.

At the nursery. *Helleborus* 'Nigra'.

Seed trays with various perennials, ferns and grasses.

Noses of *Hosta* 'Halcyon'.

A nursery with *Festuca* and *Astilbe hybrids*.

Nature at a Glance: The Urban Scenery in the Work of Inside Outside
Gaston Bekkers

Landscape in the Urbanizing World
At the end of the eighteenth century, Irishman Robert Barker was granted a patent for the painted panorama, at a time when nature also became the subject of urban expansion. He called the invention of the panorama and this new form of painting 'nature at a glance'. 'An entire view of any country or situation, as it appears to an observer turning quite round.'

The painted panorama subsequently became all the rage in and outside of England. A few years after its introduction, a reproduction of *London from the Roof of the Albion Mills* was exhibited in New York. Using its 360-degree circular horizon, the painter positioned the spectator in a new hierarchy of images, in such a way that the perception of art was injected with the semblance of participation.

Throughout Europe, buildings appeared in newly built city parks, such as Regent's Park in London and Vondelpark in Amsterdam, containing successful manifestations of entertainment and illusion, later with movable stages and 'moving panoramas'. City parks, open to the public, were one of the answers to the increased urbanization during the Industrial Revolution. They were largely built in such a way that when you walked through them you were constantly confronted with a different view, a scenery, a cluster of trees, for example, or a statue. The park with varied landscaping and the panorama were both attractions that succeeded in arousing the city inhabitants' curiosity for different and strange urban landscapes, concepts of nature and forms of life. The two were initially inextricably linked and were intended to provide spectators with as much feeling of authenticity as possible.

The relocation of paintings to parks was therefore only a small step. The topographical imitation in an illusionistic decorative painting, and especially the vedute, which reproduced cities or landscapes in smaller format, preserved all the elements of surprise. The excitement that a certain place could evoke would return in the daily reality and landscaping of a city park.

The success of this nineteenth-century visual culture, which was in many ways important for the development of architecture, disappeared rapidly with the advent of moving pictures in film. The theme of the representation of nature, however, has become topical again in the *perception* of urban public space, or the daily urban landscape in front of which the theatre of modern life continuously passes by.

In the Mutation of Things Lost
Even though from time immemorial the desire for expressions of nature and historical landscape images has of course always been in contrast with technical innovation, this theme has received special focus in the work of Inside Outside. Petra Blaisse's visual solutions for (roof) gardens and landscapes reveal a tempting urban landscape. The incredibly diverse work is a response to an open architectonic world in which the relation between public and private is constantly subjected to thorough revision.

Sehsucht, perhaps the most important retrospective of the nineteenth-century panorama, showed the fascinating world behind the many means and ways of viewing (urban) landscapes. In the work of Inside Outside, dioramas and stereoscopy make way for mirrors, sometimes with transparent curtains and peepholes, and other ingenious materials that are connected with (semi-)public space, cultivated landscaping and grass gardens. There is careful attention to detail; the work is functional and refers to the rural and recreational aspects of an urban landscape.

Landscape as *Mise en Scène*

In the history of landscape architecture, one comes across a large number of (architectonic) objects and terms in which the view of and from buildings, of the landscape and in gardens, takes centre stage. The gazebo, the watchtower, the pagoda, the *jardin suspendu*, the *patte d'oie*, the rotonda, *veduta*, belvedere, the garden chair or garden bench and, more recently, the café chairs found at lively squares in the urban landscape: these are but a few examples. In addition, the encyclopaedia of garden ornaments has witnessed a wide range of scenographic developments. The architectonic objects are placed in such a way that they immediately capture the spectator's attention, and the interiors of the buildings are designed with an emphasis on the view created.

During the time when the laws of perspective were discovered, a long time before the invention of the panorama, landscape design formed a bond with stage design and theatre. As it happens, both shared the intention of changing the real world into a world of illusion and fantasy and to use symbolic elements in the creation of images. At the time, temporary theatres and mobile stages served as a kind of laboratory in which all kinds of new discoveries and techniques were tried out and tested. This resulted in a variety of different forms of 'scenes', of views and effects.

In the history of style in garden art and landscape architecture in Europe, variants can be traced back to influences from all points of the compass. The past few centuries seem to have been mostly dominated by the English landscape style, which was based on liberal thought and provided the answer to the rediscovery of the classical Renaissance garden in the eighteenth century. The vistas with winding footpaths dissolving into the infinite horizon, but also the measured height and width and the interior of garden rooms made everything an architectonic and highly cultivated landscape. Though derived from an amalgamation of historical examples and forms, the result is nonetheless very decorative garden art, with humorous and well-considered elements. A highly cultivated form emerged from the flourishing splendour of nature and was further developed. In that respect, the public park is an important norm in the development and improvement of a city's health, given shape by designers through ideals.

Since the beginning of the twentieth century, authorities in the Netherlands have been aware of the fact that public space, usually designated as nature in this country, must be conserved during the development of a city. The romantic artificiality of a landscape park, with a distant nod to nature conservation and 'picturesque' images.

The Amsterdamse Bos, an internationally known example, was laid out in the first half of the last century on old polder structures, empty meadows, ditches and canals. New landscapes were created and old peat bogs were incorporated as natural elements in the large-scale park layout. The city park was made by urban designers with the help of landscape architects, horticulturists and foresters. The different elements resulted in a wealth of individual and characteristic vistas and effects in the landscape, often an exciting, colourful and imaginative spectacle with, among other things, a high artificial hill as viewing point that has a charm reminiscent of an old English country estate. The architects of this park, which was based on a design from the 1930s, also took into

A panel comprising the 360° panorama of *London from the Roof of the Albion Mills*, Frederick Birnie, after Robert and Henry Aston Barker, London, 1792. Collection of Bill Douglas Centre, University of Exeter, UK.

View of the surroundings of Chatsworth Castle, Derbyshire, UK, ca. 1937. Van Eesteren Archive, NAi.

Section of Robert Barkers' Panorama at London's Leicester Square, drawn by R. Mitchell, 1801. (Catalogue cover, 'Sehsucht' exhibition, Bonn, 1993) © Bastius, posters and designs, British Film Institute, London

account the perception of the landscape from a moving car, later again a point of discussion in the USA and other countries. It meant a further approximation between city and landscape.

Reversed Roles

When dynamic landscapes are assigned a leading role in architecture and when landscapes are seen as the biggest challenge for contemporary architecture, an important part of landscape history takes on a whole new purpose. The rivalry between the natural and the cultivated further strengthens the urban landscape in the twenty-first century. The work of Inside Outside shows how a contribution can be made to the synthesis of architecture, nature and interior. The meaning of a gamut of architectonic landscape concepts is key in the studio's work, with the fairly literal interpretation of a far advanced cultivation of nature as the central theme.

A variety of elements and associations are brought into play and converted into another form language. The norm is determined by the choice of planting, the shifting horizons, the ornamentation derived from a natural growing process, applied in the buildings that more than anything else want to be landscapes and, at the very least, want to include an explicit choice of views of the (urban) landscape. All subtleties are brought to the surface in order to reinforce the ideas behind an open and transparent world.

The roles seem reversed. The importance of the landscape in urban development is growing; the programmatic potential of the landscape is the challenge. Architecture is further subjected to the many possibilities the landscape has to offer. The opportunity to make all sorts of less obvious connections has been amply used. In the tailor-made choices, nature in the nineteenth century has become nature in the twenty-first century, in which nature reserves, and also the natural process, can no longer be perceived without human intervention. What is generally regarded as nature landscape is in essence never the true character of a nature landscape, but at the very most a derived form or otherwise a romanticized imitation.

The Language of Green

Inside Outside's designs show clearly how the different spaces are additionally connected to each other with the help of the visualization and use of, for example, grasses, bamboos, groundcovers and other cultivated plants as most important components. In this sense, the studio creates a stronger reality than can be perceived by the naked eye.

The architectonic space is not only formed by buildings but by everything that remains in the ruralness of the city's landscape, which includes trees and shrubbery, dikes, the furniture and the infrastructure of roads and water. It is an urban context that, due to its architectonic expression, will overshadow the solely recreational function of public space of the previous century.

The idea that the green is merely a filler, a decorative surrounding or a softening in contrast to the so-called hardness of buildings has been superseded. In other words, the form language of plantings is a co-determined element of the space and influences the spatial effect of buildings. It is not merely a supplement and enhancement. The planting already has such an emphatic presence, due to its colour and the changing of the seasons, that the form deserves to capture most of the attention, by its positioning for example.

The presence of planting materials attests to a conscious spirit of planning on the part of the designer. The interpretation of nature and the conscious use of landscape elements create new possibilities. It is also the spatial continuity of the 'natural' landscape. Visual, graphic, biological, cinematic and interactive are all aspects that give this dynamic, mutually reversible, urban landscape roots in a mysterious symbiosis from which an astonishing result emerges. The gardens and landscapes are characterized by new techniques, visual programmes, by a concentration and diversity of effects, so that the botanical repertoire reflects the client as well as the designer.

Milan Park

The fact that the interior and exterior spaces are no longer divided worlds and interweave with each other in the designs and completed projects of Inside Outside seems to speak for itself. The Giardini di Porta Nuova, a 10-ha park that the Inside Outside team is constructing in the centre of Milan, will connect different parts of the city and new housing estates by means of an ingenious system of paths. Presently, the park's construction also involves the reorganization of the entire above-ground and underground infrastructure of the urban area. Prairies, botanical gardens and sports fields will be created at points where paths intersect. The Dutch plantsman Piet Oudolf, who together with a graphic designer, urban planner, architect and landscape engineer is part of the Biblioteca Degli Alberi team, has drafted a planting blueprint. 'We take a tree, by virtue of its profile, scale, colour scheme and positive influence on the environment, just as seriously as a building.' Graphically designed texts will be written on the paths. In cities such as Paris and cities in Southern Europe, it's common for public parks to be monitored during the day and closed at night. Not in the sense that they should be surrounded by a fence. No, it's better to use the ancient solution of digging a moat or, in the case of Blaisse, for example, to use a metal curtain that can be slid open during the day. This can be a productive way of preventing vandalism since maintenance is already expensive. Moreover, the experience of entering a park through curtains can be an absolute thrill. The entry is always an important moment before you navigate across paths and along special places. The area was intensely researched and the design plans were introduced by digital means. We see the future before us in images that we are not yet able to experience in person because unfortunately it is only an impression of things to come.

Apartment in London

Unlike the Milan Park, the completed project on the Thames in London can be experienced. The private apartment has a roof garden, where floating surfaces of plants and high grasses and a wooden floor pointing in different directions create a dynamic effect. The apartment and the roof garden are focused on the magnificent panorama of the Thames. As we get closer to the interior, the garden is reinforced by, among other things, magnified images of plants. This concept is also evident in the interior's details and colours. In essence, the carpets and curtains in the interior, with magnified decorations from the plant world, such as grasses and tulips, are of the same kind of artificiality as the garden landscaping in and around the architecture based on natural patterns.

Collaboration with OMA

The Seattle Central Library (in collaboration with OMA), for example, resembles a garden of books more than anything else. The colourful carpeting in variations of red and green with digitally magnified patterns of grasses and perennials, harmonizes with patterns that have been used in the interior of the building. Or the view of an elevated horizon at the McCormick Tribune Campus Center of Illinois Institute of Technology in Chicago, USA (with OMA), on top of which a courtyard garden or patio with prairie grasses is situated. In any case, almost all designs and completed projects are linked to urban (public) life and they offer, in collaboration with the architects, clients, plantsmen and graphic artists, new solutions for the ancient landscape theme of scenery, but then in architecture.

Sources:
- Ballantyne, Andrew, *Architecture, Landscape and Liberty: Richard Payne Knight and the Picturesque* (Cambridge, Cambridge University Press, 1997).
- Catalogue from the Kunst- und Ausstellungshalle der Bundesrepublik Deutschland in Bonn. *Sehsucht. Das Panorama als Massenunterhaltung des 19. Jahrhunderts* (Frankfurt, Stroemfeld/Roter Stern, 1993).
- Watkin, David, *The English Vision: The Picturesque in Architecture, Landscape and Garden Design* (London, John Murray, 1982).
- Jacques, Michel (ed.), *Yves Brunier: Landscape Architect* (Basel, Birkhauser, 1997).

Windy Zero

Garden design and carpet for apartment building for the elderly
De Plussenburgh, Rotterdam, the Netherlands, 2003–2006

Our orange garden path ends as a 'bridge' over the pond.

Production

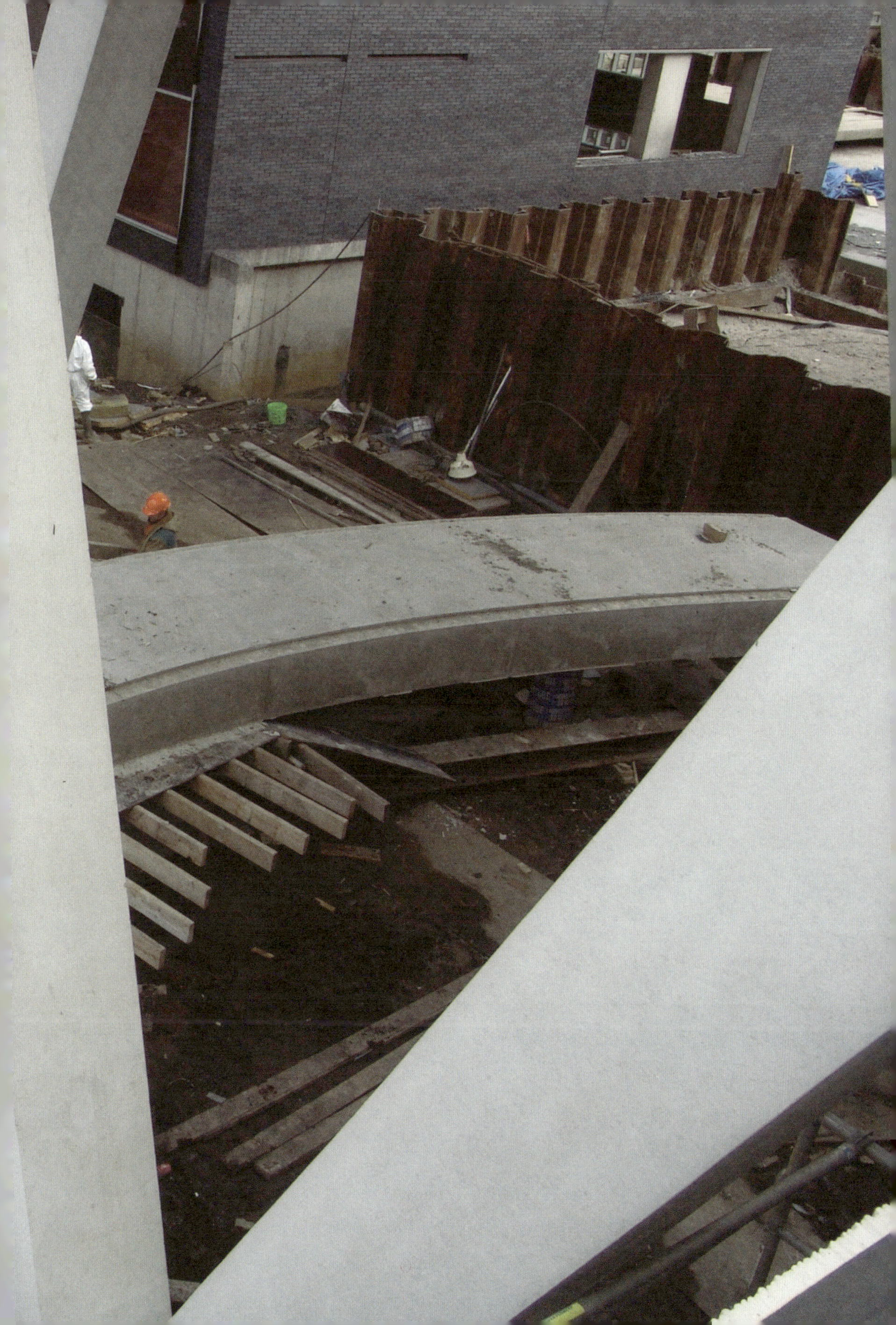

Radial Views

Roof garden and curtains for penthouse
Cinnabar Wharf, London, UK, 2002

The roof garden's wooden deck 'floats' above
the concrete structure like a ballet floor.

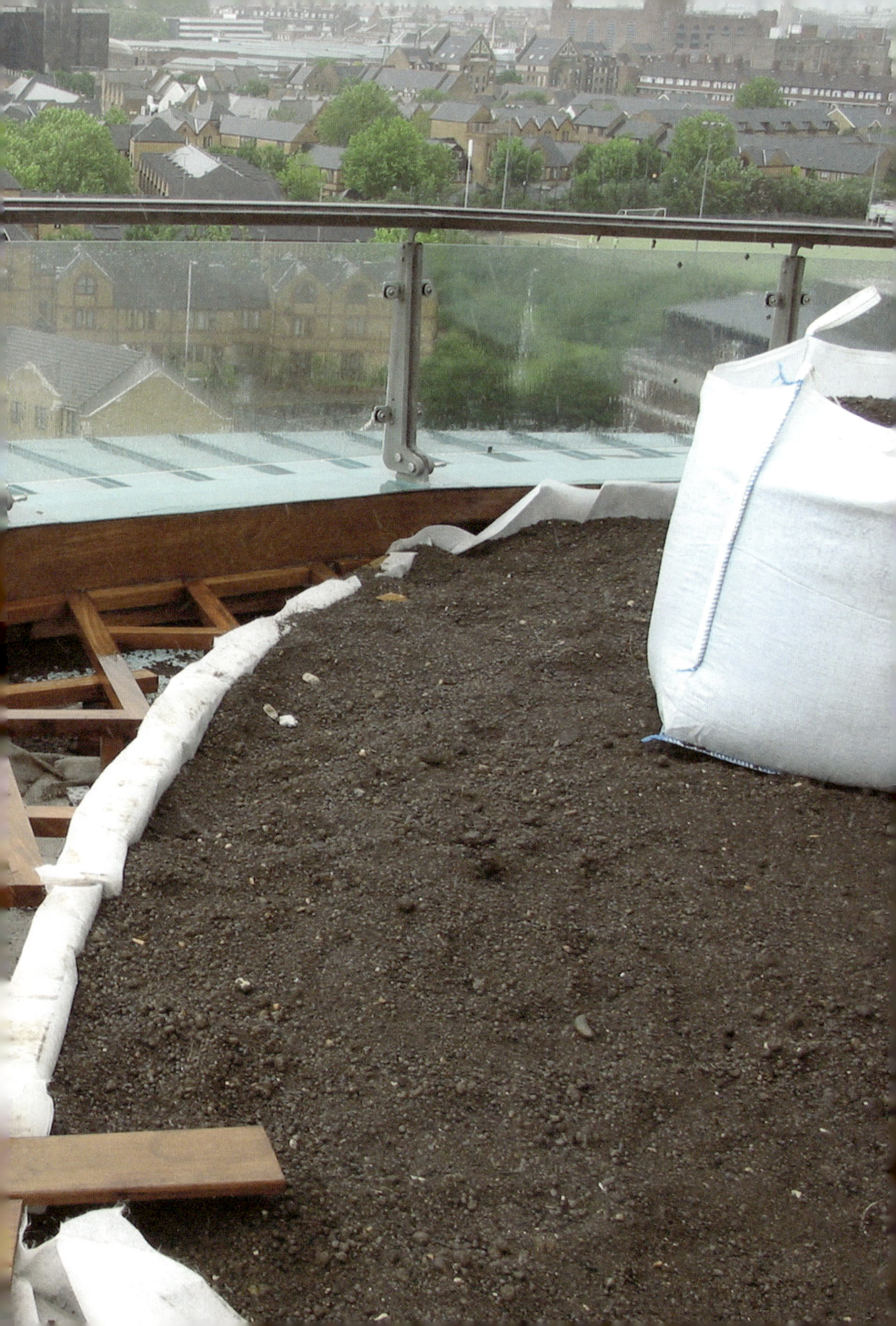

Reflection

Landscape design
McCormick Tribune Campus Center, Chicago, USA, 1998–2004

Planting the 'Mies Garden'.

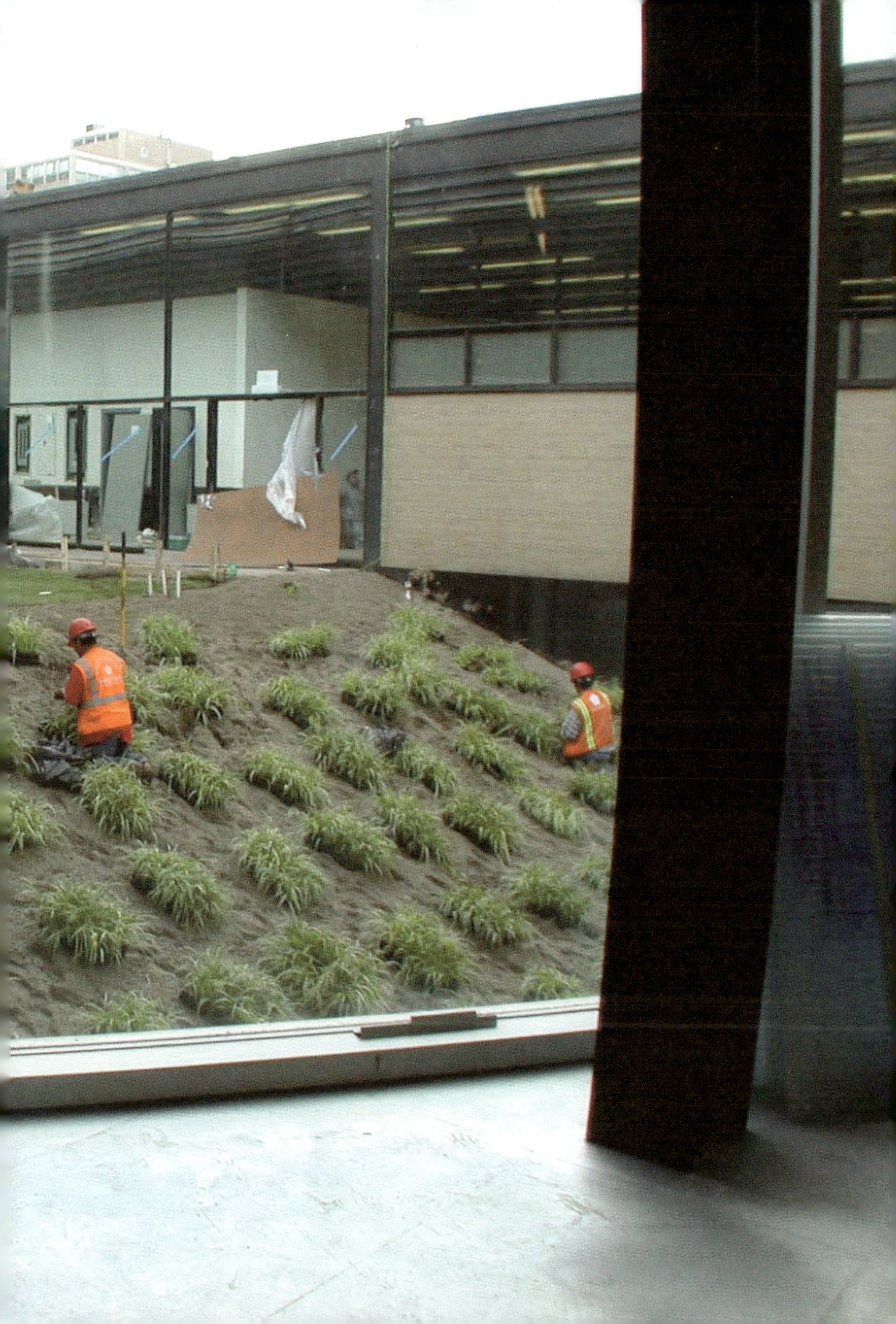

Smallest Parcel

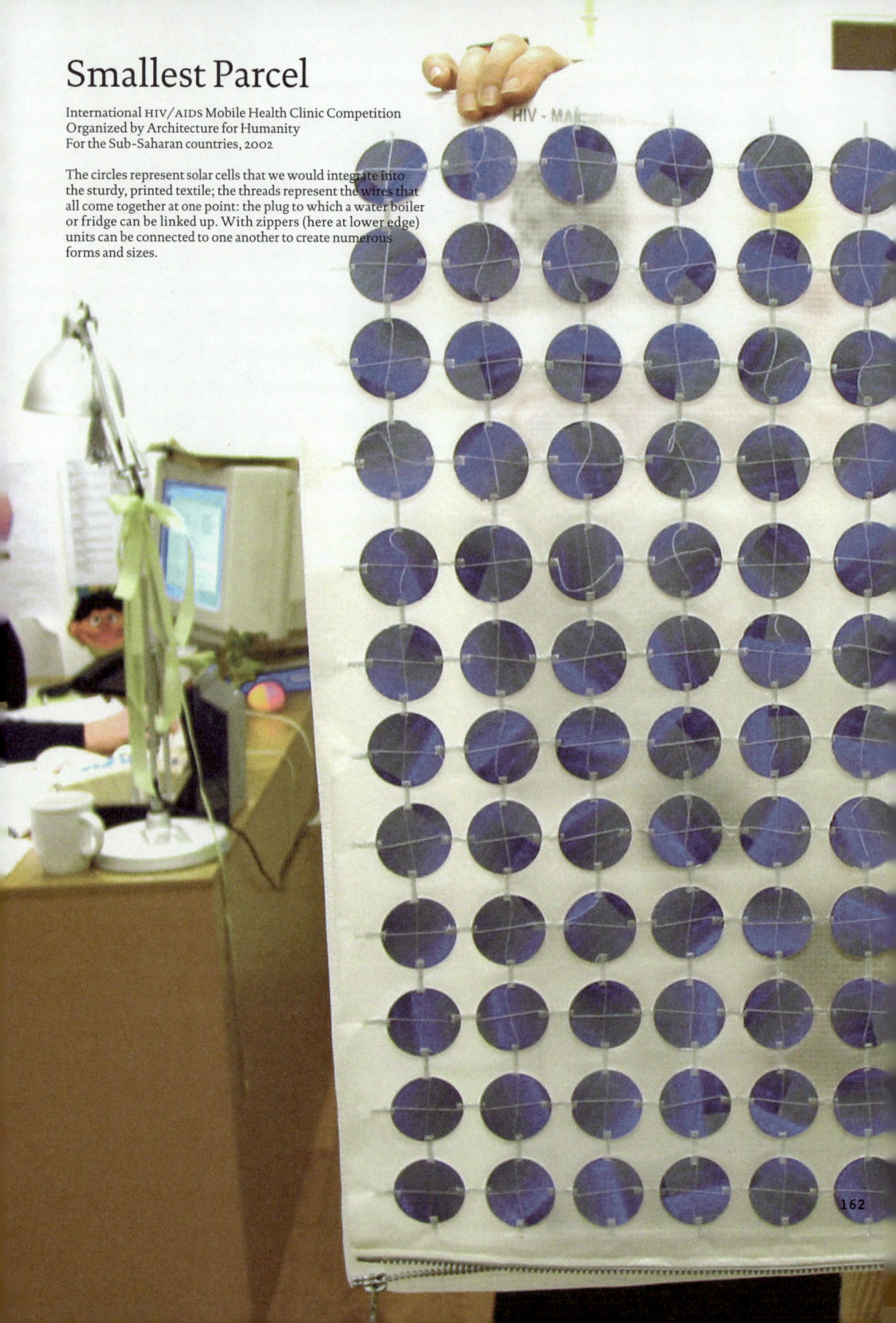

International HIV/AIDS Mobile Health Clinic Competition
Organized by Architecture for Humanity
For the Sub-Saharan countries, 2002

The circles represent solar cells that we would integrate into the sturdy, printed textile; the threads represent the wires that all come together at one point: the plug to which a water boiler or fridge can be linked up. With zippers (here at lower edge) units can be connected to one another to create numerous forms and sizes.

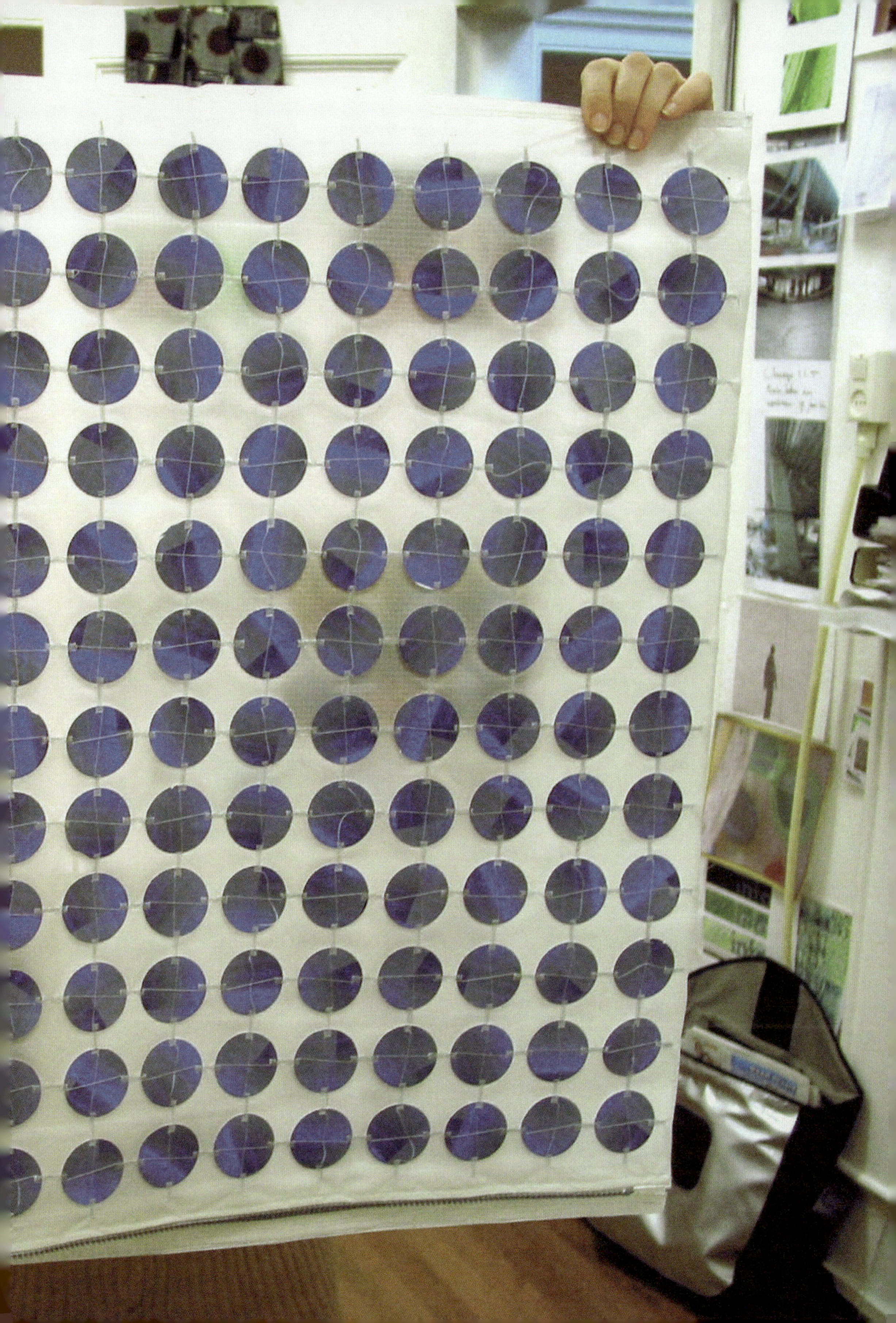

Whipped Cream with Mesh

Space- and sound-regulating curtain
Prada Epicenter, Beverly Hills, USA, 2003–2004

Eighteen women worked on the creation of the plissé curtain for the Beverly Hills Prada Epicenter: each pleat stitched separately from top to bottom, windows along lower seam, slit with overlap, plastic lining, stainless steel mesh along top edge for air and sprinklers. It arrived in Los Angeles ten days before the opening; yet it was never hung. What happened to it? . . . We all wonder.

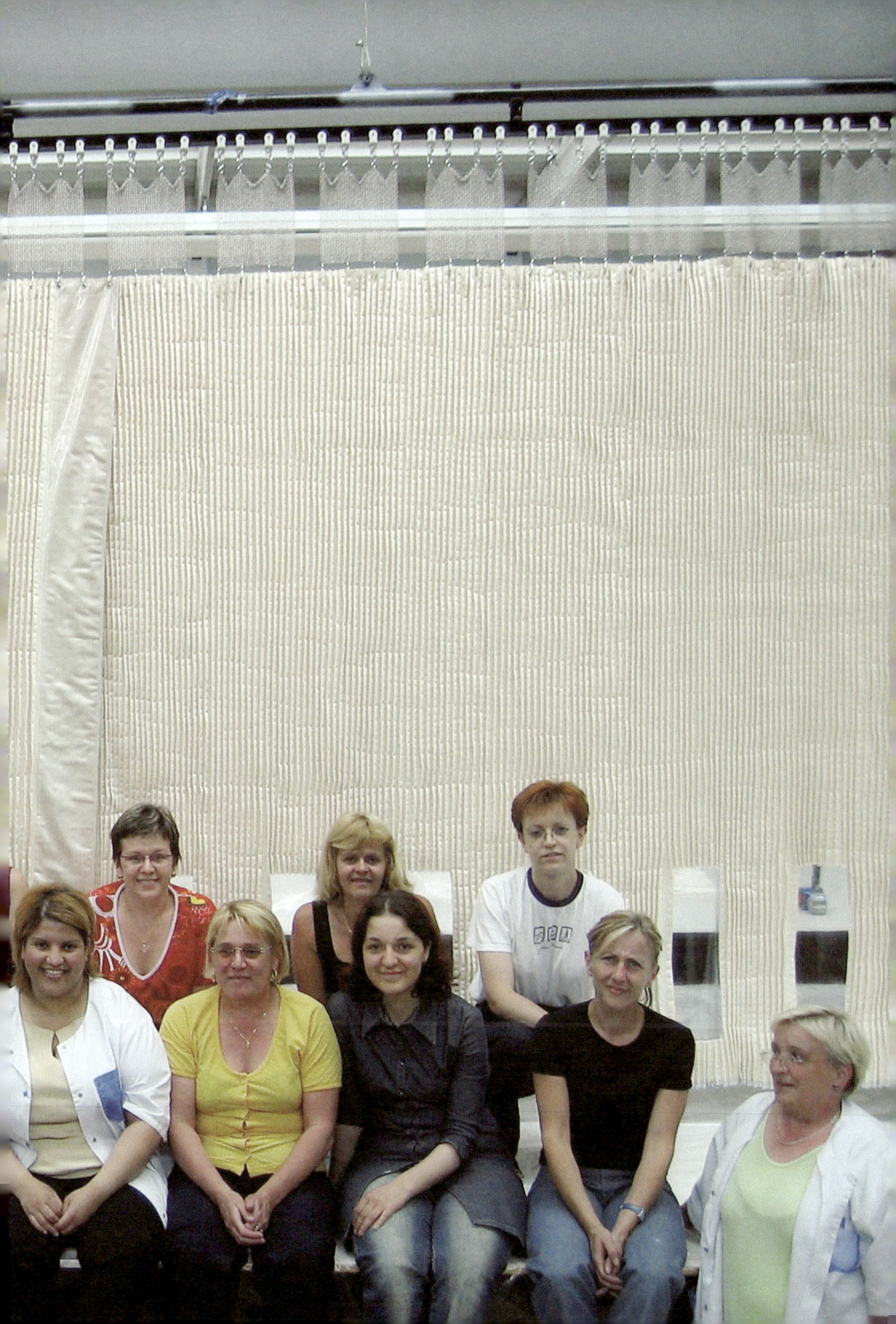

Sound Sock

Knitted protection for sound installation
Prada Epicenter, New York, USA, 2001

Six-and-a-half days of knitting at the Gramercy Park Hotel, New York: Anky and I worked from 9 AM through 8 PM with regular breaks to escape the salt dust (flame retardant treatment of voile, entering our nostrils and pores when ripping kilometres of 10 cm-wide bands) and to buy gallons of water: a landscape architect from Harvard helped to tear and knit too: thanks Kate …

The cleaning lady came every day, watching our monster grow larger by the hour, until she couldn't enter the room anymore: 10 x 5 m of knitted structure covered the floor, the furniture and crept up the walls; yet the whole thing fit into one extra-large garbage bag and we schlepped it into a taxi and drove off to the Prada store to hang it. There, of course, we found that the sound system had already been mounted, which obstructed the space and connection points we needed to mount the sock. Also: no ladders available! Ah: it's all about improvisation and ingenuity.

Reflection

Three light-regulating curtains
McCormick Tribune Campus Center, Chicago, USA, 1999–2004

At the Theatex curtain factory: matching the two-sided print of a blackout curtain at the seam.

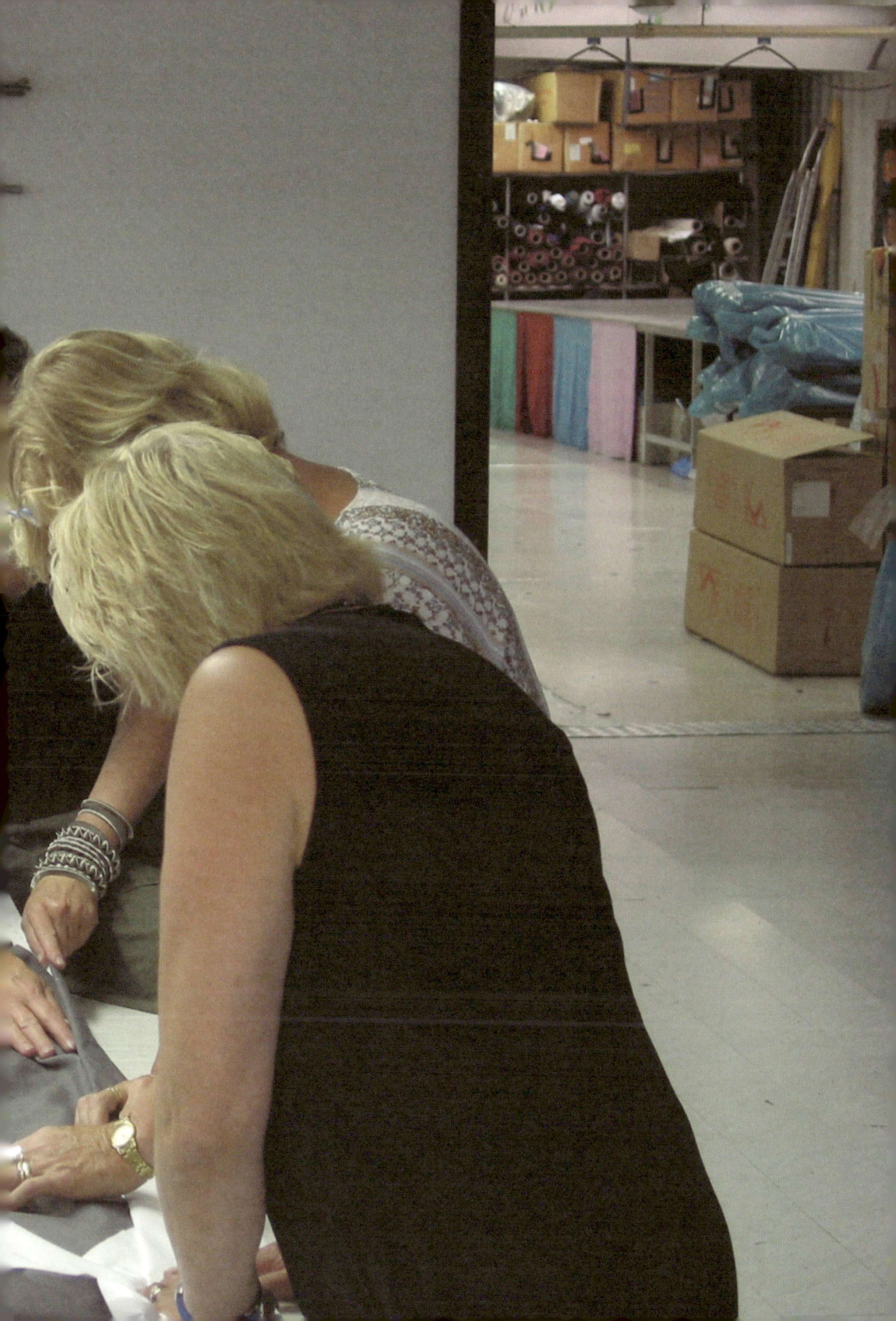

Mass

Climate- and sound-regulating division wall for entry
Heemstra/Strik House, Amsterdam, the Netherlands, 2002

Odalisque works on the 'mass' curtain.

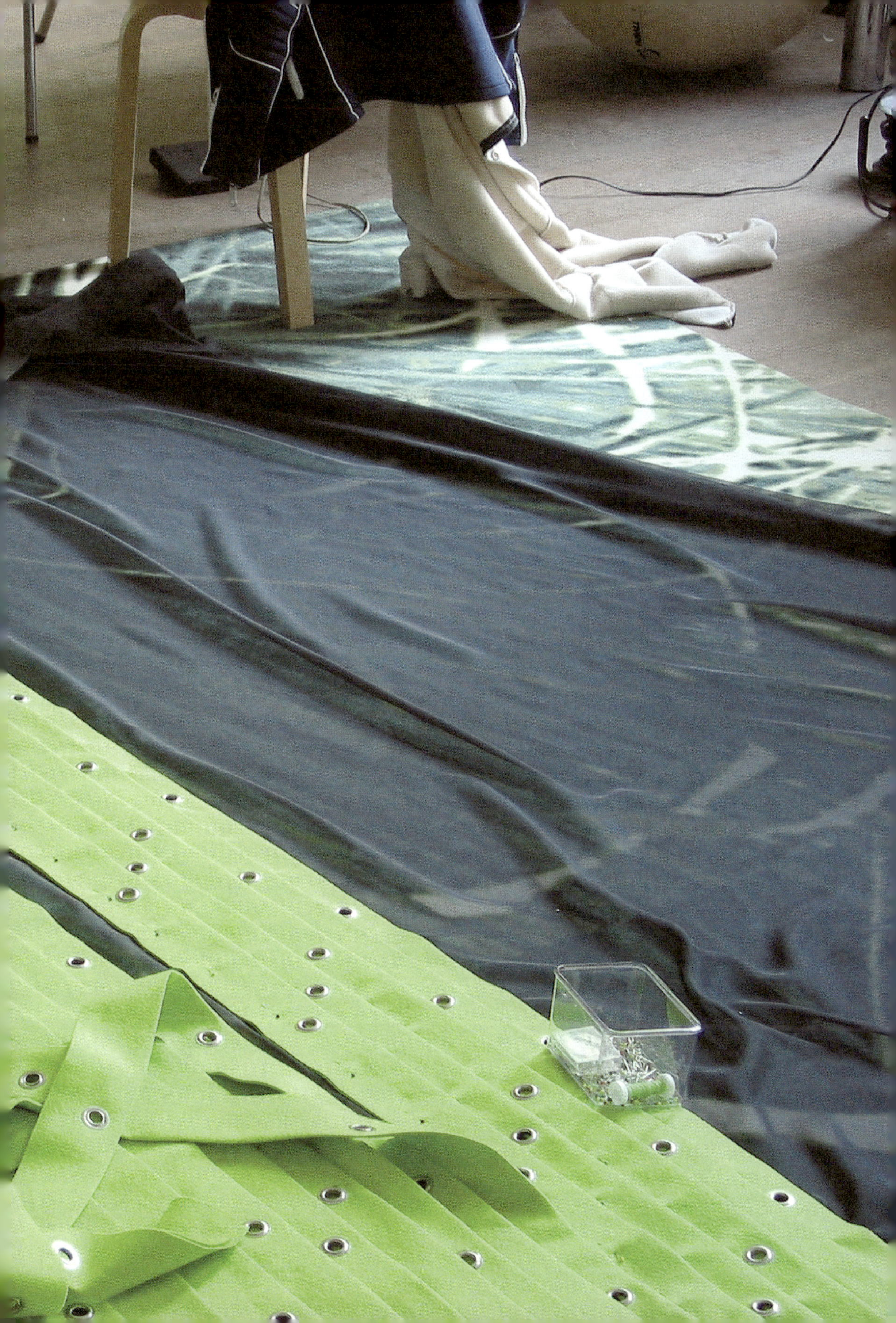

Hairs, Fins, Sauerkraut and Furs

Sound- and light-regulating curtains and wall
Mercedes Benz Museum, Stuttgart, Germany, 2004–2006

Mercedes Benz curtain in the making: hurry, we're late!
(And are the white carriers that go with the top edge and white
folded ceiling ordered according to the new eyelet distance?)

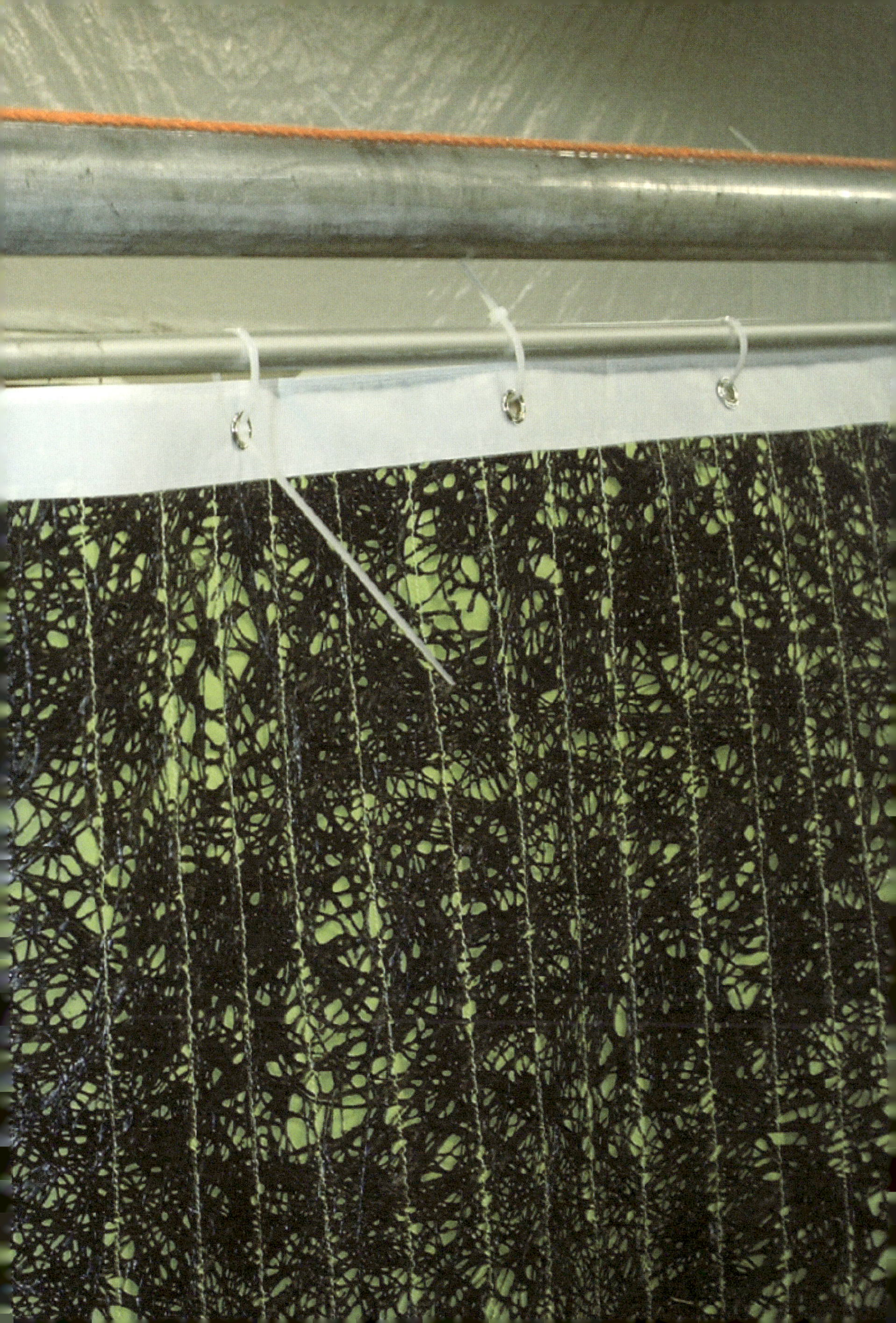

Touch

Vinyl wallpaper series
Wolf Gordon Inc., Long Island, NY, USA, 2001–2003

Our photographic images of curtain samples were etched into the copper print roll. Our first official commercial mass product. We won the prize for 'Best Mass-Produced Product 2003' of the ICFF (International Contemporary Furniture Fair) in New York, 2003.

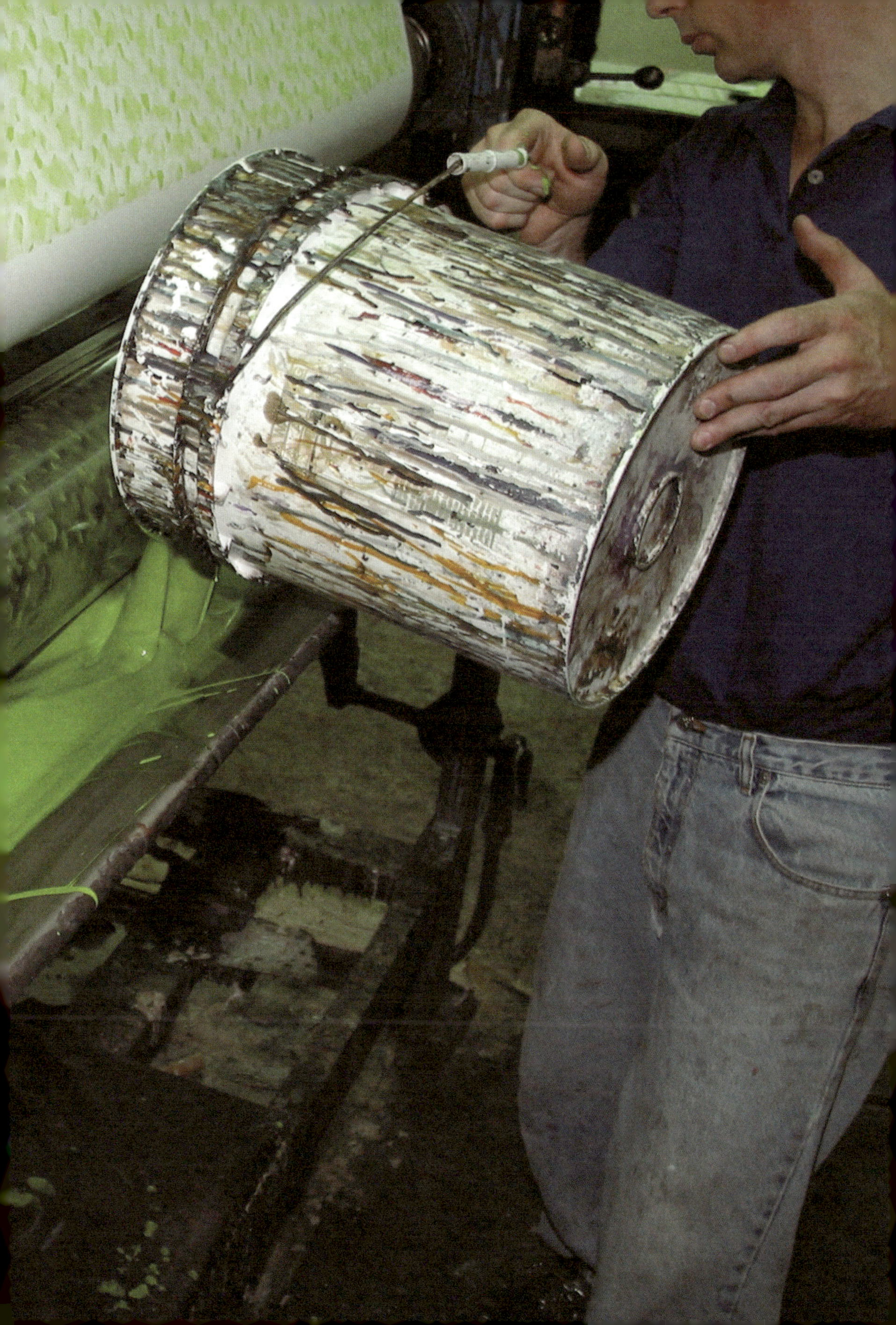

Paging through the TOUCH wallpaper sample book.

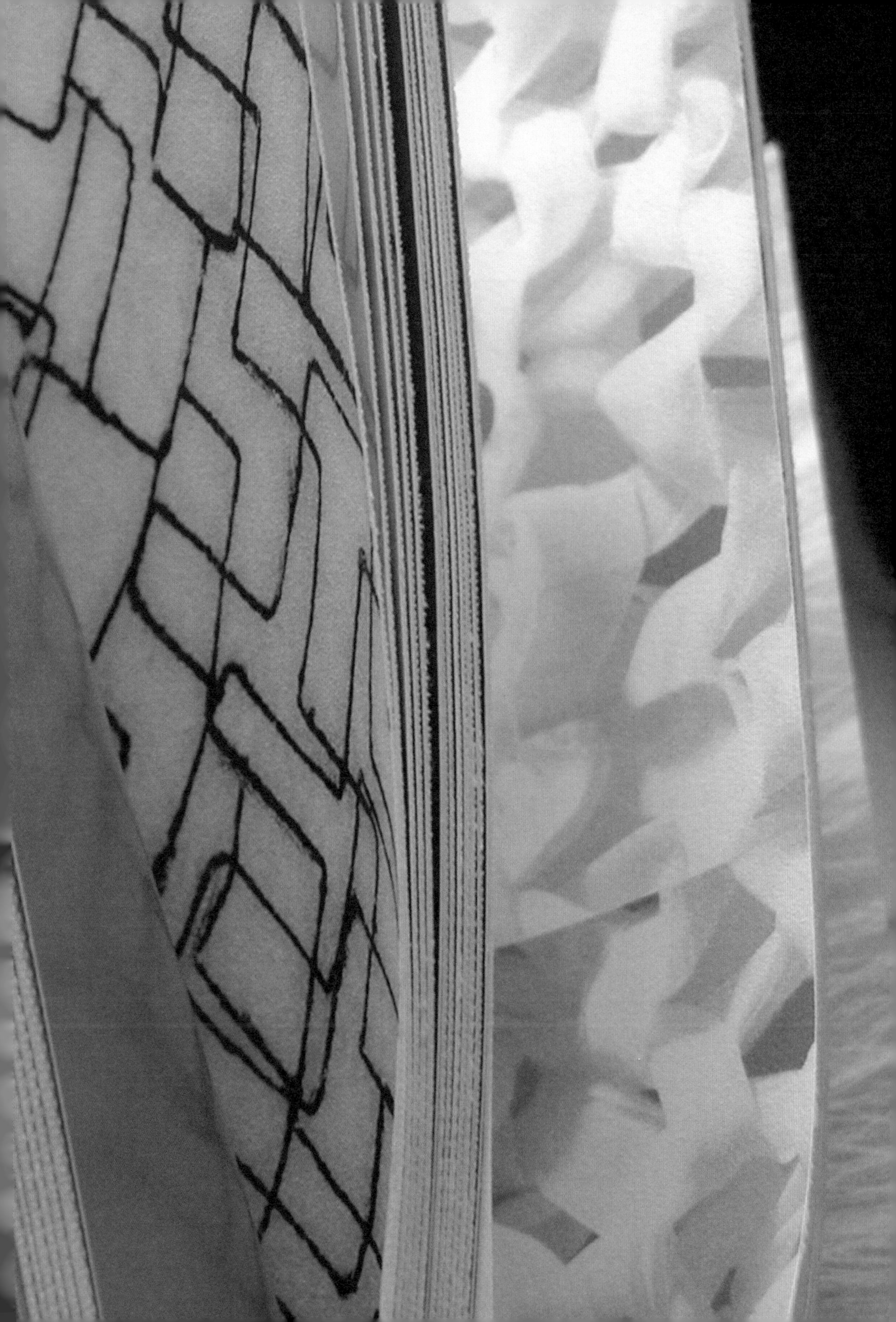

Inspecting one of the TOUCH wallpaper prototypes,
installed at the Inside Outside studio.

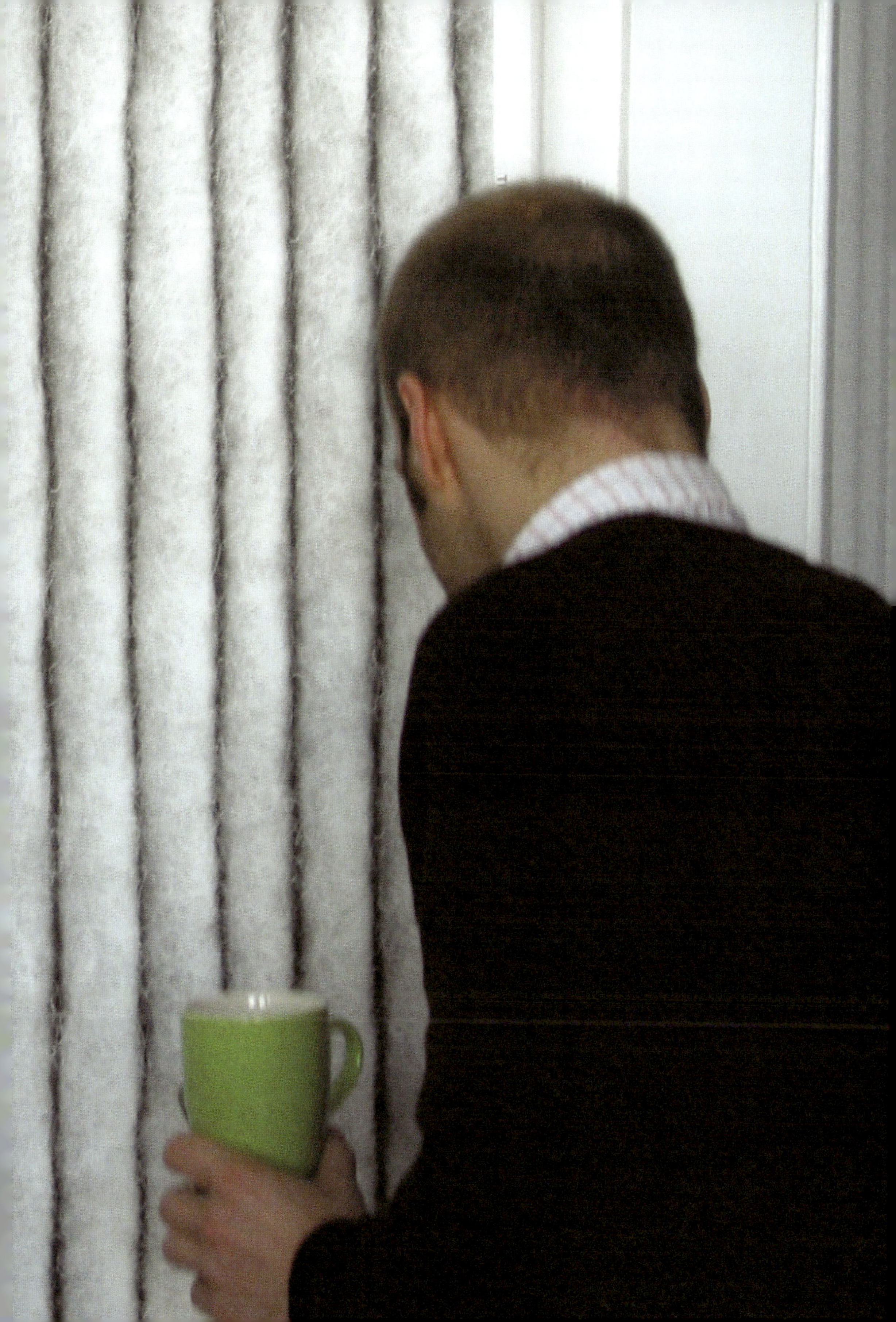

Reflection

Three light-regulating curtains
McCormick Tribune Campus Center,
Chicago, USA, 1999–2004

Print test for the IIT curtain: checking the effect
of the ink on the polyurethane coating.

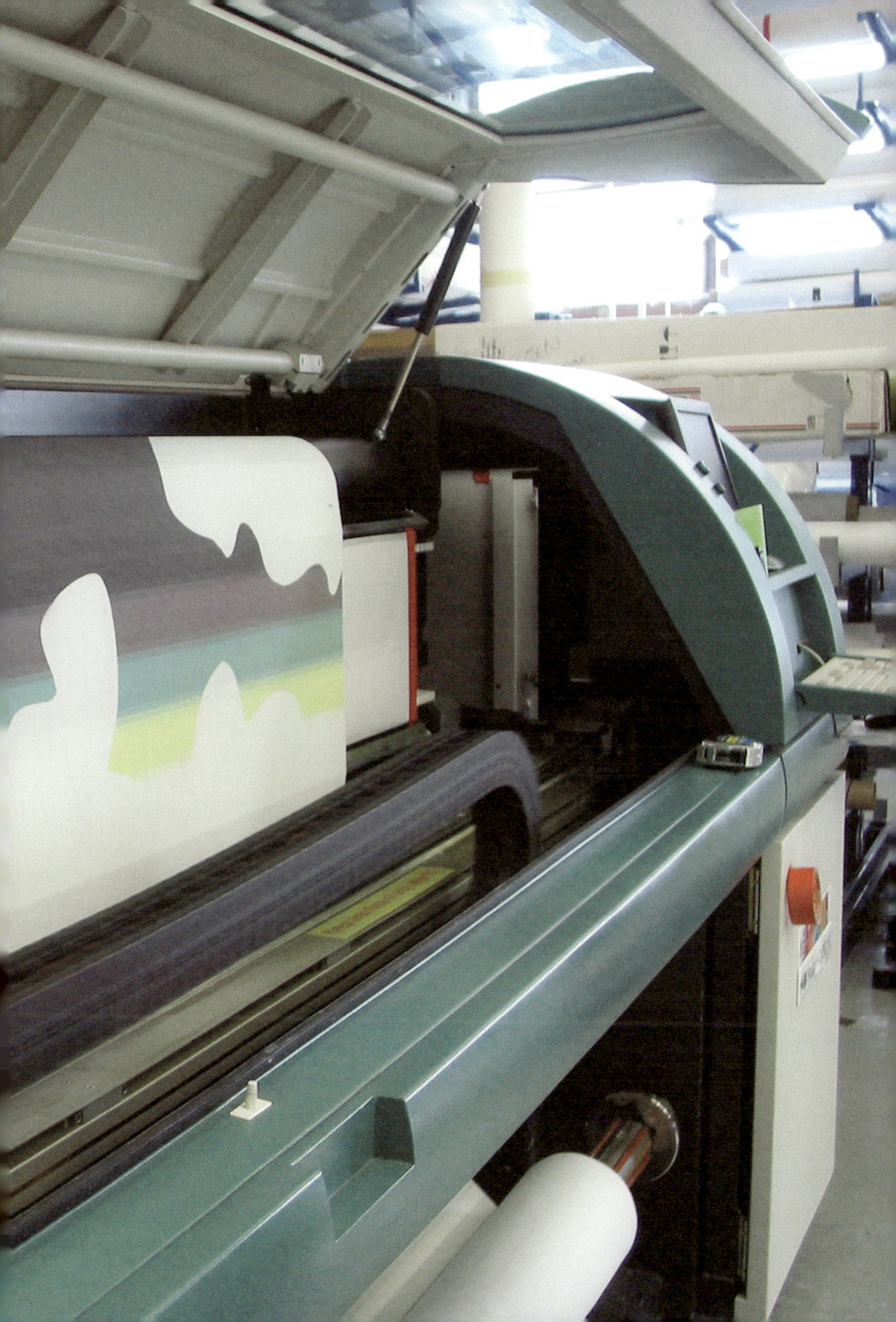

Angel Root

Light- and sound-regulating curtains
The Netherlands Embassy, Berlin, Germany, 2000–2004

Reconnecting threads in the
jacquard weaving machine.

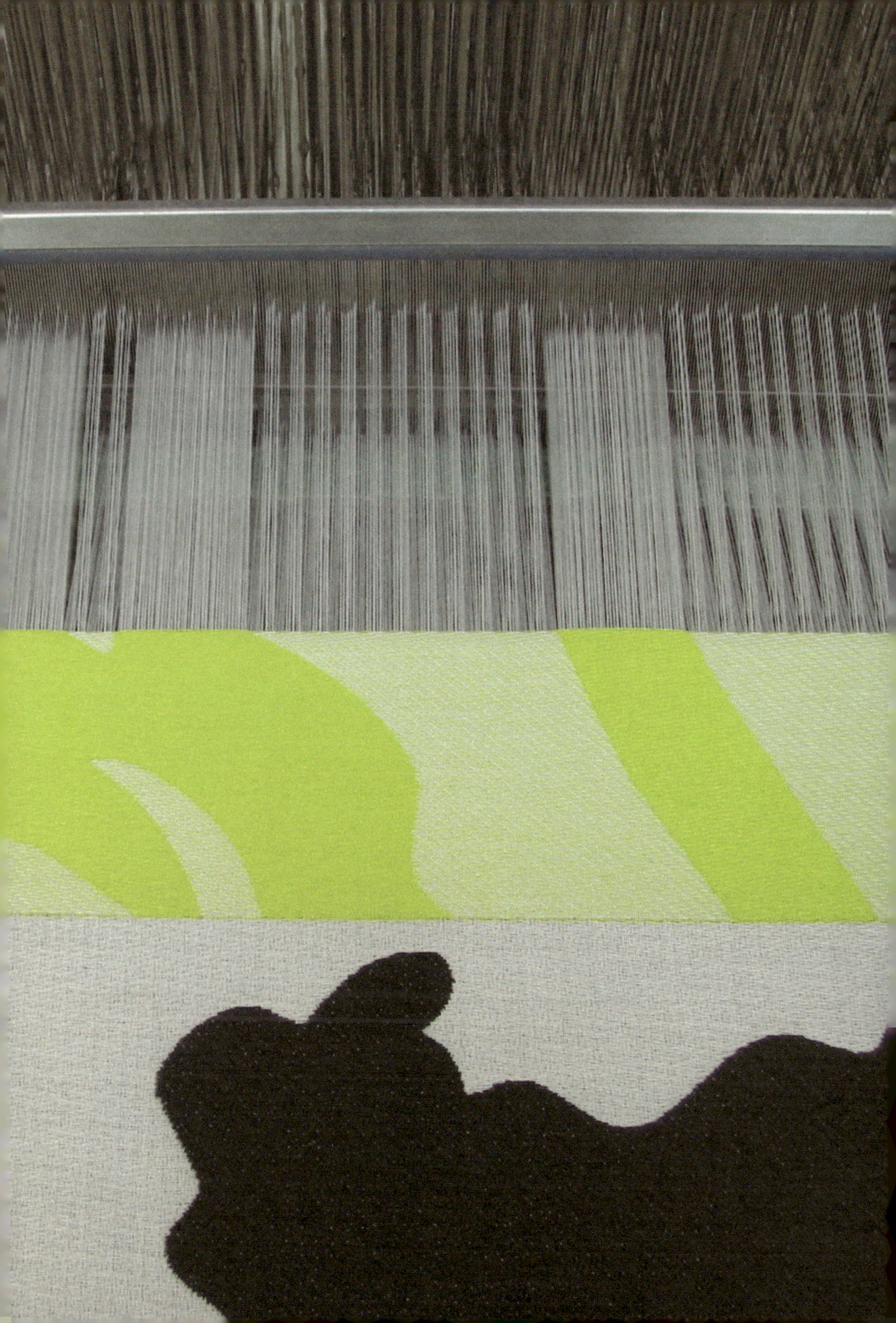

Rifletutti

Personal pavilions and mirror drop installation
Villa Manin, Codroipo, Italy, 2005

Production line at Inside Outside: 57 Riflettuti mirrored umbrellas in three weeks.

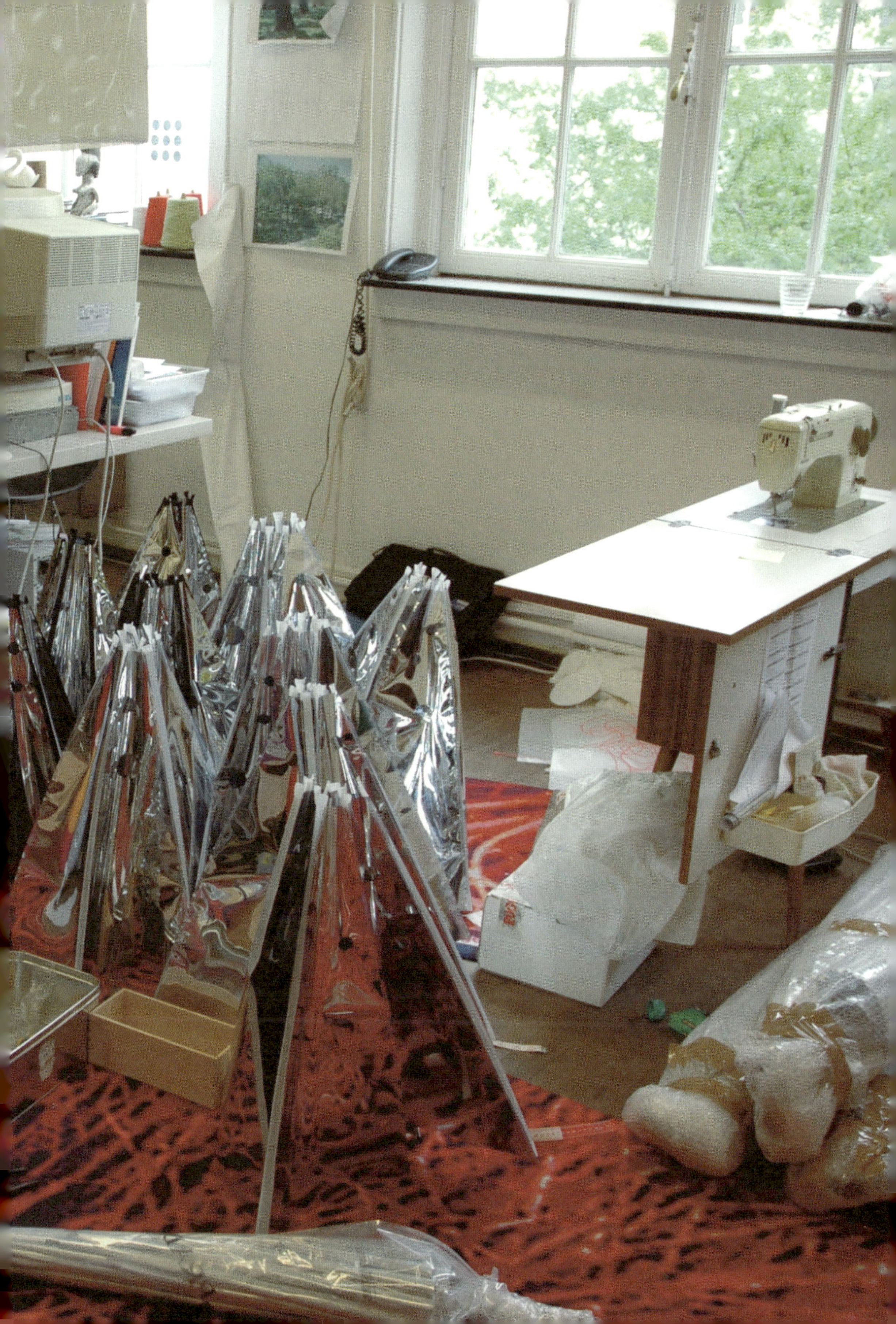

Seattle carpet reflected in an umbrella inside;

...outside revealed through the umbrella.

Inside Outside Architecture

Yellow silk curtain escapes building
Amsterdam, the Netherlands, 2003

Look at what architecture CAN'T do!

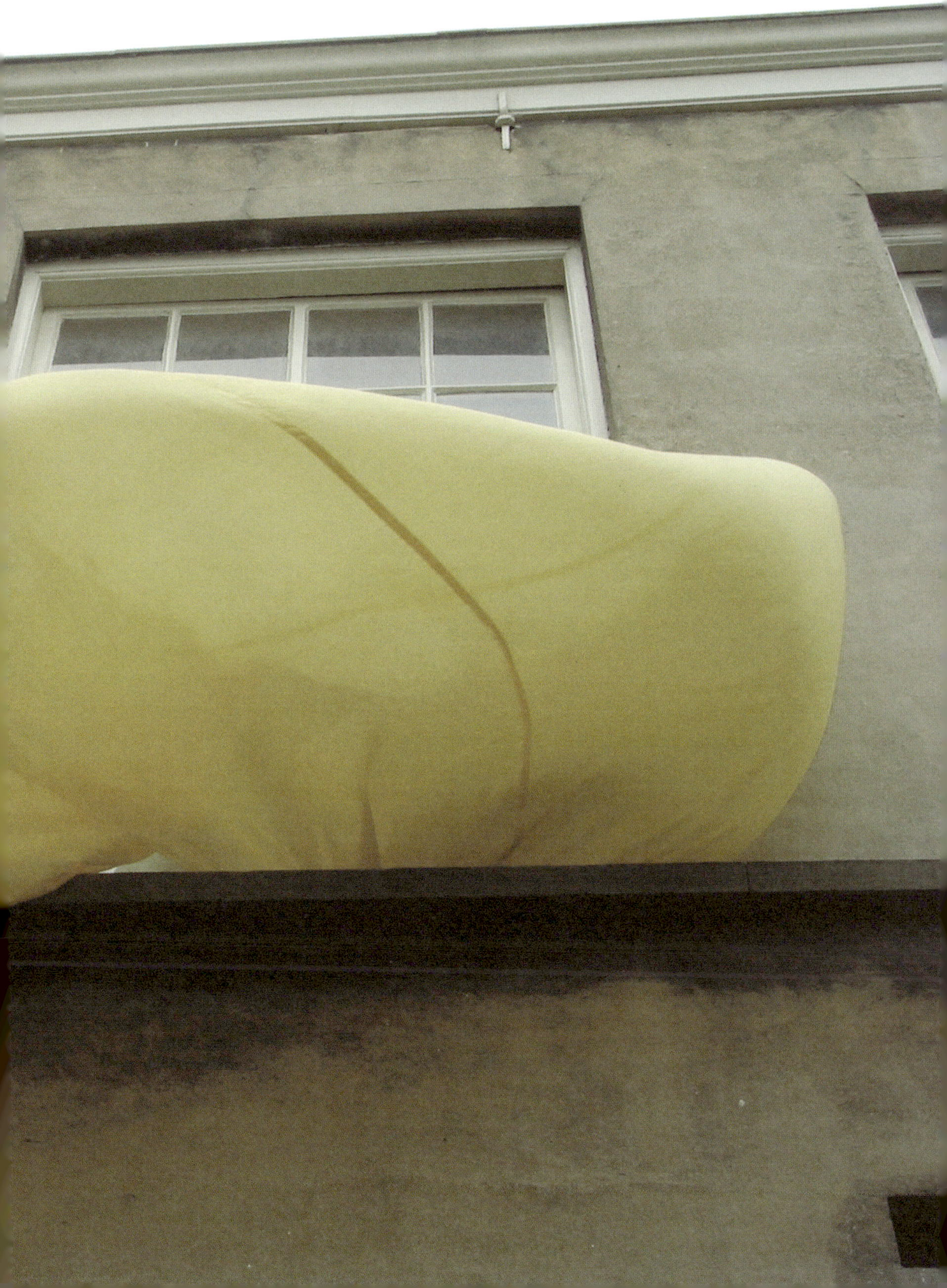

Workshop

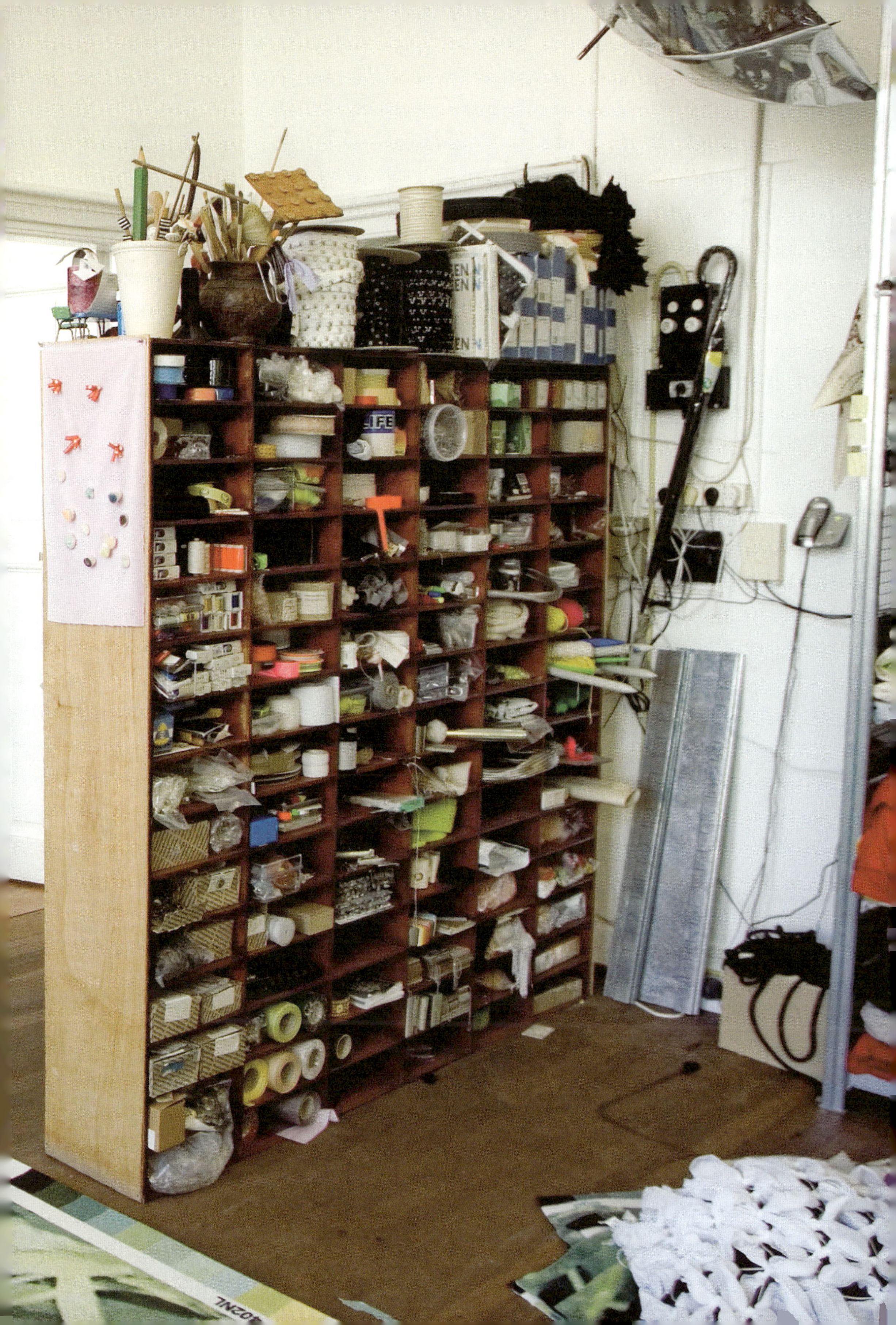
LIFE

Lunch

Inside Outside team in November 2006
F.l.t.r.: Alexandra Pander (office manager), Akane Moriyama (intern), Rosetta Elkin (landscape architect), Kim Olde Loohuis (textile designer), Aura Luz Melis (architect) and Petra Blaisse.

Inside Outside studio

Inside Outside plant-carpet installation at Sikkens Colour Fair. F.l.t.r.: Rosetta Elkin (landscape dept. IO), Marieke van den Heuvel (design dept. IO), Peter Niessen (textile dept. IO) and Petra Blaisse (IO)).

Undoing Boundaries

Seattle Central Library, Seattle, USA 2000–2004
All horizontal planes both inside and outside and the auditorium curtains

A Public Library in America

It doesn't happen very often that the client of the architect you work with asks you to cross the Atlantic for a separate meeting so they can talk to you about what they think could be crucial to the correct understanding of your task. Right after we were commissioned to do the landscape and interior design for the new Seattle Central Library, I was invited to dinner by the director of the library and a few members of the board. They wanted to explain what a public library in America is about, what the psychology and practicalities would demand of such an institution in the heart of Seattle, what their own dreams were for the building and what role they expected Inside Outside to play.

The client defined a public library as a place where everyone feels welcome and at home, where *anyone* – from old people to small children, from the homeless to schizophrenics – can go for shelter, learning and inspiration. The written word is the path to liberation, emancipation and growth, but people also spend important moments of their lives in a library. My Seattle dinner companions – all women – reflected on the fact that they all, without exception, encountered their first love, their first book or their first kiss in a library! Also, libraries in America often house sports facilities, showers and coffee shops, so just imagine: you can read, kiss, write, wash, eat, love, study, scribble, sport, discover and sleep in a library . . . you don't have to go anywhere else: this is a world in itself.

Obviously, the library was very aware of the effect landscape has on the public. Plants, trees and flowers appeal to anyone and the right configuration (prevent hiding places) – combined with seating (not to sleep on!), light effects (security!) and a bit of art – would invite people into the building and put people at ease. And no one should be intimidated by the building: It is a democratic institution, made for everyone. All interior details – whether doorknobs, toilets, walls or seats – have to work with this mentality and all entrances have to communicate a simple 'welcome'.

Words used by the library staff to describe the atmosphere of the future interior spaces were 'comforting', 'familiar', 'robust' and 'transparent'. For the garden the words 'lush', 'inviting', 'safe' and 'welcoming' were important. This was definitely the most socialistic building OMA has ever worked on, I thought . . .

The Big Team, Our Input

Working with models, we realized in an early stage that the future public spaces were so enormous and overwhelming that finishes, furniture and acoustics would play an important role in the experience of the rooms. By introducing objects of different scales, by using colour to define areas and by

1. Many people were involved: OMA's project architect Joshua Ramus was our indefatigable and precise informant and diplomat; during the execution, the very engaged New York-based architecture team and, minding every detail, Rem Koolhaas; the local architects LMN – who also offered us crucial interior architecture colleagues; furniture designers Maarten van Severen (with Chris van Duijn of OMA), the Bouroullec brothers (Vitra) and Qinze & Milan; graphic designers Bruce Mau Design – with whom we developed some of the information desk surfaces; Arup/Magnusson Klemencic structural engineer and acoustic engineers Michael Yantis and Renz van Luxemburg; lighting specialists Kugler Tillotson Associates; visual and media artists Tony Oursler, Gary Hill and Ann Hamilton; landscape architect Kate Orff – who became our spokeswoman and planting advisor on the way; the local landscape office Jones & Jones – with Else Jones and her team giving us technical and political support; and grass specialist John Greenlee (we worked on projects in and around Los Angeles); production firms Majestic Drapery (Helene helped us sew the Storefront façade curtain and produced the New York Prada store plissé curtains) and PNTA in the USA; printers Extra Large in the Netherlands; and local firms and services.

First diagrams illustrating the flow of landscape carpets/carpet landscape from interior to exterior...

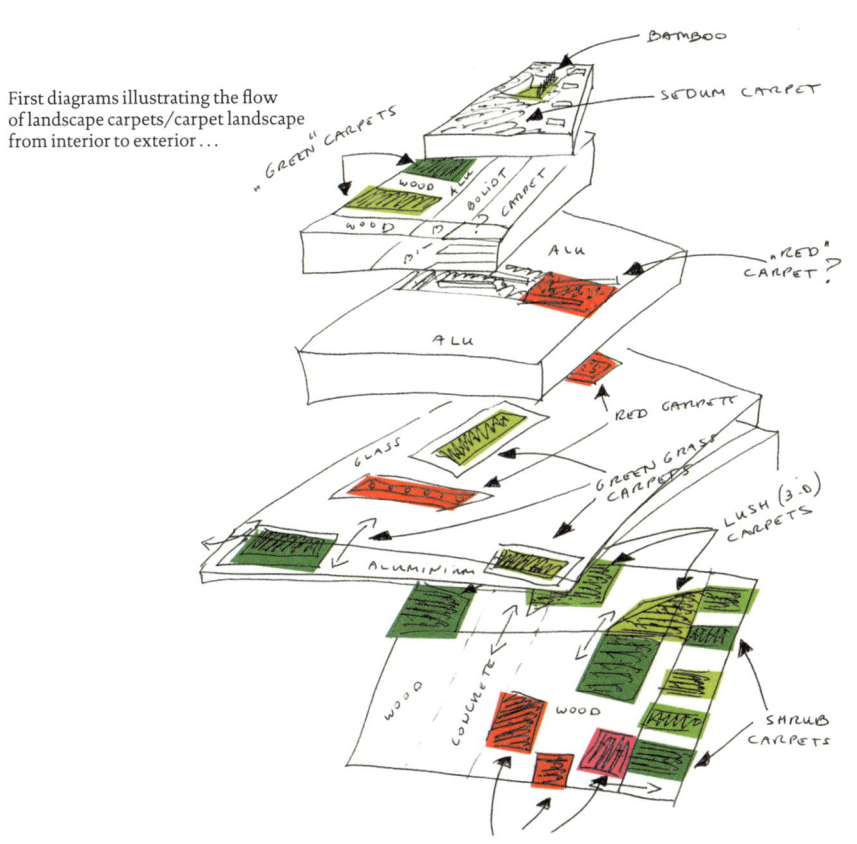

Tree families changing to 'bosquets' where the building's footprint allows more green space.

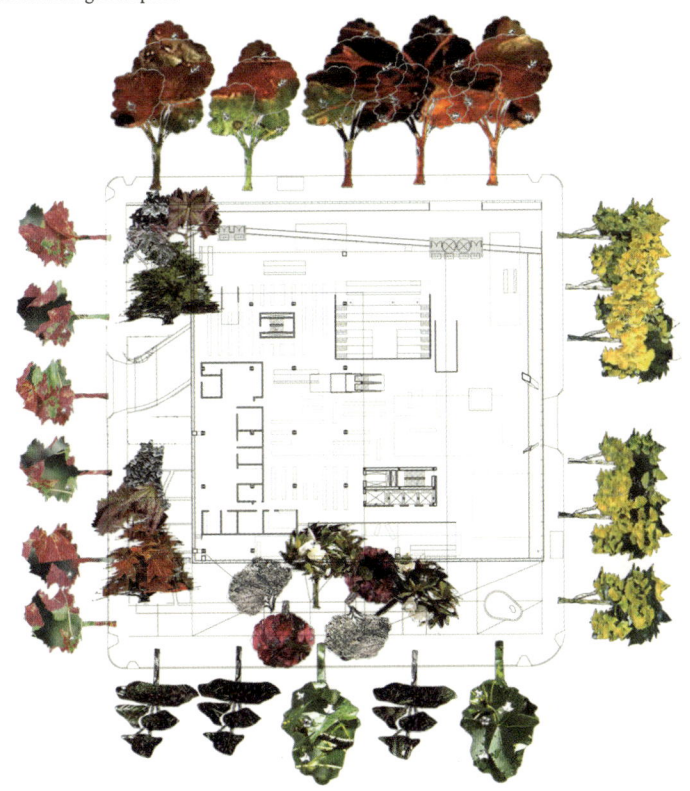

Colour and scale test: Pulmonaria carpet sample nr. 411, February 22, 2002.

modifying the acoustics from space to space, we saw that our input could make a difference.

We formed quite an international and diverse team working in numerous time zones.[1] Coordinated by the architects, all of us worked on finding the right and most innovative solutions for the technical, functional and artistic components that a public library of today implies. In the process we inspired the client's views as much as they influenced ours with their practical and financial framework.

The client demanded 'transparency' in the space in order to oversee the visitors and ensure that there is no harm or pinching of books – or of each other – done. They also wondered whether people could find their way around the huge volumes, so the team began to look at how the placement of furniture, book- and staircases could influence orientation 'subconsciously'; and if their scale and colours could become orientation points; guiding movement by their positioning; transmitting functions through their form and colour.

The furniture for the library had to be flea-, lice- and vomit-proof. If somebody urinates on the furniture, it has to be cleaned within 20 minutes – then the show must go on; and no seat should invite visitors to lie down and sleep – neither inside nor out. All three furniture designers were used to working with synthetic, plastic, rubber-like and sponge-like materials (leather was too expensive); but it took some investment to convince the client and the board that 'modern' furniture could also help bridge the gap between contemporary architecture and the broad public.[2]

The demands for a library remind me of the needs of a park today... exactly the same mottos about 'bulletproof' furnishing and transparency for safety. Parks have to be designed on very low budgets and in such a way that planting can thrive without irrigation, the maintenance can be done by uneducated staff, and that security measures (gates, staff) are not necessary. So a public park has to stay beautiful, 'inviting' and alive in the crudest circumstances.

Fluid Landscaping

Meeting the city librarians – our client – and visiting their old library, I could see how involved they were with details on a day-to-day basis. The gardens looked alive and rich with plant variations; works of art filled the entrance plaza and the interiors: fountains, sculptures and mosaic decorations, slightly dated – fifties, sixties?; a specially made wall-to-wall carpet imprinted with open books, now faded; plants and personal knickknacks on the desks; very sturdy furniture, a bit stark. But also heaps of piled-up books in the storage spaces and dark and airless work spaces in which many employees had to work day in, day out: unthinkable working conditions in my view: time for a new building!

The current building is in the exact same place in downtown Seattle, surrounded by white, grey, brown and black high-rise buildings. It was composed of what I saw as a fishnet structure that stretched around a pile of shifted and floating floor plates. Two main avenues – 5th and 4th – frame the

2.
You must understand that when a building is only a model and a digital presentation, the client and the boards, donors, commissions and government parties they have to convince from the start are always hesitant and suspicious; sometimes even afraid of what they see: so modern, so harsh, so large, so inhuman, so unpractical, so difficult to maintain, so unwelcoming, etcetera, etcetera. Part of the work an architect and his team do – assisted by advisors and specialists – is to soothe everyone's worries, finding the right iconography and language to transform not only the design itself to a certain degree, but the way in which it is perceived.

Real and translated vegetation;
the blue cage, furniture, the city...

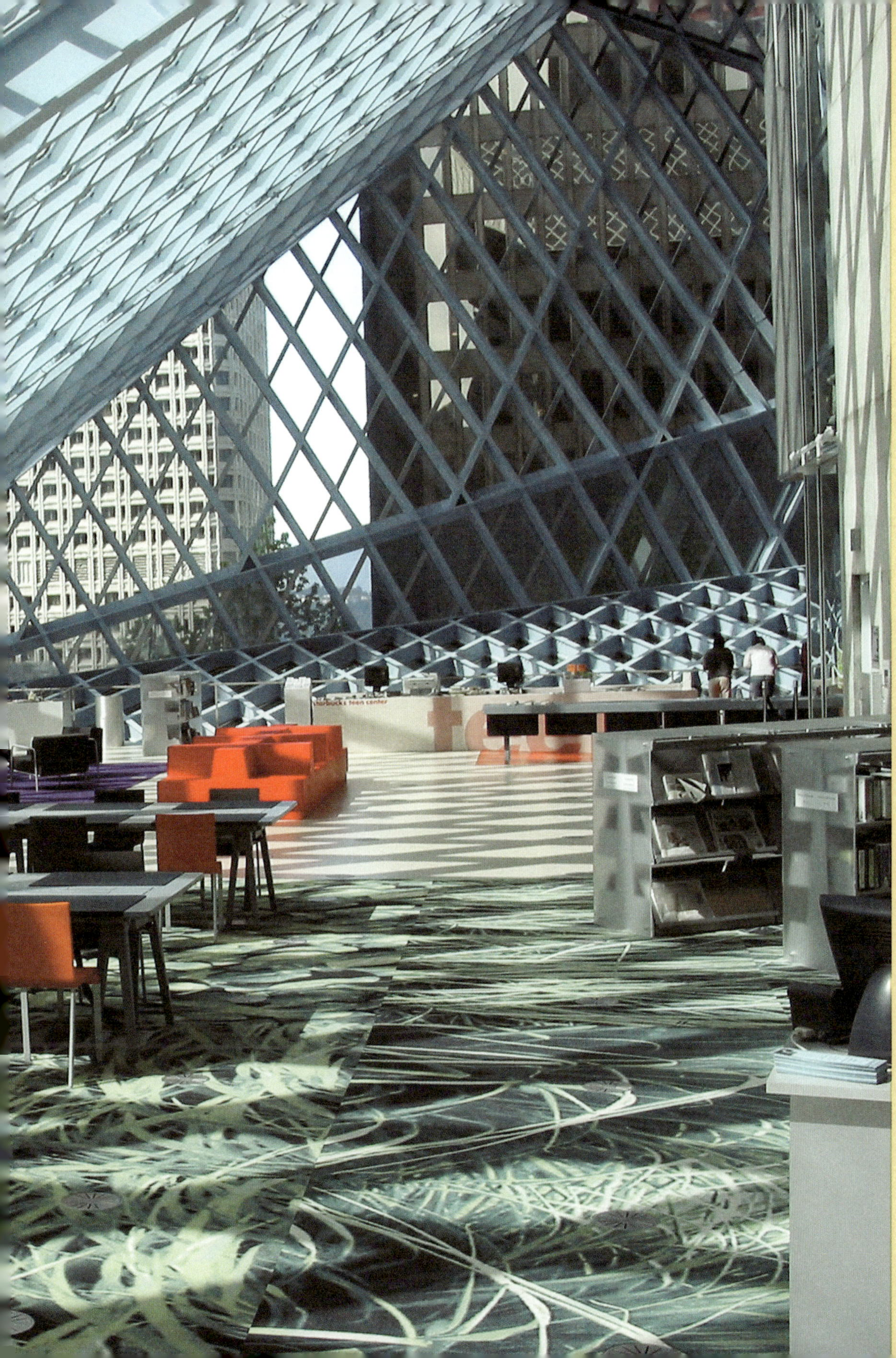

library on different levels and sloping streets connect those two avenues along the library's flanks.

The basic shape of the project must have derived from this topography; also, the building looks as if it stretches and turns itself in all directions to perceive little patches of the grand nature just beyond the city blocks: the sea down on one side, mountains and forests on the other...

As in the Kunsthal in Rotterdam, where the park flows into the building to reappear on the roof, 'landscape' is very present in this project: the library invites the outside in and makes its interiors visible to the exterior. The sloping roads of the city seem to launch the mentality of the building, its flow from one level to another.

The most important discussions we had with the architects here were about the continuation of landscape in the interior and the coherent sequence of ambiences and functions throughout the building: the choice of colours and materials; and how to coordinate this on every level.

We made diagrams to indicate the fluidity of movement from outside in, showing how to materialize and emphasize this effect with one language: the carpet; and only the horizontal plane, floor and ceiling. We also made collages to indicate colour ranges and ambiences for the different library sections: Children's Library, International Library, Auditorium, Living Room, Assembly, Mixing Chamber, Book Spiral, Reading Room and Headquarters; a bit like you would do in fashion predictions. Our aim here was comparable to the landscape-like exhibitions we designed: to keep the public alert and interested by leading them not only from one space to another but also from one experience to another.

Culture in Colour

As with each project, we were introduced to a completely unknown world of tastes and colours: our first impression was that there seemed to be great affinity with brown, beige, dark green, ochre, aubergine and burgundy in Washington State. It reminds me of hunting cabins: wood, leather, rugs, open fire, hunting and sports trophies on the walls; being one with the forest, the soil and the field; pointing to Seattle's Scandinavian inheritance more than to its Indian predecessors, I would say. No correlation with OMA, on first sight; but interesting to insert in their futuristic building! Some of OMA's architects came from Seattle and they collected images of their parents' interiors. There they were: aubergine, brown, burgundy red, dark green, white – the inspiration for the future Reading Room colours.

Since our work is partly preoccupied with the use of colour, we can't but notice that every culture and environment has its own particular colour allergies. In some countries you cannot use white, pink, beige or red. In Seattle, we were not allowed to use orange.[3]

The discussions about colour use can be heated at times, since colour is a purely emotional subject. It remains fascinating how every single person and culture interprets colour differently and how the effect of a colour changes

3. Now you know that orange is a very Dutch colour: not only does it refer to our royal family Van Oranje Nassau, but Holland, in the seventeenth century, was the largest producer in Europe of a ferocious root called 'meekrap' (Rubia tinctorum) from which orange pigment is produced. These roots grew so fast that the Dutch government insisted they be harvested at a specific root length to prevent them from puncturing our dikes. See: Victoria Finlay, Colour, *Travels Through the Paintbox* (London, Hodder & Stoughton, 2002)

...the inside of the heart...

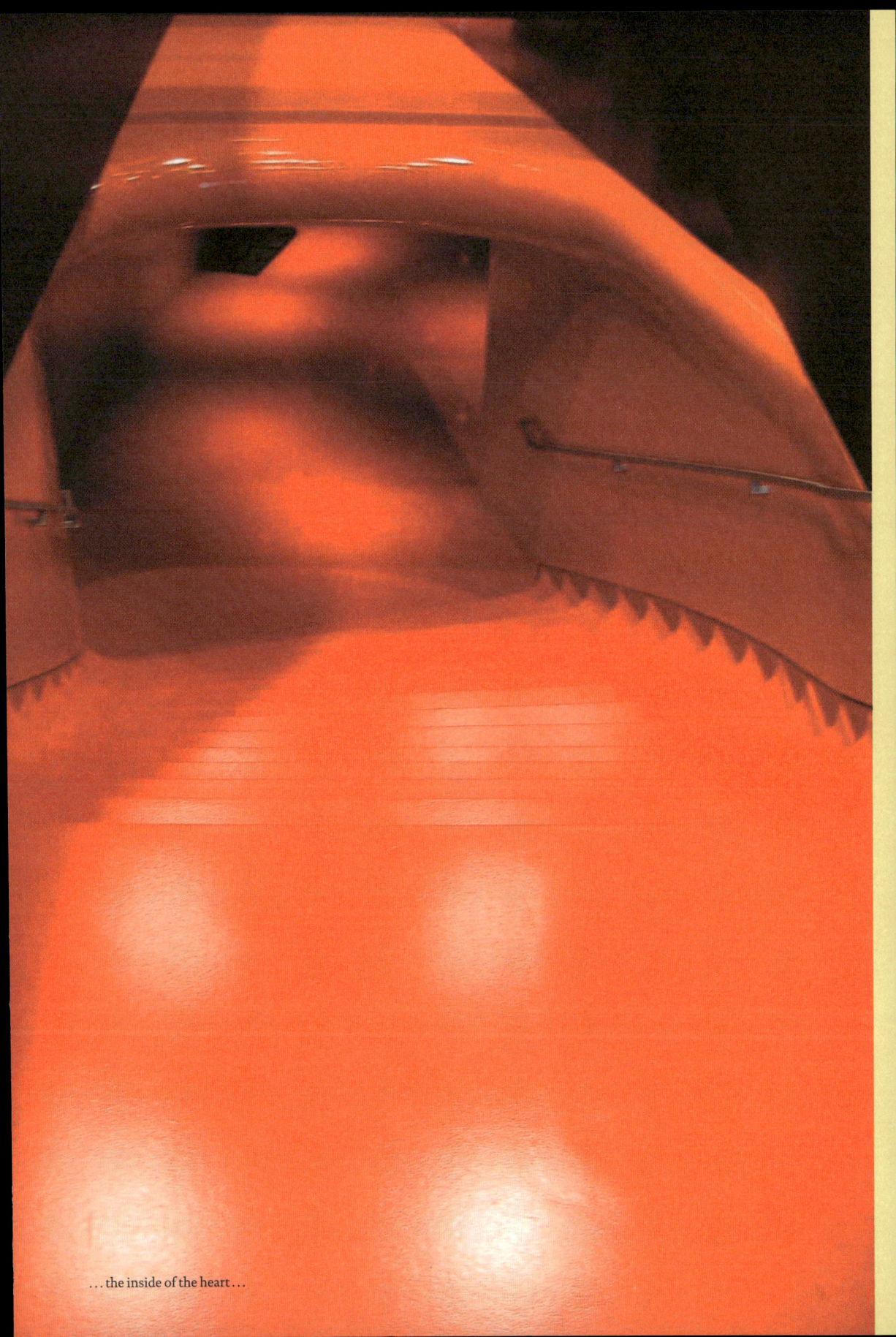

Looking up from Living Room past Assembly and Mixing Chamber and Book Spiral to the acoustic ceiling of the Reading Room.

with its environment, light temperatures, scale of surface and the volume around it. I won't go into the scientific explanations of colour, but there is a question that keeps coming back to us each time we work in the United States: why are all colours here mixed with black? From Disney World to public buildings, all colours seem muted.

Is it a cultural issue, the result of scientific theory, are there environmental regulations that forbid certain pigments; or is there an unwritten protocol that prohibits colour affront? Are colours in Europe more bright, shown more in their pure form (they are often used on a white base to make them even more lively) because of our cultural or political climates? Or does the build-up of the air here create harsh light, clarifying the blue, yellow and red of the sky, thus inspiring our tastes? Are we maybe replacing UV light with light-transmitting colours to fight depression? Or do we want to escape from our northern culture's restrictive religion-based values and morality? Why are Americans today afraid of colour?

We felt that an engaging and energetic environment would help trigger a mood of ownership and activity from the future public. Colour seemed an attractive tool with which to achieve this. At the same time, colour can help break down the boundaries between past and future, learning and enjoying between one culture and another.

Greens of Greens

Green was the colour we envisioned for the library gardens; fruitful, protective, mysterious, poisonous green; arsenic, malachite, methyl, iodine green; jade, frog back, *mi se*, celadon, emerald, sea, olive, apple, grass, mud, military, lime, spring onion and pistachio; Greek, Chinese, Van Eyck, Scheele and Lincoln green; the green of love gardens, of Persian erotic miniatures, of Mohammed's coat.

We cut up the sometimes narrow leftover spaces around the building and turned them into stepped planes of wild grasses, ferns and perennials; patches of gardens along the building's edges – sometimes covered by its folded facades – that widen towards the two entrances at 5th and 4th Avenue levels; leading – even following – the people inside . . . bringing 'flying carpets' of living green into the Living Room. Thus the carpets become gardens and gardens become carpets that catch the visitor's eye from all angles and levels.

Carpets – not wall-to-wall but loose carpets – give the floor plane colour and direction, which helps orientation and gives the room a narrative. Floor treatment was essential for the acoustics and for the soft feeling underfoot – making people feel at ease, making them want to sit and read; introducing a kind of living room atmosphere. The plant carpets, both textile and real, replace the small plant containers that you usually sea spread throughout a public building, all dusty and sad. Interesting to see how their scale and imagery influences the notion of the bookshelves and the heavy furniture: diminishing their massiveness to elegant slimness.

For the outside we included municipal trees lining the street as part of the whole, augmenting their numbers towards the building, creating small 'bosquets' on planes of grasses, flowers, perennials. Our aim was to create 'clans of trees', meaning that one genus was represented by a number of species. Fifth Avenue, for instance, is lined with one kind of oak tree; but when the line passes the library, the row changes into a small grouping, a clan of oak trees. We also wanted to preserve as many of the existing trees, shrubs and plants as possible, integrating them into the new garden. The library worked with a very outspoken and passionate gardener, and she and I went over each and every plant on site.

Green, the Afterimage

Like in Porto, the auditorium is a wooden box with a hard floor, so we considered even the auditorium to be an extension of the garden: indeed one walks into the library from 5th Avenue, past some plant carpets and almost automatically down into the performance room. And so does the earth-brown polyurethane floor that, from 4th Avenue, takes over the garden's ground palette immediately inside the glass façade, flows around the elevator shaft and into the auditorium. There, Maarten van Severen's chairs are bluish green, turning the seating plane into a grass slope. The curtain is of a yellowish apple green with cream – depending on where you stand, it changes colour and depth.

As always, we started with the configuration of the track. Here, it loops around the stage and then aligns with one side wall; a kind of S-shape; careful never to cover the entrance door. This S-shape means that the curtain can be turned around, so both faces of the curtain can be used: a heavy, pleated textile layer faces the public in front of the stage and along the auditorium wall for sound absorbance; and a thick plastic lining (imprinted with bear hairs alias rotting grass – the powerful nature that used to surround the city alias the fate of urban plantings if not kept up) appears when the curtain functions as a backdrop for the stage, reflecting the sound more than absorbing it.

Before the off-white cloth was sewn into large fins, we silkscreened it with apple-green vertical stripes; each stripe built up of a carefully drawn open grid of fine lines so as not to stiffen the cloth with a thick layer of paint. Once meticulously sewn together (one has to stitch exactly along the weave to insure that the fins don't turn), the fins have the green colour always to one side. Like the striped effect of bulb fields, the colour and depth of the curtain changes as you walk by. The fins create air rooms, acoustic absorbance and a form of climatic isolation, exactly as the millions of pleats in the white VIP curtains of the Prada store, but on a much larger scale. The curtain is divided in two unequal halves, with the centre slit positioned at the centre of the chairs when closing off the stage. This slit is marked with a bright red dot. The curtain's outer edges are each covered with an equally red, larger dot that is folded through the middle, showing half a round dot on each side. These dots are for a better grip when handling the curtain, as it is moved into all its positions by hand.

Blue versus Grey

The colour of the steel structure was a major decision for the architects. Joshua and Rem studied international colour codes for steel beams and came up with a series of greys, black, orange and ... a very light blue, used in France, apparently. The three of us stood over the final selection: the blue immediately overruled the two 'promising greys' as far as we were concerned, although it was a bit scary to imagine so much blue, spacious sky blue (though with a hint of grey, or maybe we should say: very light grey with more than a hint of blue in it ...) hovering over each space, defining every volume. We discussed the Seattle weather (mostly grey); the colour of the surrounding buildings (mostly grey and brown); the colour of the streets, objects, politics (kind of grey) ... and imagined the optimism that this light blue might bring to the building's surrounding and its interior. Tests were done on site and the light blue was chosen.

Yellow as Highlighter

The escalators had to be bright objects visible from everywhere: as a wayfinder, inviting people to move up and down through the building. They were initially orange (out of the question), then pink, then they changed to green, then finally to yellow; all Day-Glow of course, like a highlighter.

Pink and Yellow

For the Children's Library, a bare concrete volume in which large columns stand tilted like old wetland trees, we wanted to cover the irregular ceiling with millions of hanging bulbs ... clouds of light. We drew pink, red and yellow play areas for the floor, with sunken and bulging seats and m&m-shaped poufs, embedded into thick colourful surfaces – like gymnastics mattresses – that would act as play and reading fields for the youngest readers. The triangular reading room floor, naturally lit through skylights, was softened with the green plant carpet for a 'picnic read' effect.

White with Green

For the Living Room we envisioned a very light atmosphere, white with lime and greens; fresh, with undulating chains of red lounge chairs. The initial Persian carpets (that folded up and down to create seating areas) were replaced by a circular black 'water pool' (of reflective polyurethane), plant carpets and loose easy chairs.

The Red

To define the Teen's Library on the Living Room level, the floor bluntly changes from white-stained wood to red polyurethane. Moving up one floor to the 'inbetween space' called Assembly, you enter a soft and warm organic space (first imagined covered in carpet-thick textile, but countless regulations prevented this idea), the inside of the heart: red, dark red, pink, orange and orange-brown cover rounded forms and narrow, winding corridors. From

Escalator enters
Reading Room.

this boiling hot and pumping space, doors open into brightly lit, clinic-like workspaces (white, light grey and blue; with here and there a brown or black plane). Stairs climb up to the steel-cold floor above: the digital library – or Mixing Chamber.

Greens – Mauves – Reds

We tried to have the plant carpets produced in the USA – as a public building, local materials and finishes are appreciated – asking three American manufacturers to make samples with our multi-green digital plant images as base. None of the samples – and they were redone several times – met our expectations. Not only were the colours reduced to grey, beige and olive green, but the photographic images kept turning into corporate looking patterns, totally dead.

There is something strange about this language tangle. Because it can't just be about language – words – it has to be partly about psychological differences. For some reason the concept of literally printing a photograph, showing a three-dimensional image of plants on a rug, was not understood. Or let's say: surely understood by the local manufacturers, because we showed them the photographs we made, and an impression of the result we envisioned (handing them a piece of the plant carpet we made for our Storefront exhibit years earlier). But for some mysterious reason our idea didn't catch. Could it be something in the general mentality like: Why literally imitate nature, if you can show human interference in such an interesting way: by design? Or is it maybe a subconscious taboo: do not copy God's creations? Interesting...

'It's not easy bein' green' said Kermit the Frog. So we turned back to Europe, found a sympathetic representative of a Danish firm (familiar with political cartoons) and finally succeeded in translating our idea into a real product. First of all, the concept of photographic imagery was understood, and second: the Danish pigment regulations allow for even brighter colour use than in the Netherlands or the USA, so we were happy. This was essential, as we knew that sun filters would be integrated in the glass of the Library's entire façade, which would give a dark tint (here it is: typical) to all colours; and that the prominent (and varied) thickness of the steel structure would cast shadows into the interior.

The difficulty of transferring a picture onto a carpet is that a carpet, however you make it: knotted, tufted, woven or printed in some way, can only be built up of eight to twelve colours. But even a totally green looking photograph is composed of 397 colours. You can imagine the pain and sorrow we went through to reduce that amount to twelve base colours – without losing the 'photo' effect: the contrast and depth that we wanted to achieve.

We worked to create three different colour schemes (green, pink and mauve) and played with the scale, enlarging the images until we reached the size we needed without loosing too much clarity. We knew the building would allow many different distances and perspectives, so the aim was to achieve a scale that works at different levels of focus, depending on the viewer's position.[4]

4.
The work had to be realized with very tight budgets while meeting the technical, wear and tear, safety and cleaning requirements. This process of thorough research on material, technique, colours and production took two and a half years and was entirely covered by ourselves with some welcome financial help of the architects.

White

The acoustic cushion ceiling of the Reading Room was purple for a very long time. I really wanted Yves Klein blue velvet at first – which you can see in our models – but velvet is not really suitable here and when we made the 'Seattle colour scope', dark purple seemed a right combination with the dark wooden floor, the light blue steel structure, the purple and pink garden carpets, the rows of black, grey and white reading tables. But one day, as the building was going up, Joshua called me and said, 'PB, I have a problem. I'm standing here at the construction site. The building has reached its fourth floor and I'm looking up into what will be the Reading Room. I imagine this huge plane of purple cushion, visible from the street; and let me tell you: it is much larger than you think! Can you come over?'

So good to say 'stand with us here and try to understand that we need a new idea' instead of just telling us through the phone what is wrong and what to do. I went and the architects were absolutely right: purple would be really ugly and the white plane is so much better. Today, you can see from the street, but also experience in the room itself that the ceiling's reflectivity is an important asset.

Horizontal/Vertical

It's weird to realize that we work on so many commissions at the same time, and that the emphasis lies on different areas in each project: in some we are working on horizontal planes: gardens, plazas, carpets, ceilings; in others we concentrate on vertical planes: curtains, planting screens, walls, façades. In some all emphasis is on colour and imagery; in others all is about colourless structures and invisible veils; and in the next we reinterpret classic recipes for restoration purposes.

Dialogue

The realization of Seattle Central Library was a five-year process of continuous dialogue between all parties, attempting to specify everything from small to large scale. No hidden thing – not even the smallest – was accepted if it could weaken the architectural concept and the efficiency of the building.

We were asked for advice on the interior finishes, colour use, acoustic solutions and on the development of the landscape. All was contracted under the role of 'advisors'. It wasn't until much later in the process that we were asked to design the auditorium curtain. As an advisor, you mind everybody's business: you have to understand the architects' conceptual motives and to follow what each party does and what architects and clients want to achieve – or learn to want on the way – in order to 'advise' in an intelligent manner. What you need is overview, and to be proficient in the art of asking questions and gathering information at regular intervals. You learn to exchange ideas in a way that avoids imposing something; you need to make it all a process of interactions: you influence me, I'll influence you and together we'll make the work – and the way in which our mutual aims are formulated – better.

We had to keep up conversation and discussion in order to check decisions and mentality again and again, because we wanted to avoid losing the strength of the concept. This often happens unnoticed on the way, especially when processes are stretched over such long periods and over so many countries. Physical distances and differences in culture, language and mentality of the parties involved and the usual restrictions and impossibilities of public projects made it necessary for the entire team to reposition itself on even the smallest decisions and creative directions on a very regular basis.

From our side, we eventually focused our attention on the unification of the building's volumes through the manipulation of the horizontal planes – floors and ceilings – and through the one vertical structure that choreographs both sound and space in a single movement, which was the auditorium curtain.

new fiction

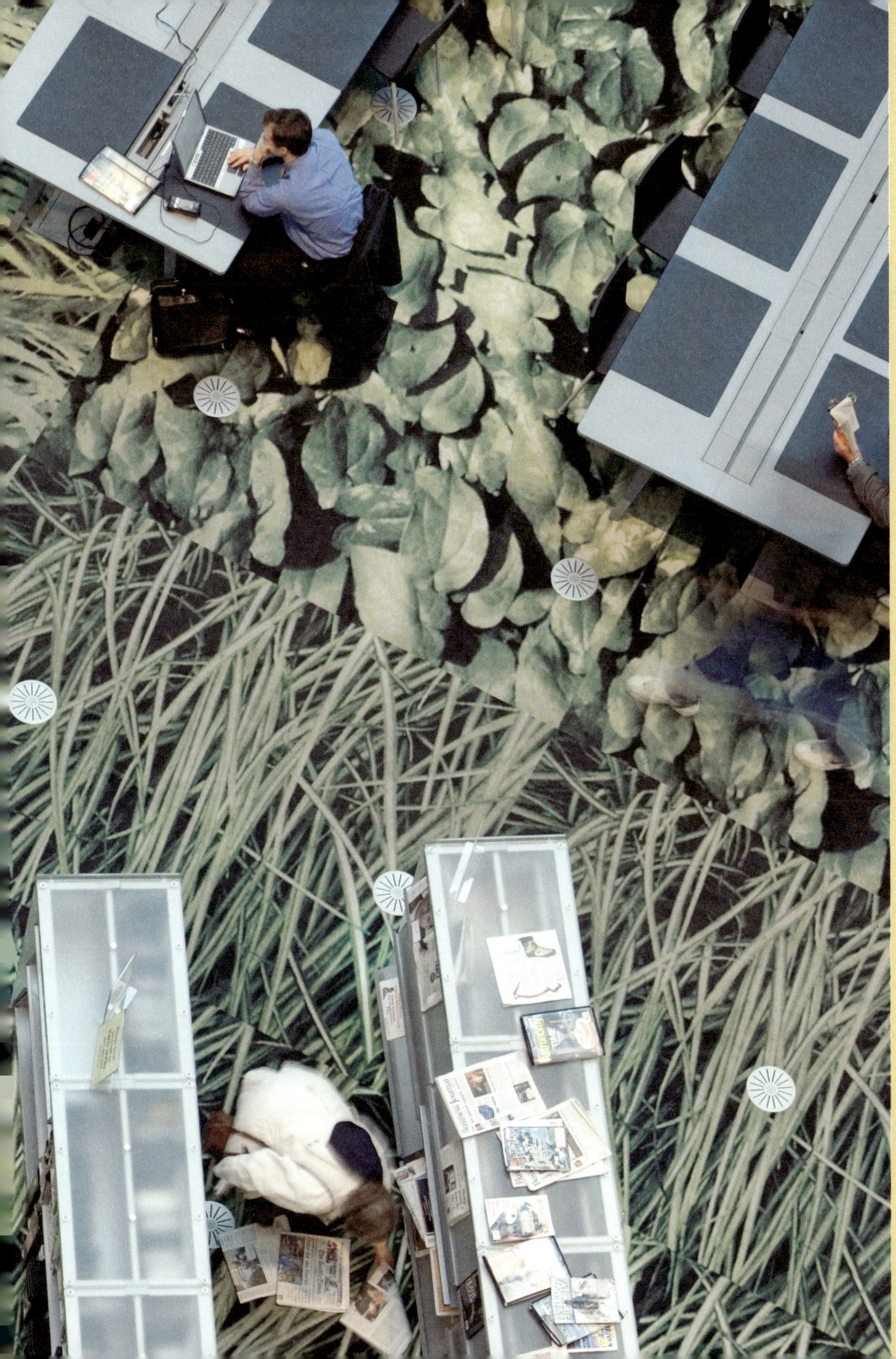

Looking down from Reading Room level

Choosing colours and materials.

Detail of red garden carpet.

Model for Kids Room soft seating areas.

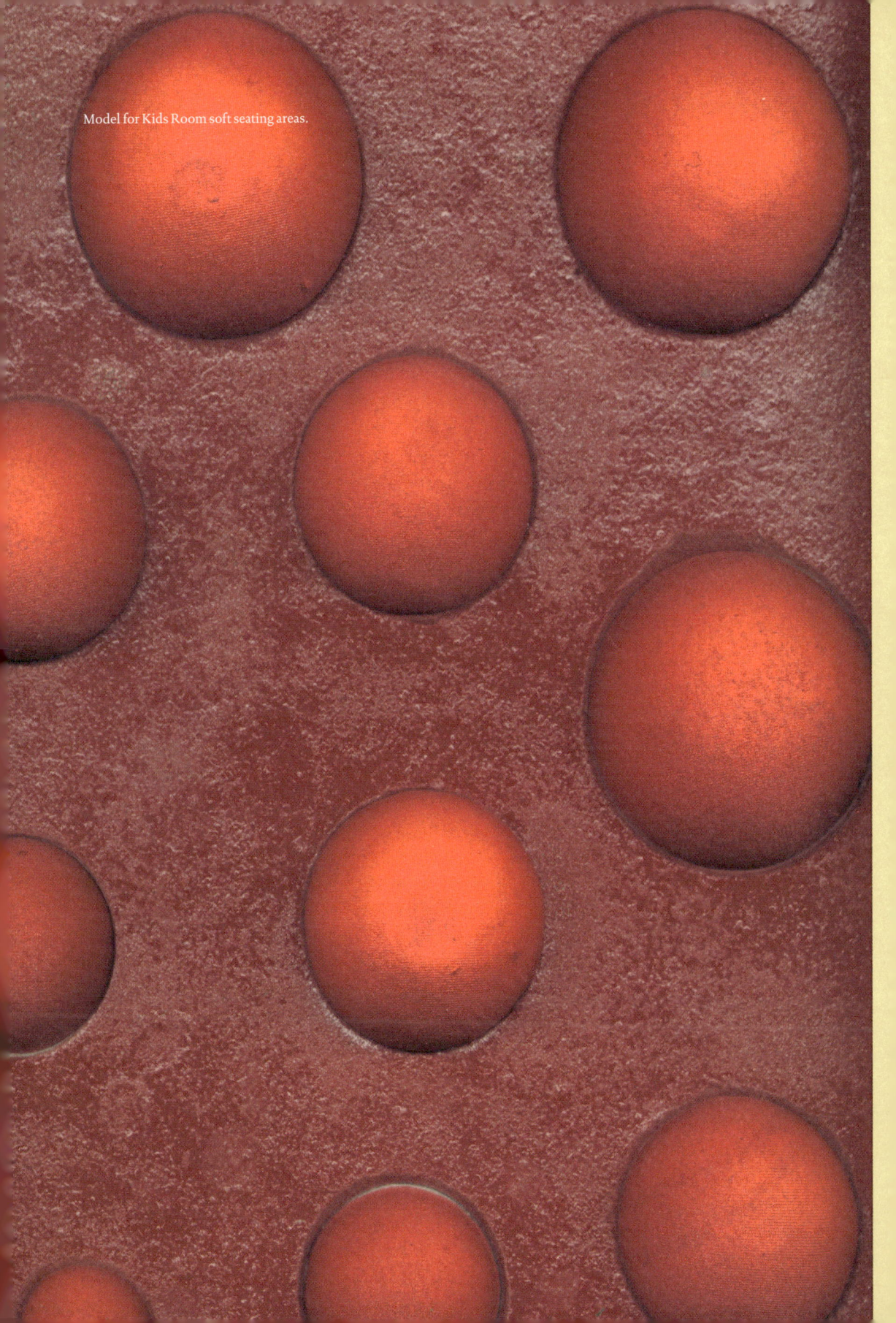

Teen's Library.

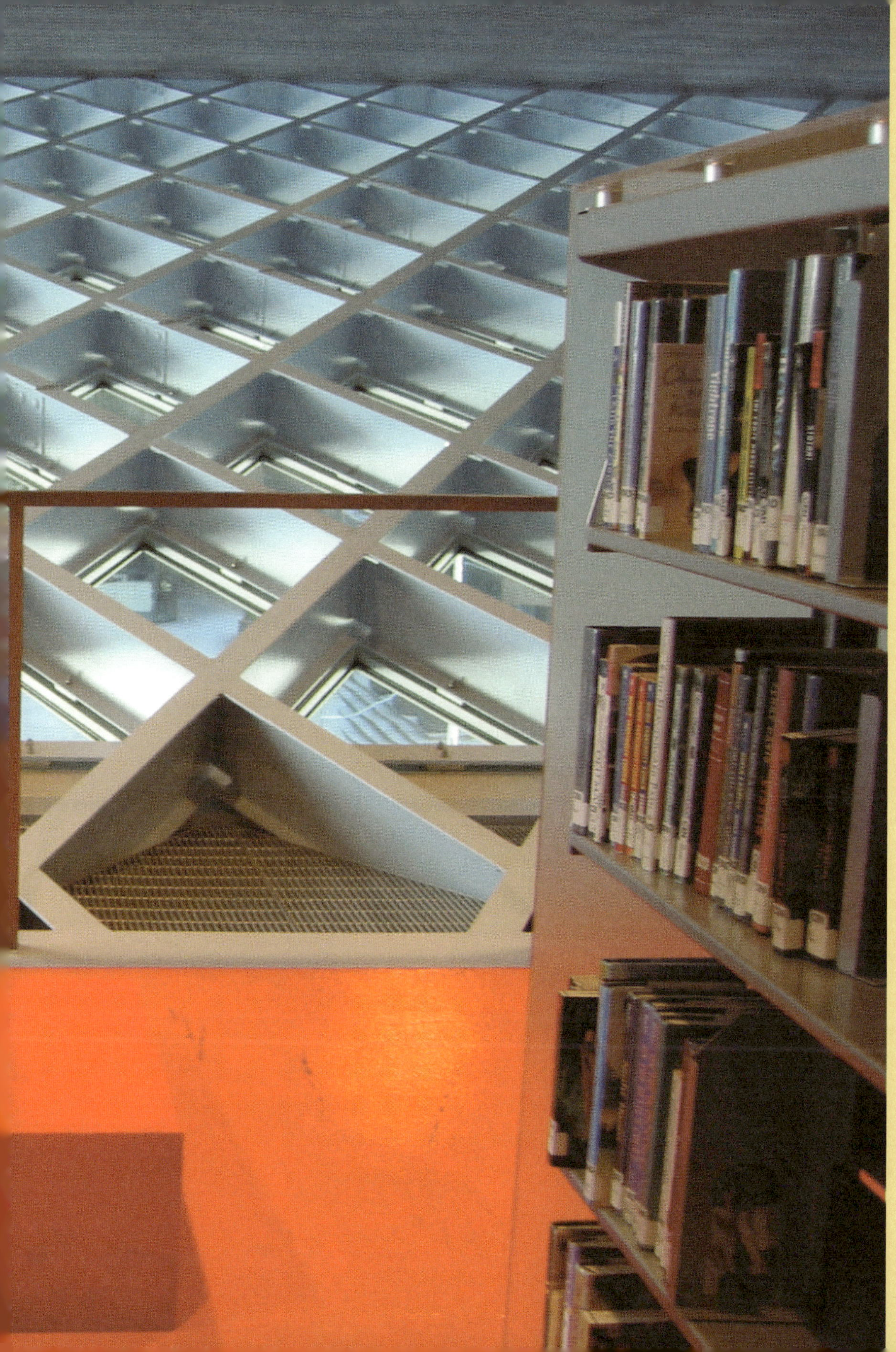

Four carpet conditions in one image:
1. plant-carpet; 2. flying plant carpet; 3. black water splash; and past the temporary screen: 4. textile carpet turns into grass carpet outside.

the norcliffe foundation living room

3

2

Design Issues of Acoustics
Renz van Luxemburg

Today, curtains are still in great demand in a variety of situations. Theatres, for example, need curtains to control light, acoustics and sight lines. In the case of the recently inaugurated Casa da Música in Porto, curtains control acoustics as much as light, while having an additional artistic value.

The first human impression of a space when entering it is visual: cool, warm, hard, exciting, and so on. Then, our ears start to check what we see, in search of its relation with the function. That is why visual and auditive perception must be in balance. Often daylight must be controlled to prevent glare and to optimize lighting levels. Curtains do this job, but ideally, besides meeting with the particular use and function of the space, they should also ensure that the acoustic condition follows the light condition as it changes.

Acoustics of space refers to the sensation of the sound striking the ear. In other words, acoustics is a matter of sound, the result of interfering sound waves being reflected or absorbed when reaching a surface. As with light, surface properties determine the amount and mode of energy reflected. Between parallel surfaces, standing waves may occur which are perceived as an echo. By treating one of the surfaces with curtains or irregular shaped bodies, these echoes are suppressed.

In acoustics, three types of sound absorption are distinguished. Lightweight panels on a closed air space absorb the sound at the low frequencies (low tones). Perforated panels absorb the middle high tones. Porous materials absorb the high tones. Heavy velvet curtains behave as porous materials. Stretched plastic materials can behave like low-frequency absorbing panels. Canvas and comparable materials behave differently.

Ask a passer-by how to improve the acoustics of a space. Nine out of ten will advise to you to use curtains, referring to heavy velvet theatre curtains. Indeed, they absorb sound at the middle and high tones, but in this frequency area the presence of people has the same effect. Petra Blaisse and Inside Outside, on the contrary, are not restricted to this one solution.

In Seattle Central Library, Inside Outside designed an auditorium curtain that has a different function on either side, which both face the audience along the intelligently patterned designed rails. One side exposes the high-frequency sound-absorbing material, while the inverse acts as a panel absorber for the low frequencies; thus performing as a real acoustic tool and expanding the functions of the curtains.

In Casa da Música, they experimented with all kinds of curtains in combination with reflective materials to control both the acoustics, as well as the light in the Large Auditorium, Small Auditorium and Rehearsal Room. Effectively using colours, patterns and textures, Inside Outside designs curtains that fulfil multiple functions.

Designing and creating spaces requires knowledge of perception, and therefore of human psychology and physiology. That is why designing always becomes research by experiment in the approach of Inside Outside. They carefully choose materials with light- and sound-reflective properties in mind, contributing to the spatial control and optimizing acoustics, thereby reinforcing the qualities of architectural space.

Eindhoven, 2005

"Bears used to live in these forests."

The perpetual platonic dance of M and P: in many OMA buildings Maarten van Severen and our interventions complement/surround each other (Bordeaux, Paris, Porto, Seattle).

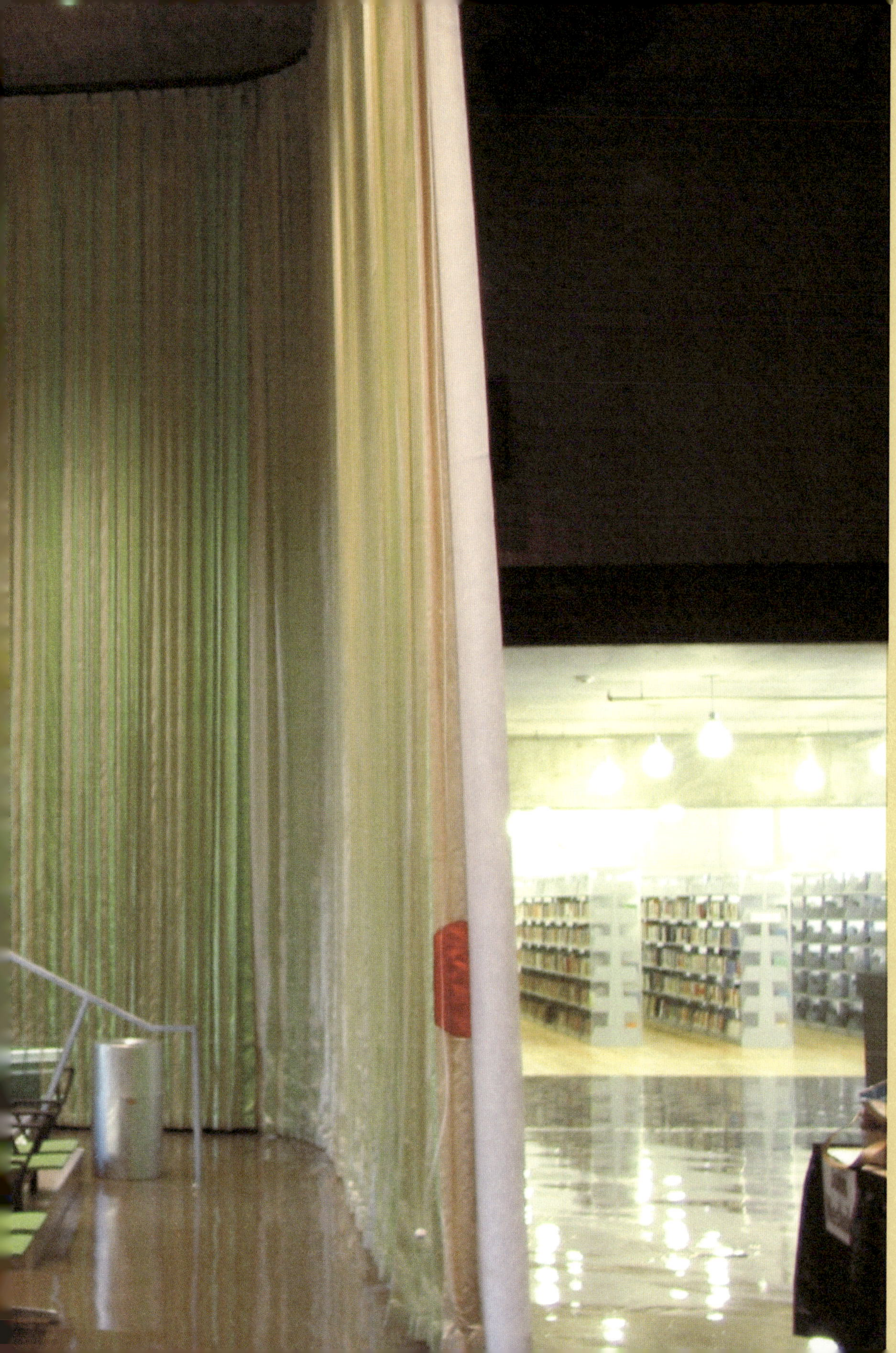

Gardens in the making.

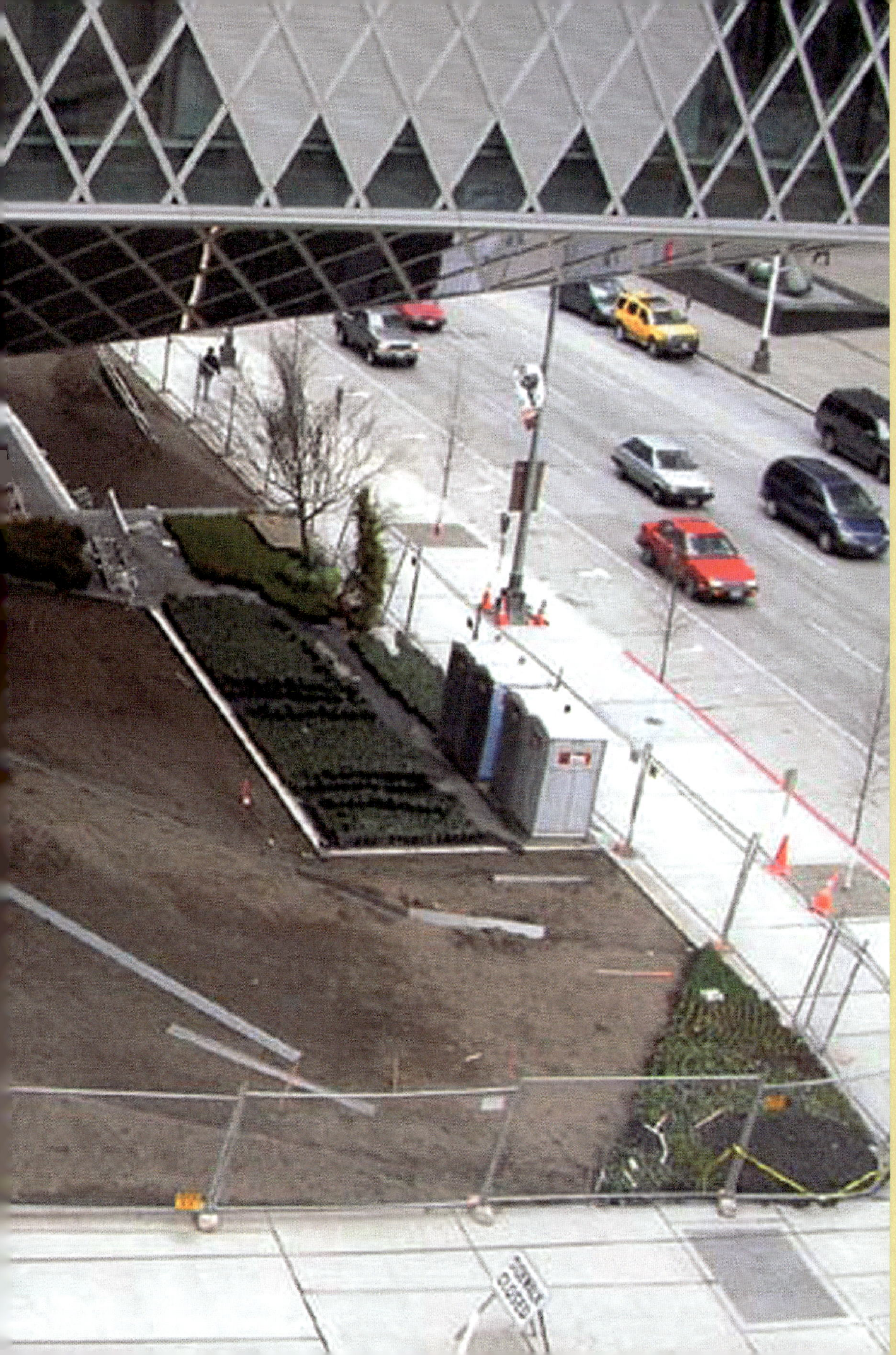

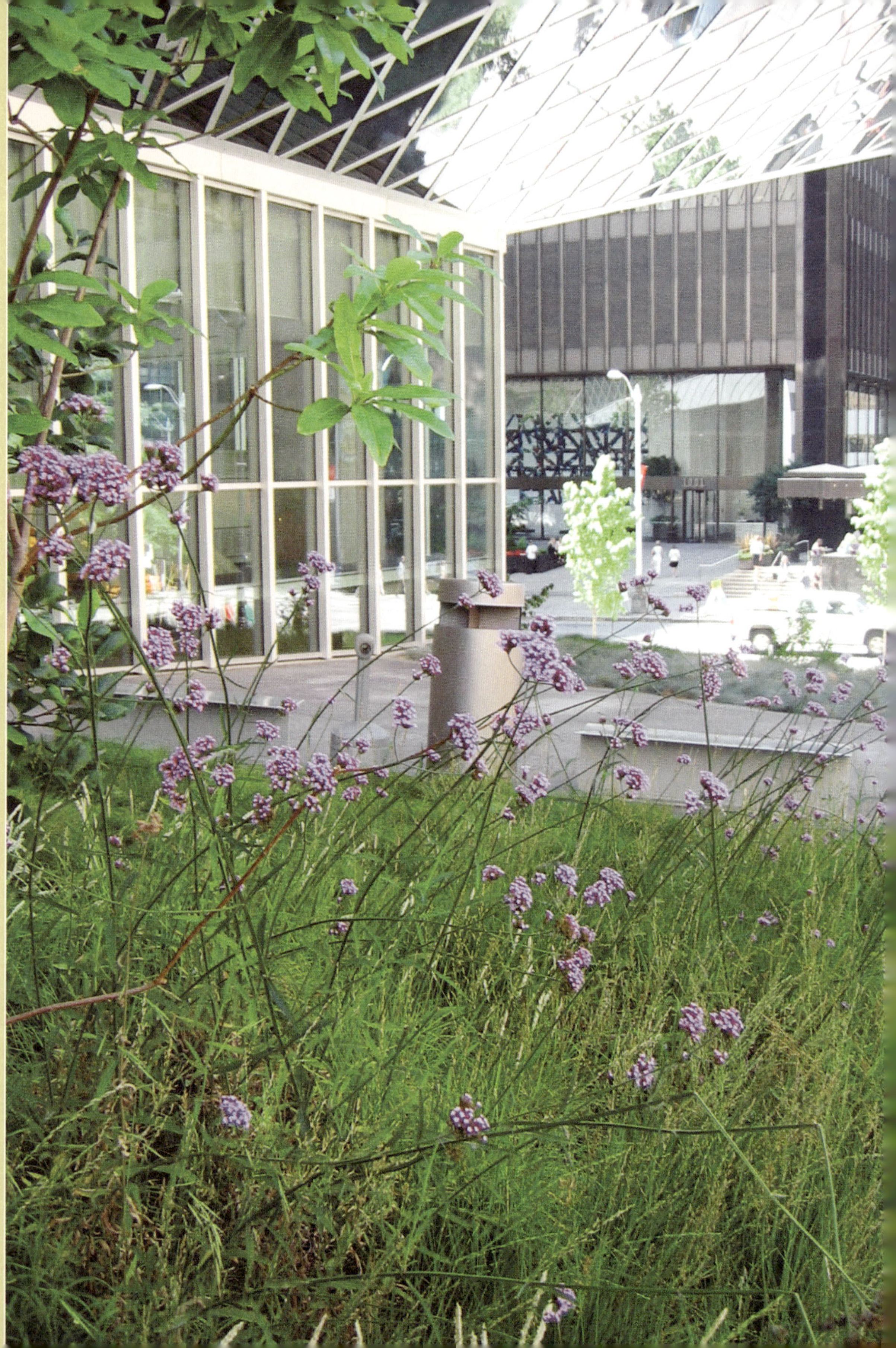

Entrance on 4th Avenue.

Entrance on 5th Avenue.

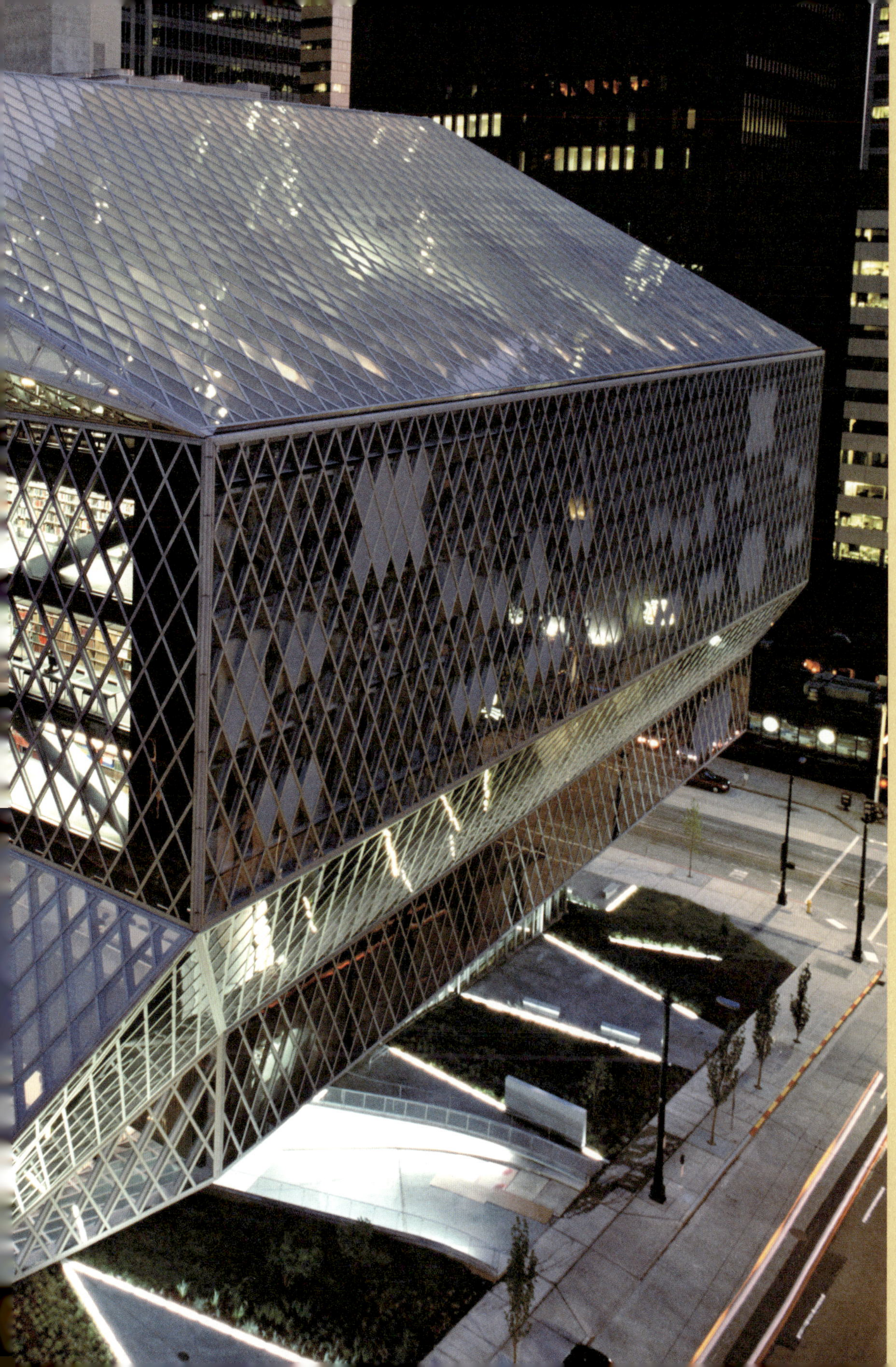

Water Fleece

Aesthetic curtain for glass façades
Villa Floirac, Bordeaux, France, 1996–1998

Like water, every breath of wind triggers the tulle curtain's movement and lets it flow in and out of the house, along the track that escapes its boundaries, from living room to outside terrace.

Windows

... and there appeared the grass circle.

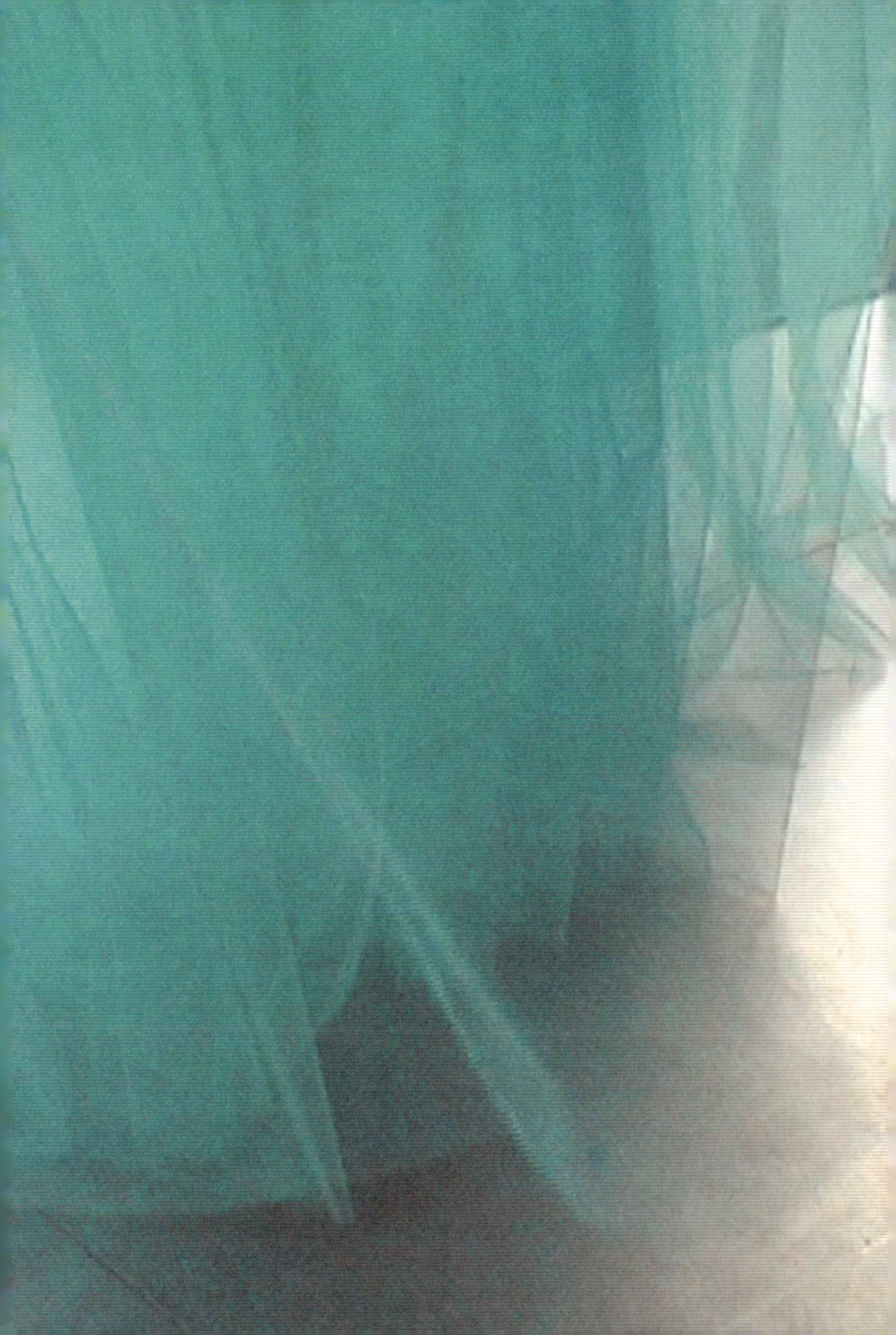

Bedroom Terrace Mirror

Light-regulating curtain
Villa Floirac, Bordeaux, France, 1996–1998

The reflective balcony curtain mirrors both inside and outside.

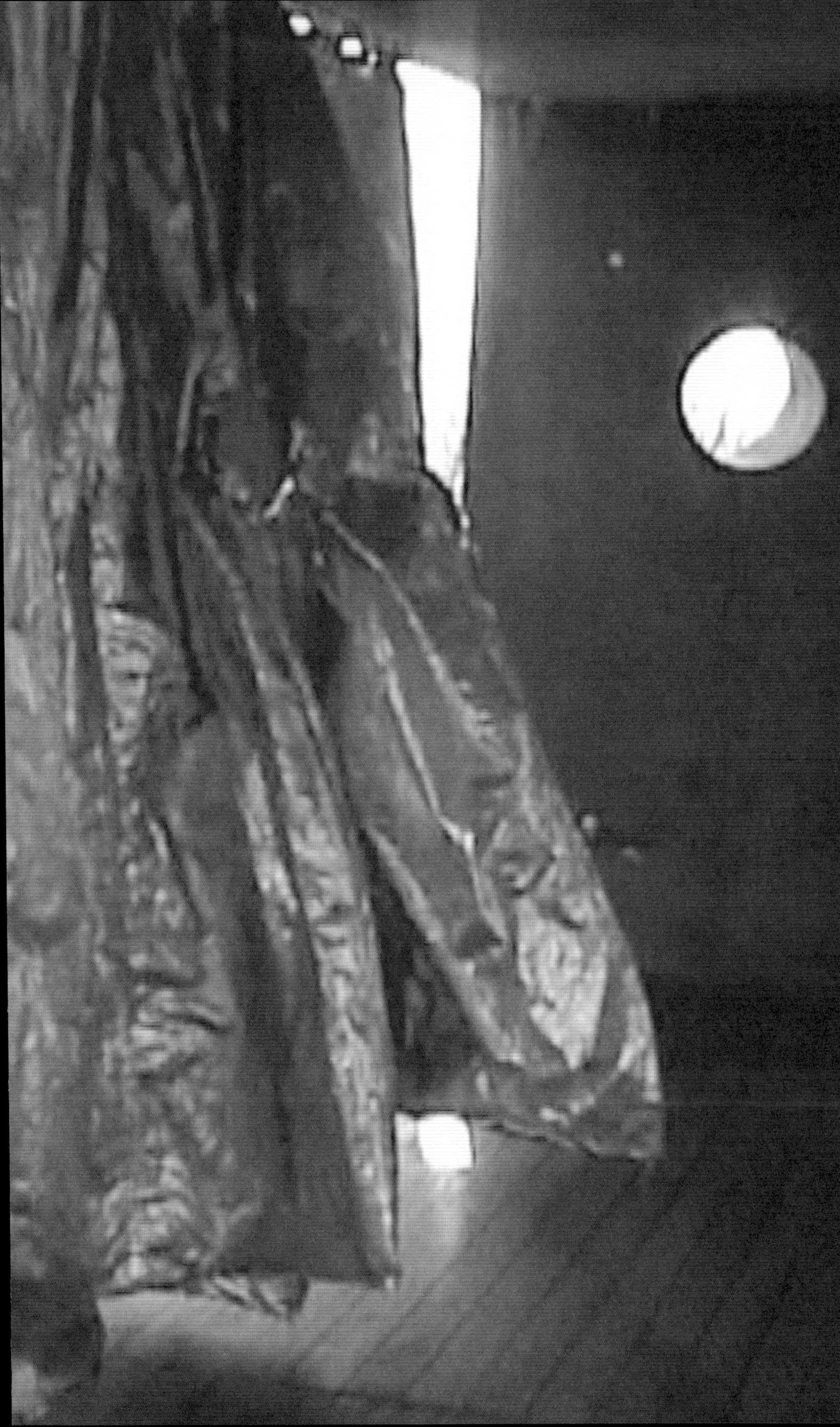

Pink Bathrobe

Space-defining and light-regulating curtains
for master bathroom and bedroom
Villa Floirac, Bordeaux, France, 1996–1998

Pink silk enveloping the naked body.

Living with Curtains
Hélène Lemoine

INSIDE
Turquoise, in tulle, through which you see the clouds and the raindrops that course down the windows. Pink, in silk, they surround me in my bath – beaming curtains, good mood curtains.

OUTSIDE
They move at the touch of the hand or the breath of the wind, surprising everybody, wrapping us in shadow on burning afternoons, in summer on the terrace while looking at the city. Silver, they shine at night in the light of the moon, closing off the bedroom balcony.

Bordeaux, 2005

Soft embrace: from bath to wash basins to (bedroom) windows.

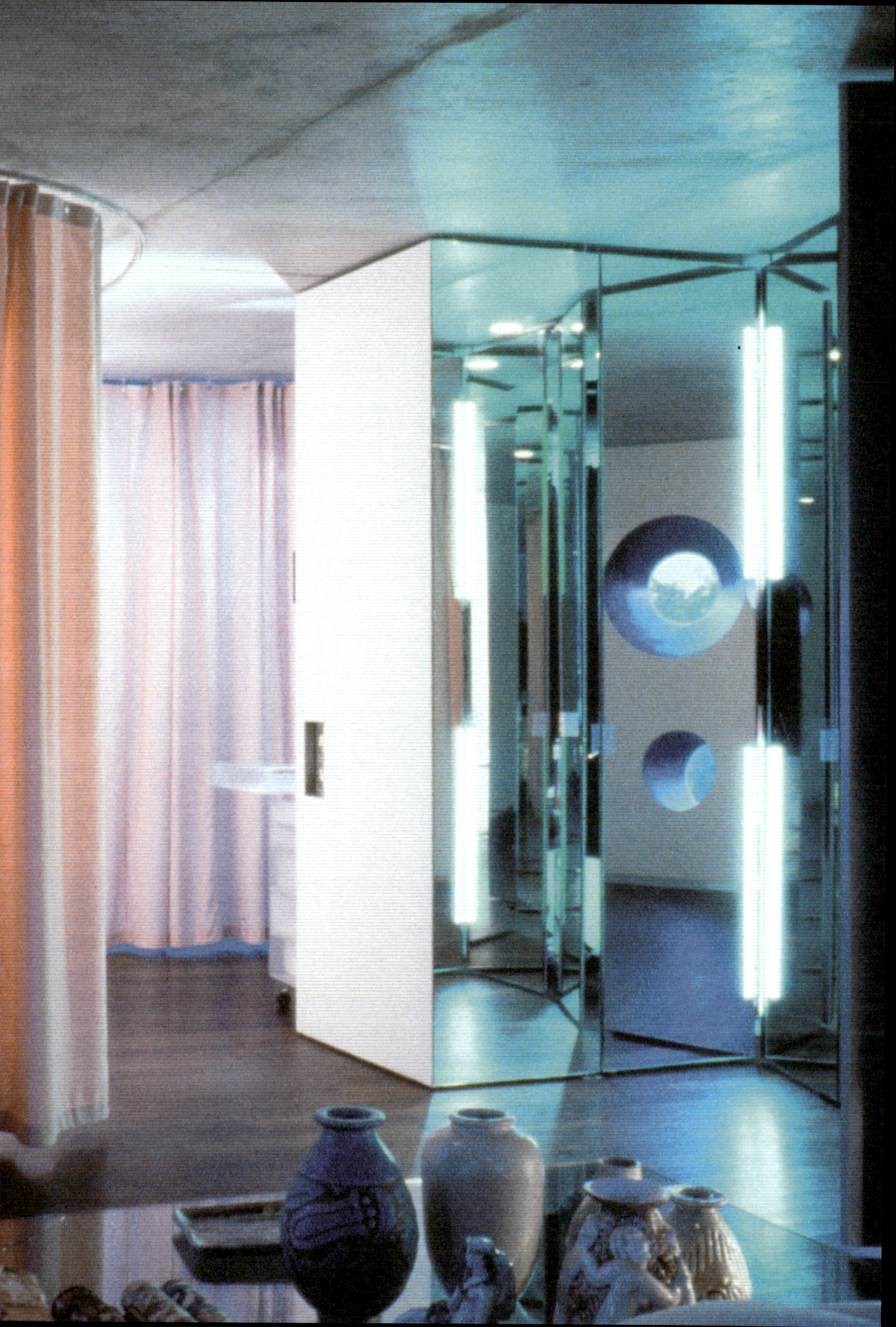

Sun and Moon

Light- and space-regulating curtains
Villa Watté, Leefdaal, Belgium, 2003–2004

Darkening but not excluding.

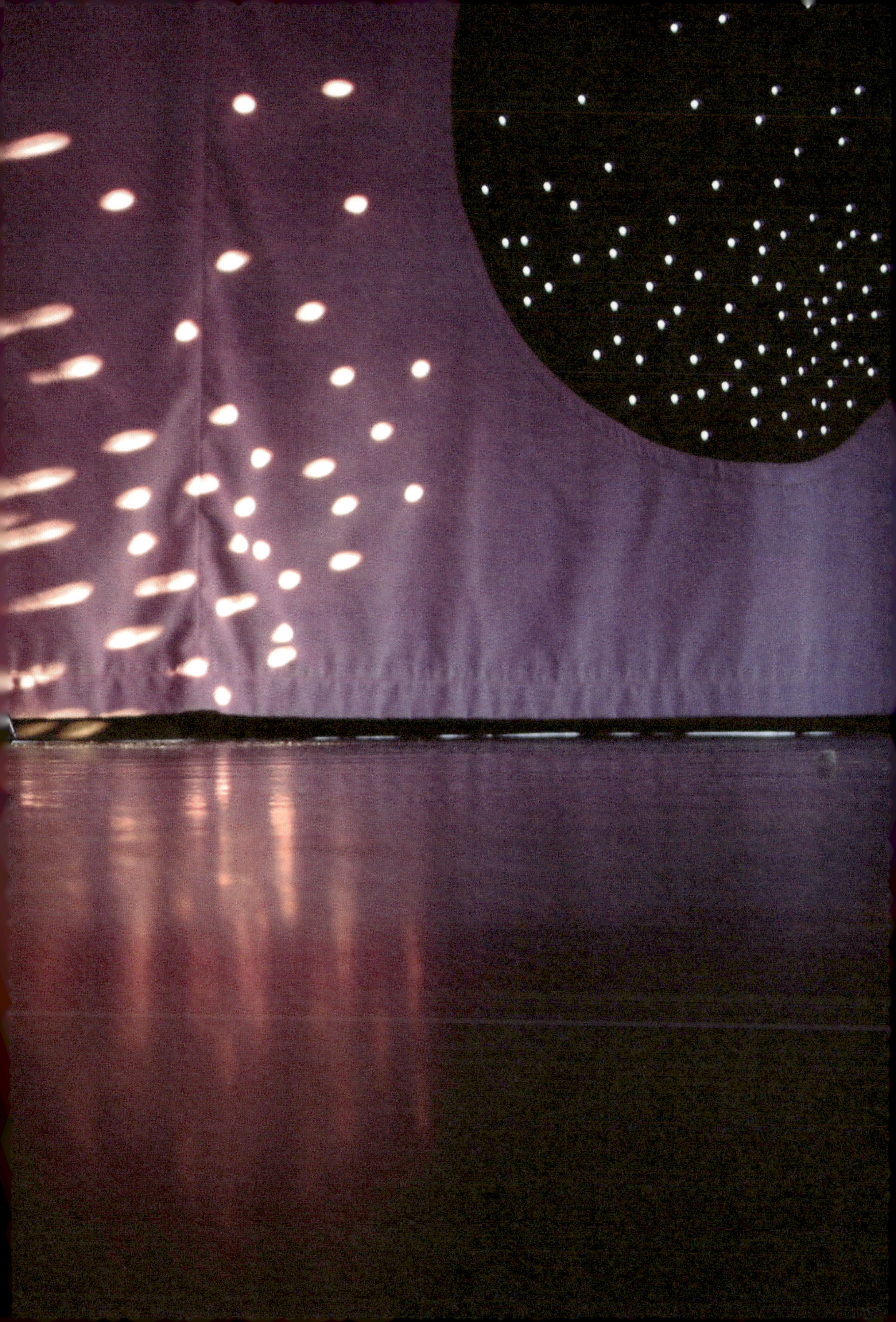

Multiple moons.

"Gentlemen, I send you by this same post a little French box of – so called – 'safe' colours. We have various scares here about scarlet-pink – girofleé – and carnation-darnation fevers; and I've just given this dozen of mortal sins to a young convalescent of six. Will you kindly analyse the temptations and see if they're – not worse than apples and currents – if only mildly licked? And if really right – will you please make me another box, like this exactly, for ten pence . . ."

(Letter from John Ruskin to Messrs Winsor and Newton, August 9, 1889. Victoria Finlay, Colour, Hodder and Stoughton, 2002.)

Shshshsh...

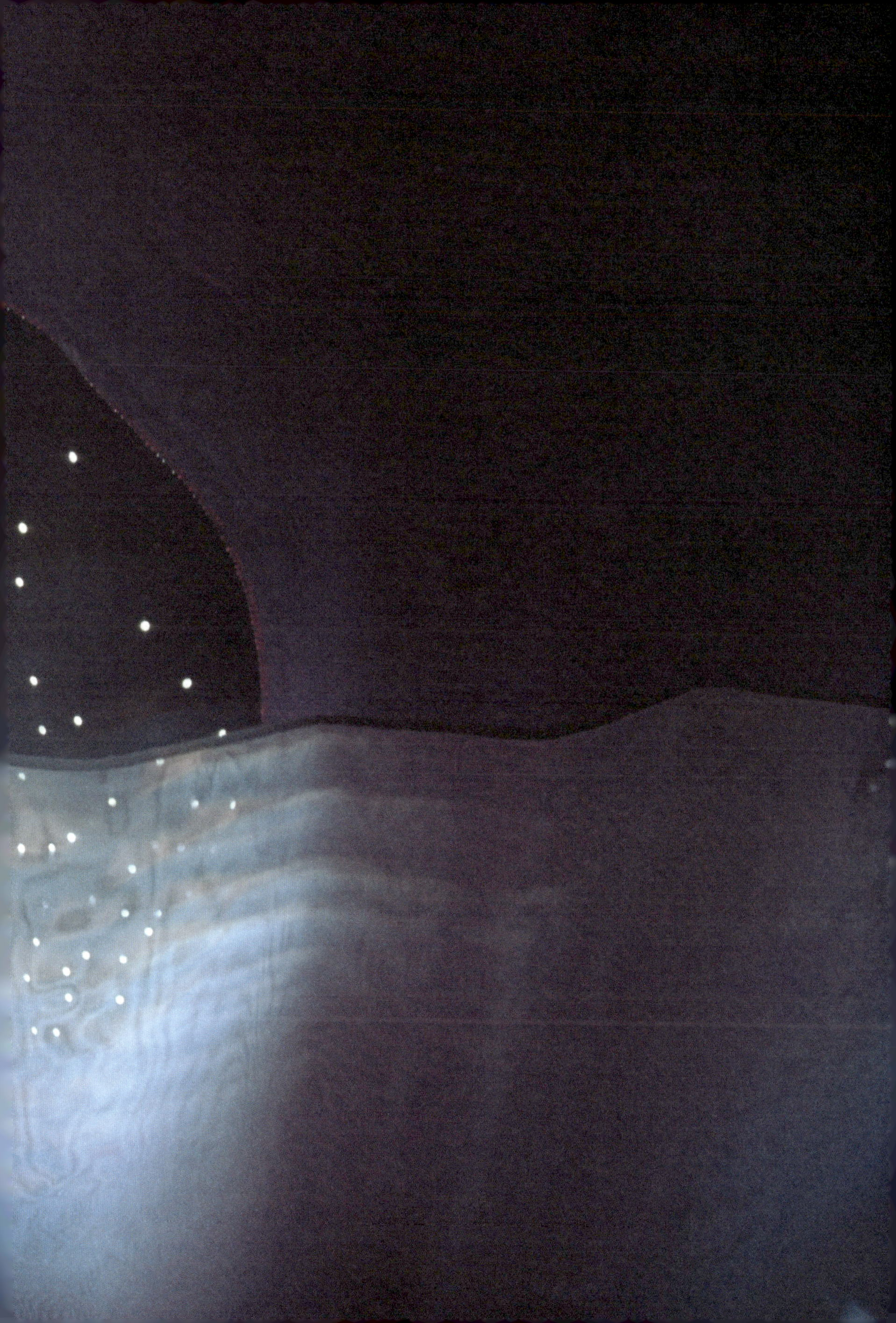

Window Windows

Sun-reflecting voile
Architectura & Natura Bookstore
Amsterdam, the Netherlands, 2003

Light damages and reveals...
books shielded and exposed.

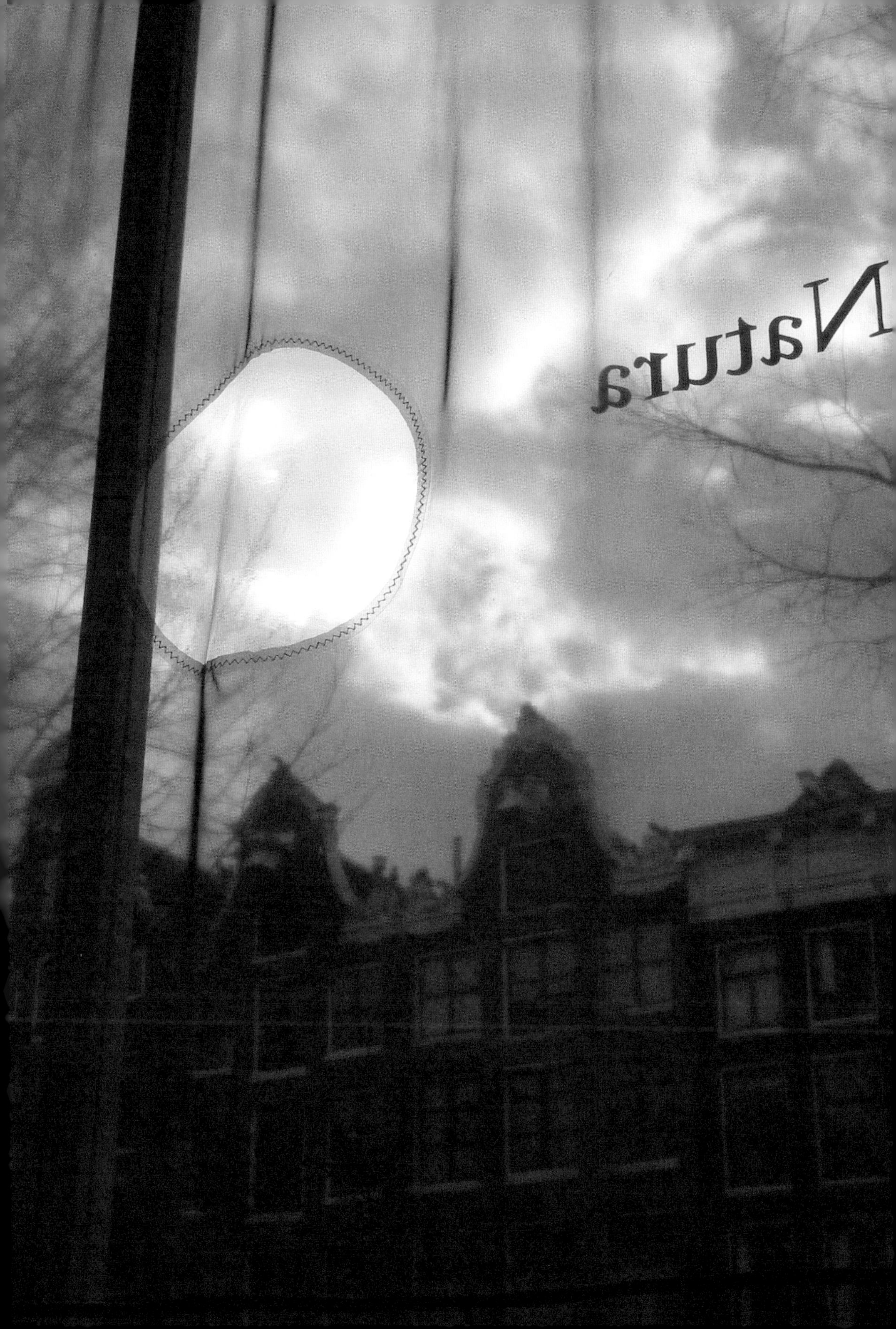
Natura

Dutch

Custom tile design for Terminal F washrooms
Schiphol Airport, Amsterdam, the Netherlands, 2006

'The repairs to Ladies and Babies look good –
Disabled will be checked this morning.'
(production company in communication with Inside Outside)

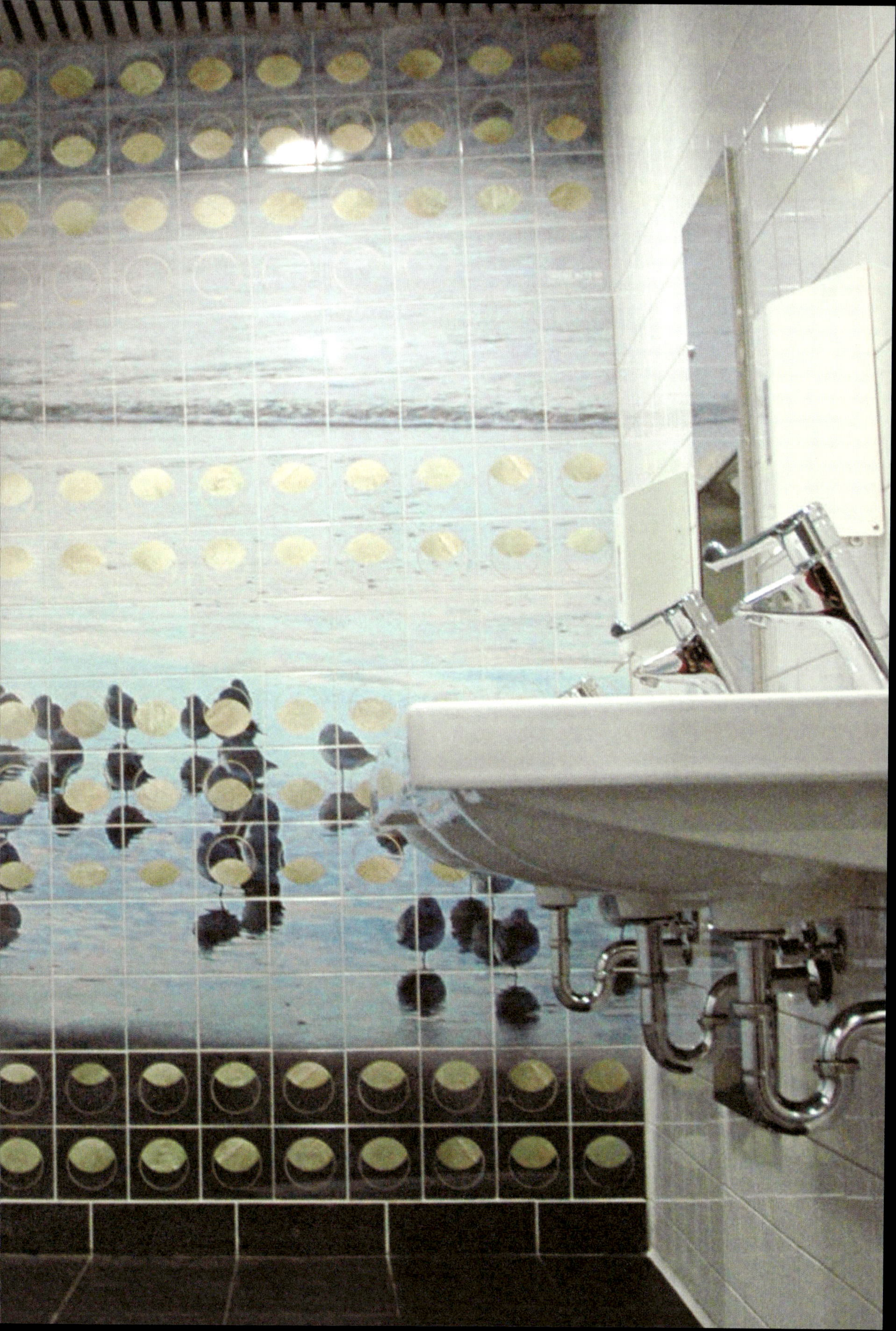

The Path as Spatial Tool

State Detention Centre, Nieuwegein, the Netherlands 1997–1999

Prison Development

Next to shopping, offices and housing, prisons are a major development sector in the Netherlands. Recognizing an imminent shortage of prisons in the early eighties, the Dutch Government Building Department initiated the construction of a huge amount of prisons all over the country in the following decades. As the pace accelerated, standards were lowered, even leading to the construction of many temporary facilities. But, typical of our country, the administration had the idea of asking a different landscape architect for every prison.

In 1996 I was invited by Max One, an urban planning office based in Rotterdam, to create a 'green plan', as we say in Dutch, for an office park along the highway near Utrecht. It was a project commissioned by the developers, Ballast Nedam. Later, they sold one plot in the heart of the area to the state, to build a prison, a remand centre. Then the government architect called me: 'Would you be interested in designing the gardens of the prison? It might be nice if there's a connection between the office park and the interior prison garden.' He said he liked my Nederlands Dans Theater curtains and interior interventions, and that he trusted my talent would prove itself in gardens, too.

To get a landscape commission because of an earlier interior design was special. It was courageous of the government architect to ask me, as I was not officially licensed. I asked DS Landscape Architects if they wanted to join me. They had just sent me a presentation of their work, and that looked good.

The business park around the prison had already been envisioned by that time. Its basic structure was developed according to the typical eighties and nineties recipe, in which land is bought by developers, divided into plots, then sold to companies who in turn hire their own architect to create a representation of their firm. You know – meaningless boxes, puddings and cakes that last a couple of decades at most – three-dimensional billboards to be noticed from the highway, nothing more and nothing less.

So, for the landscape and the infrastructural organization – the two subjects actually melt together – the architects and our team developed a very classic proposal with wide lanes, spacious sidewalks and very English planting schemes. Trimmed hedges of a shrub called *Cupressus leylandii* (Leyland cypress), with entrance gates to define each plot and at the same time bind the entire area together; giving it structure and direction, recognizable as a special composition when seen from the highway. In between the lanes, we planned unpruned trees, growing out of undulating lawns with seasonal bulbs and flowers.

Along the roads we proposed large-leaved, low-maintenance perennials – – (*Petasites japonicus var. giganteum,* or Butterbur) that thrived in the very moist and sandy soil of the region. Carefully chosen street finishes, lamps, benches, waste paper baskets and signage systems (some incorporated into the street surface) gave the area a more 'refined' finish than usual, communicating a certain status. The new State Prison was embedded in this very corporate environment with a clear organization and logic. It was as if the whole development would be breathing an atmosphere of business and success.

House of Detention

My first proposition for the prison's exterior wall was a mirroring surface that, from the outside, would make the prison seem to disappear; the outside world would only see itself reflected. The controlled, corporate, market-economy driven world would live around an optical illusion, denying or ignoring the existence and the social implications of the institution of a prison, thus also denying the prisoners as fellow citizens that occupy their own space in society.

The prison is a 'Huis van Bewaring', Dutch for 'remand centre', a prison where people go when they have just been arrested and stay from a few weeks to two and a half years at the most. Usually, they are still in a state of shock, not knowing what their future will be. Although arrested, they are legally innocent until proven otherwise. They wait for their case to be prepared, for legal steps and decisions to be taken. So there is a lot of tension among inmates. There are isolation cells and there is very high security. Intense exercise is essential as an antidote to their anxiety.

Obviously, every part of the prison, including the parking spaces for the staff and visitors, a high-security entrance, drop-off area and the gardens, had to be organized strictly according to regulations. And every detail was specified by the government regulations that were given to us concerning the sports and relaxation programmes that the 'courtyards' (they don't say gardens!) should offer: the routes prisoners were allowed to follow, and at what time of the day; the physical characteristics and transparency level of furniture and shelters; size limits and sharpness levels of landscape materials; height and density of planting, transparency of leaves, positioning of branches; shadow and topography restrictions; visibility from specified camera and window angles and security personnel standpoints; and the positioning of lamps and their light levels.

Life in Prison

The prison building was designed by Archivolt Architects, who had already designed a number of prisons more or less according to the same model. The building is a 'triple cross' with an extra lifted entrance and facilities volume in the middle. Surrounded by a perimeter wall, this form creates seven inner gardens: three for men, three for women and one large service yard where goods and prisoners are brought in and taken out.

Inside the building, passages are shut by gate after gate, with scanning machines and video cameras that aggressively follow you everywhere. The canteens, the visiting areas and the work and gym spaces are located on the ground floor. Each crossing at each floor houses a mirrored, round security checkpoint from which the guards can see every detail of every cell corridor without themselves being visible to the prisoners.

Every floor plan looks the same. Only the cell doors are of a different colour on each floor. And each floor has its own art addition: work by artists invited by the government to make a site-specific work! The women's quarters have a different organization than the men's: the men have to share showers, for instance, whereas women have their own shower inside their cell. In the women's quarters, there is room for babies and small children; but not in the men's.

The gardens are surrounded by layers of security – gate after gate, accurately spaced – leaving strips of no man's land where only security and maintenance can enter, ending at the actual stone prison wall. I saw on the drawings that there were fewer layers of gates around the women's gardens, and that they were also lower. I wondered why.

The prison director explained that there is at least one biological difference between men and women: men have enormous emotional difficulty to accept their fate; and, when they are imprisoned, they either feel aggression towards themselves – finding ways to commit suicide – or towards society, threatening inmates or trying to escape. Women are the opposite: once they are caught, they feel responsibility towards others, they think more often of the family and children that are left behind; they have a certain patience with their fate, if not acceptance. Women hardly ever try to escape, they seldom want to commit suicide: they look for solutions in a more constructive way. So you don't need to put up as many fences or take as many security and suicide prevention measures.

Very interesting.

By law, every prisoner in the Netherlands has the right to fresh air and exercise, he or she has the right to participate in sports, smoke and (inter)act in the outdoors. Doctors, psychologists, therapists and social workers must be available. The Dutch government demands that every prison has sports fields, running tracks, ball fields, gymnastic racks, workout spaces, walking trajectories, meditation and prayer areas, televisions and a view of the sky and something that grows: leaves, a tree of some kind – a form of life. Manual work and study is part of the aim, so that prisoners can create and learn, and acquire some personal income and satisfaction.

It is important, according to the government, to help people resolve their key problems and get them back into society if there is no danger of repetition or threat to society. This means that circumstances should be reasonably good for prisoners, given that their mental state is already fragile and that they are suffering enough by being taken out of active society and away from their homes. A lot of time and money seems to be invested in research, therapy and replacement programmes. Often these programmes work, sometimes they don't.

We were shocked to hear that eighty per cent of the prisoners are not of Dutch origin, but are immigrants from former Dutch colonies and other

Working drawing of prison gardens and parking lot.

1. path (orange asphalt)
2. maintenance path (black asphalt granulate)
3. drop-off court (black tarmac)
4. container storage area (white demarcating lines)
5. grass landscape
6. running track (stabilized black granulate)
7. sandbox
8. packed granulate (beige sand with concrete)
9. ball field (blue tarmac with multiple lines)
10. white carpet (washed and burnt shells)
11. terracotta carpet (red mine stone)
12. blue carpet (blue mussel shelves, washed)
13. ball field (black asphalt with multi coloured lines)
14. lawn
15. soccer pitch (50%)
16. parking lot: black and light grey brick
* stadium lightening
– Betula papyrifera
– Pinus nigra
– shelters

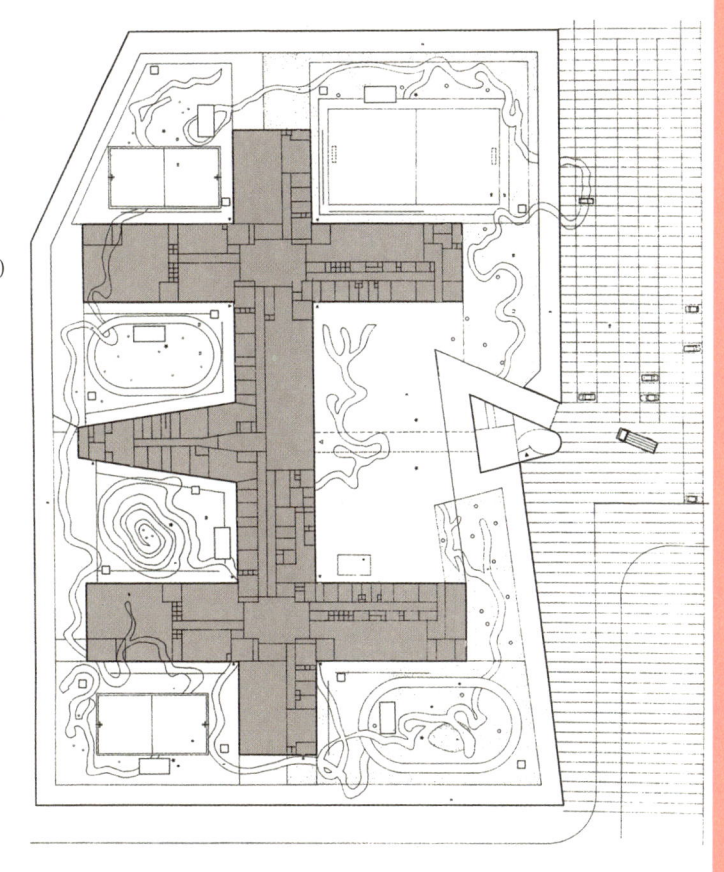

Prison embedded in business park.

countries. So we are talking about people who came to the Nertherlands to work and live recently or in the fifties and sixties, or their children or even grandchildren. This information gave us a cynical feeling about the Dutch situation: why are so many immigrants in Dutch prisons? Are they locked up because they react to the life and work situation in our country; or is our country reacting to them inhabiting our market and living space? What about Dutch criminals? Are there simply less of them, or are they just not caught? Or are they sent for psychiatric treatment or reeducation elsewhere and sooner? And what does that say about us, democratic and socially aware Northern European citizens of today?

The more we heard about the internal prison psychology and decision-making processes, the more we thought about what brings people to commit crimes and get caught, the more I wanted our design to counter, albeit in a simplified way, this over-organization with 'uncontrollable' ingredients.

Psychiatrists may say no, no, no, the brain is actually all straight lines that connect at predictable points. But my idea of the human brain is an organic and elastic form that changes all the time and which is an intricate and never-ending system, developing or shrinking according to will and circumstance. It seems we use different parts of our brain in different phases of our lives and never all of it – and certainly not enough of it, unless we're training it in all directions consciously and regularly. Such intricacy of the brain became another source of inspiration for the idea for the prison garden.

Microcosm within a Wall

We studied all the plans and sections of Archivolt Architects' building. It was extremely homogeneous and methodical: every floor was the same. Straight lines, sober surfaces, super functional. We looked at all the materials and colours, at the furniture and how space was divided into corridors and rooms, what each room's function was, where the windows were, where the bars were, what you looked out on, and which direction the cells were facing.

Realizing that the future gardens would be squeezed between two super controlled and controlling worlds – the one driven by morals, the other by the market – we could only imagine the gardens being conceived in a manner that would challenge the rigid and self-protective structure of both the inside and the outside world.

The idea of the path emerged as the main object for the garden. This path would run frantically through the prison site, penetrating the building, ignoring gates and walls, slipping out and going in, like a worm underground, or in-deed like the uncontrolled reasoning that can sometimes pester the human mind. Such an undulating, eccentric path, if executed as a strong and very visible continuous form, could orchestrate the gardens, attract the view and invite unexpected movements, creating a sense of liberating space.

We built a model of the site and the prison building, cutting coloured paper into a long and twisted organic form to decide the movement of the path. I was thinking about my father in intensive care, with an aneurysm in a major artery running through his chest. He survived, but I remember literally standing in the abandoned ammunition factory outside Amsterdam that was DS's studio on a cold and sunny day, thinking of the complexity and fluidity of the body, the brain, the soul and life itself! The movements of my hands drawing the lines of the path were the direct reflection of these thoughts.

I wondered if the garden's design could augment your insight with each level that you climb inside the building, causing the path's 'logic' to become clearer with each floor. What if, looking out of your cell window, you could not only follow little tracks of birds, mice and insects – famous companions in prison stories – but also create time and space by letting your gaze meander over the path to relax and organize your mind? I was curious if we could play with the garden's design – the colours, the path – so that your understanding of the garden would complement and reinforce the level you inhabit.

If you are *in* the garden, you cannot oversee the form of the path. You can use the entire surface of the garden, walk anywhere you like. But if you choose to follow the eccentric path, you will experience its form through your movement. Your feet will lead you through the garden in an unpredictable way and this meandering movement will take up your time and change your perspective.

Scenario for the Gardens

Each garden has a different sports programme, meaning that inmates visit different gardens at various times of the day. And as I described before: there is no way you can tell where you are in the building, unless you look outside for a reference. At the time, the buildings outside the prison walls were not developed yet; only SMART had built one of its transparent car towers overnight. So we made each garden in a different colour and with different materials. One garden is a white mound, covered with a carpet of white shells. A second garden is warm orange, made of terracotta granulate. A third garden is blue, made of mussel shells: blue with black-and-white mother-of-pearl. A fourth is ochre in colour, made of half-hard sand (stabilisé); the fifth garden is a mix of greens: fake grass (soccer field) and real grass (mixed with bulbs and wild flowers) – and the last garden is a wild flower garden with subtle topographies that catch the light in different ways.

So we created mineral and herbal carpets in different materials and colours, with a black path that cuts through each garden in a different figure. No matter how small and constrained the garden may be, you can experience different perspectives at every turn.

All the gardens are linked both by the material and the path, as if a 'carpet' is escaping the strict boundaries of a garden, changing colour somewhere around a corner. The garden is one continuous space, notwithstanding the numerous obstructions. Herbs, perennials, wild flowers, bulbs and grass will grow out of the garden surfaces in different colours – blue, green, lime green, orange, white, black, pink and ochre. Every garden has its own atmosphere. The plants may not grow tall or dense, and should not depend on trimming: they are all low-growing and self-supporting, giving seasonal effects.

The grass we chose for the blue mussel field is Dutch dune grass, which has a beautiful blue colour and is very strong. For the two grass gardens – one for women and one for men – we chose mixed flowers, herbs and bulbs which refer to wild flower fields with their natural seasonal changes.

For the white-shelled women's garden we chose spring bulbs (snowdrops and anemone) and 'lady's robe' or *Alchemila mollis* (Lady's mantle), which is a beautiful lime green plant whose leaves have furry hairs that catch every raindrop. The droplets glitter like tears or pearls, depending on how you look at them.

Trees, like all plantings, have to be very sturdy so that not much care is needed. For gardens on the north side of the prison, where people have to be visible throughout the year, we chose the Himalayan birch (*Betula jacquamontii*), a white-stemmed tree with fine leaves. We had to lift the crowns up to a certain height and over-water them for the branches to remain soft so that prisoners cannot climb up and hang themselves.

On the south side of the prison, where visibility seemed less of a problem, we were allowed to use pine trees, which are evergreen, provided that we planted each tree according to visibility and kept the logistics of videos and cam-recorders in mind.

Unusual Garden Elements

The design of 'shelters' was also part of our programme. That is, roofed areas for inmates and guards to sit outside in, regardless of the weather. These are hardly more than a transparent plastic roof on a secondhand concrete structure (that used to be a bicycle storage that we found and liked – the budget here was extremely low), but we still managed to create an elegant form that satisfies security restrictions. We had to ensure an open structure, so that prisoners are visible at all times and light is transmitted; but more importantly: the roof had to be made of breakable material to prevent prisoners from climbing onto them.

Connected to the shelters are wind screens, wooden benches, wastepaper baskets (including ashtrays), all positioned on a rectangular concrete floor slab. Guards have their own, strategically positioned shelters of the same design in a smaller size. The path runs right through these structures.

Running tracks and sports fields cut through the composition of the garden. Two gardens have basketball and volleyball fields, another has the first pitch with rounded corners for soccer and three gardens have running tracks. And there is a garden in which women and children can play and relax.

Inside the building and outside the prison wall where we created the parking areas for prison staff and visitors, art works were installed by government invitation. In the course of the garden development, our eccentric path needed extra budget to be realized. Our path was recognized as a 'sculptural element' and its financing was supported with part of the administration's arts budget.

Speaking of the budget, we had proposed that the prison wall be covered in polished metal on the exterior, but this was too expensive. The architects decided on an ochre-coloured pigment mixed into the concrete for the entire surface, both inside and outside. The wall itself has a stepped form, growing thinner from the top down – I guess they needed to make it very difficult to climb.

After Seven Years of Use
Recently, I went back to the prison after seven years, and found that the whole context has changed. The women are gone. One garden has been transformed into cell blocks. The security has become more grim . . . We were not allowed to see any prisoners and they were not allowed to see us. We were not allowed inside the gardens. We had to make the appointment months ahead of time. For exactly 45 minutes, during lunch time, we were allowed to take photographs from behind the barred windows of staff offices; or from the roof down under the strict guidance of an armed guard. No prisoner to be seen.

The ochre prison wall now looks worn and decoloured by the weather. Some trees have grown well, others have dried out and have just been replaced by the same species, one generation younger. The original planting survived but is now mixed with weeds that outgrow them in a few areas.

It was exciting to see that the gardens have been used and used and used! You see the traces and the strong graphic lines of the eccentric path while the running tracks have become fainter: the edges were powdery and, here and there, merged with the surrounding 'mineral carpets'. It was actually beautiful to see how each garden had acquired its own story. By the varying degrees of wear one could see some were used more than others. It was intriguing to look at an empty garden with all the signs of intensive use!

Then, all of a sudden and by accident, on our way back, one of the gardens that we had already photographed – the Terracotta Garden – filled with male prisoners. The guard bellowed, 'Put away your cameras! Now!' We did, but looked for a few silent minutes onto this world beneath us, where men of all skin colours and ages moved about. It was a very hot and humid day and most inmates had taken off their shirts. They all looked handsome and well trained. Tattoos in all forms and measurements had a unifying effect, making the scene almost fashionable.

Some guys were running around the track, some were slowly walking along the path, some were working out on the racks. Some were hanging around in small groups, talking, or keeping to themselves, smoking. Without exception, they all looked alert and defensive of their personal territory: their own body. You could sense they were measuring each other silently, without disturbing the peace. Then some men noticed us on the roof and waved, nodded, or stretched their arms to make the 'peace' sign. We answered their sign language and quickly moved away. It was a touching experience.

Under no circumstances were we allowed to publish any image on which security measures (walls, gates, cameras, outside world) were visible. All images were first sent to the prison staff for censuring. All recognizable structures and faces (of the guards accompanying us or their colleagues playing soccer) had to be distorted.

Collage for presentation to government,
prison staff and architects (1997).

Garden 1
Women's ball field

Garden 6
Women's philosophical garden

Garden 2
Women's running track and
children's playground

Garden 5
Men's running track

Garden 4
Men's ball field

Garden 3
Men's soccer field and running track

Garden 1
The path doesn't stop for anything (1999).

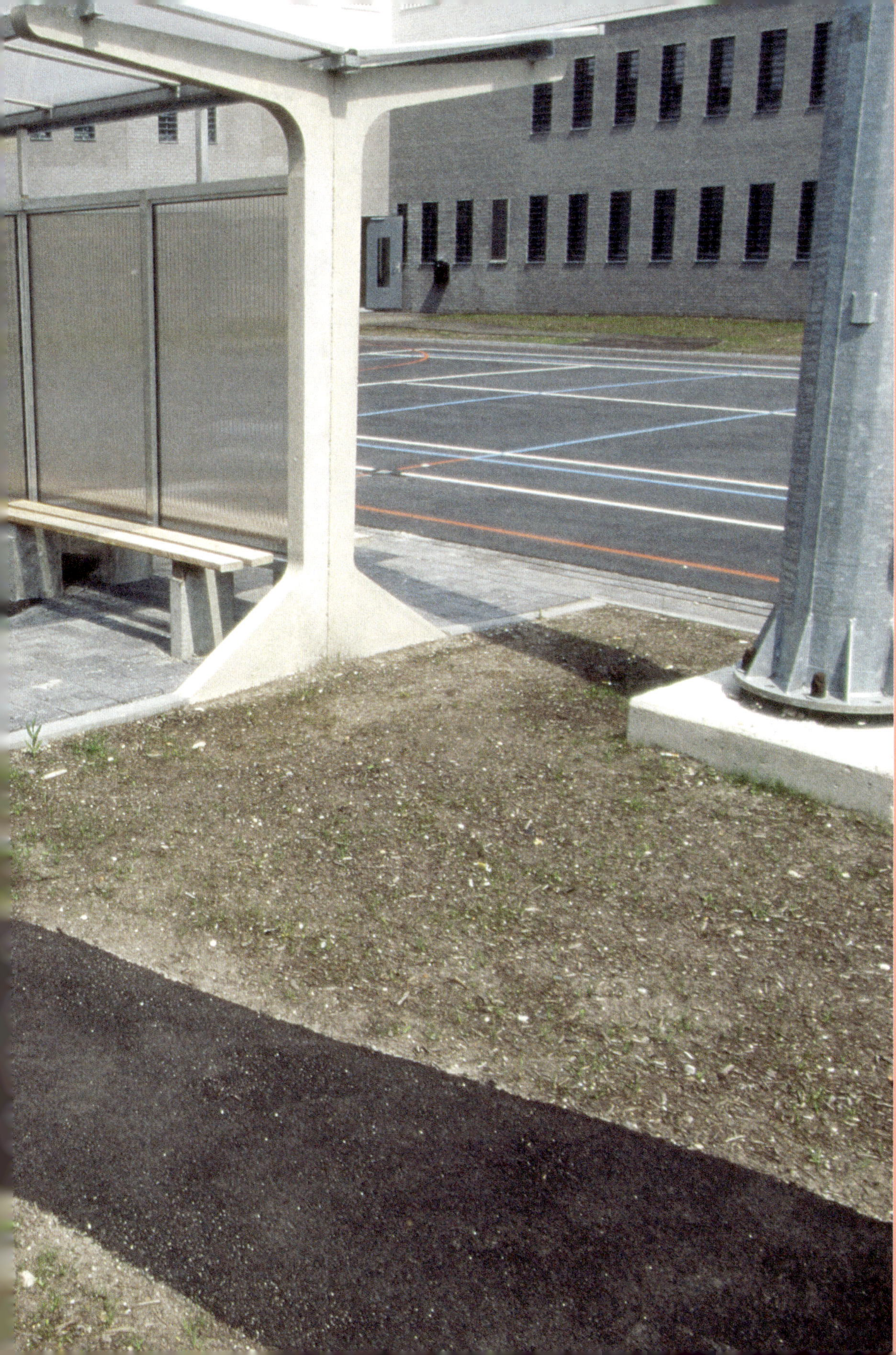

Garden 2
Orientation tool for inmates: each garden has a different colour and form (1999).

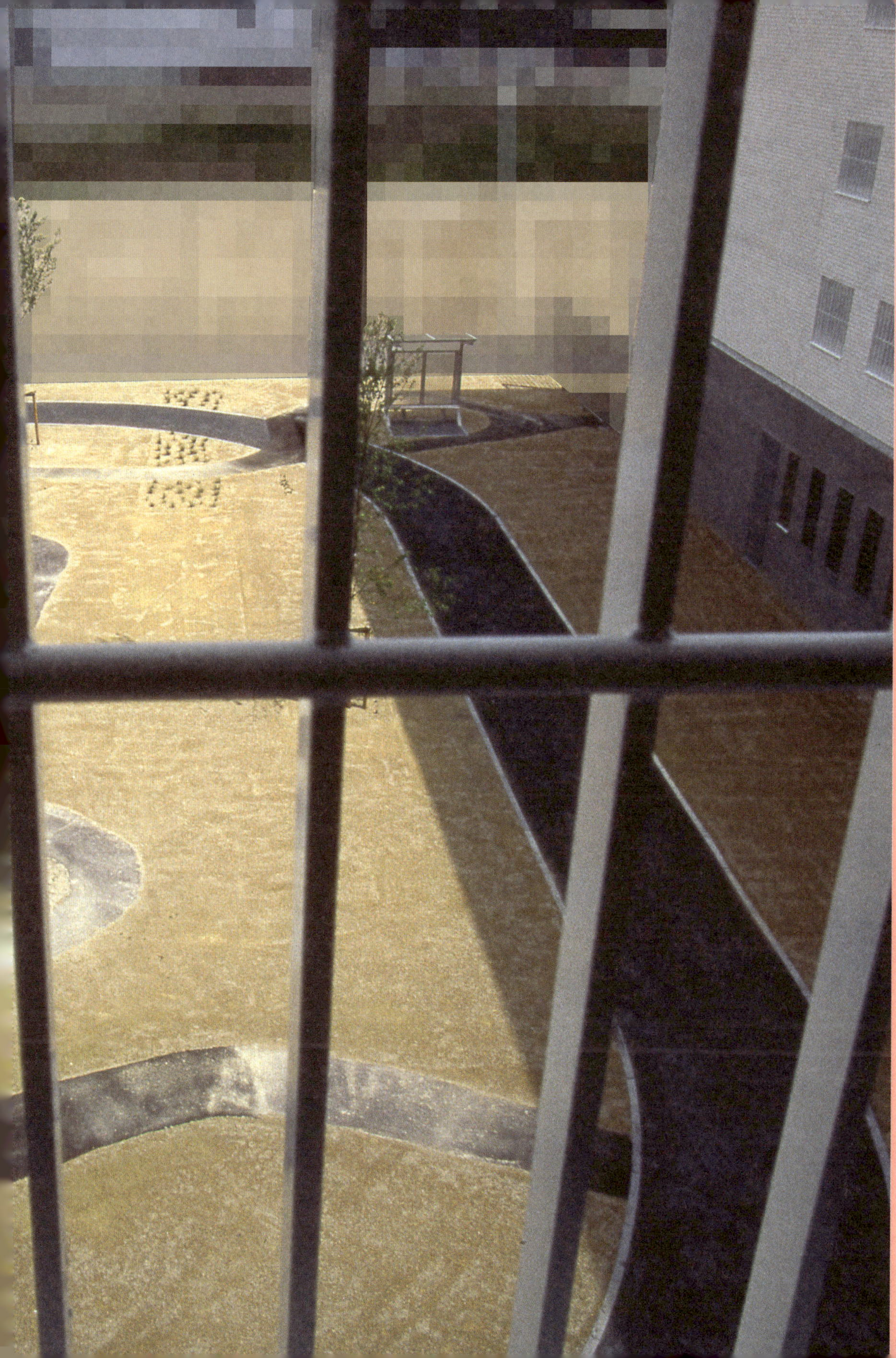

Garden 3
Ever seen a soccer field with
rounded corners? (2005)

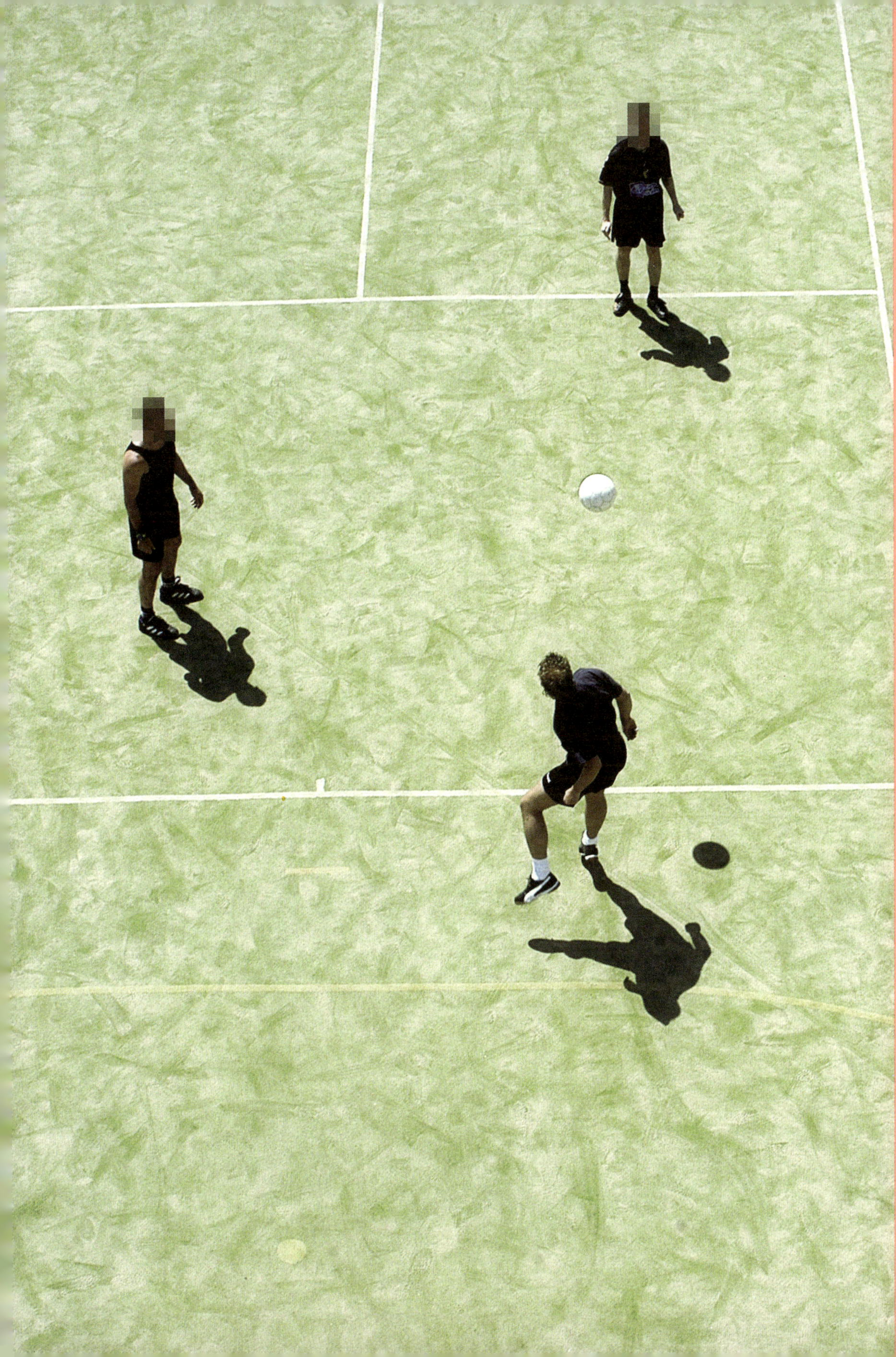

Garden 4
Garden separation: the recently seeded grass and wild flower carpet of the men's soccer garden changes to the blue mussel shell carpet of the men's ball field garden (1999).

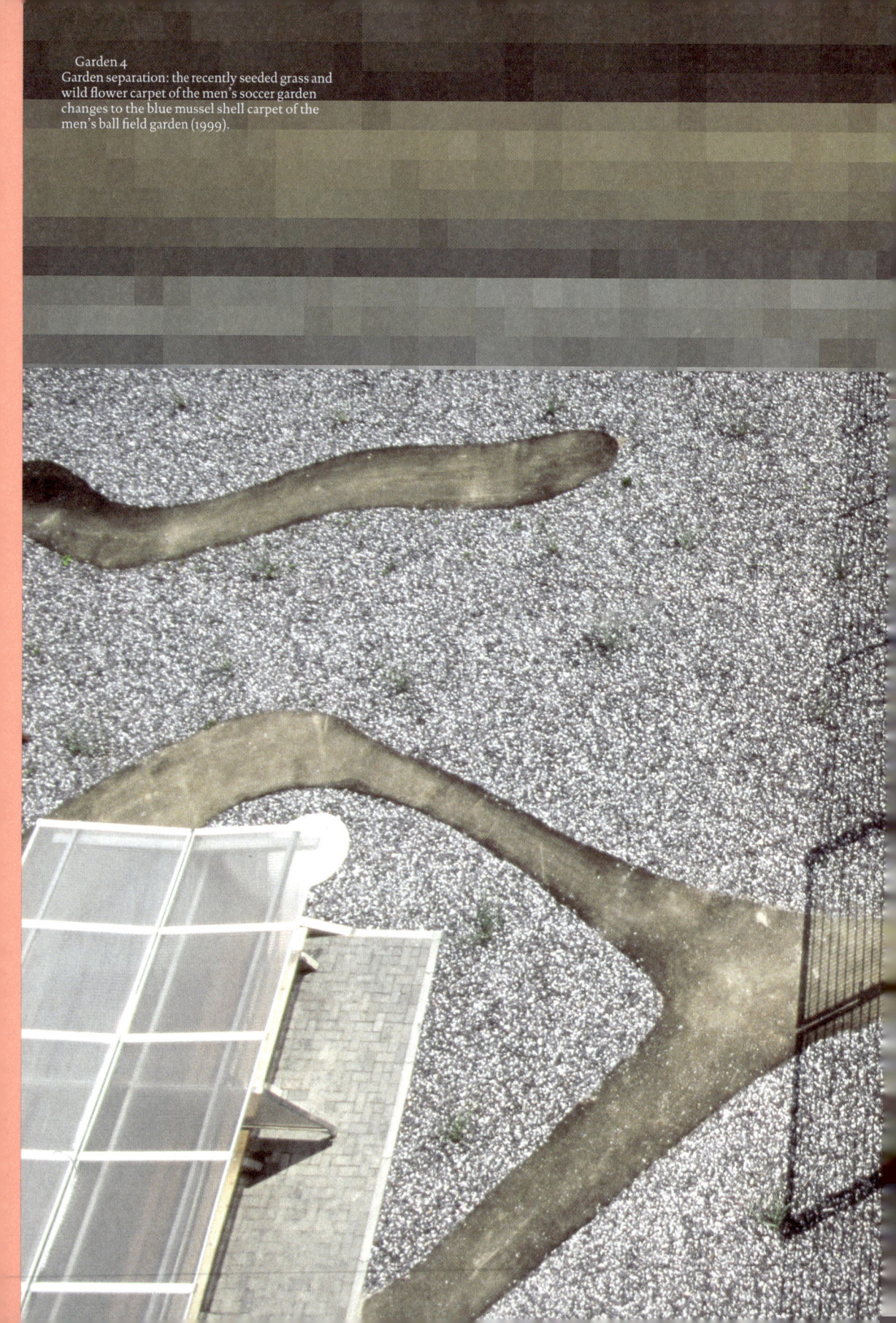

Garden 3

Garden 4
Mussel shells, dune grass, birches
and asphalt (1999).

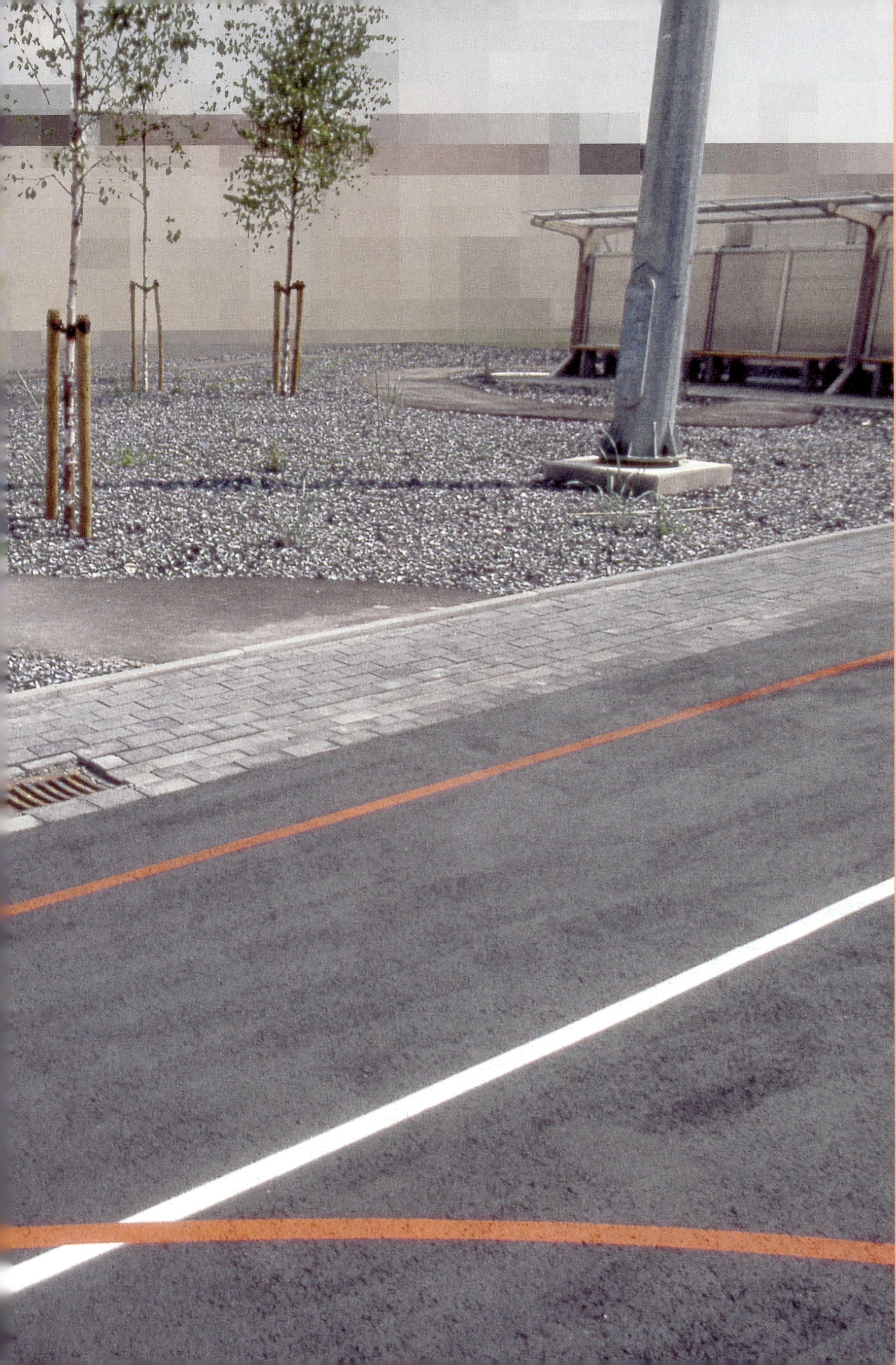

Elymus arenarius 'Glaucus' in a carpet of blue mussels (1999).

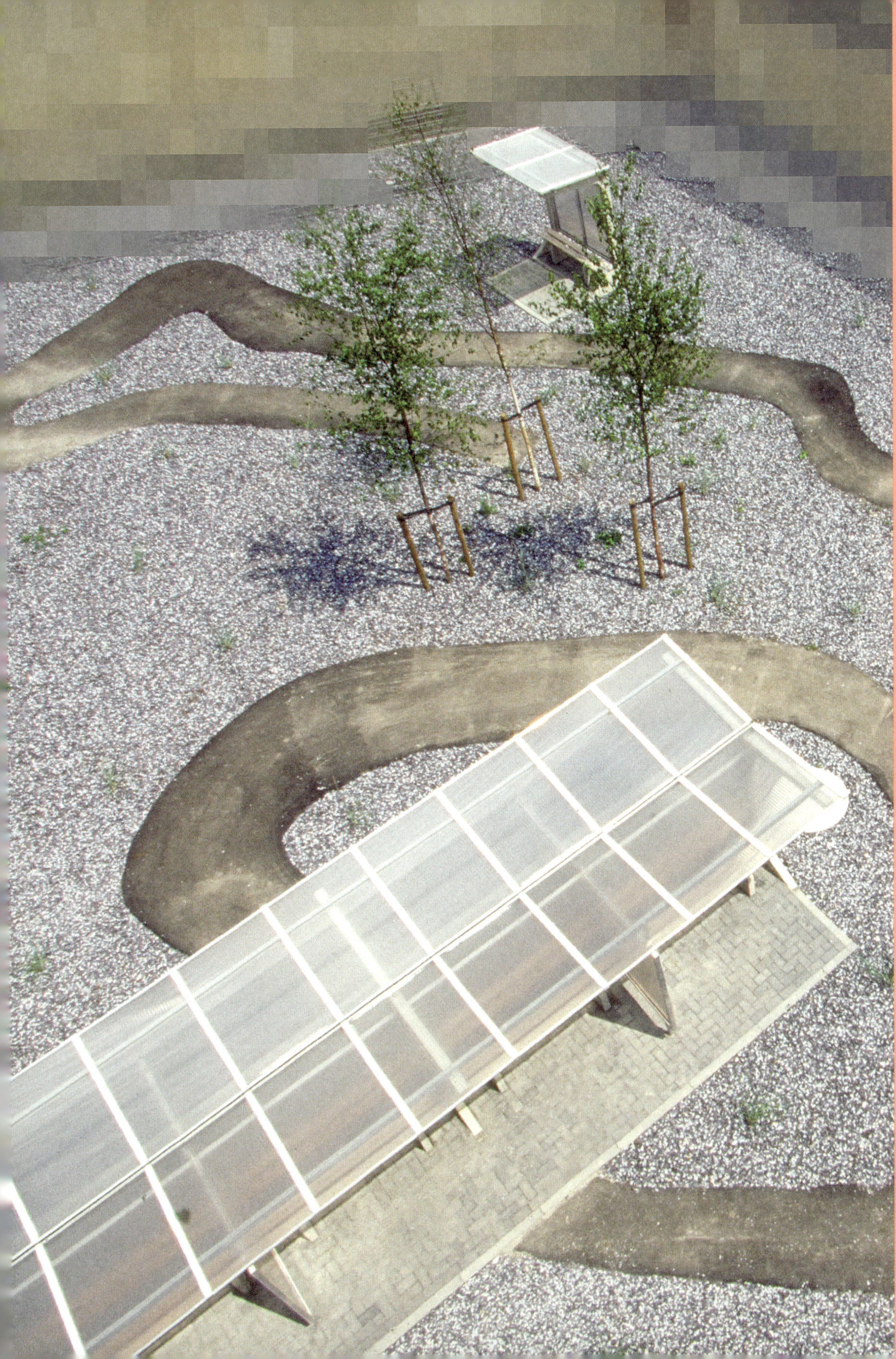

Garden 5
Men's garden: carpet of terracotta-coloured granulate, seasonal bulbs, perennials, birches, asphalt with fine blacktop layer (path), basalt granulate (running track) framed by concrete edge and shelters (concrete structure, wooden benches and plastic roof) (1999).

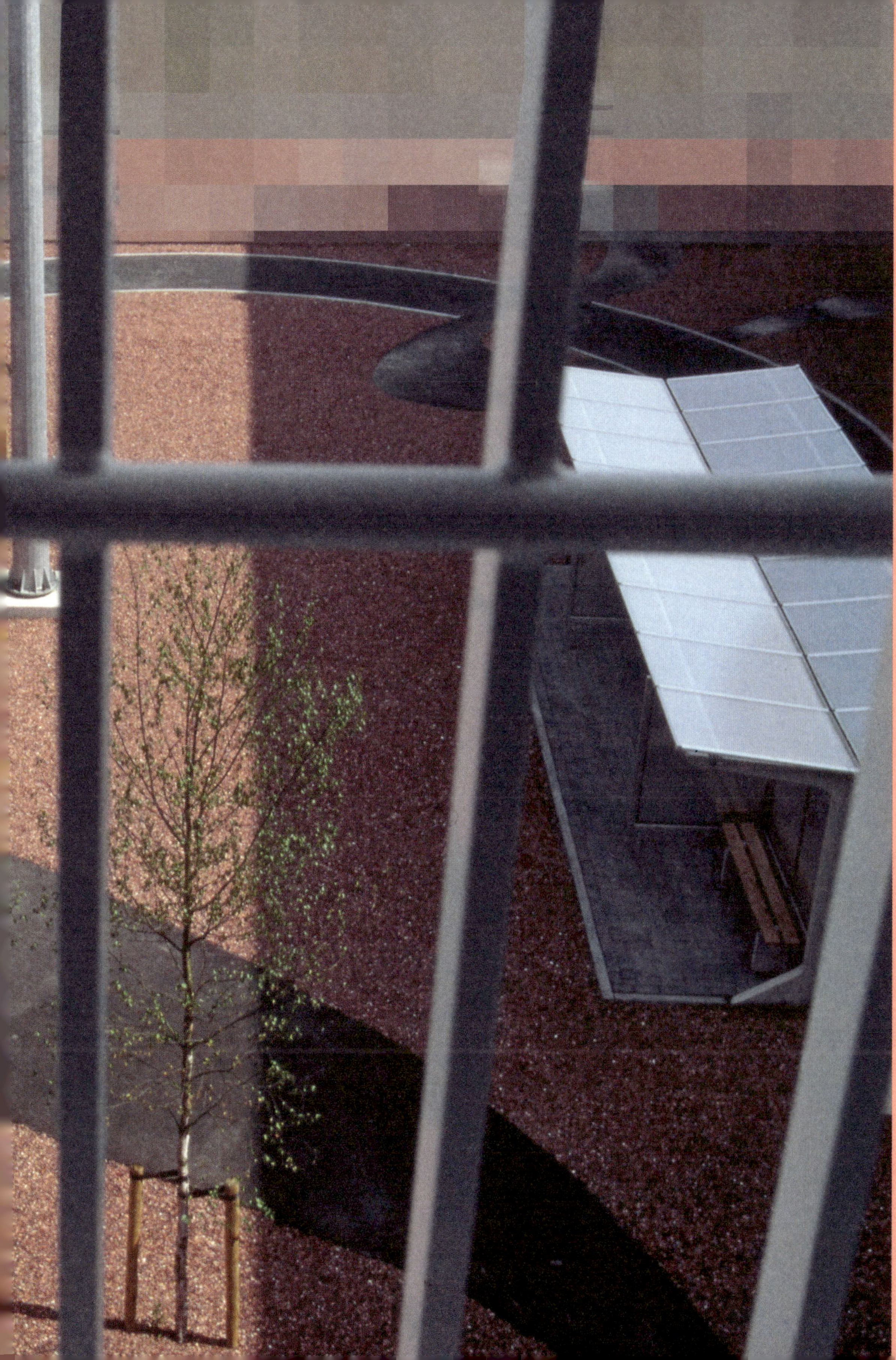

Garden 5
The right arm of the path leads to the women's 'family apartment': once every few months, husband and small children are allowed to stay over (2005).

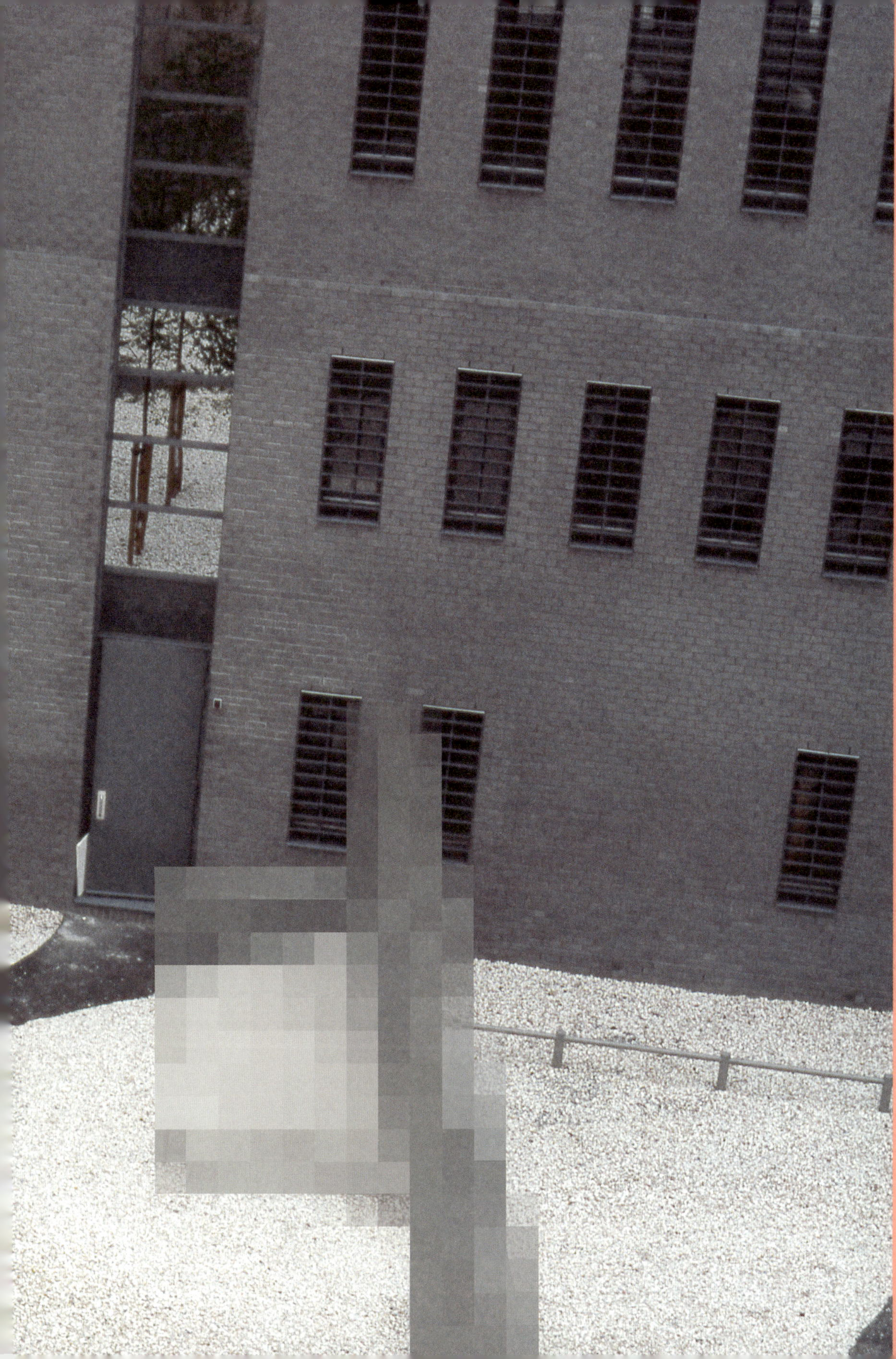

Garden 6
(1999)

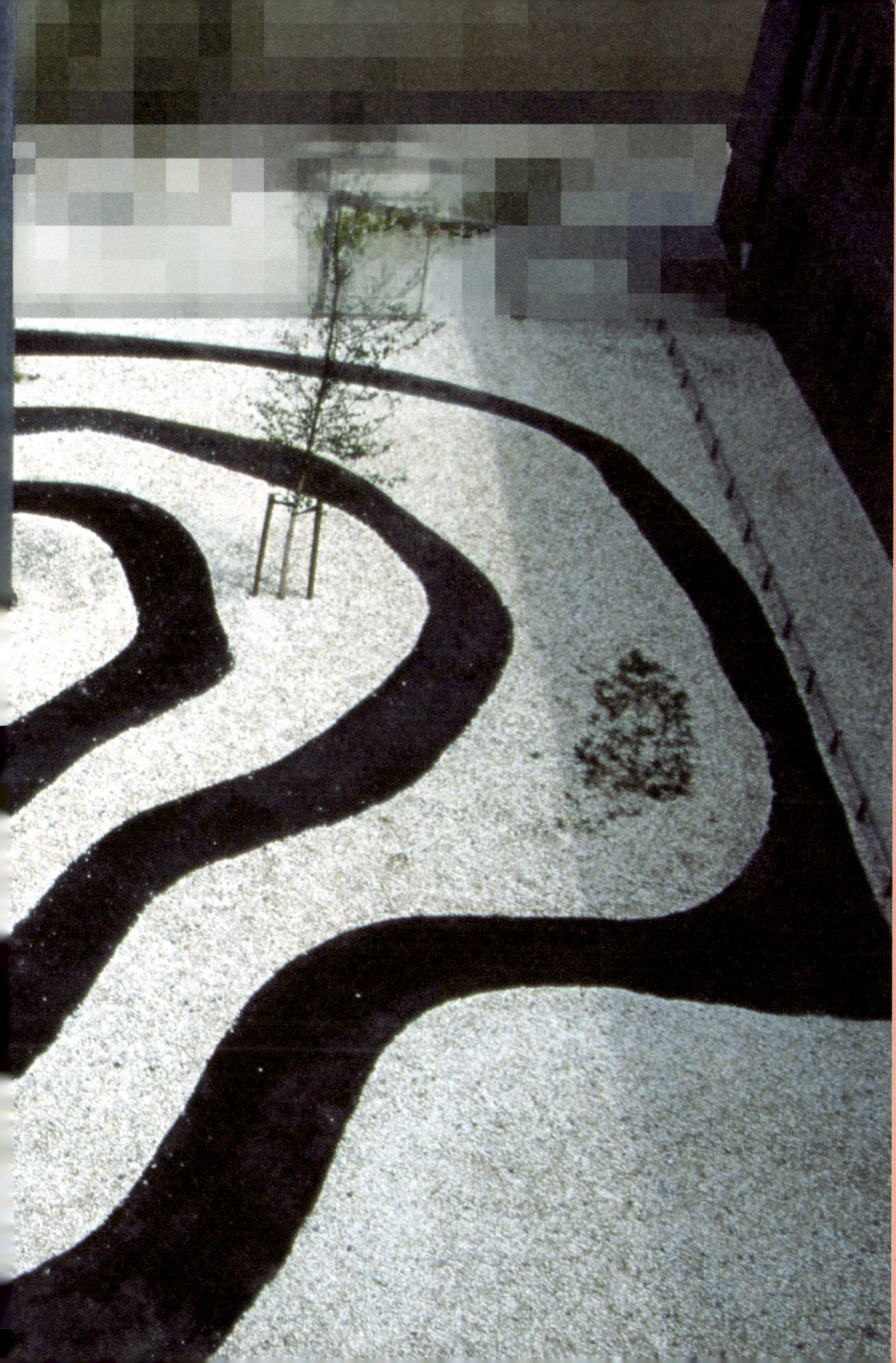

Garden 6
White shell carpet, birch trees, patches of *Alchemilla mollis* and seasonal bulbs. We were told in 1997–1999 that all trees had to be trimmed so that inmates could not hang themselves or use branches as weapons. Now that the prison is solely for men, the trees are far from trimmed and their full crowns take away the view from the video cameras. What does this mean? (2005)

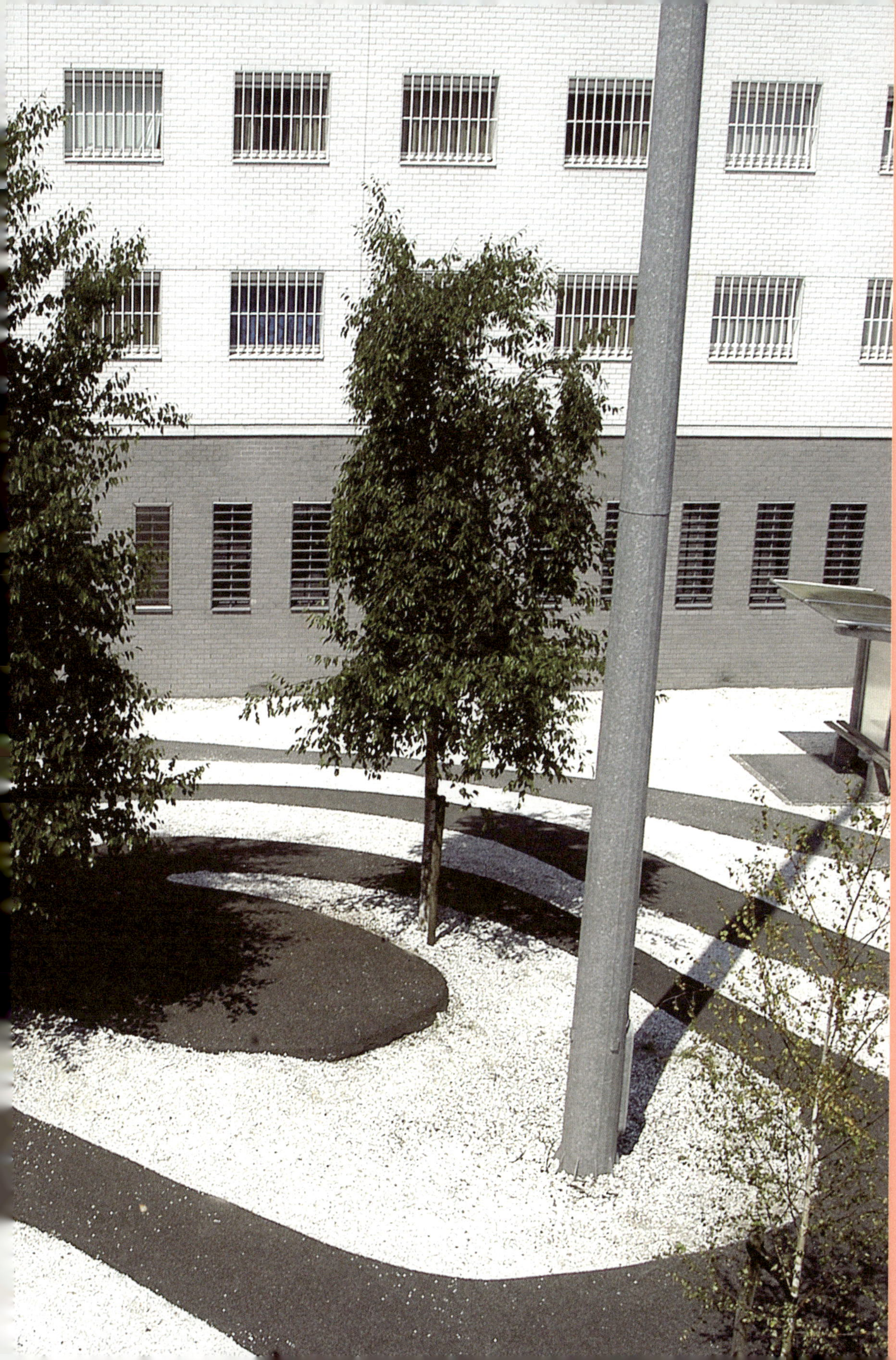

A Choreography of Reciprocities
Dirk van den Heuvel

Exploring

One of the most compelling representations of the heroic period of modern architecture is a moving image. As a moving image it is still a rarity among the canonical pictures of the architectural discourse. This image is a film sequence by Pierre Chenal, part of the 1932 documentary he made for Le Corbusier, 'Architecture d'Aujourd'hui'. It depicts the special qualities of the new architecture of Le Corbusier's white villas, which apparently could be shown only by way of moving images, and not by the more conventional static architectural media of drawing or model, or that other then recent medium of photography.

The sequence I'm referring to is that of the *promenade architecturale*, one of the decisive and constituent parts of the Villa Savoye at Poissy (1928-1930). The key element of the film sequence is the appearance of a human figure, a woman walking along the ramp up to the roof; first the camera catches her from above, then filming from inside the living room we see her from behind, walking outside. Finally, we see her from below, ascending the ramp and reaching the upper roof terrace where she sits down to enjoy the garden and views of the surrounding environment, while being shielded by curved, white screens.

These screens are not just shields, they are a double-acting device. First, the screens frame the views and thus direct the inhabitant's gaze; they create the difference between an 'inside' and an 'outside'; and yet, at the same time they 'frame' the inhabitant/viewer, too, not unlike a film camera does.

In many ways Chenal's film sequence epitomized the changes that came with the invention of modern architecture. As such it marked a new beginning in the sense of a new understanding of architecture and its potentials. It demonstrated how movement and interaction between bodies and their environment define and generate space, as well as the experience of space. By incorporating movement, another time dimension was introduced, too. Architectural space was now to be understood as a field, or territory, open to events accumulating into narratives, ever shifting and unfolding.

The filmic representation of the architecture and its surrounding landscape further emphasized the inherently ambiguous relations between inside and outside, including that of nature and domestic space. By doing so, it also called for a reinvestigation of the nature of boundaries and thresholds.

It is at this juncture that the work of Petra Blaisse and her office Inside Outside can be situated – it is an unrelenting exploration of these reciprocities between movement, space and boundaries, and it seeks the enhancement of the construction and experience of multiplicitous and simultaneous narratives.

Let's try and follow the route that Chenal and Le Corbusier offered us – which trajectories does Petra Blaisse draw? And what boundaries? What, and who, is being framed?

Lines of Movement

Looking at Blaisse's 'outside' projects – the parks and gardens – the *promenade architecturale* seems more than the logical starting point to unravel the intentions and actual projects. Indeed, it is a structuring device generating the design. It is already present in one of Blaisse's first commissions for a park, the Museumpark in Rotterdam (1992-1994) that she did together with Yves Brunier. Two paths form the backbone of the new urban space; one straight, linking two museums as directly as possible, and one meandering, leading the stroller along the more romantic and idyllic spots. The two paths connect various events, in the first place the four 'rooms' of the park – each with its own atmosphere. But the paths themselves become an event, too; the meandering one purely by its pointless winding, and the straight one by becoming a bridge over an artificial stream of pebbles and blue glazed stones, about halfway along the route.

A winding path connecting various outdoor 'rooms' was also chosen as the leading idea for the design of the outdoor spaces of the Nieuwegein State Detention Centre (1999). The project takes on a much more metaphoric meaning, though, since the path necessarily conflicts with the walls and fences of the prison. In her explanation, Blaisse refers to the concept of the labyrinth. Seen from above, it looks like a clear geometric structure, while from below, in the labyrinth itself, one loses the overall view. But something else happens as one moves through the space; a succession of encounters arises, concatenations of anecdotes and events. The space here becomes comprehensible in a narrative development. Each individual movement generates a story of its own, movements come together, cross, clash, agree, continue together, or not.

This idea of a multiplicity of movements is further elaborated in the project for a park in Milan – the 'Biblioteca degli Alberi' (2003). The design is based on the idea of regenerating the derelict urban space by introducing a web of new pathways crossing the available site. This site is nothing more than a leftover space in the middle of the city, burdened by heavy traffic and underground infrastructure. Blaisse and her team introduced paths that cross this emptiness and that connect the existing and planned urban programmes bordering it. Together the paths make up a new informal pattern of lines, crossings and fields, thus providing a new, polycentric structure to situate the various recreational activities and educational and cultural programmes, all over the site.

Here too, the paths are designed as narratives, as a set of scenarios, so to speak, that unfold while moving through the park. This is done by cleverly manipulating the already uneven terrain – the paths climb and fall; together with the slopes and a wide variety of planting and trees they create views or enclosed spaces. The resulting patchwork contains botanical gardens and orchards, squares and waters, as well as several buildings to house, among others, a fashion school, exhibition spaces and a museum, and sports facilities.

These buildings are positioned in such a way that they are embedded in the web of paths; at times paths continue into buildings, thus turning them into gates or 'connectors'. It is at such points that the differences between inside and outside are blurred, and boundaries are rendered ambiguous.

Shifting Boundaries
As mentioned before, besides movement, the notion of the boundary is essential to grasp the work of Blaisse. In Blaisse's projects, boundaries are not merely dividing devices; they articulate the reciprocities at play – such as that of inside and outside, and the fact that the one can never do without the other. Hence – as if to underpin this notion of reciprocity – most of the time these boundaries themselves are of a dynamic, shifting and changing nature. They act as screens or filters, both creating differences and allowing continuities – qualities that are made dependent of the position and movement of the visitor or inhabitant, but also of the time of day, light, sound, season or ritual.

As in the cases of the park designs, we find in the interior spaces, too, a montage of experiences, a sequencing and staging of multiple and parallel events and narratives. The basic instrument to achieve this is, actually, quite simple. As in the park designs it is about directing lines of movement and sight, and about recombining programmatic diversity. But more than in the outdoor spaces, the dressing and layering of space is important in the inside spaces. To dismiss dressing as nothing more than applying decoration is not just missing the point; it is proof of a profound ignorance of the workings of architecture and how architecture comes to be. Dressing, and especially textile, belongs to the first architectural devices used to create enclosures and boundaries.

Gottfried Semper even went as far as to call textile one of the primal sources of architecture; next to the cave and the hut, the tent belongs to the primal origins of the architectural discipline. Here, structure and construction are intrinsically connected to the provisional and transitory.

The dynamics and ambiguities of a textile architecture are at the core of Blaisse's interior work. Without any doubt, her most outstanding products are curtains. Over the years, Blaisse has designed and produced spectacular drapes for domestic spaces, shops, exhibitions, universities as well as theatres, museums and congress halls. The latter are among the most monumental, due to their sheer size.

The way these curtains are conceived, how they are positioned, and how they work demonstrates their architectural character. The intended effects relate to volume, scale and sculptural quality and division of space and time. They result from the clever manipulation and processing of the material, through folding, pleating, patterning, smart seams and hems, creating effects of depth, thickness (or lightness), translucency and transparency, reflections and movement.

In all its simplicity, Blaisse's yellow silk curtain for the Villa dall'Ava designed by OMA/Rem Koolhaas, summarizes the intentions of her work. Within the rather Corbusian free space of the ground floor of the villa, the curtain encircles the *salle de séjour* to construct its own interior within the larger space – 'to create room in the room', as Koolhaas noted. Together with the sliding glass doors – partly matte, partly clear glass – the curtain makes up the façade, forming a boundary between inside and outside that is no longer simply defined, but is transient, in motion, unstable and light by nature.

Frans Parthesius perfectly caught this transient characteristic in his videos of Blaisse's curtains. Lightly, yet languidly we see the golden cloth drag across the granito floor, then sway across the grass – nothing less than the transformation of a simple, everyday thing into poetic movement.

This idea of a room in a room is elaborated in more designs. Similar strategies are followed, for instance, in the curtains for the Villa Floirac in Bordeaux (1996-1998) and the Glass Pavilion, Toledo (2003). However, the most radical realization hitherto is the drape in the auditorium of the Rotterdam Kunsthal. As a theatre curtain it uses the techniques of the theatre, yet undermines its conventions at the same time.

The Kunsthal curtain does not hang in the traditional position between audience and stage, but is draped round one of the concrete columns in the hall, and when unrolled, it slides into the hall encircling the audience. Thus, it creates an ambiguous effect: enveloping the audience it is not just the 'stage' that is framed as the focus of attention, but also the hall full of people. The space of the auditorium becomes a situation in which interaction between the users constantly causes the redirecting of looks. The curtain itself participates in this exchange: it is active in contributing the partition and determining positions and persepectives, but through its special position it is just as much an object of being looked at. The drape itself becomes an event of its own, undermining architectural conventions and boundaries, in order to explore the limits between inside and outside anew.

Energizing Architecture
Is it proper to measure Blaisse's work against the heroic period of modern architecture? Chenal's film sequence of the Villa Savoye suggests many connections; some real, others on a more metaphoric level, most notably, of course, the new ambiguity between inside and outside.

Yet any comparison to, or inclusion in the modern tradition is complicated by the fact that this tradition is far from homogeneous. By now, it is well-known that it entails various contradictory strands – at all levels of ideology, theory and practice. Looking at Blaisse's work it is evident that if one wants to speak of it in terms of the modern tradition, one has to think of it as a certain sensibility, not a particular style, or a historical period. This sensibility is not limited to that of the canonical period, as represented by the positions of Le Corbusier or Adolf Loos. For instance, use of colour, choice of patterns and scaling techniques also point to other sensibilities at work, such as those of the surrealists and Pop Art.

At the core of this sensibility is the wish to energize architecture, to bring about an intensification of the experience of space, and to charge it with expectancy. It is in this sense that Blaisse thinks of the modern project as unfinished and still unfolding, offering fruitful possibilities to be further explored. These possibilities entail two different aspects – one is an aspect of language, or vocabulary, the other is an aspect of organization.

To begin with the latter, Blaisse's interest in models of organization comparable to those of the modern tradition – such as the *promenade architecturale* – is not so much an ideological one. Unlike other positions within modernism, Blaisse's interest lies with what she calls the 'working process' – bringing together the requirements from the particular assignment and means available. So, instead of a method for unifying and totalizing, Blaisse regards these models as a natural possibility to 'tie together heterogeneous elements', as she put it when describing her intentions for the Milan park project. In this approach singular qualities are left intact and further intensified, since this would enhance the multiplicity of events that brings about the experience of both urban and domestic space.

With regard to the vocabulary of modern architecture, it becomes clear that Blaisse regards its possibilities as highly underused, still not fully investigated and developed, and that these possibilities encompass a richness still to be discovered and enjoyed. Next to the pleasures of free movement, self-consciously undergoing space as a generous, bodily experience gathered from all senses, these also include the celebration of the inherent qualities of materials, the delight in combining heaviness with light touch, hard with soft, and cold with hot. Blaisse's interest also comes close to what Alison and Peter Smithson called 'an architecture of the enjoyment of luxury materials, of the well-made, of the high-finish', as well as a 'passion for perfection in detail'.

When trying to fully grasp the concept of space that is at the heart of Blaisse's work, one comes across a final unresolved question of the modern tradition: is space abstract or real?

To Blaisse space, events and the way they build up into narratives seem to be intrinsically intertwined. Space is not something abstract, a neutral stratum in which events come to life – something modernism has been reproached for. In Blaisse's projects space exists *in* and *as* events – in and as the individual and collective interactions between users, inhabitants and their environment. Here, the notion of reciprocity is crucial again, since such interactions are the outcome of dynamic reciprocities at play.

This understanding of space (and hence architecture) as a constellation of reciprocities can be traced throughout the history of modern architecture and its associated avant-gardes. It finds allies in Cubism, Matisse or De Stijl. It can also be found in the efforts by the Smithsons and Aldo van Eyck who aimed at such continuous regenerating of the modern tradition; and in current times we can trace it in the work of OMA/Rem Koolhaas and Bernard Tschumi.

As a conclusion – what becomes clear then in the work of Blaisse is a redefining of architecture as a choreography of reciprocities – a dynamic constellation generating a multiplicity of experiences, continuously recharging and reenergizing the tissue of events that make up the spaces we use and in which we live. And as such the architecture of Blaisse invites participation.

Amsterdam, 2006

Distant Recipe

Garden, planting scheme and curtains
Seoul National University Museum, Seoul, Korea, 2005

The Korean way of supporting newly planted trees: surgical beauty.

Gardens

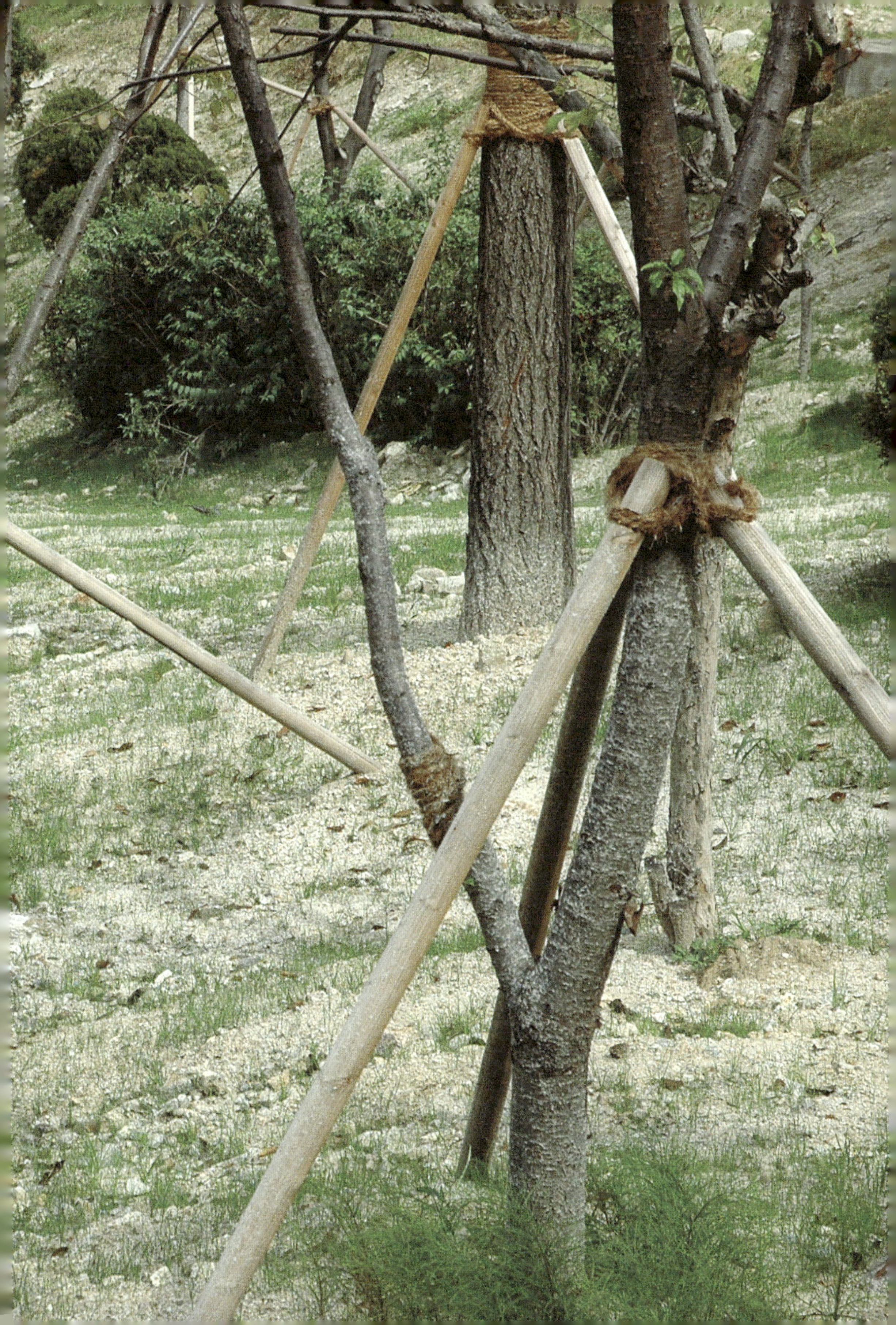

...sketches constructed: the ideas are barely sent and just two months later you can savour the result!

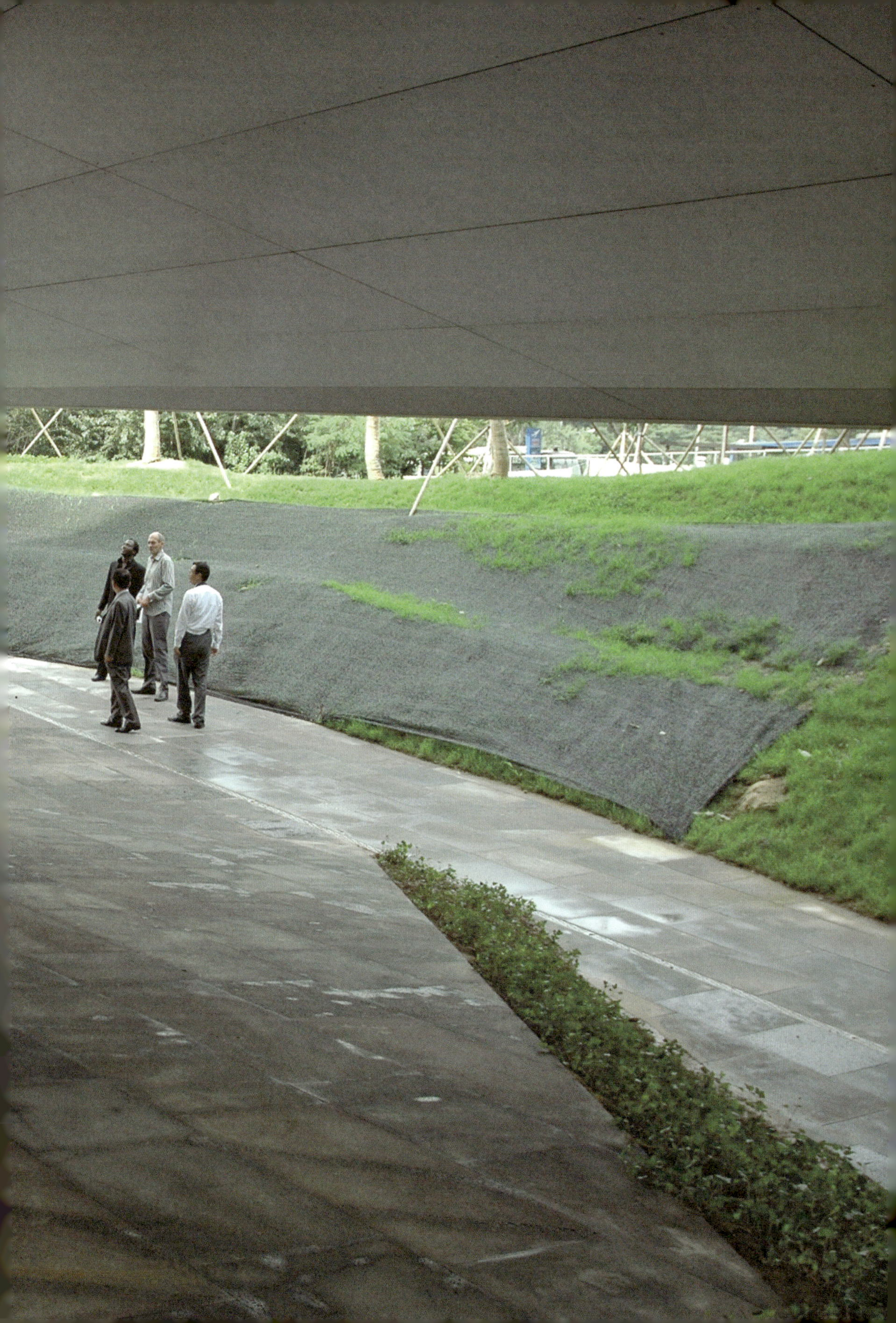

Arteries

Semi-public gardens
Park Apartments Chassée Terrein,
Breda, the Netherlands, 2000–2001

Xaveer de Geyter... connective tissue
between freestanding towers.

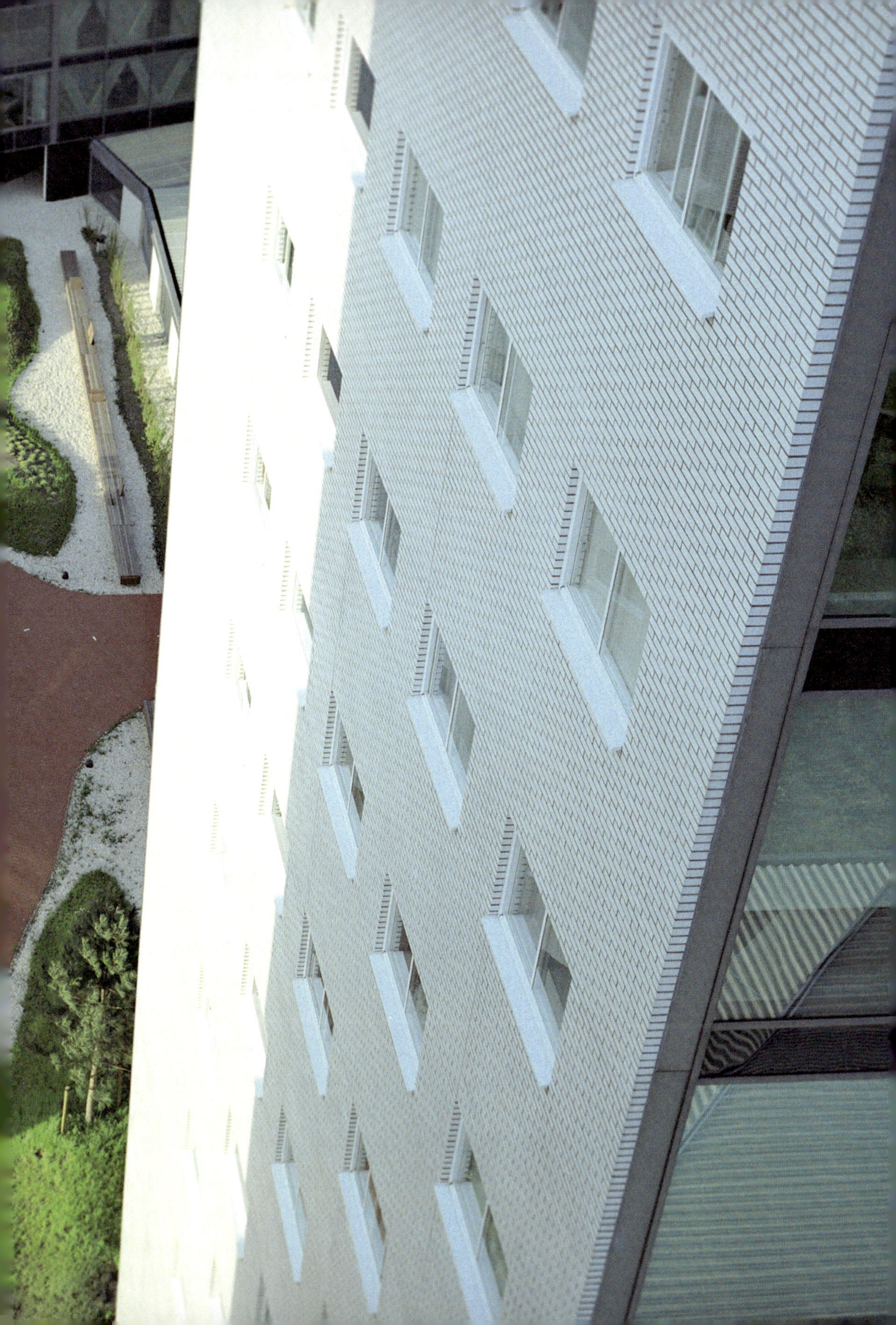

Low-placed beamers light plantings and path. In the middle of the path, bricks with reflective white surfaces lead the way …

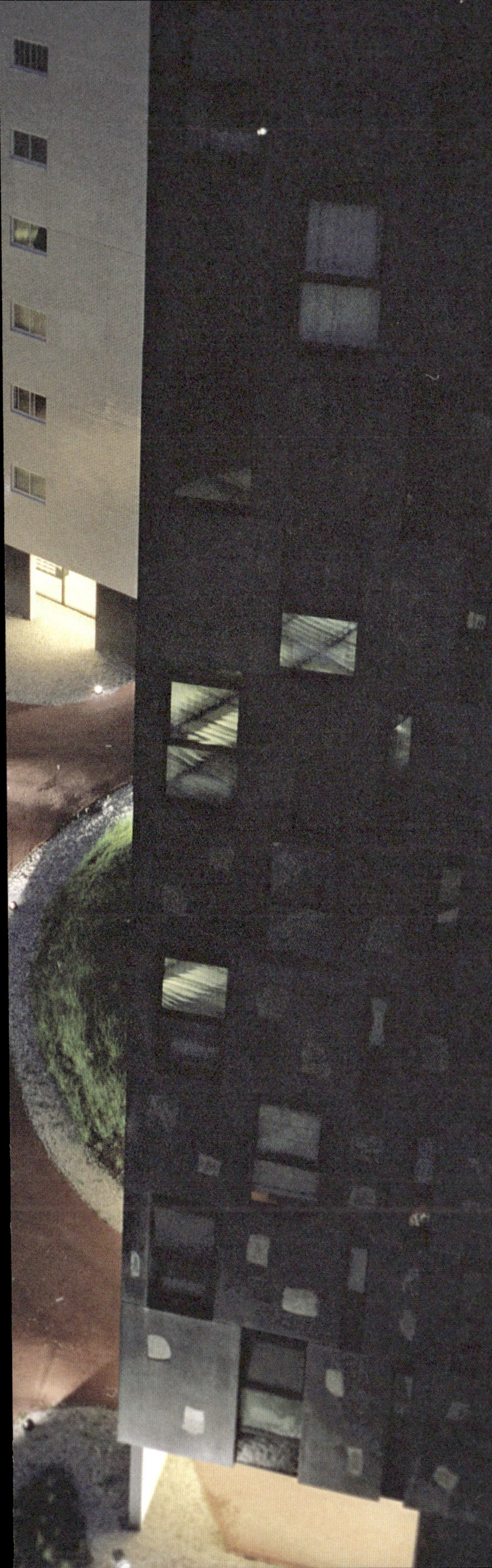

Municipal Restoration: Previous
Museumpark
Rotterdam, the Netherlands, 1992–2005

An apple orchard (85 trees composed of six ancient Dutch apple species) on white shells is reflected in a distorting mirror wall.

Glass rocks in a river of stones light up the forest: ode to the old stream that was relocated to the edge of the park.

Municipal Restoration: Current

Museumpark
Rotterdam, the Netherlands, 2005–2007

Current situation: a parking lot has been built below ground. The entire park needs revision due to maintenance and use issues among the city and adjacent museums (who now share the costs and therefore have a say in the park's organization and programme).

Oil Pressure

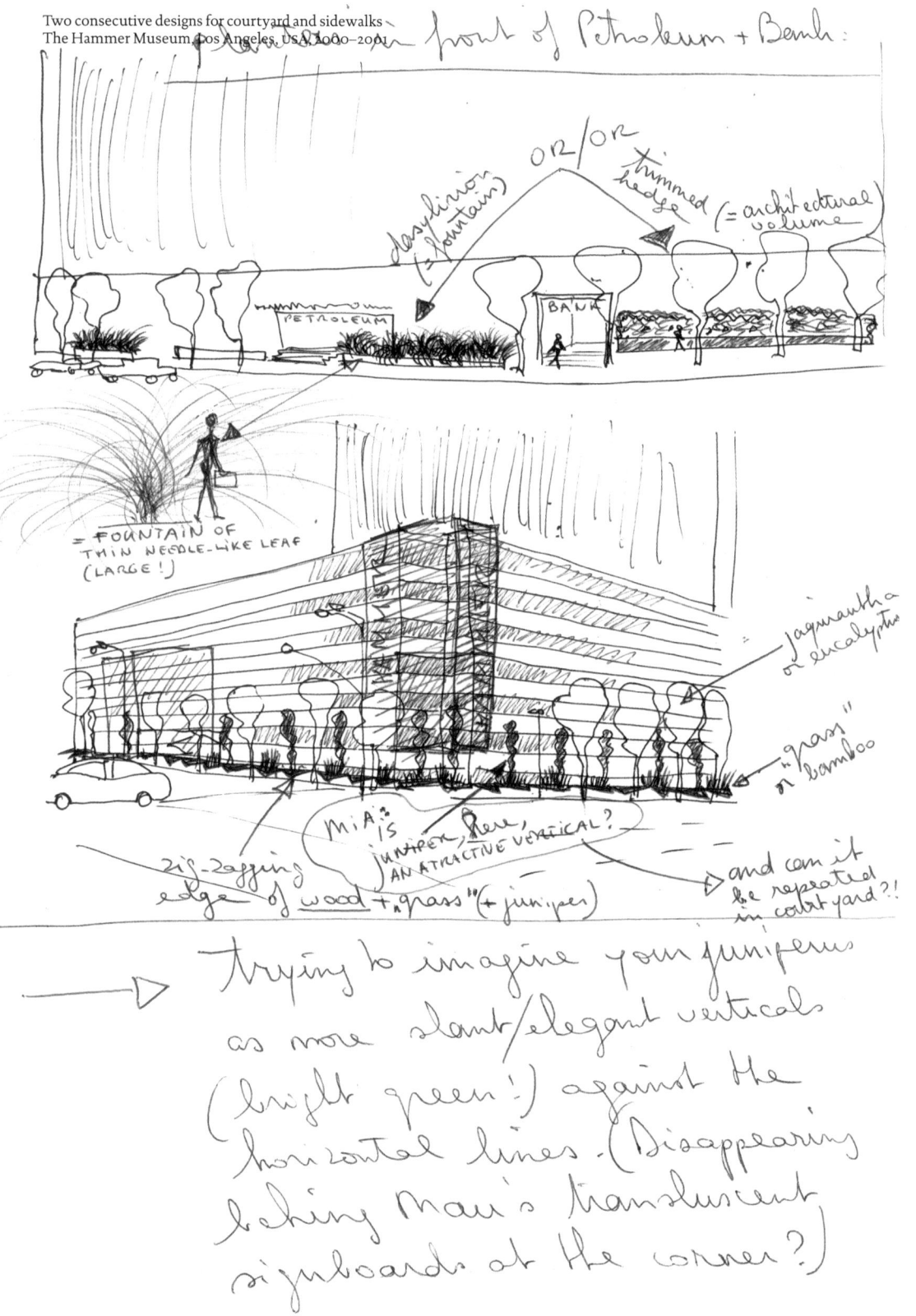

Two consecutive designs for courtyard and sidewalks
The Hammer Museum, Los Angeles, USA, 2000–2001

[Sketch annotations:]

in front of Petroleum + Bank:

desylirion (fountain) OR/OR trimmed hedge (= architectural volume)

PETROLEUM · BANK

= FOUNTAIN OF THIN NEEDLE-LIKE LEAF (LARGE!)

jaguarantha or eucalyptus

"grass" or bamboo

MIA: IS JUNIPER, here, AN ATTRACTIVE VERTICAL?

zig-zagging edge of wood + "grass" (+ juniper)

and can it be repeated in courtyard?!

→ trying to imagine your junipers as more slant/elegant verticals (bright green!) against the horizontal lines. (Disappearing behind Mau's translucent signboards at the corner?)

HAMMER:
edges of
building

August 2, 2001

between 4" - 12"

concrete with
black pigment

False Horizons

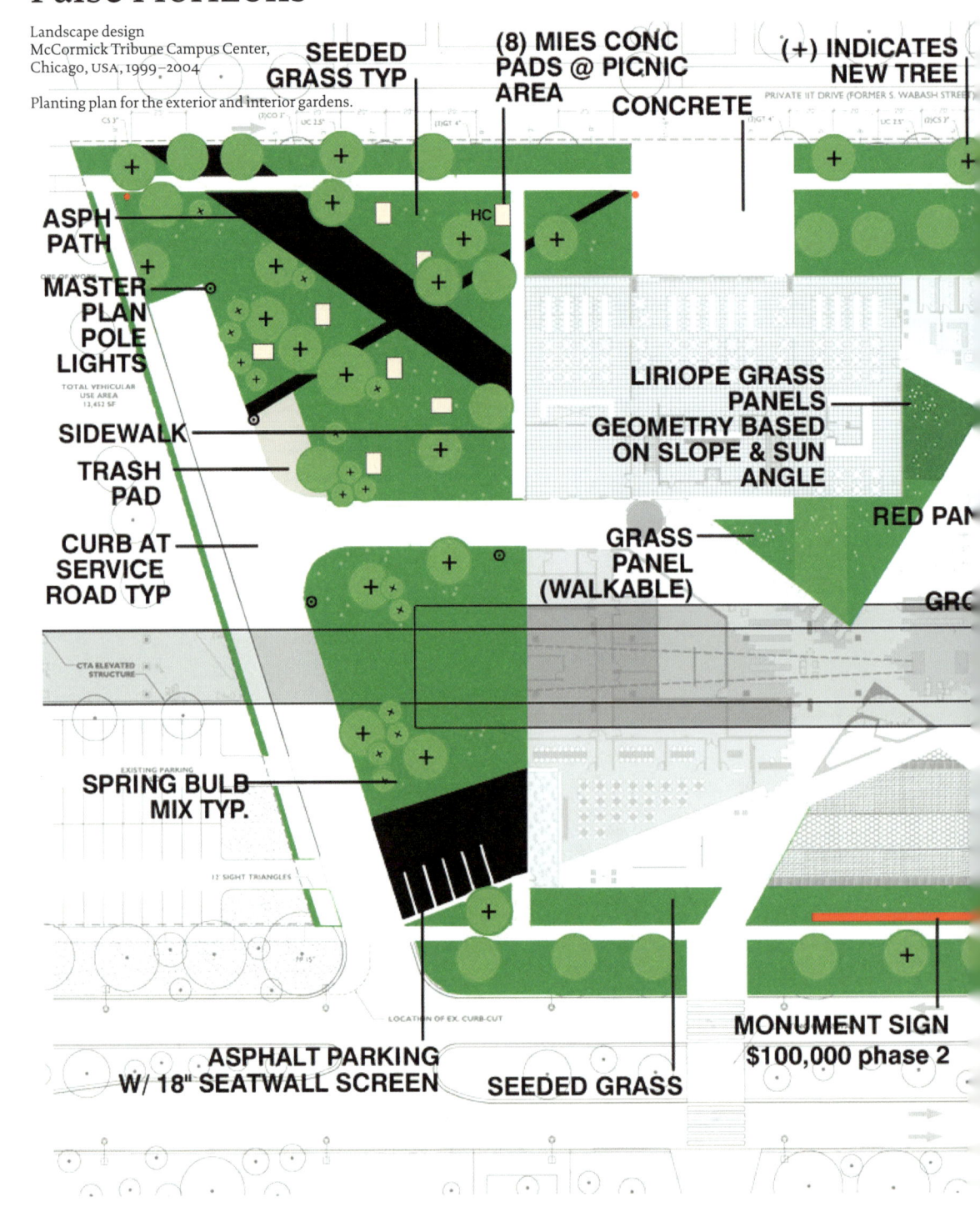

Landscape design
McCormick Tribune Campus Center,
Chicago, USA, 1999–2004

Planting plan for the exterior and interior gardens.

IIT LANDSCAPE ALL
06/30/03

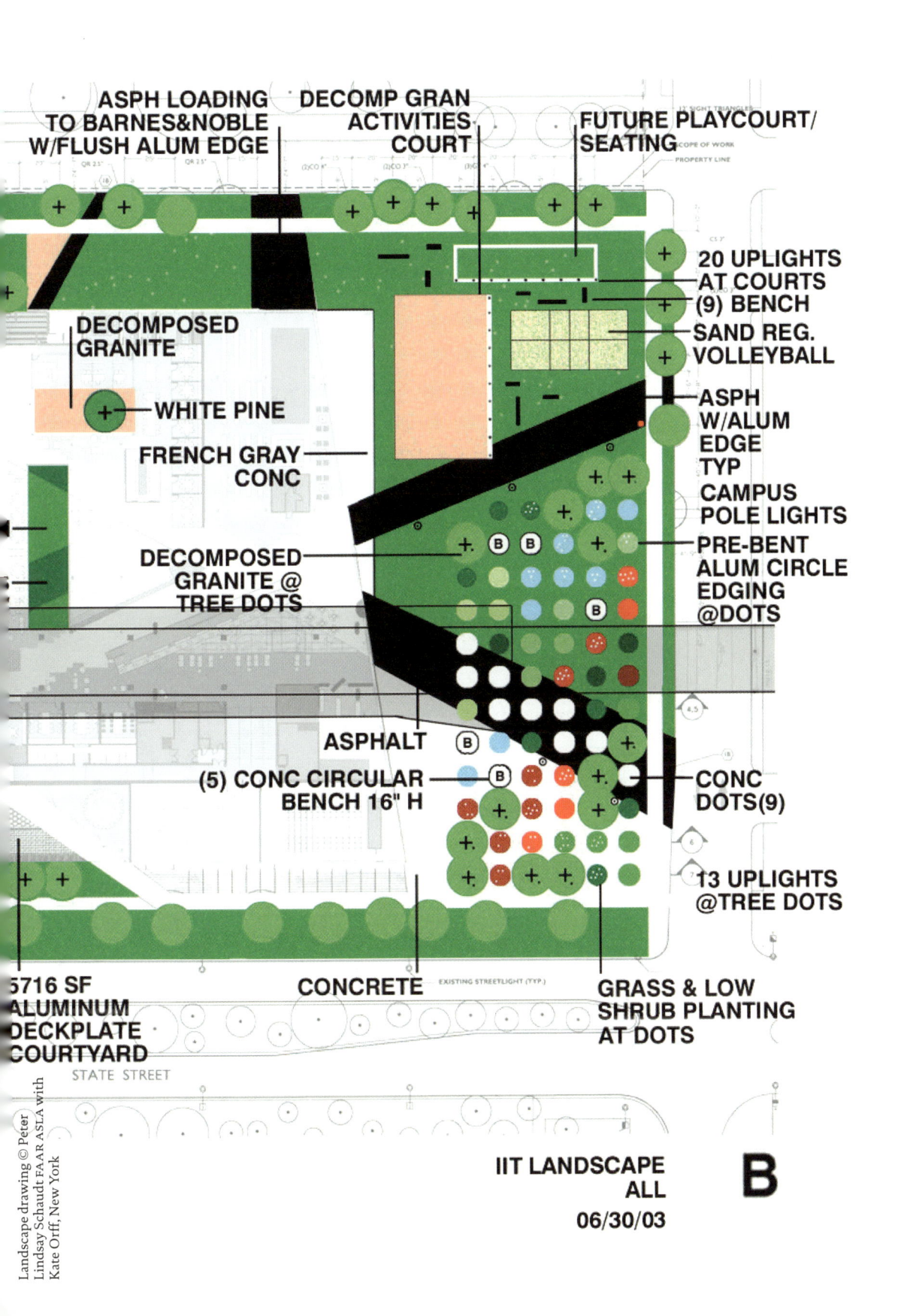

B

Landscape drawing © Peter Lindsay Schaudt FAAR ASLA with Kate Orff, New York

Former bowling bridge turned into a floating prairie.

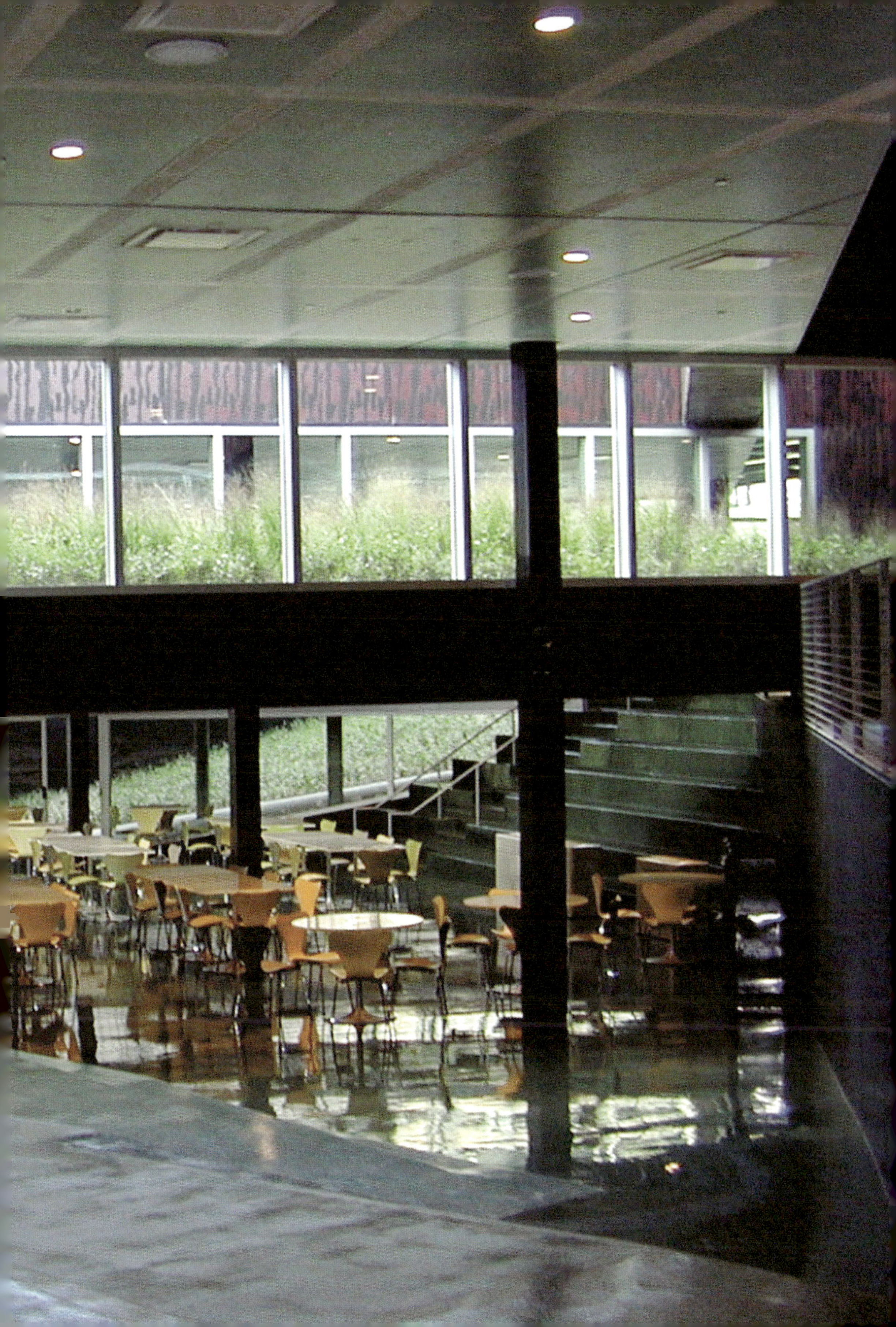

View, Movement, Protection

Garden manipulations
Villa Floirac, Bordeaux, France, 1996–1998

Looking from the courtyard through the guesthouse's patio towards the garden behind.

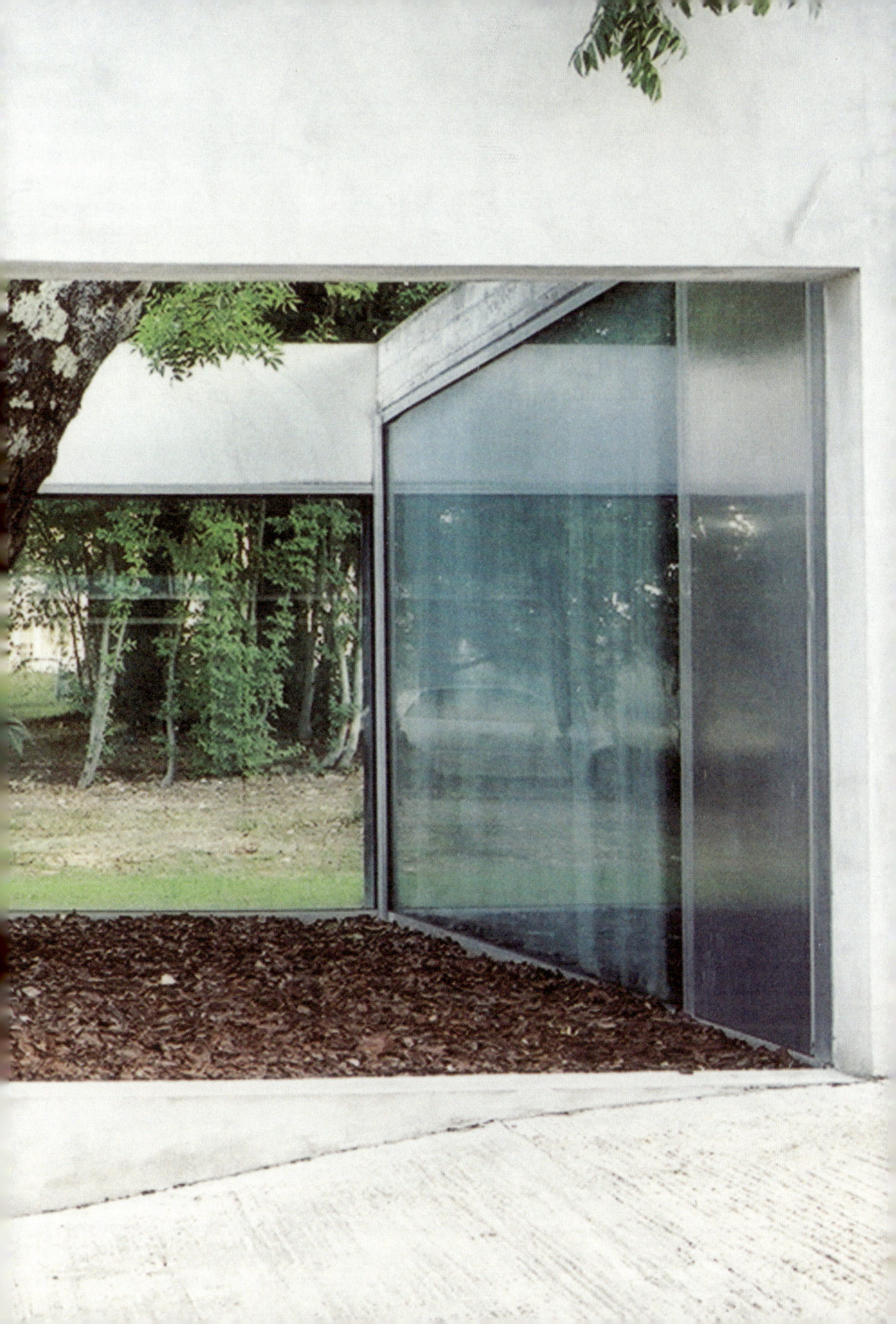

Looking from the garden through the guesthouse's patio towards the drop-off courtyard.

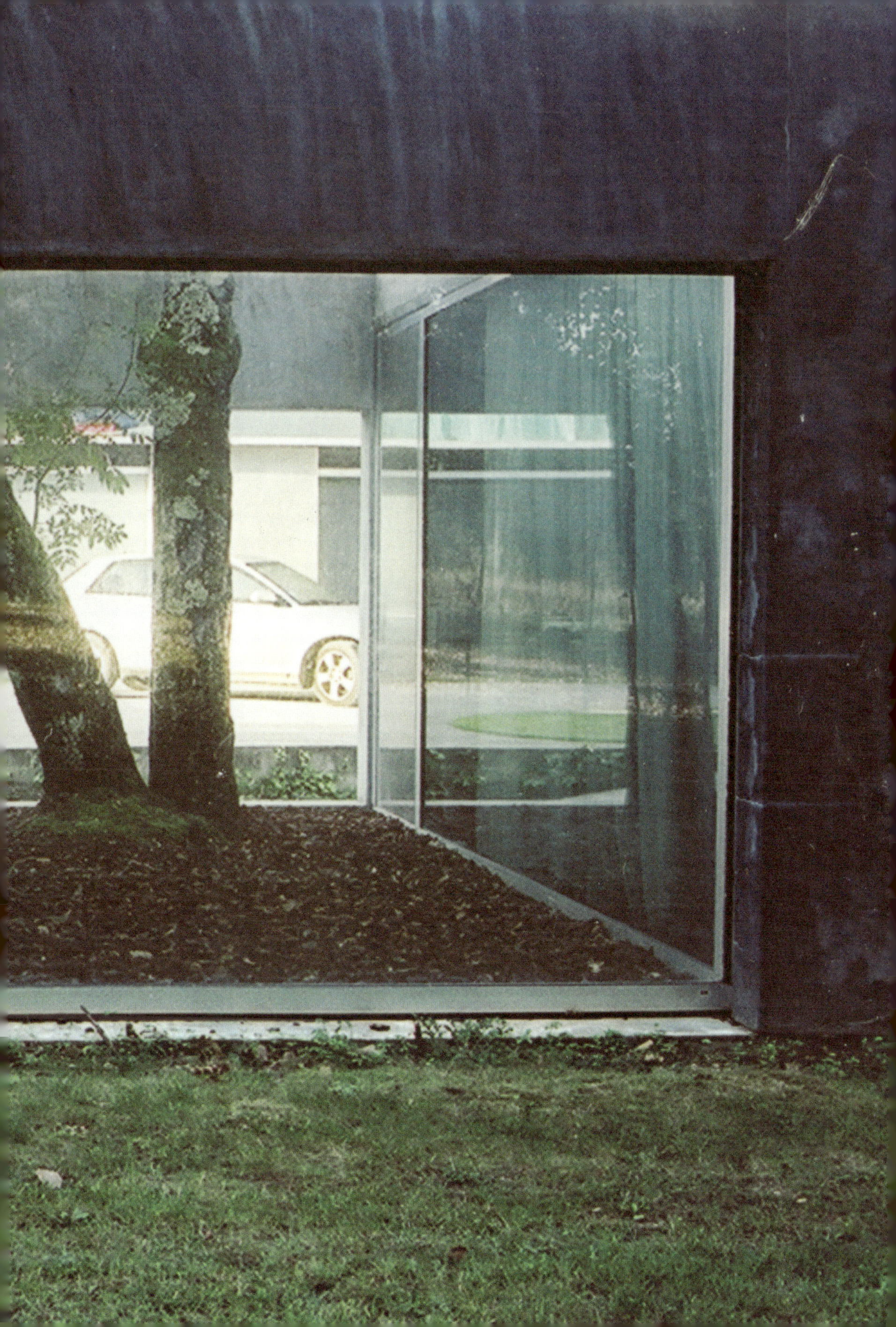

Cool Inlays

Island designs for an invited competition
Dubai, AE, 2005

Rainforest and water garden islands flank the highrise building designed by OMA. Both gardens function as grey water recycling tools for the building. They also offer recreation, culture and education to the public, generating income for maintenance.

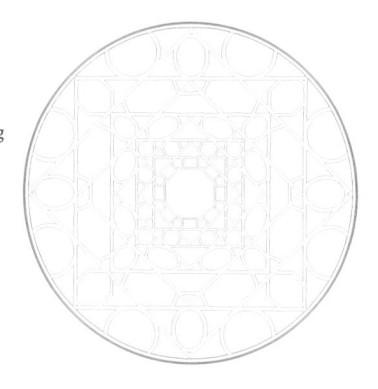

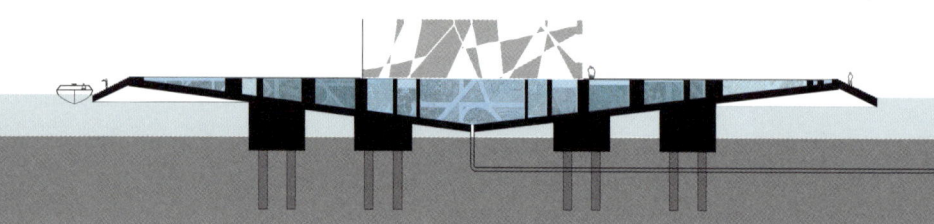

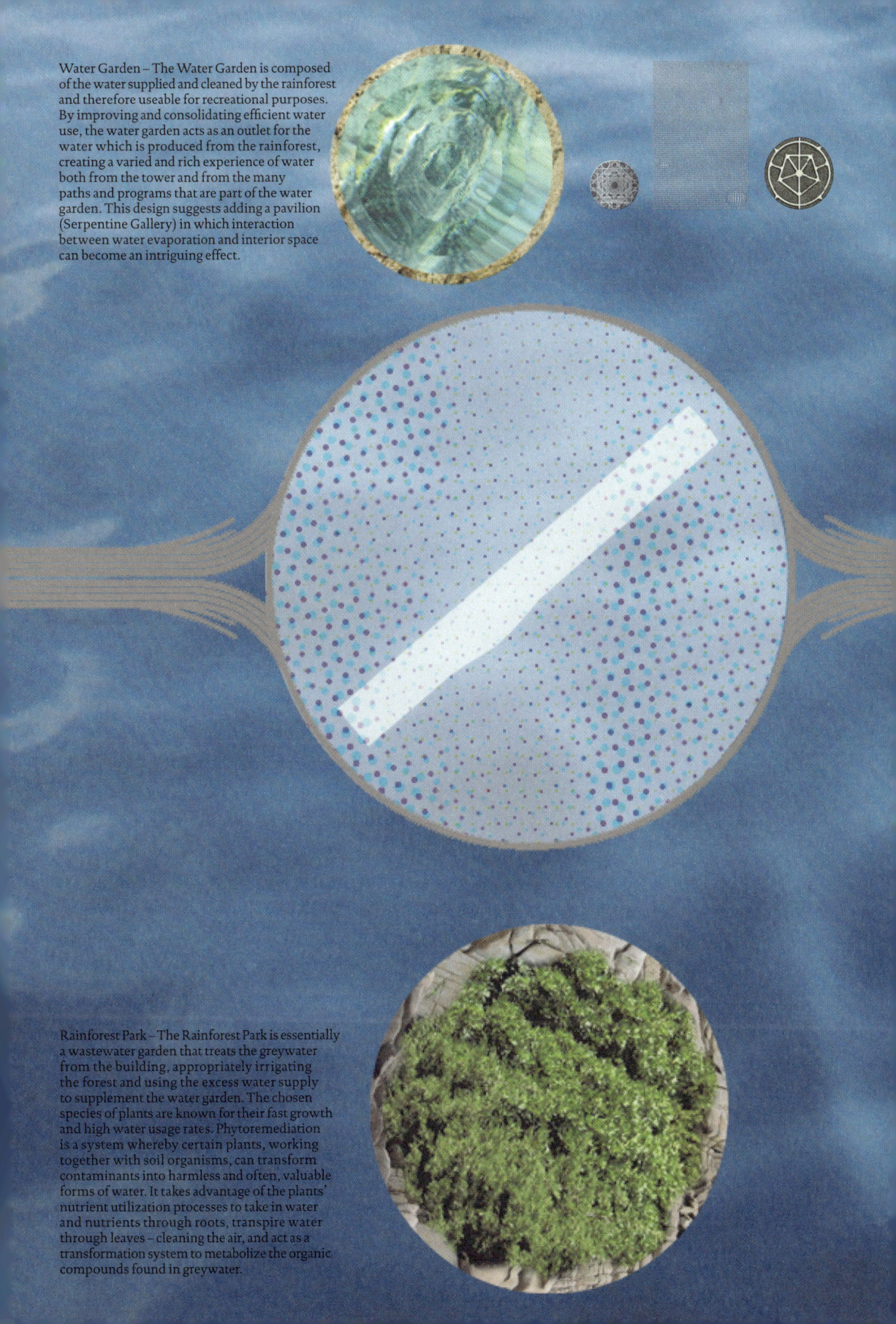

Water Garden – The Water Garden is composed of the water supplied and cleaned by the rainforest and therefore useable for recreational purposes. By improving and consolidating efficient water use, the water garden acts as an outlet for the water which is produced from the rainforest, creating a varied and rich experience of water both from the tower and from the many paths and programs that are part of the water garden. This design suggests adding a pavilion (Serpentine Gallery) in which interaction between water evaporation and interior space can become an intriguing effect.

Rainforest Park – The Rainforest Park is essentially a wastewater garden that treats the greywater from the building, appropriately irrigating the forest and using the excess water supply to supplement the water garden. The chosen species of plants are known for their fast growth and high water usage rates. Phytoremediation is a system whereby certain plants, working together with soil organisms, can transform contaminants into harmless and often, valuable forms of water. It takes advantage of the plants' nutrient utilization processes to take in water and nutrients through roots, transpire water through leaves – cleaning the air, and act as a transformation system to metabolize the organic compounds found in greywater.

Shade, Honey

Planting plan and terrace sun shades
Dutch House, Holten, the Netherlands, 1999

Sun-screen and butterfly planting envelop the floating glass house.
Adriaan Geuze/West 8 designed the garden, but after three years
Inside Outside was asked to redo and enrich the planting near the
house for colour effects, scent, animal life and flower arrangements.
We asked Adriaan first, of course.

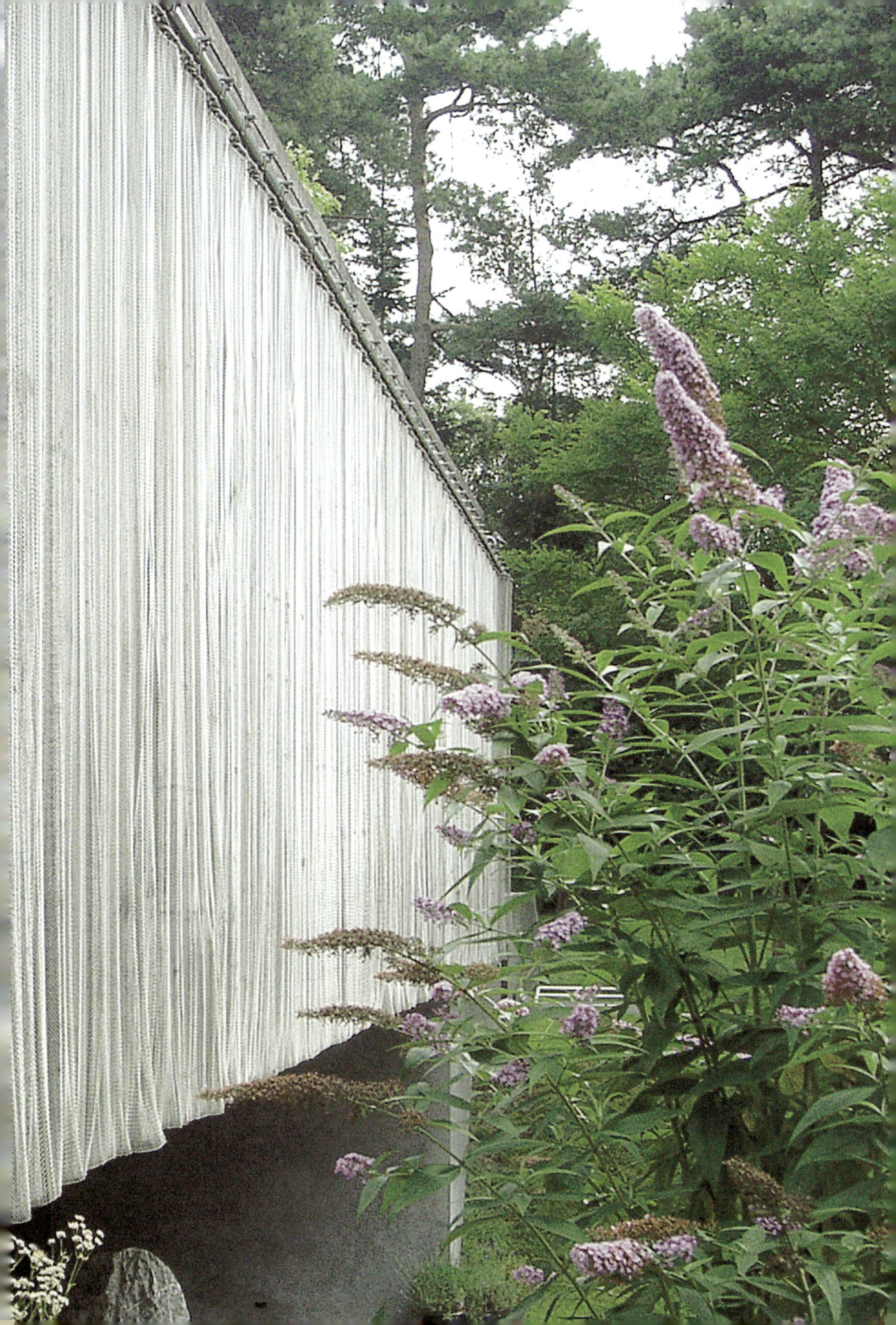

The lady of the house had asked me to attract butterflies,
but when bees and bumble bees started to visit the herbs
and flowers, I received a call: butterflies YES, bees NO!
I said we would make a sign for the flowerbeds: 'no bees allowed'.

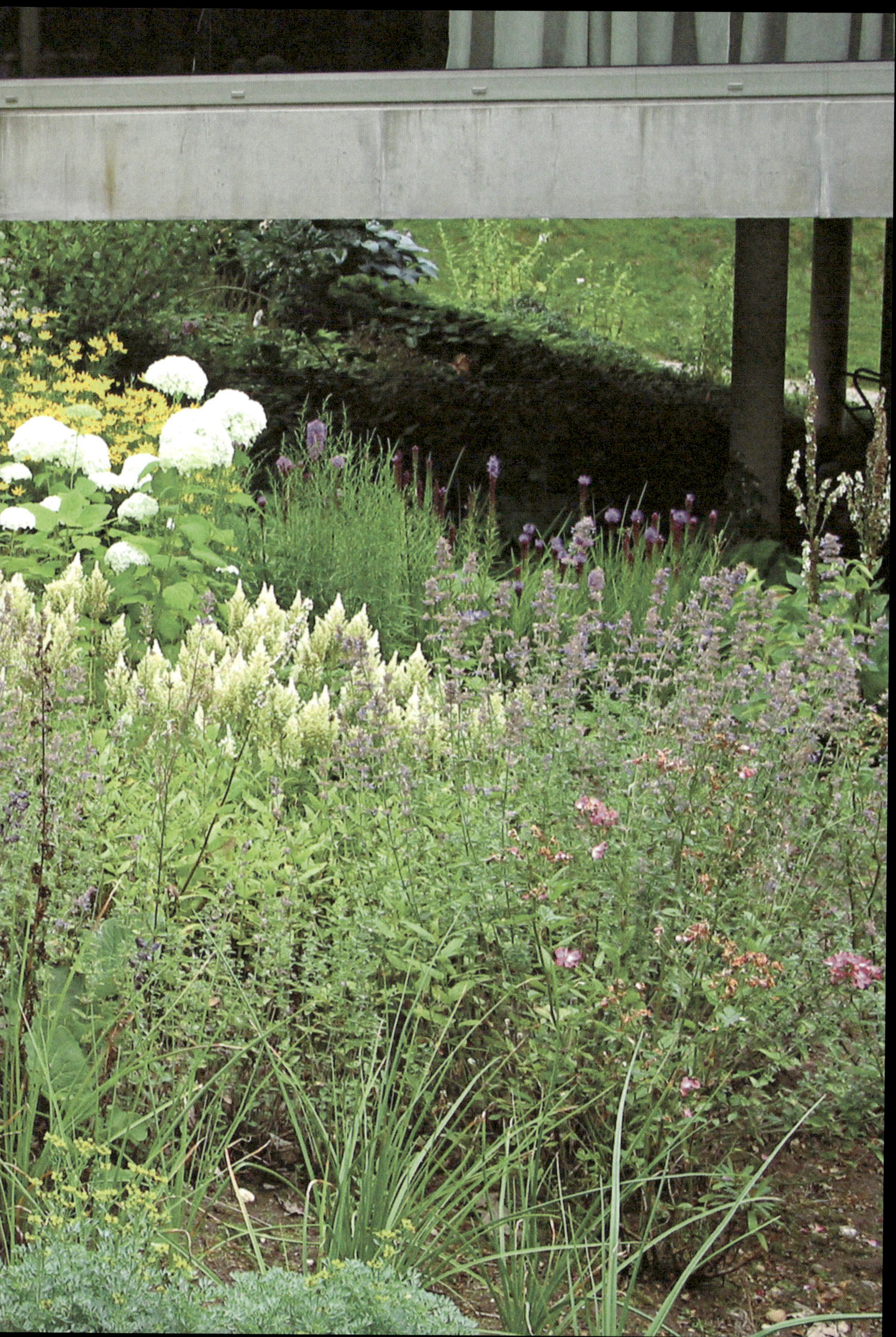

Riga Port City

Landscape masterplan
Riga, Latvia, 2006 – ongoing

Forest Cover
Latvian forests are its outstanding feature, and are spread evenly across the country in clusters. They differ from those of North America and the rest of Europe, primarily because of their relatively brush-free understory. The forest floor is none the less rich in plant and animal life and these easy to penetrate forests have provided wood, which has been a basic source of energy for Latvians and is now its most important export.

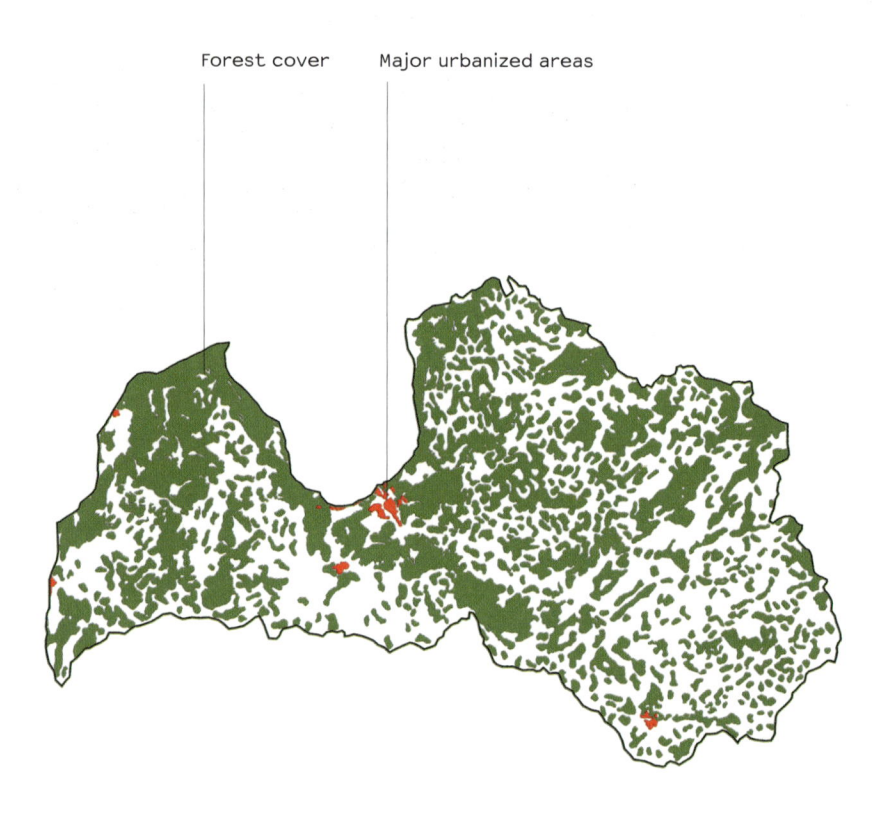

Forest cover   Major urbanized areas

Latvia has an extremely high forest cover compared to its urbanized area...

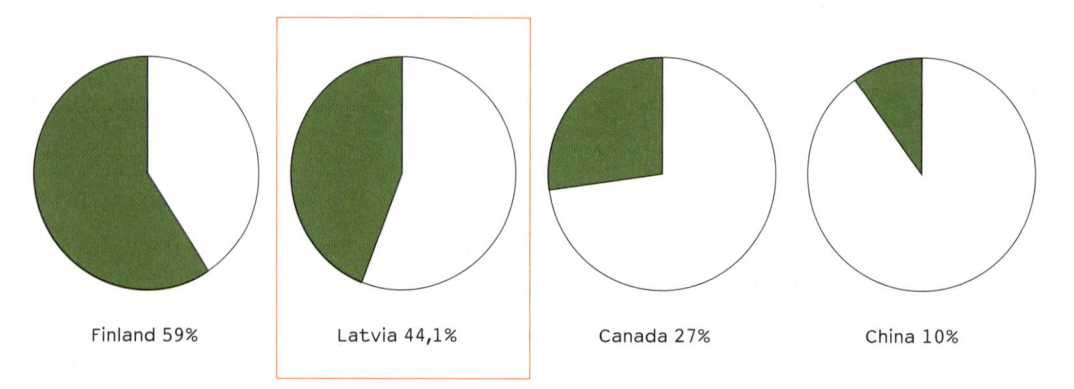

Finland 59%   Latvia 44,1%   Canada 27%   China 10%

...and compared to other parts of the world

...use country's original forest patch forms as landscape organization on new site, in reduced scale.

0m 100m 200m   500m   1000m

Museum Plaza – Cultural Park
East-West section

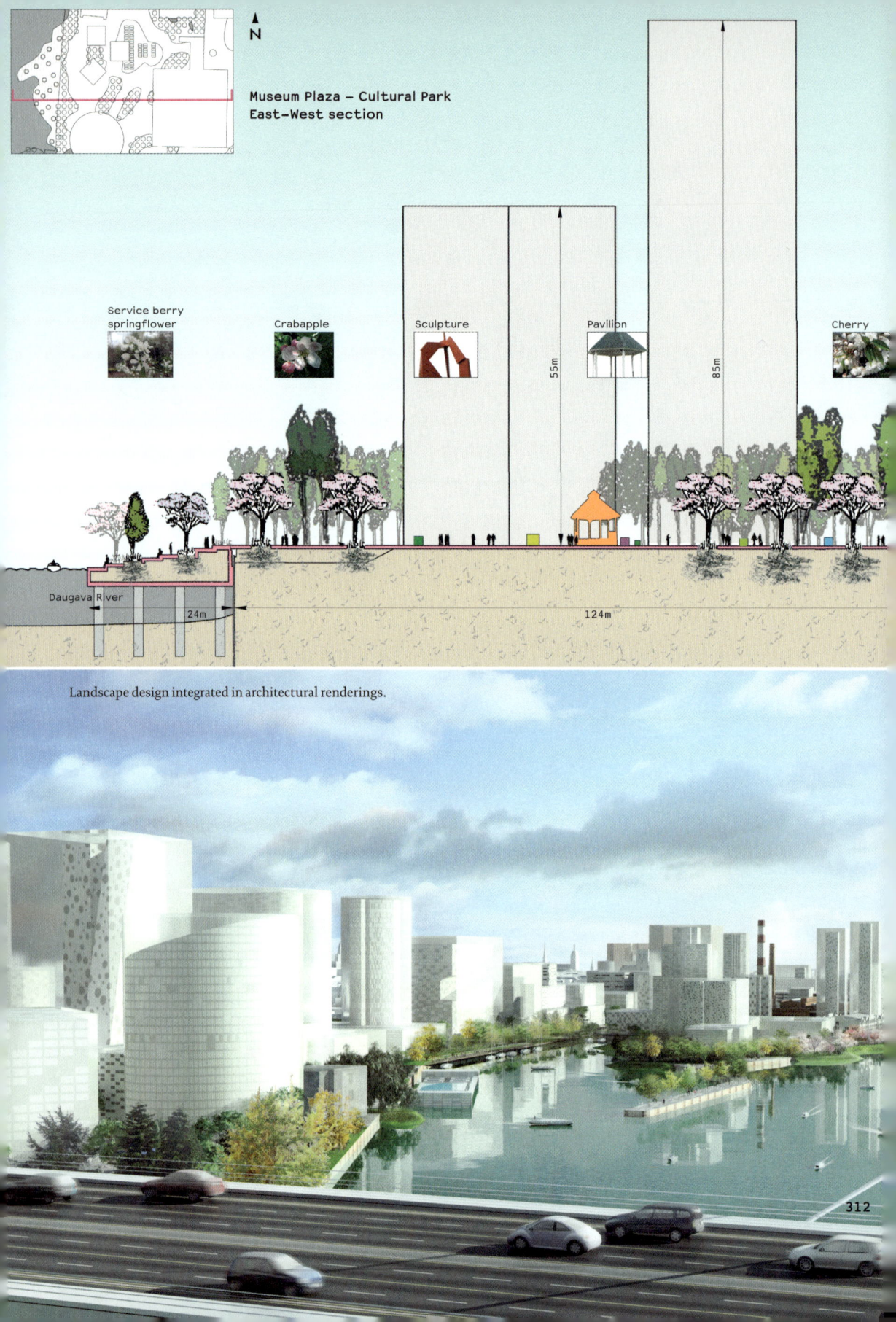

Service berry springflower

Crabapple

Sculpture

55m

Pavilion

85m

Cherry

Daugava River

24m

124m

Landscape design integrated in architectural renderings.

312

A Baltic Terminal
dark deciduous

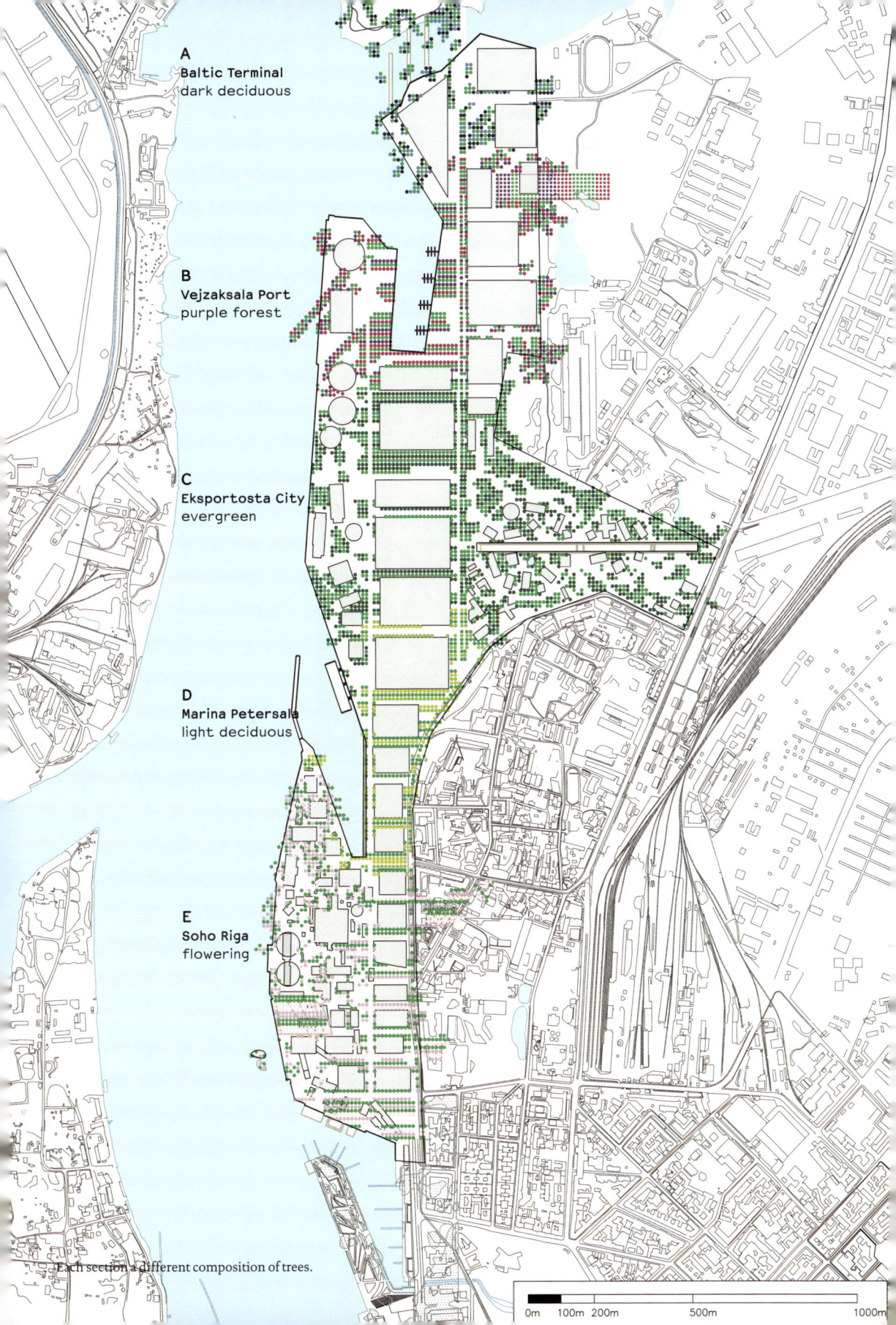

B Vejzaksala Port
purple forest

C Eksportosta City
evergreen

D Marina Petersala
light deciduous

E Soho Riga
flowering

Each section a different composition of trees.

0m 100m 200m   500m   1000m

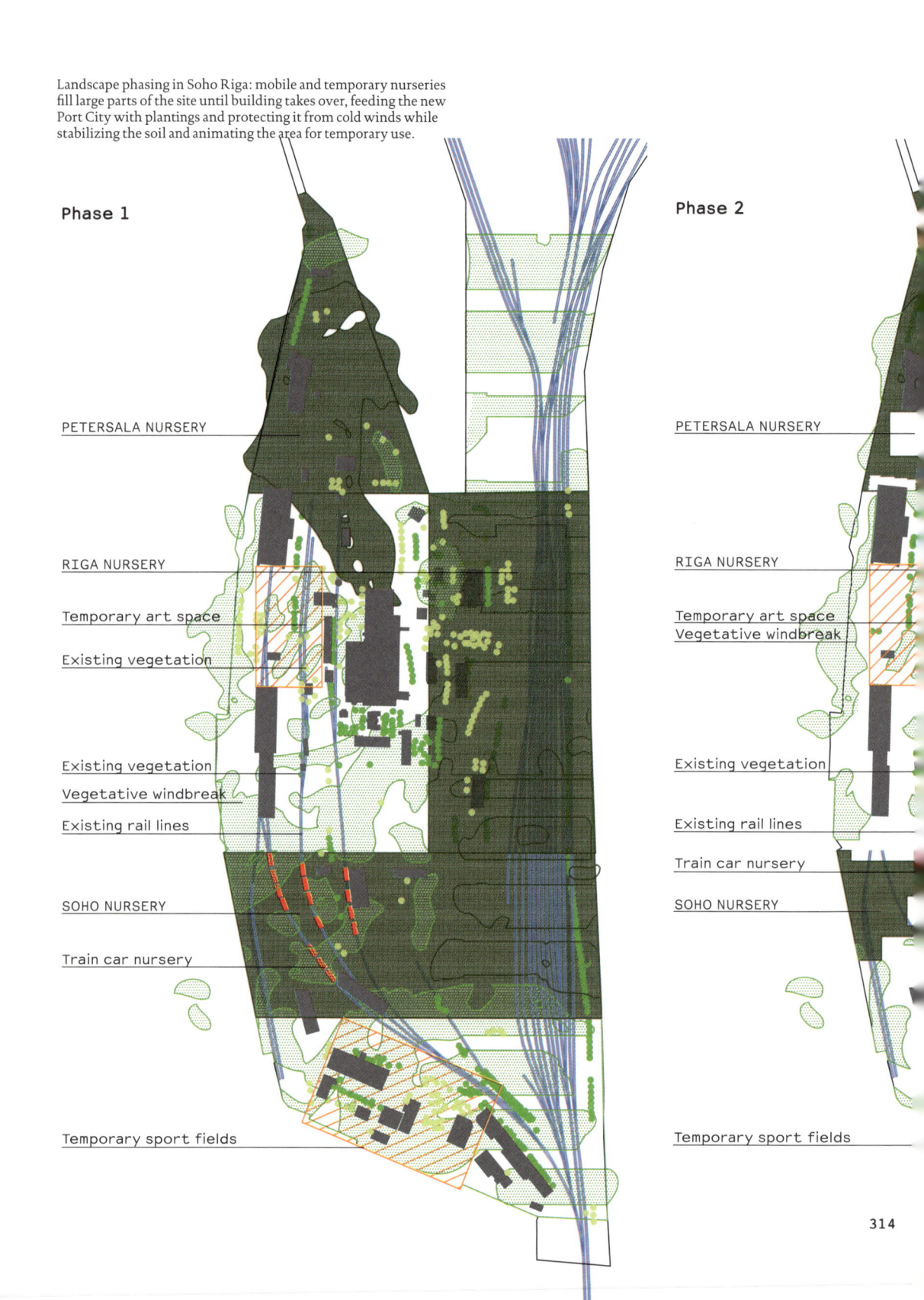

Landscape phasing in Soho Riga: mobile and temporary nurseries fill large parts of the site until building takes over, feeding the new Port City with plantings and protecting it from cold winds while stabilizing the soil and animating the area for temporary use.

Phase 1

- PETERSALA NURSERY
- RIGA NURSERY
- Temporary art space
- Existing vegetation
- Existing vegetation
- Vegetative windbreak
- Existing rail lines
- SOHO NURSERY
- Train car nursery
- Temporary sport fields

Phase 2

- PETERSALA NURSERY
- RIGA NURSERY
- Temporary art space
- Vegetative windbreak
- Existing vegetation
- Existing rail lines
- Train car nursery
- SOHO NURSERY
- Temporary sport fields

Phase 3

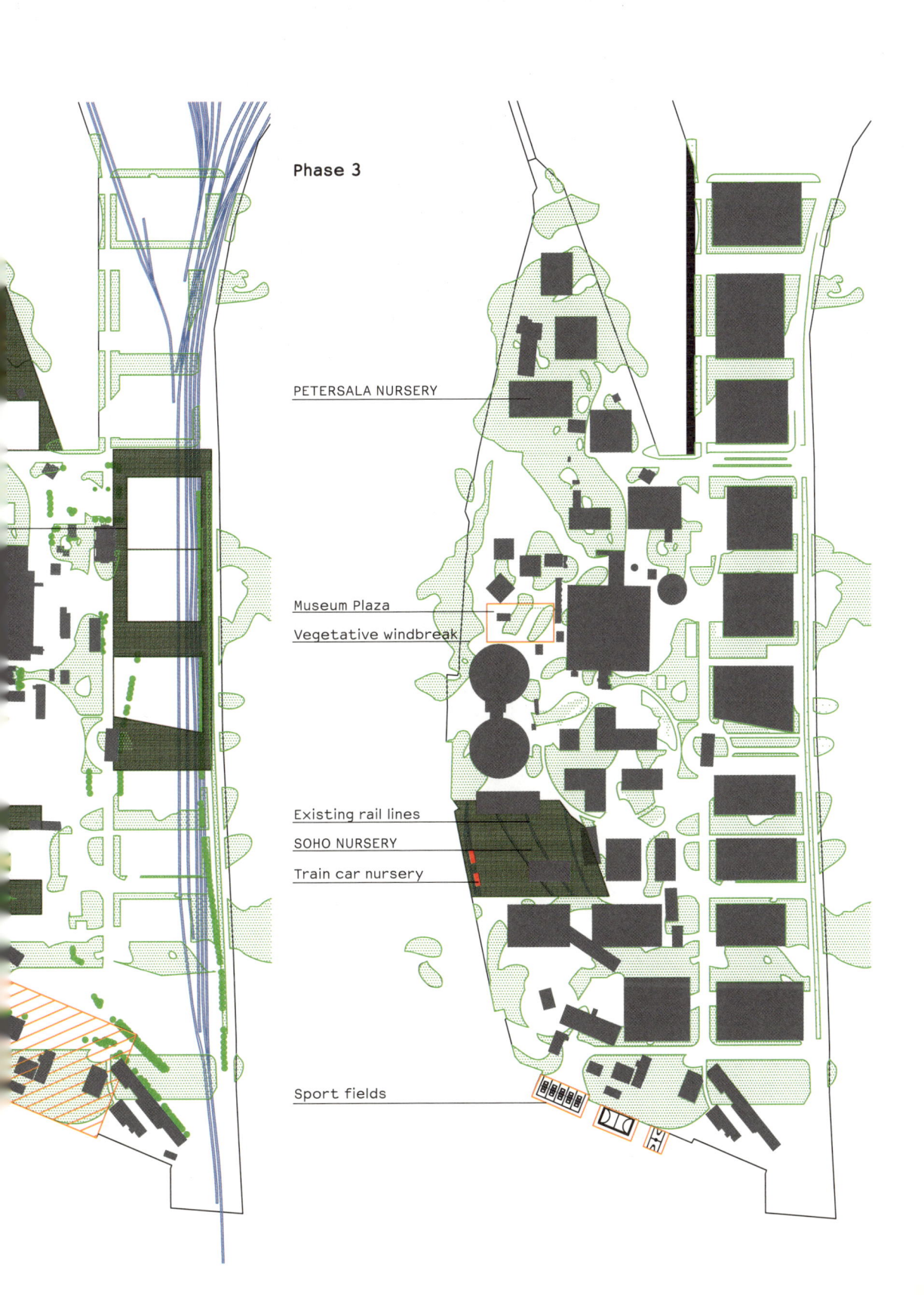

PETERSALA NURSERY

Museum Plaza
Vegetative windbreak

Existing rail lines
SOHO NURSERY
Train car nursery

Sport fields

Piranesi Pixel

Landscape design for CCTV/TVCC site
Beijing, China, 2004

At the request of OMA we assisted the architecture team with the landscape design for their CCTV and TVCC project in Beijing, introducing an intricate urban pattern based on Piranesi's reconstruction of Ancient Rome, translated into a dot grid for practical construction and maintenance purposes, at the same time referring to the build-up of the television image.

Model and drawing OMA / Inside Outside

Schematic design phase: pixelated Piranesi.

Schematic design phase: imagining the effect of the dotted landscape in a positive and negative version.

Connective Green

Landscape Design for 'H-Project', Seoul, South Korea 1995–1997

The Beauty of Topography

Anyone who visits Seoul for the first time will be struck by the beauty of its topography. The city is like a fluid tissue flowing between rounded mountains. The entire city is bathed in streaks of light and shadow. The scene is dramatic, especially at sunset, when everything turns a hot orange-pink. The mountains in Seoul are almost entirely covered with forests. They clean the air, break the wind, hold the soil, and give shelter to animal life, while the mountains provide spectacular views of the city.

The city's position, I was told, has been defined through Feng Shui: protection in the back; an open view towards the Han River from the sides and the front; and facing the Yellow Sea. The first inhabitants of the area date back to 4000 BC, but the city was founded in the fourteenth century by King Yi T'aejo – its location pointed out by the geomantic prophet Priest Muhak – and immediately grew into a busy commercial city that, still today, keeps on growing with incredible speed.

Seoul is littered with stories, religions, ancient palaces, shrines, monuments and beautiful walled gardens. City gates stand stoic in the middle of the modern and hectic downtown area, where low, traditional houses and inns are hidden just behind high-rise blocks. When we worked there, the city already had 14 million inhabitants and now it's said to have 22 million: everyone seems to want to live and work in Seoul! The sound of crows is what I remember waking up to.

The Process of Knowing

My first trip to Seoul was taken to simply understand the complex condition of the site and to gather some background information on the city. Walking up and down the alleys, I looked at what kind of trees, shrubs and grasses were growing there 'naturally'. I also observed the planting choices for public spaces and streets, how they roundabouts are organized with planting elements, in what forms hedges are clipped, and the general maintenance level. I liked the contrast between the 'unnatural' vegetation of the city services and the unplanned green areas. Of course, the traditional gardens were an inspiration in themselves, although there was no time to visit more than one...

Poplars, plane trees, birch, larch, juniper, maple, gingko and various pine trees and many forms of low, trimmed evergreens and flowering shrubs were common to the city. I visited a theme park outside Seoul with the local landscape architects we were working with and everywhere I went I noted very high levels of maintenance. I imagined a very organized, densely planted, folded landscape on our site; a bit like folded paper, entering, covering and enveloping the built structures.

As always, we started with the 'process of knowing', even though we don't necessarily translate this knowledge into something recognizable in the end. As landscape designers, we need to inform ourselves on the climate; where the wind comes from, how cold it gets. On soil conditions, how much rain falls, where underground or natural water flows to. On gardening rules: when are trees planted, cut, trimmed, used and how are they protected? On semantics: what do water, trees, flowers, colours symbolize: longevity, prosperity, death? On symbolic gestures: what flowers, dinners or presents are given on which occasion? On dress protocol: cloth, colour, cut, hat? On tradition: what role does Feng Shui play in architecture and daily life; which religions are there, what percentage of what and where most of which; and is it practiced, accepted, mixed? What superstitions survive generations? And so on.

From the architects and clients, one mostly gets to-the-point information: the firm, the history, the aims, the mentality, the regulations and restrictions of the project. But then the architects take you out to lunch or dinner and if you ask for it, they will talk about their more private lives.

'Natural beauty' means different things in every context: in a city like Seoul, everything seems focused on the value of contemporary/futuristic technology as emancipator, as tool for growth and wealth. Natural beauty seems represented by the elegant young women in traditional clothes: serene hostesses welcoming or assisting in every venue, wearing slim dresses with high waists and a bow in soft colours: light blue, white, pink; and in the carefully composed flower arrangements. Design is in everything, the hand of man is valued, and 'natural beauty' seems orchestrated through controlled sets of rules. The wildest visible ingredient of Seoul is Seoul itself, with its amazing neons, huge market buildings, spicy food places, hidden discotheques with screaming rap and harsh rock music, its student rallies and its innovative artists.

Seoul's markets, on the contrary, are so well-organized that food and articles are not just displayed but exhibited: selected by form and colour, you gape at impeccable piles of greens, blues, reds, purples, pinks, browns, blacks, whites and silvers. Vegetables, fish, meat, kitchen tools, socks, slippers, flowers, gloves, bags, aprons, textiles, herbs and sweets – objects, materials and foods are shown as vast planes or mounds, each with its own unique compositions of colour. And then there are the scents, the unbelievable peculiar scents that differ from area to area, place to place, weather to weather. Ah! The market: a never-ending inspiration. You always wish there was a place[1] where you could cook, taste, use and wear everything you see.

Forming a Landscape Team

On the slope of one of the mountains, the chairman of the global electric appliance manufacturer Samsung, who lived in that area himself at the time, bought a vast piece of ground and asked four European architects to design a group of museums, medical facilities and a special office for the chairman. These buildings, of which two were to be designed by Jean Nouvel, two by OMA/Rem Koolhaas, one by Mario Botta and two by Terry Farrell, would

1.
One day we visited a large market building and, climbing the concrete stairs, we noticed we were enveloped by the sweetest flower scent and, looking down, saw that we were walking over a soft, colourful carpet of flower petals. Following the trail, we reached the top floor and entered the largest interior flower market we had ever seen! Drunk on the scent we stared into a space filled with what seemed endless walls of colour: all flowers were stacked on top of each other on long tables, creating high, linear piles of roses, carnations, chrysanthemums, lilacs, lilies …

LANDSCAPE

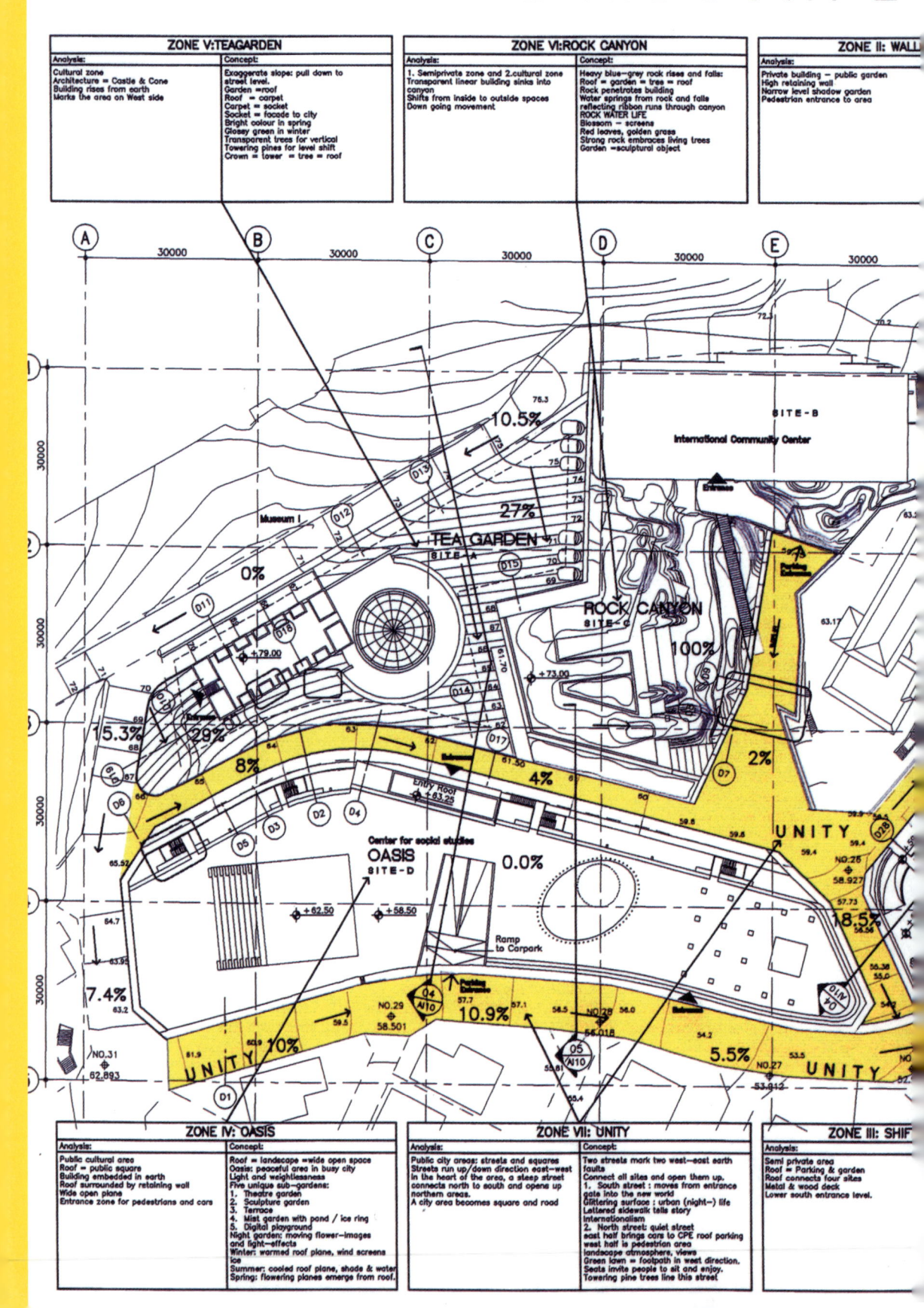

ZONE V: TEAGARDEN

Analysis:
- Cultural zone
- Architecture = Castle & Cone
- Building rises from earth
- Marks the area on West side

Concept:
- Exaggerate slope: pull down to street level.
- Garden = roof
- Roof = carpet
- Carpet = socket
- Socket = facade to city
- Bright colour in spring
- Glossy green in winter
- Transparent trees for vertical
- Towering pines for level shift
- Crown = lower = tree = roof

ZONE VI: ROCK CANYON

Analysis:
1. Semiprivate zone and 2. cultural zone
- Transparent linear building sinks into canyon
- Shifts from inside to outside spaces
- Down going movement

Concept:
- Heavy blue-grey rock rises and falls
- Roof = garden = tree = roof
- Rock penetrates building
- Water springs from rock and falls
- reflecting ribbon runs through canyon
- ROCK WATER LIFE
- Blossom = screens
- Red leaves, golden grass
- Strong rock embraces living trees
- Garden = sculptural object

ZONE II: WALL

Analysis:
- Private building — public garden
- High retaining wall
- Narrow level shadow garden
- Pedestrian entrance to area

ZONE IV: OASIS

Analysis:
- Public cultural area
- Roof = public square
- Building embedded in earth
- Roof surrounded by retaining wall
- Wide open plane
- Entrance zone for pedestrians and cars

Concept:
- Roof = landscape = wide open space
- Oasis: peaceful area in busy city
- Light and weightlessness
- Five unique sub-gardens:
  1. Theatre garden
  2. Sculpture garden
  3. Terrace
  4. Mist garden with pond / ice ring
  5. Digital playground
- Night garden: moving flower-images and light-effects
- Winter: warmed roof plane, wind screens
- Summer: cooled roof plane, shade & water
- Spring: flowering planes emerge from roof.

ZONE VII: UNITY

Analysis:
- Public city areas: streets and squares
- Streets run up/down direction east-west in the heart of the area, a steep street connects north to south and opens up northern areas.
- A city area becomes square and road

Concept:
- Two streets mark two west-east earth faults
- Connect all sites and open them up.
1. South street: moves from entrance gate into the new world
- Glittering surface: urban (night-) life
- Lettered sidewalk tells story internationalism
2. North street: quiet street east half brings cars to CPE roof parking west half is pedestrian area landscape atmosphere, views
- Green lawn = footpath in west direction.
- Seats invite people to sit and enjoy.
- Towering pine trees line this street.

ZONE III: SHIF

Analysis:
- Semi private area
- Roof = Parking & garden
- Roof connects four sites
- Metal & wood deck
- Lower south entrance level.

ASTERPLAN

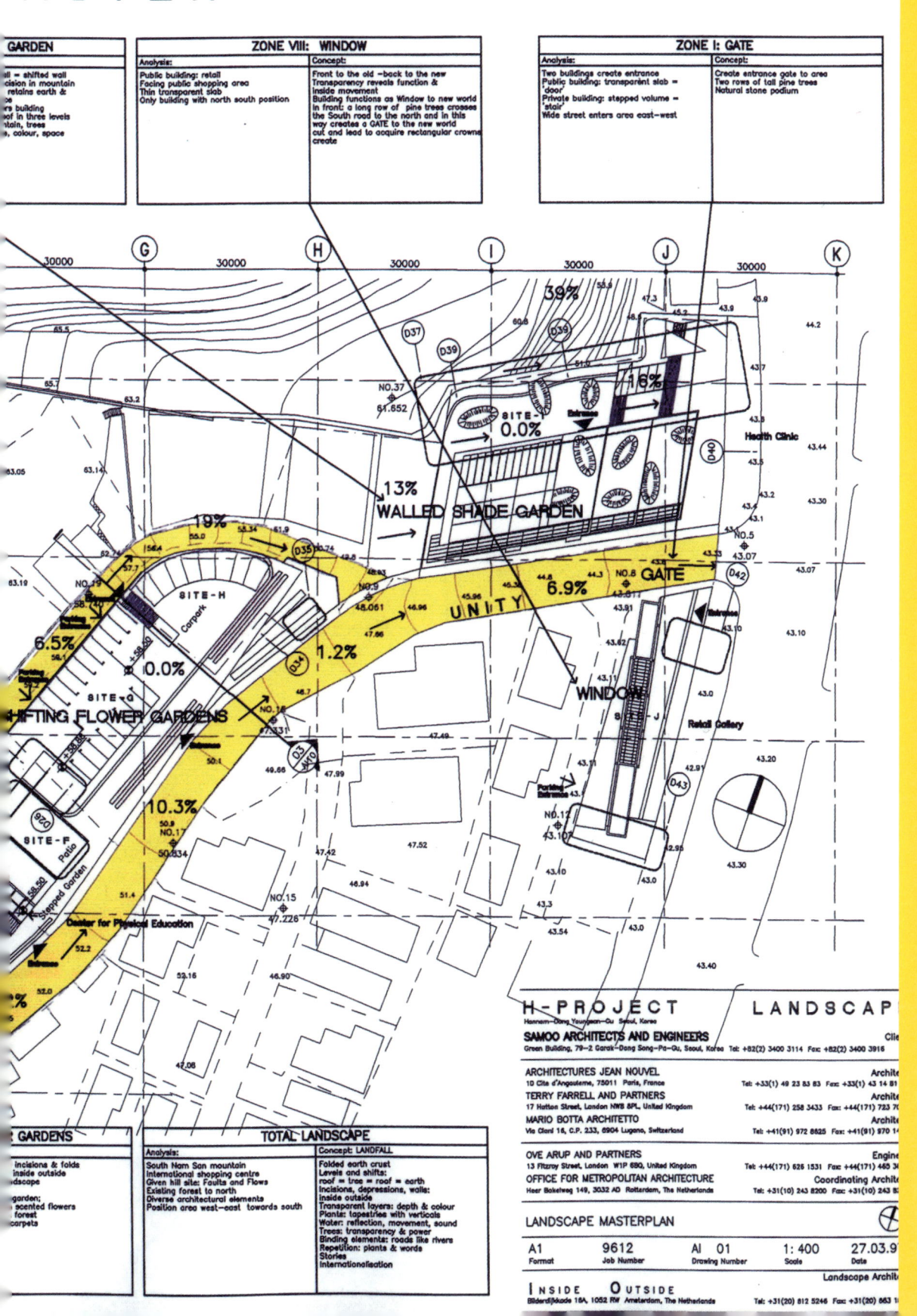

ZONE VIII: WINDOW

Analysis:
Public building: retail
Facing public shopping area
Thin transparent slab
Only building with north south position

Concept:
Front to the old – back to the new
Transparency reveals function & inside movement
Building functions as Window to new world in front: a long row of pine trees crosses the South road to the north and in this way creates a GATE to the new world cut and lead to acquire rectangular crowns create

ZONE I: GATE

Analysis:
Two buildings create entrance
Public building: transparent slab = 'door'
Private building: stepped volume = 'stair'
Wide street enters area east-west

Concept:
Create entrance gate to area
Two rows of tall pine trees
Natural stone podium

GARDEN

– shifted wall
cision in mountain
retains earth &
rs building
ot in three levels
ain, trees
, colour, space

GARDENS

incisions & folds
inside outside
dscape

garden:
scented flowers
forest
carpets

TOTAL LANDSCAPE

Analysis:
South Nam San mountain
International shopping centre
Given hill site: Faults and Flows
Existing forest to north
Diverse architectural elements
Position area west-east towards south

Concept: LANDFALL
Folded earth crust
Levels and shifts:
roof = tree = roof = earth
Incisions, depressions, walls: inside outside
Transparent layers: depth & colour
Plants: tapestries with verticals
Water: reflection, movement, sound
Trees: transparency & power
Binding elements: roads like rivers
Repetition: plants & words
Stories
Internationalisation

H-PROJECT
Hannam-Dong Youngsan-Gu Seoul, Korea

SAMOO ARCHITECTS AND ENGINEERS
Green Building, 79-2 Garak-Dong Song-Pa-Gu, Seoul, Korea Tel: +82(2) 3400 3114 Fax: +82(2) 3400 3916

ARCHITECTURES JEAN NOUVEL — Architect
10 Cite d'Angouteme, 75011 Paris, France Tel: +33(1) 49 23 83 83 Fax: +33(1) 43 14 81

TERRY FARRELL AND PARTNERS — Architect
17 Hatton Street, London NW8 8PL, United Kingdom Tel: +44(171) 258 3433 Fax: +44(171) 723 70

MARIO BOTTA ARCHITETTO — Architect
Via Ciani 16, C.P. 233, 6904 Lugano, Switzerland Tel: +41(91) 972 8625 Fax: +41(91) 970 14

OVE ARUP AND PARTNERS — Engineer
13 Fitzroy Street, London W1P 6BQ, United Kingdom Tel: +44(171) 625 1531 Fax: +44(171) 465 3

OFFICE FOR METROPOLITAN ARCHITECTURE — Coordinating Architect
Heer Bokelweg 149, 3032 AD Rotterdam, The Netherlands Tel: +31(10) 243 8200 Fax: +31(10) 243 8

LANDSCAPE MASTERPLAN

A1	9612	AI 01	1:400	27.03.97
Format	Job Number	Drawing Number	Scale	Date

Landscape Architect

INSIDE OUTSIDE
Bilderdijkkade 18A, 1052 RW Amsterdam, The Netherlands Tel: +31(20) 612 5246 Fax: +31(20) 663 1

Situation drawing by Petra Blaisse

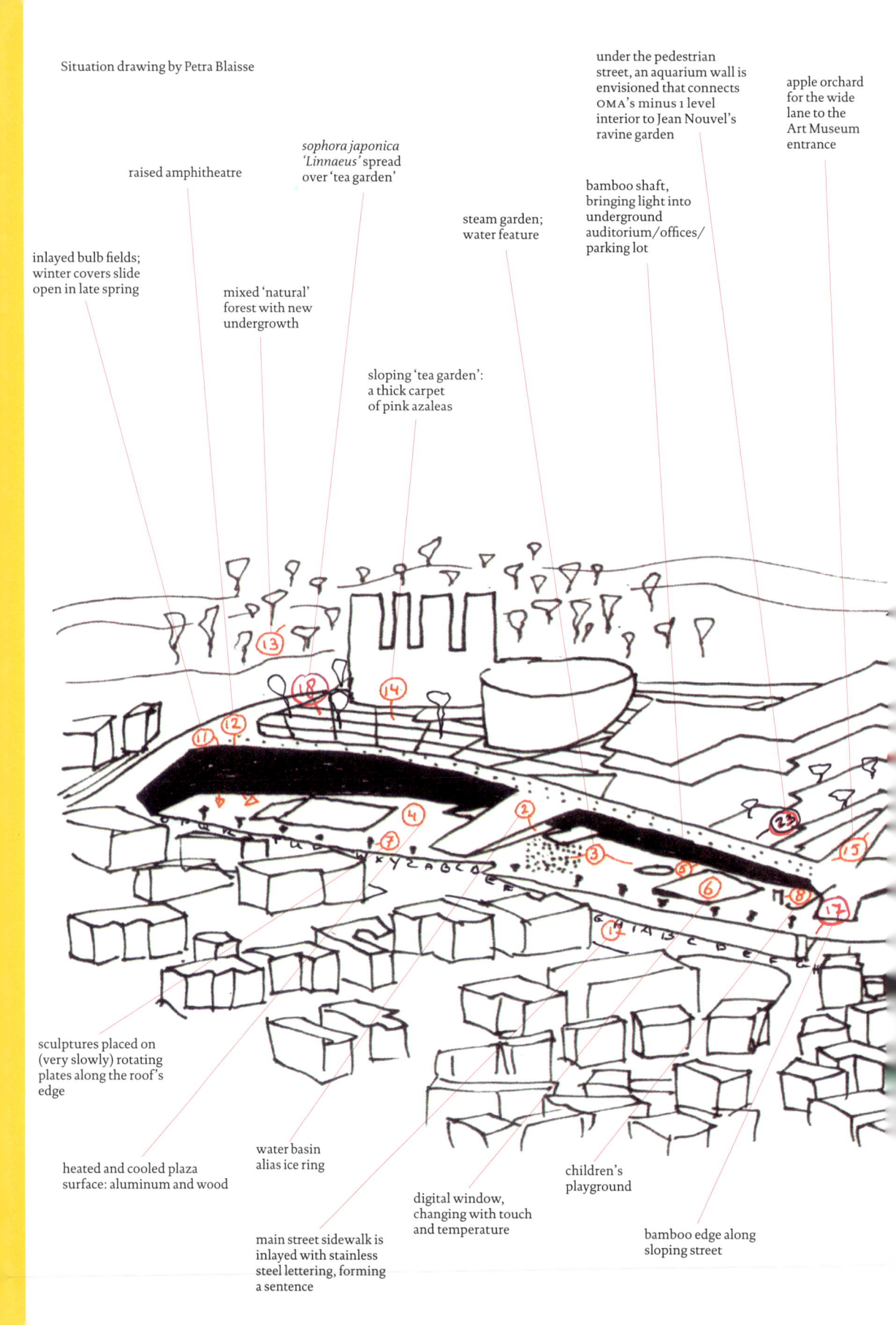

raised amphitheatre

sophora japonica 'Linnaeus' spread over 'tea garden'

steam garden; water feature

under the pedestrian street, an aquarium wall is envisioned that connects OMA's minus 1 level interior to Jean Nouvel's ravine garden

apple orchard for the wide lane to the Art Museum entrance

bamboo shaft, bringing light into underground auditorium/offices/parking lot

inlayed bulb fields; winter covers slide open in late spring

mixed 'natural' forest with new undergrowth

sloping 'tea garden': a thick carpet of pink azaleas

sculptures placed on (very slowly) rotating plates along the roof's edge

heated and cooled plaza surface: aluminum and wood

water basin alias ice ring

main street sidewalk is inlayed with stainless steel lettering, forming a sentence

digital window, changing with touch and temperature

children's playground

bamboo edge along sloping street

façade and ravine garden melt

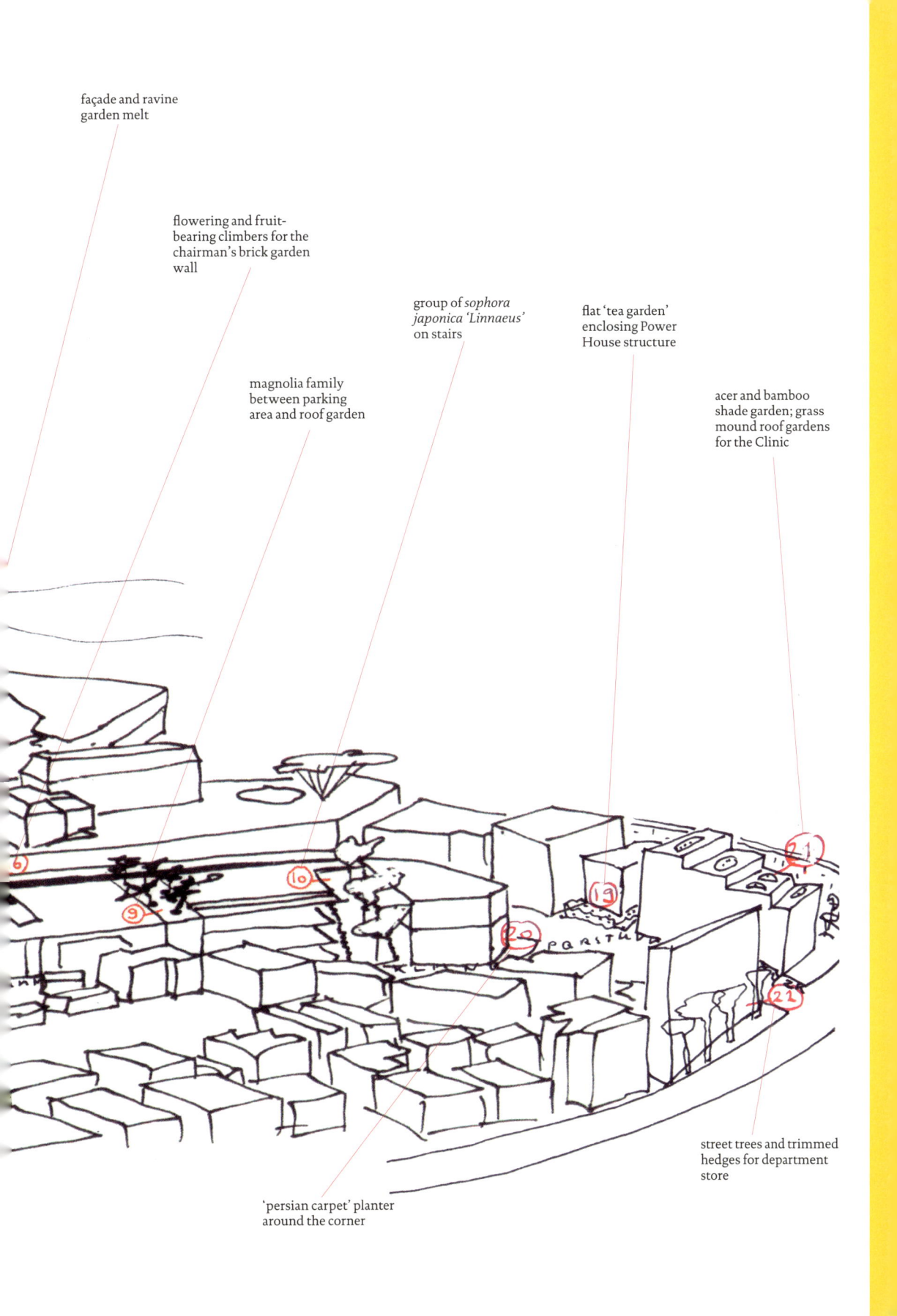

flowering and fruit-bearing climbers for the chairman's brick garden wall

group of *sophora japonica 'Linnaeus'* on stairs

flat 'tea garden' enclosing Power House structure

magnolia family between parking area and roof garden

acer and bamboo shade garden; grass mound roof gardens for the Clinic

'persian carpet' planter around the corner

street trees and trimmed hedges for department store

form a varied group, each building with its own size and form, facing in its own direction, all overlooking the city from different angles.

I was introduced to Samsung by OMA – the master planners – and became the landscape designer for the entire project after passing the usual 'exam': presenting my earlier work, describing my design mentality for this particular project, presenting a fee and cost proposal, agreeing to the given schedules and demands. At the time, this was a fairly challenging task for me. Standing at the beginning of my career, I was asked to work with four established architects, to surround and connect seven buildings in total. The landscape had to create a single, unified area with planting, streets, sidewalks and infrastructure. Having never worked in Asia, I had to learn about climate, soil conditions, culture and the traditions of Seoul and Korea and – the site being quite steep – also about road construction and water systems of which I knew nothing. Since I worked alone at the time, I always invited free-lance designers, draughtsmen, craftsmen, architects, engineers or planting specialists for every new project.[2] They helped finalize my designs and produce all necessary materials for submission.

Digging Their Own Holes

The location of the site was interesting: against the lower flank of one of Seoul's mountains. The soil was rocky and hard. Seoul's climate is harsh: extremely hot in summer and extremely cold in winter. The client wanted to insert cultural facilities into the existing calm and intimate atmosphere of the traditional neighbourhood – even though a mirror-clad Hyatt hovers over the site: a huge flat screen with many eyes. Farrel's two commercial buildings were situated at the outer edge of the area, facing a busy road. They framed the street that flowed into the quieter hinterland, forming a 'gate to the new world'.

Trees were taken down and a housing area was demolished behind wooden fences. The ochre and brown rocky soil of the site was exposed. Dogs barked.

The Hannam Dong area had strict height restrictions, and most architects had to build into the ground to accommodate the necessary programmes, so they all dug into the hard soil. Nouvel went really deep, turning one façade of his building into a rock-like structure, looking into the newly created ravine. For this garden – an exaggerated rock/crater condition that entered and accentuated the building's descending façade – he collaborated with the Belgian artist Pierre Culot. As H-Project's landscape planner, I had to communicate with them to make all conditions 'fit'. I knew Culot from when I worked at the Stedelijk Museum, in the seventies and eighties, where we acquired some of his ceramic work for the applied arts collection. Jean Nouvel and I had met a few times at dinners in Paris, and I had always appreciated that he accepted our invitation to model in the Villa dall'Ava[3] when photographer Hans Werlemann and I made a photo series there in the early nineties: a stunning Faustus with a black cape, standing, reading and sleeping in another man's creation.

---

2. With Italian architect Irene Curruli, whom I met when giving a Berlage workshop; the help of OMA architects that gave us computer support and a desk to work at; and with the backing of Amsterdam based B&B Landschapsarchitecten (for 50 per cent of our fee) – who drew up our ideas in AutoCAD and went through planting, street and lighting schemes and pricing. We also asked three independent landscape engineers to give us technical advice on a regular basis: drawing up soil, irrigation and construction details. In the last presentation phase, in 1997, American architect Andrew MacNair joined our team to help produce the final Landscape Design Development presentation book.

3. I worked on the interiors and curtains of the Villa dall'Ava in Saint Cloud, Paris, a private house on a sloped site overlooking the Bois de Boulogne. Maarten van Severen made the kitchen, Yves Brunier designed the garden and OMA's team – Jeroen Thomas, Hans Werlemann and others – were ever present to help finish every detail of the house.

Botta – who always talked about cooking and food – stayed true to his formula, creating a round, tower-like volume with trees on top, made of brick to accommodate a ceramic museum. The tower rose from a steep slope that covered a large underground foyer that connected the Nouvel, Botta and OMA buildings.

OMA's two stretched buildings lay embedded in the rock at the foot of Botta's and Nouvel's museums, their roofs forming a large podium, shaped like butterfly wings. All four sites were separated only by narrow pedestrian streets, under which buildings and lowered gardens connected.

Landscape Design as Nexus

It was interesting to see how meticulously the urban landscape was defined by local regulations and the client. Starting from what a landscape designer must undertake and present, the dossier prescribed the proportion of landscaped area versus built area for each official plot. Because they were bigger than the original houses, each building was composed of a number of registered plots, adding the obligation of locating the landscaped areas accordingly. For each built surface per plot, the minimum surface of garden, the sizes and numbers of trees and shrubs per m^2; a distinction between evergreen and deciduous; and the amount of full (natural) soil versus the amount of terrace, roof or container garden; each value was defined by law. The amount of landscape demanded for a plot was 15 percent of the total site surface. This meant that Botta's 2.333,30 m^2 plot, for instance, needed to include a garden surface of 350.80 m^2, of which two thirds had to be 'full soil' and one third was allowed to be 'other'. On these surfaces a minimum of 0.2 trees per m^2 – of which 30 percent evergreen and 70 percent deciduous – and 1.0 shrubs per m^2 – of which 30 percent evergreen and 70 percent deciduous – had to be planted.

To understand these regulations was a puzzle, and we started by breaking down the required data for each building site. Having done that, we discovered that nearly all buildings used up too much of their plot: they did not leave enough space for the required full-soil landscape; nor did all of them create suitable spaces for 'other' planting. Imagine one of OMA's sites, its 4,033.00 m^2 surface completely taken up by building, needing 604.90 m^2 of garden of which 403.27 m^2 planted in full soil!

When the architects met together at OMA, one day, we borrowed an office and, feeling like a surgery, sat with each architecture firm and said: 'Okay, such-and-such is the syllabus for your site, which shows that we need to acquire more room for both full-soil landscape and integrated gardens. How would you like to go about it? Is it possible for you to take out a piece here; shift an area there; and maybe stack a few floors to shrink your building's footprint? Sink some floor surface or ceiling to create a patio inside your building – so that we can create a garden? And, oh yes, can you adjust the structure of your roof to allow for weight and irrigation of a considerable roof garden? Do you prefer transparent or massive trees in combination with your façades? You can only have so many low trees, the rest have to be larger...!'

You can imagine what FUN we had and how hated we felt at the same time... as a discipline.

The results of these demands began to take shape: OMA created a long trench along the back side of their building – squeezed between rock wall and interior – in order to create enough area of full soil (this also brought welcome light into their interior spaces). They shortened their 'butterfly wings' on the buidlings' outer ends to give space within their site, but also thought with us about every possible pocket within or outside the building that could be filled with garden. Botta reinforced the sloping roof of the Ceramics Museum for the weight of 90 cm of soil, irrigation tubes, moisture build-up (turning into ice or snow in winter) and a closed layer of rhododendrons (a variety of the former azalea clan) over its entire surface; and enlarged the planters on the towers for larger sized trees. Nouvel had enough space to one side but needed to back off a little along the northwestern edge of his site to allow for the required 'edge planting', and he needed to adjust rockworks and build special structures to allow large pine trees to root. And Farrel had to allow our input in every slit of full soil and on every roof terrace available.

<u>Anything Can Be Landscape</u>
For mountain slopes, street edges, patios, roofs, inner courts, parking areas, sidewalks, planters, crater inclines, art- and public plazas, open air underground slots, stepped areas from roofs into interiors and for roof terraces – public, semipublic and private – we proposed evergreen and seasonal tree groupings, azalea 'tea plantations', grass and wildflower fields, acer gardens, perennial and tree planters, vertical gardens, apple orchards, magnolia libraries, seasonal bulb gardens with winter lids, stepped box hedge gardens, mounded roof terraces, thick bamboo lines both below and above ground, Persian flower carpets, etcetera – repeating plantings and forms, choosing lighting, furniture, street and sidewalk finishes that showed one signature, one world, one narrative; including words inlayed over the entire length of the main street's edge to connect the area from east to west with one stroke.

Searching for alternative 'landscape' ingredients, we also drew an aquarium wall,[4] a steam room, an ice rink, a rock garden, a shade terrace, fountains, digital playgrounds, a stepped terrace, mounds, slots, seats and 'green' street finishes. This project was really fascinating because in one single commission, we encountered every form of urban landscape one can imagine.

For roads, sidewalks and plazas we combined asphalt, concrete, glass, metal, wood, stone and pebbles – materials people in Seoul are familiar with – in a new way. We tested a number of combinations of metal with wood, concrete inlayed with pebbles, natural stone, chunks of glass or stainless steel letters. We integrated thick pieces of glass in coloured concrete sidewalks.

The driveway to Nouvel's buildings, for example, was finished in black concrete with white pebbles and then sanded flat, while driveways to other buildings had the same pebbles inlayed as a three-dimensional structure – choices depending on the amount of traffic and pedestrian flow expected.

4. We discovered that the bottom of the slit that was made for a sunken garden in the OMA building, was at the same level as the pit of Jean Nouvel's rock garden, which lies behind the OMA building; only separated by a narrow slice of soil that supports an equally narrow street. We thought, Okay, why not take away the soil that supports the street and make instead – in the form of an underground aquarium that supports the street above and creates a view from OMA's interior to Nouvel' beautiful rock canyon? Though it turned out to be too expensive to realize, the idea *was* considered. Imagine: we could have watched fish swimming in front of rocks on one side and floating through an interior on the other.

Technical Battle

As with every project, we struggled through numerous technical issues, problems that arise because of severe natural factors such as heavy rain, drought, cold winds and heat – extreme conditions following each other during the year – combined with the urban circumstances in which we worked: the fact that we had to 'weave through' each and every condition that was offered meant that the wind, drought, light, temperature and water conditions of each location – big and small, high and low, inside and outside, protected or exposed – were very sensitive issues that had to be carefully balanced out. Water gushes down the dried-out (or frozen) slopes and façade surfaces into the smallest joint or opening and onto every road, pathway and flat roof. Wind hits the shallow-rooted plantings, dries out the soil, and spreads bugs and viruses among principally strong species that grow in less than ideal conditions.

We invited three engineers specialized in various disciplines (structure, water, soil, lighting) into the team and spent hours every session throughout the project's development on solving these technical issues, drawing details of irrigation systems, root stabilizers, tree root conductors, tree trunk supporters, bamboo root containers and underground air and irrigation pipes, specially designed gutters, raised street and roof edges, façade edge details, drain pipes, lightweight soil build-ups, concrete and soil mixtures, rock grips, porous sidewalk finishes, invisible container drip systems, steam installations, stepped planter construction details, soil retaining mats, roof terrace and grass mound structures, slope stabilizers, trellises, calculating weights of snow and ice spread over given roof surfaces; and the effect of temperature fluctuations on street finishes and potted roots – details that were new to all involved, as mid-European topographic and climatic conditions are rather different from those in Seoul.

A Scientific Process

In the H-Project the entire process of designing the landscape was scientific rather than creative. If you work for a corporate client who knows exactly what they want and for a city that has a clear infrastructural and cultural policy, you are creatively limited.

And the client was tough. Everything had to be strictly formatted. I'd never had a commissioner who formulated the exact size and sequence of my presentation; for a competition this is normal, but not for a commission. I was even told how to illustrate my design, how to point out and how to position images, samples and plans on a presentation board. 'It's not your creativity that counts, but it's how easy it is for us to understand that matters', the client said. If everyone they worked with would have his own way of presenting, they would have to put a lot of energy into understanding a mentality and penetrating a proposal. It would make it harder for them to judge its quality according to their own standards. I thought this was very condescending at first, then realized it was smart and considered it a challenge. These very strict regulations and restrictions dictating one's every move forced me to develop another form of creativity – one that had to do with solving riddles and allowing systems to rule without losing a degree of personal touch – more than anything else.

I couldn't sleep before presentations and was fearful of the blunt way in which I was ordered around. I had heard that Samsung's architecture office Samoo worked on more than 400 active projects, so their patience was limited. The OMA team – Koolhaas with Gary Bates, Adrienne Fisher and others – was helpful in translating the situation and coordinating moves, but of course my team and I had to do it alone, and I was only a subconsultant who designed the landscape: hierarchy is important in Korea.

Once, when I had to present my final design, I became so insecure that I asked the creative director of B&B Landschapsarchitecten at the time, Michael van Gessel, to go with me to Seoul. I thought that an experienced, male landscape architect beside me would help our plan pass the last test. Indeed, Michael's presence helped a great deal, because we were two, a larger presence; with more to say and communicate. I remember us preparing our next-day presentation in the hotel room, and him enacting the client, bombarding me with the most difficult questions and comments he could think of! We had asked the hotel for a projection screen and a slide projector so we could practice. Piles of slides on the bed, like a miniature Manhattan, reorganizing and selecting again and again – tsjak tsjak tsjak – you get very skilful at dropping slides into carrousels.

All our presentations were translated sentence by sentence by a person standing by on the stage – as they translate, you can oversee the room and study the faces and plan your next sentence at each interval (quite a few people sleep during presentations and meetings in Asia, I have noticed; it must be because they work incessantly. You must use your voice, exaggerate intonation and create stage drama to keep your audience awake!). It is a beautiful rhythm of sound, two languages intertwined; words become detached sentences, hanging in the air like a held breath . . . to then continue again. Amazing how much longer or shorter translations can be than the original: you can say five words where the translator needs forty – or vice versa – and this creates hilarious moments.

After a deadline like this one, you fall into exhaustion – though content if things went well. Apart from a good harsh body scrub, eating and drinking together helps you relax, and in Seoul you find the best eating places ever: along the street, in little niches and in barely covered shacks, fierce women either serve you steaming hot noodle dishes that they attack with scissors; or they grill raw sliced meat and intestines (scissor-cut on the spot) on little fire-hot grills inlayed in your table, hanging over you, handing you piles of crisp salad leaves, fresh garlic toes and greens, pouring teas, beers and plum alcohol in water glasses, yelling and laughing and shooing away bums and street musicians that stand gravely insulted when you give them some change (that immediately disappears in their pockets): they are musicians, definitely not beggars.

Building and landscape as one topographic line.

Section A-A

Section D-D

Section B-B

Section E-E

Section C-C

Section F-F

Section G-G

Section H-H

Section I-I

PLANTING M

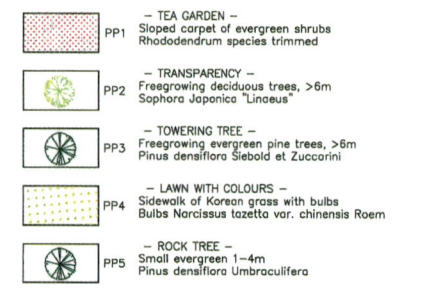

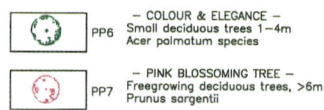

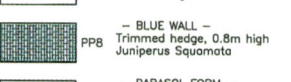

PP1	— TEA GARDEN — Sloped carpet of evergreen shrubs Rhododendrum species trimmed	
PP2	— TRANSPARENCY — Freegrowing deciduous trees, >6m Sophora Japonica "Linaeus"	
PP3	— TOWERING TREE — Freegrowing evergreen pine trees, >6m Pinus densiflora Siebold et Zuccarini	
PP4	— LAWN WITH COLOURS — Sidewalk of Korean grass with bulbs Bulbs Narcissus tazetta var. chinensis Roem	
PP5	— ROCK TREE — Small evergreen 1–4m Pinus densiflora Umbraculifera	
PP6	— COLOUR & ELEGANCE — Small deciduous trees 1–4m Acer palmatum species	
PP7	— PINK BLOSSOMING TREE — Freegrowing deciduous trees, >6m Prunus sargentii	
PP8	— BLUE WALL — Trimmed hedge, 0.8m high Juniperus Squamata	
PP9	— PARASOL FORM — White flowering tree in planter Cornus kausa Berger	
PP10	— CONTINUATION OF INNER SPACE — Various hardy bamboos with distinctive features Phyllostachis species	
PP11	— GROUNDCOVER IN Low evergreen shrubs Taxus cuspidata Siebe Mahonia japonica, Ste	
PP12	— GOLDEN TUFTS IN Grasses e.g. Miscanthus sinen	
PP13	— COLOUR — Perrenials Anemone x hybrida 'H & Polygonum affine	
PP14	— ARCHITECTURAL E Steps of trimmed eve Buxus microphylla va	
PP15	— LARGE PINK/PURP Freegrowing deciduou Magnolia kobus Magnolia denutata De	

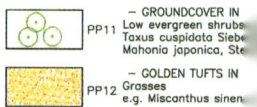

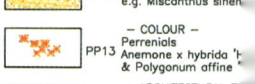

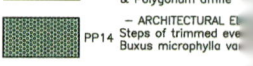

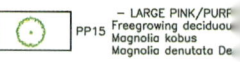

STERPLAN

Planting List

Anemone x hybrida 'Honorine Jobert'
Clematis chinensis 'Nakai'
Epimedium koreanum
Galanthus nivalis
Lavandula angustifolia 'Dwarf blue'
Lilium var.
Muscari armeniacum
Narcissus tazetta var. chinensis Roem
Polygonum affine 'Darjeeling red'
Scilla siberica
Sedum acre
   Trees (regulation 70% Deciduous 30% Evergreen)
Acer palmatum 'Aureum'
Acer palmatum 'Dissectum'
Acer palmatum 'Senkaki'
Betula papyrifera
Betula pendula
Betula utilis
Cornus kousa 'Berger'
Magnolia denudata 'Desrousseaux'
Magnolia liliflora
Magnolia sieboldii 'K. Koch'
Malus 'Schone van Boskoop'
Malus 'Cox's Orange Pippin'
Pinus densiflora 'Umbraculifera'
Pinus giganteus
Pinus mugo
Pinus thumbergii
Prunus sargentii
Sophora japonica 'Linnaeus'
Taxus baccata
Taxus cuspidata 'Siebold et Zuccarin'
   Groundcover
Euonymus fortunei var. 'Radicans rehder'
Festuca glauca
Miscanthus sinensis 'Silberfeder'
   Shrubs
Buxus angustifolia 'Dwarf blue'
Buxus microphylla var. 'Koreana'
Juniperus media 'Pfizeriana glauca'
Juniperus squamata
Juniperus virginiana
Ligustrum vulgare 'Atrovirens'
Paeonia var.
Rhododendron species
Rosa var.
Stephanandra incisa 'Crispa'
Syringa velutina venosa
   Bamboo
Phyllostachys bambusoides 'Heterocycla'
Phyllostachys bambusoides 'Siebold et Zuccarini'
Phyllostachys pubescens 'Mael'
Phyllostachys viridi 'Glaucesens'

— HILLY SCENTED GARDEN —
PP16 Grass mounds with flowering perrenial Epimedium x Rubrum, Summer flowering bulb Lilium leichtlinii, Clematis Chinensis Nakai, Syringa Velutina Venosa

— ARCHITECTURAL ELEMENT —
PP17 Mounds with various shrubs and grasses Festuca glauca and Rhododendron species

— PERSIAN CARPET —
PP18 Rows of flowers and evergreen shrubs Paeonia, rose and other species

SOIL AREA

SITE-A

	LOCAL CODE	PLAN
Site area	2,333.30 m²	
Landscaping 15%	350.80 m²	355.00 m²
Full earth 2/3	233.33 m²	237.67 m²
Others 1/3	116.67 m²	118.33 m²

SITE-B

	LOCAL CODE	PLAN
Site area	2,055.50 m²	
Landscaping 15%	308.30 m²	320.00 m²
Full earth 2/3	205.53 m²	213.00 m²
Others 1/3	102.77 m²	107.00 m²

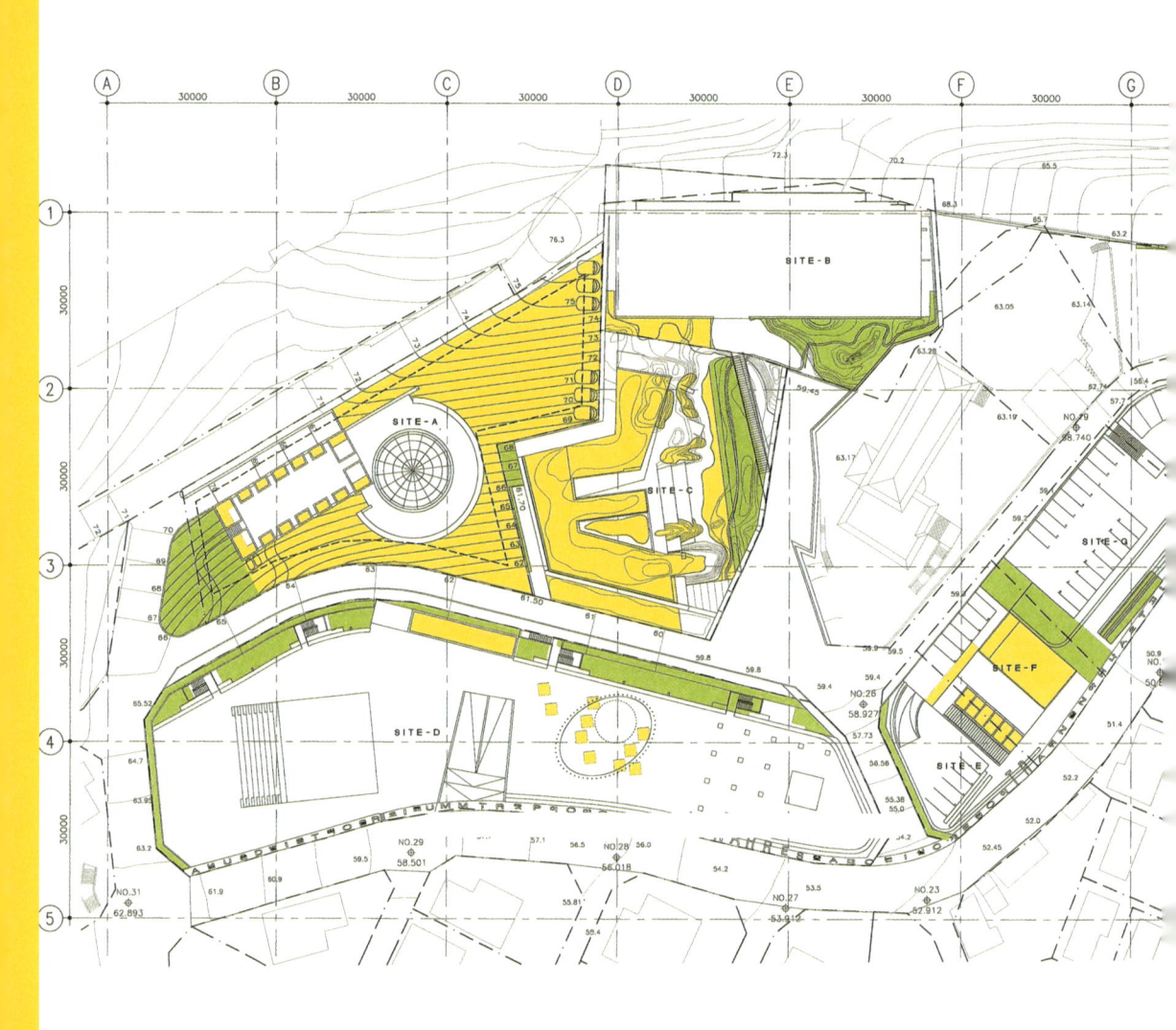

Full earth planting area

Other planting area

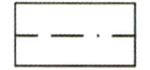

Property line

LCULATION

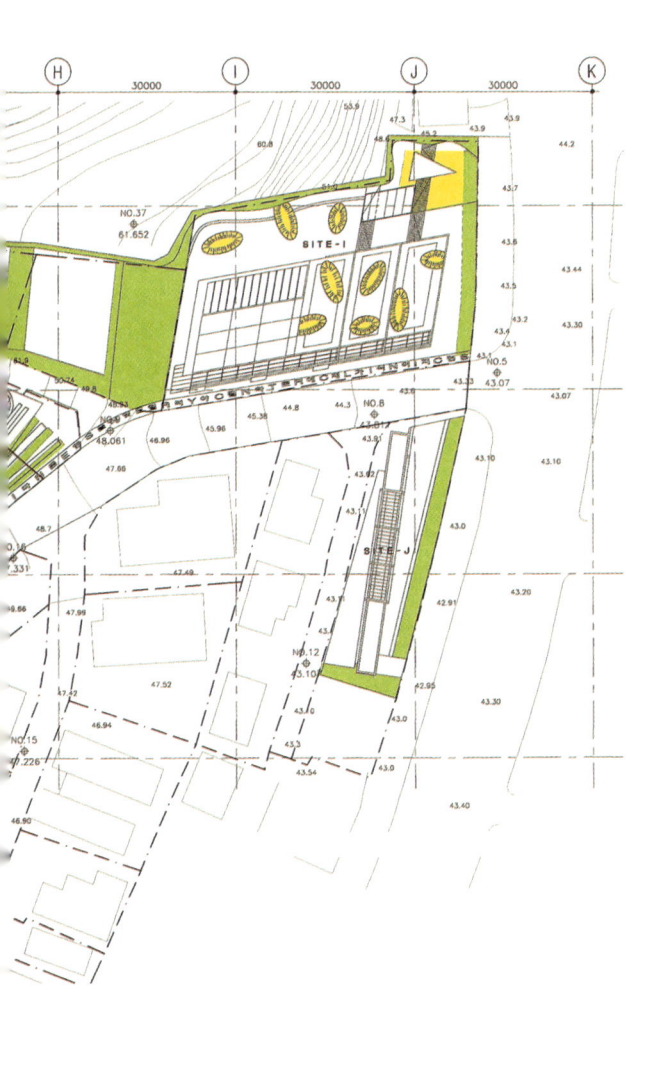

SITE-E

	LOCAL CODE	PLAN
Site area	494.50 m²	
Landscaping 15%	24.70 m²	67.50 m²
Full earth 2/3	16.47 m²	40.50 m²
Others 1/3	8.23 m²	27.00 m²

SITE-F

	LOCAL CODE	PLAN
Site area	573.5 m²	
Landscaping 15%	26.70 m²	178.00 m²
Full earth 2/3	178.00 m²	92.50 m²
Others 1/3	8.90 m²	85.50 m²

SITE-G

	LOCAL CODE	PLAN
Site area	931.30 m²	
Landscaping 15%	46.60 m²	96.00 m²
Full earth 2/3	31.07 m²	64.00 m²
Others 1/3	15.53 m²	32.00 m²

SITE-H

	LOCAL CODE	PLAN
Site area	495.80 m²	
Landscaping 15%	24.80 m²	32.40 m²
Full earth 2/3	16.53 m²	32.40 m²
Others 1/3	8.27 m²	– m²

SITE-C

	LOCAL CODE	PLAN
Site area	1,699.80 m²	
Landscaping 15%	255.00 m²	350.00 m²
Full earth 2/3	170.00 m²	233.33 m²
Others 1/3	85.00 m²	116.67 m²

SITE-D

	LOCAL CODE	PLAN
Site area	4,033.00 m²	
Landscaping 15%	604.90 m²	610.00 m²
Full earth 2/3	403.27 m²	406.70 m²
Others 1/3	201.63 m²	203.30 m²

SITE-I

	LOCAL CODE	PLAN
Site area	1,630.30 m²	
Landscaping 15%	244.60 m²	300.00 m²
Full earth 2/3	163.40 m²	164.00 m²
Others 1/3	81.20 m²	136.00 m²

SITE-J

	LOCAL CODE	PLAN
Site area	562.70 m²	
Landscaping 15%	84.40 m²	90.00 m²
Full earth 2/3	56.27 m²	60.00 m²
Others 1/3	28.13 m²	30.00 m²

PLANT CA

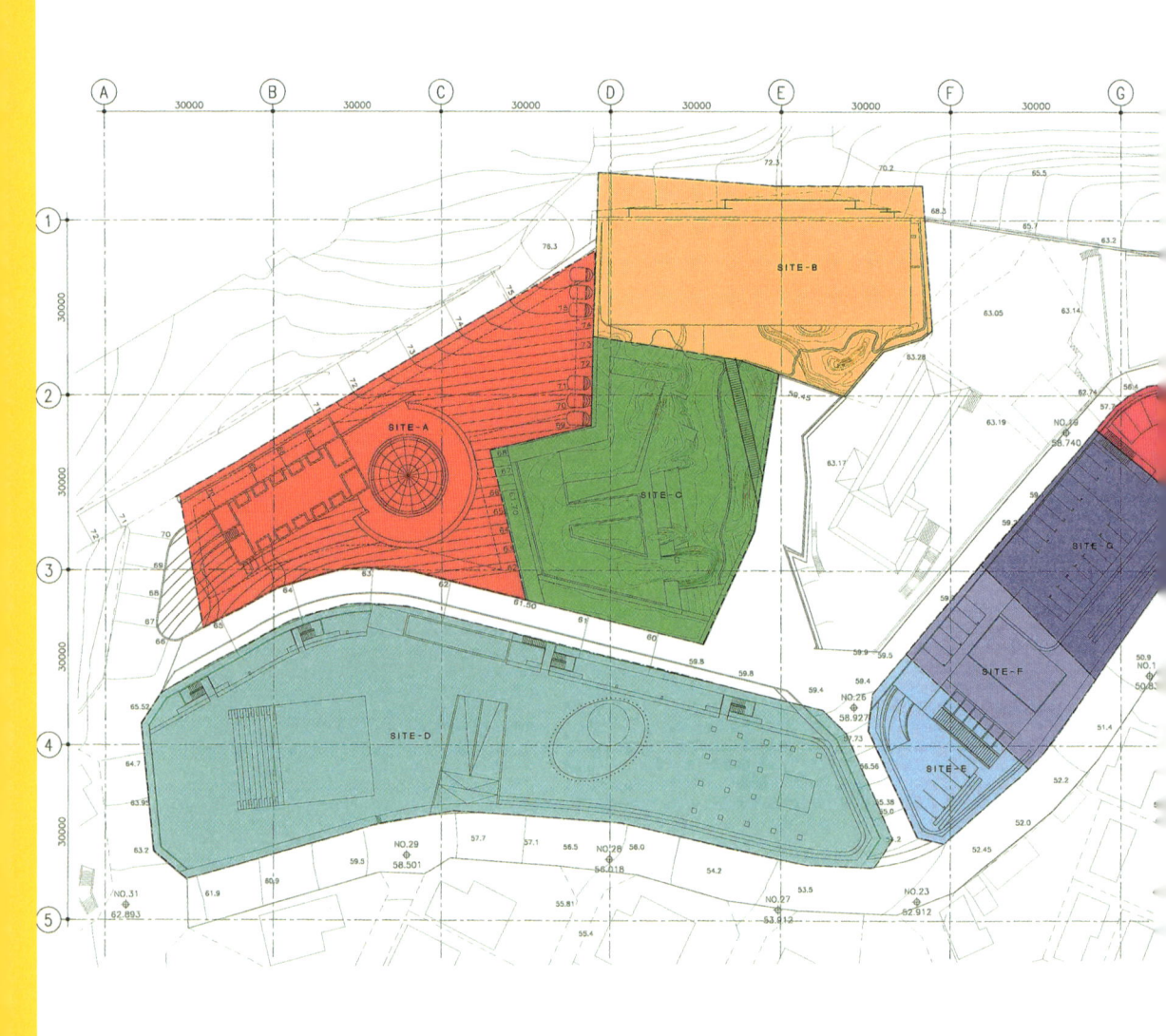

SITE-C

			PLAN
REGULATION		255m²	1550m²
0.2/ m² Trees		51	
30% Evergreen		16	26
70% Decidious		35	14
1.0/ m² Shrubs		255	
30% Evergreen		77	2913
70% Decidious		178	130

SITE-D

			PLAN
REGULATION		605m²	610m²
0.2/ m² Trees		121	
30% Evergreen		37	50
70% Decidious		84	10
1.0/ m² Shrubs		605	
30% Evergreen		183	1420
70% Decidious		427	X

CULATION

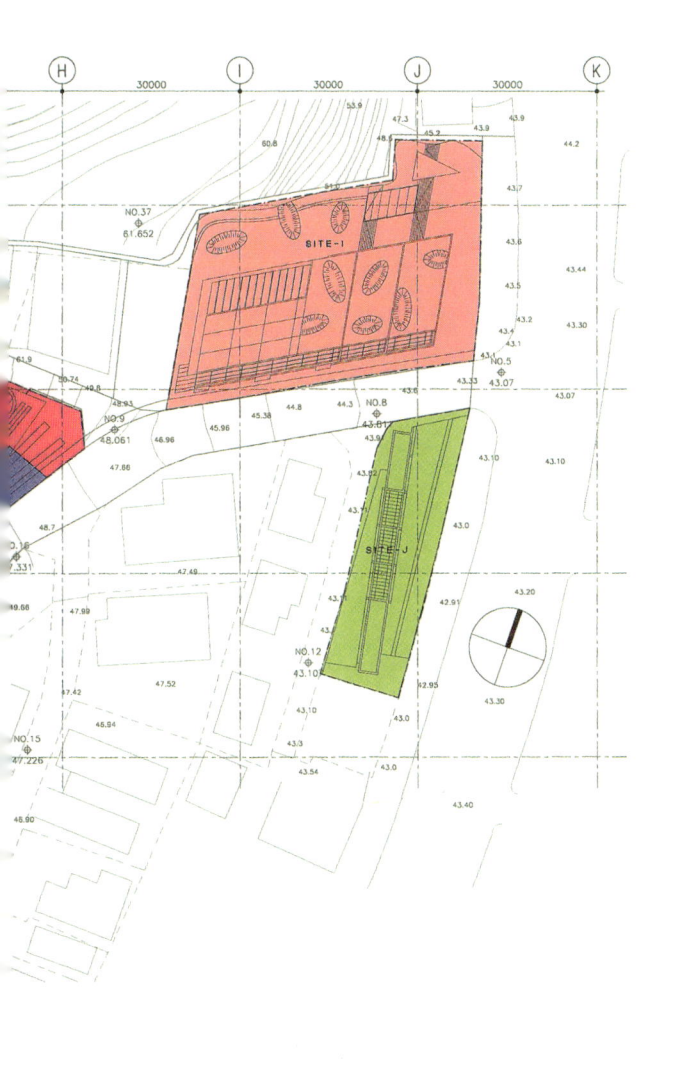

SITE-F

	REGULATION	27 m²	PLAN 178 m²
	0.2/ m² Trees	6	7
	30% Evergreen	2	3
	70% Decidious	4	4
	1.0/ m² Shrubs	27	
	30% Evergreen	8	195
	70% Decidious	19	16

SITE-G

	REGULATION	47 m²	PLAN 96 m²
	0.2/ m² Trees	9	7
	30% Evergreen	3	3
	70% Decidious	7	4
	1.0/ m² Shrubs	47	
	30% Evergreen	14	380
	70% Decidious	33	100

SITE-H

	REGULATION	25 m²	PLAN 32.0 m²
	0.2/ m² Trees	5	
	30% Evergreen	2	5
	70% Decidious	3	X
	1.0/ m² Shrubs	25	
	30% Evergreen	7.5	160
	70% Decidious	17.5	160

SITE-I

	REGULATION	245 m²	PLAN 300 m²
	0.2/ m² Trees	49	
	30% Evergreen	15	13
	70% Decidious	34	30
	1.0/ m² Shrubs	245	360
	30% Evergreen	74	108
	70% Decidious	171	252

SITE-E

	REGULATION	25 m²	PLAN 67.0 m²
	0.2/ m² Trees	6	
	30% Evergreen	2	X
	70% Decidious	4	3
	1.0/ m² Shrubs	25	
	30% Evergreen	7	490
	70% Decidious	18	X

SITE-J

	REGULATION	85 m²	PLAN 90 m²
	0.2/ m² Trees	17	17
	30% Evergreen	6	10
	70% Decidious	11	7
	1.0/ m² Shrubs	85	85
	30% Evergreen	26	272
	70% Decidious	59	X

PAVING PLAN

LIGHTING PLAN

WATER + FURNITURE PLAN

PLANTING PLAN - WEST

1997 model:
Looking up from the city road that passes the new area: through the 'gate' (lined by Farrell buildings), up the main road where all the buildings seem stacked: the embedded OMA structures, the 'Victorian' house of the chairman, the Nouvel museums and the Botta tower.

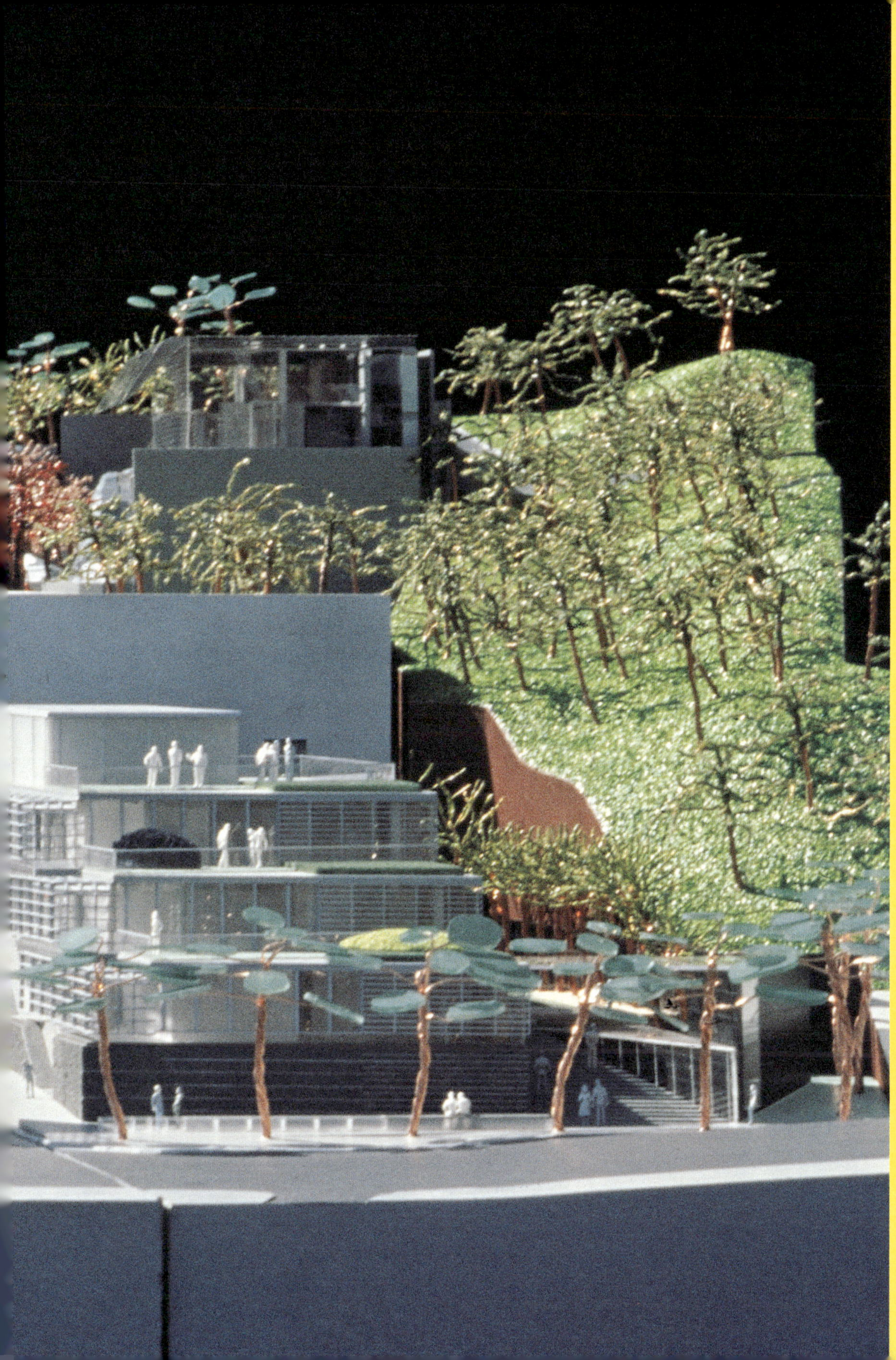

2005:
Standing in the middle of the site looking past the chairman's compound wall at buildings to the right by Jean Nouvel and Mario Botta, and to the left by OMA.

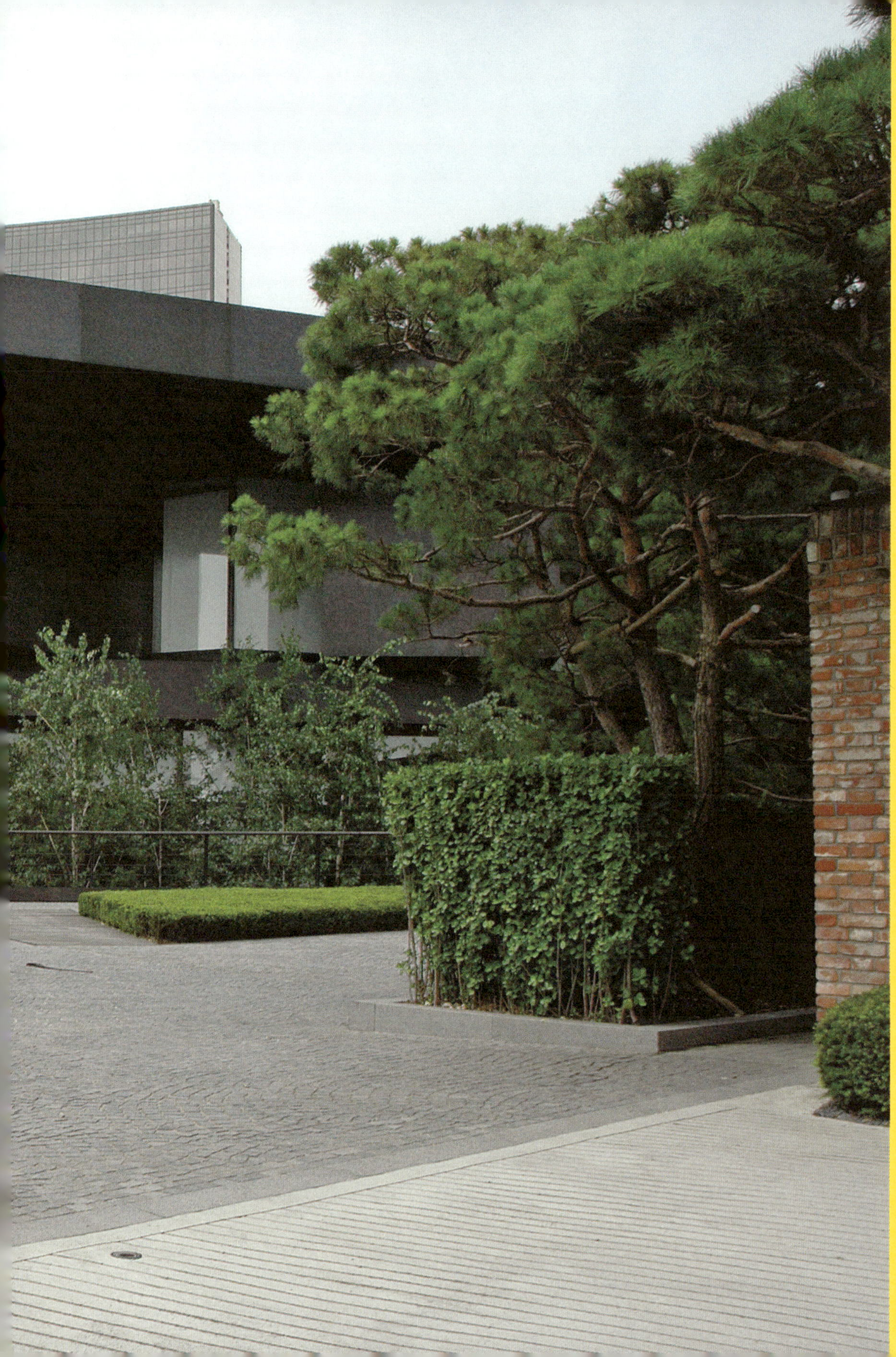

Silk Rock, Sunset

Light- and sound-regulating curtains
Lensvelt Furniture Headquarters, Breda, the Netherlands, 2000

Structures

This curtain solves both acoustic and light problems and has two faces. Velvet (flat) and silk (bulging) are connected by the top half of press studs. A tiny hole in the middle of each stud allows light to come through, creating the effect of a starry sky. With a looped track the curtain is turned around, changing the room's atmosphere in one fluid movement: three-dimensional silver or flat orange (you can choose which wall to cover). Sun-screening voile with bright green tulle hangs along the opposite wall.

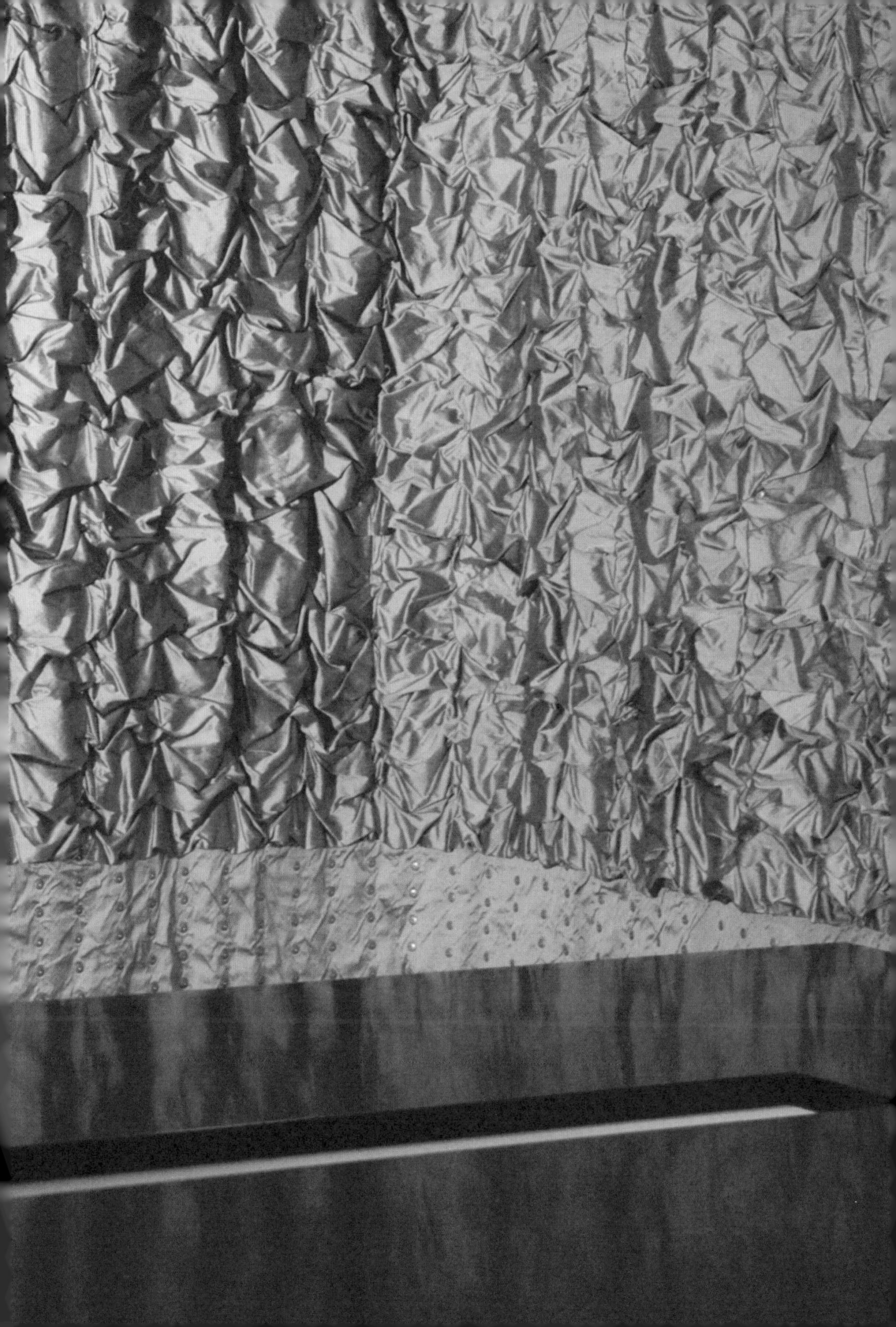

346

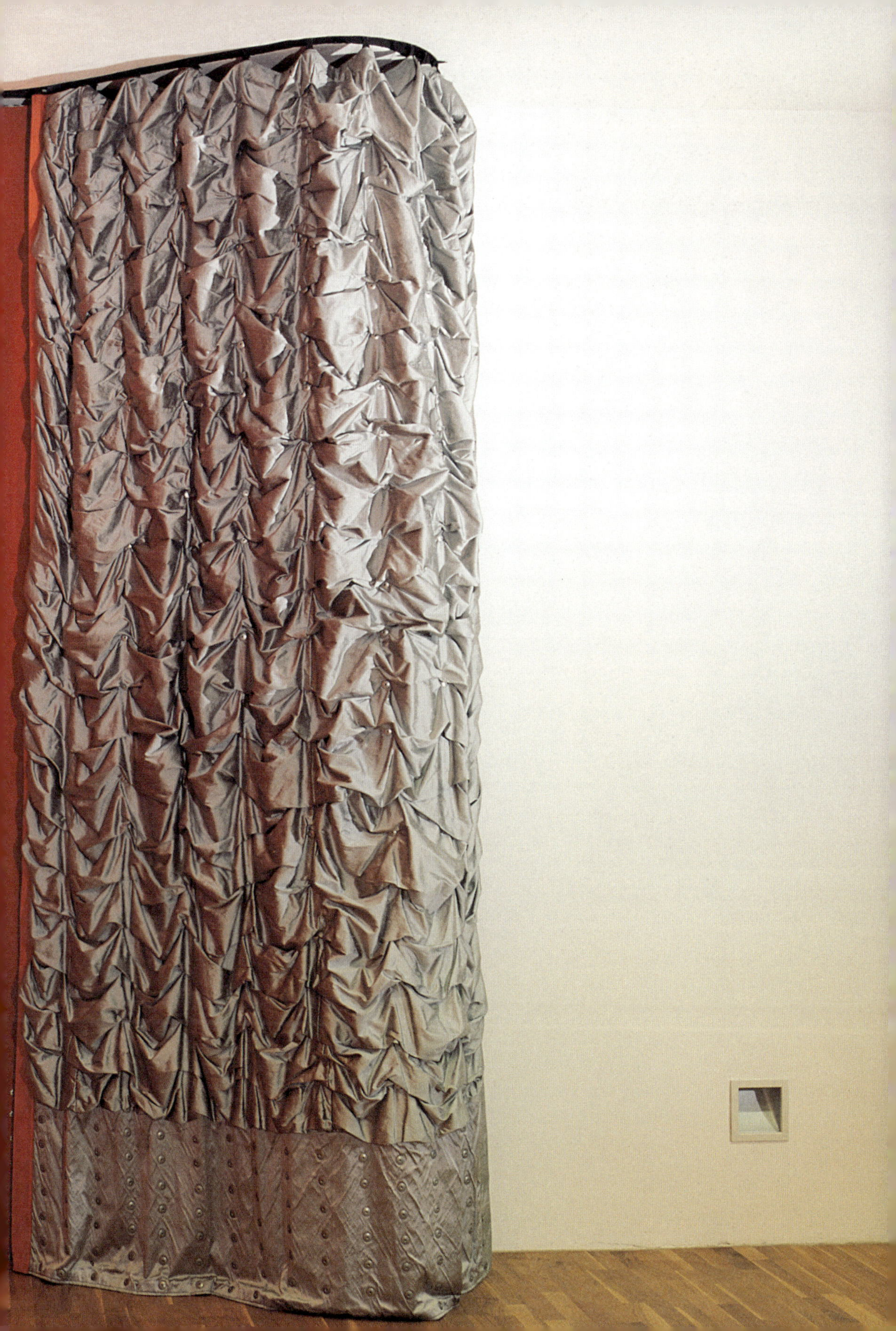

Garage Door

Light-regulating curtain
Lehmann Maupin Gallery, New York, USA, 2002–2003

This construction cloth darkens or closes off the gallery for video installations or when an exhibition is being installed. We liked to show the street number and later added the 'enter here' sign: the horizontal window notwithstanding, people tended to think the gallery was closed when the curtain was drawn.

RETAIL SPA
AVAILABL
212-334-46
THE MANHATTES GRO

540 WEST
26TH ST

... with and without window cover. As it turned out, the gallery needed to black out the space now and then, so we added a separate canvas lining to be clicked on if needed. The curtain disappears completely into a hollow side wall.

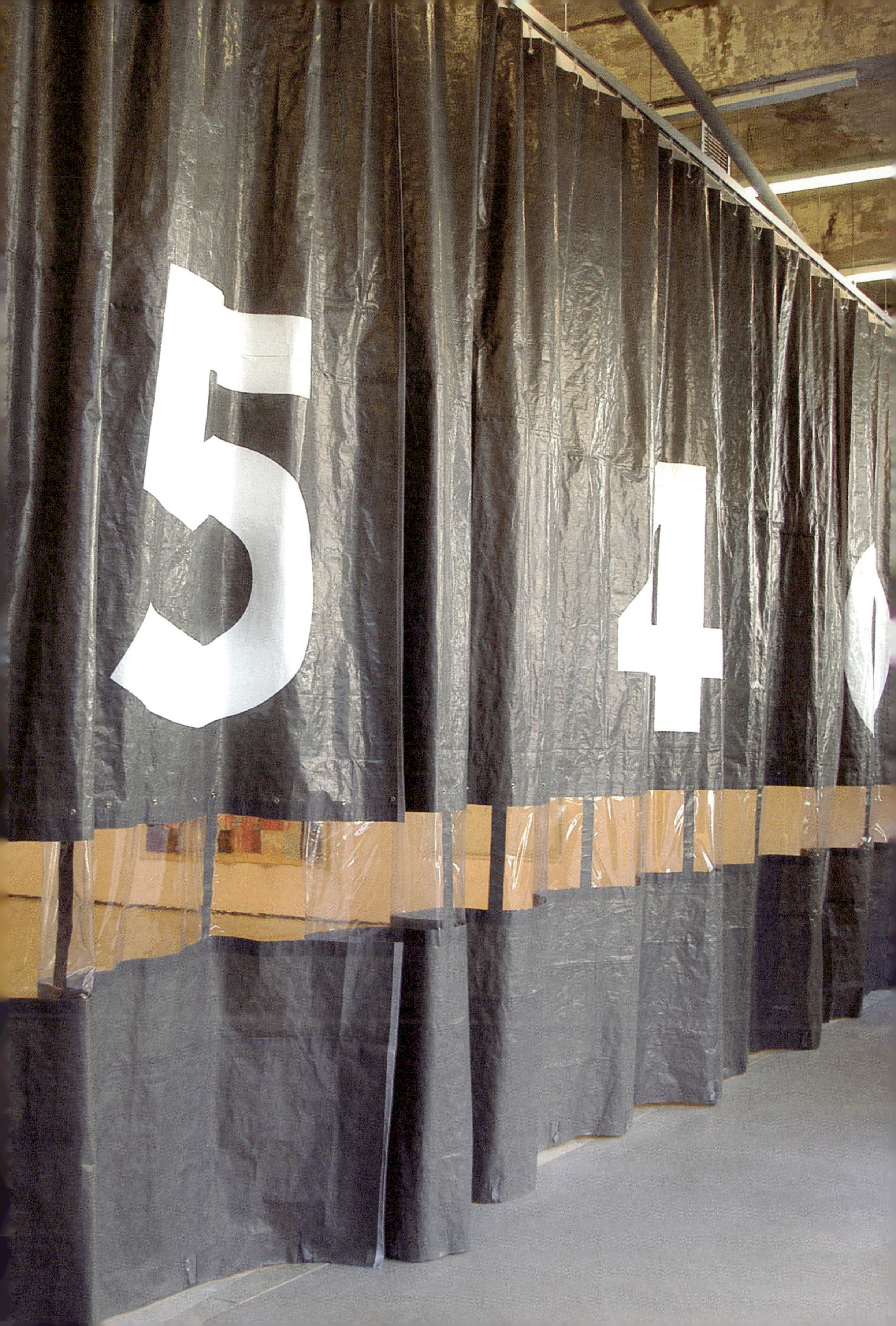
5
4

Collaboration with Inside Outside and Petra Blaisse
Bernd Baumeister

Through the Prada Epicenter, Toledo and especially Porto we have learnt to appreciate the work of Petra Blaisse and Inside Outside. We have rarely had the opportunity, in the past sixty years, to collaborate on such exceptional textile solutions.

In their projects, Inside Outside don't get stuck in design; with great professional skill and originality, they combine the most diverse materials and production methods. In doing so, their designs playfully resolve the frequent dilemma between aesthetic preference and technical necessities. Their designs are defined by the choice and mix of materials, the innovative production methods and the refinement of the detailing. For us, the unique challenge has been to physically translate – in dialogue with Inside Outside – the original designs in such a way that they appear to full advantage, in spite of the technical requirements, the often impressive dimensions and the conditions on site.

Each project is unique: For the Porto project, 14 curtains were planned, each a highly decorative object. Our task was to investigate, together with Inside Outside, the technical requirements such as acoustics, fire retardation levels and wear and tear; to find solutions for limited storage spaces; to realize particular forms of movement; and to convert the artistic designs. This succeeded most impressively with the Knotting Curtain in the large auditorium. Inside Outside first envisioned a knitted view filter made of torn strips of Trevira CS voile[1] that, due to the physical characteristics of the building, could only be folded upward to be stored inside the ceiling. They made a series of samples which were entrusted to us for approval and feasibility. It quickly became clear to us that the intended knitting technique would not be suitable for such a large curtain dimension (22 m x 15 m), also considering the mechanical stresses of raising and lowering a curtain of such weight and size. In several conversations between Inside Outside and our team, a new concept was developed.

Onto a stable net structure, 17 people knotted 6000 hours' worth of Trevira CS voile strips, on the exact instructions of Petra Blaisse that we respected throughout. The strips were torn rather than cut, each strip was equally long, the size of the knots was prescribed and the lines between the knots had to be of a certain length and looseness. Photos of our work were taken and emailed to Inside Outside on a regular basis so that they could give their comments efficiently.

What at first sight seemed overly prescriptive turned out to be necessary and important: it was this precision that generated the curtain's weightless appearance and liveliness.

The Prada project in Los Angeles was a challenge of a completely different nature. Inside Outside's design showed a VIP curtain made of white satin CS fabric[2] in two parts. The curtain was to fold like a plissé skirt, to underline its connection to the fashion house. Stainless steel mesh along the top edge and rectangular cut outs in the lower half of the curtain enlivened its appearance, and a sheet of clear plastic and long zippers to connect the layers provided additional production details. Apart from the effort to combine different materials with different characteristics into a single, functioning 'VIP curtain', the countless individual pleats were a major challenge. Inside Outside's design intent, meticulously described in their production recipe, allowed no variation in terms of pleat depth or distance between pleats. This made it extremely difficult to incorporate more than thirty cutouts and zippers into the curtain.

The solution was as obvious as it was time-consuming: Every single pleat had to be individually marked and sewn from top to bottom, folding 37 m of width into

1. Polyester voile, flame retardant.

2. White, shiny fabric of dense weave.

12.5 m of pleated surface. In the end, almost five hundred hours of work were invested into 37 m² of visible curtain. Whether Porto or Prada, each curtain that we were able to produce for Inside Outside posed considerable challenges to our workshops. But tasks such as these are the salt in the soup of our day-to-day business.

Our collaboration with Petra Blaisse and Inside Outside has taught us a great deal and we are already looking forward to the next highlights.

Umkirch, September 2005

Sound Sock

Knitted protection for sound installation
Prada Epicenter, New York, USA, 2001

We made special knitting tools, large scale and very dangerous looking, but we managed to get them through customs: it was December 2001 . . . after 9/11 . . . quite an emotional time for America. We had numerous rolls of silver voile delivered at the Gramercy from our supplier in Germany, and they didn't fit in the elevators. We got permission to unwind the cloth next to the X-mas tree in the hotel entrance lobby: huge masses of tranparent silver appeared next to people checking in. We managed to get the mass upstairs and started knitting in circles, the first few rows on each other's lap, then knitting apart as we went on.

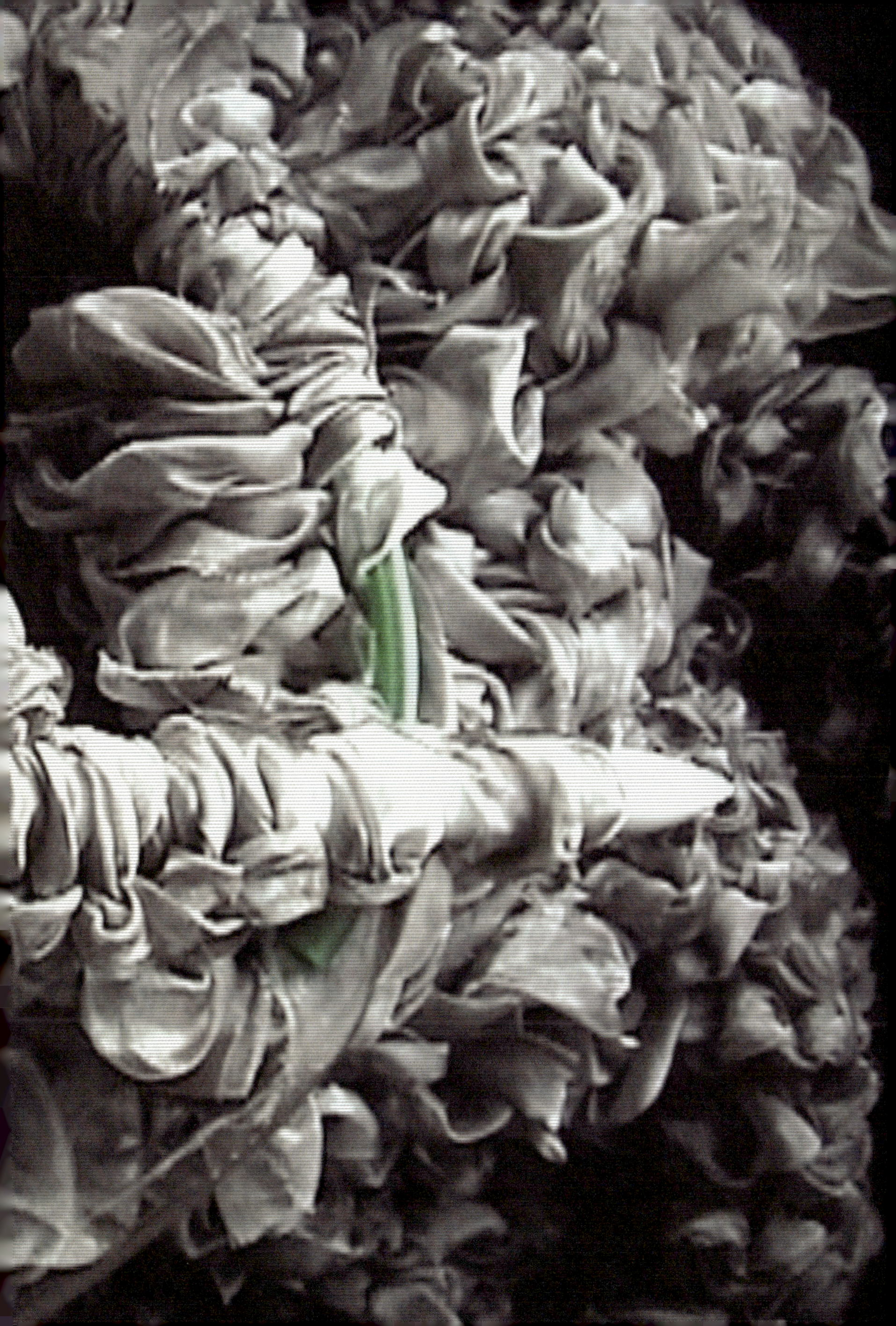

The stretched metal cupboards and the sound sock, hanging from large parallel tracks, can be digitally steered. At night, all elements collect to form a closed unity, safeguarding the collection from theft after closing time.

Pregnant sock moves to other position . . .

Surprise encounters…

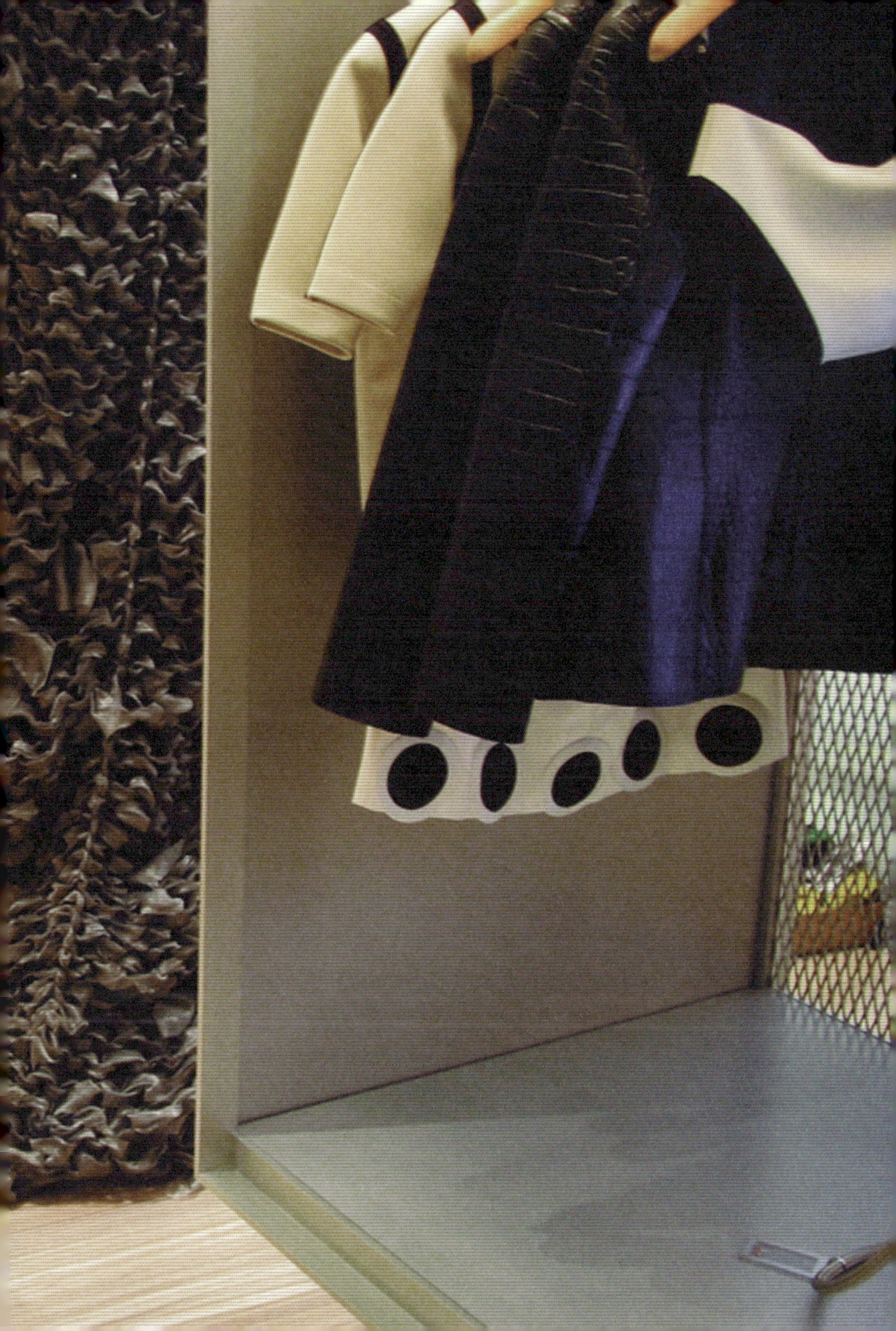

Whipped Cream

Space- and sound-regulating curtains
Prada Epicenter, New York, USA, 2003–2004

This is how you come in the service (and VIP) entrance from Mercer Street and are received by the receptionist halfway below ground. And what do you see?? The plastic lining is torn! Who can bring me a ladder? I have to fix it right here and now . . .

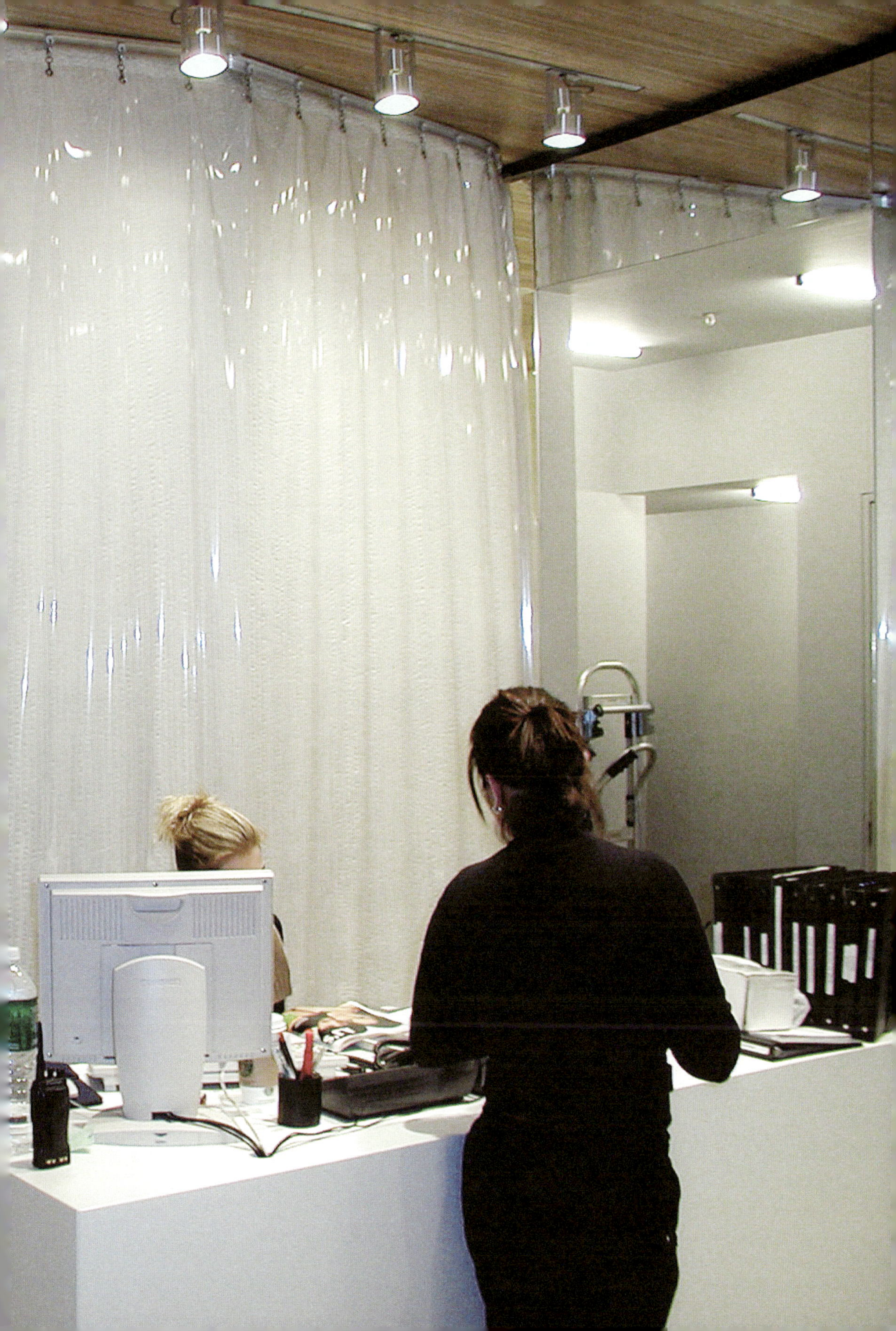

Video still of plissé being sewn in The Bronx . . . heaps of whipped cream.

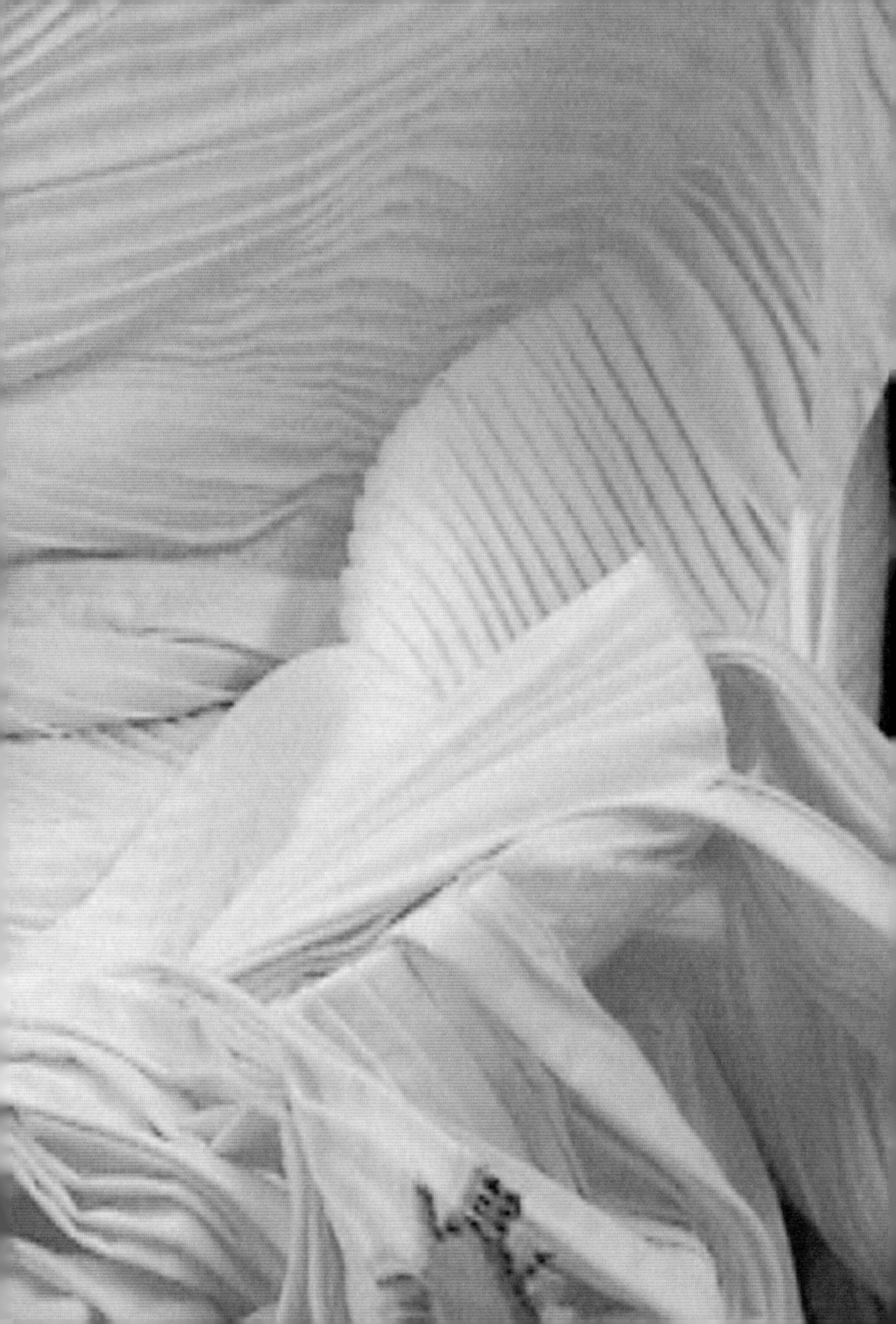

Curtain as Architecture

Casa da Música, Porto, Portugal 1999–2005
Sound-, view- and light-regulating curtains

Everyone compares the Casa da Música to a stranded body from outer space that has landed in the middle of the old city of Porto out of nowhere. It is true that every time you see people climb the large steps up to the building, you expect the stairs to fold back and 'it' to take off.

In fact, a very low slit invites you into a cathedral: an immense volume, weightless, built entirely of white concrete; its high walls, openings, the columns that fly through space, the way sound is reflected and light filters in: it is almost a religious experience. You breathe in, you're lifted up beyond gravity. You climb the countless steps and everywhere you turn you arrive in different rooms, areas, shapes with spectacular views outward, intriguing views into some other interior space, urging you on and on, up and down, steering you in inexplicable directions until you arrive somewhere – anywhere – it doesn't really matter. You want to be there.

From Storage Clump to Concert Hall

OMA suggests that the concept for the Casa derived from a private house (a massive storage clump out of which living areas were excavated) and was enlarged to the scale of a concert hall, but I never liked that story very much, as it seems very unlike OMA to make life so simple... But whatever the true evolution of this project, from the first Casa model until the building's opening, six years later, Inside Outside worked as advisor for atmospheres, materials and landscape, and as curtain designer. Roles we have played in many projects since OMA opened its office in Rotterdam in the early eighties.

Here, our exchanges eventually led to the colours and materials of the public spaces and the soft-coloured, folded travertine plaza in which the white, rock-shaped building lies embedded. No green allowed on that plaza, only curves that hide cafés, bus stops and intimate seats; all attention focused on the beautiful circular garden of the Rotunda da Boavista in front and its monumental sculpture[1] that shows a lion conquering an eagle – representing the victory of the Portuguese Patriotists over Napoleon's army in the Peninsular War (1808-1814).

Curtain as Façade

When the building was still a model and a stack of drawings, I could only understand its spatial implications by imagining an apple from which the skin was cut with flat strokes of a knife and then punctured by the same knife to take out the core. Piece after piece was then taken out, and those cavities became the public spaces and the small concert hall, all looking out over the city and, inside, connecting to the long tunnel that forms the large concert hall.

[1]. The sculpture dates from 1909 (start)-1951 (inauguration) and was made by sculptor Alves da Sousa and architect Marques da Silva.

When do you *ever* see curtains in a concert hall? Here, because both concert halls and all public spaces were 'excavated from a massive volume' and both auditoriums are dominated by huge windows, allowing a sea of daylight in from two directions! Daylight in a concert hall, music in the sun and singers in the shade of a trombone... it is unheard of.

So curtains were part of the plan from the very beginning of the project, although the true range of their technical performance was still unclear and would only develop during the process. But one thing *was* clear: windows *that* size need something, if only to soothe the client about this revolution: ... concert halls with a view.

Construction Site

During construction, the Casa da Música already felt special. It seemed somehow perfect from the first pour; down in the pit, its first idle columns stood reaching out to the sky, white and elegant as robes; countless thin, swaying steel rods shooting in all directions like fireworks. At night, construction lamps cast trillions of shadows, sliding in formations from left to right with the wind. Like seaweed washing in the waves.

Close to the hole, a medieval-looking wooden shack stood squeaking in the winter cold. Inside, barely lit but warm, booted workmen with dark and light skins, heavy eyebrows and very blue eyes ate their lunch at long wooden tables. Breathing out the smell of fish and garlic and listening to melancholy music, they prepared for the next shift: moulding and pouring, filling, fencing, scraping and weaving, folding, sawing, welding, cutting, measuring, aligning; carrying enormous bundles of rods, planks, cables, pipes, packs and tools on shoulders, climbing up and down scaffoldings, balancing on planks bridging puddles and air – apparitions of men at work in the windy wet misty cold that clouds in from the sea.

The Concert Halls

From the beginning, OMA wanted to make the two concert halls into rectangular 'shoeboxes': the large concert hall (Sala 1) with its aluminium floors and stage, rows of connected chairs as one continuous plane, as if the floor folds up and down, and a wooden 'cover' forming walls and ceiling; and the small concert hall (Sala 2), with a dark floor and loose chairs that can be taken out completely leaving an empty space, and an equal wooden 'cover' forming walls and ceiling. Both 'boxes' were imagined as surfaces of rectangular wooden plates into which all additional needs would be integrated: sound, air and light; curtain storage and machinery. Everything more or less invisibly built in, solved within that one folded plane.

Structures and Veils

At first the idea of curtains was purely a visual game in the architect's models and representations: textile scraps were inserted as placeholders, very decorative elements with large birds and flowers – a counterpoint to

Plans and sections of concert halls and, in red, the
positions of all the curtains designed by Inside Outside.
(Underground rehearsal rooms are not shown here.)

Sala 1
Layer 1a (white)
view filter

Sala 1
Layer 2a (black)
blackout and acoustic curtain

Sala 1
Layer 3a (white)
sun-reflective voiles

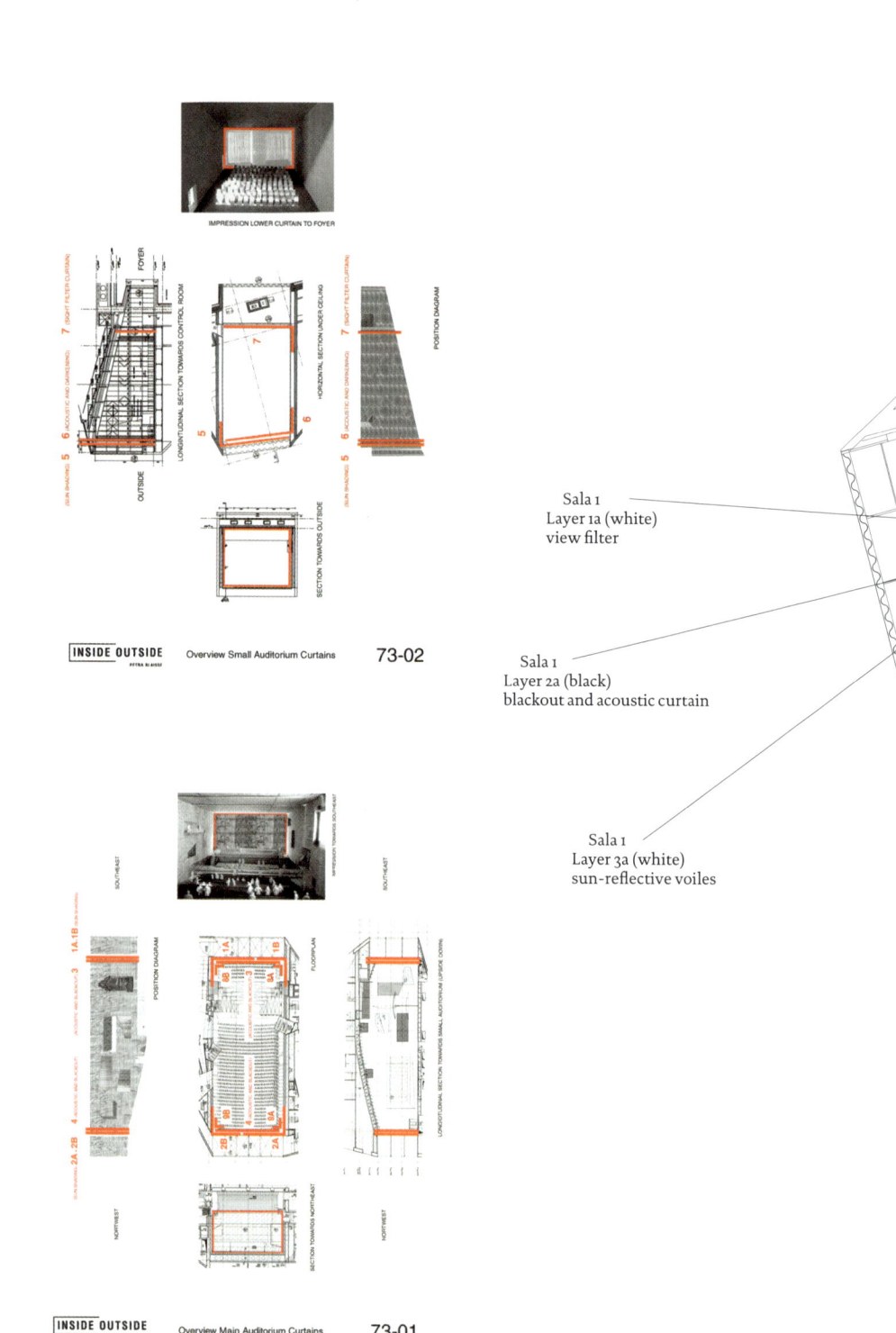

Plan showing the two main concert hall being 'punctured' by public spaces.

Sala 1
Layer 3b (black)
sun-reflective voiles

Sala 1
Layer 1b (black)
view filter

Sala 1
Layer 2b (white)
blackout and acoustic curtain

Sala 2
Layer 3 (white) view-filtering curtain

Sala 2
Layer 1 (grey)
darkening and acoustic curtain

Sala 2
Layer 2 (black)
sun-reflective and shading curtain

the clean, sculptural form of the white concrete building. We soon forgot about decorations and colours and began to interpret the curtains as walls, façades, integral parts of the architecture, structures that complete a room.

As the public rooms became more and more colourful and decorated – to radiate colour into their surroundings, to implement local culture and to imply their use – we realized that all curtains should be colourless, more restrained objects. Spatial effects would only be triggered through structure and scale, with light, weight and movement.

As the requirements and expectations of the curtains changed, we did tests for each room and each function; from one material to another; from whites to blacks, thin and thick, rigid and fluid. This process was useful because, by going through these many tryouts, the entire team learnt that even the smallest shift in position, scale, material or structure has a considerable impact on the performance and potential of a room. It is always a delicate balance: solving too many issues with textile – making them too present – could work against the stark, structural character of the building.

In the end, we made six separate curtains for the large concert hall – three layers on each side – measuring between 13 and 15 m in height and 22 m in width; three curtains for the small auditorium – measuring between 12 and 7 m high by 17 m wide; and two curtains for the rehearsal studios below ground, measuring up to 8 m high by 65 m wide.

Some of these layers hardly claim any space and disappear as quietly as they come. Others, however, have a three-dimensional rhythmic structure and take up space as much as they *are* space in themselves; walls of varying degrees of transparency and mass that fold upwards into ceilings or sideways into hollow walls. Each of them adds to the acoustic and atmospheric definition of the rooms, together with sound-reflecting and absorbing surfaces, orchestra pit and public – with all planes, forms and volumes, hard and soft, porous and massive.

SALA I

Surface

Maarten van Severen († 2005) designed the chairs in strict rows of silver, like ripples in the sea. Each rigid, transparent armrest holds a little LED lamp for reading during performances.[2] First, the chairs were to be upholstered in perforated silver plastics and leathers, but as these materials didn't react well acoustically and were too vulnerable, they were replaced with light grey mohair velvet.

We thought: here is a concert hall with a scale that emanates strength and with a sobriety that radiates integrity. Its sheer uninterrupted volume and the enormous size of each plane make the space impressive. A few elements enrich the interior: the coloured glass of the balcony windows; the organs on both sides of the stage; the transparent acoustic canopy, like a modern chandelier above the orchestra; the massive pleated windows – light green –

2. Like plankton that light up the waves on a summer night

in front and behind; the large floor plane of aluminium and silver velvet; the colourless curtains that filter light and project shadows; and the views of the ochre red city, blue sky, green treetops and bronze sculpture.

Yet something was still missing, something to add scale to the wooden, monochrome walls and link everything together. Something festive, a symbol of cultural wealth, a warm glow to embellish the visitors' complexions and intensify the colours of their clothes…

Gold then, and not mathematically placed squares or rectangles but voluptuous, large-scale, rounded forms like naked angels on old paintings, like trumpets and tuba's, like the hairdos of opera singers.

We suggested imprinting the entire wooden shoebox with an enlarged version of the wood's own grain: a shimmering layer of organic shapes, flames of gold, that reflect the light.[3]

Hanging Walls and Reflective Veils
(2x) 22 x 15 or 13 m of façade

The large auditorium has three types of curtains: sun-screening, blackout/acoustic and view-filtering.

Directly aligning with the glass façades on both sides of the hall, light and transparent grey voiles with large, white, weighed-down seams screen the glare and reflect the sun. Fluorescent slits point the way to security doors. They disappear into the hollow wooden side walls.

The two blackout curtains – one behind the orchestra and the other behind the audience's seats – had to be heavy and porous, so that they could also absorb sound. Positioned a few metres away from the glass façades, they fold out from the ceiling: a lid folds open, out the curtain comes, and 'hop!' the lid closes again without a sound. I had never imagined that folding and unfolding movements could be so like tai-chi: in perfect harmony and very sloooow.

These blackout curtains are made out of two connected layers. One of the two layers (looking inward) is made of thick wool to secure the right acoustic absorbance. The second layer (facing out) is made of a dense, coated cloth to block out the smallest bit of daylight from the room.

Behind the public seating area the same build-up is applied. The acoustically absorbent layers (looking inward) are made of bleached wool behind the orchestra – acting as a projection screen for light and moving images; and of matte black wool behind the audience, fulfilling the opposite role of the projection screen – absorbing light, creating a large black hole.

As both of the backsides of these blackout drapes would be visible from the city and from the foyer spaces (pressed between the two corrugated glass layers on both sides of the large concert hall), we had many discussions as to what additional role these large surfaces could have: they could provide indirect light or digital information to the foyers; they could be large paintings addressing the city – sea battle paintings of old masters, Gobelin tapestries

---

3.
Like so many ideas that pass by between OMA and their advisors (we are one of many satellites that invest specific know-how into their projects at their invitation), this idea would have remained an idea if it would not have been taken up by Koolhaas and his team. Sure, Inside Outside made a start by sketching wood-grain patterns and suggesting the scale and materialization of these forms, but it was thanks to OMA's true-to-size samples, their PhotoShop interpretations and their conviction to show it again and again in presentations to the client, and then finding the right people to realize this idea that it survived all phases and became real. In the process, the golden wood-grain form was 'digitized' on the architect's request, meaning that its rounded forms are built up of small squares instead of fluid lines. Architectural language managed its way into this *one* organic form; the only voluptuous decoration in the building! Actually, the digitizing made me think of censored porn: sexual organs as blobs of beige, pink, white and black.

Voluptuous stone landscape.

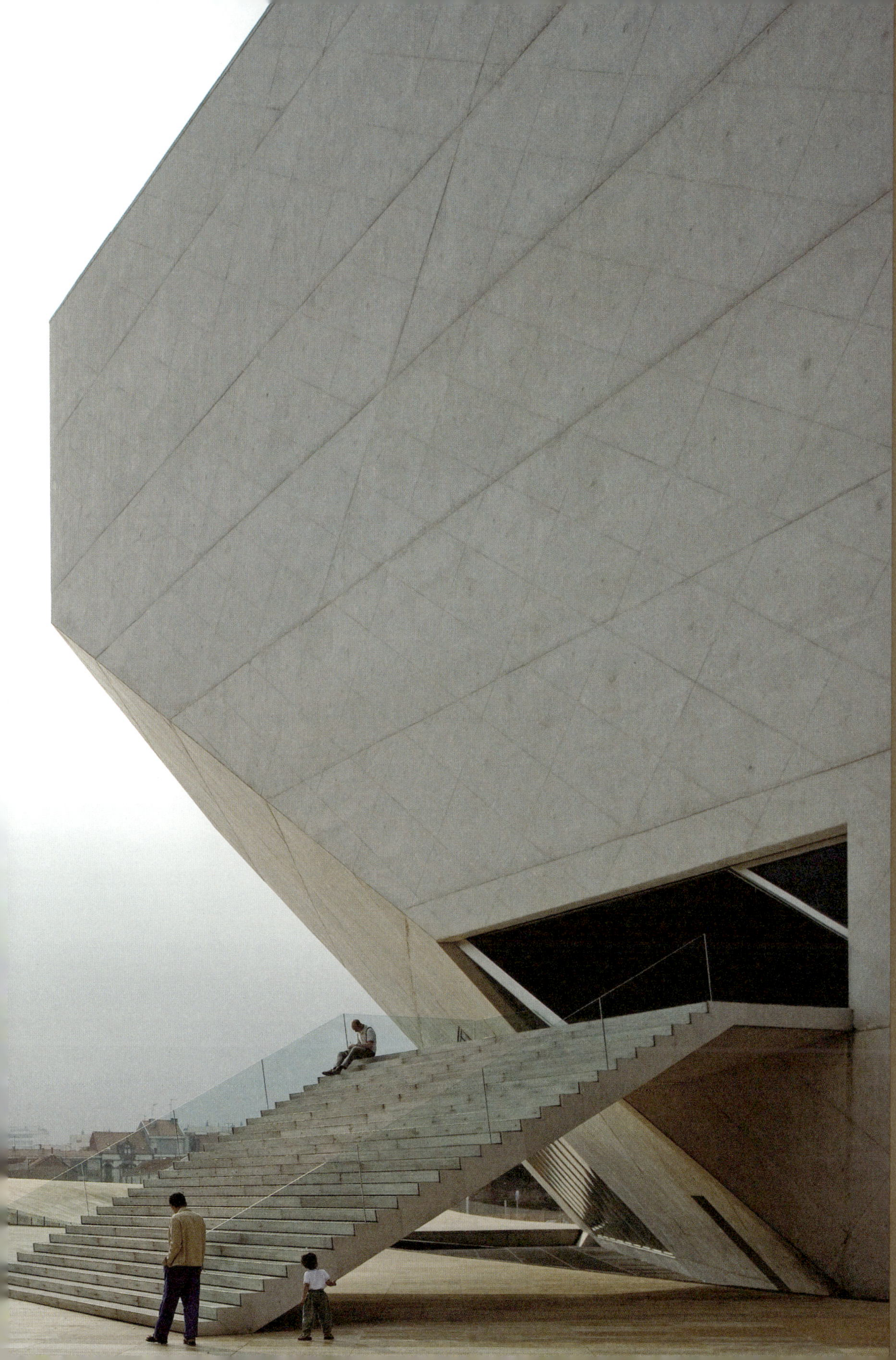

Sala 1 – view filter 1b and blackout curtain 2b
Large concert hall naked – but for the golden fleece.

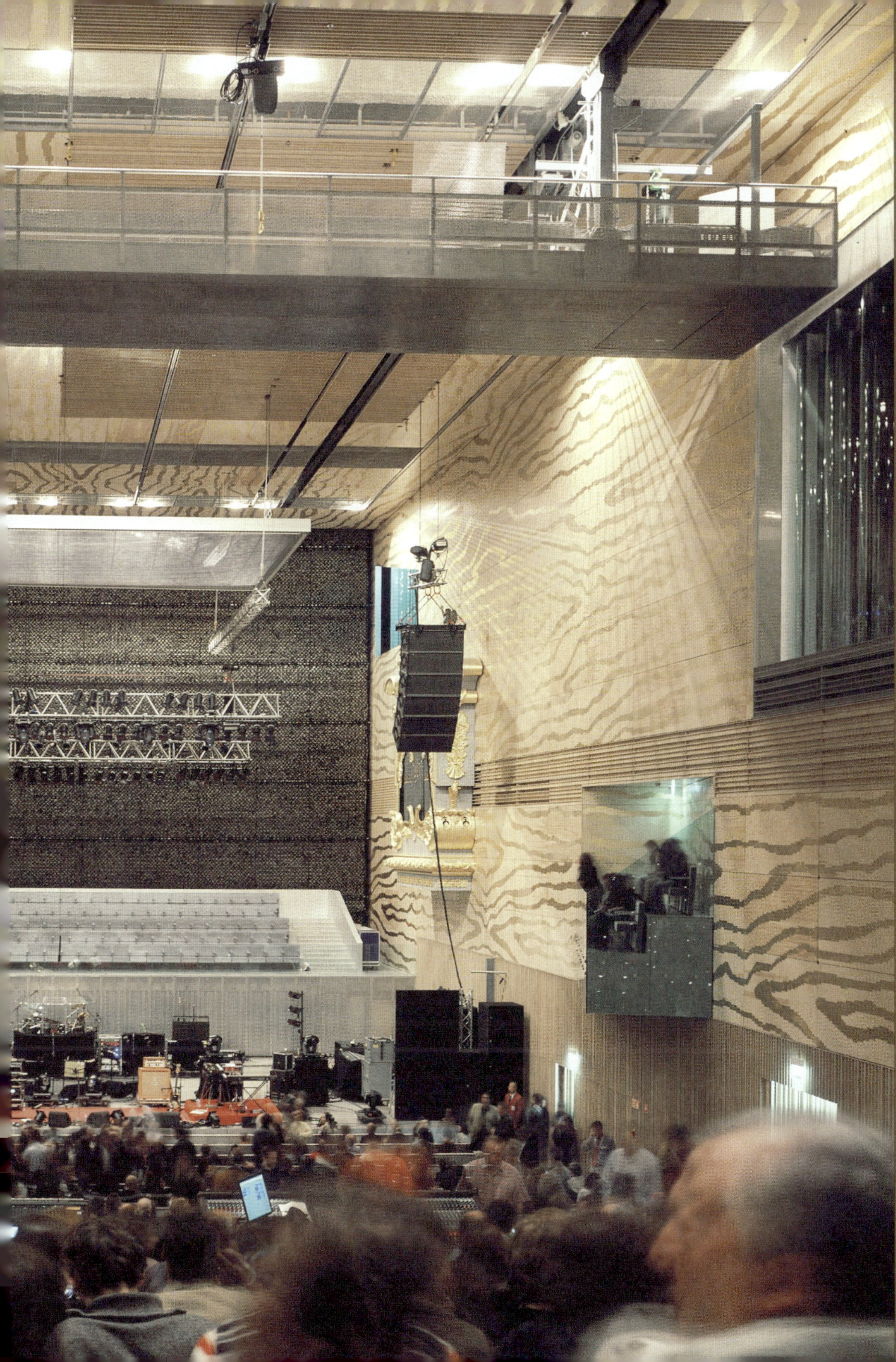

representing nature, scientific drawings of medusas or shellfish (the sea is near!). Hard to make a convincing choice here, until someone suggested using Inside Outside's construction drawings of the actual knotted curtains inside…

We enlarged our drawings fourfold and digitally printed the blackout cloth for each side of the hall, using a different working drawing for each side in different shades of greys and whites.

Open Structures
(2x) 22 x 15 or 13 m of façade

In addition, Rem Koolhaas wanted a 'view filter' on each side of the hall. The term 'view filter' felt totally obvious yet also very vague: a view filter to what degree, with what purpose? To filter out, to tone down, spread light, obscure, fade, blur what is visible behind it? Or to envelope the room, create an aesthetic backdrop for the orchestra, allowing the gaze to sense the outside, to see sky, trees, sculpture and city?

Since this curtain was meant to be used randomly, it was not allowed to have any acoustic effect on the space. To realize this 'acoustic non-existence', we needed a weightless and open structure: a giant piece of lace. Since almost everything has an acoustic effect, we needed to do many tests and calculations in order to arrive at the right answer for a concept that was inspired by the lace voiles that Portuguese women wear over their hair in church: black for married, white for unmarried women; which we enlarged and simplified.

I thought of the many churches I saw when we lived in Portugal and Austria when I was a child. I remember my mother and other women covering their hair with white or black lace before entering church with those special expressions that only mass brings about: alternating between serenity, grief, concentration, boredom, dozing off until the singing brings everyone back to life. Large or small, all churches then were sober structures in themselves – except for the Stephan's Dome in Vienna – but filled with choir and organ music, littered with gold leaf or the gold thread appearing on the priest's robes, the objects on the altar, the domes and fresco's and paintings of Christ and Jesus and the apostles, sculptures of terror-struck male, female and animal figures with Mary in light blue and white robes, her veiled head surrounded by a golden halo, innocently in their midst. The stained windows spread patches of coloured light through the space, gliding over all objects in the course of mass. We were not allowed to have breakfast on Sundays and mass seemed endless, so we looked around while the Latin rhymes and flows filled our ears and soothed our minds. Communion was a welcome distraction, and the host welcome food that we glued to our palate and sucked on at length.

To achieve the lacelike effect that we wanted for the view filters, we used the technique Inside Outside had developed for the Prada store in New York: knitting bands of very thin material (zero acoustic effect) into a complex but very open structure. In our studio, we did knitting test after knitting test, trying to achieve the right recipe and scale … each test more beautiful than the other.

Sala 1 – view filter 1a
The blackout goes down;
the view filter follows.

Sala 1 – blackout curtain 2a
The end of the day... time to open up.

scale of actual cu al curtain

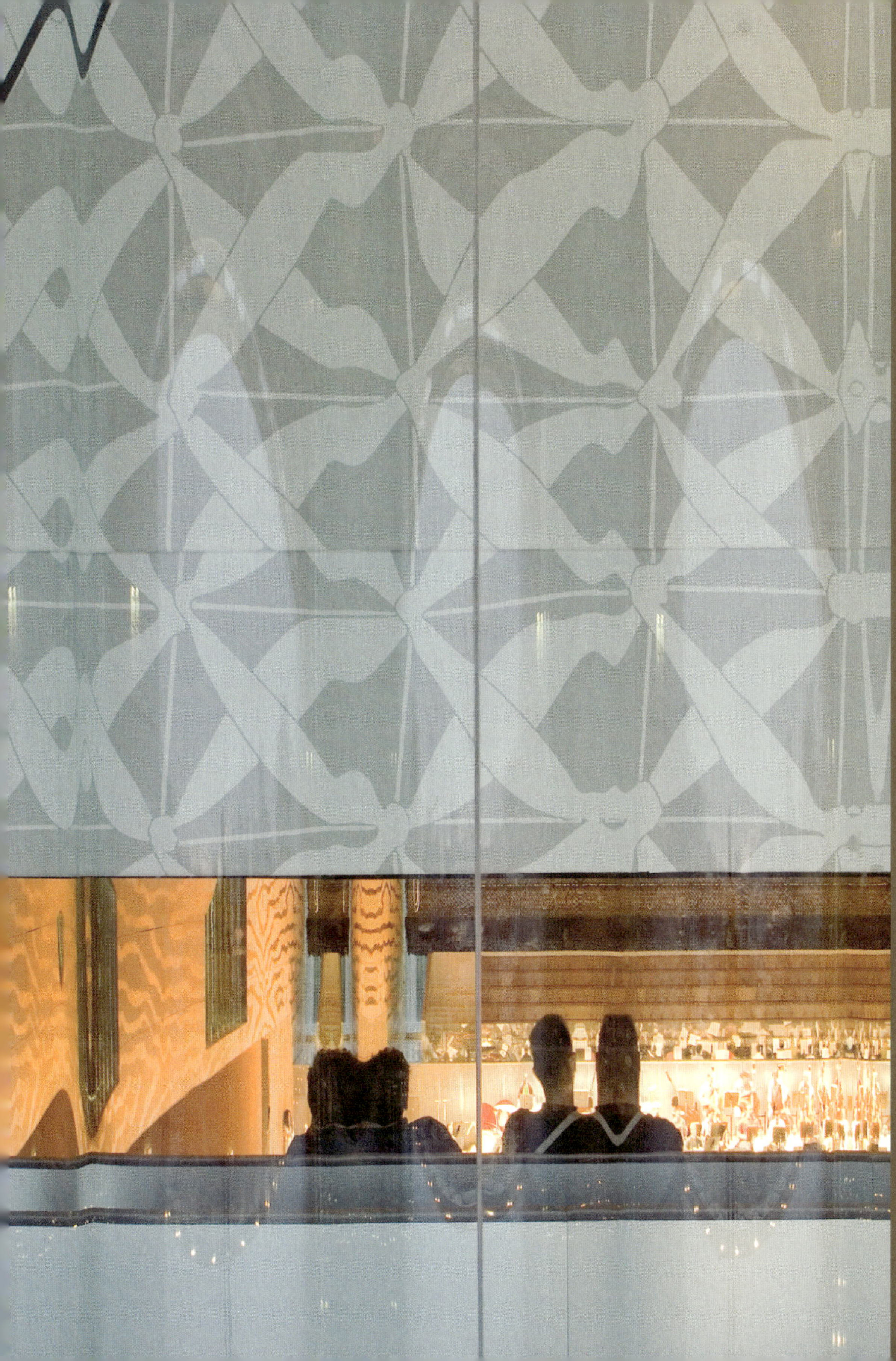

We used a very thin and transparent voile; in itself an insipid cloth that through manipulation acquires a totally different character. But it became clear that, however ingenious the loop and knot combinations we tried were, knitting would never be stable enough at the anticipated scale. We needed a skeleton, flexible enough to move with the curtain and fold in and out of the ceiling. We found strong, large-scale fishing nets – plunging into the Dutch fishing industry, which was surprisingly interesting – and then crocheted bands of voile into them with our hands, moving from 'knit' to 'knot'.

We drew recipes and made one-to-one (1:1) samples of the knots. The cloth had to be knotted loosely yet not too much so; and the pieces of cloth that appear at each end of its width – little rectangular flags where your tear stops and you turn to start tearing in the opposite direction – had to be pulled to one side of the curtain, creating an extra three-dimensionality.

Gerriets GmbH from Germany eventually got the commission for the production of the curtains and they worked with us to refine technique and materials. They hired seventeen people in Germany and France – mostly women – to tear the white and black voile cloth into bands of 10 cm width, zigzagging their way through an entire bale and then knotting these endlessly long bands into the netting; all materials fire proof of course. Side by side, these women worked their way through six white and seven black bands of 22 x 2.5 m, knot by knot and often reknotting areas if they were too loose, too stretched or too different from the adjacent knotted areas. It took them 700 hours.

Since no two people knot the same, the whole thing had to be meticulously orchestrated. We asked Gerriets to mail us photographs of the process at regular intervals, so that we could follow the knotting from afar and react to 'impurities' if necessary. Quite a military operation!

The two view-filtering curtains – one white and one black, each appearing out of the ceiling at the outer ends of the concert hall – were composed of seven or eight knotted bands of 22 x 2.5 m. Each band was slid into an aluminium profile – two bands fit into each profile – to create one knotted plane of 22 x 15 or 13 m. Each aluminium profile, horizontally aligned, has thin steel cables attached in a vertical direction, connecting the lowest beam to each following beam and to the motor hidden inside the roof; allowing the curtain to fold up and down evenly. Eight-hundred and fifty linear metres of voile, 300 centimeters wide, was used for these two curtains: 2,550 square metres of cloth to produce 616 square metres of knotted surface.

Weight, Sound and Storage Effect

In each curtain project, we have regular discussions with the architects to review storage and motor spaces and to ensure that they are included in the construction drawings. The same goes for structural adjustments: we provide the engineers with the necessary information to make sure that ceilings can carry the curtain's load. A curtain can occupy from 2 to 100 m^2 of architectural space in storage and can weigh up to 500 or more kilos.

Sala 1 – view filter 1b
The lowest band folds over following
band as the curtain folds up.

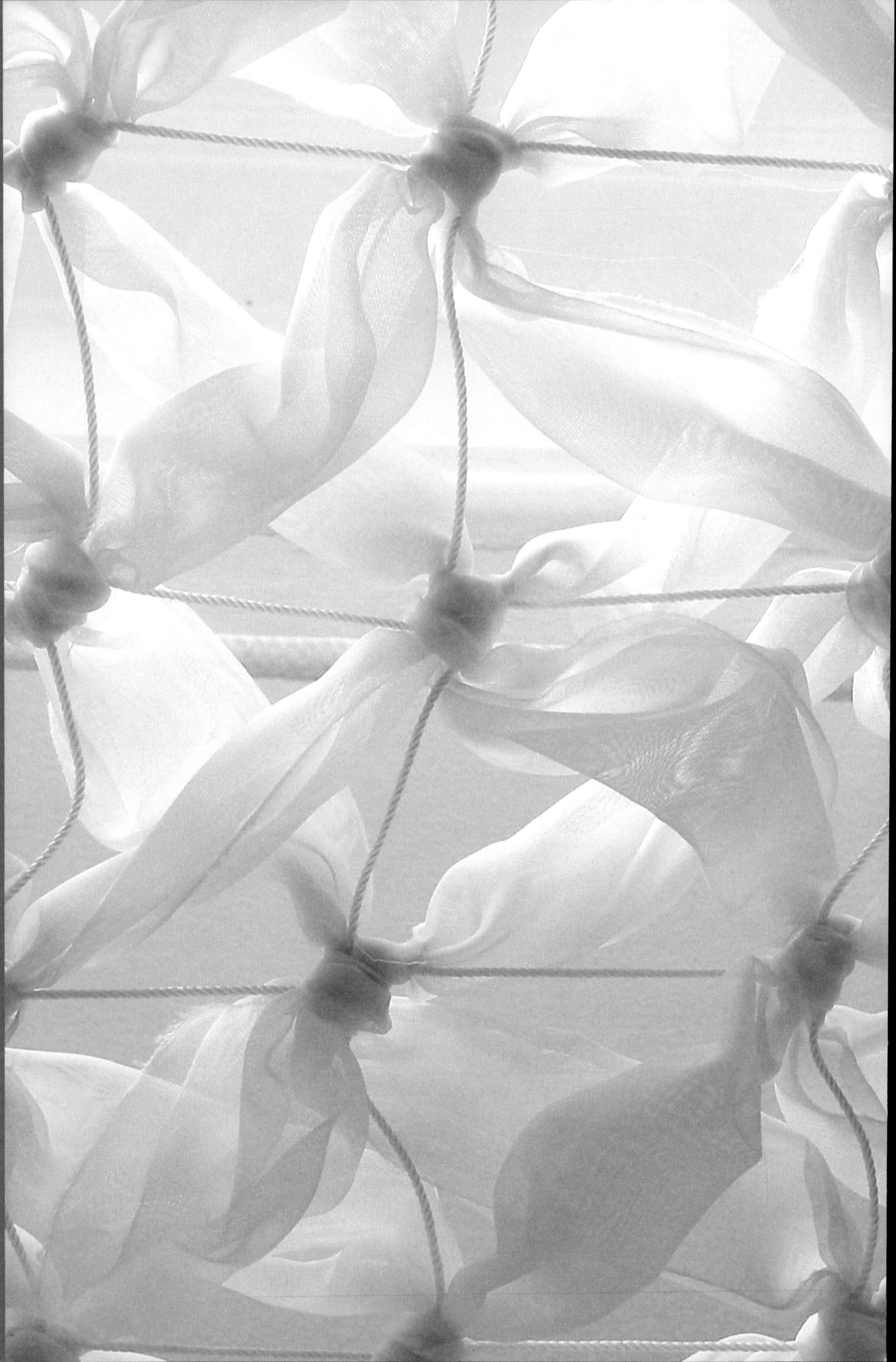

Motors can be large, heavy and noisy; but also tiny and flexible, running along with the curtains within the tracks. Checking structural drawings and exchanging information up to the very last stage is essential.

In the end, slim doors that measure up to 15 m in height open up automatically and allow curtains to slide in and out of hollow walls effortlessly and elegantly, closing without a sound. Shifting panels in the large auditorium's ceiling allow four textile structures of 22 m width to fold down or up independently, evenly and without obstruction, leaving no trace when shut. Tracks are recessed and motors[4] are hidden and silenced behind folding or turning lids: all beautifully detailed by the architects and stage engineers.

Curtain Scrutiny

Every curtain idea we develop has to be aesthetically accepted by the architects, measured and reviewed by the acoustic engineer, then technically reviewed by the architects, users, contractors, theatre engineers and production people. The objects have to answer to acoustic, weight, volume, fire, wear and tear, financial and technical demands and have to be detailed in a way that is workable and feasible within a given schedule. Very often the review meetings unleash more questions than answers, which is always good and sometimes painful. The ultimate test follows later: the local fire brigade tests the curtains on site and either accepts them or not; and if not, well...

Tender Process

Design is a negotiation and does not come with a guarantee; not to you and not to the parties that you involve in the process. You 'massage' companies into studying technical solutions or possibilities with you, do tests and calculate budgets in a much earlier stage; lots of diplomacy required. And you have to invest all the time, as there is no way a client will invest in experiments.

You must understand that working with yarn, pigments and textiles is like working with gold and metals: prices, availability and regulations can change every single day! Who knows what will happen in India, Pakistan or China, Korea, Africa, the United States or the Arab Emirates tomorrow, what new tensions terrorism, poverty and the pressure of the market economy and religious or cultural ethics will bring? What small or large natural disasters or economic decisions will not only uproot societies but also nature – the source of everything? And if you imagine that architecture projects stretch over years and years; that an accepted design is sometimes executed five years later and has to be realized for the exact same budget that has been agreed upon years before, without inflation correction... then you understand the risk designers take at each turn, and how often we have to reposition ourselves, our ideas and solutions along the way.

Mind you, we still think it's worth it.

---

4. Two motors were installed inside the roof on both ends of the large concert hall to allow the view filters to appear and disappear separately from the acoustic/darkening curtains.

Food and Surf

When you finish work in Porto, you are bound to enjoy rich red and fruity white wines and fantastic pork, salted and fresh fish, cheeses, oils and potatoes. As you walk through the city's narrow alleys, you pass buildings clad with tiles blue and white, black and mauve, blue and silver, green and grey. Sometimes – like in the small station downtown – entire historic paintings of wars and conquests are pictured in blue-and-white tiles that cover the hall from ceiling to floor. Is there a link between our Delfts Blauw and the Portuguese azulejos?

All alleys (roofed by laundry fluttering overhead) lead down to the wide brown streaming Douro River, where hundreds of fat, silvery fish fight for a place around the sewer mouths that drain the city's sanitary waters unhindered, while large boats slide under Eiffel's two-level bridge towards the sea or up river.

When you reach the strong, rocky coast you face a roaring, foaming sea, smelling of seaweed and salt. You are enveloped in white mist and you struggle against the wind. Shiny black, grey, dark green and blue shapes loom up from fog and water. Only when the sun dissolves the mist and starts to set do gold, pink, orange and light blue appear, warming the ground you stand on.

Sala 1 – view filter 1b and
gold leaf on wood.

Sala 1 – view filter 1a
Sun from the west: golden ripples on the water surface.

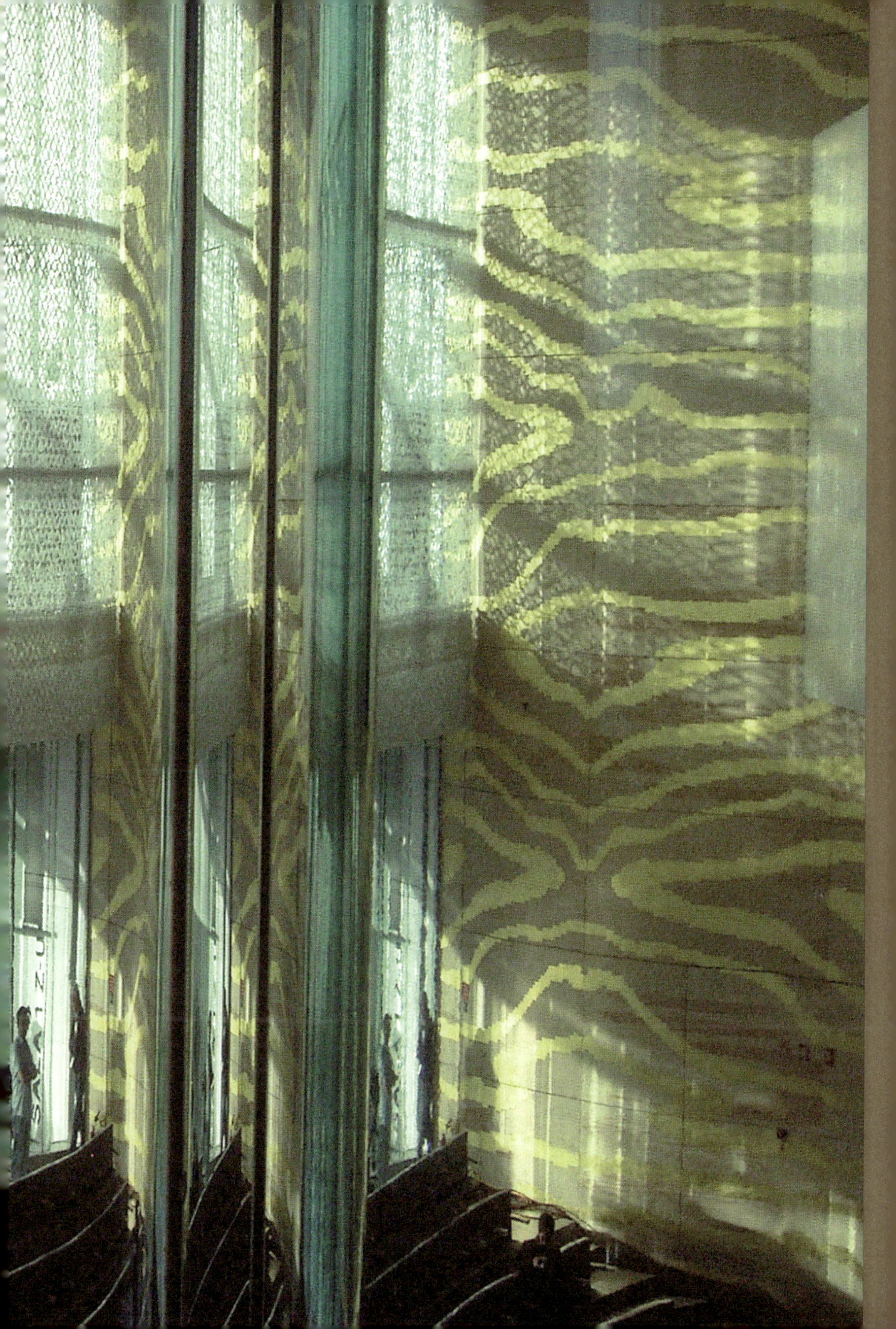

Sala 1 – view filter 1a
The two foyer levels seen through the knotted plane.

Sala 1 – view filter 1b
… standing in one of the foyers,
looking in through the glass waves.

"The human skull comprises only a small number of bones, with which only limited variation can be achieved. But a cichlid's* skull is made of at least 100 tiny bones that are linked – more or less in a floating state – to each other, and can each be lengthened or shortened or made lighter or heavier. In principle, a great deal is possible; one architectural feat after another is realized."

(Interview with Tijs Goldschmidt, "Every species is the embodiment of experience with the world", Feelings Are Always Local, V2_Publishing/NAi Publishers, 2004.)

*Fish family in Lake Victoria, East Africa.

Sala 1 – blackout curtain 2b
The large concert hall's blackout/acoustic curtain is down!

170 mm

20 mm

SALA 2

Sauerkraut and Velvet
14 x 12 and 14 x 7 metres height

The red auditorium is sandwiched between windows, one corrugated, one not; one looking out over the city, one overlooking the large concert hall. A bright, red-stained wooden box with a black floor, it has an ambivalent scale: sometimes you think it's small and intimate, the next time you enter you feel like a midget when you see people move under the windows.

The curtains we made for this room really are curtains, in the sense that they obediently follow the glazed façades, hang from tracks, pleat, move and are soft and swirling. They roll sideways and disappear – one curtain to the left, the others to the right – into the hidden storage spaces in the side walls.

Facing south and looking over the city, two curtains cover a large window 16 m wide and 11 m high: a sun-screening and a darkening curtain (this curtain does not block out the light – like a blackout curtain would do – but darkens the space); one thick, one thin. Each curtain enters the space from a different side, and each on its own track, so that the two layers can interact.

Facing North, a view-filtering curtain covers the glass wall to the foyer.

Reflective Voile

Because the window faces south, we had to make the sun-screening layer less transparent than the voile in the large auditorium. We added an extra layer to the voile: bands of so-called Contra-H (*choucroute* for insiders), a stiff open material made of rope and glue, normally used for scenery or costumes that need volume. I like the round, wild spaghetti of its structure; it looks active in itself.

We cut the stiff sheets into bands of 20 cm and then sewed those with regular distances onto the voile, creating vertical lamellas with soft areas in-between for pleating. The pleating here is organized with metal sticks that are integrated into the upper seam and connected to the carriers, folding the curtain exactly right when the curtain shuts and shifts into the storage. We made a black version of this curtain on the south side and a white, finer version along the inner north window.

We discovered that the *choucroute* could best be sealed inside voile. We 'bloused' white voile loosely over the bands of *choucroute* and saw that the material projects beautiful shadows onto the voile.

Darkening Velvet

The second layer is a grey velvet curtain that enters the room from the opposite direction. This curtain is heavy and pleated with an acoustic function, allowing a bit of light to come in – we're always happy if we don't need to create complete darkness – but darkening the space enough to allow light or image projections. The cotton velvet material, its pleats and the lining absorb sound to adjustable degrees, depending on how far the curtain is moved into the space.

The 11 m-high bands of velvet with the pile in alternating directions trigger an effect of light and shade. We inserted vertical rows of large stainless steel rings in the velvet, creating rows of round holes. The curtain is lined with white satin: a fine, translucent weave that catches and spreads daylight. Inside, the holes look like small lamps during the day; at night, they look that way from the outside.

Filtering Structure

The third curtain, placed on the opposite side of the room, filters the view to the adjacent foyer and softens the acoustic reflectivity of the corrugated glass wall. It is made of voile with bands of white *choucroute*.

During the entire design process, no slits were requested for this curtain which covers the exit doors (trusting the motorized system to regulate its position), but when the fire commission came by on the day before the opening, slits had to be made on the spot! In intense communication with the Gerriets team on site, we decided to cut the slits with scissors right there and then, and to line the edges with orange 'Day Glow' bands, that had been sent to Porto by FedEx within hours.

Sala 2 – view filter 3
The small concert hall seen through the view filter curtain that lines the glass wall between the foyer and the hall's interior.

Sala 2 – Sun reflective & shading curtains – 2

Sala 2 – darkening & acoustic curtain – 1

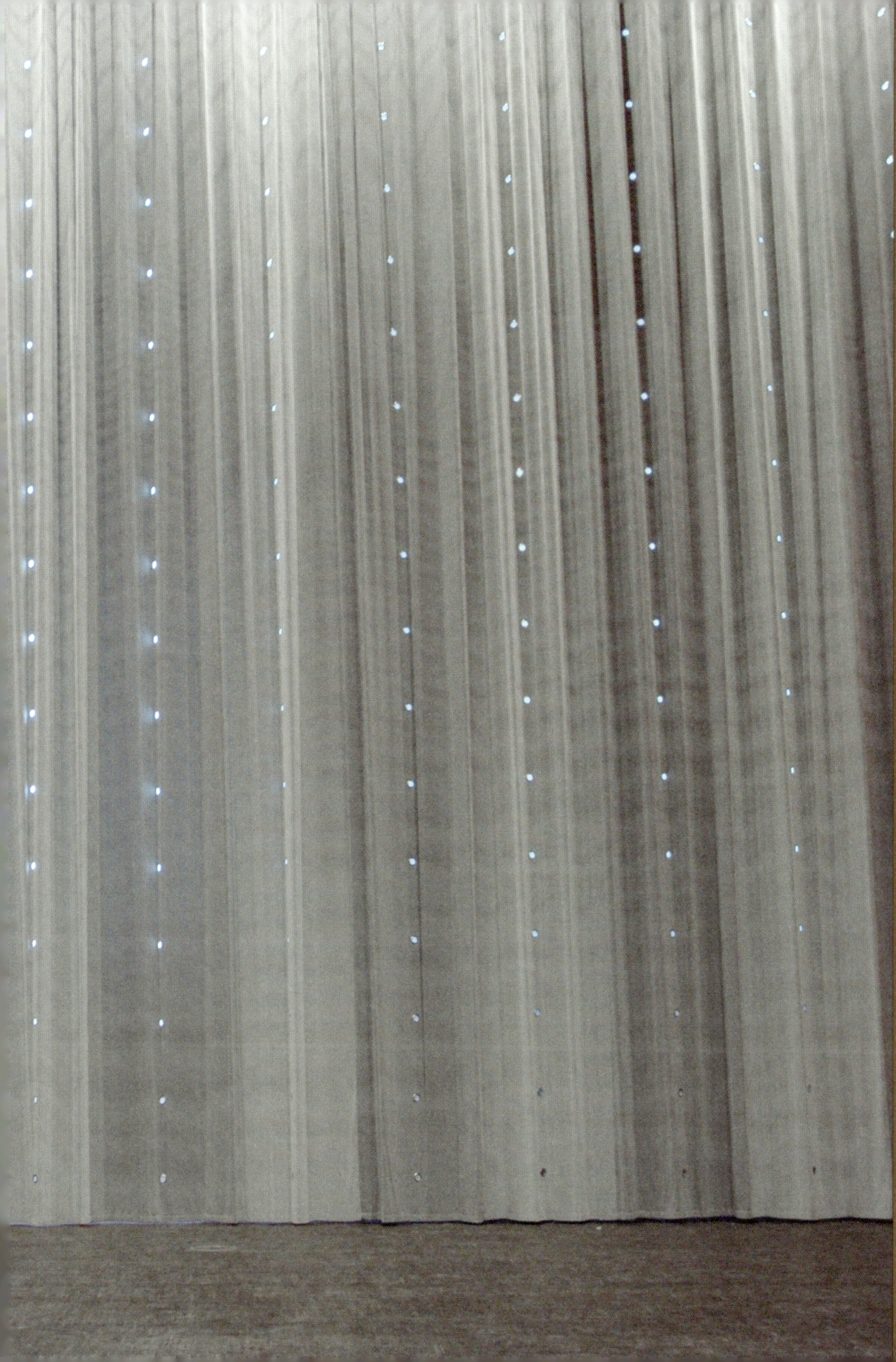

REHEARSAL ROOMS

<u>Blankets for the Dungeons</u>
<u>Curtains of 65 and 27.5 x 7.7 m</u>

In the two voluminous subterranean rehearsal rooms, both 8 m high, curtains were to be completely in the service of variable acoustic requirements. The rooms themselves are careful and sober compositions of dark wooden floors, plaster board and mirrored walls, bare concrete columns, walls and ceilings. Tracks were drawn as continuous loops, allowing the curtains to be shifted into any position, pulled by hand.

The architects insisted on 'heavy duty' material and dark green, brown or red canvas (like the sails of old wooden Dutch sailboats), but apart from their acoustic inadequateness, we persisted in our belief that all curtains should be colourless and so we made one white and one black room. Both curtains are made of woolen serge (a heavy open weave for maximum acoustic absorbance) with, along the top, round plastic windows that enable visitors and technicians in the control booth to look inside the hall, even when the curtains are closed. A transparent slit along the lower edges shows life behind the curtains: important for people who step inside during rehearsals. Slits are marked with coloured bands to show entrances and exits at strategic points.

Black-and-white woolen curtains for acoustic absorption; with windows for a view from the control booths and public window; a transparent slit in the seam announces visitors and occupants.

Rehearsal rooms
Sound-absorbent curtains regulate
the acoustic quality of the rooms.

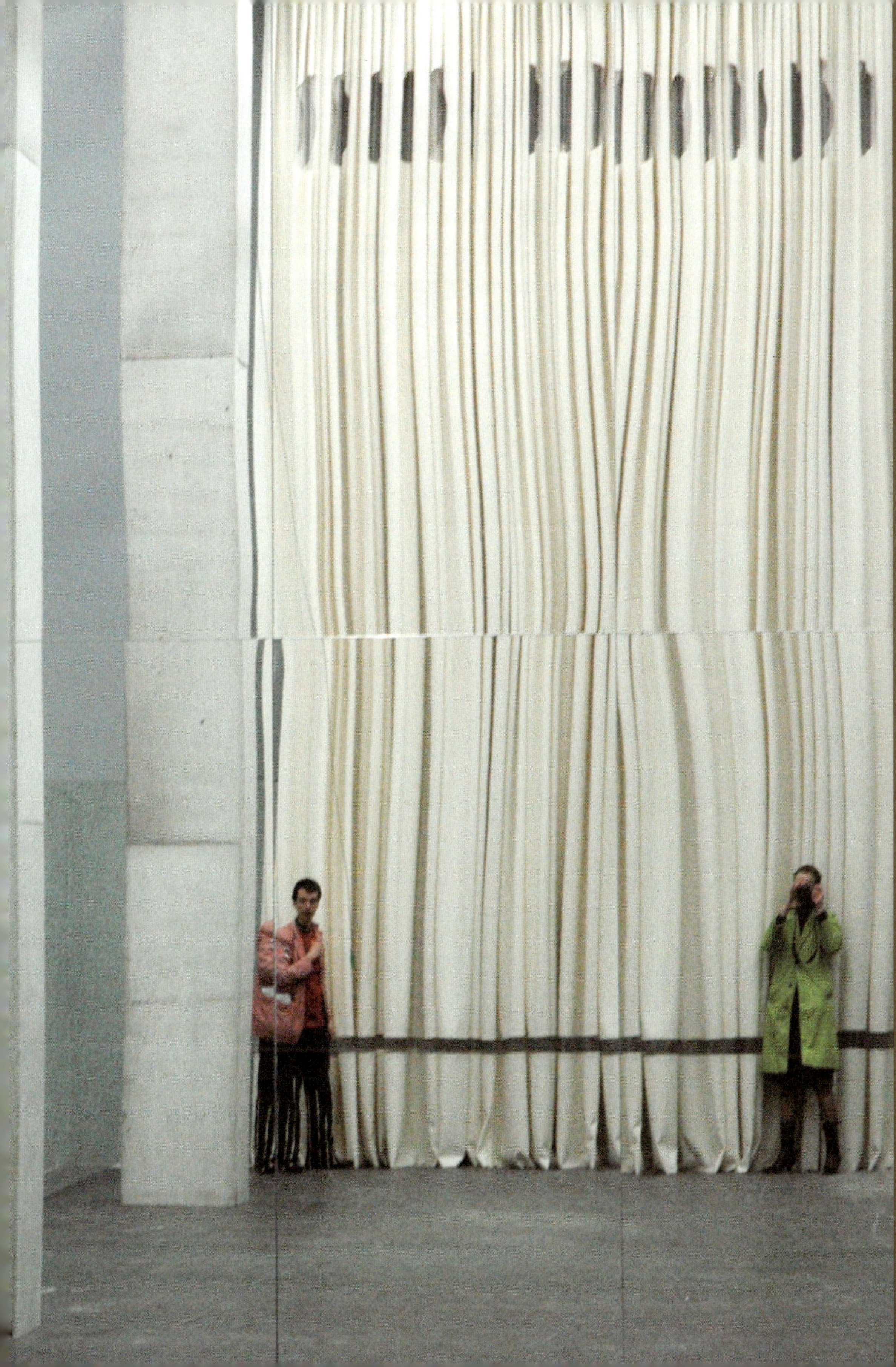

White rehearsal room:
the wool serge curtain pulled out.

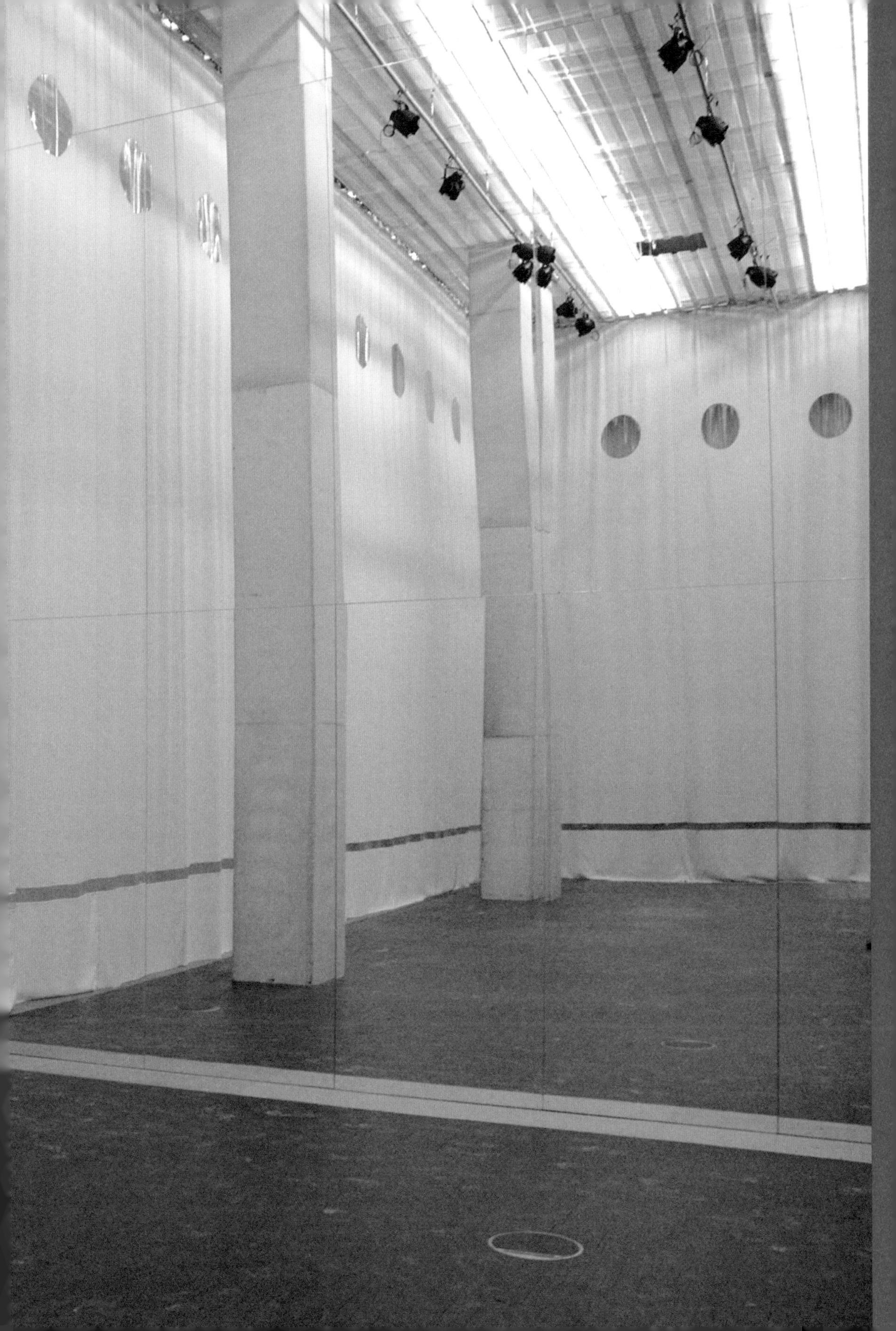

One of the large concert hall windows looks out over the circular park, with the monument as vertical object in its centre.

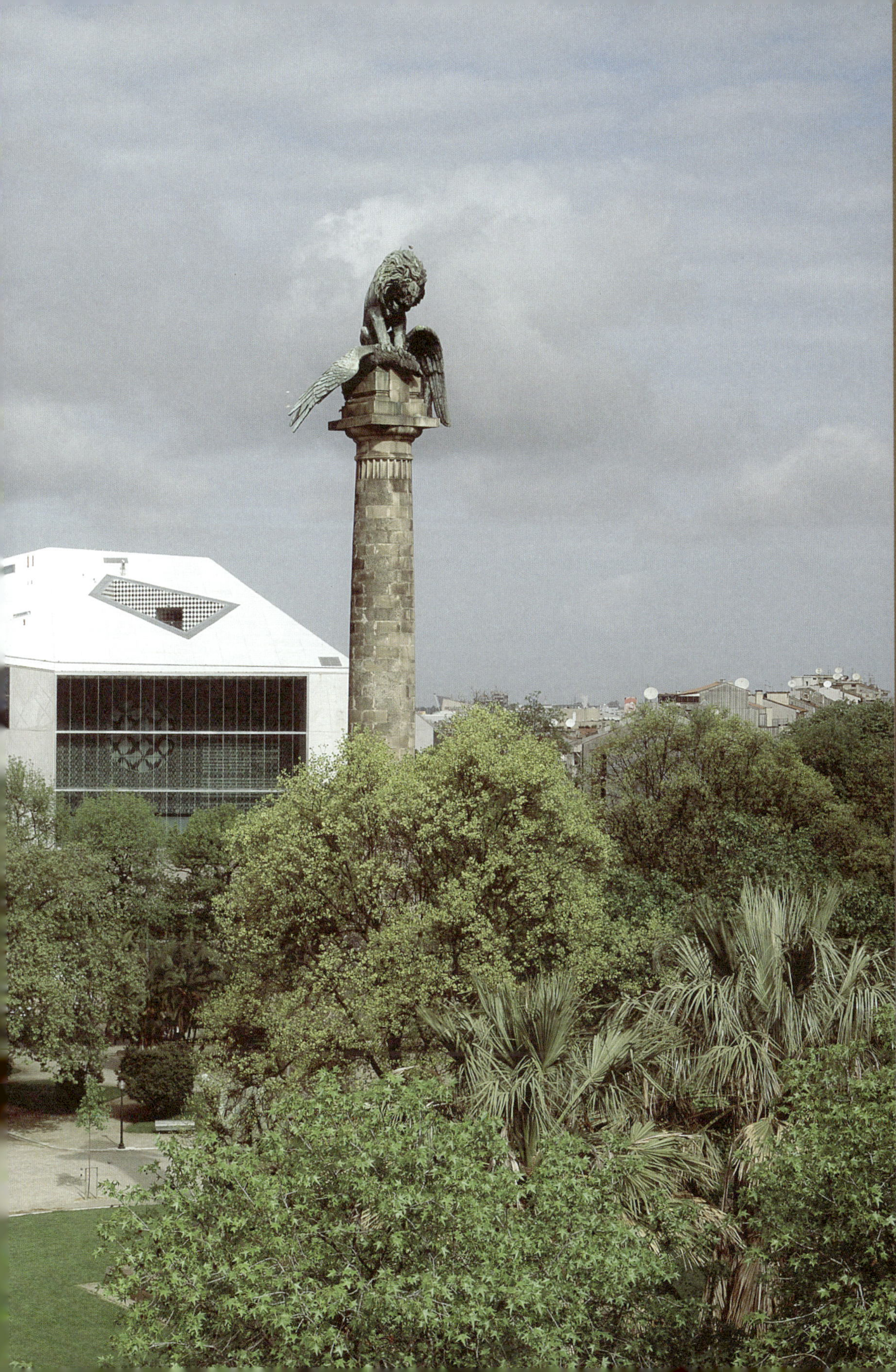

Dialectics of the Tangible and the Intangible
Cecil Balmond

Space Is Alive
My practice is about the structure of organization. I believe that, in terms of organization, the rather simplistic world we have inherited is only a small subset of a much larger and more complex world. The generic is serial, it unfolds and has various qualities to it. It's just that, in the past, we have simplified it into an architecture where Cartesian recta-linearity repeats rhythms.

I believe space is alive, it has qualities the moment we act in it – until then it has a sort of a nascent, infinite potential to react. The moment we act, things happen. And as a design moves on, whether it's a piece of landscape, a painting or a piece of music, certain rules come into play, certain innate senses of balance and equilibrium we've got in ourselves.

I am interested in this aesthetic. And I'm interested in what new rigours are put into the unfolding of space when you are into an area of flux on the surface. Pieces of architecture drop out of the structure of organization, out of which in turn drop structures that can then be engineered.

Patterning of Space
For me, structure in architecture is a sort of catalyst and a vibrant thing that marks rhythms, punctuates space and produces episodes. These structural qualities are highly architectural. The Kunsthal is a classic example. So is the Bordeaux Villa – in a simple way, with just a few movements of displaced columns and beams acting in an extreme equilibrium.

From the curtain and interior works of Petra Blaisse that I have seen in Seattle and Porto I can see her strong interest in spatial qualities that come from colour, rhythms of pleats, folds, knots, loops and density. I'm interested in the same things, but in my work they turn into hard tectonic features that then become pieces of structural elements.

My starting points concerning space are intuitive. I think of the human eye travelling through that space and a nascent or phantom pattern begins to form. Later, the act of geometry materializes the dynamics of what I sensed. The Serpentine Pavilion that I worked on with Toyo Ito was a radical moment for me – realizing that the wall and the roof need not be a wall and a roof in the conventional sense. Triggered by Ito's initial proposal for a roof plane with random lines, I started thinking about a complete self-generating pattern that could be folded.

I have studied music keenly, including Western harmony and Indian ragas. The structure of the music that has fascinated me is probably the source of my interest in organization. A ratio of certain two numbers I used in the Pavilion – an algorithm that makes a rule repeat itself – gave the whole network of crossing lines that turned into material steel that was then folded like origami into a structure or piece of architectural space. It was post-rationally that I found that ratio was actually the fundamental ratio in Western harmony for music.

Crossing lines in space, the planes and right angles would lose all definition. It was like travelling in a time capsule. The walls and the floors and the roof would lose direction and defy a sense of enclosure. I usually see a column as a punctuation point, a wall as a diaphragm. Then these 'structural elements' put into space or an architectural piece suddenly gain certain dynamics and the eye starts to relate around these things.

For the bridge I am designing in Philadelphia, I let three landscape lines move into the reality of a structure, as if a narrative of landscape turns into a tectonic art piece that crosses a river line, and unfolds into a car park. To me, that's structure.

Dynamically Virtual versus Physically Real

In the Casa da Música curtains there is a whole movement of textures – from dark to light. Fabric is interesting because it gives immediate surface, and it gives structure through its colour or fabricating technique. When I was working with Anish Kapoor at the Tate Modern, the key move that gave that form solidity was choosing the deep red. It became like steel and suddenly took another depth beyond its own structural characteristics. The colour supercharged the form.

The fold of the fabric, the way it hangs, the way it catches light – all work together to give a complete spatial effect. The curtains are structural open cells that carry light and transparency, floating with gravity, compared to the more solid direct concession a concrete wall would make. The cellular nature of the curtain structure allows a cascade effect.

The inherent qualities of folding and pleating that you have to do with fabrics are two of the fundamental ways of making structures work in the real world, from the universe down to the atom. Folding, pleating, branching, overlapping, knotting (weaving): all of those come from the language of fabrics. In Casa da Música, Blaisse used knot and fold, then in the Prada Store she used knit – also a kind of weaving – and pleat.

For me cloth and curtains are real structure. Only by touching or probing fabric can you say it's not a literal, conventional, narrow definition of structure. But it is a potential template for structure.

There seems to be an increasing degree of structure and depth growing in Blaisse's work. I feel that she is exploring the third dimension. Her fabric takes on aspects of volume through her own intuition. If fabric is only used as a surface, it remains a pattern in the literal sense of the word, which is fine, very pleasurable, enjoyable, but it never takes on another life, or what I call a higher interpretation. When the work feels volumetric in some way or begins to define its volumes locally to its own surfaces, the work is truly dynamic.

If you dismiss the definitions of the architecture, you feel more structure with Blaisse's work. And architecture should be liberated by what Blaisse does – like the architecture is liberated by what I do – if we do it well.

I think we are very similar. The commonalities are both structures. It is curious that she is dealing with an almost intangible world whereas I deal with a completely concrete world. And yet, we are perhaps achieving the same kind of effects.

London, 2005 (based on an interview by the editor)

Serpentine Gallery Pavilion, London, designed by Toyo Ito with Cecil Balmond, 2002.

Anish Kapoor's Marsyas shown at the Tate Modern, London, 2002–2003.

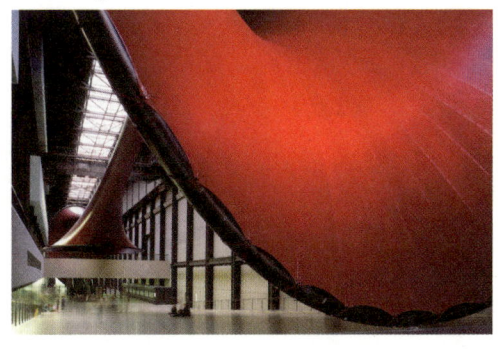

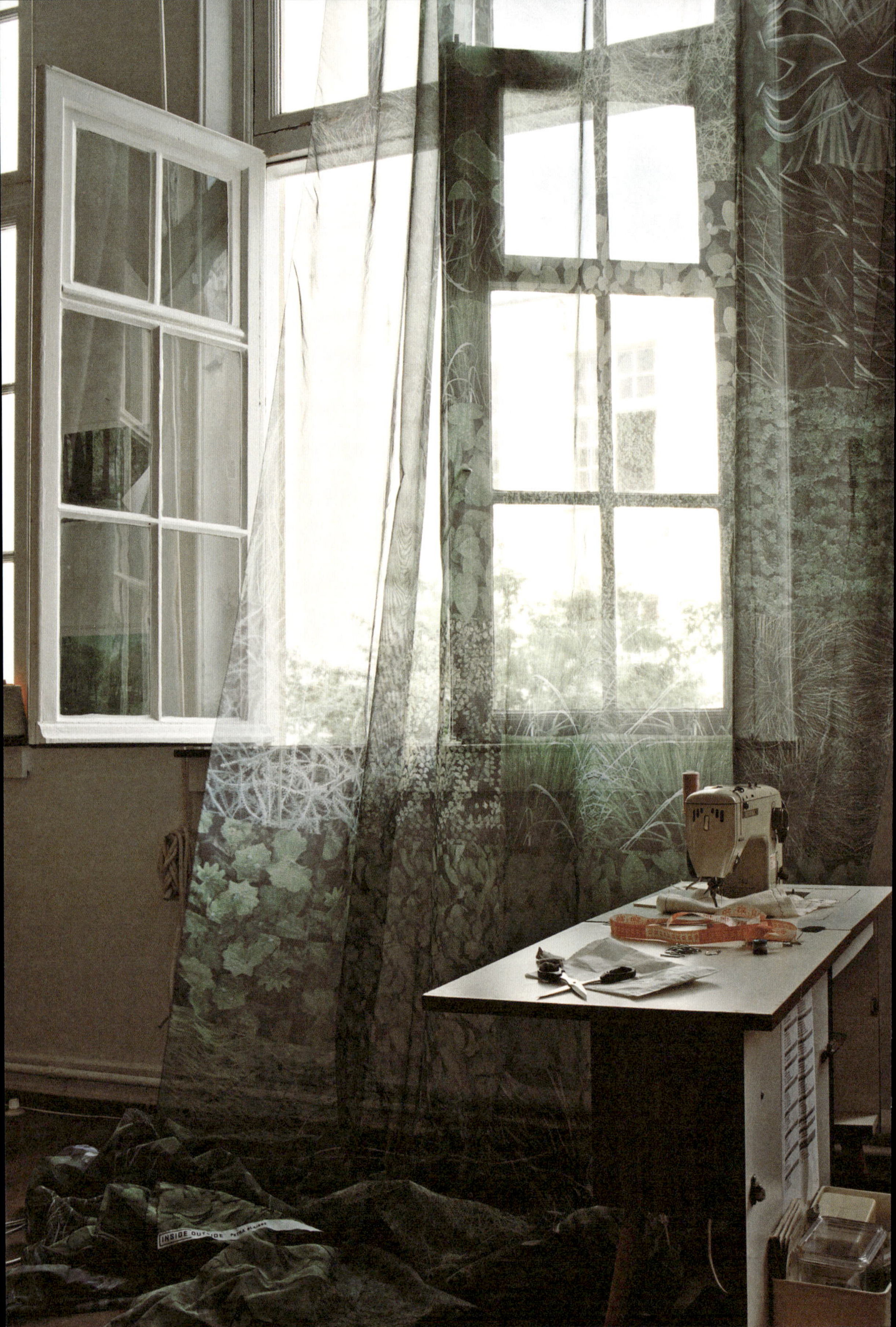
INSIDE

Title
Invisible Presence

Location
The Glass Pavilion, Toledo, Ohio, USA

Site
Park adjacent to the Toledo Museum of Art

Client
Toledo Museum of Art

Status
Commission 2003
Completion of 80% design development 2005

Architects
SANAA: Kazuyo Sejima and Ryue Nishizawa, Tokyo

Team
Inside Outside, Amsterdam
Harvey Marshall Berling Associates, New York (acoustic consultation)
Arup Lighting, New York (lighting consultation)
Transsolar, New York/Stuttgart (climate engineering)
Paratus Group, New York (financial management)
Robiflex, Beverwyk (assistance on sample production)
Zeebra, Ede (silk-screen test printing)
Twentebelt, Hengelo (steel mesh sample provision)
Gerriets GmbH, Umkirch (rail, runner and motor testing)
HELM, Frankfurt (rail and runner testing)

Scope of Work
Designing of a space-defining, darkening and acoustically absorbent curtain for the multi-purpose room, and a series of climate- and light-regulating and sun-reflective curtains for the rest of the building; technical consultation on textiles in relation to light and climate requirements.

The project
In first instance Inside Outside was asked to create a multi-purpose room curtain that would have a very imminent, colourful presence and would fulfil a representative role for the Glass Pavilion as an institution. In the second instance, the team discovered that many light and climate issues could be solved with flexible, thin textiles. Our commission expanded and we developed designs for a darkening, space-dividing and sound-absorbing curtain for the multi-purpose room and for a number of shading and sun-reflective, translucent and transparent curtains for the rest of the building. We designed track configurations so that each curtain could appear and disappear, and proposed curtains of a very thin quality with minimal creative interventions that could be manipulated into different positions and pleat configurations to achieve gradations of shading. Our aim here was to leave the transparency and sobriety of the architecture intact.

Specifications

1. Primary Exhibition Space 1
Curtain size (width x height): 75.3 x 4.0 m (incl. 15% pleat)
Total cloth surface: 301 m^2
Material: Verosol 812,000 FR. Polyester weave (Trevira CS) with an aluminium powder coating, 1.50 m width, 95 gr/m^2, colour: grey front, silver back. Flame-proofed to NFP A 701.

Programme: Sun-screening curtain; translucent, grey on the inside, silver on the outside (aluminium powder coating). The curtain was designed with a minimum 15 cm air gap for airflow along the top of the curtain and weighed down seams (changeable position, visible storage). Daylight-filtering, darkening up to 90%; exhibits should be readable and visible; permanent status.

2. Primary Exhibition Space 2
Curtain size (width x height): 34.0 x 4.0 m (incl. 15% pleat)
Total cloth surface: 136 m^2
Material: Verosol 812,000 FR. Polyester weave (Trevira CS) with an aluminium powder coating, 1.50 m width, 95 gr/m^2, colour: grey front, silver back. Flame-proofed to NFP A 701.

Programme: Sun-screening curtain; translucent, grey on the inside, silver on the outside (aluminium powder coating). Minimum 15 cm air gap for airflow on top and bottom of the curtain (changeable position, visible storage). Daylight-filtering, darkening up to 90%; exhibits should be readable and visible; permanent status.

3. Hot Shop/Cafe
Curtain size (width x height): 60.4 x 4.0 m (incl. 15% pleat)
Total cloth surface: 241.5 m^2
Material: Verosol 816,000 FR. Polyester weave (Trevira CS) with an aluminium powder coating, 1.50 m width, 72 gr/m^2, colour: grey front, silver back. Flame-proofed to NFP A 701.

Programme: Sun-screening curtain; Translucent, grey on the inside, silver on the outside (aluminium powder coating). The curtain was designed to have a minimum 15 cm air gap on the top and bottom and a 'special' treatment on the bottom (changeable position, invisible storage). Cooling and filtering, sun-screening, light control, warmth insulation; (partial) openings for view in and out, permanent status.

4. Multi-purpose Room
Curtain size (width x height): 95.0 x 4.0 m (incl. 50% pleat)
Total cloth surface: 380 m^2
Material: To be specified. Flame proofed to NFP A 701.

Programme: Representational curtain for event space, minimum of 15 cm air gap for airflow on top and bottom of the curtain. Darkening (not blackout), acoustic absorption, enabling flow of conditioned air, shading indirect sunlight in the northeast corner of the building (cooling), privacy, and space organization.

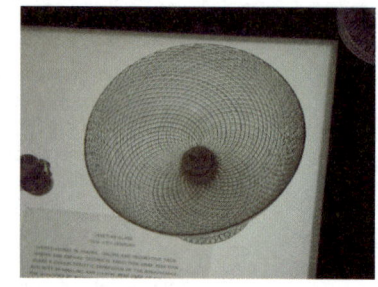

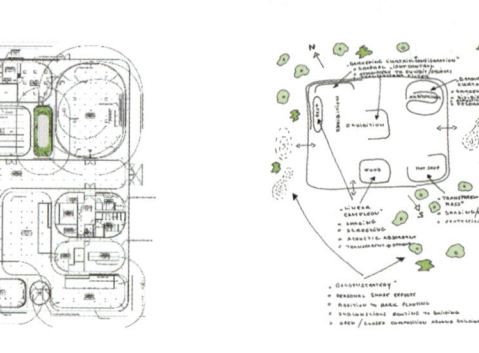

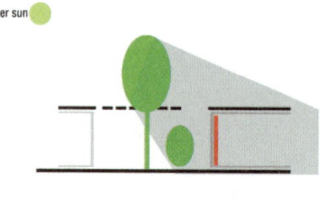

INVISIBLE PRESENCE
The Glass Pavilion, Toledo, USA, 2002–2005

Arts Museum Glass Centre, Toledo

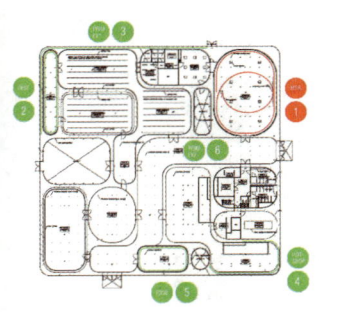

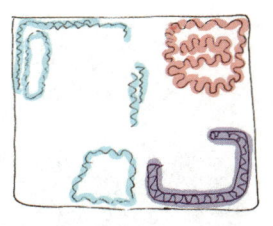

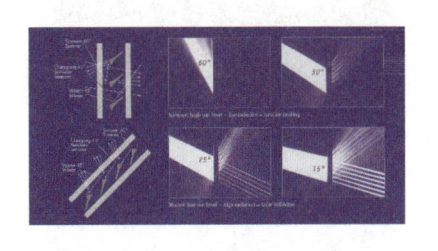

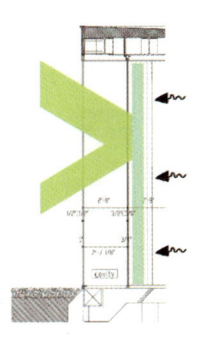

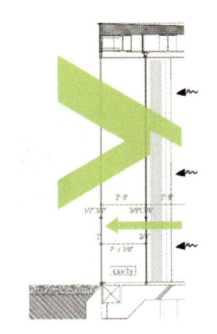

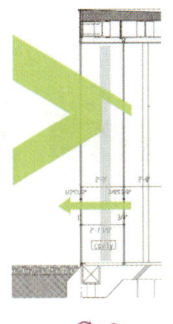

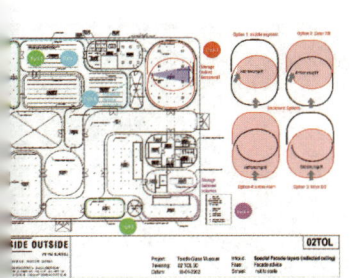

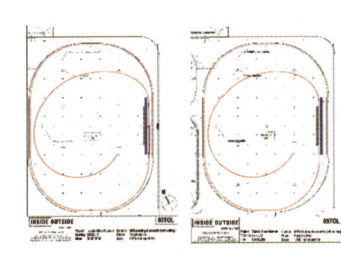

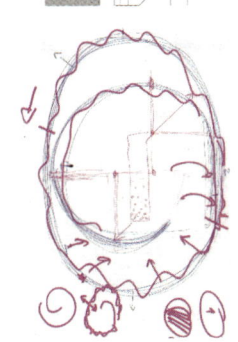

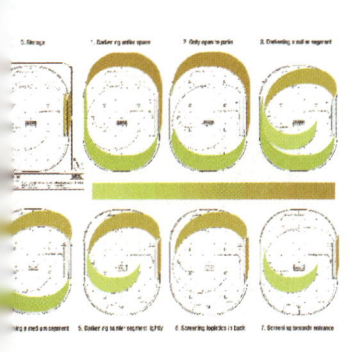

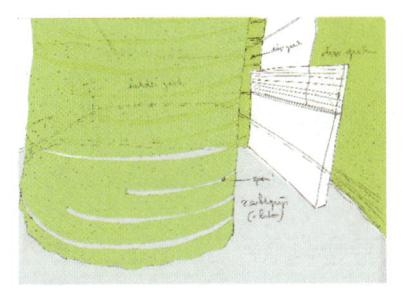

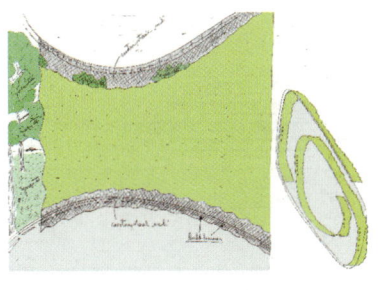

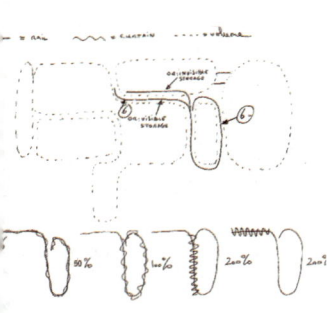

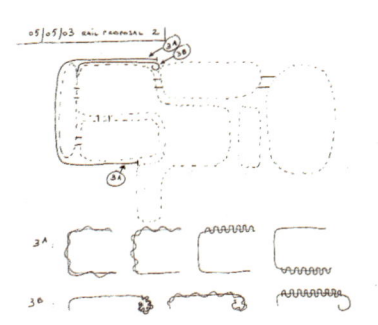

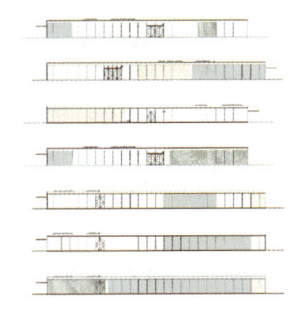

- - -▷ Light filtering
⤳ Sound absorption
▶ Light reflection
▶ Sound reflection

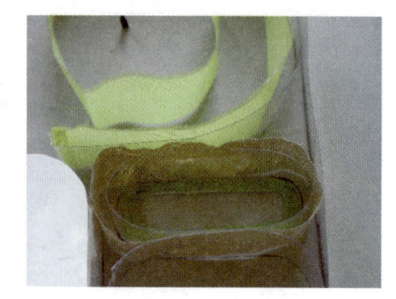

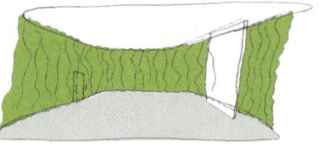

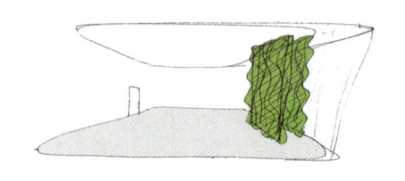

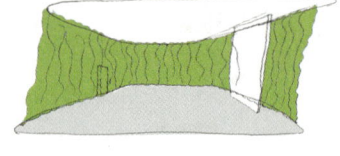

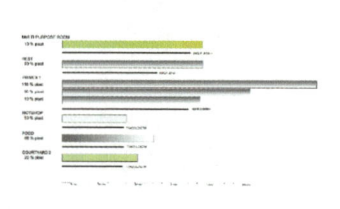

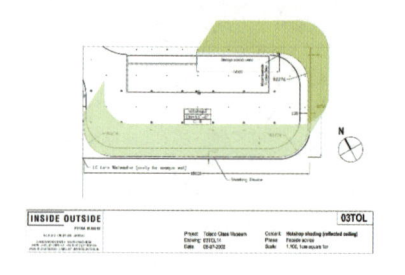

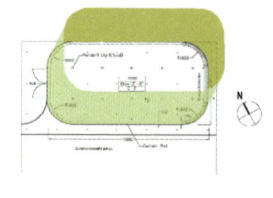

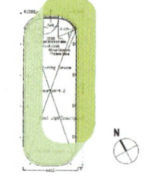

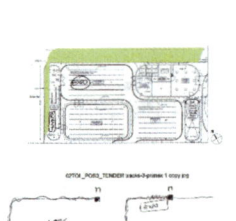

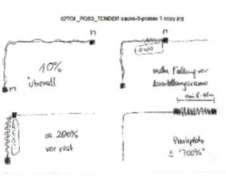

INVISIBLE PRESENCE The Glass Pavilion, Toledo, USA, 2002–2005

413

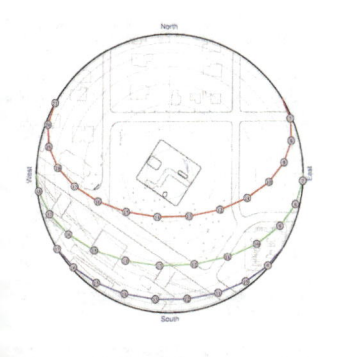

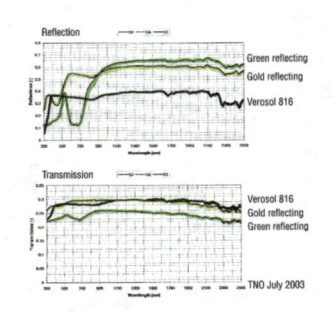

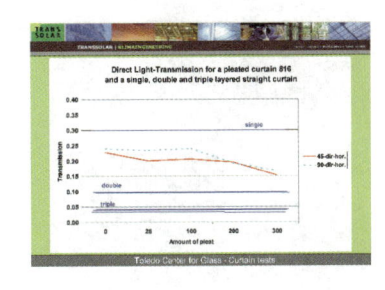

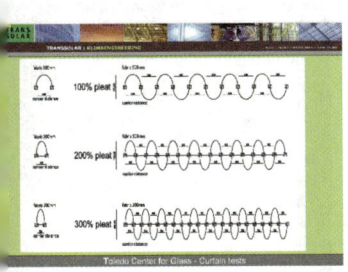

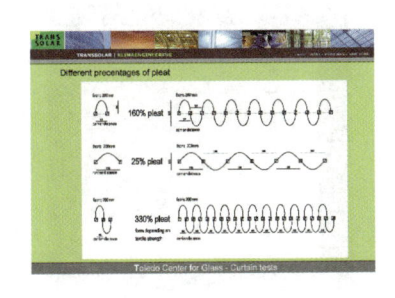

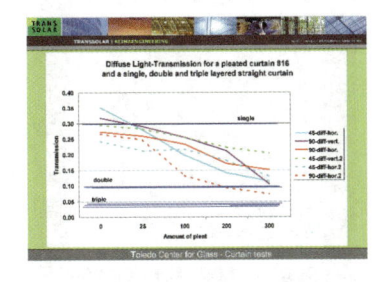

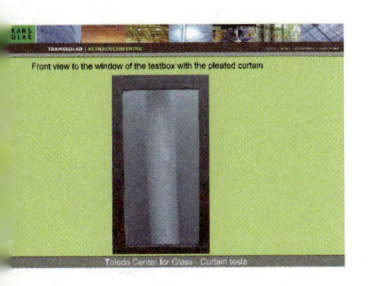

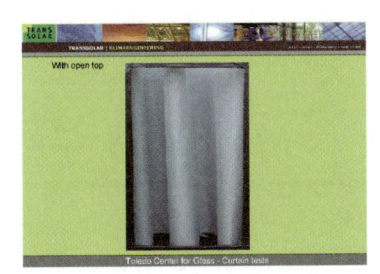

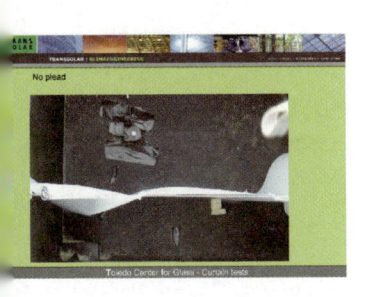

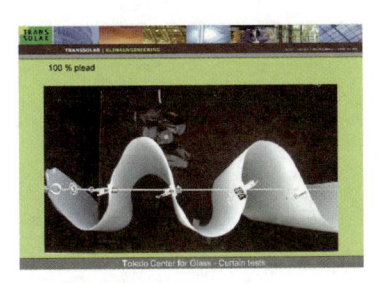

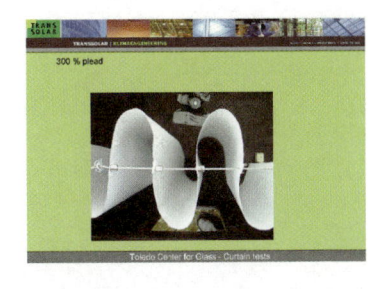

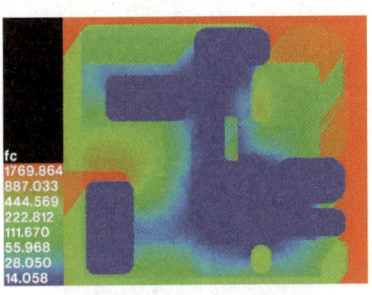

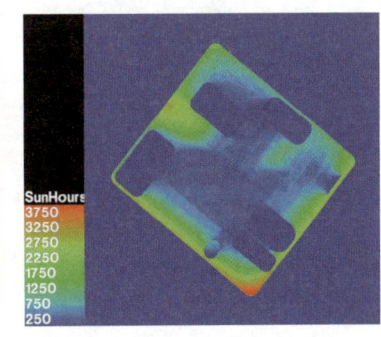

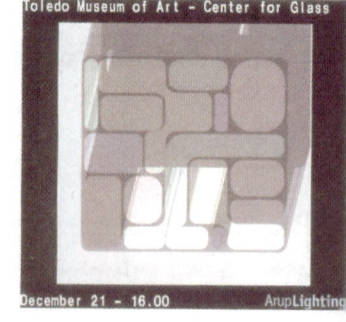

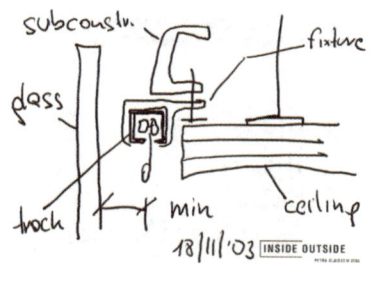

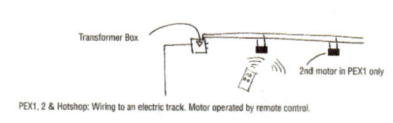

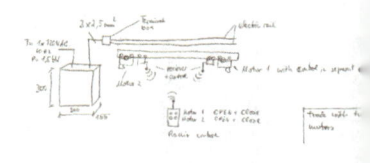

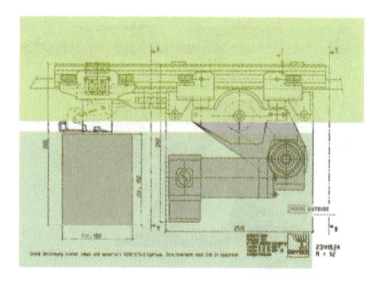

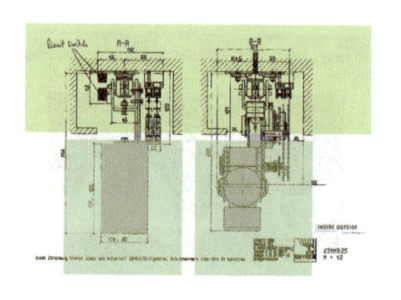

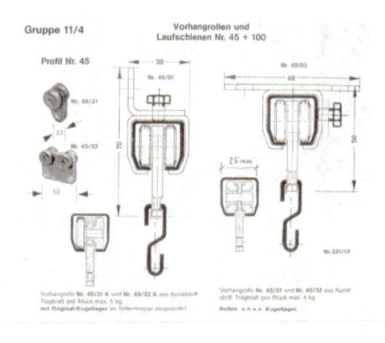

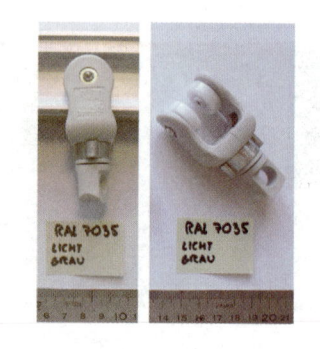

INVISIBLE PRESENCE The Glass Pavilion, Toledo, USA, 2002–2005

415

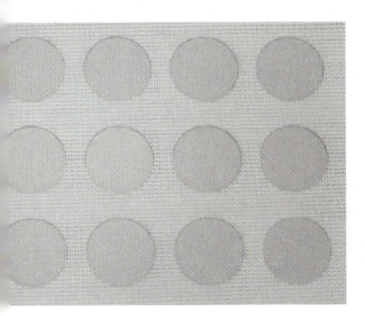

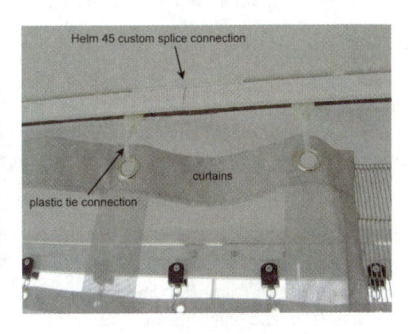

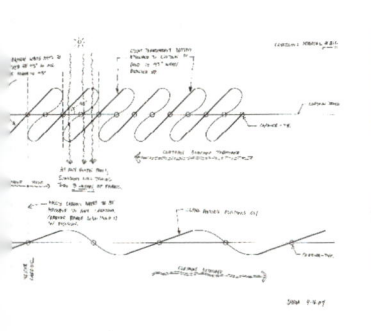

Title
Restoration Revised

Location
The Hackney Empire Theatre,
291 Mare Street, London, UK

Site
Landmark theatre in central London

Client
Hackney Empire Theatre
The Heritage Lottery Fund
The London Arts Council

Status
Commission 2000
Completion 2005

Architects
Tim Ronalds Architects, London

Team
Inside Outside, Amsterdam
Tim Ronalds Architects, London (colour consultation)
Arup Acoustics, Cambridge (acoustic consultation)
Ken Creasey Ltd, London (production and installation)

Scope of Work
Main auditorium: stage curtain, side drapes, acoustic and light-excluding curtains
Educational space: space-defining voiles, darkening curtains
Pepy's Bar: acoustically-absorbing and muting curtains, stage backdrop curtain

The Project
For this renovated variety theatre in London, Inside Outside designed the stage curtains and acoustic drapes for the main auditorium and space-, acoustic- and light-regulating curtains for the new rehearsal studio and the theater café. The classic forms and the overwhelming number of colours that dominate the old building provide a stimulating contrast to the newly designed portion of the building. Inside Outside's work reflects this contrast with a number of distinct designs that vary in colour, materiality and technique, depending on the history and function of each space.

Specifications
Auditorium:
Stage Curtain:
Stage opening: 10.4 x 9.4 m
Curtain size (width x height):
  in situ: 10.85 x 10.2 m
  flat: 44 x 10.2 m
Total cloth surface: 448.8 m²

Weight red velour: 570 gr/m²
Overall cloth weight: 290 kg
Total weight: 480 kg (including all the extra tunnels, cords, etcetera plus the steel frame that stretches its width)

Felt sticks: 1,000 m
Gold metallic cord: 4 mm x 5,000 m
Eyelets: 4,735 total (single connection)

Pink moiré fabric behind the centre slit.

Pelmet:
Size (width x height): 10.8 x 3 m (height is measured in centre)
Fabric used: 38 m²

The pelmet was made in three sections with a wooden framework and bolted together; covered with burgundy red velvet and gold metallic cord.

Upper Circle Curtains:
Curtain size (width x height): 9.0 x 5.6 m (2x)
Total cloth surface: 100.8 m²

Weight of velour: 380 gr/m²
Weight of serge: 400 gr/m²
Weight of glass cloth: 280 gr/m²
Total weight: 1,060 gr/m²

New Annex:
Education Space: Rainbow Voile
Curtain size (width x height):
  in situ (incl. 15% pleat): 35.9 x 3.95 m
  flat: 41.3 x 3.95 m
Total cloth surface: 163.1 m²
Material: Digitally printed voile; 54 gr/m²

Education Space: Darkening Curtain
Curtain size (width x height): 47.6 x 4.5 m max. (3.8 m min.)
Total cloth surface: 214.5 m²
Material: Burgundy coloured serge; 420 gr/m²

Pepy's Bar: Acoustic Curtain
Total cloth surface: 113.2 m²
Total surface of voile: 78.7 m²
Material: Mother of pearl cotton velvet 560 gr/m²; Trevira CS satin 54 gr/m², Trevira CS voile; 220 pieces of silver metal press-fasteners (snaps)

Pepy's Bar: Metal Mesh Backdrop
Total surface of mesh: 50.85 m²
Material: Stainless steel spiral mesh positioned vertically, spiral diametre 5 mm, thickness of thread 0.8 mm, 4,500 gr/m².

417

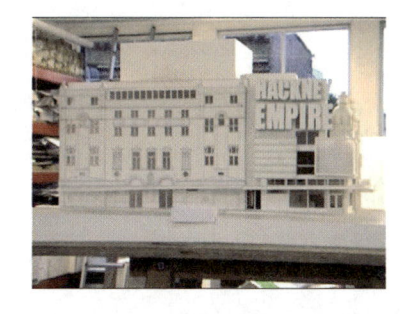

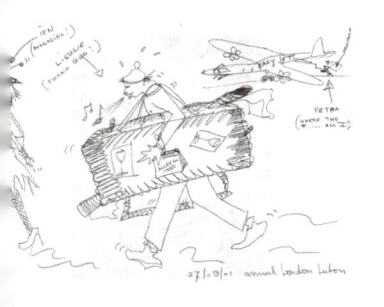

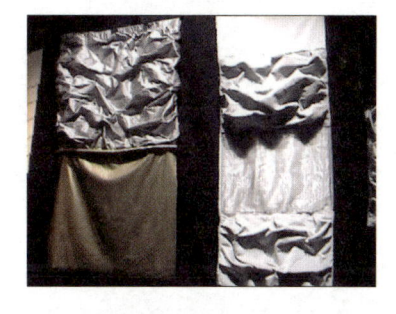

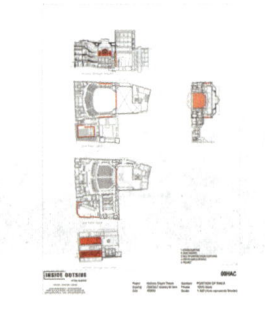

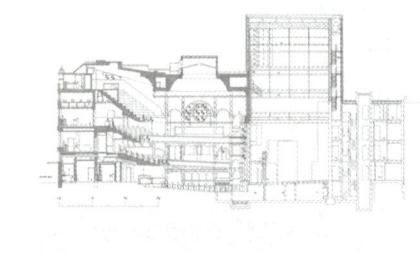

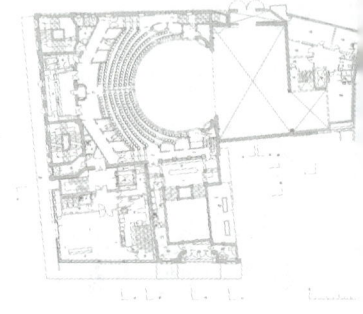

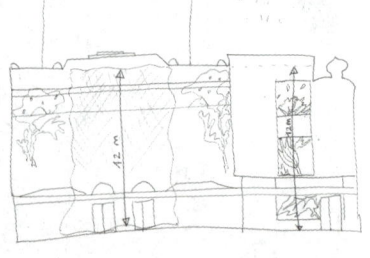

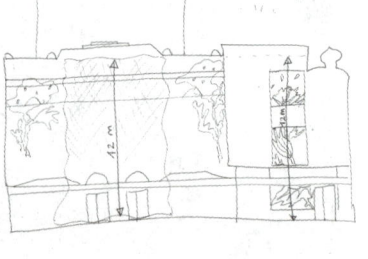

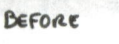

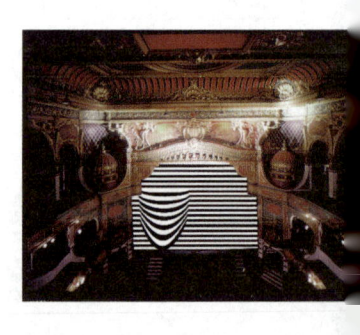

RESTORATION REVISED Hackney Empire Theatre, London, UK, 1999–2005

BEFORE · AFTER

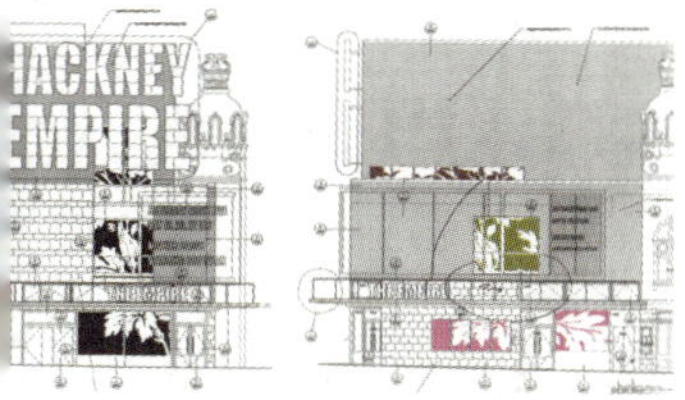
HACKNEY
EMPIRE

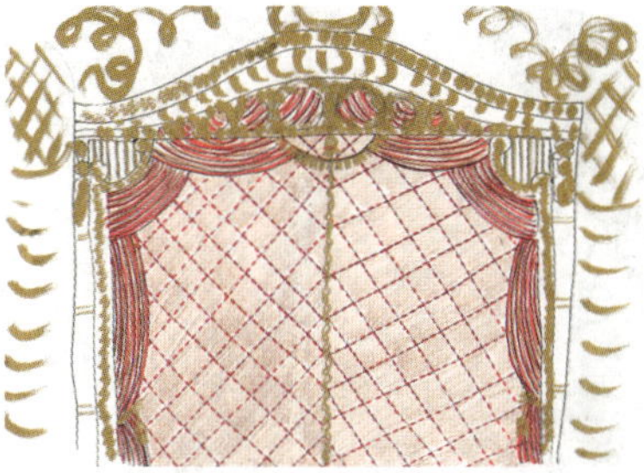

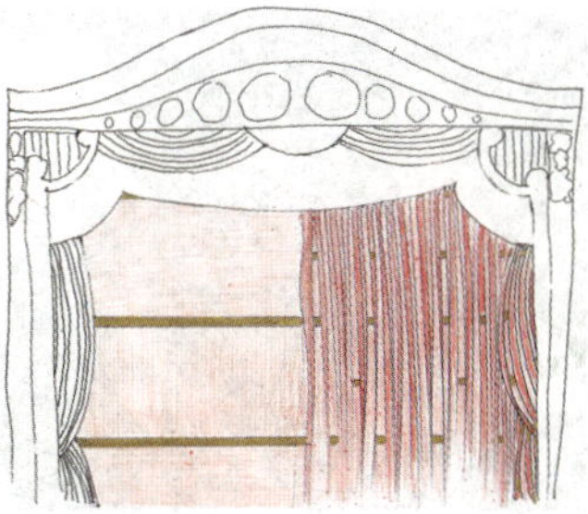

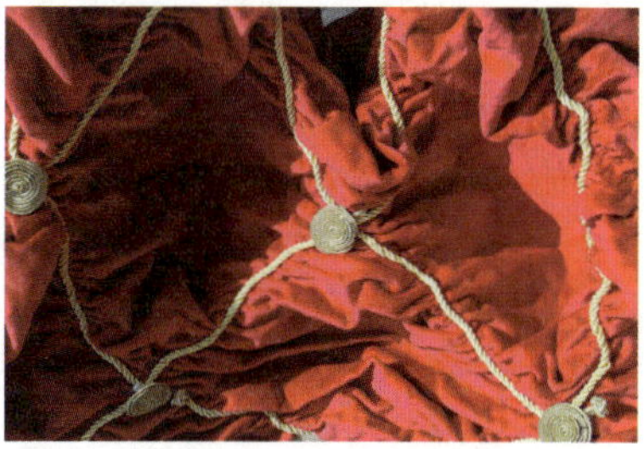

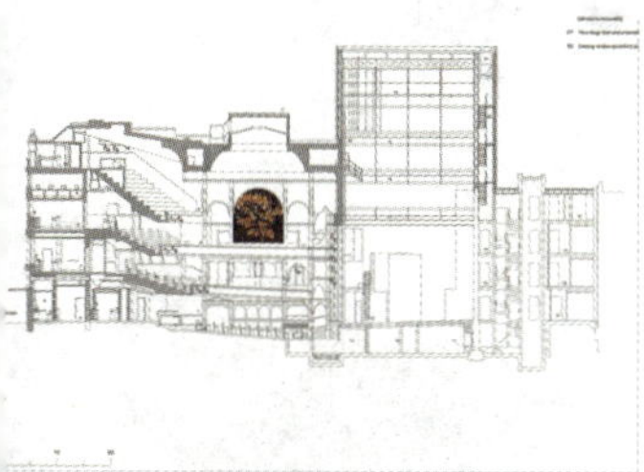

A1
D1
E1
F1
A2
A3
E3
F3
3A
3B

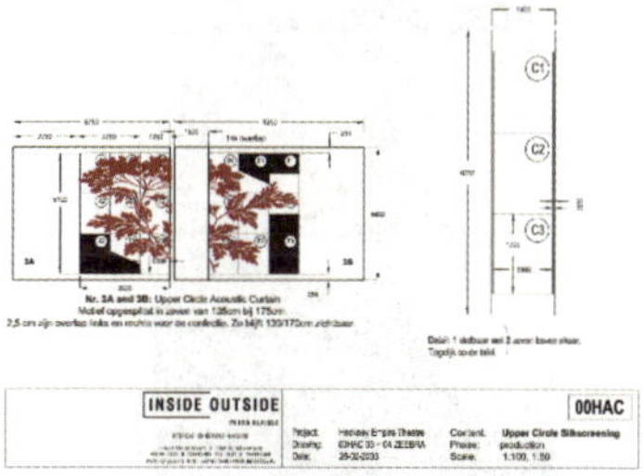
INSIDE OUTSIDE
00HAC

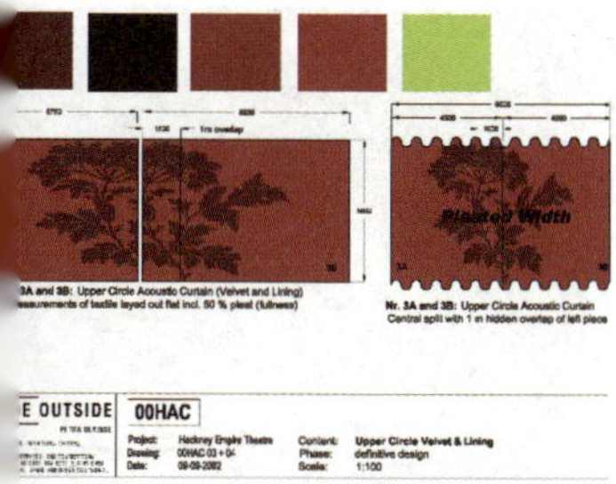
3A and 3B: Upper Circle Acoustic Curtain (Velvet and Lining)
Nr. 3A and 3B: Upper Circle Acoustic Curtain
Central split with 1 in hidden overlap of left piece
E OUTSIDE
00HAC
Project: Hackney Empire Theatre
Content: Upper Circle Velvet & Lining
Phase: definitive design
Scale: 1:100

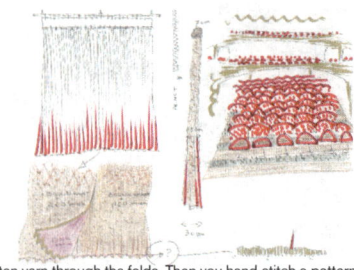

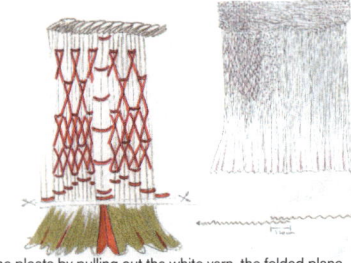

I was taught, once, to sew a little girl's dress with a smocked top: you had to fold the cloth into hundreds of tiny pleats, fixing them together by roughly sewing a thread of white cotton yarn through the folds. Then you hand-stitch a pattern of small stitches over the pleats, connecting two pleats at each turn – with different colours of thread. Then, releasing the pleats by pulling out the white yarn, the folded plane changes into an elastic, three-dimensional surface of diamonds overlaid with a rich pattern of colourful stitches.

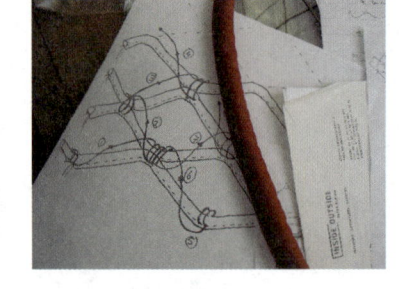

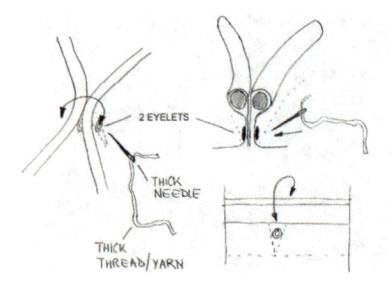

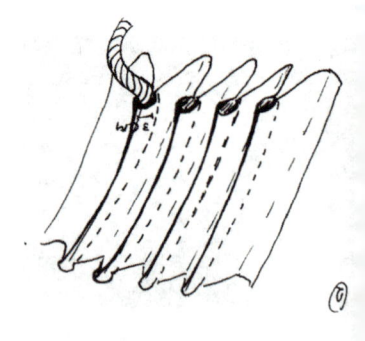

RESTORATION REVISED Hackney Empire Theatre, London, UK, 1999–2005

421

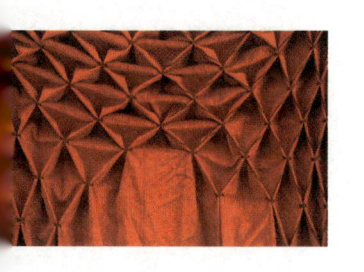

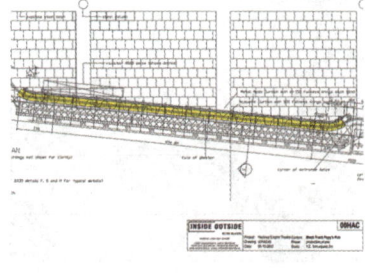

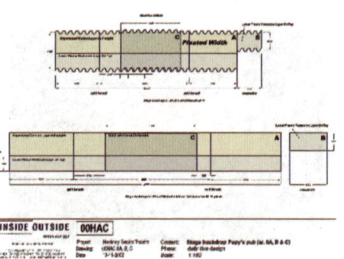

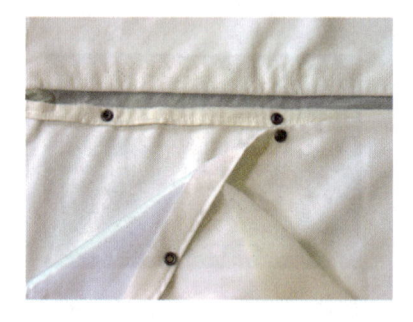

RESTORATION REVISED Hackney Empire Theatre, London, UK, 1999–2005

WHITE ROOM & RAINBOW CURTAIN + DARK BROWN/FLOWERS
±475
GREY ROOM & GREEN/FLOWERS + TRANSLUCENT PLASTIC
±323
BLACK ROOM & PINK/FLOWERS + STAINLESS TRANSPARENT CHAINMESH
±450
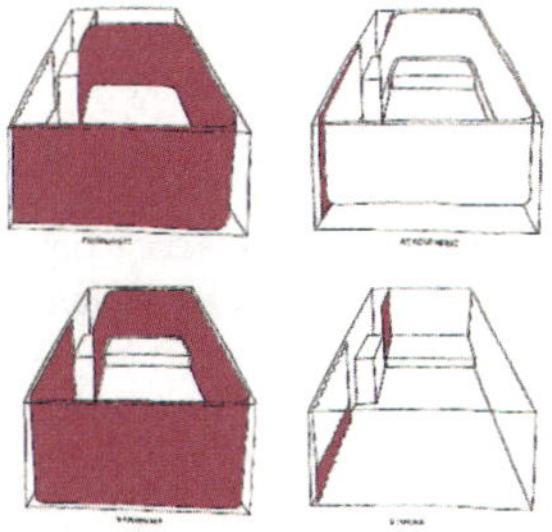
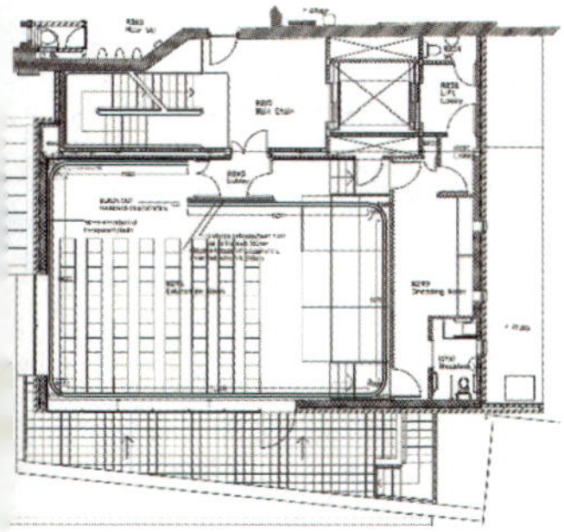
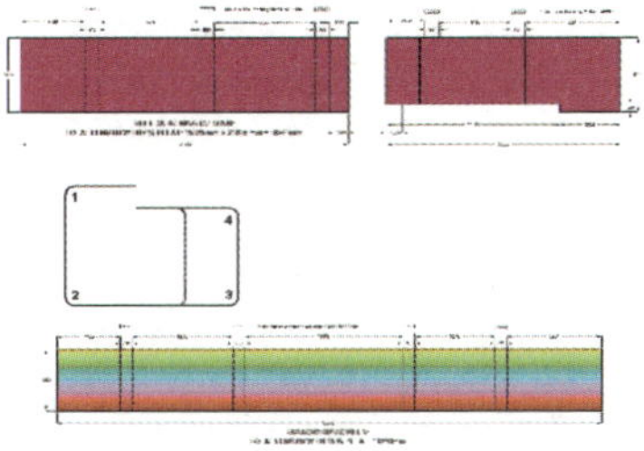
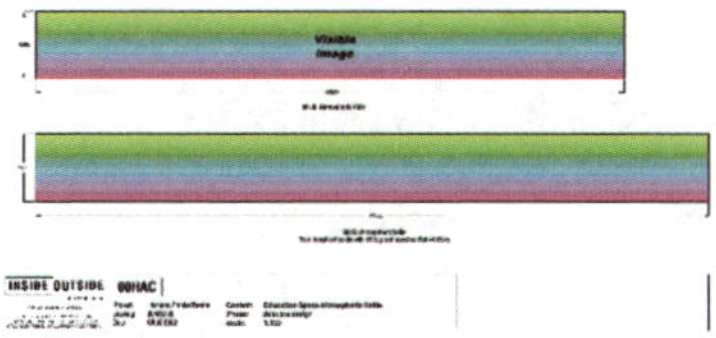
INSIDE OUTSIDE
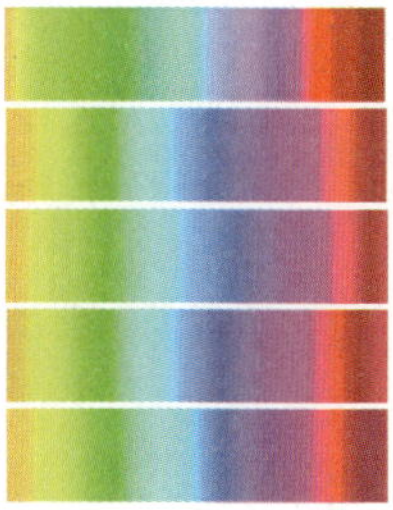

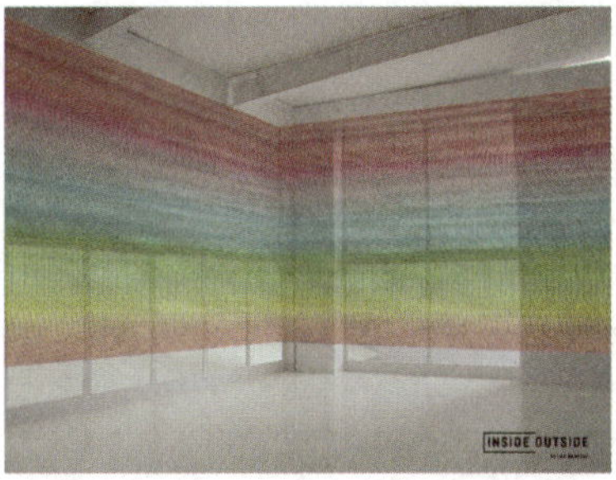
INSIDE OUTSIDE

INSIDE OUTSIDE
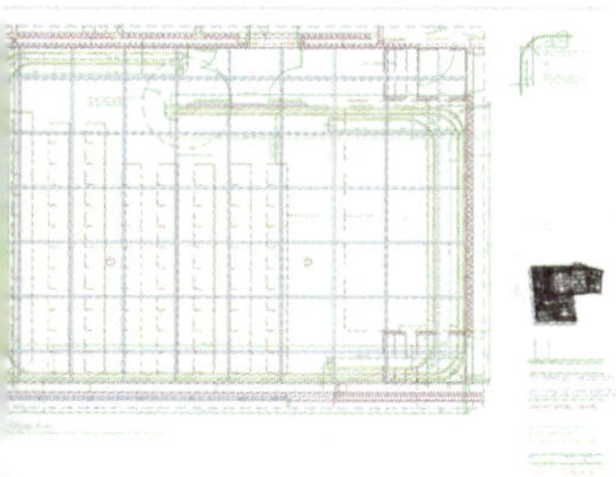

COMPLEX URBAN PLANNING — Giardini di Porta Nuova, Milan, Italy, 2003–unknown

Title
Biblioteca degli Alberi (Library of Trees)

Location
Giardini di Porta Nuova, Milan, Italy

Site
Infrastructurally bounded open space between *Stazione di Porto Garibaldi* and *Stazione Centrale*

Client
The City of Milan

Status:
Competition entry 2003
Laureate of the First Prize 2004

Team
Inside Outside, Amsterdam
Mirko Zardini, Milan (city planning)
Michael Maltzan, Los Angeles (architecture)
Irma Boom, Amsterdam (graphic design)
Piet Oudolf, Hummelo (planting design)
Rob Kuster, Utrecht (landscape engineering)

Scope of Work
Urban park methodology and design

The Project
The park acts as an urban connector, organizer of infrastructure, cultural campus and botanical garden. Paths are drawn from one point to another, connecting different areas (residential, commercial, governmental) around the site, creating a web of paths. This web generates irregular plots that represent different types of gardens. By folding them up or down, both paths and plots can overcome height differences and bridge roads and underlying traffic tunnels; create sound walls and downward slopes. Circular forests are scattered over the site and will grow into interior spaces with vegetal canopies of different colour and structure that float above the park. A series of cultural, educational, social and commercial buildings are placed in the park and along its edges, triggering interest and income for the area and thus securing a high-level maintenance program for the park.

Specifications
1. Areas and Budgets
Site area: 100,000 m² (ca. 400 x 250 m)
Building area: 23,400 m²
Budget for park redevelopment: 20,000,000 euros
(200 euros per m²)
Budget for a pavilion and the restoration of the existing building included in the competition program: 4,000,000 euros
(1,000 euros per m²)

2. Planting List
Perrenials
Alcea 'Parkallee'
Amsonia tabernaemontana
Aster divaricatus
Aster lateriflorus horizontalis
Aster x frikartii 'Monch'
Aster 'Sonora'
Aster 'Twilight'
Aster 'Violetta'
Astilbe 'Purpurlanze'
Astrantia 'Claret'
Baptisia australis
Baptisia 'Purple Smoke'
Calamintha nepeta
Centranthus ruber
Cietra barbinervis
Crambe cordifolia
Discanthus cercidifolius
Echinacea purpurea
Echinacea 'Jade'
Echinacea 'Rubinstern'
Echinacea 'Rubinglow'
Elsholtzia stauntonii
Epimedium var.
Eryngium alpinum
Eryngium alpinum 'Blue Star'
Eupatorium mac. purpureum
Foeniculum 'Bronze Giant'
Fothergilla monticola
Gaura lindheimeri 'Whirling Butterflies'
Gaura lindheimeri 'Siskiou Pink'
Geranium nodosum
Geranum phaeum 'Springtime'
Geranium psilostemon
Gillenia trifoliata
Helleborus var.
Helenium 'Kupferzwerg'
Helenium 'Rubinzwerg'
Heuchera 'Purple Palace'
Heuchera villosa
Hemerocallis 'Gentle Shepard'
Hosta 'Blue Angel'
Hosta 'Halcyon'
Inula magnifica
Kalimeris incisa
Lavandula 'Munstead'
Liatris spicata
Limonium latifolium
Lippia citriodora
Lunaria rediviva
Luzula 'Waldler'
Lythrum salicaria 'Blush'
Lythrum 'Zigeunerblut'
Mertensia virginica
Monarda hybrida
Nepeta 'Walker's Low'
Origanum leavigatum
Origanum leavigatum 'Herrenhausen'
Papaver orientale
Papaver 'Flamingo'
Perovskia 'Little Spire'
Persicaria amplexicaule 'Firedance'
Persicaria polymorpha
Podophyllum peltatum

Polygonatum multiflorum
Potentilla 'Etna'
Salvia 'Blauhügel'
Salvia 'Dear Anja'
Salvia 'Evelyn'
Salvia 'Ost Friesland'
Salvia 'Purple Rain'
Salvia 'Rugen'
Sanguisorba tenuifolia
Scabiosa columbaria
Scutellaria incana
Sedum 'Bertram Anderson'
Sedum 'Matrona'
Sedum 'Munstead Red'
Sidalcea 'My Love'
Smilacina racemosa
Stachys officinalis 'Rosea'
Thalictrum delavayi
Thermopsis caroliniana
Trifolium rubens
Trollius 'Lemon Queen'
Veronica 'Evelyn'
Veronicastrum virginicum 'Fascination'

Vines

Clematis youiniana 'Praecox'
Hedera helix 'Arborescens'

Shrubs

Amorpha canescens
Amorpha fruticosa
Caryopteris x clandonesis 'Dark Knight'
Ceanothus 'Marie Simon'
Clerodendron trichotomum
Hamamelis 'Arnold Promise'
Hydrangea aspera 'Mauvette'
Hydrangea 'Blue Bird'
Hydrangea heteromala
Hydrangea involucrata hortensis
Hydrangea 'Mauvette'
Hydrangea petiolaris
Hydrangea veitchii
Indigofera ambiyantha
Indigofera heterantha
Lavatera 'White Angel'
Lonicera x purpusii
Paeonia delavayi
Phlomis italica
Rosa glauca
Rosmarinus officinalis
Thymus lanuginosus
Viburnum dilatatum
Viburnum dilatatum 'Asian Beauty'
Viburnum farreri
Viburnum lentago
Viburnum nudum
Viburnum plicatum 'Lanarth'
Viburnum plicatum 'Mariesil'
Viburnum 'Bodnatense Dawn'
Viburnum sargentii 'Onondago'
Vitex agnuscastus

Trees

Acer palmatum 'Atropupureum'
Acer saccharinum 'Lutescens'
Betula nigra
Calocedrus decurrens 'Columnaris'
Catalpa bignoniodies 'Aurea'

Cercidiphyllum japonicum
Cercis canadensis
Chaenomeles 'Apple Blossom'
Cornus kousa 'Satomi'
Cornus kousa 'Milky Way'
Cornus kousa 'Norman Hadden'
Fraxinus americana
Koelreuteria paniculata
Liriodendron tulipifera
Malus sylvestris, syn. M. pumila
Magnolia x soulangeana
Phellodendron amurense
Populus balsamifera
Prunus dulcis

Groundcovers

Athyrium opponicum 'Metallicum'
Calamagrostis brachytricha
Calamagrostis 'Karl Foerster'
Carex muskingumensis
Ceratostigma plumbaginoides
Chasmantium latifolium
Deschampsia cespitosa
Deschampsia cespitosa 'Goldtau'
Dryopteris erythrosora
Eragrostis curvula
Euonymus coloratus
Euonymus planipes
Festuca mairei
Hakonechloa macra
Imperata cylindrica
Miscanthus 'Flamingo'
Miscanthus 'Heiku'
Miscanthus 'Krater'
Miscanthus 'Malepartus'
Miscanthus 'Yakushima Dwarf'
Molinia caerulea
Molinia 'Moorhexe'
Molinia 'Transparent'
Panicum 'Dalla Blues'
Panicum virgatum 'Heavy Metal'
Panicum virgatum 'Rehbraun'
Pennisetum 'Woodside'
Polystichum varieties
Sesleria autumnalis
Sesleria heufffleriana
Sesleria nitida
Stipa gigantea
Stipa tenuissima
Stipa turcestanica
Vinca minor

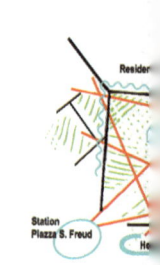

COMPLEX URBAN PLANNING Giardini di Porta Nuova, Milan, Italy, 2003–unknown

Phase 1

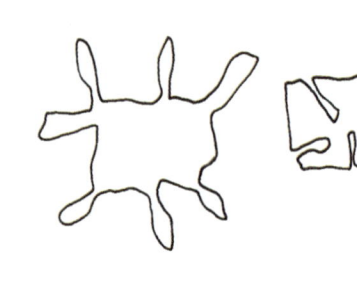

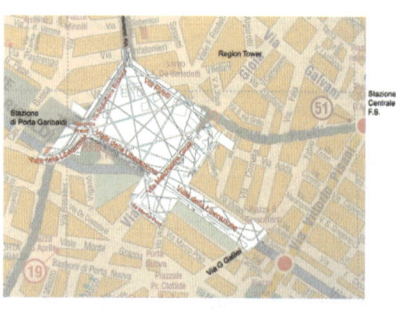

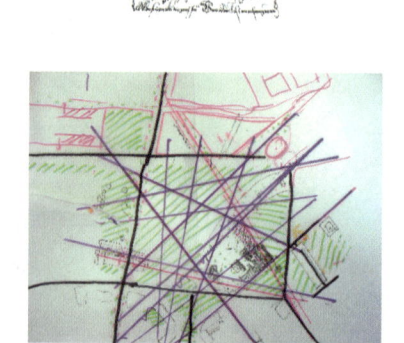

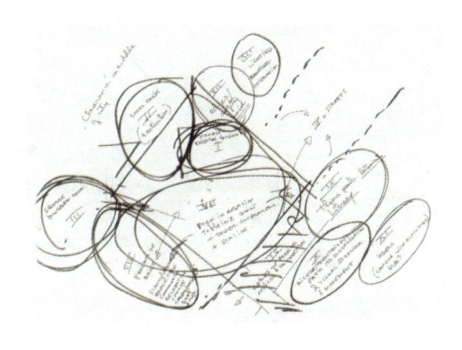

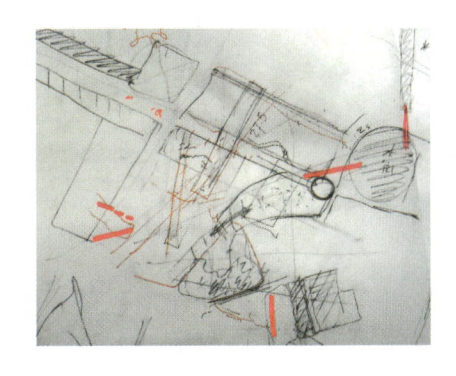

O3GAR_5-CONIOTTICI Model (1)

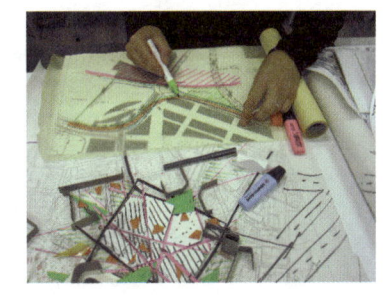

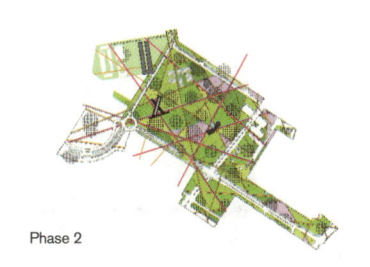

Region Tower
Municapility
Piazza Luigi Einaudi
v. liberazione

Phase 2   Phase 3

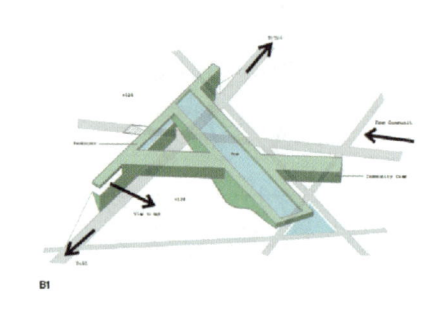

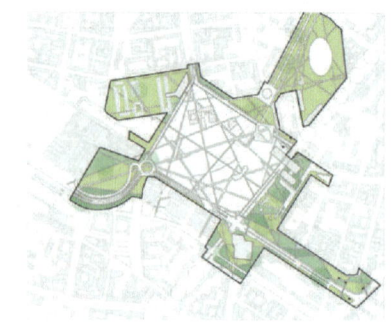

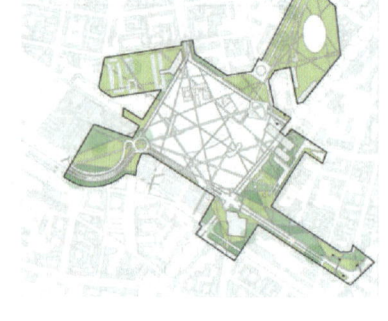

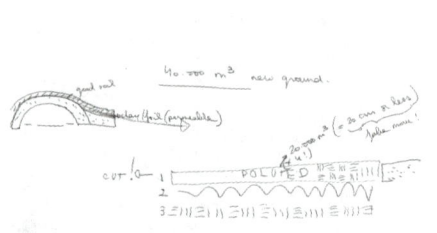

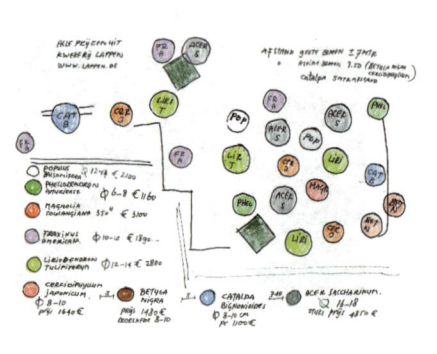

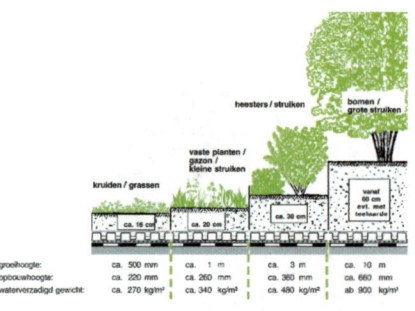

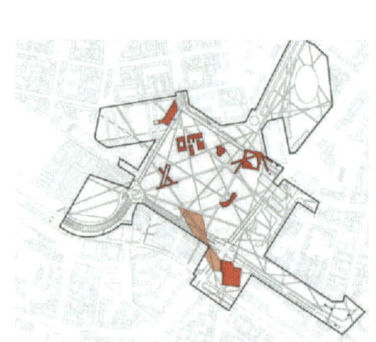

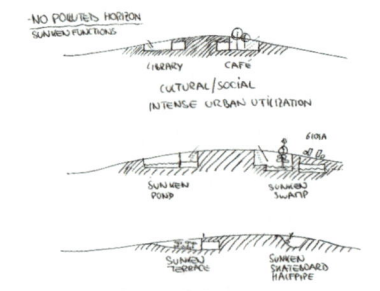

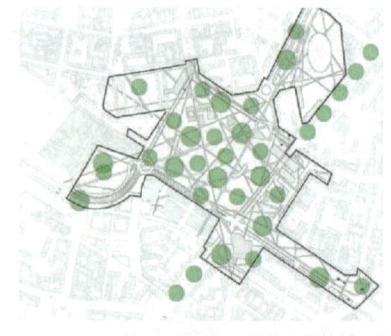

COMPLEX URBAN PLANNING
Giardini di Porta Nuova, Milan, Italy, 2003–unknown

429

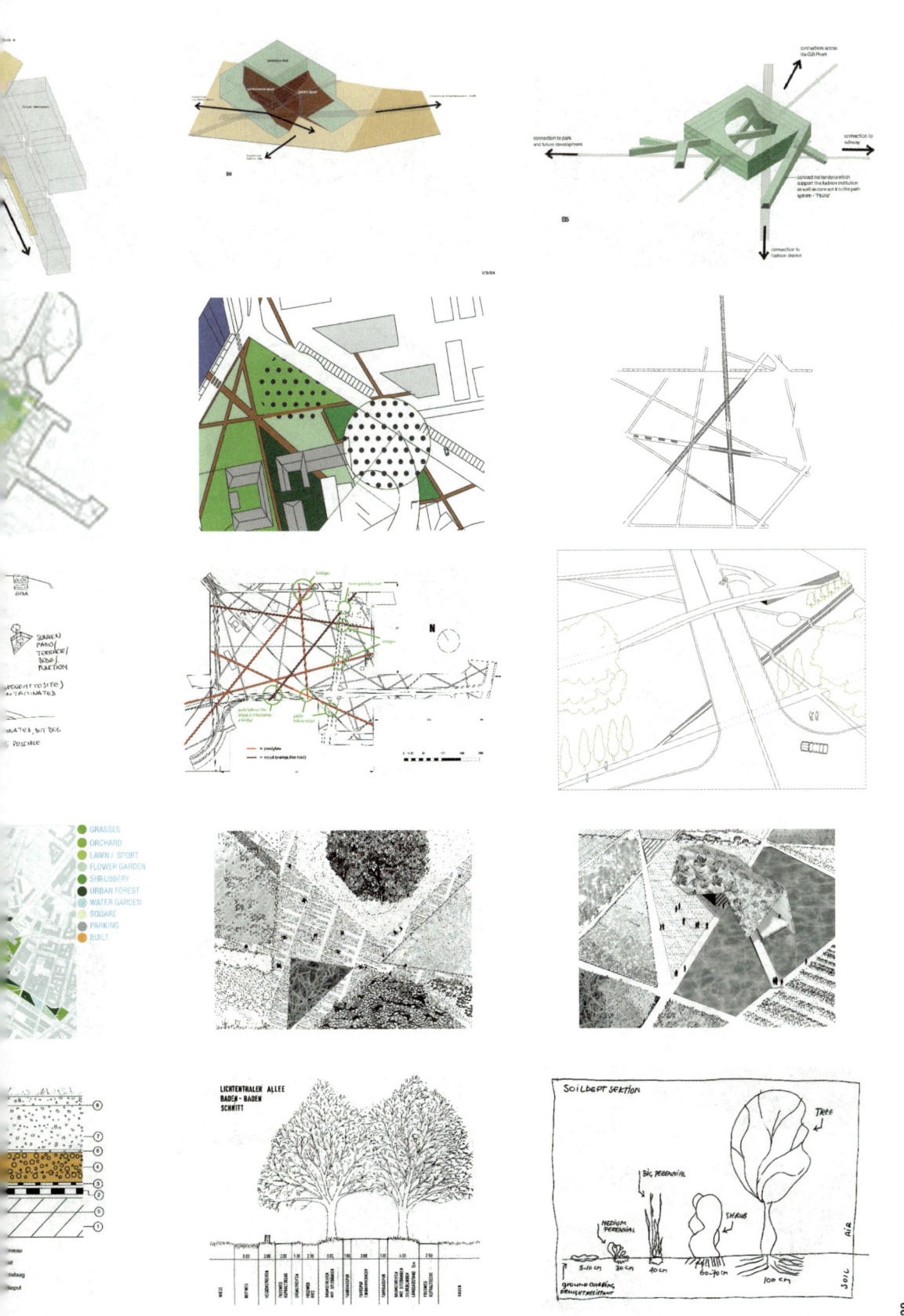

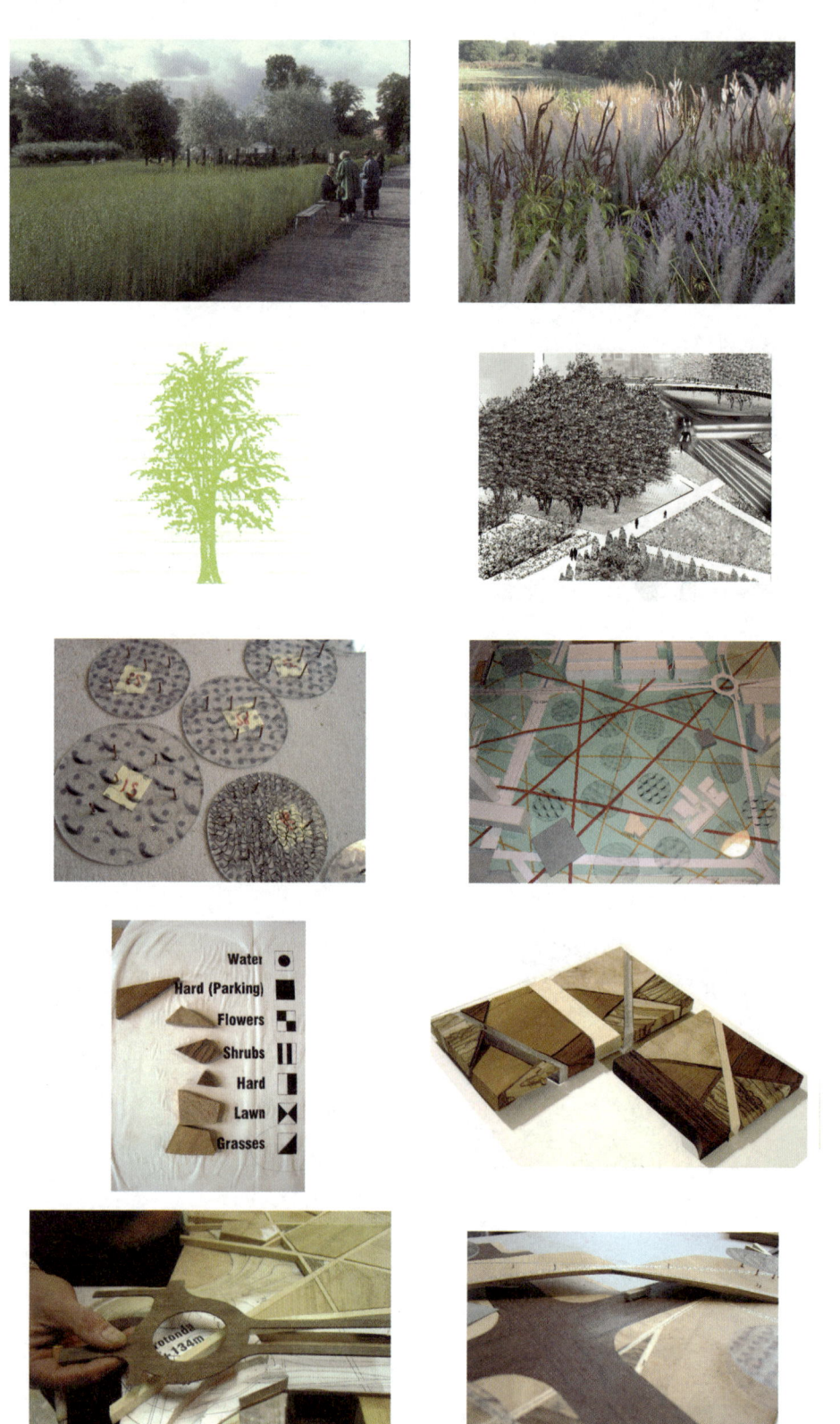

COMPLEX URBAN PLANNING Giardini di Porta Nuova, Milan, Italy, 2003–unknown

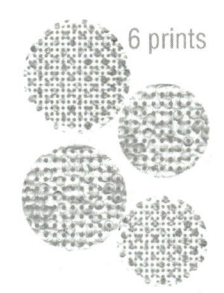

FRAXINUS AMERICANA
UP TO 40M HIGH
EXCELLENT WOOD
EMERGENCY BUDS
LEAVES UP TO 40 CM LONG
WITH 7-9 LEAF PARTICLES

ACER SACCHARUM - UP TO 35M HIGH
RED & WIND AUTUMN COLOURS
SUGAR JUICE IN WOOD, SPRING COLLECTED FOR SYRUP
5-12 × 8-12 CM RADIUS - EMBLEM FOR CANADA

6 prints

431

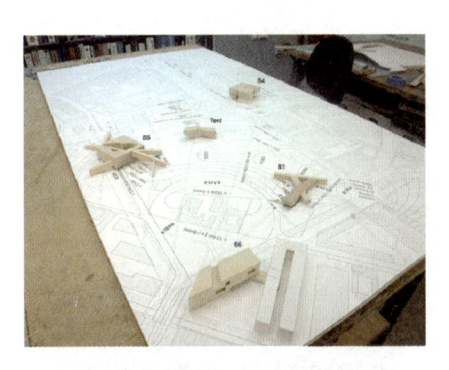

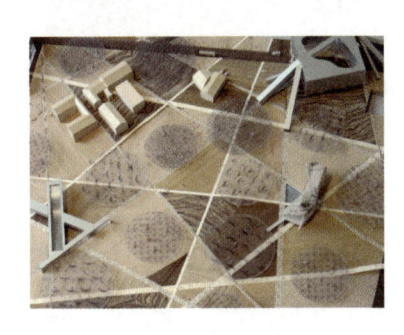

Title
Undoing Boundaries

Location
Seattle Central Library, Seattle, Washington, USA

Site
An entire city block located at 1000 Fourth Avenue in the Central Business District.

Client
The Seattle Public Library
The city of Seattle

Status
Commission 2000
Completion 2005

Architects
OMA, New York/Rotterdam
LMN Architects, Seattle

Team
Inside Outside, Amsterdam
Arup, London (structural and mechanical engineering)
Jones & Jones, Seattle (local landscape architects)
Kate Orff, New York (supporting landscape architect)
EGE, Herning (carpet production)
Helene Kierulf, Majestic Drapes, New York (curtain production)
Vertical Vision, Weesp (digital printing)
Zeebra, Ede (silkscreen printing)
Silas Morse PNTA, Seattle (curtain and track installation)
Michael R. Yantis Associates Inc., Seattle (acoustics)
Renz van Luxemburg, Eindhoven (acoustic advisory)

Scope of Work
Landscape design and planting plan for two entrance plazas, all street borders and transitional spaces; design, tender documents and supervision of production, transportation and installation of the auditorium curtains and carpets, advise on the interior finishes and colour scope, especially focusing on all horizontal planes, floor and ceiling surfaces.

The Project
The most characteristic part of this design is the way in which the landscape infiltrates and folds into the interior. The transparent façade of the building is surrounded by native tree species that are inter-planted with grass and plant fields, which slope, fold and overlap as planes of various greens.
Inside, these green fields transform into carpets, printed with large-scale plant patterns.
In the auditorium, our white-and-green finned curtain with its PVC imprinted 'bearskin' lining connects to the field of green chairs designed by Maarten van Severen and the brown polyurethane floor surface, and creates another garden-like space in the heart of the building.

Specifications
1. Areas
Site area: 38,276 m^2
Landscape area: 1,600 m^2
Carpets: 895 m^2
Curtains: 410 m^2

2. Carpets
Carpet No. 1 (large), Living Room
Images printed full scale in greens
Install size: 19.50 x 10.70 m
Order size: 5 bands of each 4 m width x 10.80 m length

Carpet No. 2 (medium), Living Room
Images printed 50% scale in greens
Install size: 7.80 x 5.20 m
Order size: 2 bands of each 4 m width x 5.40 m length

Carpet No. 3 (small), Living Room
Images printed 50% scale in greens
Install size: 1.75 x 6.90 m
Order size: 1 bands of 4 m width x 8.10 m length

Carpet No. 4, Reading Room
Images printed full scale in greens
Install size: 13.65 x 9.30 m
Order size: 4 bands of each 4 m width x 13.50 m length

Carpet No. 5, Reading Room
Images printed full scale in reds and pinks
Install size: 11.75 x 11.60 m
Order size: 3 bands of each 4 m width x 13.50 m length

Carpet No. 6, Reading Room
Images printed full scale in mauves and blues
Install size: 18.40 x 11.60 m
Order size: 3 bands of each 4 m width x 18.90 m length

3. Auditorium Curtains (a) + (b)
Curtain size (width x height): 16.3 x 8.13 m (incl. pleat)
Slit with an overlap ot 30 cm

Material: (a) Heavy off-white Trevira CS, acoustically absorbent sati with a surface treatment (silkscreen print) composed of green vertical stripes. (b) White flameproof plastic with a surface treatmer (digital printing) depicting enlarged brown fur.

Total surface area of Trevira: 375 m^2
Total surface area of plastic: 140 m^2

4. Planting List
Perennials

Acorus gramineus 'Ogon'
Acorus graminus 'Pusillus'
Allium cernuum
Astilbe 'Sprite'
Coreopsis verticillata 'Moonbeam'
Hosta 'Bizarre'
Hosta 'Blue Bush'
Hosta 'Zounds'
Iris virginica
Luzula sylvatica 'Aurea'
Tradescantia x andersoniana
Verbena bonariensis

Trees

Acer rubrum 'Armstrong Fremanii'
Acer rubrum 'Autumn Flame'
Acer rubrum 'October Glory'
Betula jacquemontii
Cedrus deodara
Cornus kousa 'Chinensis'
Liquidambar styraciflua
Liriodendron tulipifera 'Fastigiatium'
Magnolia kobus
Magnolia soulangeana
Magnolia stellata
Magnolia x loebneri
Magnolia virginiana
Quercus coccinea
Quercus rubra
Quercus shumardii
Styrax japonicus

Groundcovers/grasses

Adiantum pedatum
Athyrium filix femina
Athyrium nipponicum 'Pictum Crested'
Brachypodium sylvaticum
Carex comans 'Bronze'
Carex elata 'Bowles Golden'
Carex glauca
Carex morrowii 'Ice Dance'
Carex nigra
Carex glauca
Carex texensis
Carex testacea
Chasmantium latifolium
Deschampsia cespitosa 'Goldtau'
Dryopteris erythrosora
Elymus magillenicus
Festuca glauca 'Elijah Blue'
Festuca mairei
Hakonechloa macra 'Aureola'
Liatris spicata
Molinia caerulea 'Moorflamme'
Rumohra adiantiformis
Sesleria autumnalis
Stipa gigantea
Uncinia edgemontiana
Uncinia unicinata

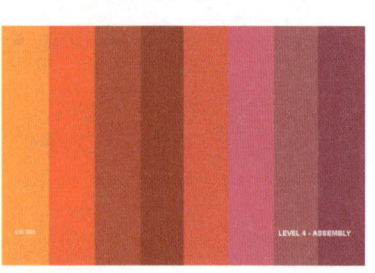

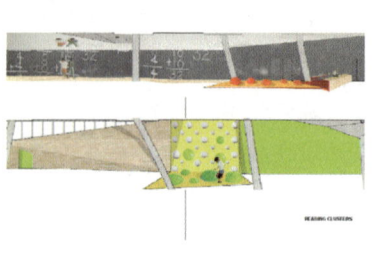

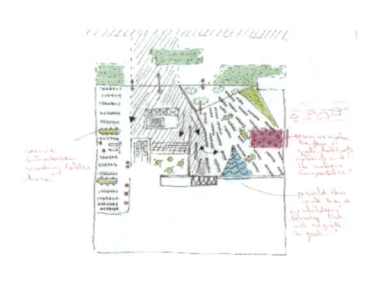

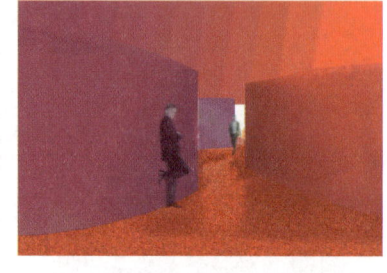

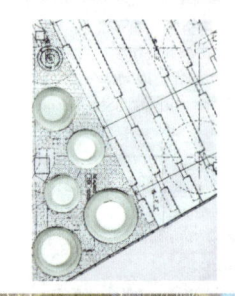

UNDOING BOUNDARIES Seattle Central Library, Seattle, USA, 2000–2004

435

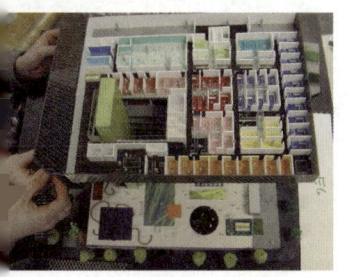

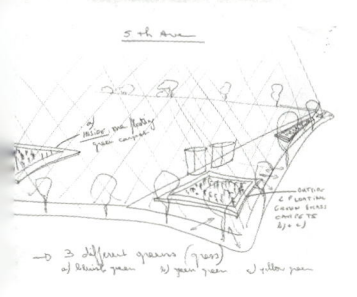

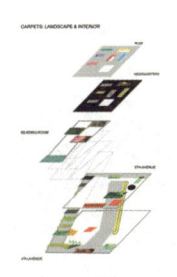

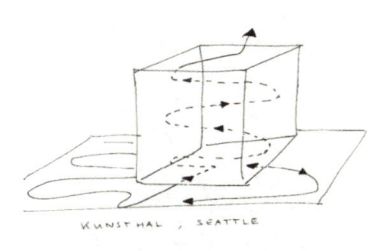

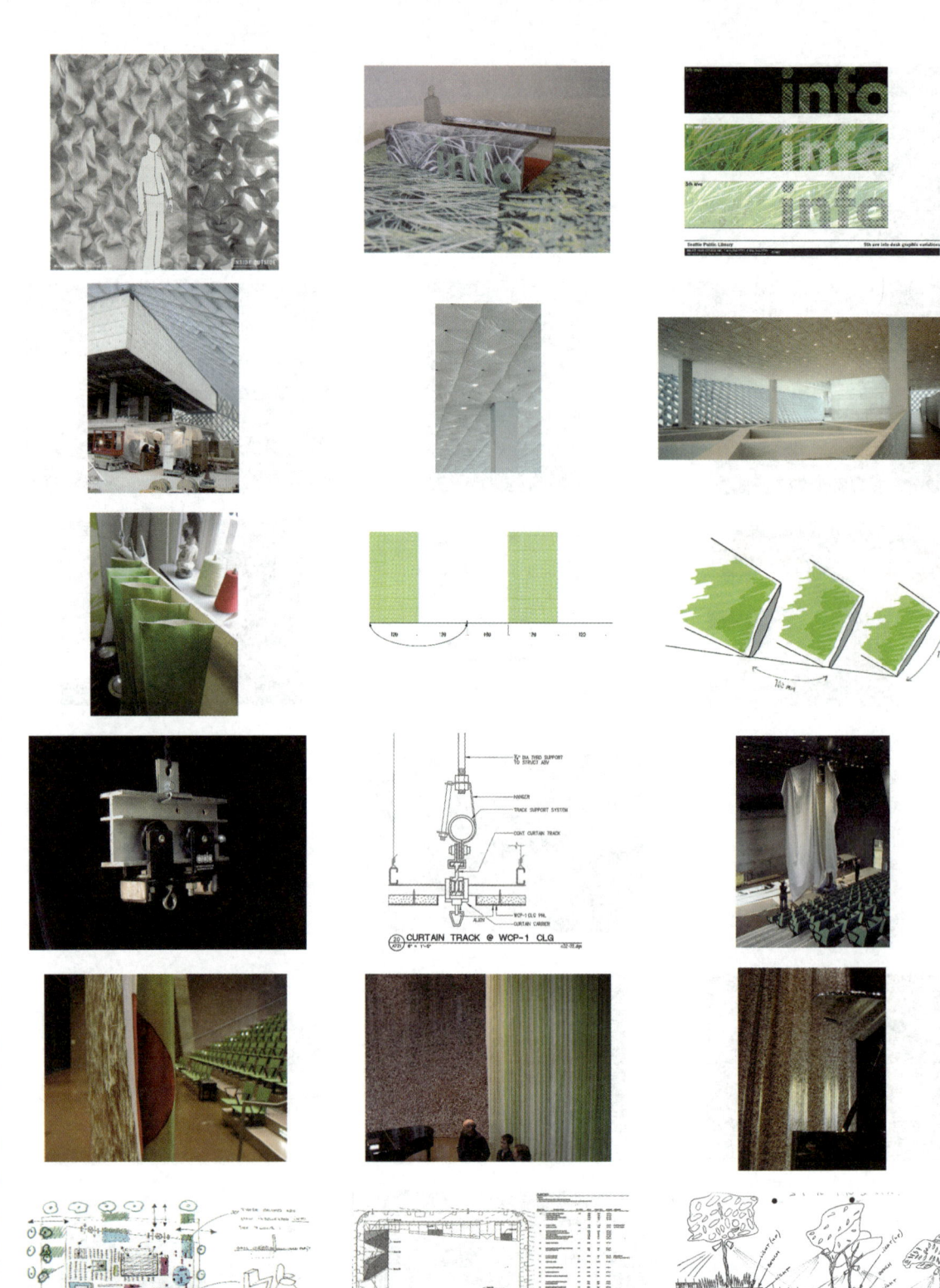

UNDOING BOUNDARIES Seattle Central Library, Seattle, USA, 2000–2004

437

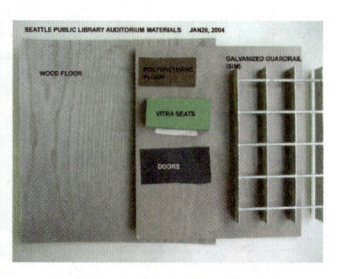

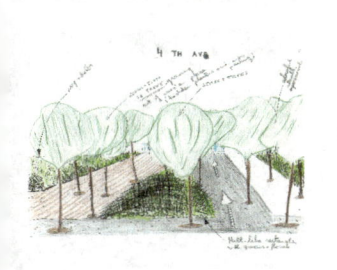

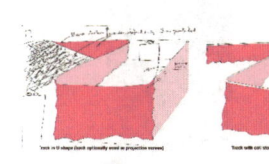

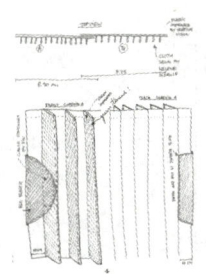

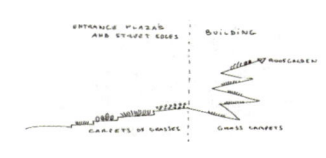

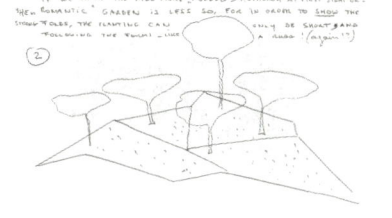

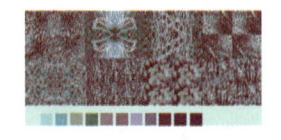

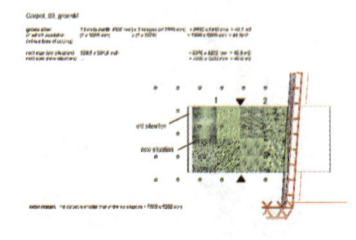

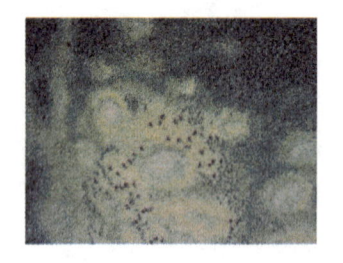

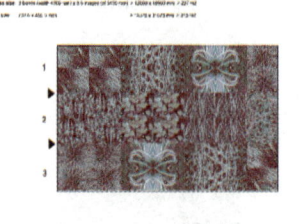

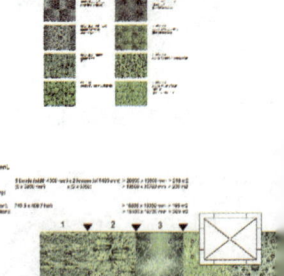

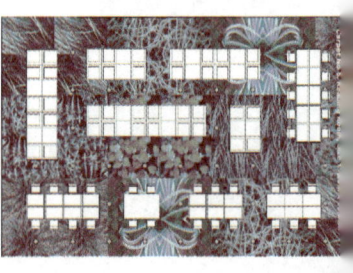

UNDOING BOUNDARIES Seattle Central Library, Seattle, USA, 2000–2004

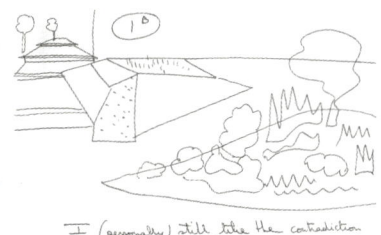

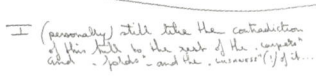

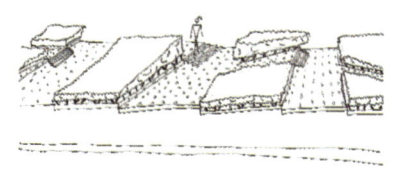

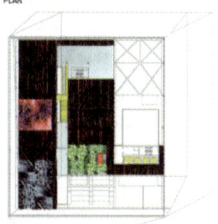

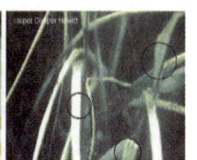

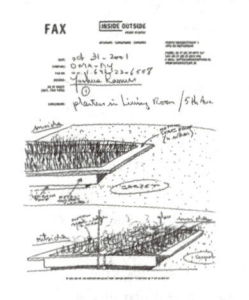

I (personally) still take the contradiction of this still to the spirit of the "carpets" and "fields" and the "meadows"(?) of it...

LEVEL TEN: READING ROOM
PLAN

Title
The Path as Spatial Tool

Location
State Detention Centre, Nieuwegein, the Netherlands

Site
A small town outside Utrecht, 33 km from Amsterdam

Client
Dutch Government Building Department

Status
Commission 1997
Completion 1999

Architects
Archivolt Architecten, Diemen

Team
Inside Outside, Amsterdam
DS Landscape Architects, Amsterdam (technical support)
Ank van Peski, Stompwijk (planting advice)

Scope of Work
For a new, triple-cross State Detention Centre: design and planting plans for six gardens; design for the main drop-off area and a parking area outside the prison walls; design for 12 shelters for inmates and guards. (This commission was part of a larger landscape and planting plan for the new business area between the State Detention Centre site and the highway, with Max One as city planners and Ballast Nedam as developers and contractors).

The Project
The landscape was conceived as a reaction to the strict urban design of the commercial area surrounding the prison, and to the equally strict and repetitive floor plans and interior circulation of the prison building. The six prison gardens represent the inscrutable human brain: a complex swirling path embedded in a range of different topsoil and surface treatments. Each garden is defined through its colour and composition, which allows inmates and staff to orient themselves from within the building. Prisoners and guards can walk, play, train and sport in the different gardens, while choosing the meandering path adds a meditative, spatial landscape experience to their daily outside routine.

Specifications
1. Total Site Area
2.5 ha

2. Path Material
Black asphalt (walking); black granulate (jogging)

3. 'Carpet' Materials
White shells, blue mussel shells, ochre dololux, terracotta granulate, grass mixtures, fake grass (soccer field), asphalt (ball courts).

4. Planting Plan
Perennials and Bulbs
Elymus magellanicum
Pennisetum alopecuroides
Iris sibirica
Ajuga reptans 'Atropurpureum'
Epimedium x rubrum
Tropaeolum majus
Galium odoratum
Fragaria vesca
Colchicum spp.
Alchemilla mollis
Pulmonoria longifolia
Mentha raripila 'Rubra'
Anemone hypemensis japonica 'Horine Jobert'

Trees
Betula jacquemontii
Pinus nigra
Robinia pseudo accacia

bloementuin

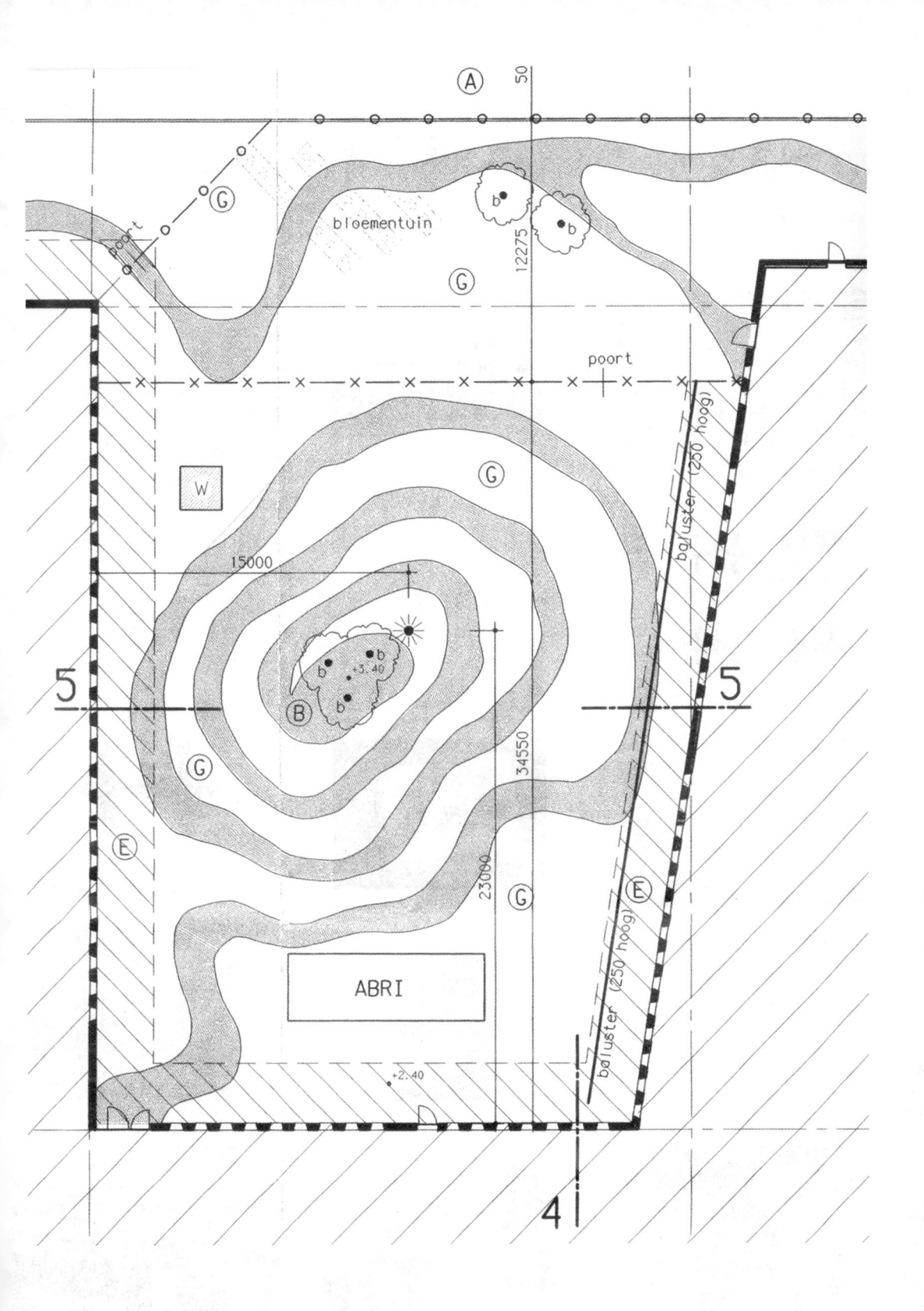

poort

baluster (250 hoog)

ABRI

baluster (250 hoog)

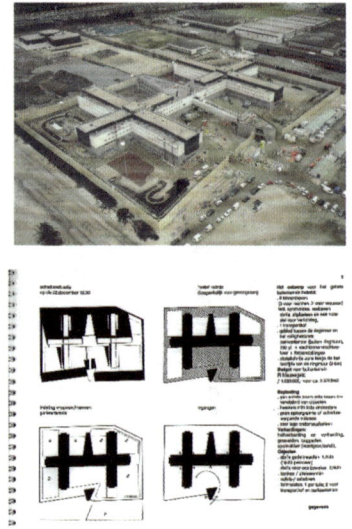

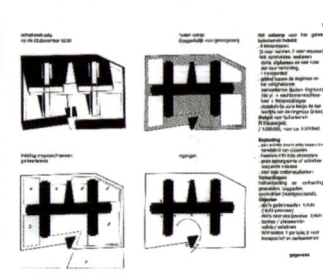

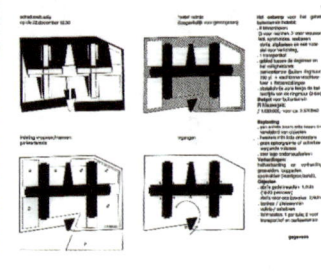

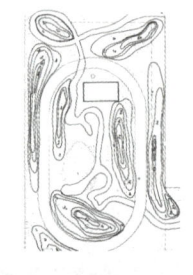

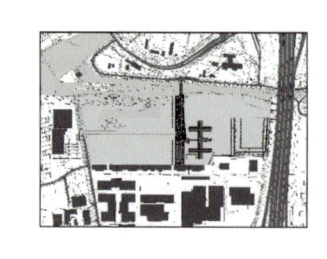

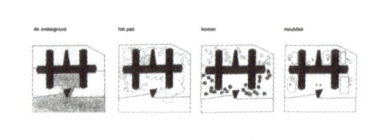

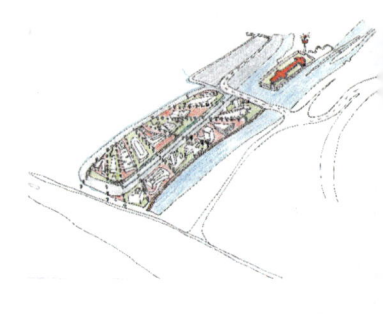

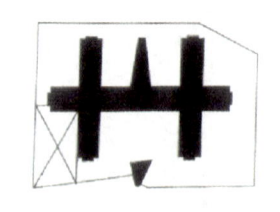

THE PATH AS SPATIAL TOOL State Detention Centre, Nieuwegein, the Netherlands, 1997–1999

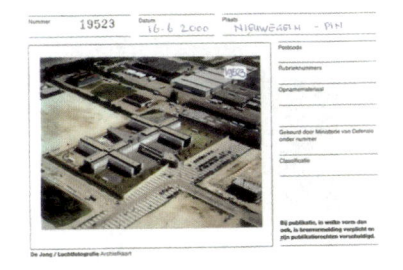

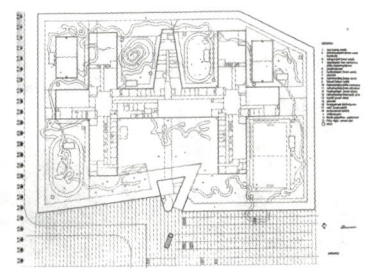

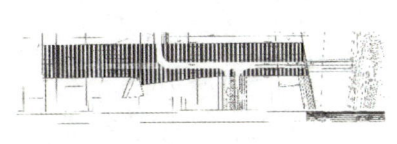

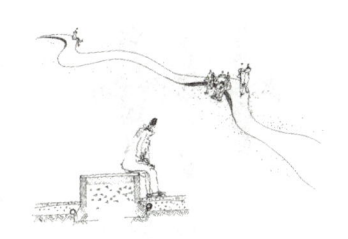

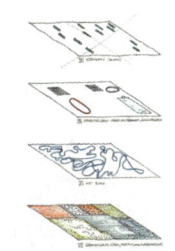

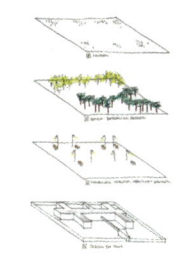

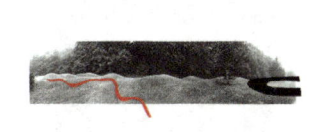

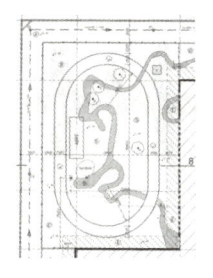

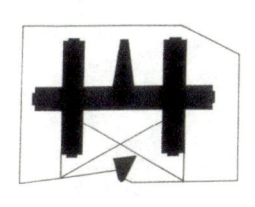

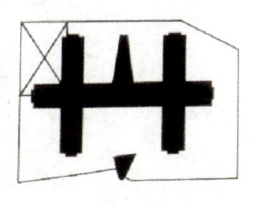

transporthof

het zandhof

443

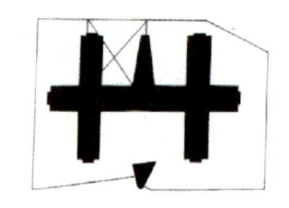

THE PATH AS SPATIAL TOOL State Detention Centre, Nieuwegein, the Netherlands, 1997–1999

het witte hof

het terracotta hof

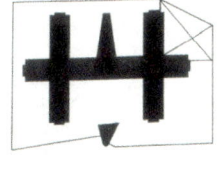

het blauwe hof

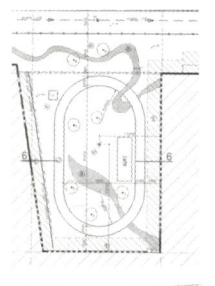

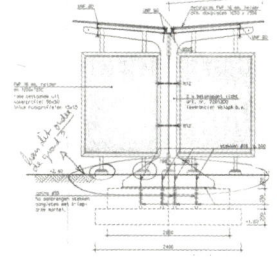

Title
Connective Green

Location
Hannam Dong District, Seoul, Korea

Site
A mountainous urban area embedded between mountains to the north and the city to the south.

Client
Samsung

Status
Commission 1995
Completion 2005

Architects
OMA, Rotterdam (city planners and architects)
Ateliers Jean Nouvel, Paris
Terry Farrell and Partners, London
Mario Botta Architetto, Lugano
Samoo Architects and Engineers, Seoul (local architects)

Team
Inside Outside, Amsterdam
Arup, London (structural and mechanical engineering)
B+B Landschapsarchitecten, Amsterdam (supporting landscape architects)
Joong-Ang Landscape Development, Seoul (local landscape architects)
Rob Kuster/Ro'Dor, Utrecht (landscape engineering)
Bruno Doedens, Amsterdam (advising landscape architect)
Wim van Krieken, Utrecht (technical detail drawings)

Scope of Work
Concept and design for connective landscape including four public areas, six gardens, general planting, furnishing, irrigation and maintenance with technical details for the entire area.

The Project
The landscape was programmed to connect, open up and enhance the movement in and around a series of heterogeneous cultural and commercial buildings. The rocky terrain created a building area with steep slopes and sharp folds, allowing both the built form and the landscape to follow, enter, integrate or bridge the irregularities of the built and natural topography. Inside Outside's design includes a wide variety of urban conditions which change position and function at every turn while generating a continuous overall effect binding the entire area together.

Specifications
<u>1. Surface Area per Block</u>
a: 350.80 m²
b: 308.30 m²
c: 255.00 m²
d: 604.90 m²
e: 24.70 m²
f: 26.70 m²
g: 46.60 m²
h: 24.80 m²
i: 244.60 m²
j: 84.40 m²
Landscape area: 1,970,80 m²
Site area: 13,111.60 m²

<u>2. Planting List</u>
Perennials
Anemone x hybrida 'Honorine Jobert'
Clematis chinensis 'Nakai'
Epimedium koreanum
Galanthus nivalis
Lavandula angustifolia 'Dwarf Blue'
Lilium var.
Muscari armeniacum
Narcissus tazetta var. chinensis
Persicaria affine 'Darjeeling Red'
Scilla siberica
Sedum acre
Trees (regulation 70% Deciduous 30% Evergreen)
Acer palmatum 'Aureum'
Acer palmatum 'Dissectum'
Acer palmatum 'Senkaki'
Betula papyrifera
Betula pendula
Betula utilis
Cornus kousa 'Berger'
Magnolia denudata 'Desrousseaux'
Magnolia liliflora
Magnolia sieboldii 'K. Koch'
Malus 'Schone van Boskoop'
Malus 'Cox's Orange Pippin'
Pinus densiflora 'Umbraculifera'
Pinus giganteus
Pinus mugo
Pinus thumbergii
Prunus sargentii
Sophora japonica 'Linnaeus'
Taxus baccata
Taxus cuspidata 'Siebold et Zuccarin'
Groundcovers
Euonymus fortunei var. 'Radicans Rehder'
Festuca glauca
Miscanthus sinensis 'Silberfeder'
Shrubs
Buxus angustifolia 'Dwarf Blue'
Buxus microphylla var. 'Koreana'
Juniperus media 'Pfizeriana Glauca'
Juniperus squamata
Juniperus virginiana
Ligustrum vulgare 'Atrovirens'
Paeonia var.
Rhododendron species
Rosa var.
Stephanandra incisa 'Crispa'
Syringa velutina venosa
Bamboos
Phyllostachys bambusoides 'Heterocycla'
Phyllostachys bambusoides 'Siebold et Zuccarini'
Phyllostachys pubescens 'Mael'
Phyllostachys viridi 'Glaucesens'

447

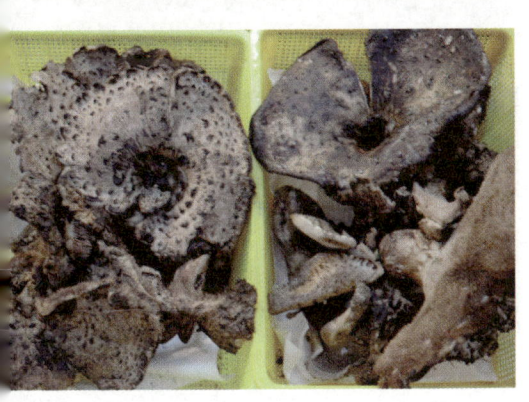

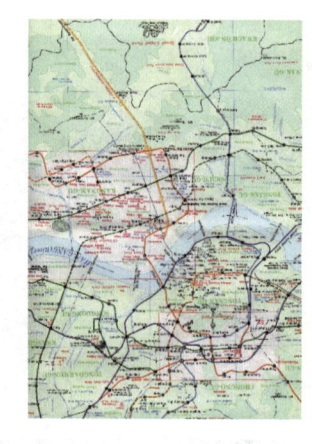

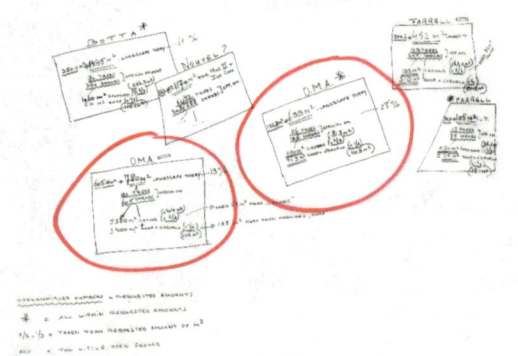

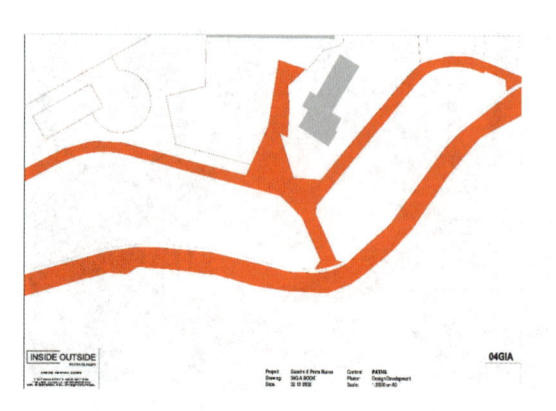

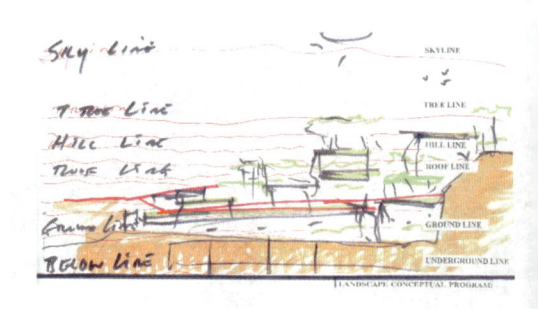

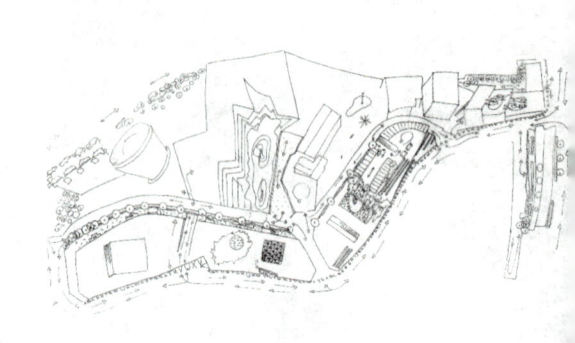

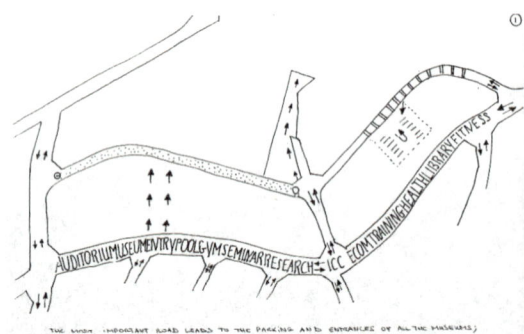

CONNECTIVE GREEN Landscape Design for 'H-Project', Seoul, South Korea, 1995–1997

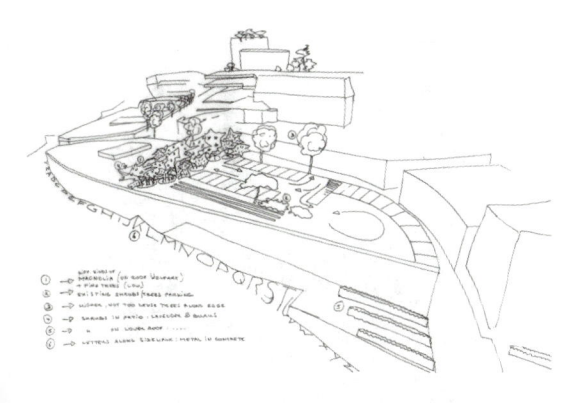

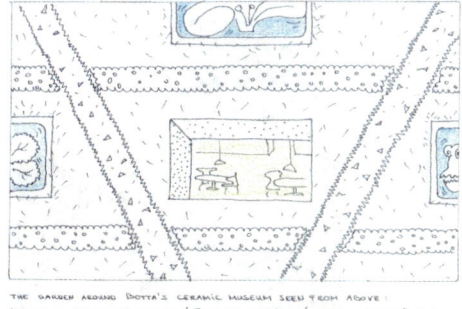

THE GARDEN AROUND BOTTA'S CERAMIC MUSEUM SEEN FROM ABOVE:
HEDGES OF "BUXUS MICROPHYLLA" & "TAXUS CUSPIDATA" CREATE "ROOMS" WITH
SCREENS OR WINDOWS (TO THE INNER SPACES SUCH AS THE "MIXING CHAMBER")
EMBEDDED IN GRASS; THREE COLORS OF GREEN FRAME THE MOVING
IMAGES OF FLOWERS FILMED AT HIGH SPEED.

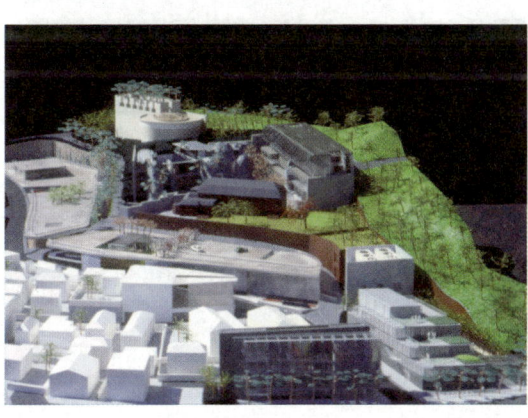

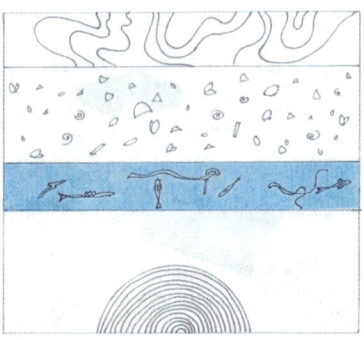

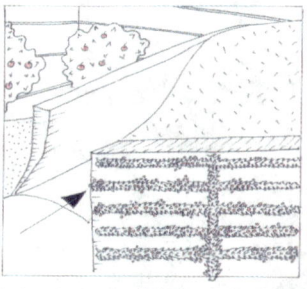

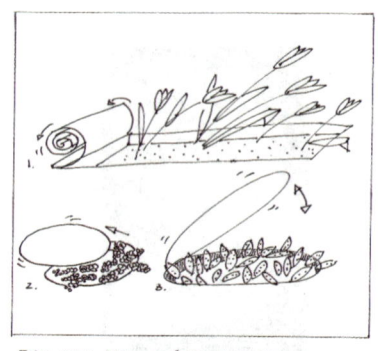

CONNECTIVE GREEN Landscape Design for 'H-Project', Seoul, South Korea, 1995–1997

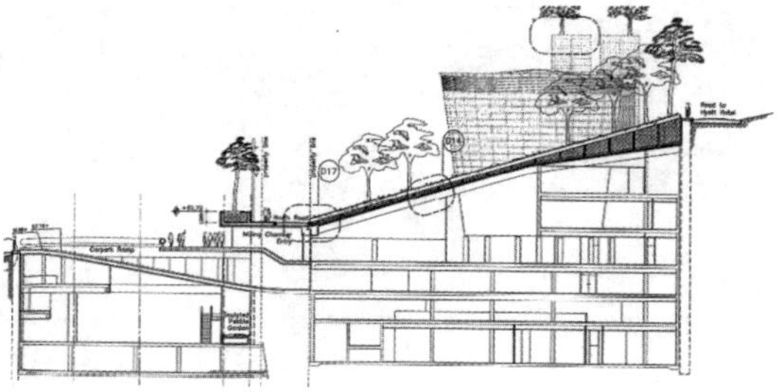

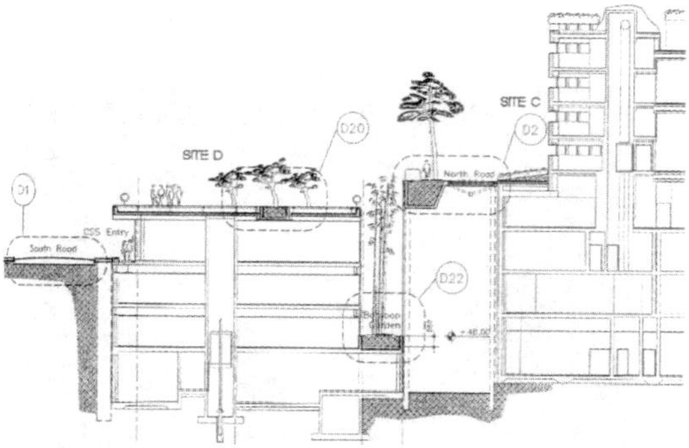

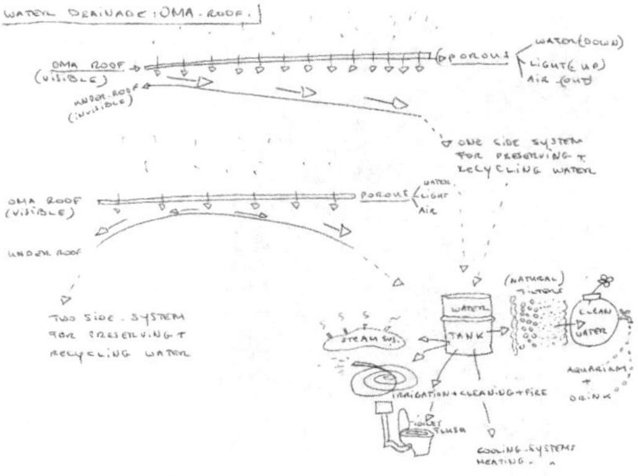

A ROAD LAYERS:
- 50 mm closed asphalt with sparkles
- existing concrete

B PAVEMENT LAYERS:
- 80 mm concrete with metallic letters
- 140 mm reinforced concrete
- watertight foil
- 100 mm sand

C Kerb Belgian hardstone size 1000 * 120 * 300

D Concrete haunching (min. 100mm)

DILATATION JOINTS:
- shrinking joint 5 mm every 4 m
- dilatation joint 10 mm every 20 m
- between kerb and asphalt 5 mm
- between pavement and building 10 mm polystyrene plate

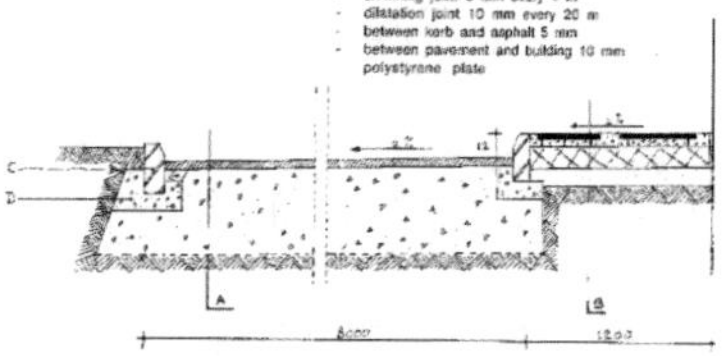

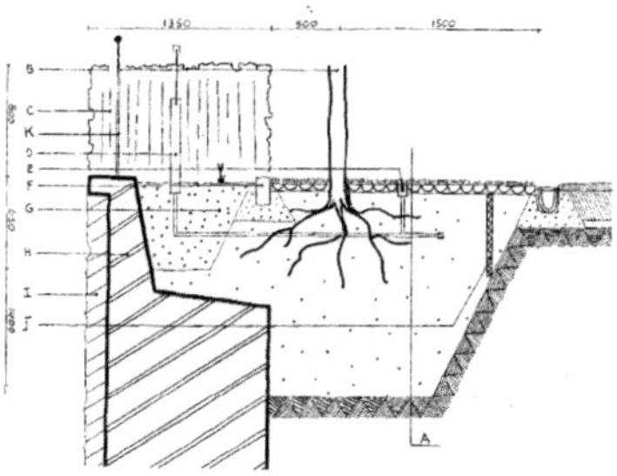

A Layers pavement
- Korean grass in honeycomb mash (syn.. size 380 * 560 * 50
- tree soil 2 m

B *Pinus densiflora* Ø 16/18
10 m high

C *Juniperus squamata* or *Taxus 'Hikaii'*
size 60/60

D Pop up sprinkler system on pole of 60 cm ('nvisible)

E Pop up sprinkler system under ground

F Concrete kerb 1000 * 150 * 300
colour grey

G Fertilized soil

H Retaining wall

I Sprayed concrete

J Deep root system 600 * 600 * 2

K Handrail of stainless steel tube, hight 1050

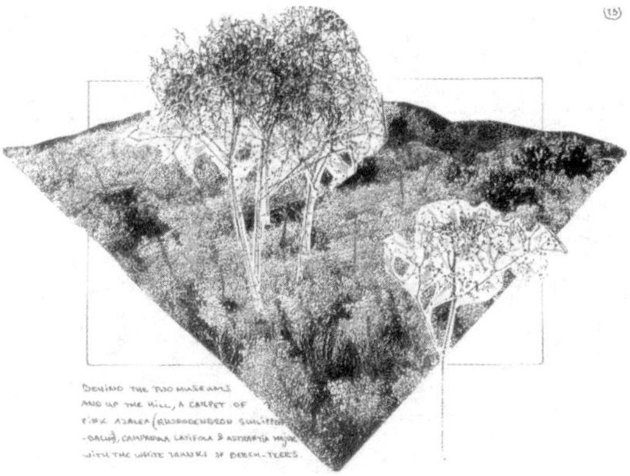

DETAIL 22
BAMBOO GARDEN CSS
CROSS SECTION
SCALE 1 : 20
10 MARCH 1997

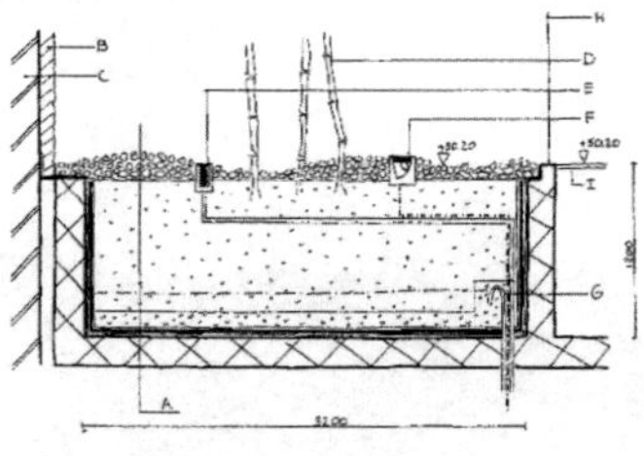

A Layers of planter
- 100 - 200 mm white pebbles size 20/40
- sand tight foil
- 850 mm growth medium
- root resistant foil
- 150 mm drainage
- watertight foil
- 100 mm insulation
- anti-vapour barrier

B Sprayed concrete

C Retaining wall

D Bamboo
- *Phyllostachys bambusoides Sieb. et Zuc.*
- *Phyllostachys pubescens Mazel*
- *Phyllostachys bambusoides heterocycla*
- *Phyllostachys virid. glaucescens*

E Sprinklers under ground

F Recessed lamps (BEGA 7488)

G Drain pipe (water level on 300 mm)

E Floor auditorium

H Glass facade

Data growth medium :
60 % flakes 40 % earth
max 15 % organic material in soil
PH = 6-6.5

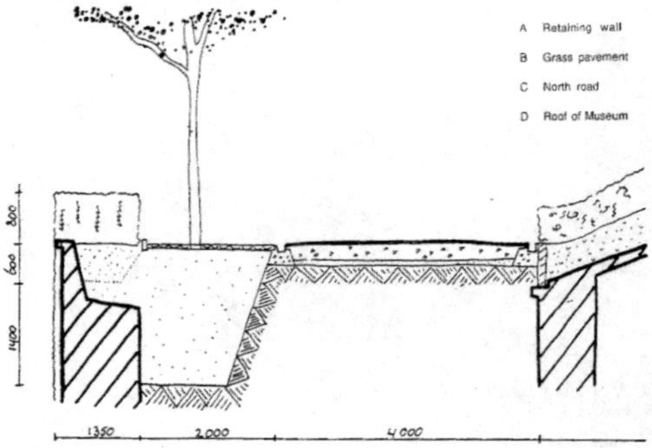

A Retaining wall

B Grass pavement

C North road

D Roof of Museum

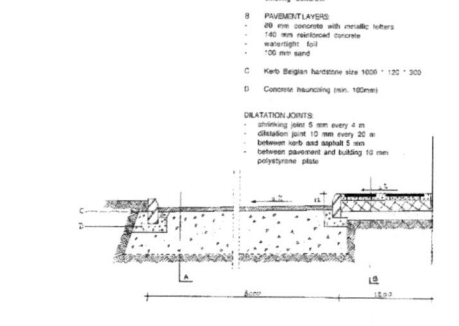

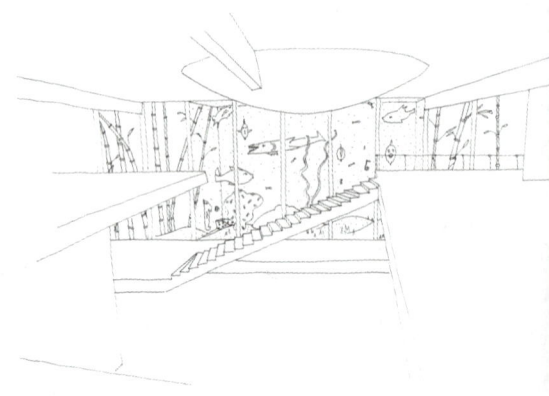

CONNECTIVE GREEN Landscape Design for 'H-Project', Seoul, South Korea, 1995–1997

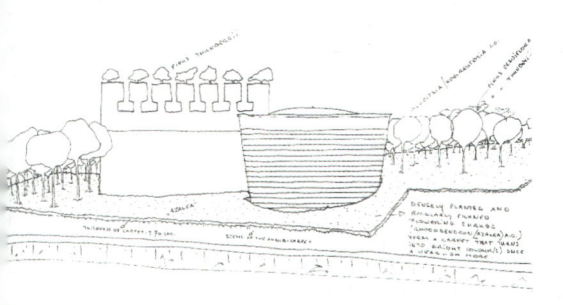

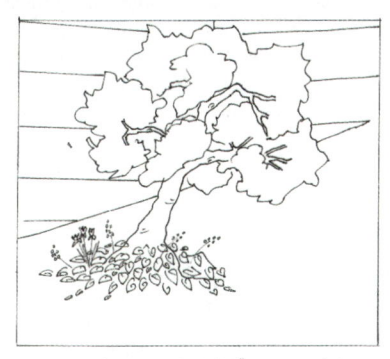

FRUIT TREES IN THE "PUBLIC GARDEN": MALUS PUMILA - OR CYDONIA OBLONGA - OR CRATAEGUS LAEVIGATA. AROUND THE TRUNK: THE IVY HEDERA HELIX "HEISE" WITH BULBS.

Title
Curtain as Architecture

Location
Casa da Música, Porto, Portugal

Site
A solitary building facing the historical park, on the Rotunda da Boavista

Client
Casa da Música

Status
Commission 1999
Completion 2004

Architects
OMA, Rotterdam

Team
Inside Outside, Amsterdam
Gerriets GmbH, Umkirch (curtain tracks and motors; curtain production and installation)
Vertical Vision, Weesp (digital printing)
Ducks Scéno, Vaux en Velin (scenography)
Thyssen, Carregado (mechanical installations)
Renz van Luxemburg, Eindhoven (acoustics)

Scope of Work
Design and supervision of the production and installation of 11 sound-, view- and light-regulating curtains for the large concert hall (1,300 seats), the small concert hall (350 seats) and 2 rehearsal rooms (total floor area: 22,000 m²); designing of the wall finishes of the large concert hall; advising on the interior and exterior atmosphere and finishes of the entire building including colour scopes. Total surface area of the 11 curtains is 2,622 m².

The Project
Nine of the eleven curtains are suspended over the four massive, corrugated glass windows of the two concert halls, which look out over the city in all directions. These curtains are used separately or in combination with one another, organizing light, visual and acoustic issues. The other two curtains cover walls in the underground rehearsal rooms for acoustic purposes. Here, integrated windows allow views from director booths and public areas into the spaces. All the curtains are colourless, with the emphasis on texture, structure, and degrees of transparency, movement and the effects of layering. Their sizes vary from 22 x 15 m to 65 x 8 m. In the concert halls, all curtains are mechanically operated and all are stored in hollow walls or in cavities above the auditoriums' lowered ceilings.

Specifications
Large Concert Hall
1. Behind Orchestra:
White Sun-Shading, 2 Parts
Curtain size (width x height):
(A) *in situ* (incl. 15% pleat): 13.5 x 15.0 m
    flat: 15.5 x 15.0 m
(B) *in situ* (incl. 15% pleat): 9.5 x 15.0 m
    flat: 10.95 x 15.0 m
Total cloth surface: 396.75 m²
Material: Verosol (upper segment sun-shading) and black voile (lower segment sun-shading)

2. Behind Orchestra:
(A) Black View Filter;
(B) White Absorbent Projection Screen;
(C) Blackout and Acoustic Absorbent Curtain
Curtain size:
Layers (A)-(C): 22.0 x 15.0 m (visible height)
22.0 x 16.0 m (incl. part hidden in mechanism)
Total cloth surface: 352.0 m² (3x)
Material: (A) black voile knotting layer;
(B) bleached Calmuc, acoustic absorption;
(C) coated blackout fabric, digitally imprinted blackout (dark grey, towards the outside)

3. Behind Audience:
White Sun-Shading, 2 Parts
Curtain size:
(A) *in situ* (incl. 15% pleat): 13.5 x 12.0 m
    flat: 15.5 x 12.0 m
(B) *in situ* (incl. 15% pleat): 9.5 x 12.0 m
    flat: 10.95 x 12.0 m
Total cloth surface: 317.4 m²
Material: Verosol (upper segment sun shading) with white voile (lower segment sun shading)

4. Behind Audience:
(A) White View Filter;
(B) Black Absorbent Projection Screen;
(C) Blackout and Acoustic Absorbent Curtain
Curtain size:
Layers (A)-(C): 22.0 x 12.0 m (visible height)
22.0 x 13.0 m (incl. part hidden in mechanism)
Total cloth surface: 286.0 m² (3x)
Material: (A) white voile knotting;
(B) black wool serge, acoustic absorption;
(C) coated blackout fabric, digitally imprinted blackout (light grey, towards the outside)

5. Behind Orchestra and Audience:
Blackout Aprons
Curtain size:
(A) *in situ:* 2.0 x 15.0 m
    flat: 3.0 x 15.0 m
(B) *in situ:* 2.0 x 12.0 m
    flat: 3.0 x 12.0 m
Material: Wool serge blackout gap

Small Concert Hall

6. Sunscreen: Copper-Coloured Voile and Black *Choucroute*
Curtain size:
  in situ (incl. 10% pleat): 14.0 x 12.0 m
  flat: 15.4 x 12.0 m
Total cloth surface: 184.8 m²
Material: Verosol sunscreen towards the outside.
Black *choucroute* (in-between) with white voile sealing
(towards the inside)

7. Grey Sound Absorbent and Darkening Curtain
Curtain size:
  in situ (incl. 50% pleat): 14.0 x 12.0 m
  flat: 21.0 x 12.0 m
Total cloth surface: 252 m² (2x)
Material: Grey cotton velvet (acoustic absorption and blackout);
stainless-steel rings (diameter 6 cm); white satin lining

8. White Foyer View Filter
Curtain size:
  in situ (incl. 10% pleat): 14.0 x 7.0 m
  flat: 15.4 x 7.0 m
Total cloth surface: 107.8 m² (2x)
Material: Laser scrim (towards the foyer); white *choucroute*
(in-between); white voile sealing (towards the auditorium)

Rehearsal Rooms

9. (A) White and (B) Black Sound Absorbent Curtain
Curtain Size:
A) 27.5 x 7.7 m (covering half the room)
B) 65.0 x 7.7 m (covering the entire room)
Total cloth surface: 712.25 m²
Material: (A) off-white wool serge (absorption), Glasklarfolie
(windows and open seam), cotton (slits), cord;
B) black wool serge (absorption), Glasklarfolie (windows
and open seam), cotton (slits), cord

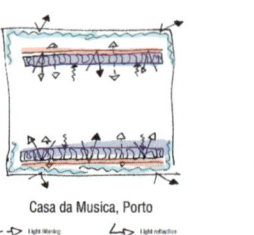

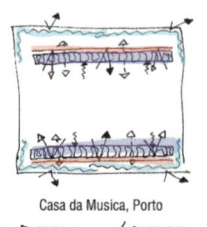

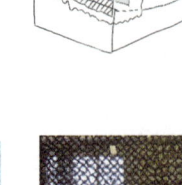

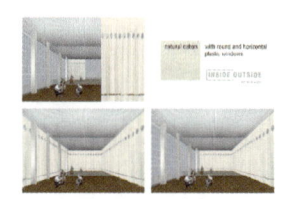

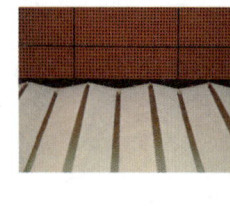

CURTAIN AS ARCHITECTURE Casa da Música, Porto, Portugal, 1999–2005

457

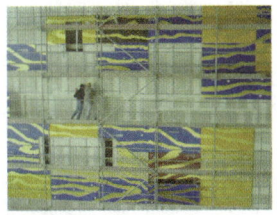

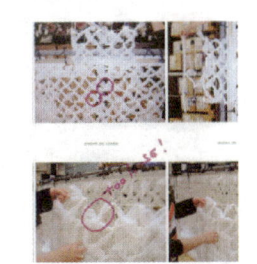

CURTAIN AS ARCHITECTURE

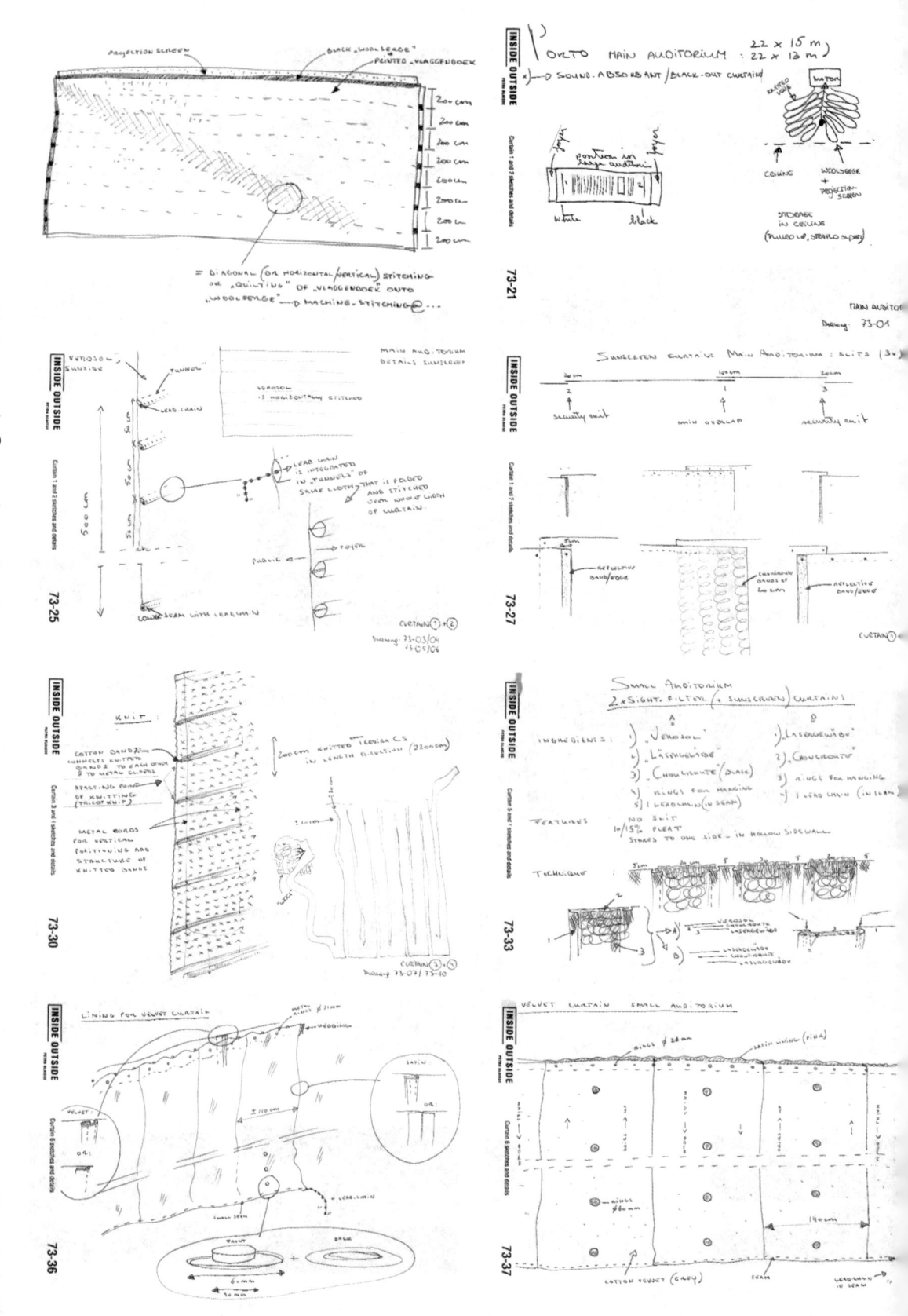

Casa da Música, Porto, Portugal, 1999–2005

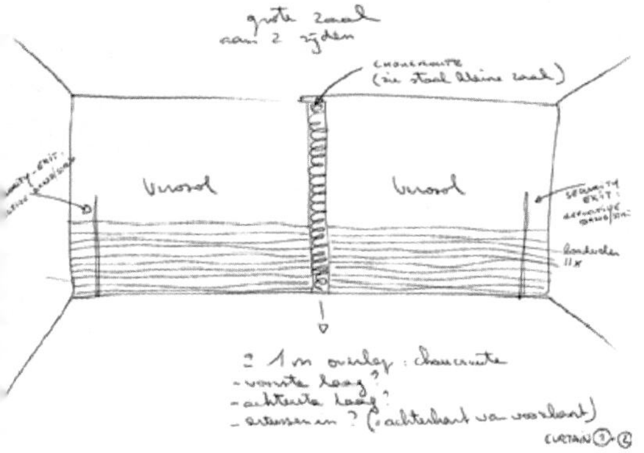

INSIDE OUTSIDE
PETRA BLAISSE

Curtain 1 and 2 sketches and details

73-24

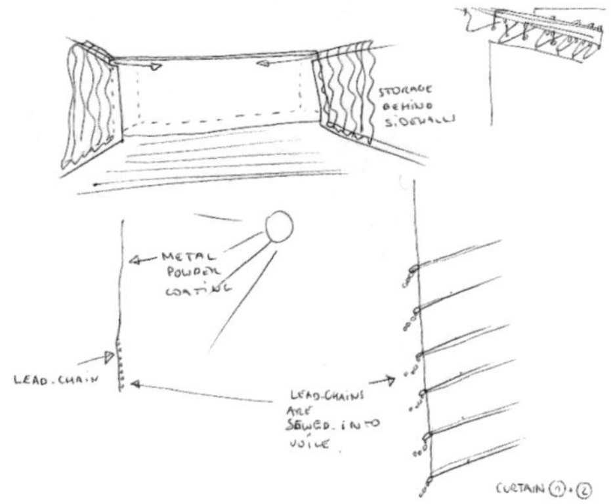

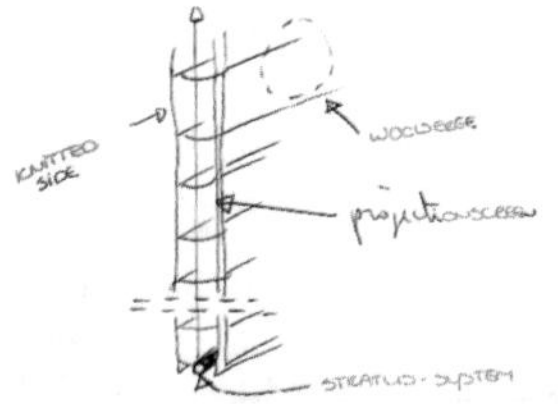

Lower end
Folding up
Completely folded up in ceiling
Folded up (sideview)

INSIDE OUTSIDE
PETRA BLAISSE

Curtain 3 and 4 sketches and details

73-29

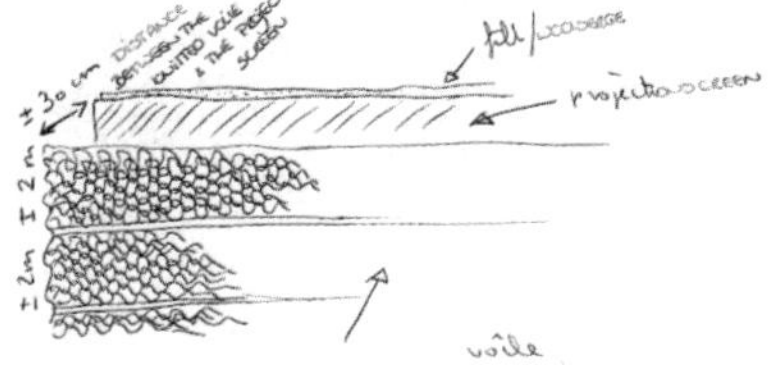

CURTAIN ③+④
Drawing: 73-07/73-10

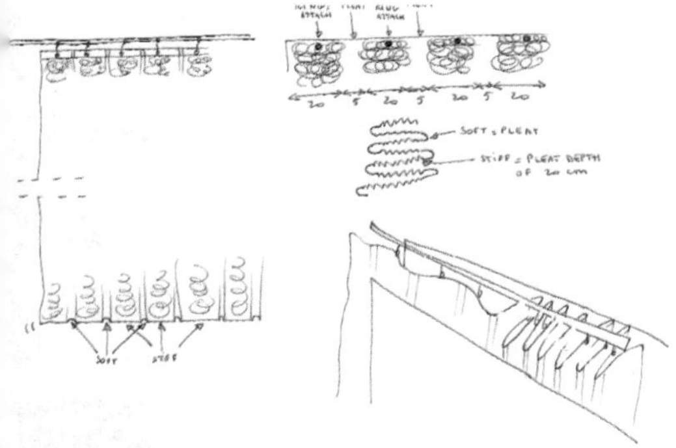

INSIDE OUTSIDE
PETRA BLAISSE

Curtain 6 sketches and details

73-35

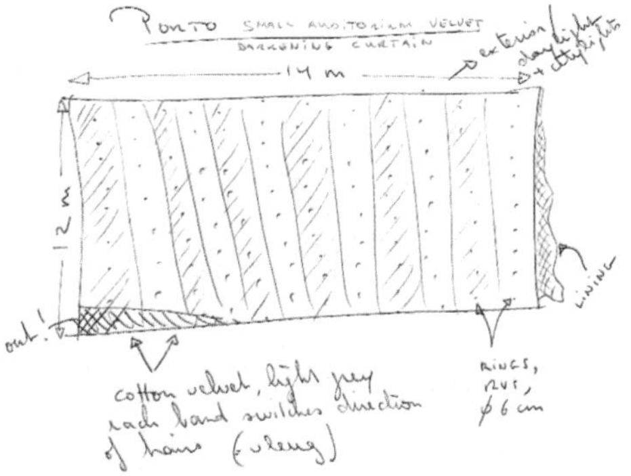

- no middle-slit or overlaps.
- cotton velvet, heaviest drape (780 gr/m²)
- vertical band.
- stored in sidewall
- lining in pink (or such)

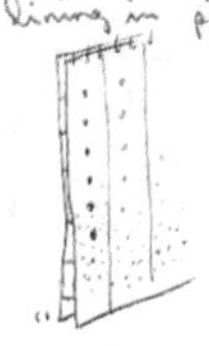

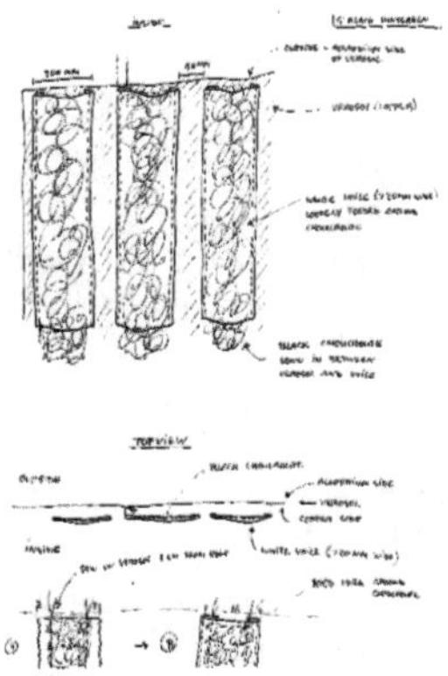

Study of Independent Screens

Inside Outside was invited by Vitra's then director Rolf Fehlbaum to research the possibility of curtains as a form of partition or private cell in office spaces. This request caught our attention, as it suggests independence from walls and ceilings: the ultimate emancipation of the curtain! We identified two object types: the curtain as screen and the curtain as wall. Both can easily create temporary, separate individual working spaces or meeting rooms. We also studied how to connect individual screens, so that shapes and sizes of working spaces could be numerous. We took the track as a starting point, but this time as a structural element in itself, bending or folding it or cutting it up in such a way that it became an independent stable object or a supporting or folding tool from which a curtain could hang; or around which a textile structure could be folded. The developments were aborted due to a shift in management and necessary economic restrictions.

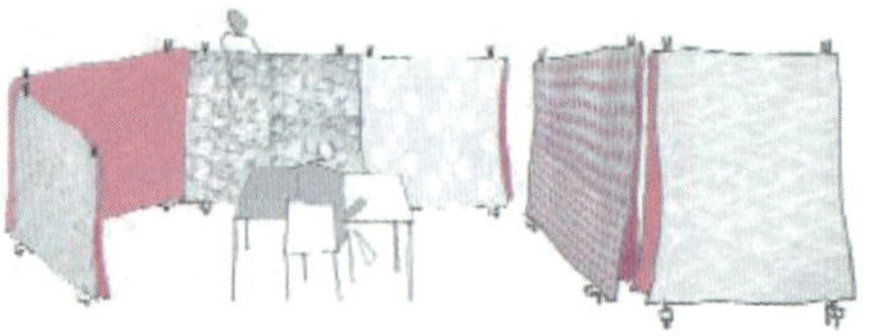

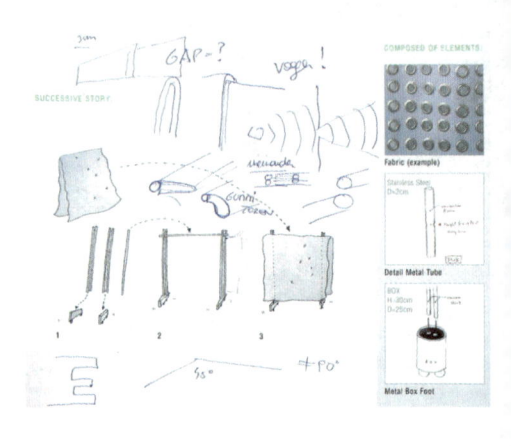

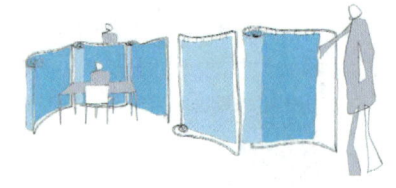

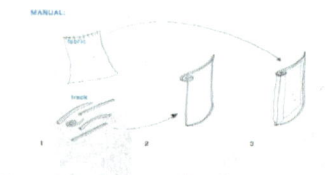

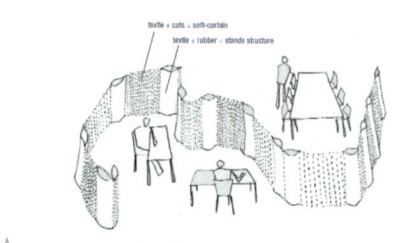

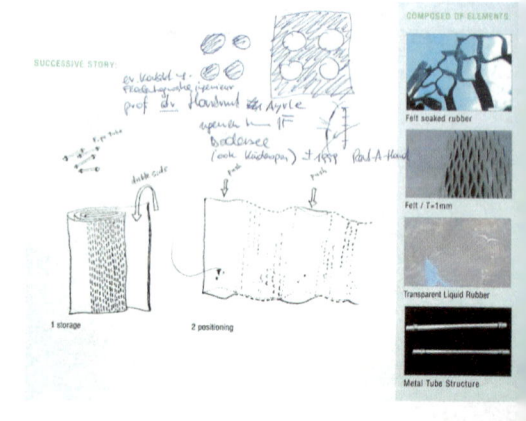

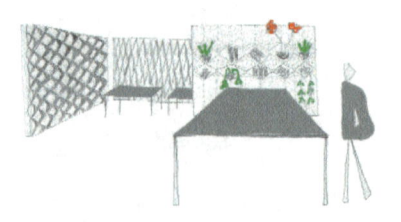

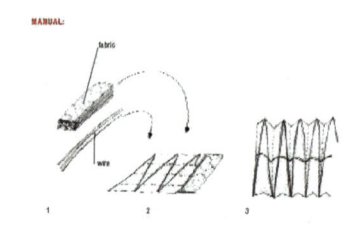

EMANCIPATION Vitra office landscape, Birsfelden, Switzerland 2004–2005

SCREEN A
SCARF

SCREEN C
TRACK-LOOP

WALL A
HARD'n'SOFT

WALL C
STORAGE

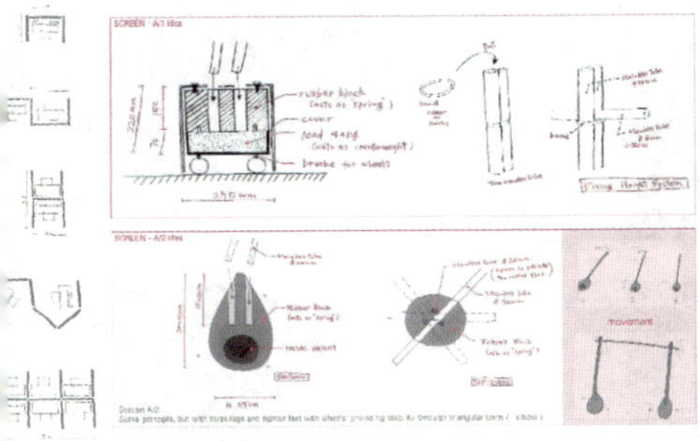
SCREEN - A/1 idea
SCREEN - A/2 idea
movement

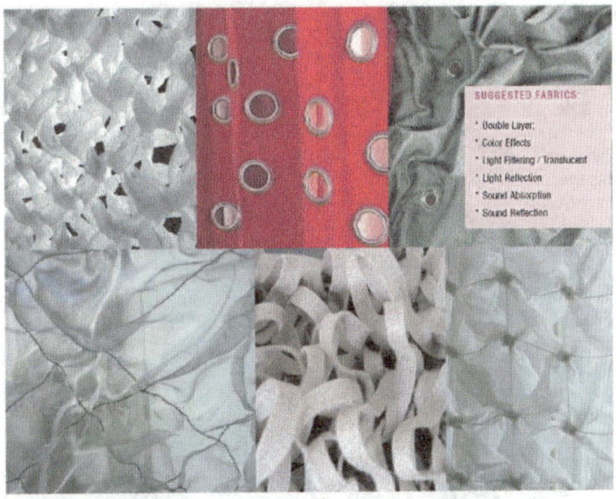
SUGGESTED FABRICS:
* Double Layer;
* Color Effects
* Light Filtering / Translucent
* Light Reflection
* Sound Absorption
* Sound Reflection

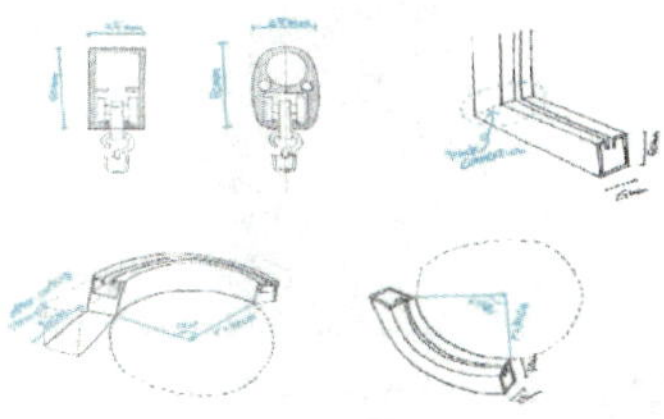

SUGGESTED FABRICS:
* Strech Material
* Weaving
* 3D Form

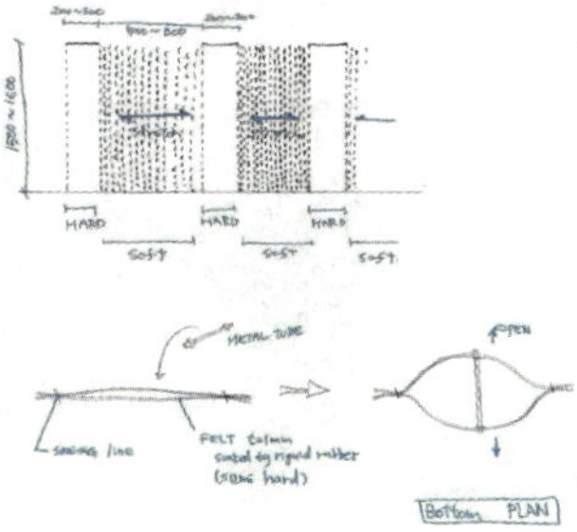
HARD
SOFT
Bottom PLAN

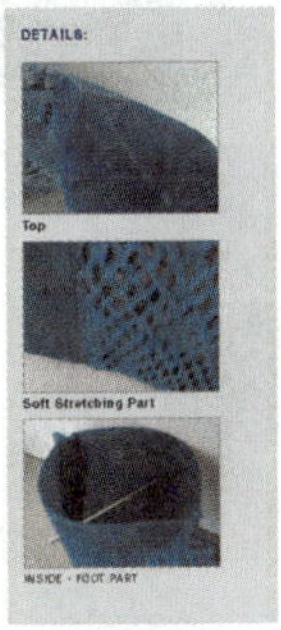
DETAILS:
Top
Soft Stretching Part
INSIDE - FOOT PART

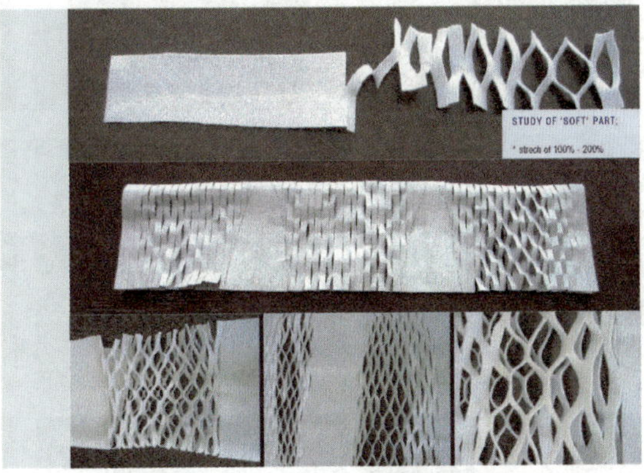
STUDY OF 'SOFT' PART;
* strech of 100% - 200%

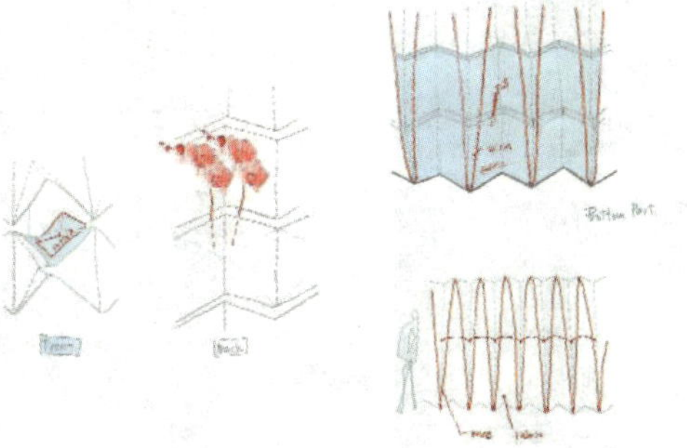
Bottom Part

SUGGESTED FABRICS:
Folding/Unfolding
Pocket
Order
Strong Material

Cover for acoustic installation

Acting as a protective hood for the store's audio system, a gigantic sock, made of a double layer of knitted silver voile, is suspended from one of the 'hanging city' metal-mesh cages. Clusters of speakers, wires and cables are hidden inside, while the sock's open structure, mimicking the expanded metal of the other 'hanging city' cupboards, allows the sound to pass unobstructed.

In the basement, two VIP dressing rooms are created using rich, white plissé curtains lined with transparent plastic. The former regulates the acoustic absorption and warms the room's interior, the latter isolates climate and sound from the outside, enhancing the customer's privacy and comfort.

SOUND SOCK Prada Epicenter, New York, USA, 2001

Architects
OMA

Flexible VIP dressing rooms

Our mission was to design a track configuration and curtains that would define two VIP dressing rooms in the New York Epicenter's basement and, two years later, on the second floor of the Beverly Hills epicenter.

In both cases, the rooms had to be acoustically muted so that conversations between clients and the staff passing by outside could not be overheard. The curtains had to be white.

We developed plissé curtains with transparent plastic linings towards the outside in order to protect the curtains from stains, prevent sound from passing through from outside and to protect the interior from the weather coming from the Mercer Street entrance door.

The millions of pleats act as air chambers, muting the sound within the rooms and stabilizing the interior temperature. Along the lower edge, rectangular windows show one behind the curtain, preventing people from entering unnoticed. Strategically placed slits form easy entrances to the rooms. The plastic linings are connected to the cloth with zippers to allow dry cleaning.

For the production of the curtains by third parties* we made 1:1 samples, drew step-by-step recipes, produced Auto-CAD working drawings and visited the workshops to discuss and test details. Textiles, plastics, curtain hooks and 'Inside Outside' labels for the lower seams were sent to the production companies and the manufacturers of tracks and carriers, and the transportation of the finished curtains was coordinated from our Amsterdam-based studio.

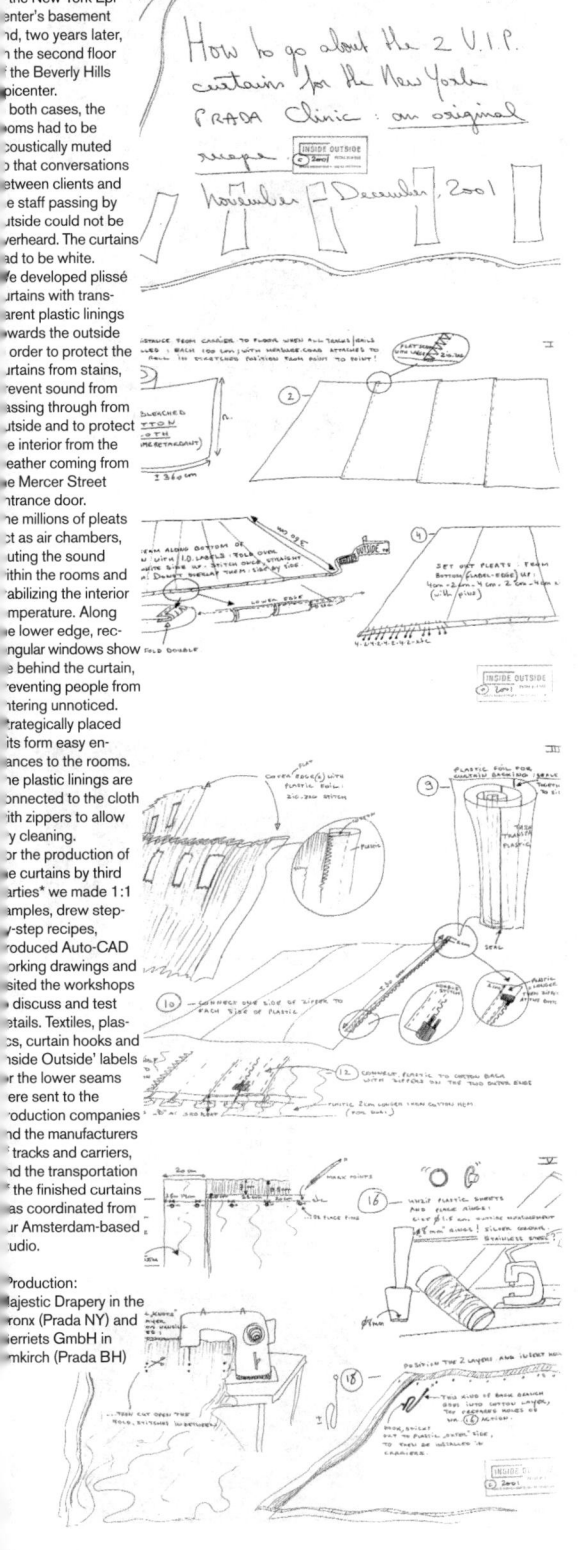

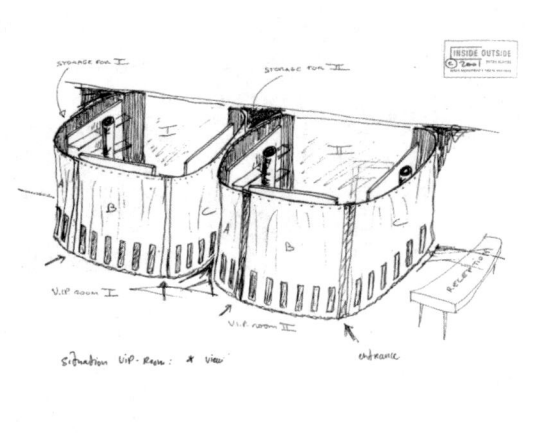

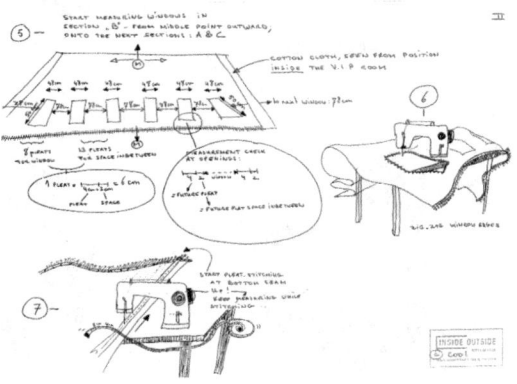

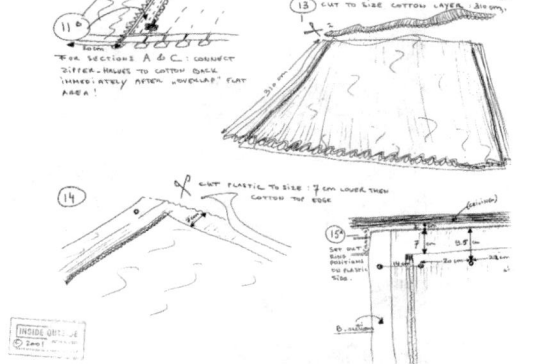

*Production:
Majestic Drapery in the Bronx (Prada NY) and Gerriets GmbH in Umkirch (Prada BH)

Architects
OMA

Penthouse garden and curtains

Roof garden, curtains and sunscreens for a round bachelor's penthouse overlooking the Thames.

In this two-storey private penthouse, Inside Outside created a spiralling, tilted garden and a system of curtains that accommodates all imaginable programmatic needs and changes inside a circular space with a sloping ceiling. The most notable feature of the architecture is the building's round shape and its location at the edge of the Thames, near Tower Bridge. The design for the roof garden exploits the given form and introduces a strong sense of unfolding drama, through floating planes and a variety of grass species that spin off in all directions.

The interior space is divided and screened using five curtains. The cocktail room looks out onto the roof garden through a semi-transparent cloth that echoes the grasses and plants outside. A second curtain acts as a blackout curtain for when the space is transformed into a screen room: an orange velvet with bright green stitch lines that refer to the plants outside. One floor below, a massive curtain with a view slit at eye level encircles and darkens the master bedroom, reflective voiles unify the segmented glass façade, an organza fleece creates a rectangular living room and a metal-mesh curtain turns the guest room into a golf green. The curtains range from bright orange and pink to silver, white, purple and gold and the materials range from silk organza to voile to velvet to sailing cloth to stainless steel.

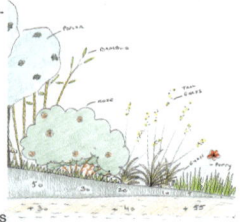

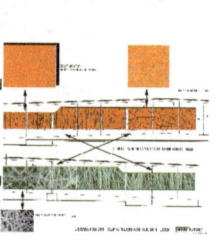

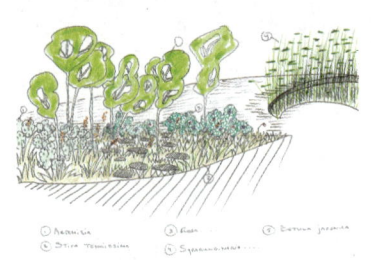

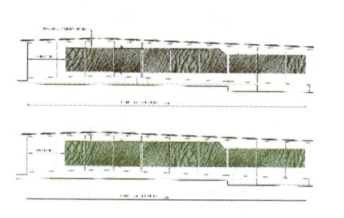

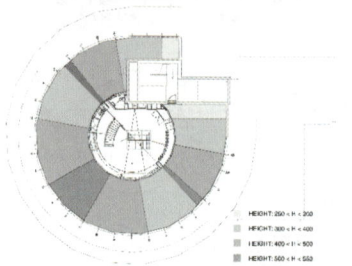

RADIAL VIEWS Cinnabar Wharf, London, UK 2002

Architects
Bushe associates
Gardeners
The Master Gardeners

VIEW FROM THE OUTSIDE

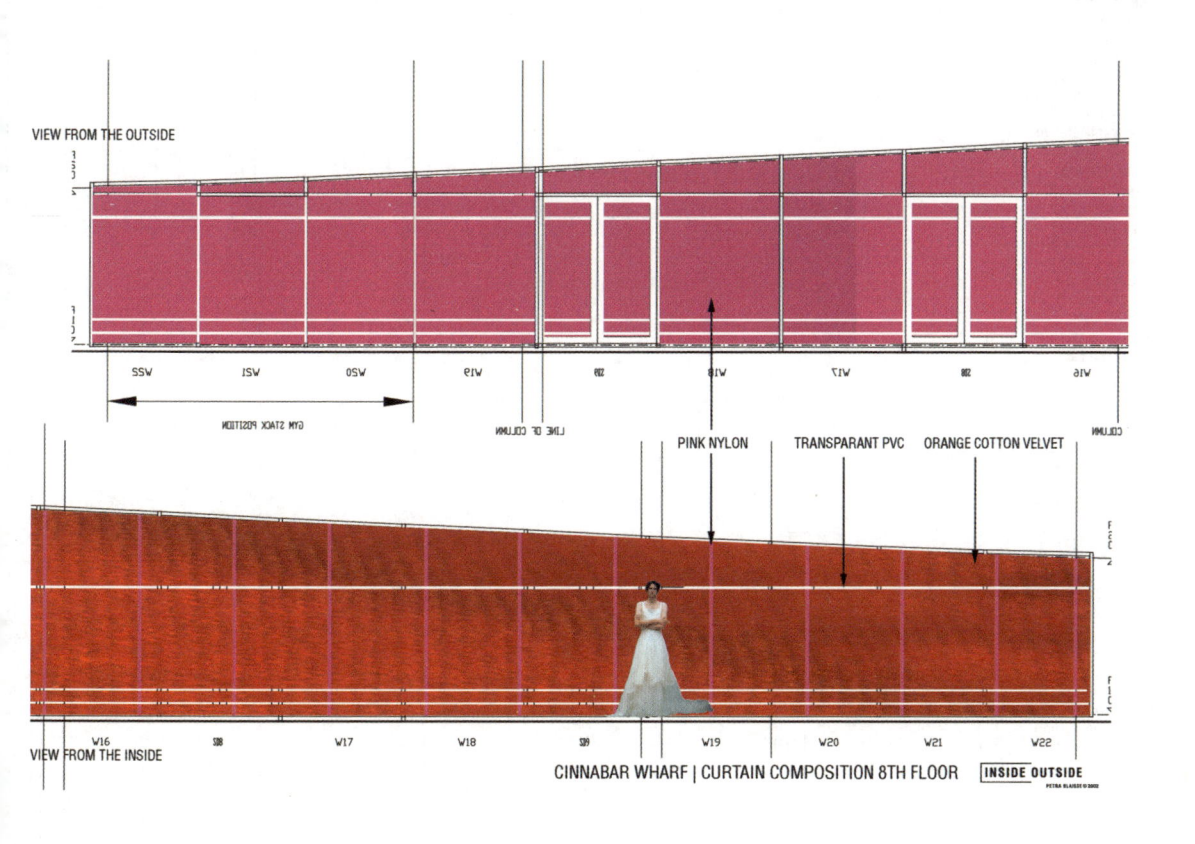

PINK NYLON   TRANSPARANT PVC   ORANGE COTTON VELVET

VIEW FROM THE INSIDE

CINNABAR WHARF | CURTAIN COMPOSITION 8TH FLOOR   INSIDE OUTSIDE

VIEW FROM OUTSIDE

VEROSOL SUNSCREEN   TRANSPARANT TREVIRA CS VOILE WITH LEAD CHAINS

VIEW FROM INDSIDE

CINNABAR WHARF | CURTAIN COMPOSITION 8TH FLOOR, SUNSCREEN IN FRONT OF THE DINING ROOM   INSIDE OUTSIDE

Thick and thin curtains for conference room

A loop at one outer end of this U-shaped double track organizes the movement and the different appearances of this dramatic cloth. One can choose between two atmospheres for the room: orange velvet (flat) or silver (blousing). The track-trajectory was cut out of the existing lowered ceiling. In reality, the track hangs from the concrete roof approximately 40 cm above. The track is stabilized with regularly placed steel tripods. The cloth's two layers of textile are only connected with large metal studs with tiny holes in their centre that allow light to pierce through. The cloth covers one entire wall when pulled out. The two-faced cloth has acoustic and darkening qualities, yet it does not express those characteristics – it looks both classic and sleazy . . . depending how you look at it.

SILK ROCK, SUNSET Lensvelt Furniture Headquarters, Breda, the Netherlands, 2000

20 cm

deur

detail 1

75mm
45mm
70mm
maten koof

31mm

3.28

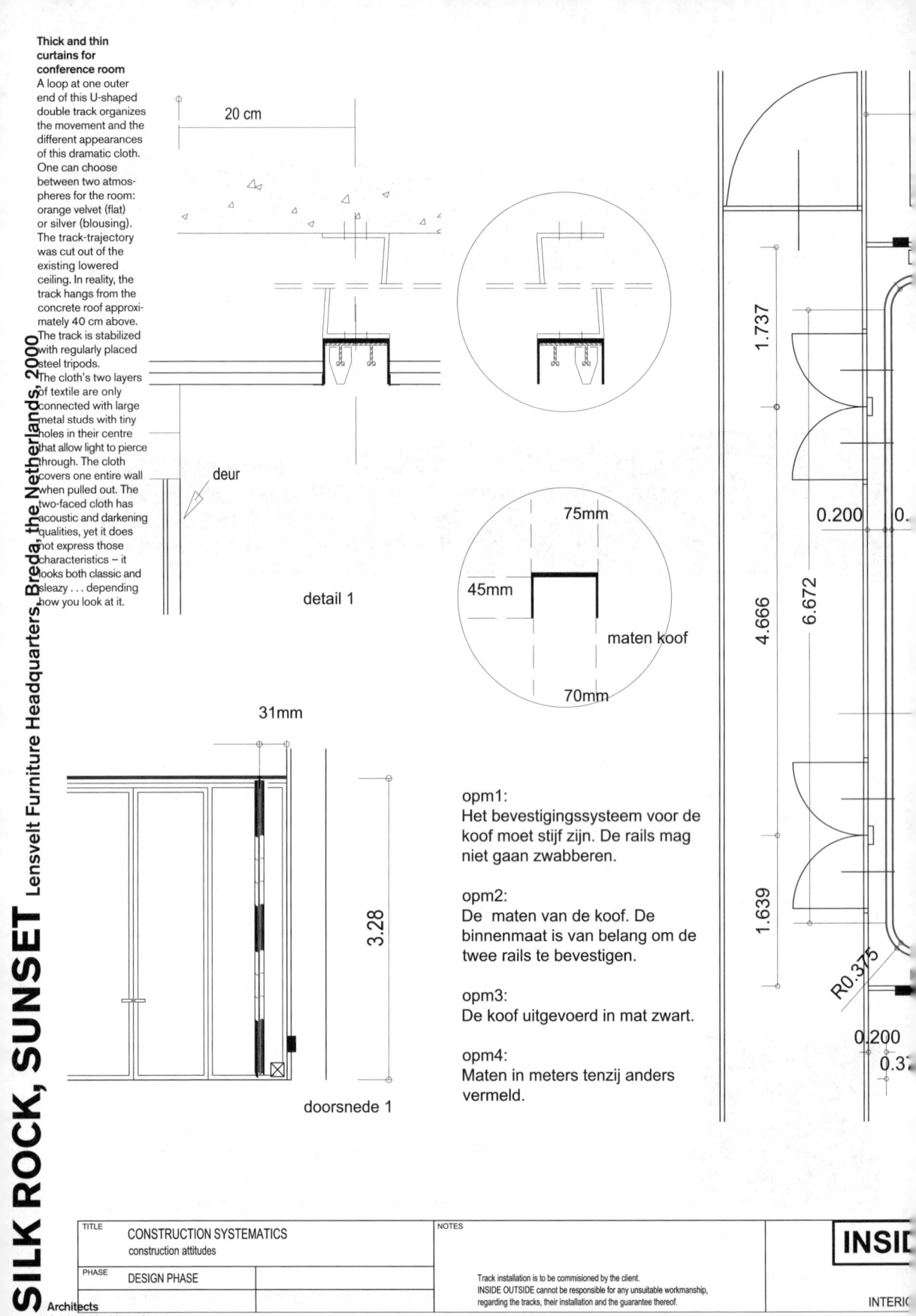

doorsnede 1

opm1:
Het bevestigingssysteem voor de koof moet stijf zijn. De rails mag niet gaan zwabberen.

opm2:
De maten van de koof. De binnenmaat is van belang om de twee rails te bevestigen.

opm3:
De koof uitgevoerd in mat zwart.

opm4:
Maten in meters tenzij anders vermeld.

1.737
0.200
4.666
6.672
1.639
R0.375
0.200

TITLE	CONSTRUCTION SYSTEMATICS construction attitudes		NOTES		INSID
PHASE	DESIGN PHASE		Track installation is to be commisioned by the client. INSIDE OUTSIDE cannot be responsible for any unsuitable workmanship, regarding the tracks, their installation and the guarantee thereof.		INTERIO

Architects
Wiel Arets Architect & Associates

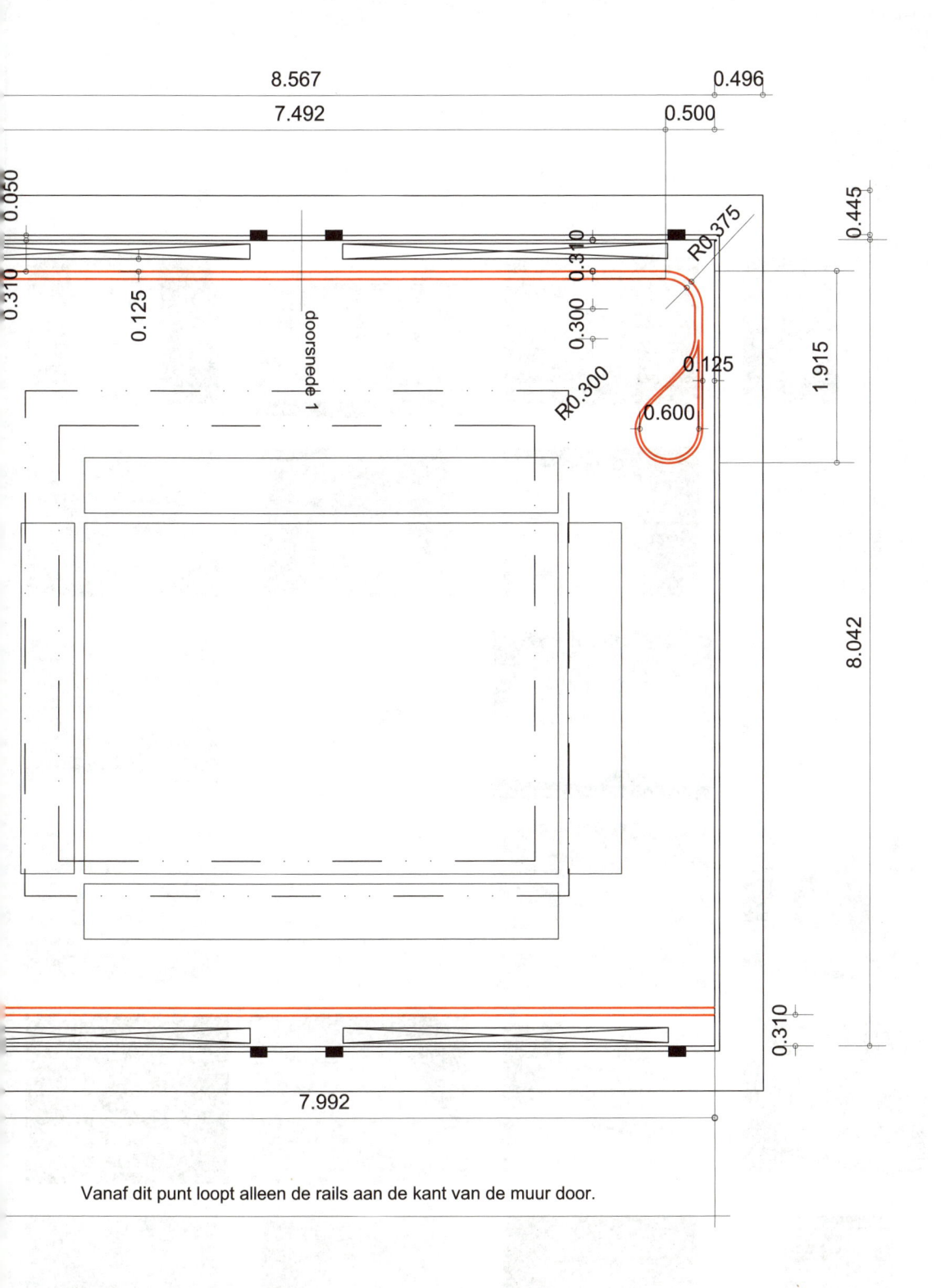

Vanaf dit punt loopt alleen de rails aan de kant van de muur door.

Sun-screen and backdrop curtain for shop window

A 'sun-reflecting and cooling' curtain for the south-oriented shop window of Amsterdam's renowned architectural bookshop Architectura & Natura. Windows of transparent plastic are fit into the sun-reflective, translucent voile. Its aluminium-coated side faces the sun, while the other side is subtly imprinted with a plant pattern, visible from the interior of the shop. The U-shaped track allows the curtain to be turned around, and to take on different positions in which it can act as sunscreen, as backdrop or as an appealing (stored) object at any point along the edges of the shop window or behind the displayed books.

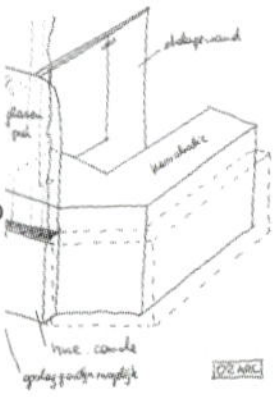

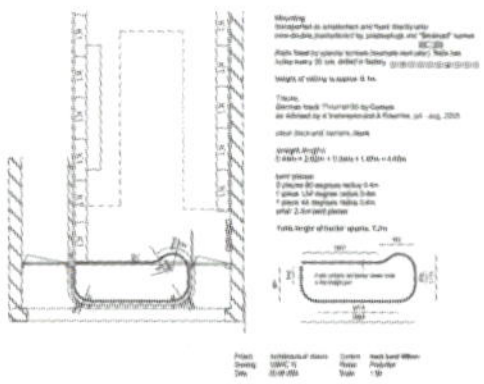

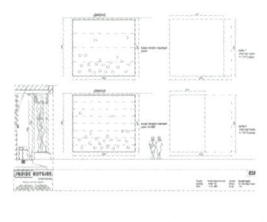

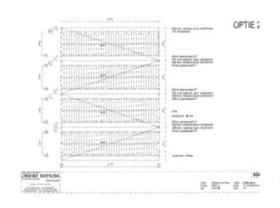

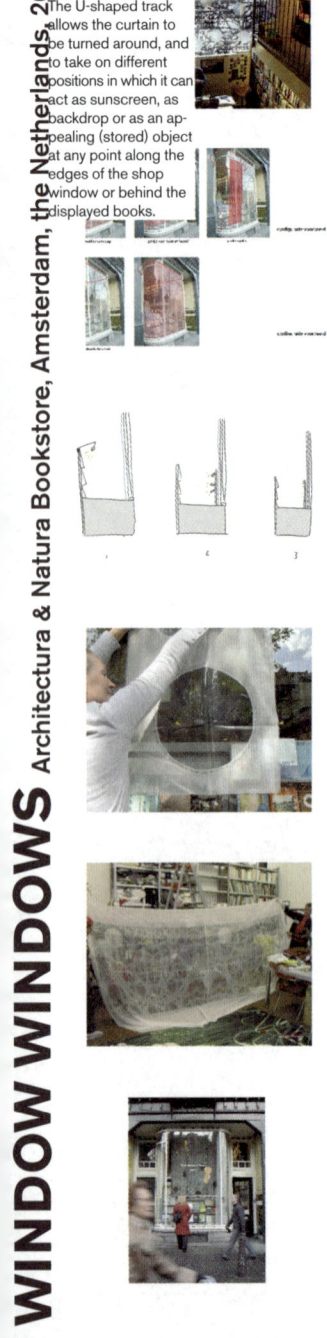

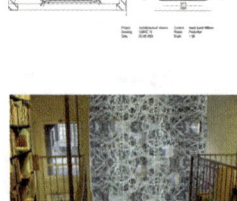

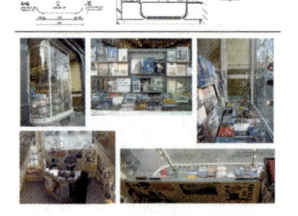

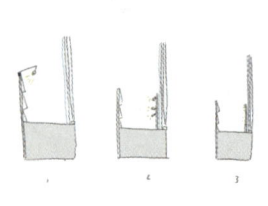

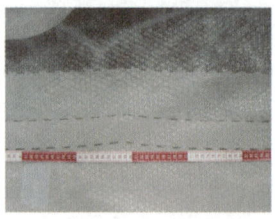

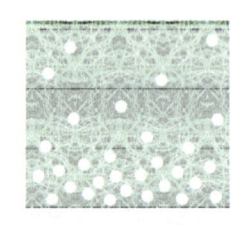

WINDOW WINDOWS Architectura & Natura Bookstore, Amsterdam, the Netherlands, 2003

Darkening façade curtains for hotel rooms

In an extremely narrow alley where Toyo Ito and his partners built a small extension to the Blue Moon Hotel, we were invited to design curtains for two of the hotel rooms. The hotel's façade is made of glass with an added aluminium 'skin': an open, 7 cm-thick structure that mimics the brick building material of the old wing, but turned in a vertical direction. The rooms behind this façade, placed on top of each other on two floors, need privacy from their front neighbours and a way to darken their space. The architect asked us to influence the aluminium façade in some way, adding an effect that would change its look from time to time. The rooms in question were tiny and narrow, and since we never store curtains in front of a transparent façade, we studied ways to move them through the room and its entrance area in a manner that would suit multiple purposes without taking up too much space. We found that the S-shaped track did the job: storing the curtain along the entrance wall, screening the room from its transparent entrance door and the wall behind, and creating privacy and darkness when pulled in front of the façade. Its bright orange colour and its large black forms (outgrowing the two floors) give a suggestive sheen to the aluminium façade, while transcending the idea of a tree shadow through its white and silver textile interior layer; giving the illusion of growth outside, thus creating a spacious effect in a truly minimal space.

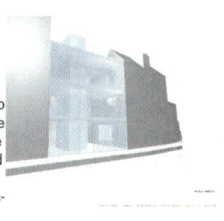

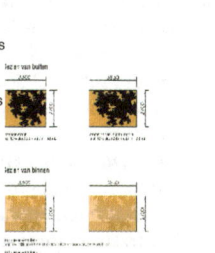

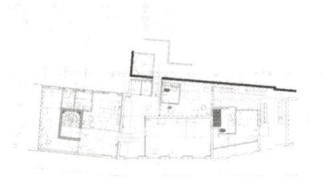

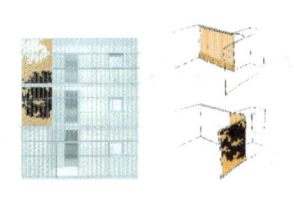

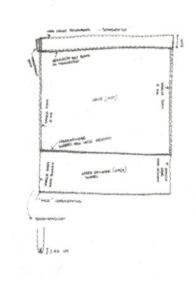

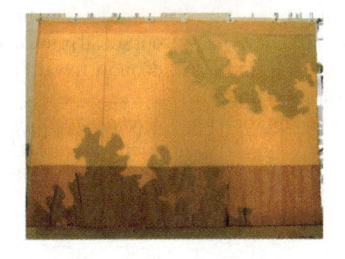

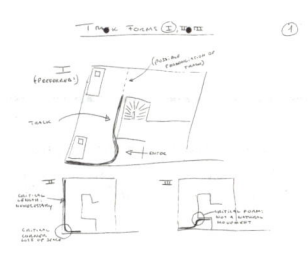

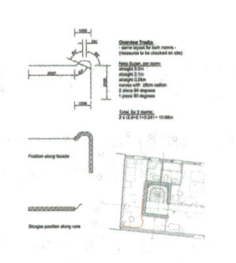

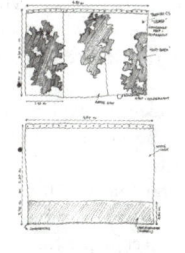

Architects
Toyo Ito Architects, Associates; Hosoya Schaeffer Architekten

Skeptic

These good acts give us pleasure, but how happens it that they give us pleasure? Because nature hath implanted in our breasts a love of others, a sense of duty to them, a moral instinct, in short, which prompts us irresistibly to feel and to succor their distresses. —Thomas Jefferson, 1814

Unweaving the Heart

Science only adds to our appreciation for poetic beauty and experiences of emotional depth   By MICHAEL SHERMER

Nineteenth-century English poet John Keats once bemoaned that Isaac Newton had "Destroyed the poetry of the rainbow by reducing it to a prism." Natural philosophy, he lamented, "Will clip an Angel's wings/Conquer all mysteries by rule and line/Empty the haunted air, and gnomed mine/Unweave a rainbow."

Does a scientific explanation for any given phenomenon diminish its beauty or its ability to inspire poetry and emotional experiences? I think not. Science and aesthetics are complementary, not conflicting; additive, not detractive. I am nearly moved to tears, for example, when I observe through my small telescope the fuzzy little patch of light that is the Andromeda galaxy. It is not just because it is lovely, but because I also understand that the photons of light landing on my retina left Andromeda 2.9 million years ago, when our ancestors were tiny-brained hominids. I am doubly stirred because it was not until 1923 that astronomer Edwin Hubble, using the 100-inch telescope on Mount Wilson in the hills just above my home in Los Angeles, deduced that this "nebula" was actually a distant extragalactic stellar system of immense size. He subsequently discovered that the light from most galaxies is shifted toward the red end of the electromagnetic spectrum (literally unweaving a rainbow of colors), meaning that the universe is expanding away from its explosive beginning. That is some aesthetic science.

No less awe-inspiring are recent attempts to unweave the emotions, described by anthropologist Helen Fisher of Rutgers University in her book *Why We Love* (Henry Holt, 2004). Lust is enhanced by dopamine, a neurohormone produced by the hypothalamus that in turn triggers the release of testosterone, the hormone that drives sexual desire. But love is the emotion of attachment reinforced by oxytocin, a hormone synthesized in the hypothalamus and secreted into the blood by the pituitary. In women, oxytocin stimulates birth contractions, lactation and maternal bonding with a nursing infant. In both women and men it increases during sex and surges at orgasm, playing a role in pair bonding, an evolutionary adaptation for long-term care of helpless infants.

At the Center for Neuroeconomics Studies at Claremont Graduate University, Paul J. Zak posits a relation between oxytocin, trust and economic well-being. "Oxytocin is a feel-good hormone, and we find that it guides subjects' decisions even when they are unable to articulate why they are acting in a trusting or trustworthy matter," Zak explained to me. He argues that trust is among the most powerful factors affecting economic growth and that it is vital for national prosperity for a country to maximize positive social interactions among its members by ensuring a reliable infrastructure, a stable economy, and the freedom to speak, associate and trade.

We establish trust among strangers through verification in social interactions. James K. Rilling and his colleagues at Emory University, for instance, employed a functional magnetic resonance imaging (fMRI) brain scan on 36 subjects while they played Prisoner's Dilemma. In the game, cooperation and defection result in differing payoffs depending on what the other participants do. The researchers found that in cooperators the brain areas that lit up were the same regions activated in response to such stimuli as desserts, money, cocaine and beautiful faces. Specifically, the neurons most responsive were those rich in dopamine (the lust liquor that is also related to addictive behaviors), located in the anteroventral striatum in the middle of the brain—the so-called pleasure center. Tellingly, cooperative subjects reported increased feelings of trust toward, and camaraderie with, like-minded partners.

In Charles Darwin's "M Notebook," in which he began outlining his theory of evolution, he penned this musing: "He who understands baboon would do more towards metaphysics than Locke." Science now reveals that love is addictive, trust is gratifying and cooperation feels good. Evolution produced this reward system because it increased the survival of members of our social primate species. He who understands Darwin would do more toward political philosophy than Jefferson.

> Science and aesthetics are complementary, not conflicting.

Michael Shermer is the publisher of Skeptic *(www.skeptic.com). His latest book is* Science Friction.

Darkening, sun-screening and sound-absorbant curtains for concert hall

Two parallel, U-shaped tracks embrace stage and audience and line the windowed façades of the rectangular concert hall that can house up to 1000 people. The two layers of curtains (four separate designs, each 22 x 7.5 m) meet in the middle of the back wall (sometimes hidden behind a projection screen), fold out to cover the windows and form single- or double-layered curtain walls that answer to acoustic, lighting and atmospheric requirements. Each curtain measures around 200 m² and each curtain – opaque velvets or transparent voiles – has its own colour, material, sheen and behaviour. The curtains can be combined, creating astounding colour shifts and dramatic effects. Inside Outside advised on the colour composition of the auditorium chairs.

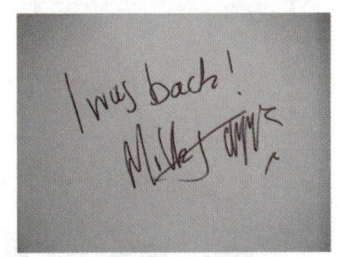

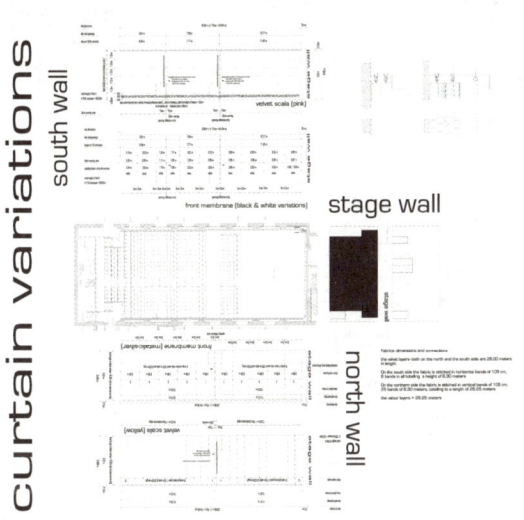

Architects
… Ronalds Architects

Cooling and darkening curtains for private house

This doughnut-shaped house needed sun- and light-reflecting voiles and a means to influence the interior's acoustic quality. Also the client asked for a form of wellbeing and privacy in this very modern and partially transparent space, especially at night. Looking at the overall situation and the garden design, we proposed white voile curtains, printed with Hydrangea photographs I had taken in the fall, years ago: pink flowering hydrangea, with here and there withering, golden areas where the Fall had set in. This print is envisioned as a gradient, changing the voile slowly from white to bright pink in a horizontal direction. The flowers themselves grow in scale at the same time from small to ever larger – ending in a bright pink velvet cloth. The curtain continues over the entire inner circle of the house, enveloping the inner courtyard and ignoring space divisions. The print disappears during the day and reappears at twilight, becoming more and more visible as darkness falls.

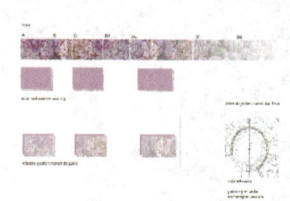

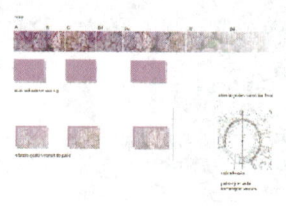

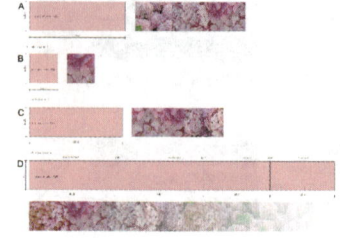

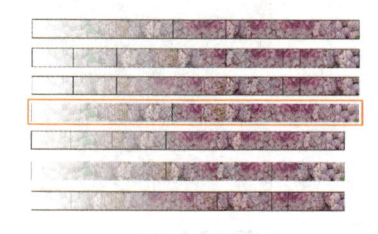

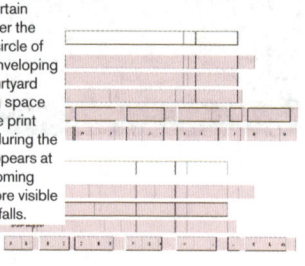

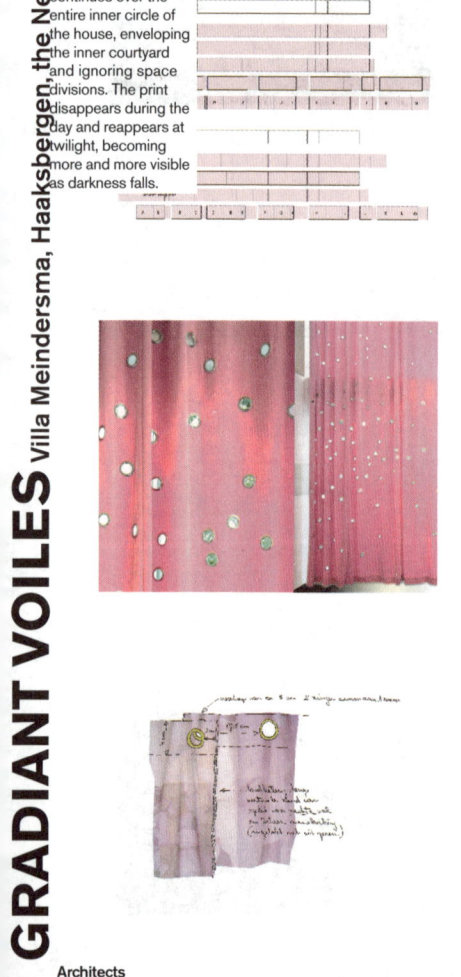

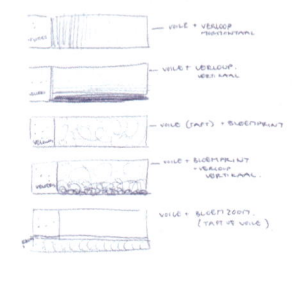

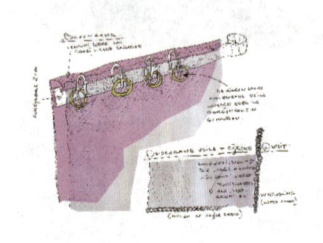

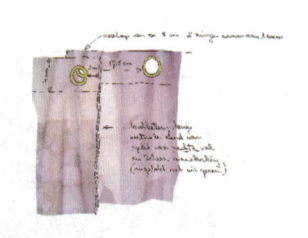

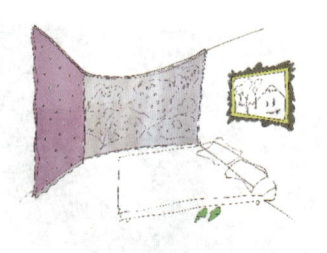

GRADIANT VOILES Villa Meindersma, Haaksbergen, the Netherlands, 2005–2006

Architects
Architecten Cie

Darkening and sound-absorbent curtains for multi-purpose room

For our embassy in Berlin, we collaborated with the architects from the conceptual phase onwards. We studied the way the movement runs from the Spree river and the city, through the park and over the sidewalks into the building and how the views from the building over the city and river could optimally be translated and emphasized by the use of colour, light, finishing materials and the thinning or placement of planting around the building. These studies, and the need for darkening, light-filtering, sun-reflecting and acoustically-absorbent elements along the building's glass façades, led to our proposal for a series of curtains. One set of curtains solved 'glare' issues in the offices and covered three façades. This idea didn't materialize, because the costs for the production of voiles with enormous images of nineteenth-century tulips) outgrowing the building's floors were over the Embassy's budget and the maintenance demands (placement and replacement) were too impractical. Monochrome yellow and silver curtains were hung instead.

For the multi-purpose room, however, we were able to realize two large woven-to-size linens that answer to the requested light and sound programme and, at the same time, emphasize the connection and reflection of the exterior to and in the interior space. The natural shape of the large-scale image and the strong colours (lime and cream; black and white), cause the curtains to form a strong counterpart to the aluminium, square-shaped building; they are clearly visible from a distance. For the first time since 1987 we had our own cloth produced, woven at the Textile Museum in Tilburg in a classic Jacquard technique, creating a double-sided, damask linen. The lime green refers to the spring leaves of the acacias in the park, the angel root to Holland's moist soil and vegetable garden tradition, and the horizontal lines to Holland's flat and spacious horizons.

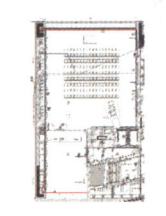

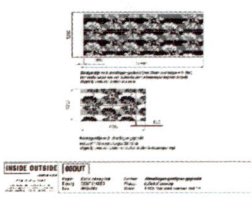

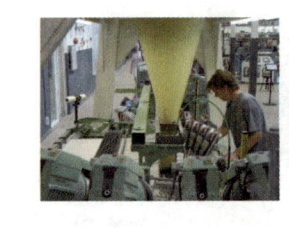

Architects
OMA

Darkening and space-defining curtain for art gallery (90 m²)

The design consists of a monumental curtain made of dark grey truck plastic, forming the partition between the street and the new gallery, a refined white box implanted into the rough structure of a former garage. The longitudinal window in the curtain, placed at thigh height, creates surreal perspectives from inside out onto the street and vice versa. Adjusting to the changing demands of the gallery space, the curtain darkens the room behind (with snap-on blinds), closes the space off during installation works, or disappears completely into its hidden storage space inside a wall. A remarkable detail is the huge white house number of the gallery (540), clearly visible to passers-by. A more subtle detail is the row of little transparent bags along the lower hem of the curtain, in which fishing leads are placed to weigh the curtain down – enough to prevent it from reacting to wind and temperature influences. In a second phase, we added a second layer to the curtain to actually black out the exhibition space. We also added the 'Enter Here' signs to encourage visitors to enter the gallery when the curtain is drawn and 'Exit Here' signs to clarify the position of the slits in a darkened gallery space.

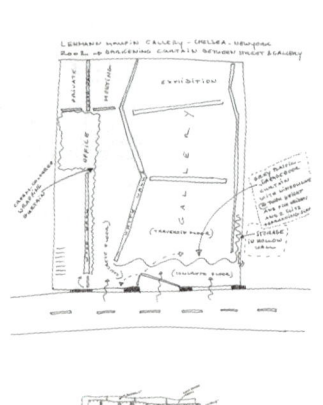

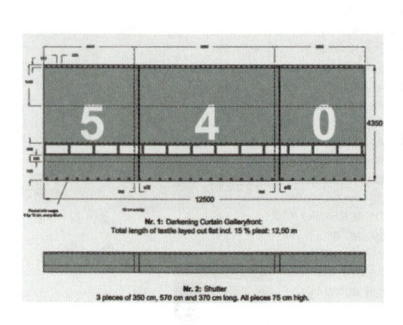

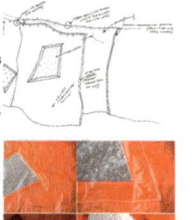

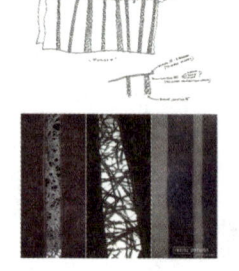

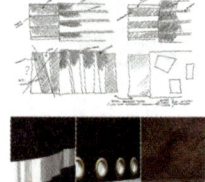

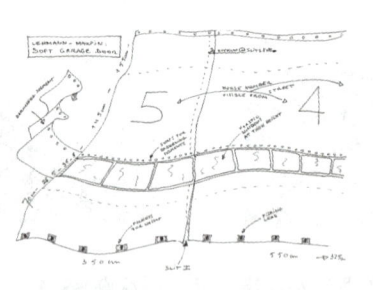

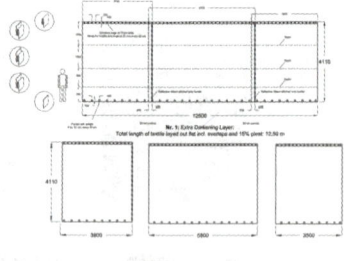

GARAGE DOOR Lehmann Maupin Gallery, New York, USA, 2002–2003

Architects
OMA

475

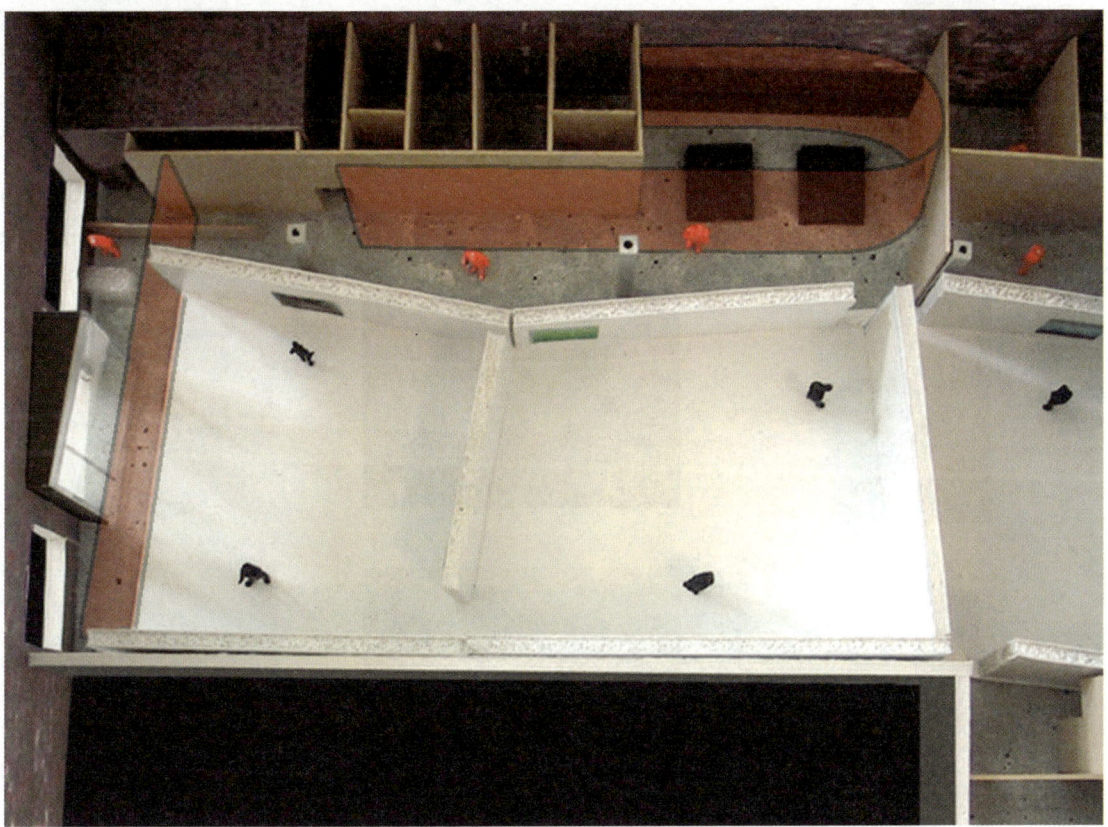

HAIRS, FINS, SAUERKRAUT AND FURS

Mercedes Benz Museum, Stuttgart Germany, 2004–2006

Multi-functional curtain and wall for car museum

Sun-filtering, darkening and acoustic curtains and an acoustical wall were developed for this new UN Studio building. Joining a rich team of designers, architects and landscape architects that had already developed their designs, we tried to complement the existing situation by inserting curtains and a wall finish that were more about structure than about colour, except for the restaurant curtain on the eighth floor, that became a colourful, three-dimensional cloth. Forming one of the walls around the multi-purpose room, we placed a heavy, grey, long-haired mohair-velvet curtain with a 'Sauerkraut' (*choucroute*) seam, lined with a transparent plastic sheet with a black-lacquer seam. On parallel tracks, sun-reflective silver voiles with broad, white seams encircle the entire space. In the Espresso Bar, a concave brush wall acts as the backdrop to the concrete interior, adding a three-dimensional 'veil'. The brush hairs scatter sound waves for a better acoustic atmosphere. The white brush hairs are inserted into panels that are covered with gold-coloured metal foil. Seven floors up, a lime green finned curtain with a black 'Sauerkraut' backing lines an open balcony and envelopes restaurant and lounge. Its design reacts to the folded white ceiling and its opacity secures the dim lighting conditions of the exhibition space below; while allowing the public to peep through its half-open surface.

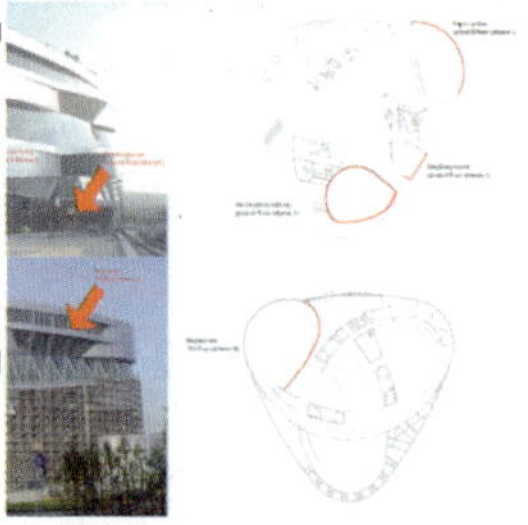

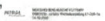

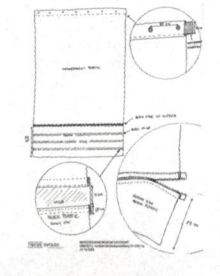

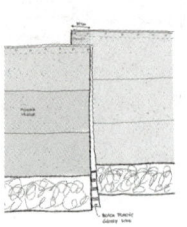

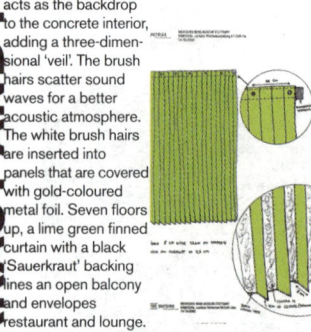

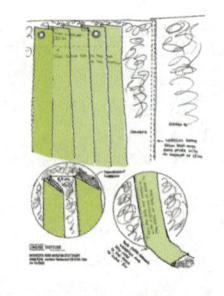

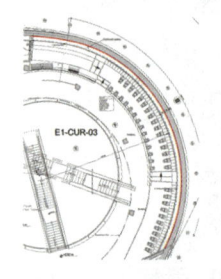

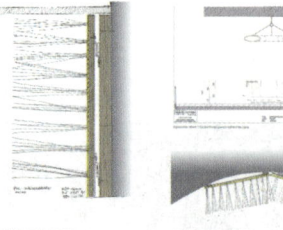

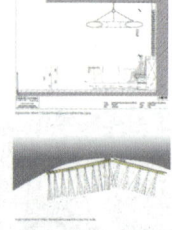

Architects
UN Studio

study panel with brushes
scale 1:20

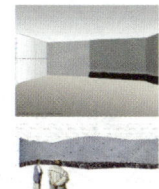

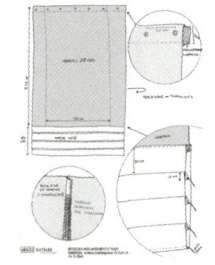

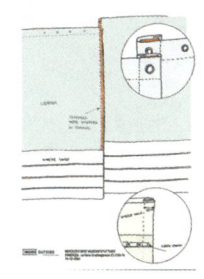

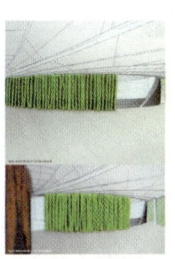

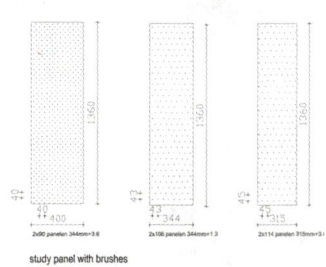

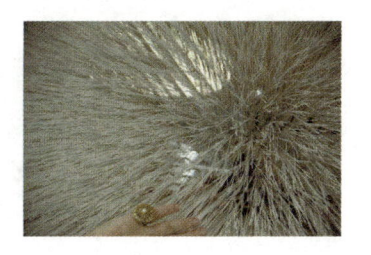

Gardens and curtains for an IIT campus building

Walking towards the new student centre, a series of strong visual effects immediately catch your attention: spacious gardens with cut-out planting circles, Mies's portrait etched onto the glass façade, spectacular bright orange walls, huge curtains imprinted with white 'tree crowns' and a train that dives into the belly of the building and comes out on the other side. What you're seeing is OMA's McCormick Tribune Centre at the Chicago's IIT Campus. Inside Outside advised the architects on the interior finishes and colour use, designed the landscape and the large darkening curtains that mark the entire west façade. A further stroll into the building reveals three interior gardens of different size and shape: a hanging garden over the students' cafeteria area; a patio with an enormous pine tree, reflecting its beautiful green colour inward; and the Mies Garden, a sloping inner garden that flows into the green cafeteria space. The gardens around the main building will be executed in the spring of 2007.

REFLECTION McCormick Tribune Campus Center, Chicago, USA, 1999–2004

Architects
OMA

Landscape architects
Kate Orff, Peter Schaudt Landscape Architecture

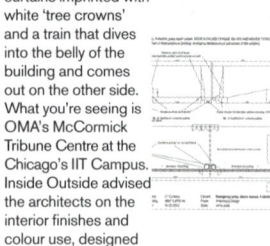

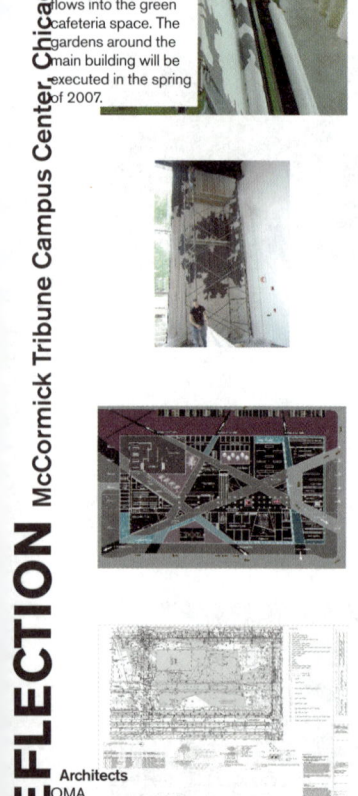

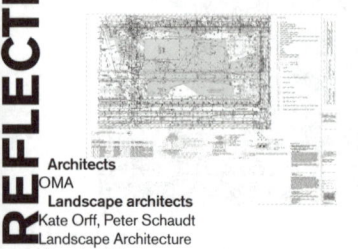

Local architects
Studio Gang

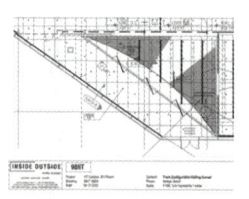

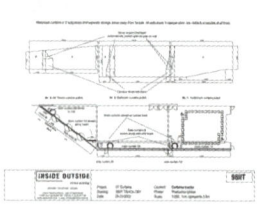

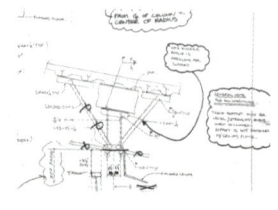

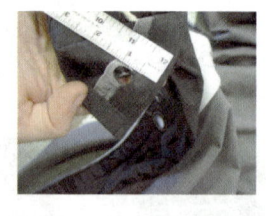

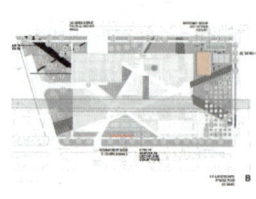

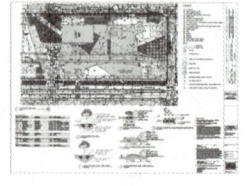

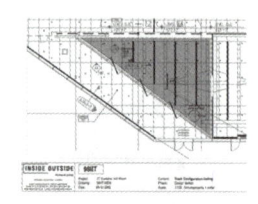

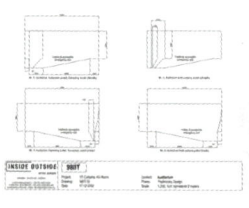

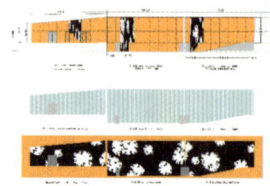

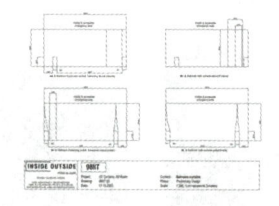

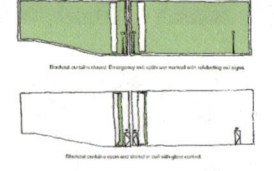

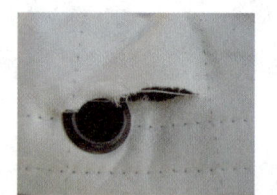

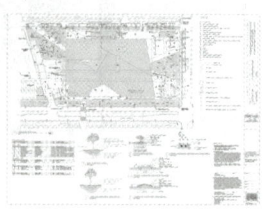

Urban garden over parking lot

This garden is situated on top of a new, underground parking lot and between an existing (1970s) nursing home and two new apartment buildings for senior citizens that stand with their 'feet' in a newly created water basin. For this urban and windy garden we envisioned a very smooth black asphalt surface to accommodate easy movement and wheel chairs) with triangular incisions, out of which moisture-loving and wind-resistant trees and grasses spring. Here and there, wooden benches in the same triangular shape pop up. An orange, meandering path runs through the garden, from the street to the main entrance and then to the waterfront, where it transforms into a pier that cuts its way through the reed and enters the water. Along the water's edge, a linear bench acts as guardrail. Inside the glass recreation space that hovers above the water, a 'garden carpet' reflects the surrounding water landscape. Inside the main building's entrance lobby, the garden is continued: two triangular cuts are made into the black floor surface, from which a bench and green plants emerge.

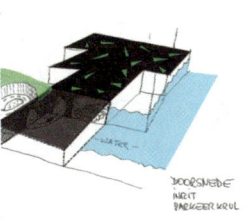

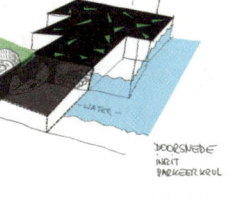

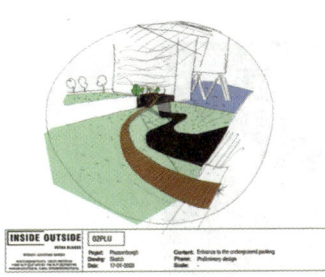

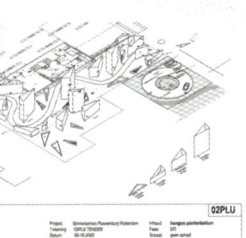

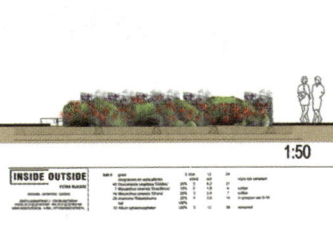

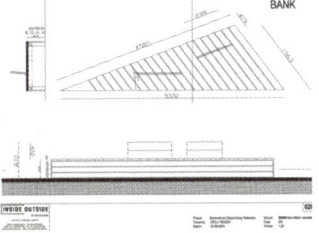

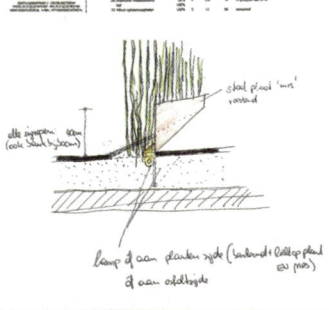

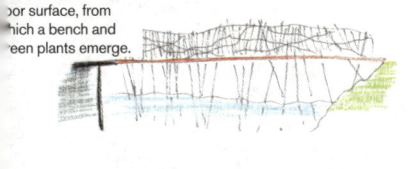

Architects
rons & Gelauff

MULTIPLE CHOICE Stedelijk Museum extension competition, Amsterdam, the Netherlands, 1992

Art Garden and Earth Garden proposals
A plan that includes a sloping garden as a connector between the new, lifted Museum entrance and Museumplein, a rooftop sculpture garden and two alternative proposals for a walled museum garden: an 'art garden', unreachable and intended only for distant contemplation from floating terraces; and an 'earth garden' that can be entered and used and in which every plant, fruit and flower is edible. In this competition presentation, we defined each plant for both gardens, illustrating their layers, profiles, heights and seasonal change with paper collages and cardboard models. The multiple choice mentality was derived from the architect's proposal for the main exhibition floor, in which three different floor plans were presented, leaving the final choice to whoever would become the new museum director.

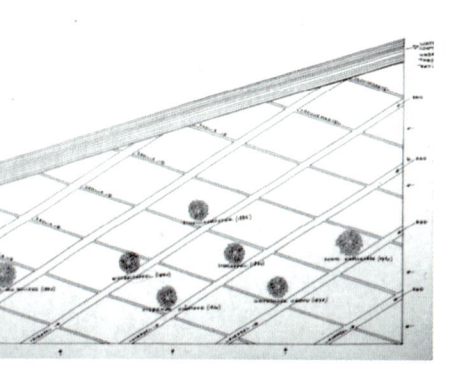

OPTIONS: GARDEN

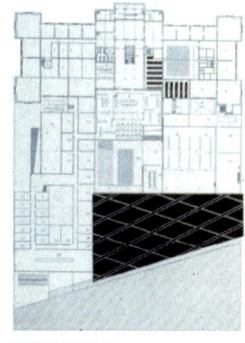

VEGETABLE GARDEN

FLOWER GARDEN

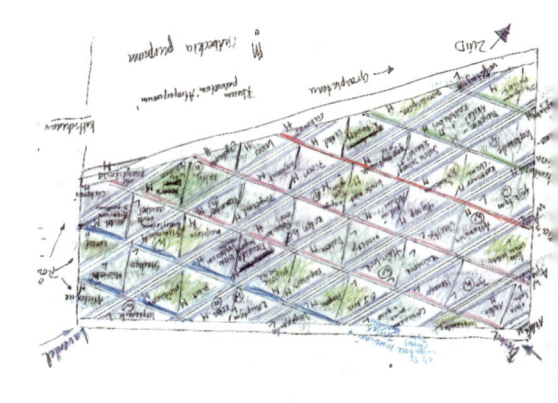

Architects
OMA

481

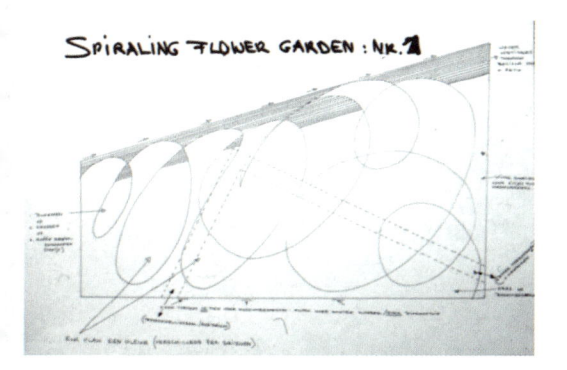

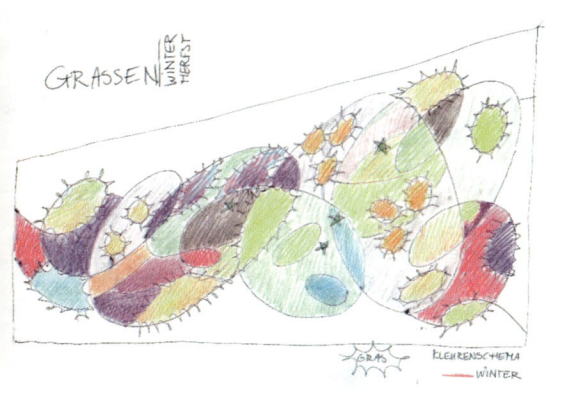

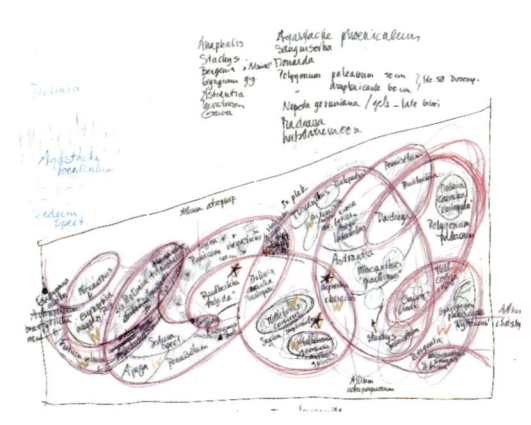

Landscaping a parking and service complex

OMA Asia was commissioned to design the buildings and infrastructure of a future service area along a highway that would open up the Taiwan Island in a north-south direction. Inside Outside was asked to design the landscape. The client was the developer of the segment of the highway. Apparently, each piece of highway is owned and developed by a different party, making logistics and planning complicated. I flew to the site with the architects, the engineers and the developer and landed in a hot, dry, hilly and barren landscape that had the colour of Spanish terracotta: a warm rusty red. It was beautiful, with tufts of green here and there: bamboo, wild grasses, thin lines of shrubbery and low trees wherever roots found moisture. Agriculture seemed to be the source of income in that area, but there was not much to see where we were walking, picking up stones, rubbing the soil between our fingers, smelling air and leaves, discovering little altars that looked out over the hills from under small and crooked trees. Typical bees live there, making small hives glued to stones on the ground – seven chambers at the most. Soon a six-lane highway would cut through this world.

Back in the Netherlands I sketched one floating oval dish after another, envisioning an oval service area; a synthetic, black-and-white plate that landed in the middle of nowhere, stuck in the flank of the hillside. On it a gas and a police station, a low building with restaurants and shops, separate washrooms, a hostel for the staff – all placed between large parking areas for busses, trucks, cars. My task was to integrate gardens that would organize the pedestrian and traffic flow and that were so attractive that people would want to stay longer. They should be gardens for relaxation, recreation, cooling, eating, playing, waiting and parking. The project was elaborated by SWA and realized in 2003.

Architects
OMA, SWA Landscape architects

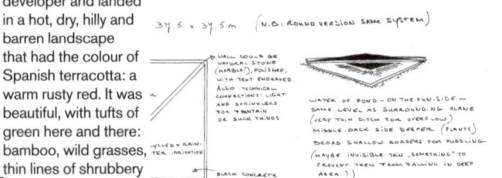

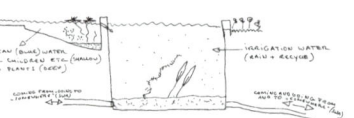

TAIWAN SKETCHES Chen Sui Service Area, Taiwan, 1999–2004

Outside the restaurant a circular pond would function as rain and grey water tank; pumps were placed at the edge of the 'plate' to guide the collected water through layers of sand, pebbles, rocks and back to the pond.

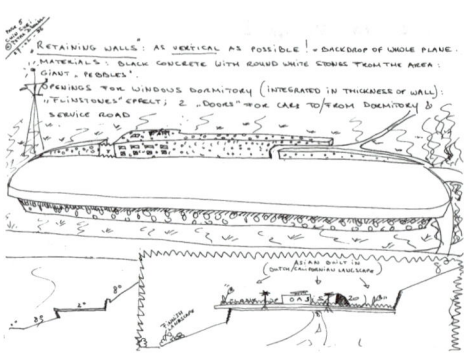

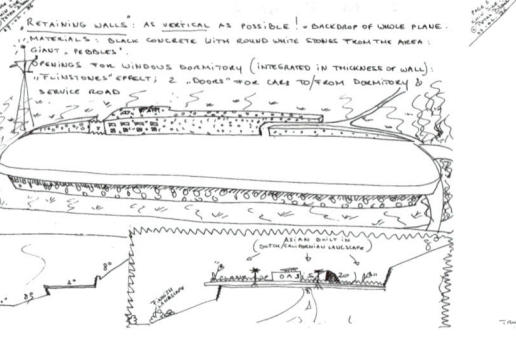

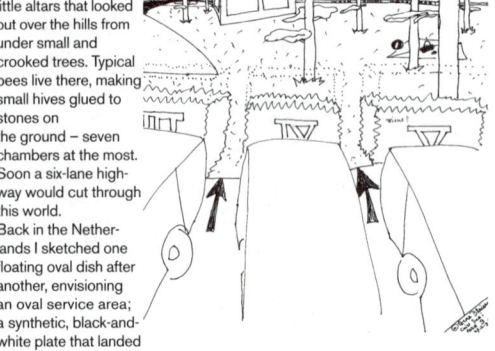

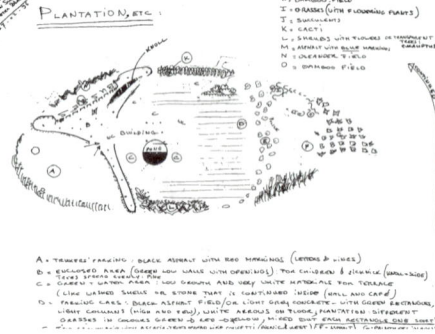

Cacti and succulent gardens formed surreal groupings between areas.

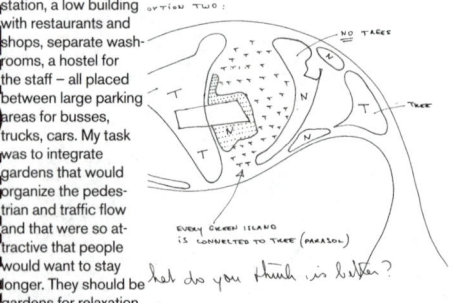

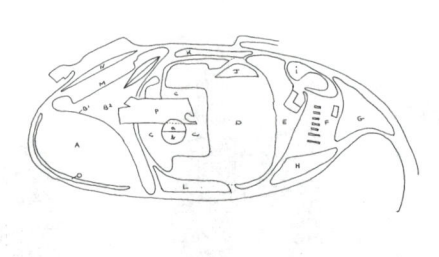

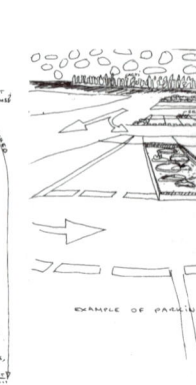

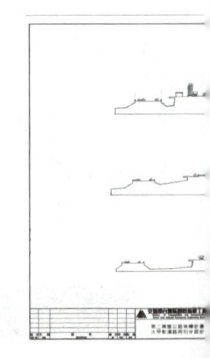

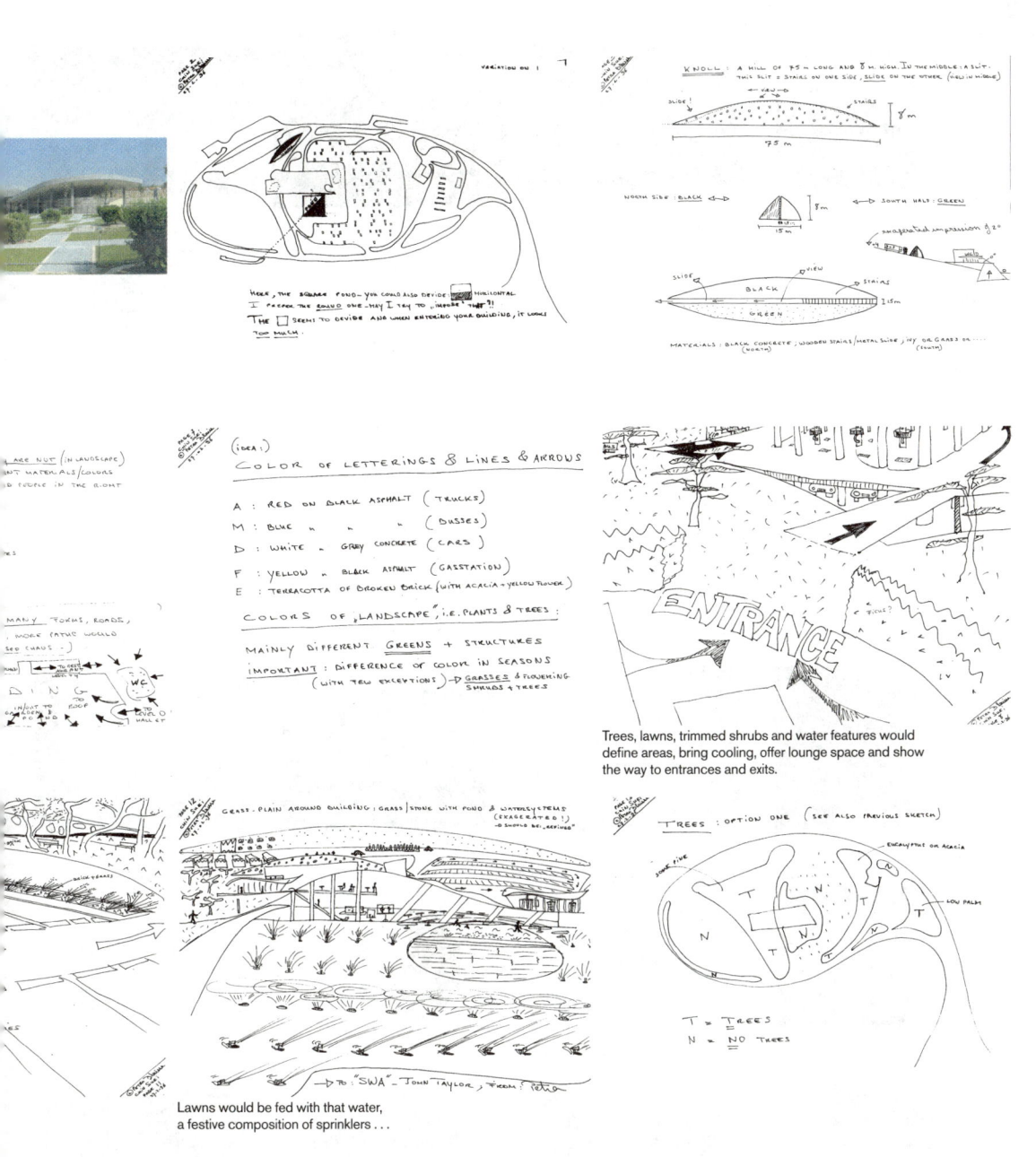

Trees, lawns, trimmed shrubs and water features would define areas, bring cooling, offer lounge space and show the way to entrances and exits.

Lawns would be fed with that water, a festive composition of sprinklers . . .

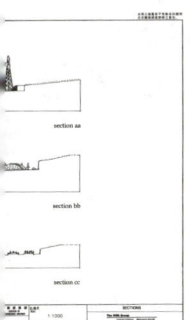

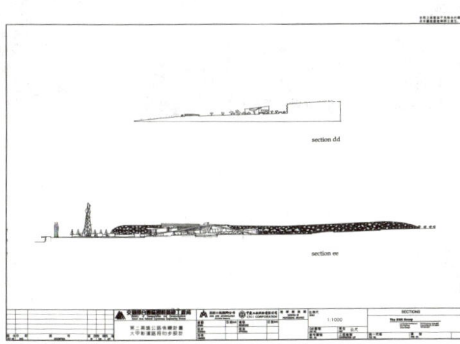

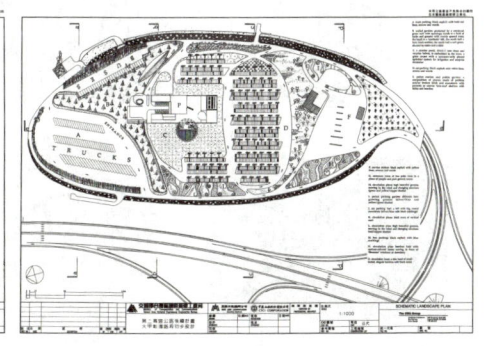

Two parks in the water

We proposed two circular parks to flank the architect's rectangular building, which itself stands on a circular plateau. All three circles 'float' in the salt-water creek, built as a meandering water feature running from the seashore, through Dubai and back to the sea again, introducing long quays and water-edge locations to the city. One round park is a sunken, sweet-water rain forest, where trees and moisture cool the environment and the temperature sinks to an agreeable level. Tree roots clean the grey water of the building through the soil, pumping it through their leaves; and this filtered water is recycled to the water garden, where a collection of conditions offers a variety of gardens for people to use and enjoy. Temporary art pavilions (managed by the Serpentine Gallery, London) cover part of the water garden, part of the year. The design considers the fact that the parks are visible day and night from the surrounding high-rise buildings and lifted highways. The emphasis, therefore, is on the bold yet decorative path structures; the diversity of planting (with which intriguing profiles, colours and seasonal changes can be achieved); various water, steam and fountain configurations; and strategic light installations that animate both gardens when natural light slides slowly into darkness.

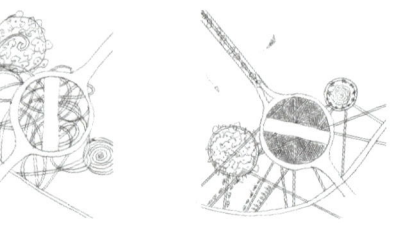

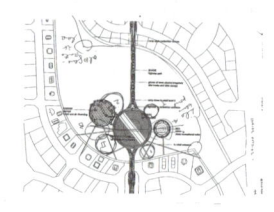

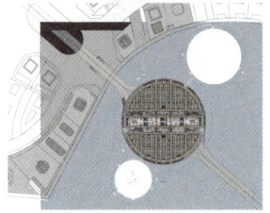

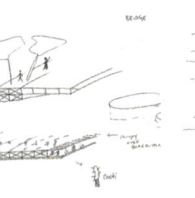

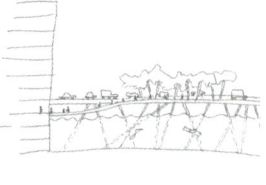

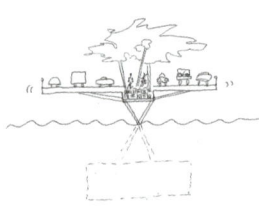

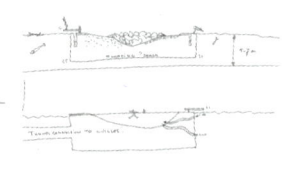

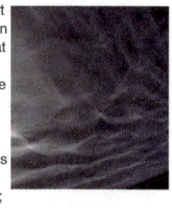

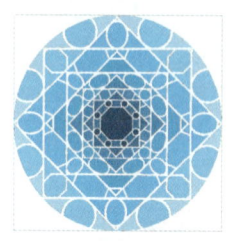

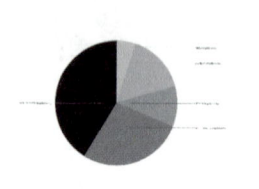

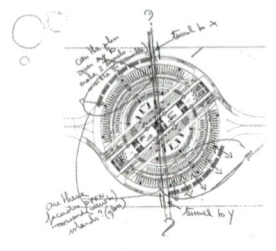

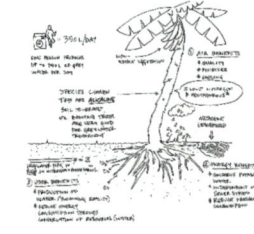

COOL INLAYS
Dubai, UAE, 2006

Architects
OMA

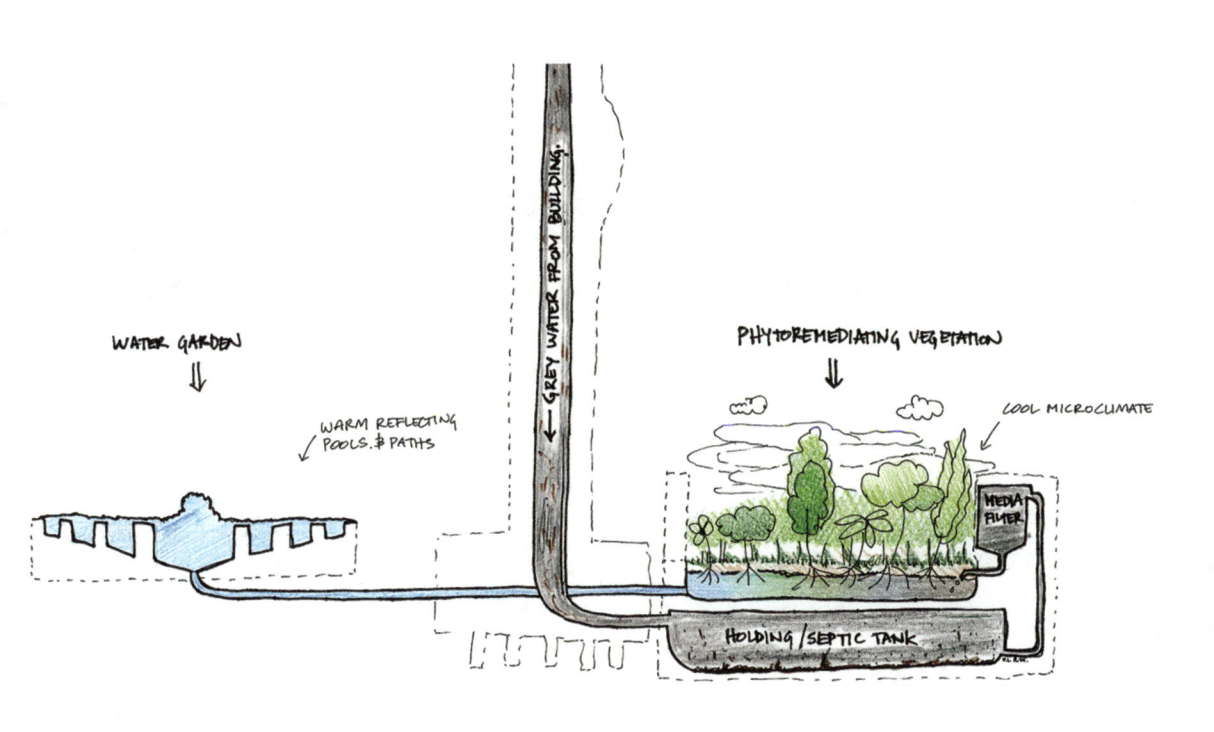

WATER GARDEN ⇓

⇐ WARM REFLECTING POOLS & PATHS

← GREY WATER FROM BUILDING

PHYTOREMEDIATING VEGETATION ⇓

COOL MICROCLIMATE ⇙

MEDIA FILTER

HOLDING/SEPTIC TANK

Planting and water system for campus city

A large new university campus is planned outside Abuja, the capital of Nigeria. The site is barren and dry, but it slopes down to a meandering river that draws a trace of thick green along its edges. The built structure presented by OMA covers only a quarter of the site and looks like a torn piece of cloth through a magnifying glass: a weave of long, two-story linear buildings, all interconnected, that create numerous open pockets – patio gardens – in-between its structure.

Our proposal for the landscape addresses water shortage, heat and work. It presents a water and planting strategy that supports the university buildings, the private households and the landscape around it. The endless roof area of the design creates enormous potential for rainwater collection. We propose to use the collected rainwater for the households (cleaning and sanitary use) and to filter and reuse grey water for the irrigation of gardens, nurseries and orchards and the maintenance of sports fields. We make use of the cooling effect of water and shade trees and use the roots of plantings for the prevention of erosion and dust formation. By proposing a gradation of green levels we try to create a fluid transition between wetter and dryer areas and between natural and more cultivated landscapes, into which agriculture is also integrated to supply the university, its users and inhabitants with fruit, cereals and vegetables.

With this landscape strategy (in combination with the university institution itself), many jobs are created to service gardens, orchards, sports facilities, car parks, water systems and wells, cafés, food stalls, small markets, and so forth.

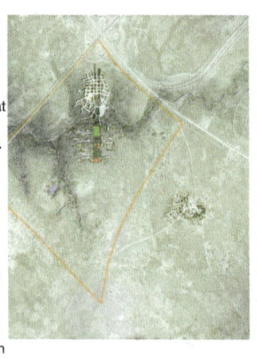

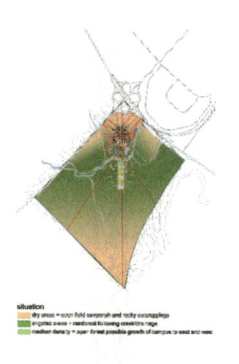

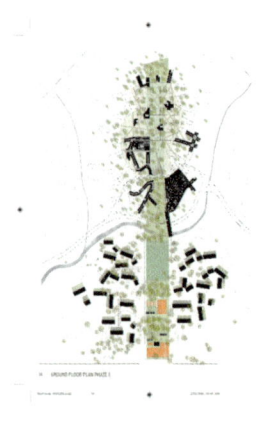

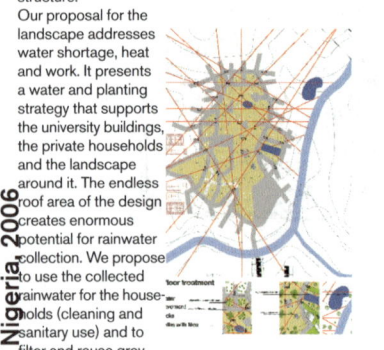

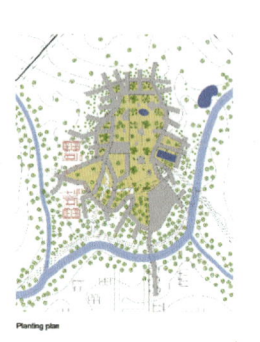

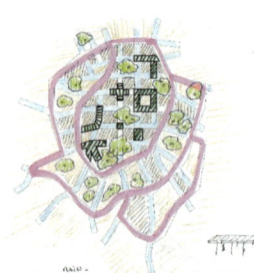

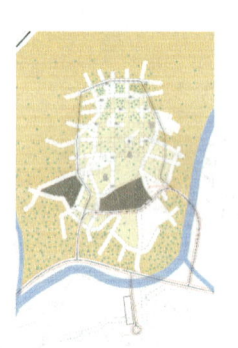

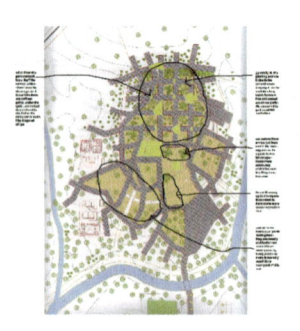

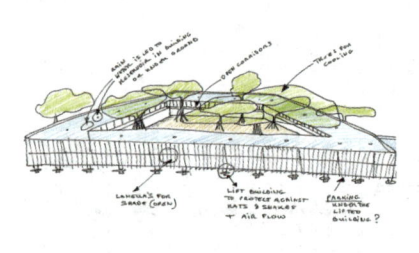

Architects
OMA

JOB CREATION — University Campus Competition, Abuja, Nigeria, 2006

487

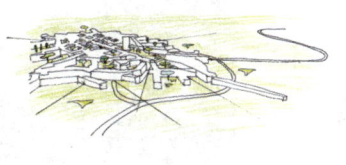

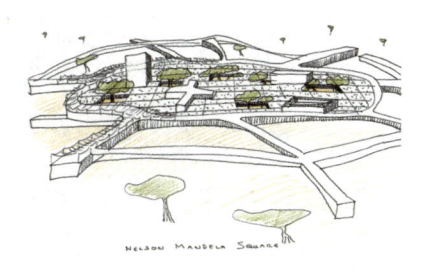

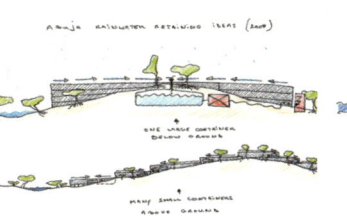

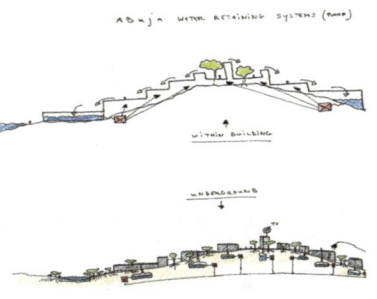

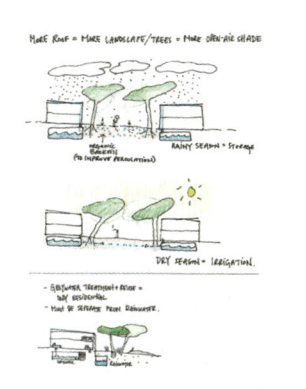

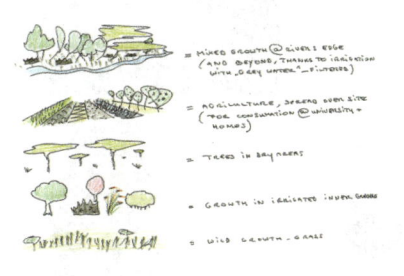

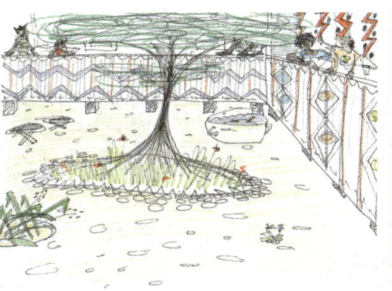

Landscape and planting plan for a new city within a city

For the master plan that is being developed by OMA for the city of Dubai, Inside Outside plays an advisory and designing role, joining the process of thought about public space, street and water-edge profiles, a 'language' with which to define different areas and the way in which planting, the use of water features, furniture and finishes can reinforce the new city planning strategy and characteristics. The methods and effects we suggest are on a larger scale – going into detail to show typical plots and the effects of specific (planting) conditions. Our proposal is to superimpose a regular, dotted grid over the entire area and to use a black-and-white language both in the planting and finishes, defining the different areas and giving each its own ambiance using planting typologies: evergreen, groundcover, flowering, aquatic, palmetum, xerophytic, prairie and allee.

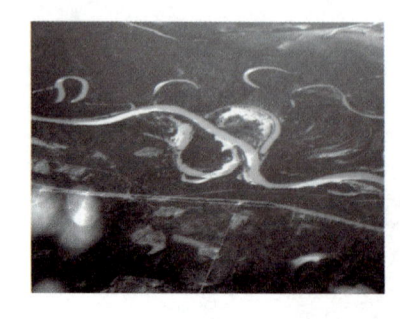

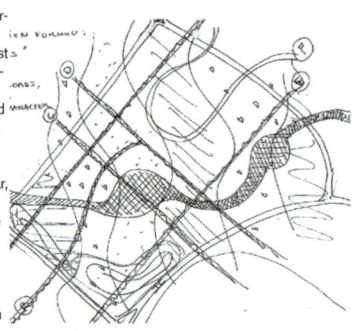

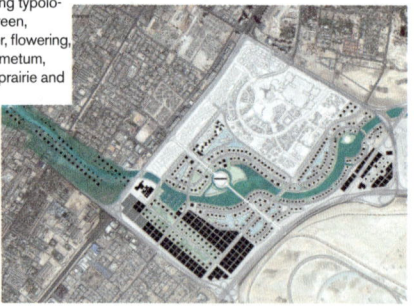

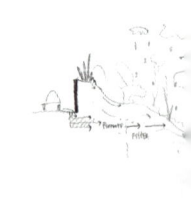

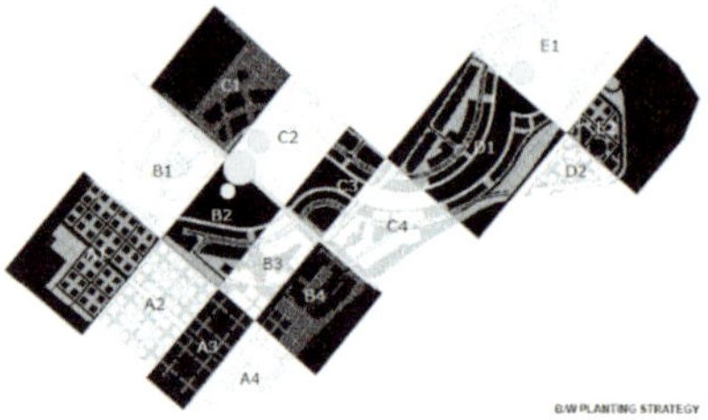

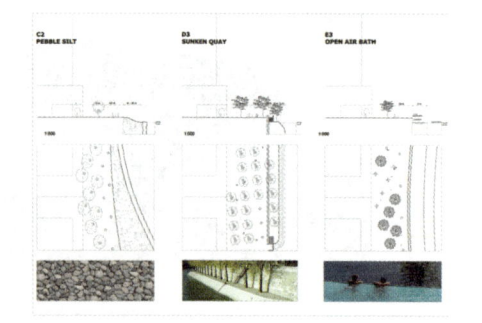

BLACK-AND-WHITE LANDSCAPE
Business Bay Master Plan, Dubai, UAE, 2006

Architects
OMA

489

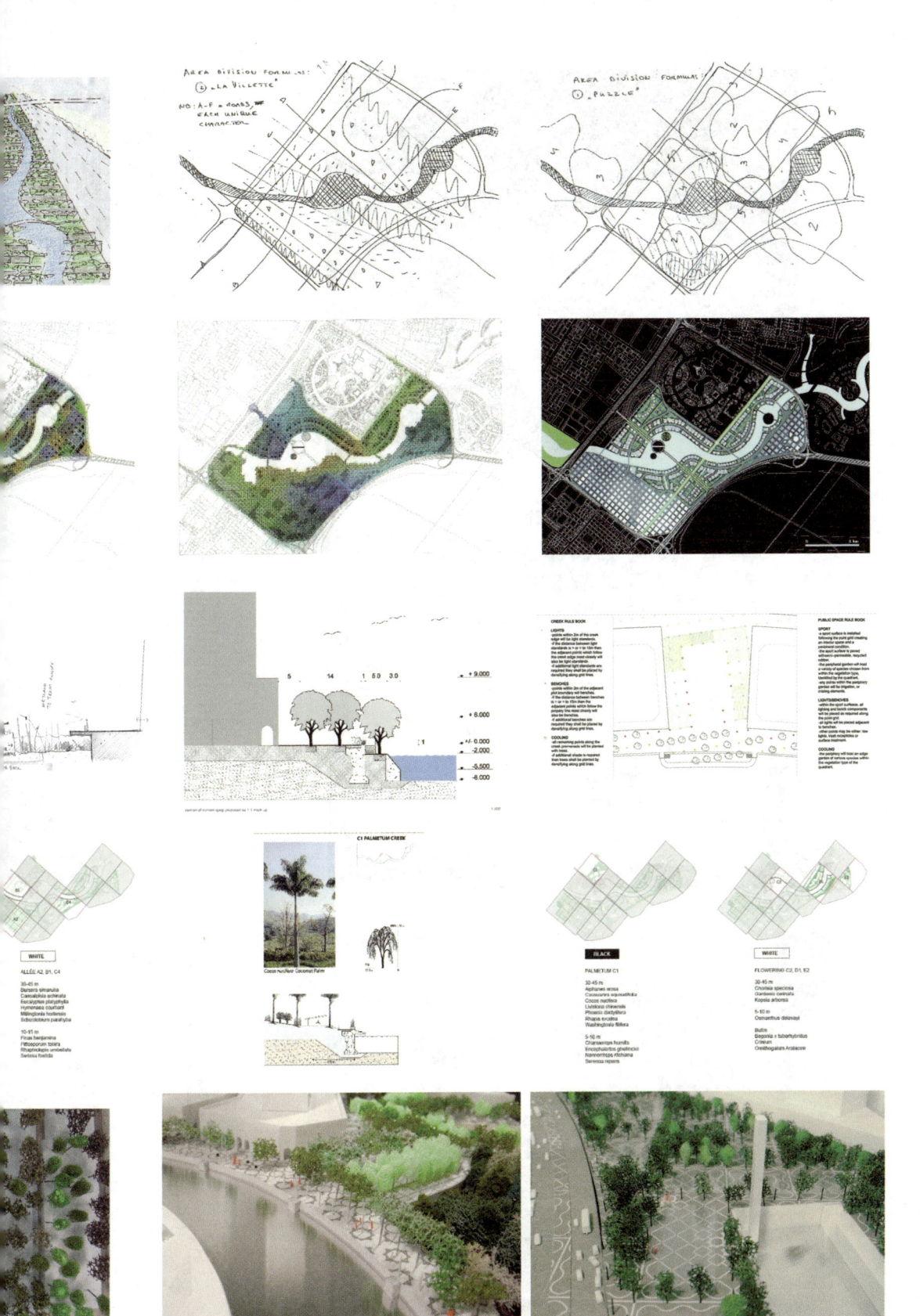

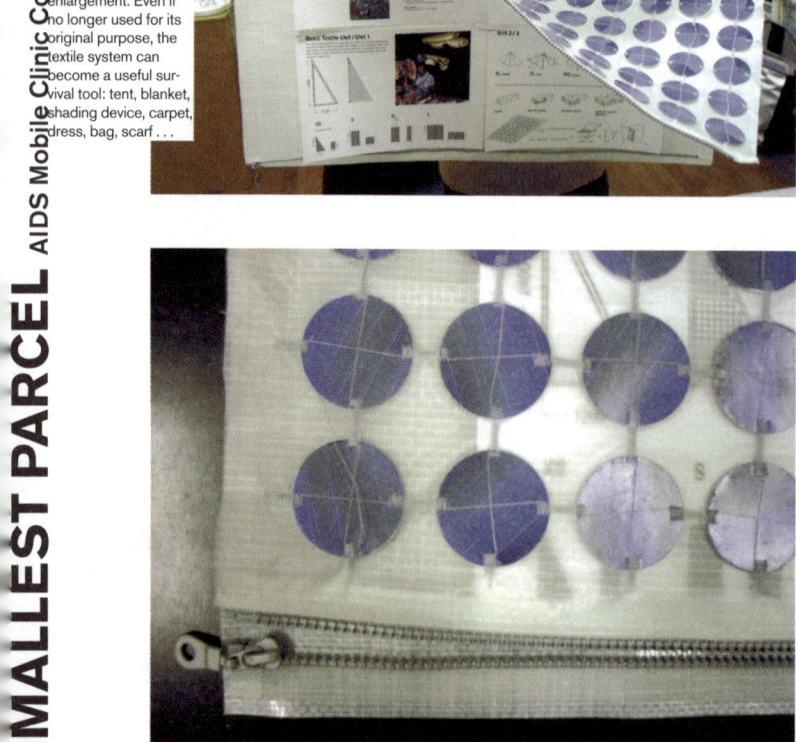

SMALLEST PARCEL AIDS Mobile Clinic Competition for Sub-Saharan countries, 2002

Mobile HIV clinic system

This sun-collecting and educational textile unit is a tool to prevent the spreading of HIV and to provide treatment to those already infected. For our mobile unit we proposed to use the characteristics of the virus – its system of dismantling, copying and multiplying – as the basic principle for our design; thus fighting the virus by using its own strategy. We designed the smallest and lightest possible element: a piece of cloth that can be rolled up and transported by one person (by bike, car, camel, scooter, horse or on foot) and into which everything needed is integrated: solar cells are woven into the cloth to collect energy, their thin cables ending in a plug for a water boiler or Frigidaire; numerous small pockets for condoms and larger ones for tools cover the other side of the cloth and all is printed with a large and colourful image narrative showing sanitary prevention and medical treatment methods. Each textile element has zipper edges that connect to any other element, allowing endless enlargement. Even if no longer used for its original purpose, the textile system can become a useful survival tool: tent, blanket, shading device, carpet, dress, bag, scarf . . .

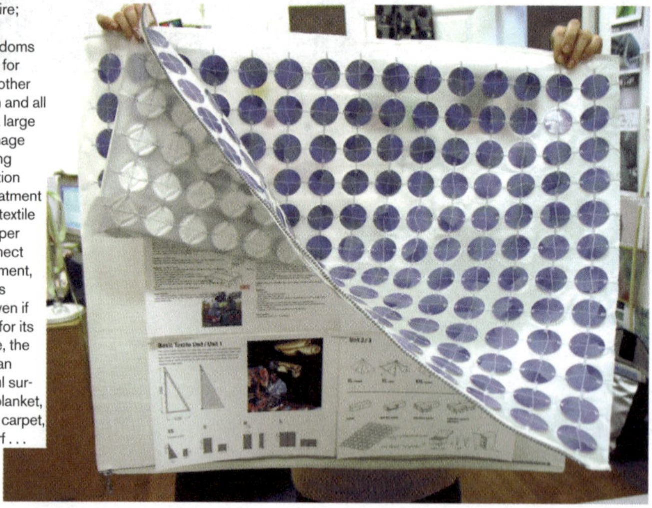

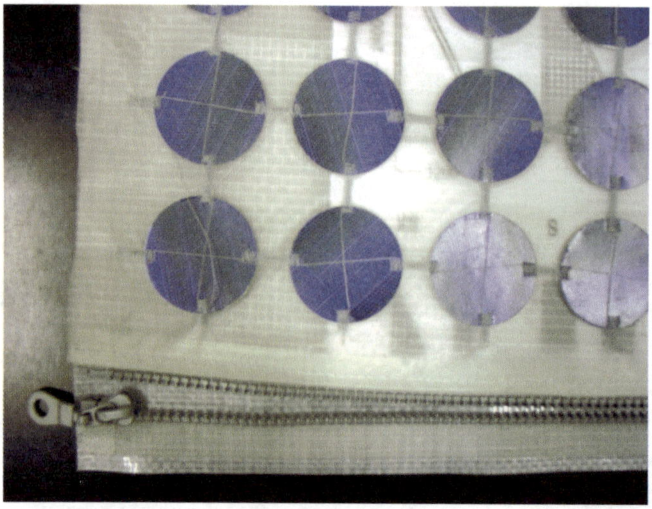

Team
Inside Outside,
Terra Firma,
Women on Waves

HIV - MA mature form

The HIV virus is the leading cause of death in sub-saharan Africa. It spreads through blood, sperm, vaginal discharge and breast milk

Once the virus enters the human body it invades CD 4 cells. In the CD 4 c
and then built into the DNA of the human cell's nucleus. Here the viral RN

Unit Network

Unit 1:

Concept: Through distributing the smaller units 2 (the daughter units)Unit 1 functions as the infected human CD 4 cells (the mother unit) that produce daughter HIV particles.

The main unit that holds and transports all other units is the container. It travels from a given point in Europe or the United States to a sub-saharan country, where it is placed in a context that has a basic form of infrastructure. The unit in itself, once emptied of it's 40 smaller units (that each contain 10 even smaller units) can, by unfolding it, be transformed into an open workspace, information and training centre and laboratory. Unit 1 will organise the transport of Unit 2's to their own destinations support the work done in the 40 units 2. In its basic form the container measures 12 x 2.5 x 2.50 meter. It can extend its volume with the 'survival blankets' that can act as roofs or walls. Because these blankets are imprinted with the HIV 'logo' and story-telling animation figures, they communicate the function and purpose of the initiative to the passer-by in a very direct manner. The unit generates its own energy with a second textile sheet: the solar cell blanket. Armed with materials, tools and only a few staff members, Unit 1 can serve a population of 20.000 to 80.000 people.

Functions of the mother unit:
Information, education, training (health workers for unit 2 and local shamans for unit 3), diagnostics, treatment, storage (medicines, tools etc.), research.

Equipment connected to this unit:
- Small laboratory to do the Western Blot test (final HIV test) and CD 4 count (to establish the effect of the treatment provided in unit 2)
- Space for training, educating the health workers of unit 3 and 2
- Storage space for packages of unit 2, HIV medicines, condoms, other
- Computer for research purposes
- Solar electricity blankets that can be zippered onto or used separately fo
- Information blankets with printed-on education about HIV/Aids and condoms in sewn-on pockets.
- Watercooler and water storage cans, light, refrigerator etc.

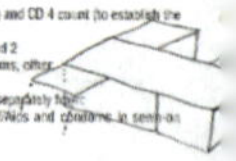

Human resources:
- 1 or 2 laboratory specialists, 1 midlevel health provider, 1 special trainer to educate the health workers that will work with unit 2, and 1 researcher to analyze the data. Backup ... a local medical doctor

Basic Textile Unit / Unit 1

Two layers zipped together, one solar net, one wind and cold shield wit
tion and condom-containing pockets. With zippers on all three sides, t
gular sheets can be connected in countless ways and to countless size
small wraps in which medicines or tools can be transported safely, to s
blankets to large tents.

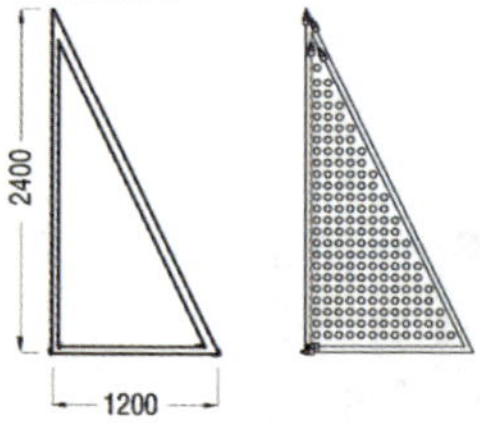

XS S

Transport wraps

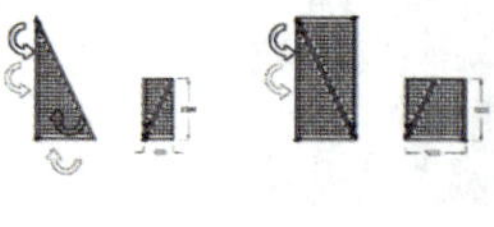

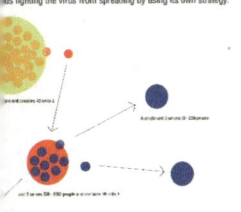

Concept

The Mobile HIV/Aids clinic we propose here consists of 3 units, whereby each smaller size unit fits into the larger unit, like a Russian doll, although here in multiple quantity.

The basic material for our units is TEXTILE with integrated SOLAR ENERGY COLLECTORS (in themselves flexible and paper thin), sewn-on pockets for male- and female CONDOMS, and imprinted ANIMATION INFORMATION, images that tell about HIV and AIDS prevention, identification, action. This means that even in dismantled form, each unit or particle beholds function and attains its aim: the spread of information as the most urgent necessity.

Daughter HIV virus in: Sperm, Blood, Mother-milk

Infecting new human CD 4 Cell

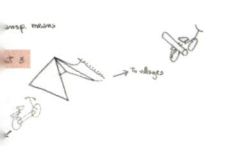

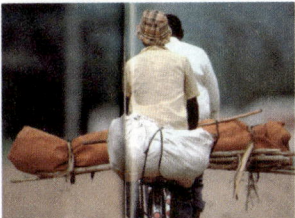

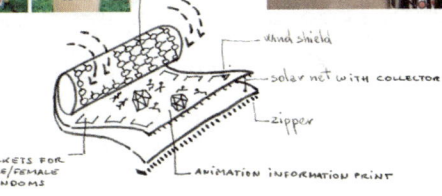

Unit 3:

Concept: Unit 3 functions like the primary HIV virus that infects a human for the first time.

It is a rolled-up package of 4 double-layered triangular sun-collecting and information-spreading textile sheets (each double layer connected onto each other by zippers) that can be seperately or together used as tent, roof, blanket, dress, hat, belt, bed, base, shelter (sticks added). To prevent HIV transmission, the most basic tools are information, education and condoms. Cartoons and texts about HIV/Aids transmission and prevention are printed on the survival blanket. With this water cooker and light attached to the solar energy blanket, the generated electricity can be used for basic hygiene such as clean water that is needed to diminish the chance of other (opportunistic) infections. Condoms (for men and women alike) and milkpowder can be used to prevent the further spreading of the HIV virus and new infections. The condoms function like the viral envelope. The solar electricity and survival blanket function like the viral RNA. Each unit can serve 50 to 200 people

Function:
- Information, shelter, assistance, prevention.

Equipment:
- Solar electricity blankets, zipped onto - or separate from:
- Survival blankets with animation information about HIV/Aids and sewn-on pockets containing condoms and milkpowder.
- Water cooker, light, -etc

Human resources:
- local village heads, medicine man/women or inhabitants.

Unit 2:

Concept: Unit 2 functions like the daughter HIV particles after being released by the CD 4 cells.

This is a box-like unit that fits onto or into a jeep or medium sized car. This aluminum and textile box unit contains information- and medical tools, solar electricity blankets, a fold-up bicycle & 10 smaller units for distribution. In this unit, people can get a HIV fast test with a blood drop from finger tip or sputum. Where the HIV fast test is positive, extra blood will be sent to the laboratory of Unit 1 for the first HIV test, the Western Blott. If this test is positive, medication will be transported back to unit 2 where the patient will receive the treatment. To follow the effect of the treatment, blood is drawn in unit 2 and then transported to Unit 1 for a CD4 count. To prevent transmission of the HIV virus, condoms and milkpowder with boiled water (mother-child transmission) are distributed.

Each unit 2 will serve 500 to 2000 people. Unit 2 will distribute 10 packages of unit 3 (that is slightly smaller than unit 2) to local medicine men or heads of the villages.

Function: Provision of information, diagnostics, treatment, distribution and coordination of 10 unit 3's.

Equipment:
- HIV fast tests
- Bloodtubes, needles, needle-containers
- Small fridge, water cooker, light, -etc.
- Bicycle (foldable). To transport blood samples to and medicines from unit 1. To transport Units 3 to destination
- Solar electricity blankets for the unit itself, with zippered-on or separately used.
- Survival blankets with information animation about HIV/Aids and sewn-on pockets that contain condoms and milkpowder
- 10 packages of unit 3 that will be distributed to the local population.

Human resources:
1 trained health workers, with local assistance.

Multiplying 1x40 x10= 400 units 3

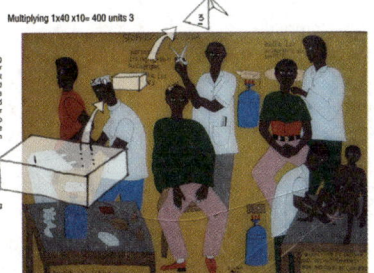

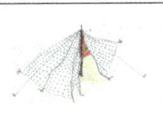

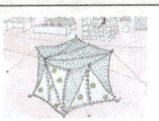

Even in dismantled form, each unit or particle beholds function and attains it's aim: the spread of information as the most urgent necessity.

Unit 2 / 3

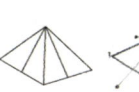

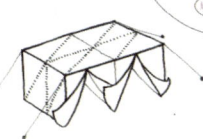

XL closed   XL open   XXL closed   XXL open

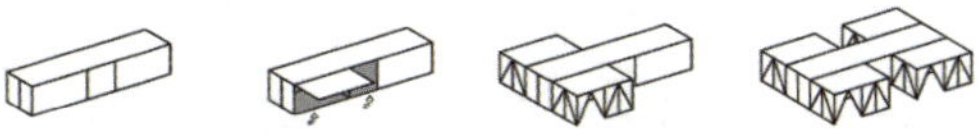

closed   opening: shade   education space   education space & laboratory

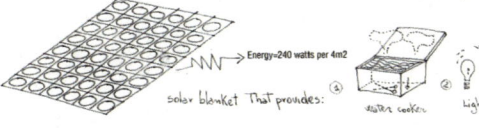

Energy=240 watts per 4m2

solar blanket that provides: water cooker, Light, Fridge

L

PROJECT CREDITS

Project	Inside Outside Design														Office						Advisors (Inside Outside and project)													Architects			
	Anky Adriaanse (NL)	Petra Blaisse (NL)	Marnix van den Broek (NL)	Lieuwe Conradie (NL)	Irene Curulli (IT)	Rosetta Sarah Elkin (CDN)	Simão Fereira (RSA)	Marieke van den Heuvel (NL)	Mathias Lehner (AU)	Yukiko Nezu (JA)	Peter Niessen (NL)	Martina Prokop (AU)	Angelique Rijk-Fokker (NL)	Floris Schifferli (NL)	Kim Uyting (NL)	Christine Zadlowski (USA)	Irma Koopman (NL)	Jeannette Kruseman (NL)	Shane van Lunteren (CDN/NL)	Alexandra Pander (NL)	Marleen de Vries (NL)	Jaap de Vries (NL)	Monique Wieman (NL)	Gaston Bekkers (NL)	Wim Beining (NL)	Tineke Blok (NL)	Fred Booij (NL)	Francois Delhay (FR)	Bruno Doedens (NL)	John Greenlee (USA)	Michael van Gessel (NL)	Rebecca Gomperts (NL)	Renz van Luxemburg (NL)	Rem Koolhaas (NL)	Ove Arup & Partners (UK/USA)	Ank van Peski (NL)	Matthias Schuler (DE)	Julie Sfez (FR)	Lily Terkuile (NL)	Michael Yantis Associates Inc.(USA)	Frits Veenis (NL)	Ien Wiegers (NL)	Architecten Cie (NL)	Archivolt Architecten (NL)	Arons & Gelauff (NL)	Boei Studio (IT)
London, Hackney Empire Theatre	X	X		X			X	X	X																																X					
Milan, Giardini di Porta Nuova, Competition		X		X				X	X													X																								
Nieuwegein, State Detention Centre		X																							X											X									X	
Porto, Casa da Música	X	X					X	X		X																					X	X														
Seattle, Seattle Central Library		X			X	X	X	X					X															X			X	X						X								
Seoul, Landscape Design 'H-Project'		X			X																			X	X																					
Toledo, The Glass Pavilion		X					X	X		X																						X														
Africa, International AIDS Mobile Unit, Competition		X	X		X			X	X											X											X															
Abuja, Landscape Design, Competition		X			X				X																																					
Amsterdam, Heemstra/Strik House		X										X																																		
Amsterdam, Stedelijk Museum		X																																												
Amsterdam, Architectura & Natura		X	X	X			X	X		X																																				
Barcelona, Paris, Rotterdam, OMA Exhibitions		X																																												
Birsfelden, Independent Screen Study for Vitra		X						X	X																							X														
Beijing, CCTV/Mediapark		X		X			X	X	X														X										X													
Berlin, the Netherlands Embassy	X	X	X		X		X	X	X	X																														X						
Bordeaux, Villa Floirac		X																																												
Breda, Lensvelt Headquarters	X	X		X														X																						X						
Breda, Chassé Terrein		X		X	X	X										X																														
Chicago, IIT/McCormick Tribune Campus Center, Reflection		X	X				X	X		X																																				
Chicago, IIT/McCormick Tribune Campus Center, Post-Occupancy		X			X				X																																					
Codroipo, Villa Manin	X	X			X				X																																					
Dartford, Mick Jagger Centre		X					X																																			X				
Delft, Faculty of Space Technology		X	X		X		X	X																																						
Dubai, High-Rise Building Competition		X			X																																									
Dubai, Master Plan		X			X						X																																			
Groningen, Blue Moon Hotel		X					X	X		X																																				
Haaksbergen, Private House	X	X					X			X	X			X																		X													X	
The Hague, Nederlands Dans Theater		X																																								X				
Holten, Dutch House		X																																												
Leefdaal, Private House		X					X	X			X																																			
Lille, Lille Grand Palais		X																										X											X		X					
London, Cinnabar Wharf Penthouse	X	X		X			X	X													X																									X
Los Angeles, Hammer Museum		X		X			X																							X																
New York, Lehmann Maupin Gallery		X			X			X	X																																					
New York, Storefront for Art and Architecture	X	X		X	X											X																														
New York, Vinyl Wallpaper Collection		X					X																																							
New York/Beverly Hills, Prada Epicenters	X	X		X					X																																					
Paris, Villa dall'Ava		X																																												
Rotterdam, Museumpark		X			X																																									
Rotterdam, Kunsthal		X																																												
Rotterdam, De Plussenburgh		X		X		X		X	X															X																					X	
Schiphol, F-terminal		X				X																																								
Stuttgart, Mercedes Benz Museum	X	X					X	X		X		X			X																															
Seoul, SNU Museum		X		X			X	X		X																																				
Taiwan, Chin Suei Service Area		X																																												
Toronto, Downsview Park		X																																												
Other Competitions and/or Collaborations																																								X			X		X	
Support Inside Outside											X			X	X	X	X	X	X	X	X	X		X		X		X				X														

| | Landscape Architects / Planting Designers | Graphic | Contractors / Specialists |

Collaborators (columns):
- Rudy Uytenhaak Architectenbureau (NL)
- Samoo Architects (KR)
- S333 (NL)
- SANAA (JP)
- Studio Gang / Mark Schendel (USA)
- Tim Ronalds Architects (UK)
- Toyo Ito (JP) & Hosoya Schaefer Architekten (CH)
- UN Studio (NL)
- Xaveer de Geyter Architecten (BE)
- Mirko Zardini (IT)
- Yves Brunier (FR)
- B&B landschapsarchitecten (NL)
- Robert Coulon (FR)
- DS Landschapsarchitecten (NL)
- DS+V (NL)
- Jones & Jones (USA)
- The Master Gardeners (UK)
- Mia Lehrer & Associates (USA)
- Rosemarijn Nitzsche (NL)
- Kate Orff (USA)
- Piet Oudolf (NL)
- Nancy Goslee Power (USA)
- Ro'Dor / Rob Kuster (NL)
- Peter Schaudt Landscape Architecture (USA)
- Liesbeth Sillem (NL)
- SWA Landscape Architects Los Angeles (USA)
- Toong-Ang Landscape Development (KR)
- West 8 (NL)
- Irma Boom (NL)
- Hard Werken (NL)
- Bruce Mau (CDN)
- Meat Productions (NL)
- 2 x 4 (USA)
- 3M (NL)
- Art on Tiles (NL)
- vd Berk en zonen (NL)
- Bolidt (NL)
- Claudie Cornasz (NL)
- Ken Creasey Ltd (UK)
- Ducks Scéno / Michel Covas (FR)
- EGE Teapper O/S (DK)
- Gerriets GmbH (DE)
- Grand Stage Chicago (USA)
- Anthony Goossens (NL)
- Harrison B.V. (NL)
- Johan Jumelet (NL)
- Ton van Kemenade (NL)
- Helene Kierulf (USA)
- Lammerts en Van Buren (NL)
- Mosterd en de Winter (NL)
- Nederlands Textiel Museum (NL)
- Nuansol (FR)
- De Punt (NL)
- Robiflex (NL)
- James Rubery (UK)
- Silas Morse PNTA (USA)
- Texoprint (NL)
- Theatex (NL)
- Twentebelt (NL)
- Vertical Vision (NL)
- Van Vlaanderen (NL)
- Hans Werlemann (NL)
- Wolf Gordon (US)
- Zeebra (NL)

PROJECT LIST OF INSIDE OUTSIDE

Work in Progress

A.R.T.E.M. (competition), Nancy
Campus landscape which coordinates three university departments: engineering, art and management
BUSINESS BAY, Dubai
Landscape master plan and planting system for CBD within the city
CCTV/TVCC, Beijing
Landscape site plan: further development
CORDOBA CONGRESS CENTER, Cordoba
Landscape plan; exterior and interior curtains
DUBAI LAND, Dubai
City Park, a green heart for a new city in the desert
HAUS DER KUNST, Munich
Curtains encircling Main Hall
McCORMICK TRIBUNE CAMPUS CENTER, Chicago
Second phase: design and construction of three gardens. Post occupancy: interior consultation
MEDIA PARK (competition), Beijing
1st Prize with EDSA, Beijing. Next phase: Landscape Design Development
MERCEDES BENZ MUSEUM, Stuttgart
One curtain
MUSEUMPARK, Rotterdam
Renovation of a city park (with OMA and Rotterdam Municipality)
NPR BANK, London
Roofscape and patio designs
PRIVATE HOUSE, Hummelo
Shading system for terrace
PRIVATE VILLA, Mexico City
Schematic design uniting garden and interior
SEOUL NATIONAL UNIVERSITY MUSEUM OF ART, Seoul
Garden and curtains for lecture hall
RIGA
Masterplan
RAK
Masterplan
Tblisi
Cinema City
Vlaams-Nederlands Huis deBuren
Interior intervention

Realized Projects

2006
DE PLUSSENBURGH, Rotterdam
Garden, parking, bridge and carpet
MERCEDES BENZ MUSEUM, Stuttgart
Three curtains and a brush wall
PRIVATE VILLA, Haaksbergen
Interior and exterior curtains
SCHIPHOL AIRPORT, Amsterdam
Tiled walls
PRADA EPICENTER, New York
Restoration of flexible VIP dressing rooms

2005
'RIFLETUTTI', Codroipo
Art installation for the Villa Manin gardens: flexible personal pavilions and 'water drops'
CASA DA MÚSICA, Porto
Sala 1: acoustic, shading and filter curtains; gold leaf wall. Sala 2: acoustic shading and filter curtains. Rehearsal room acoustic curtains; advisory on landscape and interiors
THE GLASS PAVILION, Toledo
Designs for tracks, shading and MPR curtains (not realized)
BLUE MOON HOTEL, Groningen
Interior façade curtains for two bedrooms
HACKNEY EMPIRE THEATRE, London
Main stage curtain and all other curtains for theatre and new annex
VILLA WATTÉ, Leefdaal
Space-defining and shading curtains
PRADA EPICENTER, Beverly Hills
Flexible VIP dressing room
BUTTON & TULIP TILES
A new ceramic tile series for Art on Tiles

2004
SEATTLE CENTRAL LIBRARY, Seattle
Landscape, carpets and auditorium curtains; advisory on interior finishes
THE NETHERLANDS EMBASSY, Berlin
Darkening acoustic curtains for MPR; advisory on interior and landscape
McCORMICK TRIBUNE CAMPUS CENTER, Chicago
Second phase: design and construction of three gardens. Post occupancy: interior interventions
H-PROJECT, Seoul
Landscape plan connecting seven buildings by four architects (design 1997)

2003
'TOUCH' WALLPAPER
A new vinyl wallpaper series for Wolf Gordon
LEHMANN MAUPIN GALLERY, New York
Space-defining and darkening curtain
FACULTY OF SPACE TECHNOLOGY, Delft
Polyurethane floor for cafeteria and public spaces

2002
ARTIST'S HOUSE, Amsterdam
Flexible climate wall
CINNABAR WHARF PENTHOUSE, London
Penthouse roof garden and all curtains

2001
PRADA EPICENTER, New York
Acoustic 'sock' and flexible VIP dressing rooms
CHASSÉ TERREIN, Breda
Semipublic garden connecting five apartment buildings

2000
LENSVELT HEADQUARTERS, Breda
Acoustic darkening curtain and sun screen for conference room
MICK JAGGER CENTRE, Dartford (London)
Light- and sound-regulating curtain layers for concert hall
HIGHWAY SERVICE AREA, Chin Sui
Landscape plan for Parking and Service area

1999
STATE DETENTION CENTRE, Nieuwegein
Prison gardens and parking lot
BUSINESS AREA, Nieuwegein
Landscape plan for new business area
UNIVERSAL HEADQUARTERS, Los Angeles
Landscape design and interior gardens
DUTCH HOUSE, Holten
2nd Phase planting plan for West 8 garden; shading systems for house and terrace
PARKING LOT GARDEN, Almere
A swamp garden inside a parking building (to be executed in 2007)
SECOND STAGE THEATRE, New York
Curtains

1998
VILLA FLOIRAC, Bordeaux
Interior and exterior curtains and landscape interventions
PRIVATE HOUSE, Amsterdam
Patio garden

1996
FREUD HOUSE, Amsterdam
Roof garden, bookcases and curtains

1994
MUSEUMPARK, Rotterdam
Co-design of city park (with Yves Brunier)
LILLE GRAND PALAIS, Lille
Auditorium and Main Hall curtains; floors; furnishing plan (with Julie Sfez); interior finishes

1993
KUNSTHAL, Rotterdam
Sound curtain and sloping roof garden; advisory on interior finishes

1992
VILLA DALL'AVA, Paris
Curtains and interior advisory
STEDELIJK MUSEUM EXTENSION (competition), Amsterdam
Designs and planting plans for Art Garden and Earth Garden

1991
'OMA Barcelona'
Exhibition design and installation for OMA at Collegi d'Arquitectes de Cataluña

1990
FIN DE SIÈCLE, Paris
Exhibition design and installation for OMA at Institut Français d'Architecture

1989
THE LAST DECADE, Rotterdam
Exhibition design and installation for OMA at Museum Boijmans van Beuningen
OMA, Basel
Exhibition design at installation for OMA at Architektur Museum

1988
VILLA LINTHORST, Rotterdam
Garden design and installation; shading curtains; advisory on interior finishes
ROTTERDAM '88, Rotterdam
Exhibition design in temporary Kunsthal
RESTAURANT CHRISTOPHE, Amsterdam
Patio garden

1987
NEDERLANDS DANS THEATER, The Hague
Stage curtain, furniture selection and interior finishes
CITY HALL COMPETITION, The Hague
OMA's City Hall design installation (selected team) at Gemeente Museum Den Haag

Selected Competitions

2006
MEDIA PARK, Beijing
Urban park design, 1st Prize for I.O./EDSA Team: Inside Outside, EDSA (Orient); with Charles Waldheim, Brian Eno, Atelier Markhoff, Piet Oudolf and Ro'Dor

2003-2004
GIARDINI DI PORTA NUOVA, Milan
Urban park design, 1st Prize for I.O. Team: Inside Outside, Mirko Zardini, Michael Maltzan Architects, Irma Boom, Piet Oudolf, Ro'Dor

2000
DOWNSVIEW PARK, Toronto
Urban park design, 1st Prize for Bruce Mau Team: Bruce Mau, Rem Koolhaas, Inside Outside, Oleson Worland Architects

Solo Exhibitions

2006
'Curtain Catalogue'
Vlaams-Nederlands Huis deBuren

2000
'MOVEMENTS'
Storefront for Art and Architecture, New York with a catalogue by Irma Boom: 'Movements; Introduction to a working process – 25%'

Group Exhibitions

2005
LUNA PARK, Codroipo
Installation 'RIFLETUTTI'
NEST, Amsterdam
Stedelijk Museum

2004
AMBIGUITY OF SPACE, Los Angeles
University of California
CONTENT, Rotterdam
Kunsthal

2003
CONTENT, Berlin
Neue Nationalgalerie

2002
Schatten/SHADOWS, Frankfurt
Deutsches Architektur Museum

2001
'WHAT'S COOKING' on Current Californian Architecture, Los Angeles
MOCA
SKIN, New York
Cooper-Hewitt Museum for Modern Art

1987–1991
Several Exhibition Designs

Image copyrights
Inside Outside and

American Univeristy in Cairo: 49
Arons & Gelauff: 156-157
Arup: 407
Baan, Iwan: 210-212, 218, 375
Bald, Diane: 501
Binet, Hélène: 86-87
Crommelin, Claude: 120-123, 293 (top)
Cummins, Richard/Corbis: 501
Duplan, J.P.: 106-107
Finotti, Leonardo: 370-371, 376-377
Floto+Warner: 226-227
Haan, Douwe de: 192-193
Hommert, Jens: 384-385
Horowitz, Ted/Corbis: 501
Koolhaas, Rem: 118-119, 473 (bottom)
Meech, Philip: 84-85, 90-92, 96, 98-99
Misrach, Richard: 503
Musch, Jeroen: 60-61, 344-347
OMA: 224-225, 435
Orti, Gianni Dagli/Corbis: 501
Oudolf, Piet: 146-147, 150-151, 160-161
Parthesius, Frans: 62-63, 110-111 (from video)
Pauly, Andreas/Nest: 471 (middel)
Prevot, Marc: 108-109
Powileit, Inga: 408
Ronalds, Tim: 97
Ruault, Philippe: 54-55, 228-229, 372-373, 404-405
SANAA: 410-411
Shanks, James: 174-175
Sitton, H./zefa/Corbis: 501
Smith, Grant: 471 (top)
Stavast, Petra: 288-291
Termeulen, Kai: 164-165
Tilly, Nico: 226, 437
Werlemann, Hans: 72-73, 126-127, 262-263,
268-269, 271-279, 292 (bottom), 293 (bottom),
340-341, 348-349, 351, 444-445, 448-449, 456
Zeebra: 95

PHOTO CREDITS

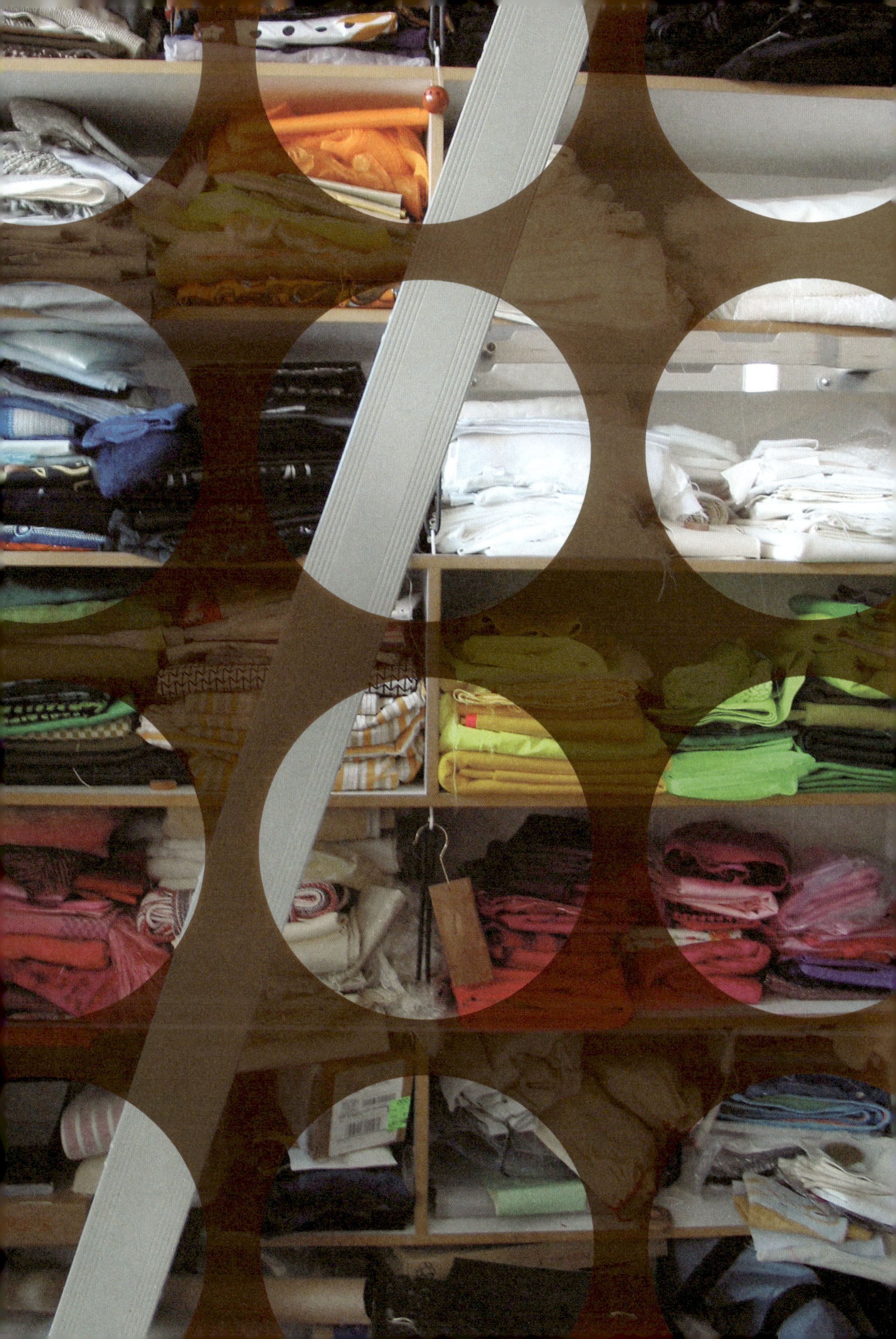

Biographies

Petra Blaisse (London, 1955) grew up in England, Portugal, Austria, Sweden and the Netherlands, and studied at art schools in London and Groningen. In the seventies and early eighties she worked at the Stedelijk Museum in Amsterdam, in the Department of Applied Arts. From 1987, she worked as freelance designer and won distinction for her installations of architectural work, in which the exhibited work was challenged more than displayed. Gradually her focus shifted to the use of textiles and finishes in interior space and, at the same time, to the design of gardens and landscape architecture.

In 1991, she founded Inside Outside. The office currently consists of about ten team members from different disciplines. Blaisse's studio is working globally on projects of increasing technical sophistication, ambition and scale.

Throughout the years, Inside Outside has collaborated with various architects and designers. Blaisse has lectured and taught extensively worldwide. Her work has been included in numerous design and architecture exhibits in Europe and the United States. In 2000 a solo exhibition on Inside Outside's work was organized at the Storefront for Art and Architecture in Soho, New York, for which Dutch graphic designer Irma Boom created Blaisse's first publication, the *Movements* catalogue.

In the past years, the opening of a number of public and private buildings in which Inside Outside implemented interior and landscape interventions brought the work of Blaisse's studio to the attention of a broader public. Examples are the McCormick Tribune Campus Center in Chicago (gardens and curtains, 1999-2004), the restoration project for the Hackney Empire Theatre in London (all curtains, 2000-2005), the gardens, carpets and finishes for the Seattle Central Library (2000-2004) and eleven theatre curtains for the Casa da Música in Porto (1999-2005). In 2004, Inside Outside and a high-profile multidisciplinary team won first prize in the 'Giardini di Porta Nuova' landscape competition with their entry 'Biblioteca degli Alberi' – a new urban park for the centre of Milan.

Cecil Balmond is a structural engineer and writer, specialized in designs for buildings with innovative structures. Since April 2004, he is deputy chairman of Arup, a global firm of designers, engineers, planners and business consultants providing a diverse range of professional services to clients around the world.

Working with some of the world's most influential architects, he continues to promote engineering as a totally creative activity. His particular interest lies in promoting an animate sense of geometry using numbers, mathematics and music as vital sources. His recent projects include the Battersea Powerstation redevelopment, the 2002 Serpentine Pavilion in London, New York's World Trade Center, and the CCTV building in Beijing.

Cecil Balmond lectures and teaches at architecture schools all over the world. He is the Crét professor in practice at the Architectural School of the University of Pennsylvania. He is also an external examiner at the Architectural Association in London, and Senior Design Fellow at the London School of Economics.

He is the author of several books and has written editorials for a wide range of external publications. His work explores the creative approach to engineering, using pattern, mathematical reasoning and advanced technology to create unconventional design. Notable books include *Number 9* (Munich: Prestel, 1998), a story about the hidden world of numbers, and *Informal* (Munich: Prestel, 2002),which explores structure as catalyst in architecture.

Bernd Baumeister studied business commerce in Freiburg. He is responsible for the personnel and operational part of the business at Gerriets International. Gerriets is a German firm, expert in textile materials and (art) curtain finishings. Baumeister's mains tasks and challenges lay in the conversion and realization of designs into technically feasible or practiceable (art)works, all in dialogue with the customer or designer, while fully meeting all technical requirements of the curtains. Project highlights, besides numerous national and international projects, include Santiago de Chile, the first main curtain; Royal Opera House London; and Casa da Música in Porto.

Gaston Bekkers, art historian and researcher, is a specialist in the landscape and garden architecture of the early twentieth century. He has published several articles and books. He is also the owner of the bookstore and publishing house Architectura & Natura in Amsterdam.

Irma Boom is a graphic designer based in Amsterdam. She worked for five years at the Dutch Government Publishing and Printing Office in The Hague. In 1991 she founded Irma Boom Office, which works nationally and internationally in both the cultural and commercial sectors. Clients include the Rijksmuseum, Inside Outside, Museum Boijmans Van Beuningen, OMA/Rem Koolhaas, NAi Publishers, Royal Tichelaar Makkum, SHV Holdings, Zumtobel, Ferrari, Vitra International, Camper and the United Nations. Since 1992 Boom has been a senior critic at Yale University in the USA. She has received many awards for her book designs and was the youngest laureate to receive the prestigious Gutenberg prize for her complete oeuvre.

Chris Dercon was born in Belgium. He was the programme director of PS1 Museum at the end of the eighties. In 1990 he moved to Rotterdam, where he was the first director of Witte de With Center for Contemporary Art. In 1996 he became director of the Museum Boijmans Van Beuningen. In 2003 he took over the directorship of the Haus der Kunst in Munich, where he organizes exhibitions with architects and designers including Droog Design, Rem Koolhaas, Konstantin Grcic and Herzog & de Meuron.

Tijs Goldschmidt is a biologist and writer. After obtaining his PhD from Leiden University, he continued to work there as a researcher until 1993, when he left to dedicate himself fully to writing. His first book, *Darwin's Dreampond: Drama in Lake Victoria* (published in Dutch in 1994 and English in 1996) was nominated, among other things, for the major Dutch AKO Literature Prize. It has since been translated into many languages. In 2000 a collection of essays (*Oversprongen*, Crossovers) about the parallels between culture and nature was published, for which he was awarded the Dutch Jan Hanlo Essay Prize in 2001. Among his other publications are 'The Angel's Balls: Reflections on the Naturalness of Culture' (*Kloten van de Engel. Beschouwingen over de natuurlijkheid van cultuur*, 2007) and 'Pretending You're Pretending' (*Doen alsof je doet alsof*, 2008), an essay on the evolutionary significance of playing among animals, including human beings. In 2009 he compiled a collection of poems and essays (*Ademgaten*, Breathing Spaces) by the Dutch poet, writer and biologist Dick Hillenius (1927-1987). Goldschmidt characteristically interweaves subjects from nature and culture in his writings, as in his essays about the 'right/left' distinction in evolution and culture, the complex emotion of shame and the significance of playing and cooking.

Dirk van den Heuvel is an architect and researcher at the Faculty of Architecture, Delft University of Technology, and is preparing a dissertation on the work of Alison and Peter Smithson. He is the co-author of *Lessons: Tupker/Risselada, A Double Portrait of Dutch Architectural Education 1953-2000* (Amsterdam: SUN Publishers, 2003), and *Alison and Peter Smithson—From the House of the Future to a House of Today* (Rotterdam: 010 Publishers, 2003). With Max Risselada, Van den Heuvel co-edited *Team 10, In Search of a Utopia of the Present* (Rotterdam: NAi Publishers, 2006). He has published articles in various magazines, including *L'Architecture d'Aujourd'hui* and *Volume*. He was formerly an editor of the architectural journal *Oase*.

Sanford Kwinter is a New York-based writer, editor and associate professor at Rice University. He is co-founder of Zone Books and ZONE, a serial publication of philosophy and contemporary culture. He has written widely on philosophical issues of design, architecture and urbanism and was a member of the series of ANY conferences and publications, and member of the editorial board of Assemblage. Kwinter was part of the exhibition and book *Mutations* in Bordeaux (2000) and Tokyo

(2001). He is principal of Studio !KAZAM, a content and communications design firm in the USA, through which he published *Pandemonium: The Rise of Predatory Locales in the Post-War World* (New York: Princeton Architectural Press, 1999). He is author of *Architectures of Time: Towards a Theory of the Event in Modernist Culture* (Cambridge: The MIT Press, 2001) and the forthcoming *Far From Equilibrium: Essays on Technology and Design Culture* (The MIT Press).

Hélène Lemoine in 1978 moves to Bordeaux with Jean-François Lemoine; 1989 Meets Rem Koolhaas and Petra Blaisse for their private house project; 1991 Jean-François Lemoine has accident; 1995-1997 Realization of the 'Maison à Bordeaux' by Rem Koolhaas and conversations with Petra Blaisse on curtains, textiles, garden, well being and femininity; 1999 Skis with Petra Blaisse in Celerina, Switzerland; 2000-2006 Uninterrupted friendship and continuation of conversations with Petra Blaisse.

Renz van Luxemburg studied architecture and building physics at the Eindhoven University of Technology (TU/e). After graduation in 1976 he started his career in architectural acoustics at the Institute for Applied Physics TNO in Delft. From 1980 to 2000 he was responsible for an affiliation between TNO and TU/e. In this period he was involved in projects including the Music Centre Eindhoven and Grand Palais, Lille. In 2000 he joined DHV. Current projects include OMA's Wyly Theatre in Dallas, Calltech University in California, Museum Plaza in Louisville Kentucky (USA) and CCTV Headquarters in Beijing (China), and the Palacio del Sur in Cordoba (Spain). In the Netherlands, he is involved in the design for the new city theatres in Almere (SANAA), in Amsterdam (Jonkman and Klinkhamer) and in Eindhoven (En En Architects). He is also involved in the design for the Muziekpaleis in Utrecht (Hertzberger) and the New Opera House in Enschede (Hoogstad). He was responsible for the acoustics of Casa da Música in Porto and the new theatre in Portimao (Portugal). He has given lectures on building acoustics at the universities in Eindhoven, Ghent, Mendrisio and at Harvard University (USA), and has written four books on the subject.

Kayoko Ota studied international law at International Christian University in Tokyo before she co-founded *Telescope*, a magazine on architecture and urban issues in 1987. She is editor and curator at OMA and AMO since 2002. She curated the major exhibitions 'Content' at the Neue Nationalgalerie, Berlin (2003) and the Kunsthal, Rotterdam (2004), and 'Waist Down', mutating exhibitions of skirts created by Miuccia Prada in Tokyo (2004), Shanghai (2005) and New York (2006). She recently co-edited with Rem Koolhaas 'Post-Occupancy', the first signature edition of *Domus*.

Tim Ronalds studied architecture at Cambridge and at MIT. He established his practice in 1982, combining it in the early years with teaching at the Architectural Association and at Harvard. A series of small projects, including Jackson's Lane & Hampstead Poolhouse, established the reputation of the practice and it was included as one of the 'Four British Architects' exhibition in London in 1990. Notable projects since include several theatres and arts centres - Chequer Mead (1997), The Landmark, Ilfracombe (1998), Mick Jagger Centre (2000) and The Hackney Empire Theatre (2004). The practice now specializes in arts and education projects, working on complex projects for clients with social agendas. Current work includes a new school/community music centre, a circus training school and the development of The Old Vic Theatre in London.

The Garden and the Veil
Sanford Kwinter

...ungodly reality gives us the beautiful either not at all or once only. Yet the world is overfull with beautiful things only poor, very poor when it comes to beautiful moments and unveilings of these things. But perhaps this is the most powerful magic of life: it is covered by a veil interwoven with gold, a veil of beautiful possibilities, sparkling with promise, resistance, bashfulness, mockery, pity, and seduction.
Friedrich Nietzsche

It is said that the Greeks prayed to their gods to give them everything beautiful not once but twice, even three times, that theirs was a culture that celebrated *appearance* and surface above all, and that in this one could glimpse their profundity. To grasp what is deep about surface, one must understand the Greek cult of appearance not as a fetish of the literal aspects of things, but of the *action* of their coming into the light, of their *passage into form*. For the Greeks, truth and beauty were in this way intimately linked and, as Nietzsche pointed out, always flirted and beguiled at the very threshold of what can be perceived, grasped or possessed, like a woman deft in the use of distance, masks and veils. The philosopher must understand first and foremost that the approach to truth is fraught with the agonies of seduction, where revelation and dissimulation are compressed with exquisite economy into a single gesture, making the revelation of truth a task at once hopeless and inescapably erotic. Living, philosophizing and making space are arts of promise, not possession.

In our own design tradition, perhaps we, too, have been long duped by the cult of the masculine – the load-bearing column, the impregnable wall, the 'dictatorial' path, the false precision that issues from fixity. To paraphrase Nietzsche's now famous question we can ask: 'What if *space* too were a woman?" and our design methods till now but error and illusion? An electrifying body of evidence over the last decade suggests that there may be something to this, thanks to the general emergence of what one might call a 'Dionysian tectonics', an assembly logic that favours the musical and the moving, the interval over the integer, and the ductile over the solid line (one need search no further than the confident architectural cosmologies of Zaha Hadid, Kazuyo Sejima or Lindy Roy). Nowhere are these tendencies more fully developed than in the Inside Outside projects of Petra Blaisse. 'Columns', for example, can be discerned everywhere in her work, formed by billows and drape and the natural fluting of textile gathered and compressed, but nowhere are these made to support 'Newtonian' loads. Indeed, one could argue that the age-old concept of 'work' itself (displacement of mass over distance and time) is here overthrown entirely in favour of something far more like the child's variable free play, the motific movements of song, the control and cyclic variation of optical, informational, thermal, and naturally, *libidinal* flows. This is living structure, put at the service of homeostasis and active regulation of the environment; space is conceived through and through as an active and especially excitable medium, literally protoplasmic. The universe of Petra Blaisse is composed of tissues and fluid devices – membranes, valves, apertures, diaphragms, pores, filaments, filters, channels and scrims – that move, constrict, dilate, rarefy, condense or form vortexes in response to cues, rhythmic patterns, or simply the intoxications of whim. Blaisse's architecture expresses better than any other I know the critical difference between the old space of physics and the one, more pertinent to the world and habits of mind of today, of chemistry. Chemistry is concerned with processes, probabilities, interactions and transformation, physics with unambiguous dispositions and states. In chemical space one bit of matter – an acid for example – *acts on* another – a solid – and produces solution

Ludovisi Throne: The Birth of Aphrodite

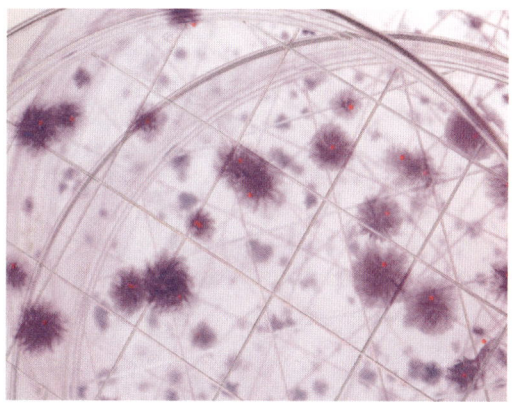

Culture

Lake

Weed

501 Woman in Purple Dress (Taj Mahal)

Alembic

(liquid), precipitation (particles), and vapour (clouds), but also a palpable, measurable rarefaction of the original solid that suffered the action so that it now transmits – through engraving or perforation – where previously it merely impeded. No other architecture today concerns itself as thoroughly with every resultant by-product, nuance and effect of chemical or thermodynamic action on space, matter or form. For Blaisse, every surface is one that acts or is acted upon, every surface is made to serve as a lens that either amplifies, suggests and withholds, or places into abeyance a part of reality that we no longer have any power to resist. The use of the frame, the lens and the passe-partout evokes the inherent – non-optical – expressionism of Proclusian metaphysics (a prominent feature of twentieth-century cinema) in which light and dark struggle with one another to both give place to a world and to structure its passions. Think of the *film noir*, and its reliance on the filtering 'curtains' and Venetian blinds to project diagonals, alternating blinding dazzle and murk, to produce mood and knowledge about the world, and then withdraw its certainties, leaving only the vertigo and vulnerability that is the landscape of fatal (feminine) seduction. *What if the truth of space could be revealed only through a veil?*

Make no mistake, however, Blaisse's universe is by no means cinematic: its task is never to create the illusion of solidity through the use of light, but the other way round: it produces 'chemical' light by mobilizing matter into controlled configurations – micro and mobile architectures – that propagate luminescence, phosphorescence and iridescence themselves. Blaisse's architecture is not only about fabric and matter in motion, or alchemically in situ, but about the infinite combinability of pathways, punctures and tracks (it is fascinating to learn that Blaisse's curtain tracks have 'points' to be switched at will, like the rail master does, to direct the traffic of transiting matter to manifold destinations on a map). Blaisse's architecture both generates and suspends desire – note the obligatory foreplay of the acutely meandering paths that seem to distance one as much as they bring one forward to the building's 'breach' – by making the desire coextensive with matter and form. In the dance of veils there is no longer negative space, there is nothing opposable to form; everything is situation and movement and the dance of propinquity and chance. Here, as in every future architecture, interval is no longer something simply between, it has become substance itself.

Inside Outside describes a seizure of power, a *coup* of sorts, in which architecture is first annihilated by a deliberate metaphysical omission – there is posited an 'outside': field/nature/landscape, and an 'interior': textiles, furnishings and their choreographed scripts, and to this is added the 'miscegenation' of their encounter, but nothing else – and then revived as the by-product only of this wedding, of the continuity of inside and out. Nowhere is the effect so dramatically visible as in the Casa da Música in Porto where the rigid, virtually neutral matrix of the building serves as no more than a passive armature for the operatic play of layers, fabrics, patterns, moirés, weaves and drapes (even a cursory glance at *Inside Outside Petra Blaisse* reveals an atlas of inventions, styles and 'moves' that have for years shaped the form-language of Blaisse's most frequent collaborator, the Office of Metropolitan Architecture). In the Porto project there simply is no independent building to be discerned once the 'anima' of the micro (inside) and macro (outside) landscapes is deleted. This is not to say that OMA contributed but a supporting part; it is merely to affirm that the dancers are finally no longer separable from the dance.

And this is how it must be, and indeed will be in the era that is opening itself up to us in the design world today. The agents of change – witness this book – are just now being drawn into focus, separating themselves from the flux of indistinct but highly radical forces, crystallizing into discernable practices, programmes, styles of action and thought. One of the most remarkable things that can already be discerned is that *space is back*, not in the old connoisseur's sense of essential, static traits distinguished through psychological experience and taste; but space as something that *erupts* within the infinite chain of actions-upon-things that is our world. The business of Inside Outside is to orchestrate physical, material (chemical) reactions which in consequence – and thus by design – provoke novel 'forms' of released movement, heat or light. Space is what happens when matter is made volatile, forced into extreme states of 'expression'. Space and matter do not separate as they once did. In the project of Inside Outside one bears witness, by historical necessity, to something very akin to the foundations of modern metaphysics itself: to the reconstruction of a space in which opposites coincide without obliteration (Nicholas of Cusa). This process entails, then just as now, the invention of a graduated path of Being in which, along one direction – outside to inside – things are 'complicated', contracted, or folded up, and along the other – inside to outside – things are 'explicated', relaxed and unfolded. While these developments once supplied the sinews of what would become known as Pantheism and the self-creating universe, they seem particularly important today when glimpsed anew through the cosmos of Petra Blaisse, because they suggest the emergence of a space-making practice deeply in tune with the philosophies of nature that tantalizingly dot our horizon and whose unbearable pressure to appear can be felt everywhere today.

New York, 2006

Outdoor Dining, Bonneville Salt Flats, Utah, 1992